Gathering up the Crumbs

Celebrating a Century
of Accredited, Ordained,
Baptist Women in Ministry in the UK

Published by the Baptist Union of Great Britain
The Baptist Union of Great Britain
Baptist House, 129 Broadway, Didcot
Oxfordshire, OX11 8RT, United Kingdom

Registered Charity 1181392

www.baptist.org.uk

British Library cataloguing in Publication Data

Data Available

ISBN 978-0-901472-86-1

Contents

Introduction

This collection of writing by women in Baptist ministry in the United Kingdom is inspired by the story of the Syro-Phoenician woman whose encounter with Jesus is recorded in Mark's Gospel. Dismissed as a 'dog' (a derogatory remark) she didn't miss a beat in her reply, 'even the dogs gather up the crumbs under the table.'

The Bible is full of stories of equally amazing women - feisty, determined, called of God to serve in diverse ways, times and places. Some were wives; others were widows, divorcees and singletons. Some were mothers or grandmothers, others were childless. Some were Hebrews, many were foreigners. So it is with us! Our editorial team, and our contributors, reflect the wonderful diversity of women in Baptist ministry and, whilst not every aspect of that is expressed here, we delight in each other, negotiate our differences with grace and aspire to honour the one who calls us.

This anthology is a 'grass roots' collection and we are thrilled that more than thirty women, around 10% of those currently in ordained Baptist ministry in these islands, have chosen to share their work.

In this collection you will find lots of exciting material, all of it original, and all of it offered by women who have first used it in some form of public worship in their own context. With such riches, it has been a very difficult task to collate and order the material, so please just dip in, savour the variety and discover material you can use or adapt, that may just inspire your own original material.

Our desire for this book is that it's sized to fit into a pocket or handbag, and will open flat so that you can use it easily. Beyond that, our hope is that your copy becomes tatty from use, with alterations, annotations, bookmarks and whatever else makes it truly yours.

As well as the editorial team, and the contributors, we'd like to thank our proof-readers, Carolyn, Jenny, Liz, Ruth W, Sarah and Steff.

Finally, we would like to express our thanks to the Revd Stephen Keyworth, and the Faith and Society Team of BUGB, who took our tentative idea and promised to make it a reality. Without their encouragement and support this book would have remained a 'nice idea'; with their support we believe we offer something exciting to our Baptist family across these islands, and maybe beyond!

Catriona, Claire, Gale, Helen D, Molly, Ruth G and Sarah
– 'The Crumblies'

We took a conscious decision not to impose grammatical or presentational restrictions. So, for example, sometimes pronouns for God are capitalised and sometimes they are not; sometimes punctuation is very precise, sometimes it is largely absent. We hope, that, like us, you will enjoy this collection of 'crumbs' rather than a perfectly uniform (unsliced?) loaf!

Contributors, proofreaders and editors

Ali Taylor	Associate Minister, Bunyan Baptist Church, Stevenage	CBA/BUGB
Amanda Pink	Accredited Minister on Leave of Absence	SEBA/BUGB
Amanda Quick	Associate Pastor, Leven Baptist Church	BUS
Brenda Morton	Retired Minister	HEBA/BUGB
Carolyn Urwin	Minister, Latchford Baptist Church	NWBA/ BUGB
Catriona Gorton	Minister, Hillhead Baptist Church	BUGB and BUS
Claire Nicholls	Minister, New Addington Baptist Church	LBA/BUGB
Clare Hooper	Regional Minister (CYF), SCBA	SCBA/BUGB
Clare McBeath	Co-Principal, Northern Baptist College	NWBA/ BUGB
Diane Holmes	Accredited Minister; Retreat Facilitator	NWBA/ BUGB
Dinah Hargreaves	Retired Minister	SWBA/BUGB
Eleanor Kelsey	Prison Chaplain	EBA/BUGB
Emma Nash	Accredited evangelist; Mission & Community Engagement Officer for Methodist Church	EBA/BUGB
Gail Scholes	Minister in Training, Farnsorth Baptist Church	NWBA/ BUGB
Gale Richards	Minister, Zion Baptist Church, Cambridge	EBA/BUGB
Hannah Montgomery	Between roles	BUS
Helen Dare *	Minister, Broad Haven Baptist Church	SWBA/BUGB
Helen Paynter	Associate Minister, Westbury on Trym; Tutor, Bristol Baptist College	WEBA/BUGB
Jane Henderson	Regional Minister for Church Transition, NWBA	NWBA/ BUGB
Jane Robson	Minister, Tilehouse Baptist Church	CBA/BUGB

* Editorial Team   ** Proof-reader

Jeannie Kendall	Co-minister, Carshalton Beeches Baptist Free Church	LBA/BUGB
Jenny Few **	Retired Minister, Trustee, Wellspring Church, Wirksworth	EMBA/BUGB
Juliet Lloyd	Pastor at Large – Storytelling	SWaBA/ BUGB
Leigh Greenwood	Minister, Stoneygate Baptist Church	EMBA/BUGB
Linda Clack	Minister, Crewe Baptist Church	NWBA/ BUGB
Linda Hopkins	Minister, Waterloo United Free Church, Liverpool	NWBA/ BUGB
Lisa Kerry	Minister, Croxley Green Baptist Church	CBA/BUGB
Liz Connelly	Lay Pastor, Barlestone Baptist Church	EMBA/BUGB
Mary Cotes	Retired Minister; Editor for Servir Ensemble	BUGB
Mary Taylor	Regional Minister, Yorkshire Baptist Association	YBA/BUGB
Molly Boot *	Minister in Training	SCBA/BUGB
Ruth Gouldbourne	Minister, Grove Lane Baptist Church, Stockport	NWBA/ BUGB
Ruth Wood	Minister, Dewsbury Baptist Church	YBA/BUGB
Sally Fox	Lay Pastor, Crown Road Baptist Church, Sutton, Surrey	BUGB
Sandra Crawford	Minister, Leyland Baptist Church & Wigan Baptist Church	NWBA/ BUGB
Sarah Bingham	Minister, Green Lane Baptist Church, Walsall	HEBA/BUGB
Steff Wright **	Minister in Training	SEBA/BUGB
Vikki Bunce	Minister, Romford Baptist Church	EBA/BUGB

Abbreviations

BUGB - Baptist Union of Great Britain
CBA - Central Baptist Association
EMBA - East Midland Baptist Association
LBA - London Baptist Association
SCBA - Southern Counties Baptist Association
SWaBA - South Wales Baptist Association
WEBA - West of England Baptist Association

BUS - Baptist Union of Scotland
EBA - Eastern Baptist Association
HEBA - Heart of England Baptist Association
NWBA - North Western Baptist Association
SEBA - South Eastern Baptist Association
SWBA - South West Baptist Association
YBA - Yorkshire Baptist Association

Illustration by Ali Taylor

Celebrating Women in Ministry

Poems, reflections and prayers written in celebration of Women in Ministry

Sing a Song of Edith by Catriona Gorton

*This was inspired by the song 'There is a line of women' by John Bell.
I chose Edith Gates, as the first Baptist woman to be ordained. It
could easily be tweaked to include Violet Hedger, Marie Living-Taylor
or even the names of other women...*

There is a line of women
Which carries on through time
Continuing to persevere
In living for their LORD.
And though the church moves slowly
And trips over its feet
Yet still they keep on trusting
God's call upon their lives.
So sing a song of Edith [Gates]
Who pioneered the way
And sing a song of others
Who do the same today
And sing of all the women
Who strive to do their best
As people called to serve God
In every time and place.

The Day you called My Name by **Catriona Gorton**

I remember the day you called my name -
So clear, so urgent, so undeniably real.
I remember the bewilderment and delight,
The anxiety and the certainty.

I couldn't know then what I know now -
Could only dream of what the future might bring,
And fear how it could all go horribly wrong.
But I offered you my unhesitating, trusting 'yes'.

I walk in the shadow of your mother -
A woman who risked everything for you,
A woman to whom you entrusted everything...
A woman who said 'here I am, at your service.'

Jesus, Son of God,
Jesus, Son of Mary,
Help me serve you too. Amen

Let us now Praise Disobedient Women by **Mary Cotes**

Suitable for any service celebrating women, including Mothers' Day. It is probably best presented using two readers. However, it could be done by just one, so italics are not essential.

Let us now praise disobedient women:
Our mothers who broke the rules
And who never would do as they were told.

They were taught they were made in the image of man,
Yet still they believed they were made in the image of God.

They were told they were irrational,
Yet still they continued to reason.

They were taught their place was in the home,
Yet still they went out to work.

They were told they should be submissive,
Yet still they dared to answer back.

They were taught they were subordinate,
Yet still they claimed equality with men.

They were told they had no rights,
Yet still they got up and asserted them.

They were taught they should be pretty, not clever,
Yet still they committed themselves to study.

They were told they should be silent,
Yet still they answered God's call to preach.

We praise God for the vision and faith of these women,
Giving thanks that our lives are different because of them.

We pray that following in their footsteps,
We might hold fast to what they gained through struggle,
And hand on faithfully to those who follow us
The same godly tradition of defiant hope and prophetic
courage.

In Homage to a Star by Amanda Pink

Though her light,
Too often,
Is obscured by the prominence of inferior but numerous street
lamps;

Though the benefit of her illumination
Seems systematically relegated
To the outlands of supposed inconsequence;

And though by those who don't know better
Her influence is restricted
To the inspiration of whimsy and romance;

Do not be fooled
By that gentle warmth of her twinkling glow:
Do you not know?
She is a brilliant fire;
Bright and hot
She burns;
Life-giving,
Ferocious
In equal measure.

Under-estimate her not.

Made in the Image of God by Sandra Crawford

Competing from the beginning, to be heard, to be recognised,
to succeed, the youngest of three.
A grammar-school girl who didn't quite make it, that competitive
spirit lost in academia.
Failure, not good enough, bruised but not broken.
The seeds of perfectionism sown; could do better, I can, I will,
striving,
inadequate, unsatisfied.

Made in the image of God... created

Called into a man's world, stepping into shoes that don't quite
fit, role models, mentors, forerunners,
speaking a language nonindigenous, a male voice, describing
a map I cannot follow.
Self-doubt, should I be here? I can, I will, driven.
Striving to find a place in a jigsaw, but I'm the wrong shape:
silenced, subdued.
Called, created, chosen, really?

Made in the image of God...called

I take the stand, a woman chosen, created in his image, called.
Relationships sour.
God's voice rings clear, "with integrity, stamp upon injustice", the
competitive spirit rises.
Broken, bruised, devalued, isolated,
my value stripped away, I'm worthless. Sadness, despair,
anxiety, fear, consume me.
A smouldering wick, but not snuffed out.

Made in the image of God... chosen

Competitiveness, birthed in one so young, I choose to fight for me, for others, for women.
Arms held high by a husband who watches the destruction and devastation of the one he loves,
He stands, he prays, he weeps, he supports, he cares.
He speaks the promises of God, 'the rivers will not sweep over you, the fire will not consume'.
Friends take their turn, holding my arms up high.

Made in the image of God... His masterpiece

Then, out of the blue, "It is finished", an audible voice, time to walk away, God knows.
A great moment knocks on the door of my heart, no louder than the beating of my heart, I listen.
God calls, quietly, persistently,
a burning bush moment, holy ground, a chance conversation, a quickening of hearts,
Called, created, chosen, really!

Made in the image of God... And he said 'it is very good'

Rebirth, renewing, reawakening, his Spirit alive, burning within like I've never known.
My value restored, my worth rediscovered. Called by name, a masterpiece, loved, cherished, renewed.
Colleagues walking as one, friendship, partnership.
Free to be me, creativity, woman of God, honesty, vulnerability.
The call of God irrevocable.

Made in the image of God... The work of His hand

Made in his image, called by name, for a purpose, at this time, in this place. Your Kingdom come, your will be done.
Marred by life, scarred by conflict, wounded by valleys.

But in the hands of the Potter moulded, shaped, re-formed,
crafted by the master, beauty from ashes.
Courage to be vulnerable, putting on 'my' shoes, celebrating
'my' puzzle shape,
Walking in the unforced rhythms of grace.

I know I'm made in the image of God.

A Risen Woman by Sandra Crawford

This poem is inspired by Nicola Slee's poem of the same name, and Psalm 63 in The Message paraphrase.

A risen woman
It's time to sing a new song, a different melody.
So here I am in the place of worship, eyes wide open,
drinking in your strength and glory.
In your generous love I am living at last!
With my lips I will praise you; with my very breath I will bless you.

A risen woman
Putting on shoes designed for me by the one who calls,
neither the stiletto heels of culture,
nor the ill-fitting patriarchal shoes of my forebears.
But shoes that fit, shoes of purpose,
shoes created for long journeys and rough terrain,
but made for me; a woman, for my personality, colour, sparkle,
and creativity.

A risen woman
Letting go of a lifestyle with status symbols of
comparison, anxiety, exhaustion,
perfectionism, productivity, drivenness, control.

Purposefully turning
towards another way of being; seeking God's path,
learning to live out of Sabbath, releasing control, embracing
God's yoke, embracing my uniqueness.

A risen woman
Learning to sit in his presence, waiting, listening.
I have sacked my negative voice, it's gone.
I'm grasping the truth that I am enough, more than enough.
Ready now to take my place,
a new phase of life; shaped yet not held by the past
I step into the arena, and join the team who dare greatly,
prepared for the dust, sweat and tears.

A risen woman
Walking again in the footsteps of the one who calls,
bearing the marks of my dyings and risings,
but wanting to fling myself full tilt into living.
Leading into the impossible,
the place that without God would be pure foolishness.
No longer striving for human success, but looking for what God
is doing and joining him in it

A risen woman
But I don't want to rise alone, come sisters, join me.
Realise your potential; yes we are afraid,
vulnerable and imperfect, but we are also brave,
worthy of love, and we are enough.
Escape the captivity of a denied life,
no lies about the cost of rising, no easy answers, just obedience
to the call, walk by faith

A risen woman
it's time to sing a new song, a different melody.
So here I am in the place of worship, eyes wide open,
Drinking in your strength and glory.
In your generous love I am living at last!
With my lips I will praise you, with my very breath I will bless you.

And Ain't I a Woman?

These reflections arise from women's experiences, and the editors salute the courage of those who have shared them.

In His Image – Who am I? by Dinah Hargreaves

"What's wrong with me?", I scream inside,
as I return from "Women's Day".
"Who are you?" was the theme, I think;
a wife, a mother, a widow? Just say.
"A woman" is what I'm supposed to reply,
but "a person, just me" is what I want to cry!

I affirm what I do for my family's needs;
I'm complete, in a way, with my roles.
Yet, myself, I'm not made of what roles I fulfil.
I'm a person, with all of my soul.
A person, just me, neither woman or man;
created by God - His image, His plan.

No wonder I'm cross, for I know there are those
pushed aside by the church as lepers, as vermin;
not "people", accepted, because they're not quite
"all male", or "all female", but part undetermined.
Their roles cross the norm. Their hormones are muddled.
They're thrown out on their ears, unaccepted as "bungled".

Me? - yes, I'm a woman, and I thank God for that.
My roles? - the traditional. I wear the hat,
occasionally trousers, more often a dress.
So why, you may ask, do I feel distress?
Because I'm affirmed, loved by God, as just "me".
So why get so cross, and even angry?

Because I know Genesis, so very abused.
(We read what we like into all of His Book!)
But, "made in His image, (both) male and female"
says clearly to me what I know very well,
we are all quite a mixture – not "normal" - not one!
And he loves us as "people" - not woman or man.
We are all quite a mixture, and in God's image too,
means he loves us as people as we also should do.

Creation by Dinah Hargreaves

Pain, ache, gnawing at my loins.
Dull, sickening, gripping pain, removing peace,
                                     removing calm.
It passes, raising hopes of ease;
returns again to greater depths and heights...

Suddenly an awareness that I am not in control -
this pulling, tearing of my innards,
this overwhelming surge
is taking me into its very pulse.
Pain, urgent need to push,
breath drawn and used to maximum effect.
Pushing, pushing – breath expelled,
then rest – rest – I am now myself...

The pain returns, increasing yet again,
      surging, pulsing ever more -
Myself – drowning in the waters of birth pangs...

There could be heavenly choirs,
    there could be fire bells ringing,
a riot inside my room, the neighbours all come calling!

I do not know, nor do I care, nor can I think or reason.
A voice calls out, my voice, yet somewhere from the earth -
Only for me the rhythmic pattern of pain,
effort,
rest,
pain and rest,
increasing in immediacy,
increasing in intensity,
myself, my life decreasing as new life fights for birth.

Push, push — more, now rest. Push, then hold, then push again.
My body does it for me, not my brain.
Hearing commands, so far away, yet wanting
so much for the end that is a new beginning.
The end has come in a slithering, screaming second.
Now is the peace.
Now the completion.
Now the fulfilment of months of waiting, giving, hoping.
Now — the sound of a cry is heard.
My child is born, as no child ever before.

Was it like this God for you,
at the birth of creation, when there was light
bursting into being, coming out of the night;
buds, leaves appearing from under the earth,
a flower in the desert, a shoot of new birth?
Was there that pain, Lord,
an urgent compulsion
to bring into being life, full and various:
snails, worms and ladybirds, rabbits and terrapins,
deer, stoat and antelope, goat, sheep, an elephant?
Birds too, and butterflies, bats flying eerily,
yet completion, fulfilment in the birth of humanity.

Was there that pain, not recorded, because
at the sight of that birth,
at the time of completion, all else before was forgotten and
ended,
for life was now made — and that life was good?
For all that had passed was light years away
as you rested, creation completed that day.

Perhaps pain did not come until man had fallen,
in sheer disobedience, turning away
from all that the loving relationship meant
twixt Creator, created — all vanished that way.
Yet not lost forever, for Love is your name.
Love is your nature, your being, your self.
You could not leave us so distant, so separate.
Birth could be re-birth, creation rebonded,
remade, through a Cross, as you sought us again.

That act of creation, blood spattered and gory,
the agony there as your life ebbed away;
the words "It is finished" not the end of the story
but the gift of new life on that victory day.

As I lay with my infant, warm flesh against flesh,
in mute adoration, in wonder and quiet -
no wonder you love your creation, O Father!
No wonder you came to be born of a woman,
involved in your world, however much pain
rebirth may still cause you
— for Love is your Name.

Haiku – Dolls by Helen Paynter

A lament for named and un-named women: their agony climbs to heaven. And is heard.

Hagar
Requisitioned womb –
Bitter slave of owners' drive.
Cheap commodity.

Jephthah's daughter
Sixty days to weep –
Floods the hills with virgin grief.
Child of folly's vow.

The Levite's concubine
Nameless surrogate –
Slain by cowardice and vice.
Useful still, though dead.

Michal
Voiceless toy of kings –
Expediency's puppet.
Pass-the-parcel wife.

Tamar
Meat to Amnon's greed -
Tossed aside like well-chewed bones.
Ruined, loveless, lost.

The others
Hundreds, thousands more –
Suburb, slum or throne-room bound.
Lust and power's dolls.

Come, Lord Jesus, come –
Sound the note of Jubilee.
Dry your daughters' tears.

No more mourning, then –
Banish weeping, death and pain.
Come, Lord Jesus, come.

Change of Life by Diane Holmes

Three reflections on the experience of hysterectomy

Fear of the hollows (before the operation)

Last night
I sat with you in a garden
It was dark
You had called into the night
'Will no one watch with me?'

Because I was scared
I heard your call
I didn't want to be alone either
So I came and sat with you
I felt with you
Your fear
I shared with you
Eternal moments of desperation

All was quiet

No Father spoke

We shared
The utter aloneness
Together
We watched.
The stars fell from the sky
The sky fell from the stars
And crushed us
Under its heavy coat.

I sat with you in a garden
Crushed
Beneath the heavy sky
No secrets uttered
No words of comfort
Spoken
No hope discerned
Just darkness

I fell asleep against you
And woke into
A world uplifted
Knowing I had shared your fear
I had touched
The root of the love
That saves the world
And was filled
Through all my echoing hollows
With trust in you.

Naming the weeping (after the operation)

Have I the right to grieve?
Shouldn't I just be grateful?
But how can I be full...

Of anything
I say hello to hollow

Barren soil is still soil
Dry ground is fertile when the rains come
But what am I?
The tide moves in and out
At moon's behest
Clouds move across the sky
But I am a stagnant pool
Reflecting nothing
Both drained
And dammed
What you give me
I cannot keep
No longer a vessel
What you pour in
Leaks out
There is no way
To the sea through me
A human cul de sac
Dead end

The bowl
Holding
Resplendent
With rotting fruit
Is more of a tree than I
It may be still-life
But it's still life.
While the apples roll from my grasp
The seeds fall through my fingers
No longer Eve
It's the only rain I have

Accepting
Should I mourn
Being
Tied to the moon
When
There's a host of stars
Out there?
When
Just one glance
From you
And
I'm a meteor shower?

I close the door gently
Slowly
Softly
So as not to wake the sleeping child
The worn-out grief
And tiptoe
Quietly
Away
Down the stairs
To where the light is on.

The Haunting Eyes of Pain by Dinah Hargreaves

This reflection arises from supporting those who have experienced abuse

Eyes, those eyes staring out at me -
out of a too small face,
swallowing me in a lake of unshed tears.
The hurt. The pain. - "help me, help me". -
I look. I look away.

What do they mean?
What do they say?
What do I do?
Where do I go?

Shall I run away, shut myself in my chapel,
protect myself with the armour of hymnody?
Shall I laugh, poke fun, change the subject, move away,
bring some light-heartedness back? Quick! Do something.

Or, shall I look back -
taking the pain into my very self -
absorbing, drowning with the agony?
It hurts. It hurts. O God, why do you allow it?
The agony of a shrieking, aching world
that's locked behind silent orbs of tears.

Forgive me Lord. Forgive me too -
for I bring pain and hurt with me.
I too am guilty, with the world.
I too need cleansing – my reluctance;
my own careless, helpless, inadequacy;
my own abusive, thoughtless encounters.
I too am part of that wounding hatefulness.

It hurts. It hurts. O God, but you hurt too;
the pain that's here, that's mine, that's hers, is yours.
The agony of your shrieking aching world
that's locked behind so many silences.

We hold her – and she hangs on to love,
to caring, hurting, to hope - to me.
We weep, we stay, aware of you our God,
holding, resting, waiting for peace.

Help – forgive – your strength Lord, yours -
   where our eyes together
         meet with you.

Han (Anger) by **Diane Holmes**

Inspired by reflection on social justice

I lay my hands upon the stone
And touched another's there
Turning it
She traced my life
Clean-lined
Through rounded cushioned hills
Placed my pink-flexed fingers
On her own dry palm

I felt a scar
So deep
It pulled my soul's plug
From its soft-loamed moorings
Water
Draining every tear
Parched the planet

Sun-lit
Resurrection garden leaves
Turned
Swirled dry throated
Withered windblown
Broken
Against Gethsemane's gates

Voiceless
She beckoned
Come
Walk the gnarled narrow garden
Of my han
Drink from my empty cup
My yoke crushes me
I am angry and desperate in heart
Learn from me

I sewed your jeans in a sweatshop
Worked nightshifts for your weekend trainers
Your words are the wood
I need for heat and light
One frustrated torn up page searching for expression
Another barefoot mile for me
Your spirit's dry reaches
The place I sow my seeds
Your freedom of choice is my subsistence
Your anger – my drought
Your convenience – my flashflood
Your coloured crayons – my blood
Your poetry – my screams
Your violated, silenced history
My every waking moment
Your nightmares
My nights

The world has folded over
Into one
God's hands fold flat in prayer
Whenever you speak your story
You speak mine
Wherever you place your hand

Mine will be there
She gave me back my hand
My han
Recognise the marks
Of your own nails
She said
And

I lay my hand upon the stone
And touched another's there

Prayer inspired by the Parable of the Lost Coin by Mary Cotes

Searching God,
As in the parable
A woman swept her whole house to find a lost coin,
Sweep away the dust of our lives
And bring what truly shines to light.

Sweep away our fear of being rejected,
Until you find our capacity to love and be loved.

Sweep away our fear of being judged,
Until you find our readiness to forgive and be forgiven.

Sweep away our fear of failure
Until you find our humble strength and determined hope.

Sweep away our fear of letting go,
Until you find our desire to lose all to win abundant life.

When you have brought these precious coins to light,
Enable us to rejoice, with you and with the angels,
That what was lost has been found,
And what was hidden has been revealed.

(Luke 15:8-10)

The *Yeast of the Kingdom* by **Mary Cotes**

Baker-woman God,
As you mix the yeast of your kingdom
Into the dough of all your world,
Mix us, too, into the fabric of our communities.
May the yeast of your kingdom be at work in us.

As the yeast is hidden in the mixture,
Grant us the faith
To believe that you are mysteriously at work
In the most unlikely of settings
And the most unpromising of people.
May the yeast of your kingdom be at work in us.

As the yeast takes its time to act,
Grant us the trust
To wait un-anxiously
But pray unceasingly
For the signs of your presence to be known.
May the yeast of your kingdom be at work in us.

As the littleness of yeast
Transforms the mountain of dough,
Grant us the humility
To believe that the tiniest deed or the shortest word
Can have the most powerful effect.
May the yeast of your kingdom be at work in us.

Baker-woman God,
As you prepare enough bread
To feed a whole multitude,
Grant us the love
Not only to throw our own table open
But to sit as guests at others',
Building a fairer world together,
Faithfully believing
That the abundant life of your Kingdom is for all. Amen.

(Matt. 13:34)

To those who are called, who are beloved

in God the Father and kept safe for Jesus Christ

JUDE 1:1-2

may mercy, peace and love

be yours in abundance

Illustration by Jane Henderson

Seasons of Life and Seasons of Loss

Seasons of Life

Infant Affirmations for Non-Religious Parent/s by Sarah Bingham

I believe every child has potential and I commit to helping mine explore theirs to the full.

I believe every child needs stability and I commit to work hard to ensure mine has/have it.

I believe every child needs unconditiona love and I commit to showing that love to my child(ren).

I believe every child needs to learn right from wrong and I commit to living as a good example to mine.

I believe every child needs boundaries until they learn self-discipline and I commit to finding the balance between having too many rules and too few.

I believe every child is a unique gift and I commit to allowing mine to be themselves and not smaller versions of me.

I believe every child has needs wider than physical provision and I commit to helping to provide whatever my child(ren) need(s).

Hymn for Infant Blessing by Liz Connelly

Possible tunes: if sung as 6 verses: Aurelia (The Church's one foundation); if sung as 3 verses: Wolvercote or Thornbury (O Jesus, I have promised) Metre 76 76 six verses, or 76 76 D three verses

Jesus look upon this child
And take *him/her* as your own
Help us all to share with *him/her*
The love that you have shown.

We would have *him/her* come to you
And live *his/her* life your way
Show us as a family
Your will from day to day

Thank you for the freedom that
We have to worship you
Help us all to teach to *him/her*
How *he/she* may worship too.

Thank you for your living word
Through which we learn of you
May *he/she* know you for *him/herself*
As *he/she* follows you *his/her* life through.

Give *him/her* your protection, Lord
And remain close by *his/her* side.
Keep *him/her* in your tender care
With the Spirit there to guide.

Thank you for the power of prayer
We pray for *him/her* this day
Welcome *him/her* into this church
And bless *him/her* now we pray.

A Wedding Blessing by Amanda Pink

May God grant *us/you*:

Time	to ponder life's beauty,
Strength	to bear all its tyranny,
and Humour	to laugh at its folly;

Love	to cherish *our/your* friends,
	to be open to the stranger,
	and to pardon *our/your* enemy;

Hope	to envision God's Kingdom come,
with Confidence	to play *our/your* own part
and Humility	to let others play theirs;

Discipline	to resist what is evil,
Anger	to challenge injustice,
Compassion	to mourn with the broken;

Tenacity	to stand in adversity,
Patience	to live with *our/your* limits,

and ultimately,
even when all else fails,

Faith	to trust in the Saviour.
Amen.	

Blessing a Garden by Mary Cotes

Loving God,
in the beginning you made humankind
from the very dust of the earth,
and placed us in a garden
to share and enjoy its life.

We pray for this garden
that it may become a focus
of meeting and welcome,
where community is nourished
and true humanity revealed.

Creator God,
in this garden,
may your life be made known.

Loving God,
you rejoiced in your creation
and called us to be your partners in its care.
We pray for this garden
that those who come here to work
might learn to treasure your world,
live responsibly
and protest at all that destroys and pollutes.

Creator God,
in this garden,
may your life be made known.

Loving God,
you gave vision to prophets
who compared to a beautiful garden
your faithful people who rebuilt ruins
and cared for the needy.
We pray for your church here,
that its garden may be a special place
of ministry and witness,
and that season upon season
it may offer new images
of the changing seasons of our lives.

Creator God,
in this garden,
may your life be made known.

Loving God,
when fear and hatred loomed,
your Son came to a garden to pray,
and longed for the trust and support of friends.
We pray for this garden
that it may be a haven of peace and solace,
where those who come with heavy hearts
may find others awake to their need.

Creator God,
in this garden,
may your life be made known.

Loving God,
in the face of death,
one who grieved came to a garden to weep
and there encountered the risen presence of Christ.
We pray for this garden,
that here new hope may take root,
falsehood may be weeded out,
that they who sow in tears may reap in joy.[1]

Creator God,
in this garden,
may your life be made known
through us and in us
as it is in the life of the earth we touch.
In the name of Jesus Christ we pray.
Amen.

---

1   Psalm 126:5-6

Seasons of Loss

There are lots of ceremonies to celebrate marriage but few resources for people experiencing breakdown of relationships. There are plenty of liturgies to celebrate birth or adoption, far fewer that recognise the pain of stillbirth, miscarriage and neonatal death. Aging, ill-health, dying and death remain all too often taboo topics, yet they affect all of us, or those we love. These reflections and prayers are offered in the hope that they will help women (and men) whose life experience brings such pain and losses.

Known Unto God by Catriona Gorton

This was inspired by a request to conduct a funeral for someone with no known relatives or friends. It could also be used at All Souls.

Is it enough to say of her, 'known unto God?'
What is expressed when I say of him 'known unto God?'

What were her girlish dreams,
His boyhood ambitions?
Known unto God.

What made them laugh?
Did they dance or sing?
Known unto God.
What was her proudest moment,
His greatest day?
Known unto God.

Who did they love – and who loved them?
Who broke their hearts – and whose did they break?
Known unto God.

What secret longings were never fulfilled?

What painful regrets were never addressed?
Known unto God.

Who now will mourn them, and who is left?
Who will remember the life that was theirs?
Known unto God.
Inadequate sufficiency,
Essentials fulfilled:
Known unto God.

'Jim' and 'Mabel,'
John Doe, Jane Doe,
Unknown soldier,
Unnamed foetus:
Known unto God
For ever - Amen.

Remember at Christmas by Vikki Bunce

Christmas lights, carol singers,
Bands playing, exhausted shoppers,
Endless lists, things to do,
Presents to wrap, excited voices.

The looming dread of the day to come
The sadness of the missing one
The empty chair, the lack of noise
The pain of grief that hurts so much.

Christmas movies, food to order
Baby sitters needed for endless parties
Last minute shopping, the tree to buy
The grotto to visit, the endless mince pies.

Family breakdown, the children have fledged
Dinner for two instead of for ten
Nowhere to go, nothing to eat
No-one to visit, no-one to treat.

Emotions are mixed as we face Christmas Day
Traditions are different with loved ones away
Or missing or married or just gone forever
Let's cancel this Christmas, let's wish it be gone.
But you're never alone, God wants to come in
To share in your pain and your long-suffering
He loves you and cares, however you feel
Just open your heart, His peace will flow in

God loves you so much, He'll comfort you still
in the pain and the heartache and the hurts that you feel
As Christmas approaches just look to the One
who brings hope through His Son, with His peace and goodwill.

The candle you light, the card that you write
The time to reflect and acknowledge this fact
That Christmas is different for this year we know
But God is with us, He's there for us still
It's hope that He gives us, that babe in the manger
So let's open our hearts so Christmas joy can come in
Through the peace and the presence of God in our lives
As He comforts us still this coming Christmas time.

Because I Love You by **Amanda Pink**

An unborn baby came to God in prayer:
Her words were unformed, her body still a handful of cells,
but her maker understood her silent, unspoken question:
"What is happening to me?"

God breathed life into her tiny body.
Because I love you,
God said,
You will have life.

A growing child came to God in prayer:
"Who are you?" the child asked, curious and inquisitive, ready
and open to learn.
And God surrounded him with people who would help him
discover the answer:
Parents and siblings,
Nannys and Grandpas,
Aunts and Uncles,
Teachers and Scout leaders,
friends,
and enemies,
and a church family.
Because I love you,
God said
I will teach you.

A nervous bridegroom came to God in prayer:
"I can't believe we're really doing this," he whispered,
astonished,
as he pondered the significance of what they were about to do,
awareness and mystery knotting themselves together into a ball
of nerves and energy in his belly.
And God saw all that was to come -
The thrill of intimacy and the joy of companionship,
the making of memories and the living nightmares,
the blazing rows, the working it out, the lessons learned,
the losses mourned and the blessings celebrated -
And, smiling, God blessed their union.

Because I love you,
God said,
You will know the richness of loving, and the richness of being
loved.

A busy family forgot to come to God in prayer:
"So much to do!", they exclaimed,
as they dashed and darted between things to do, places to be,
and people to see.
And God missed their company.
But still,
Because I love you,
God said,
I will send you many blessings to enjoy,
and even though you do not see they are from me now,
I will give them anyway,
and perhaps one day you will look back in thanks, and know.

A doubting disciple came to God in prayer:
"How could you let this happen?" she half challenged, half
lamented,
as she tried to make sense of what didn't make sense,
and suffered the mindless explanations offered by the well-
meaning
but not-understanding people around her.
"It isn't right, it isn't fair. Aren't you supposed to be good?"
And in loving mercy, God listened to every question and every
objection.
Because I love you,
God said,
You can be honest with me. I can take it.

A grieving widow came to God in prayer:
At first there were no words, just a stunned numbness, as she
waited for reality to kick back in.

And then it hit her - a tsunami of sadness and loneliness and fear and regret,
Wave after wave taking her by surprise
just as the previous one subsided, and she had thought it was over.
"How can I go on?" she sobbed, desperate for something to cling onto.
And God held her.
Because I love you,
God said,
You will be hard pressed but not destroyed.

A dying man came to God in prayer:
"Living God, have mercy on me!" he begged.
"For my days are numbered, and my sins are many".
And God pointed to the cross, where Christ had paid the ultimate price of love,
so that all who believed might not perish,
but have eternal life.
Because I love you,
God said,
You can rest in peace.

A congregation came to God in prayer, as they remembered those whom they had loved and lost.
They sang, and they remembered, they lit candles and they wept.
And God saw them, and had compassion on them.
Comfort, comfort, my people,
God said.
Because I love you,
You are never alone, for I am with you.
Because I love you.

Years' Mind by Catriona Gorton

In some Christian traditions, the weekly intercessory prayers will include an opportunity to name those "whose years' mind falls around this time". This calling to mind of those who have gone before us – at least in living memory – can be powerful and pastorally helpful. The form of words suggested here could be used within the context of a (monthly) Communion Service, or readily adapted for an annual service of remembering those whose 'years' mind', or anniversary of death, occurred during that calendar month or year.

At a Communion Service

Loving God, we recall with gratitude those who have gone before us, and whose years' mind [anniversary of death] falls around this time, thinking especially of [names] who we have known and loved.

We give thanks for the life of N who has recently died, asking you to comfort those who mourn their loss.

May our memories comfort and console us

And may your promises give us hope and strength for our own continuing lives
Amen

At Communion or at an Annual Service

Loving God, we recall with gratitude those who have gone before us, and who we call to mind at this time, thinking especially of those who we have known and loved.

In the quiet of our hearts, we name them before you...

We give thanks for their lives asking you to comfort those who mourn their loss.

May our memories comfort and console us

And may your promises give us hope and strength for our own continuing lives.
Amen.

Service of Blessing of a Memorial Bench by Carolyn Urwin

Statement of the Occasion
This *morning/afternoon* we come together in a special act of worship to bless this bench in memory of N, who is sadly missed by us all.
It is now... *length of time*... since N died and so we gather as *his/her* close family and friends to share in this short act of remembering and dedication.

Why a blessing?

Saying a prayer isn't some sort of magic act that will prevent this bench from aging or protect it from accident or vandalism.
It is an acknowledgement that there is more to life than meets the eye – that behind the beauty of this place and the love we share is God our Creator who loves us and wants the best for us.

The beauty of the different seasons everyone who uses this bench will be able to enjoy is a reminder of God's goodness and continuing providence in sustaining the earth year on year.

The rest and refreshment it will afford to all who use it reminds us of a God who himself rested after his work of creation.

And the love and companionship shared on this bench points us back to God who also wants to share his life and love with us.

So a prayer of blessing is simply asking that God will use it for good in the lives of all who use it.

Remembering N
So now we come with joy to remember *N*,
to give thanks for *his/her* life and all *he/she* meant to those who knew *him/her*,
and to bless this bench in *his/her* memory.

[A few words on the life and character of the deceased.]

So let us thank God for *N*.

Prayer of thanks
Loving God,
Our Creator, Sustainer and Redeemer,
      we give you thanks for the gift of life.
We thank you for *N*,
      for the person we knew *him/her* to be
      and the special place *he/she* continues to hold in our
      hearts.
Thank you for all the memories which we treasure.
And thank you for being with us here
      as we remember *him/her*.
We thank you for all your gifts
      those who use this bench will enjoy,
        for the beauty of this place,
        for times to rest and enjoy the life you give us
        and the love and friendship of one another.

The Lord's Prayer may be said.
So now we come to dedicate this bench in *N*'s memory.

Act of Dedication
Eternal God,
we call to mind our friend *N*,
remembering all the happy times we had
and the friendship and love we shared.

Now that *he/she* is gone from us,
we dedicate this bench to *his/her* memory,
a sign of remembrance,
and a sign of your goodness and hope.
May it bring pleasure and refreshment to all who use it
and remind us of you, the maker of all things beautiful,
and the source of all the love we share.

And now a prayer for ourselves:

Prayer
Loving God,
comfort us as we remember those whom we have loved.
Give us strength and courage for the days ahead,
compassion for others who grieve,
and hold us always in your eternal love,
through Jesus Christ the Lord.
Amen.

And to close, a blessing on you all.

Blessing
The Lord bless you and keep you,
The Lord shine his face upon you,
and be gracious to you,
and give you his peace.
Amen.

Stillbirth, Miscarriage & Neonatal Death

To the child I'll never know by Ali Taylor

Perfect one,
I'll never know you
A gift from God
Seemingly so cruelly taken away
I'll never understand why He took you
But though my heart is full of pain
I will trust that His reason is good.

I know He holds you
Forever in His arms
And I'll hold that forever in my heart
You'll never know the pain of this world
You'll be perfect forever
And your memory will stay
In my heart and mind
For all time.

Never Forgotten by Ali Taylor

Before you were here,
You were loved
As you entered this world
Our hearts were torn
We never wanted to say goodbye
Before we could say hello
How impossible to do a lifetime of loving
In time that was all too brief

And we have not just lost you,
But all our shared tomorrows

And in times yet still to come
When future stolen moments leave us breathless
May our treasured love for you
Sustain us still

May we stand together
United by our shared remembrance
Of our love for you
Knowing that you,
Our innocent one,
Is held forever safe
In the Father's arms.

Relationship Breakdown

Unravelled by Ali Taylor

The fabric of our relationship
Took half a lifetime to create
Two lives woven together
With love
All that we brought from our singleness
Entwined into one

And as we grew together
All that we experienced
Became knitted in
Our joys and sorrows
Our fears and failures
Our hopes and dreams
All that we shared in unity
Created pattern
Created texture
In the fabric of our life

But this creation,
This cloth,
Was easily destroyed
You undid the thread of love
And with a sharp tug
Row by row
Our relationship unravelled
The memories so intricately intertwined
Now cast aside
Without our love to hold them together
They lie abandoned
No longer bringing richness
To the material

Of our affinity
The thread of my love remains
But without the warp,
The weft lies useless
Unable to hold the substance
Of the fabric together
And my dismay
As this unique cloth is ruined
Is immeasurable

How come it takes so little to destruct
Something that took so long to create?
How could you destroy
Something of such rich beauty
And incalculable worth?
So many years so quickly reduced
To a jumbled mess
And all I can do is watch helplessly
As everything we have worked together
To create
Is reduced to nothing.

But I will gather up the memories
That you have so carelessly discarded
And I will take them to the master weaver
Who, in His infinite wisdom,
Will interlace them into a richer tapestry
Of my own
That bears witness to this unravelled past
But will also encompass
All the experiences
Of my future that are still to come.

Dementia

For a Lady whose Elderly Husband needs to Live in a Care Home due to Dementia by Sally Fox

I let him go... from our old life into his new life; a new life that will one day give way into eternal life.

I let him go... into the care of others. One day I will let him go into the care of the eternal God who had cared for him since before the dawn of time.

From the fullness of our past life together... I let him go into the smallness of the life he must now live alone. I let him go into the place I can only visit; unable to know where his soul waits or what is the purpose.

I let him go... but I feel left behind. He now dwells alone beside 'The Lethe River'[2] while I am stuck alone in the old world of our normality; still living among the familiar things and watching the garden grow.

---

2 The Lethe River is the mythical river of forgetfulness.

May God bless him in his new home while his future home is prepared; the place where he will fully understand just as he has been fully understood. (1 Cor 13)

The place where he will realise the love we shared even when we didn't fully understand each other; the place where he will realise the need to forgive just as he has been forgiven, the pain-less, tear-less place where God will make all things new. (Rev 21: 4-5a)

Loss before loss by **Ali Taylor**

I see you
I hear you
But it's like you're behind a pane of glass
There, but not quite there
Visible, but I can't reach you
So close, and yet so far away

There is so much I want to share with you
So much I want to say
But you can't really hear me

You're fading into a world that I can't touch
And so, my heart aches and the tears fall
Because I am losing you

I'm losing all we had
As the memories of the past we share
Are left lonely in my mind
And I'm losing all we could have
In a future not yet here

I'm losing you

And in a way
As I lose you
It feels like part of myself is lost with you

My Mother by **Catriona Gorton**

*Written for Mothering Sunday, when my mother had moved into a
care home as she had early vascular dementia and was no longer
able to live independently.*

This is my Mum, the person within whose womb I was conceived
My Mum, at whose breast I suckled
Who bathed and clothed me when I could do nothing for myself.

This is my Mum, the person who taught me to walk and to talk
My Mum, who allowed me, aged five, to take her favourite blue
glass jug to the school jumble sale (and it was gone before she
could arrive to buy it back)
Who listened to my reading, my tables, my spellings,
encouraging me to excel wherever I could.

This is my Mum, the person who went without so that I didn't
My Mum who baked a birthday cake shaped like a cottage, took
me to piano lessons and failed to teach me knit!
Whose help was the cause of my one disastrous French
homework, who steered me to subjects that should lead to
employment.

This my Mum, who never understood why I left it all to follow a
call to ministry
My Mum, who proudly spoke of her daughter, the engineer, the
minister
Who cheered from the side-lines as best she could, worried,
cajoled, and, yes, criticised.

This is my Mum, a widow for over a quarter century, many of whose friends have slipped away through death
My Mum who now finds her memory fading, time collapsing in on itself, independence stolen
Who must depend on those she nurtured to step up and care for her.

This is my Mum, who has grown old
Has been taken by the hand and led where she did not want to go.
Whom I love, and whom I cannot protect from the inevitability of old age and frailty.

The circle spins round, carer becomes cared for, child becomes as parent
This is my Mum...
God help me to be the daughter of whom she dreamed all those years ago.

Last Suppers and other Rememberings by Catriona Gorton

This was written after clearing my Mum's flat and leaving for the last time the town where I grew up. On that day I went to a café ate a strawberry flan and drank tea...

Whenever you do this, remember me:
In broken bread and poured out wine -
Or pots of tea and strawberry flans -
Take a moment to pause
Deliberately call to mind this moment
And what it meant
Live the memory
Re-live the memory
Remember the meaning

Re-member the meaning
Because every time you do
You restore the moment,
Renew the promise
Recreate the meaning
Until the day when all things are made anew in God's Kingdom
of Shalom.

Stardust and Hopes and Dreams by Sarah Bingham

Written for my mother's burial

She was made of stardust and hopes and dreams. She had a
life of joy and disappointment, laughter and tears, sweetness
and bitterness. Now there is no more confusion, frustration or
fear. She has been disappearing slowly within herself for years
and now is gone. Only the atoms remain. In line with her wishes,
to earth she is returning, to nourish and sustain life in other
forms.

She lives on in our hearts and minds and in the way she has
shaped our thoughts and actions. So we say goodbye to this
outer form and goodbye to her immediate presence with our
own mix of relief and sorrow and differing hopes of what may be
yet to come.

Endings in Church Life

Rightly, we are excited about new beginnings and create wonderful liturgies for them. The liturgies shared here are born of the lived experience of women ministers who have created them in response to challenging contexts and endings that are poignant or painful for the church communities in which they were shared.

Permanent Closure of Building, with gratitude to Hugglescote Baptist Church, Leicestershire by Catriona Gorton

This service took place on a Saturday afternoon and was followed by tea.

Welcome - Church Secretary or other Deacon

Call to Worship - Minister

Hymn or Song(s)

Prayer
> "Living God, in this building, used to the sound of singing", *Gathering for Worship*, page 297, then:

> Holy and faithful God, whose love knows no limits and upon whose grace and mercy we depend, as we gather today to give thanks for what is past, to hear your words for today and to commend to you our future: fill us afresh with hope and vision so that having shared in worship we may live to your glory.
> In Jesus' name we pray. Amen.

Hymn/Song(s)

Reading - chosen by preacher, read by a member

Sermon - we invited our Regional Minister to preach

Hymn/Song (we used the congregation's 'signature tune' – most churches have one!)

Recording our memories
>   People write a memory on a piece of good quality paper that will later be pasted into a book to form a lasting record of the day. (After time allowed for this, they were collected up by members)

Song/Hymn

Prayers of Intercession

Symbolic act of moving on
>   A Bible, a cross, chalice and communion plates are placed in a box in readiness to be carried out of the building at the close of the service. This was done by some of our longest serving members, male and female – a sign of faithful witness

Hymn/Song

Prayer
>   Lord of the years, as we leave this building to go into the future, we once more thank you for all that is past and commend to you all that is to come. May we who have encountered your love here share it with the world; we whose lives have been changed by Jesus share the Good News in word and deed; we who are refreshed by your Spirit grasp the vision you set before us. Walk with us, we pray, turn our sorrow to joy and above all grant us your peace, today and always. Amen.

Blessing

>The box is carried from the building by e.g. children, young people or newest attenders or members – a sign of hope.

Leaving the Building

>The people follow and leave the building via the front door, which is symbolically closed and locked after the last person has left. A final prayer is spoken and the people then go to for refreshments OFF SITE. To re-enter the building at this point destroys the symbolism!

Closure of a Building for Redevelopment – with gratitude to Hillhead Baptist Church, Glasgow by Catriona Gorton

This was a 'normal' Sunday morning service and coincided with the first Sunday of Advent. On the spur of the moment, as we left the building, I lifted the lit candle and carried it out of the door, a sign of defiant hope on a windy November day!

Welcome and Notices - Church Secretary or Deacon

Call to Worship - Minister

Hymn/Song

Prayer and Lord's Prayer

Anthem, Hymn or Song

Remembering

>This is our Story – by a Church Member, outline of congregation's history

And/Or...

I Remember When...

Groups visit various spaces/rooms and talk about activities that took place there

And/Or

Slide show of photos of happy events e.g. weddings, baptisms, etc.

Hymn/Song

Reading(s)   We used Hebrews 11: 1-3, 8-10, 38-12:2 and Matthew 28: 16-20

Reflection/Sermon – Minister or invited preacher

Hymn/Song

Responding:

We are the church – adding our faces to a model/outline of the church

And/or

Looking back, looking forward - recording our memories & naming our hopes on cards

Hymn/Song

Prayers of Intercession

Offering (included gathering of memory cards)

Symbolic act of moving on

> Cross, Bible, communion plate and chalice placed in a transit box by Members of long-service, closed and ready to be carried out.

Hymn

Prayer

Leaving the Building

> Leave the church singing a simple song such as 'We are marching in the light of God', led by young people carrying the transit box. The door is locked once all are outside.

Final prayer of blessing and then process to lunch venue.

Closure of a Church with gratitude to the former Kingswood Baptist Church, Watford by Jane Robson

This service, which involved a rather wonderful cake, was shared with many ecumenical guests

Welcome - Minister

> One last time... in the name of Jesus Christ... welcome!

Worship songs
Prayers – ecumenical guest

Hymn

Prayer for Worshipping Community of Kingswood - Minister

> Faithful servants of our Lord Jesus Christ in this building and in this community, we join with the saints of Kingswood Baptist Church who have gone before to pray for the blessing of God to rest upon each one of you here and wherever he leads you in the days that lie ahead.

> May the fruit of the Spirit be seen in your lives: the fruit of Love, Joy, Peace, Patience, Kindness, Goodness, Faithfulness, Humility and Self-control.

> And we pray that being rooted and established in love, you may have power, together with all the Lord's holy people, to grasp how wide and long and high and deep is the love of Christ. And may you know this love that surpasses knowledge - that you may be filled to the measure of all the fullness of God; this significant and special day - and always. Amen.

Reading and message on behalf of 'Christians across Watford' – ecumenical guest

Hymn

Prayers – ecumenical guest

> Giving thanks for the fruits of this congregation and seeking blessings of courage and strength to go forward in His service as well as praying for the work of the one united church in Watford.

Message - Minister

Cake

We shared cake together – it was cut up on the communion table and everyone had a piece which was eaten there and then... during that time people chatted and then we moved into the closing act of worship.

Photo: Jane Robson

Closing act of Worship

We explained that at the end of the singing of the next hymn the pianist would continue playing and then, led by the Church Secretary, we would all file out of the front door and gather in front of the church... everyone would need to take all their belongings with them.

Hymn

The longest serving member of the church and the Minister were the last out of the church. The Minister turned out all the lights as we left and closed the doors. The member locked one of the locks and the minister locked the second and final lock.

Final Benediction

People remained to take photos and left when they were ready.

(The following day many of the church's contents were then collected by other churches that were going to be able to make good use of them).

An Ecumenical Communion Service for Closure of a Building
by Catriona Gorton

The congregation I serve in Glasgow has for almost two decades shared evening worship with neighbouring churches of other traditions, taking it in turns to host. This is the outline of the service we shared the evening we closed our premises pending redevelopment.

Welcome and Call to Worship

Hymn

Prayer
> Loving God, who was and is and always will be,
> It is strange to realise that this is a "last time"
> The last time we will sit on these old red chairs,
> > Arranged in a ring, expressing inclusion and equality
> The last time we will sing our praises and speak our prayers
> > Accompanied by the rattling of these heaters blowing warm air
> The last time we will break bread and share wine around this table
> > Sign of our unity, expression of our hope-filled faith
> The last time, in this place, that we will say "this is the last time"!
>
> Gentle God, who shares our laughter and our tears
> It is good to be assured that you are with us
> As we call to mind precious memories of
> > services we have shared and people we have loved
> As we lay down and let go what is ending
> And as we take up what now begins
> Hopeful God, in these moments

Help us to dream new dreams
To imagine new opportunities for worship and learning
To continue to encourage and empower each other
As we seek to grow in grace and love,

In these moments where the meeting of past and future is palpable
Show us the memories we may cherish and the values we must continue to live
As we journey with Jesus, in whose name we pray.
Amen.

Looking Back in Gratitude – the Story of the Shared Evening Services

Recording our memories / Music for reflection

Bible Reading(s)

Looking Forward in Hope – a Reflection

Hymn We used 'For everyone born a place at the table'

Communion

Invitation

For everyone born there is a place at this table
Denominational niceties over who may preside and who may partake
Are set aside in the name of the one who broke down humanly constructed barriers
Of race and status and gender and more

For everyone who has come, and does come, and will come

To share in this experiment in worship and learning
Where style and content, theological position and tradition
are set aside
In the name of the one whom each of us attempts to follow

For everyone who is curious, questioning, certain,
doubting
Who hears in their heart a word of welcome
An invitation to share in a symbol, or a mystery, or a
sacrament
There is a place at the Table of the Lord

So come, for it is Christ who invites us
Christ who whispers our name
And draws us into the circle of unending love.

Institution

We hear the old familiar words of the apostle Paul, as he
wrote them to the church in Corinth...

For I received from the Lord what I also handed on to you,
that the Lord Jesus on the night when he was betrayed
took a loaf of bread, and when he had given thanks, he
broke it and said, "This is my body that is for you. Do this
in remembrance of me." In the same way he took the cup
also, after supper, saying, "This cup is the new covenant in
my blood. Do this, as often as you drink it, in remembrance
of me." For as often as you eat this bread and drink the
cup, you proclaim the Lord's death until he comes.

Thanksgiving

It seems strange, Lord, this last Lord's Supper in this place
in which we have shared so much.

The symbolism hangs heavy in the air and perhaps we risk expecting too much, risk being disappointed because it is not, or cannot be, what we imagine it might.
So, as we offer our thanks for this bread and for this wine, and for all they mean to us
As we remember other times and other people with whom we have shared
We acknowledge the bitter-sweetness of this moment and offer that to your care

May we who share discover our needs to be met and our souls refreshed for whatever the future may bring.
Bless this bread and wine to our bodies and our lives in your service.
Amen.

Sharing

Acclamation
Your death we commemorate
Your rising we celebrate
Your coming in glory we anticipate
Glory be to you, O Christ.

Hymn

Blessing

We left the building singing, and crossed the road to a neighbouring church for refreshments

Intercessory Prayers for Building Closure (Hugglescote) by Catriona Gorton

Faithful God, who inspired the formation/planting of a congregation here in *[town/village/etc]*, we bring our thanks for what is past...
for the vision and courage of those pioneers who met in *[place]*,
for the faithful witness of those who laboured to establish a meeting house in *[street name]*,
able to serve the village nearby;
for the sacrificial giving of those who built this/these buildings to continue the mission to which they believed you had called them.

We thank you for those whose names are recorded on plaques, in minute books or tombstones – and for those names we will never know – each playing his or her part in the story of your church here...

We thank you too for the many organisations within the church that have provided fellowship and opportunities for service: (if you name present and past organisations, do so carefully so none get missed)...
In a moment of quiet, we bring you thanks for our personal memories...

Holy God, who has remained faithful throughout the story of this church, we bring our regrets and sorrow...

For the opportunities allowed to slip by,
For the times when we have allowed differences of opinion to grow into enmity,
For the decisions that, with hindsight, were neither wise nor helpful...
Forgiving God, we admit that we have not always acted in accordance with your will and on occasion have failed even to

reach our own standards. As we each silently confess to our failings, grant us assurance of your pardon...

Loving God, as our time of meeting in this building nears its close, we bring to you our emotions – some keenly aware of a sense of loss, others strangely calm, some bemused or confused, others with a sense of liberation... As you surround each of us with your love, we ask your help in seeing beyond our own reactions to those of others so that we might support one another not only at this time but also in the weeks and months ahead...

Living God, at this new beginning, as our journey moves from the known into the unknowable, we commend ourselves once more to your service. By your Spirit's indwelling, may we be granted wisdom and discernment in the decisions we make about our future life.

May we be willing to die in order to rise anew, just as Christ died and rose for us. Give us courage to take risks and live sacrificially in your service. Open our eyes, hearts and minds to see and understand the work you have for us to do as we play our part in your mission in this place. May our lives individually and together be totally centred on Christ and committed to the incoming of his Kingdom...

Eternal God, as we have prayed for ourselves, we remember that we are but a small part of your creation. We cannot know or name every situation where your help or healing is needed. In our troubled and disordered world, we simply pray for your peace and justice, so that all people might begin to grasp the amazing truth of your love. We gather our feelings, thoughts and prayers together as we join in the familiar words of Jesus... our Father...

Intercessory Prayers for Building Closure (Hillhead) by Catriona Gorton

God of all times and all places,
We come to you, as we do week by week, with our prayers for others and for each other.
We come to you with a sense that this is, in some senses, a hugely significant moment
And in others it is just another Sunday
We come to you having looked back in grateful remembrance
And forward in hopeful anticipation.
And now we centre ourselves in the moment
In the here and now
Of a disordered and troubled world in which your love, and the hope of Christ, are sorely needed.

We look back and recall how this church has always had a pioneering spirit, moving from the centre to the edges, both literal and metaphorical, planting new congregations, sending missionaries overseas, and serving the poorest and most marginalised people on our doorstep. And so today, as we give thanks, we also call to mind in our prayers some of the organisations and charities we have supported, influenced and served, asking your blessing on those who continue their work [e.g. BUS/BUGB/BMS and local charities]:

We pray for new energy and a renewed sense of purpose as we continue to play our role in providing a distinctive Christian witness in this part of the city. Help us to hold fast to our values, aspiring to be a community that is worshipping, inclusive, missional, prophetic and sacrificial.

Give us courage to name and to speak out against injustice, and the determination to work for change

Show us the timeless truths that we must cherish, passing them on to a new generation, and timebound practices that we must relinquish if we are to move forward.

Inspire us with exciting ideas and daring dreams of what we might yet become as your Spirit works within us.

Amidst the recalling and recording, celebrating and dreaming, we pause, aware that this is a community of real people facing rea challenges in their everyday lives.

We pray for those who grieve the loss of loved ones, remembering especially...
We pray for those who carry a burden of care for those who are ill, infirm or aged, especially those whose lovec ones are far away.
We pray for those whose daily work is arduous, stressful or unrewarding, and also for those who are energised and fulfilled in their chosen careers.
In a moment of stillness, we name in our hearts those precious to us in whatever circumstance, that your love will surround them and your peace fill their hearts...

Lastly, we cannot pray for ourselves and ignore the world around us. So many complex situations, so many bewildering and confusing news reports, so many places and people hurt and hurting, all longing for peace and safety and love... Words fail us; we fear that to name one is to overlook another; to pray for one infers a preference we do not intend; to focus on this is to suggest that that is less important. So, again, we pause, quietly calling to mind the situations that have moved us, asking for your wisdom, grace, mercy and love to transform fear, hate and anger to love, joy and peace.

God of all times, and of all places, accept these prayers, which we offer in the name of Jesus. Amen

Retirement of a Minister: Prayers of Thanksgiving, Confession, and Intercession by Brenda Morton

Thanksgiving and Confession

Minister   We come to this special service with mixed feelings about past and future – feelings of thankfulness and failure, feelings of anticipation and trepidation. Let us bring all these thoughts and feelings to the Lord.

People: *Lord, graciously hear us.*

Minister: Lord God, for all the blessings I have received in this place,
For all the love and hospitality,
For all the grace and forbearance,
For all that I have learnt,
Even for hard lessons that have helped me grow,
I thank You.
For all that I have been able to give,
For all that I have achieved,
For all the friendships made and people helped and healed
Through this church and our ministry together,
I thank You, Lord.

People: *Lord God, for all the blessings we have received during this ministry,*
For the love, patience and pastoral care shown to us,
For the fruits of study and prayer in teaching and preaching,
For new thoughts and a widening of our horizons,
We thank You, Lord
For opportunities taken together as a church and minister

> *To show Your love to the community,*
> *For those we have seen come to faith,*
> *For growth in faith and understanding,*
> *We thank You, Lord.*

Minister: For all I have left undone,
            For hurts I have caused unwittingly,
            For failures of ideas, projects and plans,
            For missed opportunities,
            For all I have failed to achieve through lack of
            inspiration or vision,
            For moments of impatience and lack of grace,
            Father, forgive me

People: *For what we have failed to receive*
            For hurts we have caused unwittingly,
            For missed opportunities and failure to grasp new
            ideas,
            For failures of vision, enthusiasm, or energy,
            For moments of criticism or lack of love,
            Father, forgive us.

Statement of Absolution:

Intercession

Minister: For these people, Lord I pray that they may be united
            in faith and vision as they face a new chapter in this
            church's life.
            Grant an outpouring of Your Spirit to guide and
            overrule as they seek a new Minister, and grant that
            he or she will love and enthuse them as they love
            and support him or her.

People: *For our departing Minister, ...*
              Lord we pray for wisdom and guidance
              as she begins this new phase of her life.
              Pour out your Spirit upon her, and on .... and their
              family,
              And bless them in their life together.
              Help them to find a new spiritual home
              where they will find love and support.
              And guide them into new ways
              in which to use the gifts you have given them.

Minister: Lord God, I pray for this community,
              that this church will shine like a beacon on a dark
              night,
              to draw people to Your light, our Lord and Saviour
              Christ Jesus.
              I leave them with my love and my blessing.
              Please grant them Your blessing

People: *Let our light shine in this place.*
              May our departing Minister's light shine in the place to
              which You have called her.
              We let her go with our blessing.
              Grant her Your blessing.

Minister: Past put behind us, for the future take us,

People   *Lord of the Years, to live for Christ alone! Amen!*

A Release of Covenant at the Conclusion of a Pastorate by Catriona Gorton

Minister:
On [date], before God and in the presence of many witnesses, I declared that I believed in my heart that I had been called by God to serve in pastoral oversight of this church and congregation. I now believe that call has been fulfilled and that God has brought us to a parting of the ways.

People:
On [date], before God and in the presence of many witnesses we declared that we believed you had been called by God to be our Minister. We, too, now believe that call has been fulfilled and that God has brought us to a parting of the ways.

Minister:
At my induction I promised to carry out this ministry with enthusiasm and dedication, to set God's word before people, to lead in the conduct of worship, to work in partnership with deacons, members and attenders, and to encourage you all to carry out Christ's mission in the local community and in the world.

I have done my best to keep my promises.
For the ways in which I have succeeded, I give thanks to God.
For the ways I have failed, I apologise and seek forgiveness.

People:
*For the ways in which you have succeeded in keeping your promises, we give thanks to God.
For the ways you have failed, we accept your apologies and forgive you.*

At your induction we promised to encourage and support you, working together cheerfully and humbly in extending the work of the kingdom of God

We have done our best to keep our promises.
For the ways in which we have succeeded, we give thanks to God.
For the ways we have failed, we apologise and seek forgiveness.

Minister:
For the ways in which you have succeeded in keeping your promises, I give thanks to God.
For the ways you have failed, I accept your apologies and forgive you.

We have declared before God our belief that this ministry is now complete, I ask you therefore to release me from my covenant to you.

People:
We release you to God's safekeeping
May you continue to walk in Christ's footsteps and grow in maturity as his faithful disciple.

We have declared before God our belief that this ministry is now complete, we ask you therefore to release us from our covenant to you.

Minister:
I release you to God's safekeeping
May you continue to walk in Christ's footsteps and grow in maturity as his faithful disciples.

All:
We have declared our belief that this ministry is now complete and have released one another from the covenant that bound us. We now pray God's blessing for one another:
May the Lord bless us and keep us
The Lord make his face to shine upon us and be gracious unto us
The Lord lift up the light of his countenance upon us and give us peace
Now and forevermore. Amen.

Advent, Christmas and Epiphany

Reflections, Meditations and Prayers for Advent, Christmas and Epiphany

Advent Liturgy: Longing and Belonging by Clare McBeath

Originally used in a college setting
NB some theologians use the word kin-dom as a non-patriarchal
alternative to kingdom.

Opening Prayer
Advent God
We come bringing with us
the busyness of the season
the lists of things to do,
things to buy, wrap, make
friends and family to visit.

We come bringing with us
the angst of a world
that is not at peace
wranglings over Brexit,
armed conflicts
reports on climate change.

We come bringing with us
the tiredness of the end of term
assignments still to be written
church services to plan
people to pastor.

Advent God
We come because we long
for a moment of calm

We come because we long
for a deeper relationship with you

We come because we long
to celebrate this end of term with one another

We come because we long
to reflect on the meaning of Christmas

Above all we come bringing our longing
to belong to you
to belong to one another
and to belong to your kin-dom
of peace, justice and joy.

Blessing
God who dwells in the margins and the least likely places
Keep us awake and alert
And bless us with the surprising and the unexpected
Because we long to belong

Jesus, born as one of us, baby small and vulnerable
Help us balance our own needs with the needs of others
And bless us with your gentleness and mercy
Because we long to belong

Holy Spirit, who brings the margins to centre stage
Help us turn the tables on injustice
And bless us with your gift of radical welcome and hospitality
Because we long to belong

Meditations and Reflections

An Angel Came To Mary by Liz Connelly

An angel came to Mary, "Peace" he said,
"The Lord is with you, and you are blessed!"
Mary was troubled, she did not understand,
"Fear not," said the angel, "The Lord is at hand.

Blessed are you among women, the Lord has been gracious to you.
You are His precious servant, and will conceive and bear a Son
Who will be named Jesus, and called Son of the Most High.
He will be King, and His Kingdom will have no end."

"I am the Lord's servant, may it happen to me
As the Lord has commanded, but how can it be
That He should remember me and make me glad?
My heart praises the Lord, men need no more be sad.

Blessed am I among women, the Lord has been gracious to me.
I am His precious servant, and will conceive and bear a Son
Who will be named Jesus, and called Son of the Most High.
He will be King, and His Kingdom will have no end."

God so loved the world that He gave His Son
To save all believers now the victory is won.
It was while we were still sinners that Christ died, says God's word.
So now we're redeemed, we are cleansed by His blood.

Blessed are those who follow, God pours out His love through His Son.
We must all be like servants, and believe in the One
Who is named Jesus, and called Son of the Most High.
He is King, and His Kingdom will have no end.

Liz and Zech by Catriona Gorton

Imagine Liz waiting at home for Zech to get home, wondering how his day has been, and making sure that his tea was ready on the table. Did neighbours come to her door with rumours of what was happening at the Temple? Did she wait anxiously for her beloved Zech, who could so easily have divorced her for her failings as a wife, wondering if he was ill? Did she stand in the doorway scanning the horizon?

Was Zech, when he arrived home, a little more amorous than usual, anxious to play his part in fulfilling the promise? Or was he too bewildered and too befuddled to find a way to communicate to Liz, the woman who had shared the highs and lows of their long lives? Was there a kind of 'chemistry' or 'telepathy' that led them to understand each other without need for words?

And as the days passed, was there renewed intimacy for this couple, mysteriously rejuvenated by hope? Did Liz laugh as Zech tried to explain with hand gestures what he needed to say? Was he able to continue to work at the Temple, or was he forced to endure solitude as well as silence?

How did they feel as Liz woke one day and dashed from the house, compelled to vomit? Did they dare to believe it was beginning, that new life filled her arid womb? A gentle hug befitting the years, or a crazy, if a little stiff, dance? And as the weeks passed, her belly swelled and the first flicks of life confirmed their dreams, did their smiles grow wider, the glow of love shine brighter?

And fear... they were old, their bodies were worn, could Liz successfully carry this precious life to term?

And Zech, unable to speak, unable to say how he felt as he watched and dreamed and dreaded...

Nine months of silence must have worn thin at times. Frustration that feelings and information could not be spoken or acknowledged. The rest from conversation, at first perhaps strange, briefly welcomed, must have been a real nuisance at times. Yet other ways of communication must have emerged... the touch, the glance, the facial expression... did they discover new ways of expressing their love, their fears, their needs?

And then the labour. Young midwives supporting this old woman who had seen so much of life. Neighbours wondering how it would all come out. Hearing Liz scream, did they fear this would destroy her? Watching Zech stand, silent, outside the house, did they ache to see the concern in his eyes? Did they see that despite this there was joy, hope, anticipation?

A baby's shrill cry cut through the air. A smile spread across the wrinkled face of Zech as he rushed in to embrace his beloved Liz. Tired, aching, tears of joy streaming down her wizened face, and a gentle smile that said 'God's promise has been kept.'

Suddenly the air was filled with the sound of a deep chuckle... then a hearty laugh, and the neighbours looked round. The silence was broken and Zech let out a cry of praise! God had remembered after all.

Taking his new son in his arms, Zech welcomed John the Joy-bringer, John the Path-clearer, John the Herald of hope, with a smile and a new kind of silence... awe and wonder. And Liz, exhausted but thrilled, reached out to draw her son to her breast, assured that something new was just beginning. New waiting, new wondering... a silence to be filled.

The First Christmas Eve by Catriona Gorton

What was the first Christmas Eve like, Lord God?
A heavily pregnant girl going into labour in an overcrowded
house in an overflowing town.
A man watching, helpless, as his young wife moaned and
pushed, assisted undoubtedly by the local stool-woman

And all around them life (and death) carrying on just the same as
ever:
Beggars begging
Soldiers soldiering
Bullies bullying...
And, beyond neat alliteration, people starving, weeping,
cheating,
Hoping, waiting, cooking, drinking, cleaning...

Unseen
Almost unheard
A tiny waif slipped into the experienced hands of the midwife
Opened his tiny mouth
Filled his infant lungs
And let out a mighty yell...

And the man wiped sweat from the young girl's brow
And the girl drew the infant to her heavy breast
And you, God, you nestled safe and content in her arms...
Emmanuel, God with us.

Contemplation of a Pregnant Teenager by Sarah Bingham

They say you forget the pain
When the baby is in your arms.
I don't know if it's true –
I'm still waiting.
But even if it is, I know
I won't forget the fear;
What if Joe rejects me?
What if people don't believe me?
What if this child means my end?

And though my fear was unfounded
Even to my ears my story just sounded
Too crazy not to be confounded.
But here I find myself surrounded,
By creatures, with warm hay deep mounded,
And Joe by my side, still astounded.

They say you forget the pain
When the baby is in your arms.
I don't know if it's true –
But I will remember
All this;
The glory of a visiting angel,
The kindness of a stranger,
Joe's love and care,
Hints of heaven in my every-day.

Count Me In by Juliet Lloyd

One … Two… Three…
I'm counting … Four … Five … Six
I'm counting off the days until my baby is due …
Start again…One … Two …
And I'm counting the days…Three… before I leave my home …
…my safe place … Four … my familiarity…
… and the care of my Mother…
… and I can't make the numbers tally.
How will we ever make it work out… alone in a strange city?
I was counting, the day I heard the news – heads of maize at
the edge of the field.
How many to feed us that day, and the rest to put in store.
Numbering the leaves as I peeled them back…
…making each count for my true love's devotion … naming the
days till two would become one. Till the stranger told me I'd
been 'counted worthy' … by Heaven's reckoning … to bear a
son.
Not any son, mind you,
('though, by my figuring, any son was not on the cards!)
…but Heaven's Glory, a tiny child,
"And you shall call his name 'Jesus' – the rescuer'"
… And somehow, I found myself saying, "Count me in."
Of course, I hadn't counted on the sideways glances,
Neighbours who filled in the gaps,
Joined up the dots … added two and two and made five.
"It stands to reason," they said. "It's the way of the world." (Or
assumed worse – this is occupied territory – dangerous
country).
Nor telling my parents (or my bewildered boyfriend) my news… I
hadn't yet put that into the equation.
Dad's reaction was hard to take – rocking backwards and
forwards, Sadly recounting for all the lost purity and innocence
of my childhood

- mine wasn't an easy tale to take in ...
Mum said she couldn't bear to look at me – sent me away:
"Go see your Aunt Elizabeth: we can count on her to know what
to do with you."
And the wise old woman, way past counting days of child-
hoping, knew my words were true:
The babe in her womb bounced in rhythm to the heartbeat of
mine!
And Joseph ... well... finally, hours passing, visions shared would
bring us back in step... ... but the waiting was hard.
So, now I'm counting ...
... counting the days until I step out ... feeling unprepared...
.. on an unknown road to Bethlehem ...to be ... counted
.. together with my husband, Joseph,
... and God's Son, Jesus, who will, of course, be travelling with us
... just as we were told.

21st Century Shepherd by Juliet Lloyd

*[Adult in rough clothing, sits as though sleeping alongside bundles,
implying sleeping children under blankets next to boxes/crates, in low
lighting. Suddenly, sound of angelic singing ('Hallelujah Chorus'?) and
bright light from above (bright spotlight?) appears. She jumps up and
grabs a nearby stick to use as protection for her and children against
unseen assailant.]*

Leave us alone! Clear off! We're not doing any harm here – just
trying to get some kip. You touch these kids and I'll ... *[voice
trails off and she stands gob-smacked, looking around her]*

[Gradually putting stick down, steps back]

Okay, okay, look - we don't want any trouble . .
I'm just looking out for my family ... you took me by surprise ...

I didn't see you come...

[Suddenly aware of how many angels there are, spins around bewildered]

How many of you are there?! How are you doing that? That's amazing!!

[A possible interpretation starts to dawn on her]

Oh, I get it! You're one of those floats for the carnival – that's brilliant! Those lighting effects and the flying bit – it's out of this world! And the choir! Man – you must have been practising for months! And I'm really gutted for you, 'cos you've missed it! Yeah, the carnival parade was at three, and the judging at six – I know, because I took the kids for a ganders. Wish they were awake now – 'cos there wasn't anything a patch on this ... but I daren't wake 'em. They're sleeping now after I blew everything on a Supersize Burger meal, so that they wouldn't notice the cold. But for what it's worth, I'd have given you the prize. Shame that...

[Hugs herself with cold]

Man, it's a cold one...
What do you mean news? For me? But you don't even know me! Nobody does ... we slip under everybody's radar – no reputation to live up to ... no labels to trace us.
Haven't even got my watch anymore - my Dad gave me that before I left home. I had a name then – Dad engraved it on my watch – someone might have had a message for me then but not recently.

[Gives sheepish grin and shrugs regretfully]

It should have been worth more than a burger meal – even a supersize one – but when you've got kids, you take what you can get.

[looks back again … intrigued]

You say it's all going to change? Someone's come who'll change things? And there's a place in town where I'll start to find hope again? Yes, I know that hotel in the centre … but if you think they'll let me and my family in there, you're havin' a laugh! Oh, not in there? In the old warehouse round the corner… are you serious? How will I know … what does the sign say? 'House of Grace'? Maybe … you know, I think I could believe anything tonight …
Just one thing … the people at this place … are they likely to be as loud as you?

The Depressed Donkey by **Ruth Gouldbourne**

Life, don't talk to me about life. Just when you think it can't get any worse – it does. And it doesn't stop there. It goes on getting worse. In my experience, anyway. Take this last couple of days for example. It was bad enough in Nazareth.

That's where I'm from by the way. Rotten place – no life in it all. Not so much a one-horse town as a two-donkey town – and both of us depressed. Gloomy and dull, that's the best you can say about it. Not exactly on the tourist track of course.

Nothing of any importance there of course. Why should people come and look at us. Not as if there's anything special to see. Just ordinary people doing ordinary dull jobs – and a very bored donkey, doing a very dull job. Not wildly exciting being a donkey in the hill country. Nowhere to go except up and down –

or sometimes down and up if you fancy a change. But that's the way it is.

Can't change it — must just endure it. Not getting you down, am I? Oh good!

I was going to tell you why I was depressed, wasn't I. As if living in Nazareth wasn't enough? Normally it is, but just to make sure, I had to live through the last two days. It started with a notice from the Emperor. Always bad news, in my experience, when something comes from the government. Usually means life's going to get tougher.

This one came — must have been a week ago. Just like that, no warning, no gentle breaking of the news. Just — go to the family home and get registered. OK for donkeys, you might think. Doesn't apply to them. Well, that's as maybe, but we still get involved.

Nobody asks our opinion. Nobody offers us an incentive. All I got was the master coming into my stable — not much to write home about in itself, if I could write, which I can't but you never know — anyway, in he came and announced, calm as you like, that I was going on a trip to Bethlehem. And you can be sure it wasn't for the good of MY health. No. For hers, more like.

Nine months gone, she is, and off to Bethlehem because the government says so. Typical of course. No thought of checking if their census — whatever that is — is at a convenient time for folk. Oh no — just off you go and get registered. And if she's to get there, who's to take her. Who do you think. And me with a bad back too. Hardly fit to carry myself let alone a pregnant woman. An unmarried pregnant woman too. I'm not one to gossip, but — well....

Anyway, I like her, and I did want to make the journey as smooth as I could, but it's not easy. Actually, that's an understatement. It was blooming difficult. The government may be requiring the census, but they aren't doing much for the roads. I suppose, to be fair, we weren't mugged or pushed off the hillside. We didn't even fall into any potholes. But smooth – no! And slow! I guess it would be fair to say I'm not the fastest beast on four legs, but the roads were so busy. I couldn't have gone any faster than a moderate walking pace even if I had wanted to. Which I didn't, but it's nice to have the option.

So we plodded on – and on – and on – and on. She walked a bit of the way, but it was clear she couldn't go far, so I carried her most of the time. Her and the packs. Actually, he carried the packs quite a lot, but I still had to carry them some of the time. What with the crowds and her condition, and the packs – well, we didn't get as far as we would have wanted last night, so we stopped over night at one of his cousins' places.

It was OK, I suppose. They weren't a very friendly lot, though. I tried talking to some of them, but they didn't seem to want to. Some folk are just plain unfriendly I suppose. All I tried to do was tell them about Nazareth and about the journey, but they kept on about some party that they'd been to, and the interesting people they'd seen. And one of them seemed to want to make people smile. Daft idea, if you ask me. I'm not depressing you, am I? O good.

Anyway, we set off again this morning, and the crowds were just as bad, and she wasn't too good. Near her time, I shouldn't wonder. Makes sense, doesn't it. Live all your life in a little town where you know everybody, everything's to hand and you've got your own home, and of course you're in a strange town without family or a roof over your head when your first child is about to be born. That's life, isn't it!

He's done the best he could though.

We got here late afternoon, and he hunted everywhere for somewhere to stay. Too late most places of course. Well, what else would you expect. Thinking ahead seems beyond them, If they'd consulted me – which they wouldn't and why should they, but you never know – I could have told them. There's never enough beds, and you've just got to make your mind up to it.

Mind you, he did find us somewhere. I suppose. A stable it is. Bit crowded too – all these extra beasts come in like us for the census. I suppose it keeps it cosy – but it's a bit smelly too. And I really don't like the look of her. That baby's on the way alright. Well, I suppose getting born here is a good introduction to the rest of what the world is.

Give them the facts right away, I always say. No good hiding things. Might as well see life for what it is. Life! Don't talk to me about life.

Oh – there's the cry – I knew the baby was coming. Poor thing.

The Haughty Camel by Ruth Gouldbourne

Join up and see the world, they said. Sign on and travel to far away and exotic places. Be the envy of your friends and family. Well, they were right about travelling long distances. But I'm not sure anybody is going to be jealous of a trip to a fly-ridden, overcrowded, hillside – town is too big a word, place will have to do. Especially when they see the accommodation. Not big enough to swing a....well, to swing anything really. And as if it's not cramped enough already, it turns out we've got to share it with humans. I ask you! And not even decent ones – this lot are young, and definitely not of the top drawer variety, and there's even a — a baby! Well, it's just not right, is it, a baby in a stable. It's not that I'm prejudiced, you know. But some people should keep to their proper place. And babies, well, babies — we all know what babies do. They make a noise, and a smell — and — other things. And I'm expected to share a stall with it — him, whatever.

Well, I suppose it's all part of life's rich tapestry, but it's definitely not what I expected when I took the contract, and I will be making that quite clear when I get home, I can tell you.

Now the other night, that was quite different. Not perfect, but definitely better. Well, you can't expect perfect this far from home, but we did have stalls, and water, and proper company; people who knew how to treat us. It's not for myself that I am bothered you understand. But my rider — he's an important man, top of his profession, and very well respected by his peers. And I don't like to see him behaving like he has here. It all seems a bit — well, a bit demeaning, really. We set out with such high hopes you see. There's a group of us. Apparently they've all been working together on studying the stars. I did tell you they were high-powered, didn't I? Anyway, what they had learnt was that there was to be a new king. So, they wanted to go and pay homage — well, you would, wouldn't you. So they got together proper gifts, and then looked for appropriate transport. That's where I come in. Quite the best I am, though I shouldn't say so myself. But why deny the truth. I can travel for miles on a single fill-up, I know how to behave in the best company, and I am well aware of the dignity of my rider, and well able to enforce respect for myself — I mean him!

So we set off. It was a long journey, but there was this star... it kept going ahead of us. It was quite impressive really. I don't suppose you will have had much chance to see such a thing.

It is only people who have studied at the best universities who know how to interpret such signs, and I don't suppose....no, I thought not. Anyway, stop me if you don't understand, but there was this star, and it seemed to keep moving, and we followed it. Very technical stuff, as I'm sure you can see, but fortunately I have enough experience and expertise to know how to cope with such things. In due course, as was to be expected, it stopped over a palace. Admittedly, it was a palace in Jerusalem, which I must confess was not the place I had expected to come. I mean, it's not exactly the centre of the world, is it — not one of the big powers. But, that was where we arrived, and as I say, at least they knew how to treat us there. Nice stall, good food, and the company was alright, given the restrictions of a provincial region.

But did we stay there — no! Couple of days later, and we're off again. Heading down some dusty track, to some fly-blown place that nobody's ever heard of. Well, I guess that's not strictly true, because there was some word of a prophecy, but not one I'd ever heard of. Anyway, that's how we came here — Bethlehem I think it's called. And not content with coming to this godforsaken place, we end up in an outhouse of a cheap inn, and it's full of people! And animals! It can't get much worse. At least, I thought it couldn't. But once we got here, the whole pack of them; these eminent men, who should have some regard for my dignity if not their own, down they get, and off with the packs and out come the treasures, and they're on their knees and offering them to this slip of a girl and her shiftless looking husband — if they're married, and I wouldn't be too sure of that — for this baby, which they say is a king.

Can't see it myself, I must say. Doesn't make sense, if you know what I mean. But then, who's going to ask me. I'm just a camel.

The House-proud Cow by Ruth Gouldbourne

Well now, I'm not one to gossip – but you should see the goings on here this evening. Last year's soldiers' winter festival had nothing on it. They just got noisy and sang in the streets; they didn't come into our home. I don't know what to make of it really. I mean – whatever happens out there, usually we're left in peace. You kind of expect it really, don't you? To be left in peace and quiet in your own home.

It's not as if the home is much really – it's a bit cramped, and it does have to be said that some of the others are a bit untidy, so it's not always showcase perfect. But it's ours, and we like it the way it is; it's warm and cosy, and it's got everything we need.

During the day now, I don't mind folk coming in then. They've got to, really. I can't go hauling my milk up to the big house easily, can I? So they need to come here and get it. But that's expected. I know when it's going to happen, and I can get things a bit tidied up and sorted. It's being taken unexpected that flusters me. I mean, what will people think if they just see the place when we haven't got it fixed up, and when we're all settled down for the night. We're used to it. We know that we're not – well, slobs, I suppose. But it might look like that to somebody coming in. I mean – there's not a lot of room, and when we're all in here for the night, it does get untidy. But I keep it clean; you could eat your dinner off the floor if you wanted to. Actually, we usually do. And the foodstall is never stale. With my lot around, no food lasts long enough to get stale! And when I can get near enough, I usually give the windows a bit of a lick, just to keep them clean. But by the end of the day, well, when we're all in here, it's a bit of a crush, and I don't usually bother. We expect the people in the big house to leave us in peace until the morning, and I'll tidy up ready for then, once everybody's up and out the way.

But today's just been mad. The streets were full of people all day, and there was constant coming and going at the big house – I think they were getting a bit frazzled up there too; they seemed to be constantly running out of milk, so I was constantly having to find some more, so I didn't really have time to get things sorted as I usually do. And then there was so much to see – I must admit I spent more time looking out into the street than I usually do – people coming and going from all over the place; all sorts of clothes too. You should have seen them – all colours and styles; some of them a bit – modern – too. Well, I suppose what else can you expect with folk coming from all over the place. Fair stirred up our little town. But it got quieter towards evening, and I was really quite pleased when the door was closed, and we could all settle down. Ok, so I was a bit lax in the clearing up, but I thought it wouldn't matter. After all, there's always tomorrow, and nobody ever comes to see us after the door is closed – at least, they don't usually.

But of course, the one day I don't tidy up, there's a knock at the door – well, less a knock truth to tell, more a pushing in as if they owned the place, by the folk at the big house. Actually, I suppose they do own the place, but that's beside the point. It's our home.

Anyway, in they come, bold as you like, and me trying to sort out the piles of bedding and push some of the food back into the stall and sweep the floor and lick the window all at the same time. But they didn't seem to notice. Just as well really! The man from the big house had two new folk with him – I didn't know them at least. I was so ashamed; bad enough people I know seeing the state the place had go into, but strangers!

Mind you, I don't think they were in any condition to notice; he was trying to be big and brave, but he's just a lad and tired out.

And as for her – well, I don't know what they were thinking of bringing her away from her own home in her condition. Nine months if she's a day, and fit to drop. In here, says the big man – it's not much – not much; it's my home! Anyway; it's not much, he says, but I can let you stay here

Never asked us mind you. But – well, what can you do. They clearly needed it, so we shuffled up, and left them some space – and off he went, the big man, muttering about needing to get things sorted out at the big house. Closed the door and left us all to get on with it.

Well! I wasn't wrong – nine months and then some, and it was obvious what was going to happen. She needed a bit of privacy, poor dear, so I stood near her, kept her shielded as best I could, and after it was all over, my youngest nudged the foodstall over so they could lay the baby there. It wasn't too bad, because we'd all given it a bit of a scrub out early in the day; chasing the last of the grain to tell you the truth. He – the young lad – piled together some of our straw bedding to line it, and they laid the wee one in. Left us a bit short of anywhere to sleep, but you couldn't really grudge them.

I thought it might quieten down a bit after that – and tomorrow I could tidy up, before I got more embarrassed.

But no! Bad enough we have people in here when it's a mess; but just half an hour ago, all this light floods in. Now all my shortcomings as a housekeeper are all too clear – no place to hide the mess. Light in every corner and everything up there to be seen. And as if that's not enough, the music – drawing attention from everywhere to our little home. I was awkward enough that all the mess was on view, but why call everybody to look at it.

Admittedly, nobody seemed that interested in the lack of a tidy floor. There were people turned up, certainly. But they wanted to see the baby, not my messy floor or dirty windows. And it was nice. They came to see the little one, and made quite a fuss of him and the parents. Presents and songs and celebrations and so on. Nice. Peaceful too, in an odd way, even with all the light and music. And nobody seemed to mind too much that it wasn't – well, as tidy as I would have liked. In fact, well, looking at that baby, strange as it sounds, I almost forgot just how untidy it was, just how dirty the floor was. I know it probably sounds a bit soft, but it didn't seem to matter quite so much – as if, well, almost as if my keeping the floor clean wasn't the most important thing in the world for a bit.

I liked that. I liked that we could think about something else, and make the little one feel safe, and care for his mum and dad. I dare say I'll go back to worrying about the floor – but maybe not quite so much.

The Sheep's Story by Ruth Gouldbourne

You know, they say of us sheep that we are silly creatures – a bit lacking in the brain department. You needn't look so innocent – I know what's said, and mostly it's true. But not always. We're not quite as daft as we're painted. In fact – and promise you won't tell, because this is very secret, but in fact, we're really quite intelligent if we put our minds to it. It suits us to appear stupid, you see – that way, nobody expects us to take responsibility. Well, who would ask a sheep to do anything which demanded concentration? So, we get left to do what we want, and enjoy ourselves without any hard work. You should try it sometime – oh! I see some of you do.....

Well, you'll know what I mean, then.

Anyway, they say we're daft, but we've got enough nous to know when things are not all they should be; when the shepherds have had a bit too much to drink like, or when one of them is pining for his lady-love, and would be rather be at home than up on the hills watching us eat. It's quite good, those days, actually – we can wander off as far as we like, and search out the really tasty places, while he's sitting mooning over her at home. Find some nice treats that way, we do. Where was I? O yes, - we know what's going on most of the time. So, I could tell something strange was going on tonight. I can't quite be sure what it was that gave me the clue – it might have been the singing choirs of the heavenly host, though you'd be surprised how often that happens and the shepherds don't see it. Out there in the hills at night, when it's all quiet, and the world has gone to sleep. You wouldn't imagine how often me and the boys catch a few of the angels out having a sing. It's as if they can't keep quiet, and want to share their praises. But on the whole, they don't appear when people can see them – either that, or the people are too busy to pay attention. Me and the others, we see them often enough not to be too surprised, though it's a treat right enough, and we make the most of it. But it wasn't that, although they did seem in particularly good voice earlier on this evening, and there did seem to be more of them than usual.

But it was something else. They seemed more - purposeful than they often are. I guess you haven't seen the angelic choir too often, have you – no, I can see that. Well, the thing is, usually, they seem just to sing and play for the fun of it – well, that's not quite right, but for the sheer joy of it might be better. You know what I mean; praise for the sake of praise. But tonight – well, they seemed to be anxious to communicate something. AND, the shepherds saw and heard them. That definitely was unusual; unusual for the shepherds too. They were terrified – fell on their faces and thought they were going to die and everything. Quite funny, really. They're supposed to be there to protect us, and there they were scared out of their socks, and we were quite calm. Well, we'd seen it before, and it's awe-inspiring alright, but – well, safe's not the right word, but at least we've learnt we'll survive it. They clearly didn't think they would – and as for thinking about us, they didn't seem to have time to do that at all. Anyway, all we heard was the wonderful music.

It really is wonderful you know. If you ever get the chance to hear the angelic choir, take it – it's something you will never forget. I can't really describe it – sheep aren't that good at music – but it sounds like the freshest grass, the clearest water, the gentlest sunshine and the brightest star- or something like that. Oh I can't describe it – you'll have to listen for yourselves. In fact, if you listen had enough, you might just catch an echo – they seem to be keeping it up a long time tonight... can you hear it?

No? Pity – it really is wonderful. Where was I?

O yes, what was different – well, the shepherds listened to all this, once they'd got off their faces, and then they had a confab. Seems like they had heard something very important. Unfortunately, I had found a tasty patch of sorrel, and was just too far away to hear what was said. But blow me, it must have been vital, because after their discussion, they all just up and left. Just like that. Never seen that happen before – usually, if one of the has to go back to town for something – or someone – there's at least one of them left here to keep us company. But not tonight! Off they all went, and here we are all alone. Not that I'm scared, or anything. Not really. Not scared, exactly. More – more jealous I guess. I mean, there's clearly something important happening, and as always, the sheep are being left out. Not wanted except for our wool.

In fact, the more I think about it, the more I think about it, the more I think this isn't right. After all, we heard the angels too – in fact, we hear them more often. And the bit I did catch was about a stable. We know stables – some of my best friends live in stables. Why should they be going to this party or whatever it is in the stable, and not us. No – I don't think I approve of that, and I don't think I'm going to stand for it.

Oy, you lot – come on – we're off. If they can go and see whatever it is in this stable, we can too. Coming?

Questions by **Brenda Morton**

A reflection on the Slaughter of the Innocents, inspired by the hymn "Your child's coming was my child's going, Mary" by Ian Fraser © Stainer and Bell 1994

Your child's coming was my child's going, Mary.

Instead of the sweet smell of baby powder, the giggles of joy
The town is bathed with the smell of **myrrh**, the stench of death,
anointing our infants for burial, and silence. Oh the silence!
Broken only by the sound of bitter wailing:
The wailing of dozens of mothers whose future hope has been
cruelly, brutally, snatched away.
I know its not your fault, and I'm glad you got away and he survived;
but it doesn't lesson my grief – or the grief of all the mothers of Bethlehem.
Why did you have to bring death to our town?
Rivers of blood, the agony of breasts that bear milk that is not drunk.
Fathers who can do nothing to ease the anguish of their wives,
Older children and grandparents who don't understand,
whole families traumatised. For what, I want to know?

Your child's living was my child's dying, Mary.

There are rumours that you were visited by star-gazers from the east, who brought rich gifts – but stupidly told Herod their business. Why, oh why, did they have to mention a king? Wise men, some call them. Hah! If they were wise they would know better than to speak of Kingship to a megalomaniac.
(Wise women would have known to keep their heads down.)
Would they had never made it to Judea.
Would they had perished in the desert, before bringing their thoughtless words to Herod's ears.
I hope their gifts were worth it. I expect the **gold** was useful to a family of refugees.
What will he be, your son, Mary? Is he a future King? Will he bring hope to our nation?

Your child's saving was my child's destroying, Mary.

We looked for a king, born of David's line to bring salvation to Israel, to throw off the yoke of the oppressor, to set us free.
Maybe your son is special – after all, it is a miracle he survived – maybe God's hand is on him.
How did you know to run? Why didn't you warn the rest of us mothers?
How will you survive in Egypt?
Will he grow up to save others, your son? I do hope so. I hope our sacrifice, our pain, will be worth it in the long run.
Take care of him, Mary, cherish him as we cannot cherish our little ones.
When you burn your **frankincense**, say a prayer for us, for our town.
One day, when he's grown, and made something of himself, will you come back and tell us?

Voices

Joseph's Mother (Matthew 1 :18-25) by Jeannie Kendall

They always say
The mother-son bond is special.
I don't know
I've loved every one of my children
Boys and girls
It felt no different.

But yes, I wanted my sons to marry well
And most did –
I'd best leave Matthan out of it -
Joseph I thought
Would be the easiest to sort
Having always
such quiet thoughtfulness
I thought no woman could resist.

We arranged a good one.
Lovely girl
Or so I thought.
The plans were well advanced
And I was looking forward to the day
And then the news.
I still feel ill to think of it.
I thought I was
Such a good judge of character.
I got that one wrong.

Well, I told him –
"Rid yourself my boy –
We'll look again"

And that was what
He was all set to do.
And then one day
He comes with some ridiculous tale
A dream from God.
He must think
 I am a fool.

"Oh really"
I said.
"You'll be telling me next
 it's God's fault
the shame
that's on our family."
He went very quiet at that.

I'm having none of it.
If he wants to keep to it
There's nothing I can do
Mothers can't interfere
But if he thinks
I'll celebrate
He's very mistaken.
God knows
Where this will lead us.

Mary's mother by Jeannie Kendall

It was not meant to be like this.
I had made her such a good match:
Looked forward to a better life for her
And, in time, grandchildren on my knee.
In time, not now.
Not now, with no wedding band
To give her status and security
Not now, with whispers as she enters
The room – or I do, come to that –
Not now, dragging her swollen belly
(Young perfection a memory
Beneath the stretch marks)
Far away from me
To give birth with his family
And not her own.
"Not now, not now",
I wept through many sleepless nights.
But now it is.
And I *will* love her child –
How can I not love a fragile life
Who did not choose the circumstance?
And I *will* love her child
And choose again – as parents do –
To hold her pain, and mine, in silence.

The female relative (Luke 2:1-7) by Jeannie Kendall

You see it all in families.
Hospitality means
You turn the odd blind eye
And smile at guests
No matter what.
It was crazy at census time.
Everyone wanting to stay
And we'd run out of any space
When Joseph and his wife turned up.

I felt bad, I really did.
But there was simply nowhere left.
And some were asleep
And others elderly.
What could I do?
Best to put them
In the corner
Where we kept our animals.
Warm at least.

I never expected her
To give birth that soon –
Not that you
Can ever tell.
But best then to stay
Not that she could have moved.

She had a hard time of it.
First time often is, of course,
But this one, well,
More like a cosmic struggle
Than a birth.

I prayed
More than I have in a while
I can tell you.
Well – family is family
Even if distant.
I didn't want the two of them
Dying under my roof.

But live they did
Much to my relief.
And I thought at last
I could look forward
To some quiet.
Quiet...
It had barely started.

The woman with Mary at Jesus' birth by Jeannie Kendall

You have a long time
To talk during a labour.
It was not how I intended
To spend that night.
A busy day with guests
Lent itself more to sleep
Than to an anxious wait
With a first-time mother.

She had seemed so very ordinary.
I'd barely glanced, except a moment's empathy,
Such a young girl, and a long journey
Far from her own people;
Husband attentive, yet with a sense of distance;

I guessed inevitable
When all that she could feel
Were the demands of her body
And the urgency of the child
Fighting to be born.

But in the end I had to help.
They were exhausted
And childbirth is always risky.
And so, seeking to distract her,
Between her waves of all-absorbing pain
I asked her for her story:
Another kind of intimacy.

At first I smiled:
Thinking the pain
Had made her fanciful
But then I saw
The quiet passion in her eyes.
And I began to wonder:
Could God – and hope - indeed be born
Among the mess and muddle of our lives?
And as one last gasp brought forth her son
I realised at last
That everything had changed
And nothing, and no-one,
Could ever be ordinary again

The shepherd's wife (Luke 2:8-20) by Jeannie Kendall

I always hated the night shift.
He would come back worn out
And less than happy
Wanting warm broth,
A warm bed, and my warm body,
Oblivious that I had been up all night
With a sickly child or a teething baby.

But this night was different.
He came back
As though the very stars
Were reflected in his eyes,
And simply sat for a long time
Saying nothing.
And somehow I knew
That our lives had changed for ever,
But had no idea how.

Wife of one of the Magi (Matthew 2:1-12) by Jeannie Kendall

I have no appetite
For politics or religion.
The first the refuge
Of the power hungry
The second for the desperate.

I married him
Because I loved him.
The rest just came with it
Like an unwelcome guest
Who would not leave
And must be tolerated.

He never talked
About his work
Which suited me fine
I knew my place
The kitchen and bedroom
My domain
But not the altar.

And then he left
On some foolish quest
And my simmering resentment
Burst into energising flame
Planning with every day
Of absence
All that I would say
On his return.
A thousand conversations
In my head

In the waking hours
Of the night.

And then he came home.
And all of them
Were silenced.

Herod's wife (Matthew 2:16-18) by Jeannie Kendall

At first I thought
That it was me:
When I saw
The unfocused eyes
That signalled
Fury beyond words.
I waited for the blows.

But this time
It was not me.
This time his rage
Was even more inexplicable:
Reduced as he was
To incandescent rage
By a tiny child.
A child!

And, as I watched,
I saw the weakness
Masquerading as his power.
And felt the fear
That someone else
Would pay the cost
This time.

Poems

Who would have thought? by Sarah Bingham

Who would have thought
That good news could come to us?
Lost in the sea of fields
Cut off from family, home, faith,
Doing a job no one wants.
Yet meeting angels and being sent
To greet that good news in a baby...

Who would have thought
That good news could come to us?
Lost in the sea of tents
Cut off from family, home, faith,
Scared people no one wants.
Yet meeting angels who've been sent
To love us in the name of that baby.

Who would have thought
That good news could come to us?
Lost in the sea...
Cut off...
No one...
Yet meeting angels...?
Loved by the baby full grown...

A strange kind of gift by Hannah Montgomery

A strange kind of gift
This Christmastime child
No tinsel adorns him
No glitter or gold
His sweet milky lips
And ten tiny toes
Are wrapped in coarse cloth
To keep out the cold.

A strange kind of gift
To give to the world
An unlikely hero
To heal and to hold –
Out to us all the mercy of heaven
As God with real skin on
Bears burdens of old.

A strange kind of gift
To even receive
An upside down kingdom
Unknown yet foretold
Promised by prophets
In poem and verse
Watching and wiling
The universe whole

A strange kind of gift
I give in return
As angels adore him
And Kings lay their gold
Christ! My hands are empty
My worship so small

But what I can give
I give heart, mind and soul.

Prayers and Blessings

Christmas Tree Blessing by Carolyn Urwin

God of love,
who came to live among us
through the birth of Jesus Christ,
the Saviour of the world,
in Bethlehem that first Christmas,
we praise you for your creation of light and life,
seen especially in this splendid tree
and for its reminder to us
of the wonder of your Christmas story.

May the brightness of its lights, shining in the darkness,
guide us to Jesus, the Light of the World;
may the greenness of its branches, and their life through the
winter,
speak to us of the eternal life that he promises to all who love
him;
and may the conversations that take place around it, and the
pleasure they bring,
point us to the love and joy that you give us through the gift of
your Son.

May everyone who sees this tree this Christmas-time
be blessed with the light of your presence shining into their
hearts,
and be filled with the love and hope that Jesus' coming brings.
Amen

Illustration by Jane Henderson

Lent, Holy Week and Easter

Reflections, Meditations and Prayers for Lent, Holy Week and Easter

Meditations and Reflections

Reading Palms on Palm Sunday by Sarah Bingham

Were I to read your palms today,
Today as the crowd waved them,
Celebrating you and the Almighty,
Were I to read them today
As you rode on a mighty donkey,
And the stones silently clamoured to praise,
Were I to read them today
As the leaders in vain called 'silence',
And you wept over the city,
Were I to read them today,
I would say that glory awaited
And the crowd would lead you to it.

Were I to read your palms on Thursday,
Thursday as you stripped garments off,
Took a bowl and towel to wash feet,
Were I to read them Thursday,
As you blessed and broke bread,
As you thanked and poured wine,
Were I to read them Thursday,
As you sweated blood in the garden,
And your friends slumbered on unawares,
Were I to read them Thursday,
I would say that betrayal awaited
And the crowd would bow down to it.

Were I to read your palms on Friday,
Friday after interminable questions,
beatings and being a whipping boy,
Were I to read them Friday,
As you were hauled from court to court,
As you stumbled weighed down with wood,
Were I to read them Friday,
As one brave woman dared the crowd,
Before you were pierced by nails,
Were I to read them Friday,
I would say that death awaited
And the crowd had left you to it.

Were I to read your palms on Sunday,
Sunday in the dawning light,
As Mary sought your body in vain,
Were I to read them Sunday
As death relinquished its grip,
And the Spirit soared anew,
Were I to read them Sunday,
With the stone rolled back,
And angels sat with good news,
Were I to read them Sunday,
I would say that the world awaited
And the crowd...

And So the Time has Come (Maundy Thursday) by Vikki Bunce

And so the time has come
When once again we stop and think
How did those disciples feel
As they came to eat and drink.

And so the time has come
When each of us can share
In the bread and cup that shows
Of just how much God cares.

And so the time has come
When we pause to stop and pray
And think about our actions
Of our past and present day.

And so the time has come
When we share like them before
In the meal that opens up for us
The gift of heaven's door.

And so the time has come
As we think about His face
And gaze upon His agony
Remember His loving grace.

And so the time has finally come
To thank Him once again
As Christ has made us clean and whole
As He's washed away our stain
Of sin and guilt and misery
To bring us hope once more
And so the time has finally come
To remember what He has done.

How did Jesus Feel? by Catriona Gorton

So how *did* Jesus feel?
Was his stomach churning as he climbed the stairs?
Did he taste the lamb prepared for his meal, or might he as well
have chewed a piece of leather?
Did his voice quiver, even ever so slightly, as he spoke words
he'd spoken many times before?
Did his hand shake, if imperceptibly, as he tore the bread?
Did the wine slop in the cup as he gave an involuntary shiver?
Did the words of the psalm pierce his heart as they foretold his
pain?
How *did* Jesus feel?

Come, Eat My Supper by Sally Fox

Come, eat my supper, eat with me,
Come, eat the lamb and bread with me.
Come, taste the lamb and sauce and wine, the taste of bitter
herbs - the sign of sacrifice.
I am the lamb, the lamb of God. I give you bread - I give you
wine.
Come, sing a song, come sing with me, come, raise your voice
along with me. Come, sing a Psalm, a sacred song, a sacred
song come sing with me. Come, sing a song of ancient praise,
a song of sadness, sing with me. Come, blend your voice with
mine and sing, with ancient words, a song with me.
Please come apart and pray with me. Come share my anguish
- stay with me. Stay close by and comfort me. This time is hard -
keep watch with me.
> *I cannot come Lord, I am not strong enough to stay with
> you,*
> *To keep awake and pray with you.*
> *I am too weak to watch with you.*

I cannot bear the whips that cut,
The jeers, abuse, the nails that pierce.
It's all too much - too hard for me.
I cannot stay to watch your pain.
I cannot bear to see the cross that takes your life and
leaves you Dead.
The only way I can look on these things is through the mist
of time; time of a long two thousand years.
The only way I can look at your cross is if it has been
planed and polished and set in a church surrounded by
flowers and candles.
The only way I can bear Easter is if it is set in Spring,
surrounded by soft sunshine and daffodils.
I'll eat a bun and a chocolate egg,
But please don't ask too much of me.

Peter's Story – I was there in the courtyard by Sarah Bingham

The first of four monologues for Good Friday

I was ashamed, in the garden; ashamed that my reaction was violence, when Jesus always taught peace. Ashamed, too, that as they moved in for the arrest, I fled with the others, fear overcoming all the fine words I'd said about staying faithful and even facing death with him. When things had quietened down a bit, and the temple guards had surrounded Jesus and moved off, I saw John trailing along behind. How could that lad have more courage than me? So, I caught him up, not thinking where we might go.

It soon became plain – we were heading to the house of Caiaphas, a fine house suited to the Chief Priest. John with his connections wangled his way in, but I was barred from entering;

no one in the city wants some rough northerner lowering the tone. Outside in the cold I wondered all sorts of things. I wondered why they had brought him here, when overnight they could do nothing. I wondered what on earth was going on in the courtyard, in the house. I wondered what Jesus was saying, doing. Was he defending himself? Was he still talking about peace and love? I wondered if there was any point hanging around, or whether it would be better to go and find the others. I'd almost made up my mind to leave; there was nothing I could do there.

Somehow, though, John persuaded the servants to let me in, his influence must have been far greater than I'd thought or imagined. Whether they were inquisitive to know who I was, or whether it was just natural wariness, I'll never know, but the servants must have been keeping an eye on me. Of course, John and I were talking – I was anxious to know what was going on. They must have overheard, because one of the serving lasses came over. "You're one of them, aren't you? One of the men who came here with that Jesus. Your voice gives you away."

I've always been proud of my accent. We're a tough lot, us northerners from Galilee. In the years wandering with Jesus, I've never changed my voice to fit in better, never tried to act more educated than I actually am. But in that moment I cursed my give away accent. John had said the guards had been handling Jesus roughly – punches and kicks once they were hidden from public view. It didn't bode well for him and it didn't bode well for me. As usual, I opened my mouth and spoke before really thinking of anything but the moment. "No, you're mistaken, I don't know the man."

Even as I said it I wanted to take it back, wanted to say, "Yes, he's my friend, he's the messiah we're waiting for, he's the holy one sent from God." Instead, I turned my face away and bundled John to another corner of the courtyard. Tears were forming, and if I'd been ashamed in the garden, that was as nothing compared to the shame I felt then. Moments later, the guards were dragging Jesus across the courtyard to another room. As he went, he scanned the crowd, looking for support or perhaps to see who else was there. And I knew he must have heard what I said, for as he caught my eye, a look of such pity and love filled his eyes that I couldn't bear to look, and turned away. If my eyes had been moist before, now I couldn't stop the tears from streaming down my face. What do you say, what do you do, when you've betrayed the best man you've ever known?

Soldier's Story – I was there on the road by Sarah Bingham

The second of four monologues for Good Friday

Well of course as a soldier, you have to follow orders and sometimes those officers ask you to do some pretty odd things. I remember, one time, I was in Britannia and my officer wanted me to go and bathe in some swamp to see if it really was a healing spring... oh, you're only interested in the gory bits? It's strange. No one ever wants to know about road building or water supplies or... alright, alright.

Sometimes, things can be a bit odd, even when you're just carrying out your regular gory duty. In my time I've crucified any number of criminals, but there was one bloke, well, I'll always remember him. His eyes, mainly, and his words. His wasn't like any of the other crucifixions I ever did, not even of the men he was crucified with. For a start, his charge sheet said he was a king, and that sort usually gets their heads cut off. Well, I suppose the charge sheet wasn't really the start.

The start was one morning, literally as the sun was rising, when we heard a commotion at the gates of the Governor's compound. Normally we couldn't get the Jewish authorities anywhere near the place – they claimed it defiled them even to go in, but that day they were determined. Along with the high ups and hobnobs were some of their temple guards – not one of them would have cut it in our army – yes, all right, I'm getting to the gory bit. Anyway, in the middle of them was some poor sod who'd obviously had an argument with a wall, if you know what I mean. I assumed he was some murderer or zealot they wanted executed. Good bit of control, taking away their rights to execute crims and force them to leave it to us.

So, we checked for weapons, 'cause it could have been a plot, then let the Chief Priest and his cronies in, along with the prisoner. God alone knows what they said to Pilate, they were in there for hours arguing, but eventually, the prisoner gets sent out to us to deal with. Apparently, he was the king of the Jews. Well, we all thought that was some bloke called Herod, but anyway, we were commanded to whip him. There's plenty of gore for you – stripped him almost to the kidneys we did. Then, just for a bit of a laugh, we dressed him up in a robe and some wit wove a circlet of thorny twigs – oh, you should have heard him swear as he made it. Anyway, we jammed this on the bloke's head. Before we could do much more though, Pilate sent for him to be shown to the crowd.

That was odd. They were shrieking away and chose to save some terrorist from the rebellion, but bellowed for this bloke to be crucified. We were about the same age, and he didn't look much like the trouble maker they were calling him out to be. Now, this was really odd, never saw this before or after, the Governor got a bowl of water and washed his hands of it. But it was still him who ordered us to march the crim away and crucify him. Poor sod, we'd made such mincemeat of his back he could hardly carry the crossbar.

And when we got there, with a bit of help from a man plucked from the crowd, this one wasn't like the other two, who were still swearing their innocence or vengeance or whatnot. No, this one was having calm conversation, even as we nailed him up. "Father forgive them", he said, "they don't know what they're doing." I thought, "Well you've got that wrong we know exactly what we're doing." But it seemed to me he was more at peace than we were, and there seemed to be real love in the things he said as they were hanging there. He told one of the crims they'd be in paradise together. And then he told someone in the crowd to be a son to his mother. I mean it was just odd. And I wondered about that charge sheet, what did it mean, 'king of the Jews'? And then the sky went dark. Yes, it was all very odd.

Mary's story – I was there at the cross by Sarah Bingham

The third of four monologues for Good Friday

It's odd how some words can haunt you for years, isn't it? How they can sit in your heart and shape your meditations and reactions. How they can sit in your mind and colour your interpretation of every event and comment that follows. When I was not much more than a girl, my love for God and devotion to my faith led to something miraculous. I had a son, a son created within me by the power of God alone, with no man intervening.

And when my Joe and I took him to the Temple, to be presented to God as the law requires, words were spoken that have always stayed with me. Only now do I fully understand what they meant. "This child will be the rise and fall of many in the land, and sorrow will pierce your own heart." They were said by an old man, a man supposedly blessing our child. But those words were more prophetic than I could ever have imagined, though I've spent more than thirty years pondering on them, seeking their meaning, looking for their fulfilment.

When Jesus was 12, my heart was pierced when we accidentally travelled home from Jerusalem without him and it took us three days to find him. Three days! Such long days – days of worry, of confusion, of loss. My heart was surely pierced, yet all he said was, "didn't you know I must be about my father's business?"

When he turned thirty, my heart was pierced when he came back from seeing his cousin John and said he was off and didn't know when he'd be back. It was more than forty days before he returned and he was so thin and drawn. I didn't have the courage to ask where he'd been or what he'd been doing, but for every one of those days, my heart had been sore at his absence, at not knowing, at wondering if he'd ever return.

His strength had recovered and then he was off again; 'Father's business', that's all he said. And the next I heard, he was teaching about the peace we could know for ourselves, with our friends, even with our enemies; how the law was fulfilled and how we need to love others just as we love ourselves, and that our love for God must be greater than every other love, even love of family. And my heart was pierced by that seeming rejection. He was so popular, people so wanted to see him. Once, when we couldn't get in, I sent a message to say the family was outside. One of his friends came out, all embarrassed and said, "He says anyone who obeys the law and loves is his mother or his brother." That hurt, I will say. That hurt a lot. But it also got me pondering again about when he was twelve and what he meant by 'his father's business' and when he was a baby and how much more could my heart be pierced.

So, here we are today and my precious, miraculous boy is nailed on a cross naked, for all the world to see, accused of I'm not sure what. The charge sheet says only 'King of the Jews'. Was this really the plan of God from the beginning? Can this really be how it ends? How can my son of peace have such a violent death? I see such deep marks of suffering on him – marks of beatings and whipping, marks from the nails, but more. In his eyes, I see the mark of loss, a look of abandonment. I hear him call 'My God, my God, why have you forsaken me?' and I know that psalm. I know how it continues. I know it does not end with abandonment, but with God helping those who call on him. Is there, then, still some hope? A soldier says my son is dead, but to confirm it, pierces his side with a spear. In that moment, my heart too is pierced.

Jesus' story – I was there on the cross by Sarah Bingham

The last of four monologues for Good Friday

We planned it; even before we started, it was planned. Not every detail, but the basics of where and when and how. What a delight it was to see things spring in to being just from a word! What fun we had designing the most intricate details and replicating those patterns at larger and larger scales through the whole of creation. Have you never noticed that frost patterns echo the shape of ferns, and you can spot spirals everywhere, if you have the eyes to see?

We knew it was a risk, to make people. To put the creative spark and our very breath into a creature, to give it a mind and heart that could choose wisdom or folly, peace or war, love or hate. We knew, too, that at some point the choice would separate them from us; that their impurity must not sully, their unholiness never mix with our utter holiness. SO, we planned how to overcome it.

We chose a people, a small, insignificant nation, one that on its own would probably have been swallowed alive by the more powerful people around them. We gave them laws so that they could reflect what we are like, shine out from the nations around them to show a different, better, way – our way. We knew they'd still mess up, that their nature meant they would fail. We gave them means to put things right – sacrifices they could make that would show the cost of harmful ways, the cost of hating over loving. But really, that was only ever meant to act as an alerting system. Of course, killing a dove or a goat doesn't actually fix the problem of the human heart.

There's only one way for the cost of sin to be paid, only one way for people to be put right with us, restored to how they should be, only one way for death to be defeated. Death had to be tasted by one it could never hold on to. We always planned that this would happen, but I never realised how much, as a man, I would struggle with it. I've spent my life following the law, obeying my father, to reveal true life to those around me. I've taught them, and demonstrated what people can do when they allow the Spirit to work in and through them. And I've loved them in a way they really do not yet understand. And sometimes, it's been frustrating, and sometimes I've wanted to throw my hands in the air and give up, but we'd talked about it and planned it. In the garden I asked that another way be found, if possible, but really, I knew there was no other way.

And now the plan is almost complete. I am broken to heal their brokenness, my blood is even now being shed to bring them true forgiveness. It hurts – it hurts physically, mentally, emotionally, spiritually. I've never been truly alone before, but the plan requires this separation. In this covenant I must take on that impurity so it can be cleansed and the impure be made pure. I could come down, if I chose, but the joy to come holds me here. The joy that in the future, all people will be able to come to us, all people find healing and forgiveness, all people live empowered by our Spirit to be as we created them. It was planned before the beginning and it is culminating now. Peace on earth and goodwill to all to whom God shows favour, right here, right now.

The Tree (Good Friday) by Hannah Montgomery

I read this poem to open a Good Friday Easter Gathering. We had dark lit the auditorium/sanctuary with candles, and projected a video on a loop of trees swaying in the wind. The reading of the poem was followed by a few moments of silence for reflection and prayer.

They cut me down in my prime
severed trunk sawn into structural seams
plank by plank
counted, numbered
now pinned
against my will -
a treason hillside for my final stand.

What hands are these flinching against mine?
Sharp metal shards
pierce through wet flesh
and thunder in my oaken veins.

I know these hands -
Christ!
The palms that shaped my soil
and coaxed my growth
To life brought height and sky and sight
now to death submits his hollow palms
And so we die, the Christ and I;
Him hostage held by my wooden heart.

We Hold a Nail by **Dinah Hargreaves**
*Written to be read during a Good Friday reflective Service, where
nails were held during the reading, and then laid at the foot of a
Cross.*

Each held a nail, and placing it
   to aching wrist, they struck a blow.
The sinews tightened, pain erupted,
   but the pain of theirs was His to know.

Peter – too ashamed to face Him;
   hidden safe behind closed doors.
Judas – the kiss still burning through him
   hanging lifeless in death's jaws.
The soldiers, careless of the moment,
   mocking, jeering to justify.
The women's pain, because they loved Him,
   their aching. "Why, O God?" their cry.

Pilate, washing still the blood-guilt;
   Herod's excuse for political sense;
Two thieves, entrapped in their own pain and destiny;
   onlookers there, just to watch till the end.

Each held a nail that pierced Him so deeply.
   We hold a nail. Can we hold it back?
Our nail – the hidden, the things too long held,
   have been piercing His heart since our world became black.

Look! Look again at the Cross, and at Jesus.
   Through the pain is God's merciful loving heart too;
and listen and take in the words said for all of us,
   "Father, forgive them – they know not what they do."

In the Sudden Darkness by Ali Taylor

In the sudden darkness
He waits.
Time suspended in the middle of the day.
Full in the knowledge of what is to come.
God's sacrificial lamb
Waits to take the blame.

The tsunami
A tidal wave of pain and anguish
The sin of all the world
Pours forth upon Him
Wave upon wave
Engulfing Him,
Swamping Him,
Drowning Him.

In my sin, on a midnight afternoon
My sinless Saviour drowns.

Holy became unholy
Good became bad
Purity tarnished.
Father and Son torn apart
And day became night.

An everlasting night.

For these wounds of Jesus will never heal.

This love, His love
An everlasting eternity
Bringing an unending forgiveness
That changes life.

This love, His love
So holy, so pure
Bringing redemption
That I might step into heaven
Where I have no right to be

He took my sin
He paid my price
That I might be set free.

The Skies Went Dark... by Sarah Bingham

And did they then fall silent, wondering,
As darkness fell across the land?
And wonder if their own spiritual blindness
Was now reinforced by God's very own hand?

And did they then fall silent, wondering,
If this might be the shadow of death?
And wonder if this was truly the Shepherd
Suffering, hanging, struggling for breath?

And did they then fall silent, wondering,
If darkness could really snuff out the Light?
And wonder if Light lost was always, forever -
Or mystery show how all is put right?

And did they then fall silent, wondering,
If darkness would always mean pain and despair?
And wonder where God was in all of these doings
Where hope was and faith was and someone to care?

And did they then fall silent, wondering,
Remembering chaos at dawn of the earth?

And wonder if darkness was only the prelude
To new work from God and a time of rebirth?

And do we now fall silent, wondering?

My Beautiful Boy by Linda Clack

I saw him there my beautiful boy. My precious beautiful Son. I
wanted to close my eyes and blot out the image of his broken
and battered body pulled and pushed onto the harsh wooden
cross. But I could not abandon him as his friends had. I could
not bear not to be with him for one single moment. I could not
betray him and leave him alone even for one second. I wanted
him to know that he was loved and not alone. And so I watched.

I watched as they fixed him to the cross. I felt the ground
shudder with each hammer blow on their ugly nails, as
they drove them through his wrist and ankles. Each blow
reverberating through my body, each grimace on his beloved
face tearing chunks out of my heart.

I watched as they dropped the cross into place and watched
the agony on his face as the jarring pain shot through his body.

I watched as they mocked and jeered at him, my poor
vulnerable beautiful boy. Who only ever loved them, who only
ever did good for them. Who even now prayed for them to be
forgiven. I watched and I wept.

I watched as finally his legs could no longer sustain his weight
and creation itself pulled him remorselessly towards the earth.
The weight of his own body making it impossible for him to
breathe. I struggled to breathe for him, and I wept.

I watched as they pushed their sword into his side. And I remembered. I remembered the words of the old man in the temple when he was first born, my beautiful boy, " .. and a sword will pierce your own soul too." And I felt the searing pain deep in my soul.

I watched as they took his broken body down from this instrument of torture, I watched as they left him alone on the cold cold earth, and I took him in my arms and wept that I had not kept him safe.

Waiting for Spring by Hannah Montgomery

I read this poem as an invitation to reflect and respond to God's promptings as I closed a preach in our Easter series. It could also be used around the seasons of winter and spring, Lent, or speaking into themes of death, mourning, and waiting.

A holy silence;
Winter arrives with
Its own kind of barrenness
Dead clay
Stubbornly refusing the
Potter's hand.

And yet,
As with every crucifixion,
Brokenness yields in the end.
Darkness eclipsed by the
Turning of the Son:
Empty palms raised in
Resurrection praise.

Psalm 24 at Easter by Mary Taylor

And Jesus said,
        'I'm done!'
And the great gates burst open.
All the tolls and barriers and checkpoints were torn down.
Even the great iron-bound doors,
the hinges and the door posts, uprooted
and lifted themselves clear from their sockets
to make the widest road, through which
the One
with clean hands and a pure heart will pass,
leading a festival crowd into the wide arena of God's heart.

She is Here by Clare McBeath

*NB while Jesus may have been born in a particular time and place
and born as male, the image of Christ in whom there is neither
male nor female, Jew nor Greek, slave nor free transcends all such
limitations and boundaries for this is the cosmic Christ. It is this idea of
the cosmic Christ that this prayer celebrates in referring to Christ as
she.*

If you want to move beyond binary concepts of gender, then we
would suggest using the words "They are here".

Prayer of Invocation

She is here...
As life breaks forth from the dark earth
She is here...
As the birds break forth into song
She is here...
As Spring is stirring all around us
She is here...
As the earth itself is reborn

She is here...
Wild, free, uncontainable
She is here...
Growing, blossoming, flourishing
She is here...
Inviting us to life in all its fullness.

In the rising of the Easter dawn
She is here...
In daffodils nodding in the breeze
She is here...
In the catkins and budding of trees
She is here...
In the ripples glinting across the water (or the rain casting ripples
across the water)
She is here...
In the greening of the grass on the hillside
She is here...
In the bleating of the new-born lambs
She is here...
In the lengthening of the days
She is here...

Blessing
Blessed be you who breaks open the Easter dawn
calling us to open our hearts
Blessed be you who dares us to be risk takers
encouraging us to try something new
Blessed be you who spreads a feast before us
Inviting us to this new community
where we taste and see that life is good...

Voices

Pilate's wife (Matthew 27:19) by Jeannie Kendall

I still remember that night.
Waking in a cold sweat
Images etched in my mind
Fear a tight band round my heart.
I dared not sleep again
Lest nightmares return.
Knowing my words
Would have no power
But I must use them anyway.
He would not heed me.
And I may never
Sleep in peace again

The Centurion's Wife by Jeannie Kendall

"Just light duties today"
He called as he left.
I felt relief
Knowing he would return
With a smile I need not fear.
Unlike other times, when,
Somehow world-weary
He would come through the door
A mix of pain and anger in his eyes
And wake at nights
With nameless horrors
He could not erase
And I could not share.

But later that day
I smiled as he came home
But saw at once in his eyes
It would not be returned;
The curious darkness
Of those daylight hours
Somehow mirrored deep within his soul.
"Light duties?"
I whispered
Trying somehow to reach him
And he began to weep.

Jesus' aunt (John 19:25) by Jeannie Kendall

'Mary's boy'
Funny how we always
Called him that.
Not Joseph's boy.
I'd always thought it was just
That mother-son
Indefinable link
And yet
As he grew
Somehow he seemed
Not quite to belong
To either of them
Or to anyone.
More his own person
Than anyone I had ever met.
Not other-worldly;
Instead more here, more fully alive
Than I could never be.

Broke her heart
The day he left.
She cried more
Than for Joseph's death.
It was if
A little of her died that day
Although she said
She'd always known
It would come to that
And the worst
Was yet to come.
"It was the myrrh"
She would say
As though that
Explained everything
But when I asked
She would just look away
As though remembering.
But now today
I remember
As I watch
Vinegar and hyssop
Run down his chin
Like tears
And I cannot comfort her
As I weep
For Mary's boy.

We Touched You by Diane Holmes

I am that kind of woman
Skilled with my hands,
My mouth.
I saw you
Alone in the rippling heat.
I touched you
My words embraced your thirst
Yours mine.
Stay awhile,
Don't go.

I washed your feet
With the living water of my tears
And dried them with my hair.
I anointed your head and feet
So precious
My hands shiny with love.
I touched you with my lips
I held your feet in my hands
Don't go, not yet.

We are women
Skilled with our hands
Preparers of perfume for the departed.
We should only touch your body
When you are dead.
But our fingers are warm
With the touch
Of the living Word.
We touched you.

I saw you
Alone

Alive, in the empty dawn
But I couldn't touch you
Couldn't hold on.
Was I already,
Were we, already
Slipping between the words?
Fading from the pages
Out of view?

Don't go
Not yet
We did
We do
Touch you

An Unnamed Woman by Catriona Gorton

So, that was it, I had bought all the special food needed for the festival. It was a busy time, as well as my own husband and three children, there would his parents and mine, my widowed sister and her two, his unmarried brother, a couple of cousins, oh yes, and my maiden aunt. A house full! It has been no small feat saving up for the extras that would have to be bought, carefully balancing my budget, setting aside a few shekels when I could for the extras, whilst paying the Roman taxes and the Temple taxes. I was proud of my achievements - we owed nothing, we had borrowed nothing, we had paid our dues and had a little left over to make the festival a celebration.

I went to the Temple to make my financial offering, having carefully calculated what could be afforded once everything essential had been paid. I met an elderly neighbour on her way, too, and we chatted. I looked away as she slipped her two tiny coins into the treasury. I didn't want her to be embarrassed;

and, to be honest, I didn't want to be embarrassed by her either. Quietly I dropped in my own offering - exactly what I could afford, well after setting aside a few coins for emergencies of course.

That evening we had been invited out to a meal in Bethany where the rabbi Jesus was being honoured. Carefully I chose which scarf to wear, which trinkets to adorn my wrists. A tiny dab of perfume, a gift from a time when money was more plentiful. We set off, hungry for conversation, eager to taste the food! It was a great evening, wonderful food, flowing wine, lively conversation... and then... Mary. It was Mary, sister of Martha and Lazarus, breaking open a jar of perfumed oil and pouring the whole lot over Jesus' feet. What a waste, I thought, just a few drops were all that was needed to tend to his dusty, travelled feet. 'What a waste' a man's voice spoke aloud, 'it could have been sold and the money given to the poor.' A murmur of agreement spread until Jesus spoke.

In one day then, two women had behaved recklessly and been commended for it. My elderly neighbour had given her last mite to the Temple, making herself dependent on the generosity of others (note to self: invite her for the festival dinner). And Mary had simply poured out a whole bottle of perfume in a rash act of devotion. I don't understand it, I've always been sensible, never spent more than I had, never borrowed. I don't understand it, I've always given what was expected of me at the Temple; I've always paid my taxes on time. I don't understand how foolishness earns approval and wisdom is overlooked...

A *Member of the Council* by Catriona Gorton

To be part of it - the Council - wow! Me? I had ong wondered
what went on in those meetings, had revered the men with
their long beards and measured tones. Now I was part of
it. It was exciting and nerve-wracking. A privilege for sure, a
responsibility undoubtedly, but an opportunity. I was, relatively
speaking, young. And I noticed how when I spoke people
would smile knowingly and shake their heads ´n a slightly
dismissive way that said, 'we were once young too; you'll learn.'
There was so much the Council could influence, could make
better, more vibrant, more Godly... but meetings seemed dry
and turgid as often as not. The biggest concern seemed to
be keeping the peace with Rome. Every now and then some
upstart looked like causing trouble and he would be quietly - or
not so quietly - dealt with.

They are good people on the Council, men who have helped
me to settle in, to learn how things work. They are not all the
same, opinions vary and a few speak out against the status
quo. I have found two good friends here - in a Council of 70 (71)
it takes time to get to know people. Nic[odemus] is a worrier,
often doesn't sleep at nights, so he tells me. He worries and
wonders about getting things right, turns over ideas in his mind.
He's been known to go out under cover of darkness to talk
with northern rabbis about philosophical ideas. He's a good
man, a thinking man, and a friend to me. And Joe [Joseph of
Arimathea]: never says much, just seems to listen intently and
weigh up what is said. A kindly man with deep, gentle eyes
and a soft voice. A friend who looks out for me, a mentor if you
like, someone who stands with me as I learn the ropes of this
responsible, confusing, powerful role.

Discussion recently has centred on one of the northern rabbis,
one who is gathering an enormous following, and who is

attracting too much attention with his talk of a Kingdom. What should be done? Various reports were brought by members who'd been out to see what he was up to - healing on Shabbat, declaring sins forgiven, consorting with women, meeting Roman centurions, touching lepers... the list was endless. Discussion flew back and forth; a decision must be made. It came to a vote - to exterminate him or not, 'better one man die than a nation perish'. So how should I vote? Nic was clear in his mind - no way was he voting for this. Joe quietly joined the 'no' vote.

What should I do? I had waited a long time to be part of this council, I wanted to make a difference, yet I wanted to be accepted. I trusted the judgement of my new-found friends but there were more and more people voting 'yes'...

A Man Servant by **Catriona Gorton**

Go and fetch some water, in fact, keep going and fetching water all day long until a couple of northerners come and ask you to show them the guest room, then bring them here. It sounds a strange command, I suppose, looking back on it, but at the time I didn't question it. In our household there were often strange commands, and you simply got on and obeyed them. It was a good household, the master was a gentle and fair man, we were treated well and rarely were voices raised against us. Yes, a good man, but an odd man - he was always hosting this or that group who wanted somewhere for a meal and a conversation. People undoubtedly whispered about us, wondered just what was going on in a house where men fetched water, but we were content.

It must have been the second or third trip to the well that day when they approached me. They looked sheepish, embarrassed as they asked me to show them the guest room.

I set down the jar, and we climbed the stairs to the room.
I showed them the long, central table, the couches - how many
cid they need? Thirteen? Yes, we could do that no problem.
We dragged the furniture across the floor and exchanged
pleasantries, then a few jokes... but we'll just pass over that...
pass over, Passover... oh, never mind, you had to be there. We
discussed the seating plan. They asked where they could buy
the bread and wine needed for the meal; we were supplying
the roast lamb, the herbs, the bitter water. So, with banter on
their lips they set off to the market...

Towards evening they returned to make final preparations. The
atmosphere was different now, as the light dimmed. Quietly, I
lit the lamps on the ledges around the room. Another servant
carried in the utensils and arranged them on the table. The men
returned. 'Do you think we have enough bread?' He looked
worried, not sure how much food thirteen hungry men would
need for a festival supper. 'Is this wine good enough?' another
wondered, 'you recall what happened at Cana!'

Time passed, and they all arrived a few at a time: Peter and
John, Thomas, Judas, Andrew... I can't recall all the names.
Somewhere in the middle of them was Jesus. The conversation
was light; they looked forward to a delicious meal, the smell of
the roast already wafting up the stairs... With my fellow servants
I stepped back into the shadows, our work now complete. I
paused at the top of the stairs... something told me that even
by the standards of our household, something unusual was
happening. So I waited...

Peter – a Sermon by Ali Taylor

It's late, and I'm cold. The darkness of the midnight hours shrouds the courtyard, a chill pervades the air. I pull my robe closer around me, edging closer to the fire. The acrid smoke fills my nostrils, the glow of the coals bathes the place with an eerie light.

Thoughts swirl through my mind. He was supposed to be king! But they've arrested him. How can he be king now? Are they going to kill him? What about us?

Vague remembrances of his past words crowd in alongside the other thoughts. None of it makes sense – it wasn't supposed to be like this.

Suddenly I become aware of questioning eyes piercing the gloom – looking directly at me and then the accusation comes: you were with him! But I'm afraid...I don't want to be arrested like him – I don't want to die... Almost before I know it, 'I do not know him' spills forth from my lips and like the smoke disappears into the darkness... Immediately I regret the lie. These easily uttered words curdle in my heart and it begins to ache.

I wait – hoping my protestations were enough. I draw my robe closer still, huddling down, trying to be invisible. But no, another voice joins the others – shattering my illusions of becoming unseen. 'You are one of them', but yet again the words of denial tumble from my lips.

I'm fearful they will drag me over and throw me down alongside him, but quietness descends, and we stay close to the burning embers, listening once more to the goings on across the courtyard.

Time passes. The hour is even later. The cold seeps upwards through the floor enveloping me and wrapping its icy fingers around my body like the fear encompassing my soul. I'd hoped they'd forgotten about me. But, in the brittle night air, another accusation snaps out. And I know I've said too much...I want to gather in the words I've spoken...for my accent has betrayed me. I'm so very afraid, but still I vehemently protest, 'I do not know what you are talking about.' As those words escape my mouth, my ears are filled with the raw sound of crowing. I look around urgently – desperate to get away. And as I look – eyes once again pierce the darkness.

His eyes.

He looks straight at me and my heart implodes with shame and guilt – for I have done the very thing that I said I would not do. It is too much. I cannot stay. I jump to my feet and flee, wanting the darkness to hide me, the bitter tears of regret stinging my face and blurring my path as I stumble away.

The Anointing – a sermon by Emma Nash

I know what we're supposed to think about this story.
We know that Judas is the bad guy.
But if we allowed ourselves to do so, we might find ourselves asking with him, "why blow a year's wages on such a fleeting act of worship?"

To understand Mary's actions, perhaps we might think of the bride getting ready for her wedding.
She may well have spent a month's wages on a dress she will wear only once.
Layers of lace, organza, silk and satin,
Dozens of ivory buttons,

Beautiful embroidery,
A long, flowing veil.
And to the expense of the dress is added jewellery, makeup, an elaborate hairstyle, satin shoes.
She has never looked so beautiful.
And it only lasts a day.
And she does all this because the occasion of her wedding makes it fitting.
She is entering into a commitment she hopes will be lifelong.
She is being joined before God to someone she loves.
A friend is becoming family.
Two families are becoming relatives.
The beauty of the occasion demands beauty.
Mary, too, created something beautiful to honour the Lord to whom she owed the life of her brother.
It did not matter that the perfume could only be used once;
It was a declaration of her love for Jesus, and he was worth the expense.

To understand Mary's act of worship, perhaps we might think of the crown jewels.
Among the many jewel-encrusted items are a golden spoon and a golden jug.
The anointing oil is poured from the jug into the spoon.
And from the spoon the archbishop takes the oil and makes the sign of the cross on the forehead of the new king or queen.
Jesus is the Christ, the Messiah, the 'anointed one.'
In anointing him with perfume Mary performed an outward sign of a spiritual reality –
A sacrament, if you will –
showing that Jesus was the anointed King of the Jews.
Only the best and most precious items are suitable for the coronation of a king.

And yet, the crown that Jesus will wear is a crown of thorns.

So, to understand Mary's act of worship, perhaps we might think of the beautiful flowers we bring to the funeral of a friend.

A costly act of love, for we want only the freshest and most beautiful blooms to honour the friend we have lost.

There is a sense in which we are wasting our money – our friend will not see the flowers.

The wreaths and crosses and bouquets will lie in the garden of the crematorium, slowly withering.

But we do it nonetheless as an act of sadness, beauty and love to honour our friend.

Mary foreshadowed Jesus' death on the cross with her act of devotion.

She anoints the living body of Jesus, perhaps knowing on one level that his triumph will come through his death.

Jesus is the king anointed for burial.

To understand Mary's act of worship, perhaps we might imagine that a church decides to observe Good Friday in a very special way.

Instead of the usual communion wine, a bottle of vintage red wine is purchased.

Perhaps a bottle of 1812 Chateau Laffite, which has been maturing for over 200 years,

Bottled in the lifetime of Jane Austen.

Just one bottle, costing £40,000, a great deal more than a year's wages for most people.

Opened, poured out into communion cups and drunk to remember the pouring out of the blood of Jesus on the cross.

A ridiculous expense – a bottle which can only be used once – just enough precious wine to go round the whole church.

It would be an act of insanity.

And yet how much more precious was the blood of Jesus poured out on the cross?

From Friday to Sunday without skipping Saturday by Sarah Bingham

Church is rarely good at lament these days. We are so caught up in celebrating our eventual resurrection, that all too often we minimise or deny the fact that life, even for believers, can be confusing, painful and downright bleak; that suffering and mourning are part and parcel of our lot.

This has a number of effects; it denies those who are suffering or mourning the liberty to express their true feelings to us and, perhaps, to God, it empties the Gospel of a vital part of its content and it tells those who do not know Jesus that He has nothing to say to them in their present state.

Yet, although common, these are blasphemous statements. They refute the very word of God. Maybe we, as Church, as God's ordinary but called people, need to grasp the nettle of facing our own confusion, fear, suffering and struggles at least one day every year, to keep us engaged with the whole Gospel.

If we accept this challenge, what better time to do this than Holy Saturday – between Good Friday and Easter Sunday. We struggle to face the reality of Christ's death because we already know he rose again on Sunday! This is the heart of the Gospel. If it isn't true, Paul says we of all people should be pitied. We should not let go of the lens of Easter. At the same time, though, we need the courage to admit we are still awaiting the return of Christ. Whilst death has been defeated, we and the whole of creation are still groaning for the renewal of the heavens and earth.

We still live in a world where things are not perfect, where 'stuff' happens. Where is God in all this suffering? This is the positive of Holy Saturday, the goodness of Good Friday. Because they show us that God is with us in our suffering. Perhaps the focus needs to be shifted to look for where God is in our own suffering, rather than the suffering itself?

How could we do this? What shape and feel might a Holy Saturday service take? Here are two models, one more 'traditional', the other more 'contemporary reflective'.

A Traditional Service
Welcome, call to worship.

Introductory hymn: Man of Sorrows, what a name

Old Testament: Isaiah 53

New Testament: 2 Corinthians 1:1-11

Hymn: Psalm 23 (any version, ancient or modern)

Gospel: John 11:17-53

Sermon: to explore the suffering of the Father – over our sin, over the loss of His Son
to explore the suffering of the Son – being human, suffering grief and pain
to explore the role of the Spirit – in bringing comfort so that we might offer comfort
to explore how the shepherd may lead us through the dark, shadowed valley which He has already walked before us, that this does not mean disapproval or rejection.

Prayers and Intercessions:

Confession   using a published prayer of confession, but
              pausing between clauses to allow time to
              recognise and release our own sin

An invitation to explore and name before God our pains, griefs,
sorrows and sufferings, either in silence or speaking them out.

Time for silently receiving from God through the Holy Spirit.

Intercession   for people and places known to us that need
               God's blessing.

If the congregation have a prayer ministry team, it may be
appropriate to offer individual prayer and perhaps anointing with
oil for all those who desire it.

Hymn: e.g. Beauty for Brokenness (Kendrick)
          or There's a lot of pain (Birtill)

Blessing

A Reflective Service may take its shape from dance

Welcome and invitation to travel together.

PowerPoint using images of the crucifixion to 'He was Despised'
from Handel's Messiah

Led biblically based meditation on Christ's emptying of himself,
his experience of being flesh, his suffering for and with us, the
coming of 'another comforter'.

Song to sing together: e.g. We have Sung our Songs of Victory
by Stuart Townend

Moving around individual stations to use symbols in aiding prayer, reflection and release:

- Using heart shaped templates and punches to signify where hearts have been broken, wounded or hardened.
- Having water poured over the hands to signify a desire for cleansing or a new start.
- Lighting a candle to demonstrate the desire for God to enter our darkness.
- Walking a mini-labyrinth stopping at marked points to pray aloud or in silence about fear, grief, confusion, disappointment, pain, suffering, sorrows, joys, triumphs, gifts, blessings.
- Putting a pin into a map of the world to identify other places of suffering.
- Reflecting on a beautiful image or calligraphy to seek God's beauty.
- Alternating turning palms down to release things to God and up to receive things from God.
- Quiet music, either instrumental like Mahler or Wellspring, or vocal, like Gregorian Chant or the Northumbria Community could play, as long as the volume is not distracting.
- This could include a station for receiving prayer ministry if appropriate.

Coming together, there might be an invitation to share what has been learned or experienced.

An appropriate poem.

Song to sing together: e.g. In Christ alone (Townend)

Sharing of 'the peace'.

Blessing and commissioning to go out.

Ideas for Interactive Worship

Good Friday 'Party Bags' by Claire Nicholls

You will need: Bags containing a small length of chain, A small cardboard crown, A nail, a cardboard red blood droplet, a length of white ribbon, an incense cone.

I used these bags as part of our Good Friday service going through the Luke account of Good Friday, interspersed with readings and reflections on the readings. Taking the bag home, the congregation could reflect on all they had seen and heard and share with their families.

The chain: Represents the chains of the wrong things we've done – link to Barabbas. Sin takes our freedom away to be who we have been created to be and holds us back. To set Barabbas free, Jesus who was innocent, needed to take on the chains that were rightly Barabbas' as he does us. I asked the congregation to hold the chain and imagine Jesus coming and removing the chains that bind us – how would they feel? Followed by a prayer of thanks.

The crown: Holding and thinking about Jesus being mocked as 'King of the Jews'. I asked the congregation some questions – how do you treat Jesus as King? Do you know him? Do you disown him? Do you mock him? Do you bow down and worship?

The nail: Talking about the pain of the cross and the crown of thorns I asked the congregation to hold the nail and feel its point and imagine what it felt like for Jesus, talking about the pain of suffering and his love.

Red blood droplet: 'Father forgive them, they know not what they do'. We used this to represent our sins, and then played some reflective music as we laid it at the foot of the cross (which was covered in white material so the red stood out).

White Ribbon: After laying our droplets at the cross we tied the white ribbon round our wrists as a sign we are forgiven.

Incense: We smelt it as we talked about the women gathering spices for Jesus' body and the myrrh from his birth. I sent them out with the bags reminding them amongst the sadness of Good Friday that the 'smell of hope' is in the air.

Journeying with the cloth – Maundy Thursday – Good Friday – Easter Sunday by Claire Nicholls

A large piece of red table cloth to journey through the end of Holy Week as part of the services....

- Maundy Thursday – use as the communion table cloth – empty the table at the end of the service (as part of the service) leaving the cloth.
- Good Friday – whilst singing 'How Deep the Father's love for us' invite people to sign their names on the cloth on the table reflecting on the words 'it was my sin that held him there' and hang over the cross.
- Easter Sunday – find the cloth, but torn up, representing the temple curtain, left in the empty tomb.

Through the Year (Special Days)

A selection of material for some of the days we choose to mark during the year

New Year

One Night – A Prayer for New Year by Ali Taylor

One night

I stand and wait
The clock ticks and a New Year will soon begin
And yet, for You, who stands outside time
In Your eternity,
This night is like any other.
Outside there is Your world
People in pain, in love, in fear and in hope
People who do not know what tomorrow will bring.

Come touch this world with Your love:
Heal broken hearts
Mend damaged bodies
Piece together fractured families
Calm angry minds
Quieten furious voices
Raise up the fallen
Comfort the scared
Bless the hopeless
Touch the lonely

Come Lord Jesus
Into Your world once again
In us and through us
Reach Your world so in need.

Help us bring Your love
Which transforms life
To begin Your eternity today.

The seconds pass
The New Year comes

You come.

Thank You Lord.

Valentine's Day

***If my love were enough...* by Sarah Bingham**

If my love were enough
I would gladly pour it out
Until your heart, mind, soul
Were filled to overflowing,
Healed, restored, made whole.

If my love were enough
I would speak out loud and clear
Until you had no doubt
Of just how much you are worth
Fears all driven out.

If my love were enough
I would show it through my acts,
Nurture this tender reed
Walk with you through your darkness
But
It's not my love you need.

Mothering Sunday

Mothering Sunday can be an especially difficult and painful time for some people, for many diverse reasons. Some women ministers are mothers, others are not – we write from our own experience and into our own contexts.

Mother God... by Sarah Bingham

Can a mother forget her child –
One she weaned from her breast?
Even if she ever could
I could not, however pressed.

How I have longed to draw you close –
Hidden safe 'neath my wing
Always, you say, 'I will not'
And turn from love I would bring.

With arms outstretched I show my love –
Still so many turn away.
Yet I show my faithfulness
Won't you turn to me today?

Always I am watching, waiting –
Longing to pour out grace.
Waiting still to see you turn
To my welcoming embrace.

Mothering Sunday Prayer by Claire Nicholls

Loving God, we come today all on different parts of our journey. Some are searching, some are feeling lost, some are hurting, some are feeling loved. Wherever we are and whatever we feel, we come to you as our parent who understands, knows and walks with us.

As we journey with you, we hear sounds of joy as families meet and celebrate being family together, children tell mothers how beautifully wonderful they are, and mothers tell children how loved they are.

We also hear sounds of mourning. We pray for those for whom today is a reminder of loss. A reminder that Mum is not with them anymore. We pray for peace. We pray for comfort. We pray that you might pick them up and carry them today.

As we journey with you, we taste the sweetness of new life. We thank you for children; the way they smile, the way they brighten our lives. Help us to welcome children into our family, loving them unconditionally as you love them.

We also taste the bitterness of those for whom today is a sorrowful and painful reminder of their childlessness. We pray for those who have desperately wanted to be parents and have not been able to be. We pray that you might bring sweetness into their lives through the blessings of others. We pray for comfort. We pray that you might pick them up and carry them today.

As we journey with you, we see the beauty in family life. We see how you have blessed and cared for us. We remember where you have led us look forward to where is next. Help us to trust you as the future unravels before our eyes.

We also remember those for whom the future is not what they expected to see. We pray for those who have lost a child – who were looking forward with joy only to have dreams shattered. We pray for peace and comfort. We pray that you might pick them up and carry them today.

As we journey with you, we remember the smells of home. The smell of freshly baked cake, a delicious meal and the familiar. We thank you for what you have provided.

We also remember that not everyone has enough, that not everyone can experience the smells of home. We pray for those children who have no home, who have nobody they can call Mum or Dad. We pray for those who do not have enough food or money. We pray that you will provide. We pray that you will pick them up and carry them today.

As we journey today, we reach our hands to you. We know that where we put our hand in your hand we can rely on your guidance, your love, your arms that carry us when life is hard.

We also remember those we love who have not reached out their hands to you or have let go: Our children who do not know you, parents, partners, siblings, wider families and the people we care about deeply. We pray that they may reach out, take your hand and choose to follow.

Loving God, we come today all on different parts of our journey. Some are searching, some are feeling lost, some are hurting, some are feeling loved. Wherever we are and whatever we feel we come to you as our parent; the one who understands, knows and walks with us.

Mothering God by Catriona Gorton

Mothering God, hold in the safe embrace of your love
Those who mourn
Those who ache with longing
Those whose hearts are pierced as by a sword

Mothering God, like a small child learning to walk, take by the
hand
Those who attempt new things
Those who are uncertain or unsure
Those who wobble and weave

Mothering God, like a dancing partner, spin with delight
Those who rejoice in success
Those whose dreams have found fulfilment
Those who dream the dreams of your Kingdom

Mothering God, grant they all may find themselves
Comfortably resting
Like a weaned child
On the parent's knee.

Mothering Sunday – I'm Thinking of You by Catriona Gorton

I am thinking of you,
Mothers that are,
Mothers that were,
Mothers that will be,

Mothers that will never be
Mothers that never were
Mothers that are not yet...
Thinking of you and praying, somehow, for you...

The new mother exhausted from labour whose new-born will not suckle

The elderly mother whose age-eroded mind can no longer recognise her own child

The frazzled mother whose children seem out of control

The mother who now nurses her own mother

The mother who longs to linger but is lured by death to eternity

The unexpected mother whose swelling belly bears witness to unplanned activity

The shamed mother, whose rapist's features stare at her from infancy's innocence

The stepmother trying, perhaps too hard, to get it right

The adoptive mother, finally holding the longed-for child

The mother who cannot be mother, life-saving drugs having destroyed her fertility

The longs-to-be mother whose body has let her down yet again

The mother who cares for her children's children, her child having died

The mother who sits alone, rejected, neglected, unloved

The mother who clings to bitterness and refuses to be reconciled

The mother who feels she has failed

The mother who dances for joy at her children's achievements

The mother who lets go of the apron strings, and delights to see her children grown

The mother who sacrificed her career to fulfil her calling as mother

The mother who...

The mothers that were

The mothers that are

The mothers that will be

The mothers that weren't
The mothers that aren't
The mothers that never will be

On this Mothering Sunday,
May the mother-love of God,
In whom we are each conceived,
Surround and fill you,
Wherever,
Whoever,
Whatever you may be.
Amen.

Rachel is Weeping by Mary Cotes

God of justice and compassion,
We pray today for mothers who are weeping.

Remembering the mothers of Bethlehem,
We pray for the women whose children have died in war or
violence,
As fodder for the bombs,
Victims of terror,
As soldiers too young to fight.

Rachel is weeping for her children,
And we lift her cry to you.

We pray for the women whose unborn children have died
because of poverty,
For lack of ante-natal care,
For want of expertise, medicine and equipment
For need of access to a hospital.

Rachel is weeping for her children
And we lift her cry to you.

We pray for the women whose children's lives are threatened
by hunger,
Whose harvests have dwindled,
Whose crops have failed,
Whose earth has become desert due to climate change.

Rachel is weeping for her children
And we lift her cry to you.

God of justice and compassion,
Help us to see mirrored in Rachel's tears
A river rising to the ears of heaven,
thundering against injustice as it flows.
May its torrent baptise us more truly
into the life of Christ's disciples
who act and pray for your kingdom to come. Amen.

(Amos 5:24; Matt.2:13-18; Rom.6:3)

Pieta at Nain by Mary Taylor

Mourning for an only son,
the widow, bereft, follows the bier.
Two crowds meet, the one alive and excited,
the other occupied with the offices of death.
And in the middle, Jesus;
moved by compassion;
moved by seeing into the future;
Jerusalem-bound with Mary, his mother.

The time scales slip.
There will be a long pieta.
And not until the third day will the son
be given back.

But for now, the widow is blessed,
'God has favoured us!'
'A prophet is amongst us!'

Pentecost

Chaos and Change by Clare McBeath

Hesitant invocation

When we survey the scene
of chaos before us
we're hesitant to invoke
the presence of God
not too sure what
we might be letting ourselves in for

Nevertheless we say
Come unsettling God
Come with your chaos
Come with your anger
Come with your passion
Come but be gentle with us

God who meets us in the chaos: opening prayer

God who meets us
in the chaos of everyday life
turning the tables on injustice

demanding that we see things
from a different perspective

we praise and thank you
that you do not allow us
to stay as we are
but you jolt us out of complacency
you challenge us to change
dare us to dream differently
and every so often
you turn our world upside down.
its exciting
its scary
its painful
its risky
but this is the journey of faith
you have called us on.
Give us the courage
to follow you
upside down God
and give us the assurance
to know
that you have travelled
the path before us
will journey with us
and will follow after us
Christ our strength
Christ our companion
Christ our guide
In Jesus' name

Playful Pentecost by Clare McBeath

This was originally written for a forest/fresh expression of church and so deliberately tries to avoid the use of churchy language instead drawing from Shakespeare and the playfulness of A Midsummer Night's Dream to introduce the idea of the coming of the Holy Spirit. NB Words in italics are intended to be said all together

Prayer of Invocation and welcome

Wake up and come and play

We welcome you
the life that stirs under the forest floor
the energy that awakens
as the leaves of spring unfurl

Wake up and come and play

We welcome you
the sparkle glinting on the water
the enthusiasm of the songbirds
as they build their nests

Wake up and come and play

We welcome you
the gentle warmth of the morning sun
the bluebells carpeting the forest floor
full of wonder and mystery

Wake up and come out to play

We welcome you
the high spirits of remembered fairy stories

awakening the child within each of us
encouraging us to play and dream.

Wake up and come out to play

For the Spirit of life and laughter
of passion and energy
of fertility and new life
of playfulness and mischief
of friendship and community
of turning things upside down
and creating chaos
is also the Spirit of Pentecost
daring us to prophesy
daring us to dream
daring us to imagine
daring us to be-with
daring us to be-long
daring us to be-come

[Read Acts 2: 17 – 19]

So do we dare?
How might we dare?
What might we dare?

[Space for sharing]

So do we dare?
How might we dare?
What might we dare?
As we say together:
Wake up and come and play

Harvest

What's Yours is Mine by Juliet Lloyd

What's Yours is mine –
Created splendour,
Patchwork fields to wave-tossed foam
Flame-flashed skies stretch into starlight
Farther than mere sight can roam.

What's Yours is mine –
The human body:
Wondrous-made and dignified
Mind inquiring, heart reviving,
Sense exploring, muscles toned

What's Yours is mine-
Each day's provisions,
In our laps and over-poured,
Wisdom's light and strength and passion
And the drive to carry on

What's Yours is mine –
Your Son, our Saviour
Love Incarnate ...... crucified
Content, it seems, His rights not grasping... (pause)

What's Yours is mine...
What's mine's, MY OWN!

Remembrance Sunday

Remember by Sarah Bingham

Remember, remember,
the fifth of November;
Distance makes us forget
Conflict and pain,
blood shed in vain,
violence without regret.

Remember, remember,
Eleventh of November;
Time now makes us forget
The gas and the tank,
Blasted field, wood and bank,
The dying man's last cigarette.
Remember, remember,
The third of September;
New conflicts make us forget
Deaths military, civilian
Both numbered in millions
The suffering still of our vets.

Remember, remember,
Day in and day out;
Complacency makes us forget
They fought and they died
Some live, dead inside
And we need to repay our debt.

White poppy and red
We remember our dead
And honour them all through our living.

Red poppy and white
We must seek to do right
By actions, as well as in giving.

Remembrance Hymn by Sarah Bingham

The original tune by Lucy Legg is available to download from
www.baptist.org.uk/remembrancehymn

Alternative tune Aurelia (The Church's one Foundation)
Metre: mostly 76 76 D

So many years have passed now
Since the war to end all wars.
We fall silent and our heads bow
Before the bugle soars.
Its plaintive notes still sounding,
Still tell of those we lost,
This Last Post still resounding,
Reminds us of the cost.

So many families shattered,
So many lives destroyed,
For causes that then mattered,
When violence was deployed
To save some far off nation
To guarantee fair play
Provoked by assassination
When terror had its day.

So many years have passed now
Still we wait for wars to cease
But rarely seek to ask how
The world can find true peace.

Stop seeing folk as other
Stretch out a friendly hand
Embrace sister and brother
Seek peace from land to land.

There is a Prince of Peace, yet,
Who lived here long ago,
How easily we forget
He said to love our foe,
To break down all division
All people to be one
United in our vision
That war will be undone.

Remembrance Hymn by Helen Paynter

Suggested Tune: Thaxted (I vow to thee my country)
Metre 13 13 13 13 13 13

In a world of pain and sorrow
Where power conquers right
We receive the fresh commission
To fight the cause of Light –
With the weapons you permit us:
Patient love, self-sacrifice;
By the stirring of the Spirit
Our fortitude will rise.
As by love and grace and mercy,
The captives we release
Most of all, our Master, teach us
The things that make for peace.

May we live the deep reality,
The realm we cannot see;
Your peaceful reign of freedom

And hospitality.
Where the government is Justice
With a bias to the poor,
Where we celebrate our difference
And hasten not to war;
Where suspicion, fear and prejudice,
The seeds of hatred, cease;
So above all, Master, teach us
The things that make for peace.

To the foes of God and humankind,
Pride and hostility
We will raise the cross of Jesus Christ:
Weakness, humility;
All the broken and fragmented
Find their purpose in that place;
Lost are found, sick find healing,
And prodigals find grace.
Here is reconciliation
Of former enemies;
Here we find our Master's remedy –
The cross that makes for peace.

And all of us, with unveiled faces, seeing the glory of the Lord as though reflected in a mirror, are being transformed into the same image from one degree of glory to another; for this comes from the Lord, the Spirit

Photo: Eleanor Kelsey

The Lord is my shepherd, I shall not want. He makes me lie down in green pastures; he leads me beside still waters; he restores my soul.

Photo: Eleanor Kelsey

Meditations, Monologues and Sermons

We invited contributions of short reflections, meditations, monologues and sermons. Whilst some are included in the thematic chapters, others did not sit readily within that structure. Here we offer a delightful pot-pourri of prose that could be used in public worship, small group or personal devotions.

Another Place Reflection by Linda Hopkins

Ebb and flow - a recurrent or rhythmical pattern of coming and going or decline and re-growth.

Read John 21: 1-19

Another Place

Along the beach 'at the end of the road' of the house where I grew up in Sefton, Merseyside and half a mile from our church building is the art installation Another Place. 100 cast iron figures of artist Antony Gormley set at various intervals along the tide line for approximately 2 miles on Crosby beach all looking out to sea. They were a cause of controversy when, originally, they were to stay for a year. The local council and various groups lobbied for them to stay permanently, whilst some locals couldn't see what all the fuss was about and wondered why people would want them there. Some think they're rude: the nakedness. Others think they are a health and safety hazard. Many love them, including me!

Catch them at different times of day and they're completely different. Sometimes submerged, or head only just visible in the water, sometimes standing still amidst unforgiving crashing waves. Others are high above the sands, their plinths in view as the sand erodes beneath them. Others covered, belly deep in the sandbanks. Barnacled, dressed-up in clothing, yarn bombed. Worn, rusted, reflecting different light. Mysterious, odd, and disturbingly naked; human.

And fellow humans interact with them, as they, the figures, interact with their surroundings; a shipping lane from the city in this otherwise ordinary suburb out to the Irish Sea.

The purpose of the sculpture for Gormley is about human interaction with the elements, how the ebb and flow of the tides and the physical elements impact this peculiar body (as he calls it). And there is no romanticism here. Gormley says of the sculpture, 'it is no hero, no ideal, just the industrially reproduced body of a middle-aged man trying to remain standing and trying to breathe, facing a horizon busy with ships moving materials and manufactured things around the planet.'

I invite you to reflect on this other encounter on the beach of a particular and peculiar unique body of the risen Jesus; the encounter of nature – fish and lots of them, for the disciples. And the ebb and flow, the coming and going, the new  and the old, that which needs to die and that which is a sign of re-growth...and reflect too on what it means to be human and a follower in an ever-changing environment.

Photo: Linda Hopkins

Use the images to aid your reflection. You can print them out. This reflection is also available on YouTube: https://www.youtube.com/watch?v=ELbVUjg-8Uk&t=12s

A re-interpretation of Acts 11 by Brenda Morton

The apostles and prophets in the Baptist Union heard that some homosexuals had received the word of God. So, when Peter went to the Council the leaders criticised him and said, "You blessed the Marriage of a gay couple".

Peter explained everything to them as it had happened. "I was in the city praying, and in a vision I saw gay couples in the wilderness walking hand in hand, arm in arm, rejoicing in their love. And I heard them praising God for it. Then I heard a voice saying 'Invite them into the Church. Eat with them. Bless them. Affirm their love. Use their gifts, listen to their pain. Let them use their experience of pain and exclusion, of love and God's acceptance to minister to others.' I replied, 'Surely not, Lord. The way I imagine they express their love is filthy, unclean, unacceptable. I cannot affirm them.'

The voice spoke from heaven a second time; 'Do not call anything impure or unclean or unacceptable that God has accepted and sanctified with his presence.'

Right then a homosexual couple came to my house, asking for a bed for the night. They told me that an angel had appeared to them and told them to come to my house and seek my blessing.

As I began to speak to them the joy of the Lord came upon them, as on us. They radiated it. They praised God aloud. Then I remembered that Jesus said "I have not come to condemn the world, but to save it. I have come that you might have life, and have it abundantly." If God filled them with the same holy, overflowing joy that He gave us, who was I to think that I could oppose God?"

When they heard this, they had no further objections and praised God, saying "So then, God has granted even to gays and lesbians the joy of knowing Him through human love!"

The Woman in Adultery by Vikki Bunce

I just wanted the ground to open up and swallow me! That had to be better than being surrounded by this pack baying for my blood, just waiting for the sign from their leader to say take me, kill me, make me suffer! I knew I couldn't escape death, it was inevitable, I was trapped. How many times have I wished that I hadn't taken that first step down the path that has led me to this point, what was it that prompted me to make that first mistake but then, once I had, it was so hard to stop, to turn back, well, I couldn't turn back, it was too late, I was already lost.

I glanced up and quickly away again, they were still there, the noise was deafening, overwhelming, all I wanted to do was curl up as small as I could and wait for the first strike. They seemed to be egging one another on and nothing seemed to be able to stop them. Once again the shame I felt overwhelmed me and, as the ground didn't seem to want to open up and swallow me, I did the next best thing, I made myself as small as possible, put my arms over my head and just waited for death to arrive.

Pause

I don't know how long I stayed like that or what it was I first noticed, was it the pain in my body, cramped for so long in one position or was it the silence, the silence like I've never heard it before. I thought maybe I'd died and not noticed but no, the pain in my limbs was so acute I realised I was very much alive. I gradually began to unfold myself trying not to cry out in pain as I did so. Eventually I opened my eyes and quickly shut them again, I must be dreaming, it can't be possible, the pack were not only silent but they had gone, but where? What was going on? I opened my eyes again slowly, blinking at the bright light and yes, it was true, they were no longer there but wait, there was something still there.

I shielded my eyes against the sunlight and squinted in the direction of the shape, it was a man bent over, a man I had never seen before, a man who, on sitting up, had the kindest eyes I had ever seen but also a look in those eyes that I couldn't quite fathom but they seemed to see right through me. I hauled myself into a sitting and then standing position and forced myself to look into those eyes, to face what it was that I could see there and then he spoke to me, 'Woman, where have they all gone? Have they not sentenced you to death?' It took me a few minutes to find my voice, I'm not sure if it was because I was still so scared of death, too well aware that I had been found guilty of adultery and knew the penalties of that, so afraid for my family who would be forever affected by my actions or because I just couldn't work out what was going on. 'No sir' I eventually stuttered back at him, still not quite believing that the pack of men who had caught me all those hours ago had finally gone. He spoke again 'Then neither will I but from now on do not sin again'.

Who am I? by Sandra Crawford
(Moses)

Shaped to be less than my potential by my voice and those of others.
Broken promises, rebukes, labels, self-limiting thoughts,
gossip and nicknames, leave a deposit which shape me,
a residue that covers me,
my greatest unbelief is in myself.
Given shoes which determine my path.

But God speaks, "Nevertheless". I take off my shoes for this is Holy Ground.
The 'I Am' of eternity confronts the 'who am I?'

Speaking to the potential he has created,
seeing beyond my unbelief,
taking me down to the spring of my life,
telling me my nature and my name.

Yet the voices that shape me to be less than my potential still protest.
All my self-doubt, fear and failure wrapped up in these three words -
'Who am I?'. A scream from within. Not me. I can't. Send him.
But God's call is to stand on holy ground.
My every-day, ordinary life,
surrendered to Him as an offering.

The start of a journey to an arena where I cannot exist without Him.
A God who can, speaks to a woman who can't.
My potential realised in my participation with Him.
"Go", he says "set my people free.
I am with you, do not be afraid".
Shoes off, God's call, Holy Ground.
All the while my inner voice continues to chip away at my character
persistently persuading me to discard myself
on my own imagined waste tip of human potential.
Whispering "hopeless, useless, failure".
Yet I seek to attune my ear to God,
choosing shoes of faith to adorn my feet.

My resilience is rooted in the regular refreshing of my call,
hearing a call to obedience not success.
Trusting him, not leaning on my own understanding.
Choosing to listen to another voice.
Who am I? A new creation, friend of God,
Come Holy Spirit embed this within.

Following a call to lead a people of ekklesia – 'the called out ones',
but discovering a spirit of enlesia, -'called in ones'.
Settled, safe and secure, looking behind,
proudly proclaiming how far they've come.
Content with their buildings and keeping them spotless.
Unsettle them Lord, let them journey again.

Lord give me an undivided heart, to seek your holy face, to be still.
To see with human eyes but perceive with divine sight.
Teach me to move beyond toleration ...to ove,
to encourage, enable, empower.
Enable me to see your pillar of cloud and fire.
Oh that they would choose life and follow

Who am I?
New creation, child of God, friend of God, His handiwork, saint, righteous, holy.
Shaped by the great I Am, who has spoken to my potential.
Called to lead wearing the shoes he designed.
To declare 'nevertheless' to the who am I's
whose potential is crushed by the voices within.
Help me lead them to your Promised Land.

Said Jesus to Martha... by Catriona Gorton

Said Jesus to Martha
Martha, sit down a moment...
No, not on that hard, kitchen chair, here in the soft welcome of the settee.

Martha, take a moment for yourself...
Put down the tea-towel, the duster, the broom; pick up a book or gaze through the window

Martha, have a little refreshment...
No, not the healthy apple or the plain biscuit, choose the
sumptuous richness of Belgian chocolate or cream-filled gateau

Martha, take a moment to indulge...
Lay aside the list of jobs to be done, people to be helped;
daydream, reflect, meditate, be

Martha this is your moment, your day...
No, not a recollection of your distractedness, but a celebration
of your authenticity
Martha, homemaker, theologian, sister, disciple...

~

We pause for a moment to see yourself in us, and to accept
ourselves as we are, image bearers of the God of Jesus Christ,
unique, loved, welcomed.

Build your House on Rock by Emma Nash

Main Road Baptist Church was a community of people who
really knew their Bible. On Sundays God's Word was preached
with great authority and the people listened well. Many brought
their own Bibles and notebooks so that they could make careful
notes of the teaching points and highlight favourite verses to
read again later. Everyone made Sunday morning a priority, so
that they could be fed with excellent teaching to set them up for
the week.

In order to build on their commitment to knowing the Bible
inside out, people met for Bible study in each other's homes
during the week. The text for the week was dwelt on and
pored over, with detailed study notes to ensure that every
nuance of translation and every cultural reference was properly
understood.

This wholesome community, well fed on the Word of God, was strong and successful. Large numbers at Sunday services meant that finances were never a problem, unlike other nearby churches which were struggling with declining numbers and crumbling buildings. The people of Main Road Baptist Church saw the struggles around them and worried that that might be them in a few years. They had large financial reserves totalling many hundreds of thousands, which they kept carefully topped up in case they were ever needed.

Sometimes there were problems when some people in the community failed to understand God's Word correctly, and others had to put them right. They would send each other letters explaining the errors they had fallen into, speaking the truth in love. Occasionally someone would refuse to heed the letter that had been sent, and continued in their error, which was very difficult and made the others, who had understood God's Word correctly, quite angry. It was so very important to ensure that everyone knew and understood the Bible.

One Sunday morning, the people of Main Road Baptist Church were enjoying coffee and fellowship after a particularly inspiring Sunday morning service, when they noticed the Lord Jesus walking by the church on the other side of the road. Some of the deacons rushed outside to greet the Lord with joy. "Lord, Lord!" they cried, "We've been waiting for your return for such a long time!" To their horror, the Lord turned to them with a blank look. "I'm sorry," the Lord said in confusion, "I never knew you."

Main Road Baptist Church was a community of people who really lived their Bible. On Sundays God's Word was preached with great authority and the people listened well, and discussed together how they might make the message a reality in their lives. Many brought their own Bibles and notebooks so that they could jot down ideas for the coming week – a person they might visit, a charitable cause they might support in some way or a new habit they might try to cultivate. Everyone made Sundays a priority, so that they could be fed with excellent teaching to put into practice during the week.

In order to build on their commitment to putting the Bible into practice in every part of their lives, people met for Bible study in each other's homes during the week. The text for the week was dwelt on and pored over, with lots of time for supporting each other in the challenging daily discipline of applying God's Word in everything they did.

This wholesome community, which got regular exercise living out the Word of God, was strong and successful, but saw struggle all around them. Other nearby churches were battling against declining numbers, crumbling buildings and little money. The people of Main Road Baptist Church saw the struggles around them and worried that that might be them in a few years. They built strong partnerships with neighbouring churches and shared their resources as much as they could. Their generosity meant that their reserves were never as high as they would like, but they trusted God for the future. They knew that he would provide them with what they needed, as they tried to supply the needs of others around them.

Sometimes there were problems when people in the community made mistakes and let each other down. Loud disagreements were common, but it was accepted that this was part of life in community, and once the problems had been aired people would forgive each other and part friends. Everyone knew that they were just as likely to make mistakes as the next person, so they were slow to get angry and quick to forgive.

One Sunday morning, the people of Main Road Baptist Church were enjoying coffee and fellowship after a particularly challenging Sunday morning service, when the Lord Jesus walked in the front door and joined the queue for coffee. Everyone rushed over to greet the Lord with joy, and it was quite some time before everyone had had their turn to shake Jesus' hand, or fling their arms round his neck for a hug, or fall at his feet. "Lord, Lord!" they cried, "We've been waiting for your return for such a long time!" "I am here", the Lord replied, "and this time I am here to stay."

The Festival by **Emma Nash**

The festival was held every year. Christians gathered from all over the country, in church or social groups, to spend a few days together worshipping God. They loved the energy that was generated by so many worshippers gathered together with one purpose.

In the mornings they attended Bible studies taught by world-renowned scholars. People got up early and queued up with their Bibles, notebooks and early morning coffee to hear the great teachers. They listened as gradually their biblical knowledge was stripped away little by little, and they left every session knowing less than they had when they went in.

In the afternoons many people attended a great marketplace in the middle of the venue where tables were piled high with books, clothing and other supplies. People brought bags of good-quality clothes to be donated to homeless charities; Bibles to be sent to countries where most Christians could not afford or even get hold of a Bible; toys and other trinkets to be sold in charity shops to raise money for good causes. Day by day the piles increased, and volunteers sifted through the mountains of stuff, sorting donations.

It was in the evenings that the really exciting things happened, however. Thousands gathered in the largest of the venues as the worship band began to play beautiful songs of lament. Everyone cried as they wept for love of God's hurting world. Then someone got up to speak about the power of prayer. People with a special story to tell were invited to step forward. They spoke of chronic illnesses; devastating bereavements; painful failures. Then a time of prayer ministry began. The happy and the whole came forward and people laid hands on them and prayed. The Spirit moved in great power, and they walked away limping.

The Syro-Phoenician Woman and Jesus by Emma Nash

*This meditation was written at a time when Donald Trump was President of the USA. Please adapt to replace his name [marked *] with that of a relevant politician for your own context.*

I wonder what Donald Trump* would make of Jesus' words?

"Let the children be fed first, for it is not fair to take the children's food and throw it to the dogs" (Mark 7.27).

America First.
Britain First.
First my people, then the others.
First Jews, then outsiders.
First children, then dogs.

It is not right to take housing and benefits from our own people and give them to foreigners.
It is not right to threaten the children's safety by letting in Yemeni dogs, Iranian dogs, Sudanese dogs.

Our safety comes before the welfare of foreigners.
Our resources feed us first, foreigners second.

Woman, you and your child are the wrong religion, the wrong
nationality – I am here for the benefit of my own people.

Did he really mean that?
Did she change his mind?

Abraham persuaded God to have mercy on Sodom and
Gomorrah if just ten righteous people were found there.

Moses persuaded God not to bring disaster upon the Israelites
for worshipping the golden calf.

Is this what is happening here?
Does just one clever riposte make the difference between
indifference and action, between misery and healing?
Is this the well-articulated protest which makes a powerful man
change his mind?

Was it all a test?

Was Jesus' apparent insult a way of finding out how much she
wanted his help,
How much she trusted him?
Like the persistent job applicant who wears the boss down;
Like the lobbyist who carries their point through sheer
perseverance?

Must we remember the profound miracle of the incarnation to
understand what is going on here?
The eternal Son, born as a human being, limited by a human
body, human emotions, human culture?
Was Jesus simply being a normal first century Palestinian Jew?

Did she come at the wrong time?
Was her arrival a few months premature?
Jesus tried so hard to keep his ministry a secret,
but the miracles kept bursting out of him,
refusing to be contained within the secrecy he mysteriously felt necessary.

A time would come when Gentile dogs would become God's children;
When Jesus would send his servant Paul as an apostle to the Gentiles;
When not even the outpouring of the Holy Spirit would be withheld from them.

Perhaps she came at the wrong time.
Like the party guest who arrives fifteen minutes before the start time, disregarding party etiquette.
Like the person who calls when you've just sat down with a glass of wine and the remote control.
Like the knock at the office door when you're concentrating on something.
Like someone else's domestic crisis that erupts and knocks your week sideways.
It's not the right time.
But she's begging for your help.

And Jesus does help.
The children may be hungry, but he feeds the dog anyway.
It may be Israel first, but here a Gentile jumps the queue.
A foretaste of the banquet to which all will be invited.
A foreshadowing of the time when the curtain will be torn from top to bottom, and even a Gentile centurion will declare that Jesus is the Son of God.

Jesus shows mercy.

He changes his foreign policy.
He recognises the desperation – and the hope – in someone
who worships the wrong gods.
He allows himself to be taken off course, to be interrupted, by
someone who needs his help

Eleven million refugees from Syria.
Many thousands attempting to cross the Mediterranean every
summer.
Hundreds of children travelling alone, we come nowhere;
They do not have valid visas;
There is no room for them here.
Our country is not a lifeboat to be swamped and dragged under.
We have our own problems, we have austerity.
Britain First.
It is not fair to take the children's food and throw it to the dogs.

In South Essex, a group of yarnbombers decide to create a 14ft
Christmas tree out of knitted and crocheted green squares.
Squares in various shades of green, from palest sage to deep
forest, arrive from all over the world.
A ball of yellow yarn adorns the top of the tree.
In January, the tree is disassembled and the squares knit
together by an army of volunteers to make blankets for
refugees in the Calais Jungle.

Elsewhere in Essex the local council have agreed to take in ten
refugees, but insist that they already have a huge waiting list for
social housing.
And so a local church agrees that, instead of looking for a
private tenant, it will offer its rental property to the council.
A family are identified who are especially vulnerable and need a
place of safety.
They are flown to the UK where they are met by members of the
church at the airport.

The family move into the church flat and they begin to rebuild their lives, assisted by their new neighbours.

'So she went home, found the child lying on the bed, and the demon gone' (Mark 7.30).

The Head Louse's Tale by Helen Paynter

(A reflection on the story of David and Goliath)

I am a head-louse; my name is Pediculus.
Most of my friends call me Pestilent Ped.
Though I look strange, do not judge me ridiculous,
Think of the itch I could cause on your head.

I stumbled once on a banquet quite sumptuous:
Beef, brawn and brave with a great shaggy head.
Three metres high (with a swagger presumptuous),
I thought Goliath would keep me well fed.

He was a soldier (with armpits malodorous),
Dwarfed all the others, who viewed him with dread.
I was content in my billet commodious,
Splendidly catered-for. 'Perfect,' I said.

Thus was the start of a partnership glorious:
Just by his helmet, I sat on his head.
Itching his scalp made the giant so furious,
No-one could vanquish Goliath and Ped.

Then came a stand-off: two armies so tremulous;
Shaking their spears but desiring their bed.
Carnage and gore seemed excessive and strenuous
Up stepped Goliath with Plan B instead.

Swaggering forth, his demeanour contemptuous,
'Send out your hero to fight me,' he said.
'Which of yon Israelite horde feels adventurous?
What? Have your nerve and audacity fled?'

Out stepped a boy, his appearance innocuous;
Fresh-faced and beardless, cheeks smooth and red.
Shrill voice denounced pagan practice idolatrous;
Marched at Goliath with valiant tread.

Girt not in armour, the boy was conspicuous;
Wool was his mantle and bare was his head.
Stooped and selected five stones (so meticulous);
Playthings for boys from the cool river bed.

Seeing the youngster, Goliath was furious.
'Am I a dog or a soldier?' he said.
Bold, the youth answered, 'By Yahweh the glorious,
He will uphold me and give me your head.

'Trusting in armour, your logic is spurious;
Size is no ally, and you should have fled.
I am on God's side; we will be victorious;
You are the one who will topple, instead.'

Puzzled, I pondered his meaning mysterious
Surely this infant could not be a threat?
Helmet and mail proved the giant was serious;
This callow youth would not live to regret

Puny of bicep, the boy was impetuous,
Into the teeth of the giant he sped.
Maddened, Goliath's reply was tempestuous,
'Vultures today will be very well-fed!'

Spinning towards me with motion vertiginous,
Stone from the sling-shot! I watched it with dread.

Doom for the man, and his vermin indigenous;
Fatal trajectory straight for my head.

Now my predicament seemed quite invidious;
Trapped as I was on the top of his head.
All of my knees knocked from misgivings hideous;
If I'd had wings, I'd have certainly fled.

Dazzling bronze made the target conspicuous;
Three metres high stood his towering head.
Narrowly missed me! The aim was meticulous –
Right between malice-filled eyes to embed.

Down crashed the giant, his end ignominious;
Felt his own sword as it cut off his head.
His last expression was less supercilious;
Dinner himself for the vultures instead.

Who should be thanked for this triumph miraculous:
Turbo-charged sling, or the giant's neglect?
Whether a weakling, or muscled and fabulous –
Ponder in depth on which side you'll select.

What of the fate of your hero, Pediculus:winging aloft on a body-
less head?
Swiftly defecting, with leap inconspicuous,
Now I'm infesting the victor, instead.

The Master Craftsman by Sandra Crawford

The Tale often told about Michelangelo forming a statue speaks of how spiritual formation takes place in the heart:

The Lion in the Marble
There was once a sculptor who worked hard with hammer and chisel on a large block of marble. A little child who was watching him saw nothing more than large and small pieces of stone falling away left and right. He had no idea what was happening. But when the boy returned to the studio a few weeks later, he saw, to his surprise, a large, powerful lion sitting in the place where the marble had stood. With great excitement, the boy ran to the sculptor and said, "Sir, tell me, how did you know there was a lion in the marble?"

I marvel as I watch the master sculptor chip away,
forming something other: His design.
As wood, marble and stone require hammer, chisel, patience and skill,
so the human spirit is shaped by the master craftsman

Is a spiritual life defined by tranquillity
or obedience? Following
God's Spirit as he draws us to the unfamiliar, the unknown.
The alternative? Distraction, busyness, emptiness.

The challenge to move from noise and mindless occupation,
to listening. Awareness of God's Spirit,
his active presence. Creation of empty spaces.
Resistance to voices that compete. Being not doing.

I choose to stop, to look at the dark days: pain, hurt, despair,
loneliness, confusion and loss,

choosing to see chipping and crafting, chiselling. Your active presence
revealing something new, something other, your new design.

As I submit my life to you as marble to be crafted,
tough and unyielding, provide me with
companions who will encourage, challenge, caution and counsel.
Lord, create a new heart and renew a right spirit in me.

Amazing Grace, Unfailing Love by Sandra Crawford

This is inspired by the song Amazing Grace, Unfailing Love by Chris Tomlin

Your value is not dependent upon your performance on the stage of your life.
You are a
 forgiven man,
a forgiven child,
a new creation.
All charges against you are cancelled .
How?
Because you have punished yourself enough?
Because you keep trying harder?
Because you are working towards perfection?
Absolutely not!
Because of the life, death and resurrection of my son.
Your shortcomings, failures and regrets
were nailed to the cross,
paid for in full,
once and for all, no further sacrifice needed.
Amazing grace. Unfailing love.

And yet you choose to listen to another voice, one who
accuses, one who sows seeds of doubt,
one who says 'you're not good enough'.
'You're not worthy'.
'You cannot be clean'.
'You must live with condemnation and
failure,
trapped and bound forever in disappointment and self-loathing'.
Why do you choose to listen to
the accuser? the one who blinds your mind?
the liar?
How long will you let the enemy triumph over you?
For these are the words of the God of this age,
making your soul downcast.
Instead, choose life.
My child I broke the power of sin and darkness.
Amazing grace. Unfailing love.

You are my beloved. You are my child. You are forgiven. You are
justified.
You are free from accusation.
Not through your hard work,
not by your striving,
but by grace.
Your self-worth does not lie in your performance
or the opinion of others,
your worth, value and ability come from me,
precious one.
So why do you listen to the voices that accuse?
My child allow me to renew your mind,
I know your past regrets,
 don't live there,
 instead step into my embrace and my promises.
Amazing grace, unfailing love.

Put your hope in me, your Saviour and your God. Rejoice in your
salvation, and sing my praises.
Trust in me with all your heart,
do not lean on your
own understanding,
but live and walk in my love, mercy
and grace.
I created you. I love you. I know you.
I have rescued you from darkness,
hear my constant whisper, 'there is no condemnation
in Christ'.
Your sin is removed as far as the east is from the west,
love keeps no record of wrongs, and I am love .
Don't live in the shadows,
walk in the light, be free.
Have confidence in me, hold unswervingly to my hope.
Amazing grace, unfailing love.

Duane and Mabel by Lisa Kerry

It's time now to tell you all of a pair
Who both loved to work in the fresh open air.
A brother, a sister, their names, Duane and Mabel
You may well have heard of their cousins – Cain and Abel.

Now Mabel was not an intelligent youth
Perhaps a bit slow, to tell you the truth
But Mabel loved sheep, and made it her plan
To have her own flock and raise her own clan.

But Duane, he was quick and really quite clever
To farm lots of fields was his own endeavour
And though he looks slick, he's not a shirker

No, Duane was in fact, a very hard worker.
And so to their separate projects they went,
To see that their time was not idly spent.

Mabel's sheep were truly a sight to behold
To her they looked like a pot full of gold
She loved every one and tended their needs
She even got up in the night for their feeds.

Duane and his fields were now spreading wide
His neat tidy farms were turning the tide –
Of fashion nearby, and soon everyone
Was standing and looking at what he had done.

Now harvest was coming and both Duane and Mabel
Looked for a gift to bring to the table.

Duane looked at his fields and couldn't decide
What to take from his crops that spread far and wide
He wanted to keep it all looking neat
Even when others had nothing to eat!

But Duane was quick and had inspiration
For how to tackle his problem donation
He gave to church funds a healthy sum,
And then with a small gift to church he would come.

Mabel too had her problems with sheep.
In fact it was making her lose out on sleep.
Her prize-winning ewe was expecting a baby-
Would it come in time for harvest – maybe?

She waited and waited to see if this ewe
Would deliver the lamb on the day it was due,
And then it arrived, at 4 in the morning

Just as the day of harvest was dawning.
And so the pair came, both Duane and Mabel
Bringing their gifts to God's holy table.

Now Duane, he looked suave and terribly neat
He'd done up his gift and it looked a real treat;
All ribbons and bows, there it lay on the table
As he tried not to sneer at scruffy old Mabel

Mabel was tired and really quite smelly
Something rather disgusting was stuck to her welly,
She humbly came forward with tears in her eyes
And gave to the Lord her Shepherding prize

God looked at Duane, and gazed upon Mabel
He looked at their gifts now laid on the table
And what do you think He made of the scene?
Did He like the new lamb, or the gift that was clean?

Well, God looked at Duane and said *"Don't you care?
That you only gave to me of your spare?
Take your gift Duane and put it out of my sight
I'm afraid that your choice was really not right"*

God smiled upon Mabel and on her prize sheep
Her wonderful gift had made His heart leap.
To Mabel He said, *"You have shown me your care
By giving your best lamb."* – Lamb said *"Baaaa"*

And now you may wonder, why tell us this rhyme?
Why should we give Duane and Mabel our time?
And what does it matter whatever *we* give?
Surely God's not bothered about how *we* all live?

Well yes, God is bothered, the reason? – here's one,
For us He gave his very own Son.

When it came to us, He gave up His best
And perhaps we had better think on it, lest
We miss out on the chance of a brand new start,
When all that we have to give is our heart

Diamond Reflection by Sarah Bingham

Think about a diamond. What is it? A lump of compressed
super-heated carbon? An industrial cutting tool – the hardest
substance known to man? A precious stone to be crafted into a
beautiful jewel?

A diamond is all of those things. Chemically, diamond is the
same as graphite. However, their appearance, qualities and
use are different. The thing that makes all the difference is the
conditions under which the mineral is formed. Diamond is only
created under conditions of severe heat and pressure. That is
why they are so rare.

Due to the conditions under which they form, diamonds have
unique properties. The internal structure makes them very hard
indeed – and allows them to be used to cut almost any other
material known to man. That same structure means that pure
diamonds will reflect and refract light in very special ways –
which makes them perfect to be carved into sparkling gems.

Zechariah 9:16 says that we will 'shine on His land like the jewels
of a crown, for they are the flock of His people'.

So, do you consider yourself to be a jewel? Or are you more
like graphite – grey and functional, rather than shining and

beautiful? Are you ready to allow heat and pressure to transform you into the jewel that God already sees? Is your vision obscured as you focus on the clay, rather than the treasure within?

I am an Alabaster Jar by Juliet Lloyd

I am an alabaster jar
I am precious to my owner
and held safe within my heart is the stuff of worship and service
I am unique ... my form designed with special attention by my creator
... my marks and blemishes are like fingerprints to him...
his fingers trace each one and he smiles ... because he intended them ...
they are part of my uniqueness ...
... like the molecules, the chromosomes and genes ... the DNA in any human
... they are no surprise to the Maker... never a mistake ... but part of his rich pattern. My curves are unnerving to some, though ... for they speak of otherness.

Too fluid ... they show unusual gentleness, and therefore, some say, weakness...
or even sensuality and passion ... and so, perhaps, loss of propriety...
or loss of control ... of emotions...of power of reason ... who knows?

I only know that I sit better in the hand and give more delight to the carrier.
... and I cause less damage to those with whom I come into close relationship.

Do they know that these curves are only achieved by the
dedicated rasping away
of hard edges and corners by a craftsman over time?
Some would bar my owner's way or deny her access to the one
she seeks,
but still He calls her forward to sit at His feet and simply know
Him.

I am an alabaster jar
My owner holds me close to her heart ... I am precious to her.
But though she, too, loves my quirky form
what she values most is what I carry inside me, for that is of
much greater worth ... that is where my true glory ... and the
essence of her fulfilment lie.
For I carry within me the stuff of worship and service.
And now that the true object of that worship is before us,
I know that I shall find myself broken ... just as she has found
herself broken ...
and in need of His compassion, restoration and recommission.
But neither of us shall be fearful of the process... because He is
the Potter... the same one who made us and so can remake us
as we need to be.
And like pieces of Kintsugi[3] pottery ... a golden thread tracing
each crack and scar... ... the signs of repair will only prove us
stronger and more precious than before.

---

3   Kintsugi is a Japanese method of repairing broken pottery using gold
     rather than glue! The resultant piece has a unique beauty in which the
     'scars' are visible and even celebrated as part of the 'redeemed' whole.

Communion – Breaking Bread

Liturgies, reflections and prayers for use when meeting around the Lord's Table

All Nations Church by Gale Richards

This Communion liturgy was used at the BUGB Baptist Assembly in May 2019, and is particularly suited to the Easter season.

Words of Approach
Acts 10: 34-35… "I now realize how true it is that God does not show favouritism but accepts from every nation the one who fears him and does what is right." (NIV)

Risen Christ, who shows no favouritism to any people group or nation, and in whom we are able to see our Creator's desire to work through people of all nations, to heal and bring heavenly peace to earth - we long to follow your example and confess our need to grow in this commitment.

Invitation
We recognise this table we eat and drink from is a table open to all who seek to follow in the ways of Christ.

In recognition of what this bread and wine has, does and will signify, we will give thanks in prayer.

Thanksgiving prayer
Creator God,
What must it have been like for the Son of Humanity to share multiple times about the suffering he was to endure, how he would be rejected by the elders, the chief priests, and the scribes, and be killed; and then go on to experience these things?

In this Easter season, as we celebrate that such suffering was not the end of the story, but after three days the Son of Humanity rose again, we pause to take in and give thanks for the body given for us, and the blood poured out for us.

We draw inspiration from the apostles' selfless response of committing themselves to your message of an all nations church, sacrificially working together, to bring your heavenly healing and peace to earth.

In awe and wonder we will eat and drink of this table as a sign of us committing ourselves to your message of an all nations church, sacrificially working together, to bring your heavenly healing and peace to earth.
Amen

The Sharing of bread and wine
We remember, Christ, that with your disciples you broke and blessed bread, poured and blessed wine;
Feed us now as we eat and drink and seek to be witnesses to your sacrificial life, death, and resurrection, as we await your promised return.
Let us eat the bread and drink the wine as we receive them...

Prayers of Intercession
Faithful God,
As we thank you that we have been fed at this table;
We pray for people, places and situations experiencing divisions.
We think particularly of...
We pray for an outpouring of your wisdom, love and peace through your all nations church to bring healing and transformation.
This we ask through Christ whose ways we seek to follow in the whole of our lives. Amen

An All Age Communion by Catriona Gorton

Invitation
We gather round a table, set for a meal
Clean linen and sparkling silver, fresh baked bread and
outpoured wine
We gather round a table, having come ill-prepared
Our hands unwashed, the dust of the day clinging to our clothes

We gather round a table, as members of one family
Brothers and sisters of heavenly parentage,
Children of God
Siblings in Christ.

The Story & Distribution
Why are we here?
Why do we take tiny crumbs of bread and teeny sips of wine?
Why do we pretend this is a feast when everything is a token?

Here is why.

Late one spring evening, at the time when everyone was
celebrating God's goodness a very long time ago, Jesus and
his friends had one last meal together. They borrowed a room
and enjoyed a good meal as they sang o d psalms and prayed
lovely prayers.
Then Jesus did something odd
As he picked up some bread, he said a prayer, then he broke it
and said, 'when you eat bread, think about me, because just as
this bread is broken, my body will be broken.'

They didn't understand.
But no-one dared ask what he meant.
So they took the bread and ate it.
And so will we!

Prayer over bread

Thank you God for bread, even this tiny little taste reminds us of the food you give us each day.

Thank you God for Jesus, help us to think about him whenever we eat bread.

Amen.

[Bread served and eaten]

After everyone had eaten their tea and was feeling pleasantly full, Jesus did something else odd

He picked up a goblet of wine and said, 'when you drink wine, think about me, because just as this wine has been poured out, so my life blood will be poured out, and there will be a new bond between people and God.'

They didn't understand

But no-one dared ask what he meant

So they took the cup of wine and drank from it.

And so will we!

[Wine distributed and cups retained]

Prayer over wine

Thank you God for wine, even this tiny little sip reminds us of the joy you give us each day.

Thank you God for Jesus, who calls us his brothers and sisters if we follow his way.

Help us to think about him whenever we drink wine.

Amen.

[Wine drunk]

After the meal was over, Jesus and his friends sang a song together before they went out, and so will we.

Story-Telling All Age Communion by Catriona Gorton

Invitation
When we read the Bible, we find stories of lots of meals Jesus shared with other people...
He shared picnics on the side of hills, and grand banquets in the homes of powerful people
He accepted hospitality from religious people and tax-gatherers, lepers and unmarried women
He even appreciated it when a woman whose reputation was a little suspect washed his feet with her tears
He cooked fish on a beach and broke bread with weary travellers at the end of a long day

Jesus shared in ordinary meals and special meals
Meals that were essential and meals that were parties
And today we pause to remember and to re-enact as best we can, the most special, simple, religiously significant, celebratory and sad meal of all.

The Story
It's a story we know well, because we have heard it many, many times.
And because we know it so well, we no longer hear it properly.
So let's try to imagine we are there, in the story, standing in the shadows watching and listening...

This is the time of the Passover festival, when Jews remember how Yahweh brought their ancestors out of slavery in the land of Egypt, led by Moses. It is a family time, a time to share in food and singing, and to give thanks to God.

Jesus is coming up the stairs with his friends. Judas is carrying the money bag, Peter is chatting to Andrew; James and John are squabbling, as usual; Thomas is asking Matthew about something or other... Soon they settle down and take their places around the low table and the food is brought in. It smells lovely and tastes even better.

Jesus reaches across and picks up some bread. Everyone pauses, and looks towards him. He holds it up and says a thank you prayer to God. Then he speaks. "Do you see this bread? Look, I am breaking it. Just like this bread, my body will be broken, so that everyone's sins can be forgiven. Each time you eat bread, I want you to remember this."

The bread passes round, and everyone takes some and chews it, wondering what Jesus means by his words.

Jesus reaches out again and picks up a big goblet of wine. Again every eye is upon him. After he has said the thank you prayer he speaks. "See this wine? It was poured out for you. Just like this wine, my blood will be poured out, so that everyone's sins can be forgiven. Each time you drink wine, I want you to remember this."

And so the goblet is passed round, and everyone takes a drink from it, wondering what Jesus is talking about.

Thanksgiving
For hundreds and hundreds of years people have carried on remembering this story. In big cathedrals and small mission halls; in tents and on beaches; in hospital wards and in prison cells; with lots of ceremony and fancy words; in secret and in silence.

And now we take our turn, so let's say thank you to God.

For this bread and this wine, we thank you, generous God. For this story and all it means, we give you praise.

As we eat and drink, and as we tell the story in our lives, help us to remember why we do so
Amen.

Distribution
[According to local custom]

Prayer Afterwards
Jesus lived among people like us, telling wonderful stories and sharing tasty food
Jesus died alone on a hillside; his friends ran away and hid in fear
Jesus rose again and made a barbecue breakfast for his followers
Jesus returned to God, but left his friends with a promise that he would come back one day
Until then, we will remember every time we eat and drink together.
Amen.

All Age Communion – Stories of Banquets by Catriona Gorton

This liturgy draws on the gospel account of Herod's banquet and the execution of John the Baptist, which is set alongside Jesus' parables about banquets, and the story of the Last Supper. The oblique reference to the Herod story makes it suitable for an all age context.

Invitation
Herod had a banquet
And he invited all the important people he could think of
And did everything he could think of to impress them
And in the end he did something very foolish
Because he didn't want to look silly

Jesus spoke of a banquet
Where all the important people said 'no thank you, I've got a better offer'
So the host invited everyone else who could be found
People of other races and languages
People who might drink too much or say the wrong thing
People who were too poor to invite him back
He did something that seemed very foolish
But God's foolishness is beyond human wisdom

Jesus had a small dinner party
Just him and his closest friends
They wanted to celebrate how good God had been
A very, very long time ago
Jesus said things that seemed very strange, even a bit silly
But his friends remembered the words
And passed them on, for a very, very long time
So that even today we can share in a special memory meal

Institution
One of the first followers of Jesus, called Paul wrote down what he had learned: [read from 1 Cor 11 GNB or other 'easy' language version]

Prayer
Party-loving God, you gave us this special way of remembering all that Jesus has done for us,
So that as we take tiny bites of bread and sips of wine it is like being in a great banquet
To which everyone who ever lives is welcome
Help us to be thankful for all Jesus has done, even though it seems strange and we may not understand it
And help us to live like him, giving ourselves for other people
Amen.

Distribution
[According to local custom]

Acclamation
It seems crazy, God, that you would allow Jesus to die
But in his death we find new life
It seems impossible, God, that Jesus would rise again,
But in his rising he shows us death is never the end
It blows our minds, God, to think that Jesus might come again
But this is the hope that we live towards
An upside-down Kingdom of justice, peace and joy.

Unpacking Communion by Claire Nicholls

You need:
- Table
- A box or picnic basket containing:
- Communion Cloth, Bible, Cup, Wine, Plate, Bread, Candle, matches

You will need to gradually unpack the box and set up the table through the liturgy, led by the headings in *italics*.

Script
As we prepare for communion let us get the room ready, as the disciples did at the Last Supper.

Read: Luke 22:7-13

Table
Here is the table. It's a table that speaks of 2000 years of history where the people of God have gathered and eaten and drunk to remember the first time that Jesus did this, on that first Thursday, the day before he was to go to the cross.

As we gather around the table we are reminded that we are not alone.

We gather with those who are part of our journey – those who hold us up when we feel unsteady and those who have inspired us and shown us God's way.

We gather with those who we love, those who are broken, those we worry about and those who worry about us.

We gather to share life and faith and love as we remember the one who came so we might live our lives in all their fullness.

As we lay the table we tell His story, which is our story too.

Cloth
This cloth represents the communion of the saints: those who have been washed clean of their sins as they have turned to Jesus. We each have a place amongst the threads and stitches of this cloth, as we can all be made clean, we can all be forgiven.
This cloth represents the grave clothes left empty, where the death we remember was overcome, and resurrection conquered all. We each have the promise of the resurrection life, and as we remember, we recall how there is more to this story than body broken and blood shed.

Bible
This Bible contains everything we need to know about this story that we remember today. It begins with nothing and ends with everything. It tells us a story of covenant, a story of love, a story that is life changing, a story of truth and a story of eternity.

As we remember the story, we remember that we are part of something much bigger than in this room, and we stand with the worldwide church as together, on this day, we remember that last supper, which once again re-centres us on Jesus.

Cup
[fill with wine]
This cup told those first disciples the story of Passover – of how God chose them and loved them and brought them out of slavery. This cup tells us the story of blood shed for us so that we might know the depth of God's love and the freedom he offers through death on a cross.

Bread
[and plate]
This bread speaks of life shared, of body wholeness, of body broken. It tells the story of how Jesus brought wholeness by breaking for us.

As we lay this table, as we prepare and get ready, let us remember how in the breaking, we are restored, how in the shedding, we have freedom and how together with the communion of the saints we can stand in hope because we know that there is more to life than the things we see around us.

Candle
This candle speaks of the light that never goes out. The Christ light: that, even in the darkest of darkest places, cannot be snuffed out. It reminds us, as we remember this story, and even on our own the darkest days, that there is still light.

[Light candle]

As we watch the candle flicker let us bring ourselves to God, in silence, as we offer our brokenness to him and ask for forgiveness.

Sharing at the Table

We're going to share bread and wine, and we're going to serve one another. When you are ready, come to the table, bring someone with you or meet someone there, and serve one another – pray and give thanks, share peace with one another, share bread, share wine. And remember that this is a feast, so eat big chunks of bread, take big gulps of wine, take your time, and return to your seats with the taste of the meal.

Read 1 Corinthians 11:23-26

[share bread and wine]

As we have gathered at the table, we have been reminded of all that God has done for us. In this story that re-centres us, that holds us together in what unites us, that speaks of restoration and forgiveness, of new life – we find life in all its fullness. The table levels us, calls us as equals; however we are feeling, whatever we have done, however well life is going right now. It takes us all to the place that child is in, who to every question in church answers Jesus.

The table reminds us that there is always hope, there is always forgiveness, and there is always something more. Christ has died, Christ is risen, Christ will come again.

A Communion for the Parting of Ways by Sarah Bingham

This could be used, for example, at the end of a pilgrimage or a shared project, at a home group when someone is leaving, or at a home communion when someone is dying.

Individuals or groups speak parts 1 and 2

1&2   We come as friends who walk together
1   We come as friends from different places
2   *We come as friends who one day will walk apart*

1&2   We come invited by Jesus to remember
1   We come because He is our saviour
2   *We come because He is our friend*

1&2   We come with all our faults, and we are sorry
1   We come knowing we are forgiven when we repent
2   *We come knowing the Spirit brings new life*

[PAUSE and reflect]

1&2   We come with all our regrets, and lay them down
1   We come with tears to be dried
2   *We come with hurts to be healed*

1&2   We come with all our joyous memories
1   We come with memories of people
2   *We come with memories of events*

1&2   We come as we are; imperfect yet loved, unfinished yet chosen, weak yet called (PAUSE)

1&2   We come to remember this parting of the ways for Jesus
1   Him knowing what was to come
2   *His friends still blithely oblivious*

1&2 We come to remember this parting of his body
1 His body broken for healing [nominated person break the bread]
2 *His blood poured out for forgiveness* [second person pour the cup]

1&2 We come to remember his departing from life
1 The skies growing dark
2 *The Temple curtain torn*
[PAUSE]

1&2 We come, even so, in hope – for death could not hold Him
1 We come thankful for reconciliation with God
2 *We come thankful for reconciliation with others*

1&2 We come to share and remember and to look forward to God's final reconciliation in Christ

[Eat and Drink and bless each other, using appropriate words.]

Remember Me by Catriona Gorton
This could be used for a communion service on Remembrance Sunday

Preparing Hearts and Minds

Remember me.
Let me not be forgotten,
Let my living have meaning,
Let my story be told...

Remember me.
Re-member me,

Put back together the fragments of my story
Let me live on in your heart, in your mind...

Here is a mystery too profound for words:
It is in the breaking, the pouring
The tearing and the spilling
That the putting back together becomes possible...

This bread for my body
This cup for my blood
Shared, consumed
Becoming part of you
As you become part of my body...

Remember me.
Re-member me
Put me back together,
Weave together the broken strands of my story
Let me be with you, if not today, then one day, in paradise...

Here is a mystery too profound for words:
It is in the remembering that comes the forgetting
The slate wiped clean, the tears dried
And life after death, life everlasting becomes possible...

Remember me
Let us not forget
Let us live the meaning of the story
Let the story once more be told...

Institution
We remember, we retell, we relive words so familiar they are
almost part of us, and we allow them to live again...

For I received from the Lord what I also handed on to you, that the Lord Jesus on the night when he was betrayed took a loaf of bread, and when he had given thanks, he broke it and said, 'This is my body that is for you. Do this in remembrance of me.' In the same way he took the cup also, after supper, saying, 'This cup is the new covenant in my blood. Do this, as often as you drink it, in remembrance of me.' For as often as you eat this bread and drink the cup, you proclaim the Lord's death until he comes. (1 Corinthians 11: 23 – 26 NRSV)

Thanksgiving Prayer
Remember me.
Remember me in bread broken and wine poured.

Jesus Christ,
We remember you
We remember your instruction to those who would follow in your way
And so in quiet gratitude and humble faith,
We receive these symbols of indestructible love.
Amen.

Distribution in Silence
[according to local custom]

Afterwards
Remember me:
We remember the horrific reality of your arrest, trial and execution
Who became sin for us

Remember me:
We remember the curious mystery of your rising and revelation
Who became life for us

Remember me:
We remember the incomprehensible promise of your coming
Who will lead us all safe home.

A Communion for Hurting People by Diane Holmes

God I was angry
I was angry, God with you
I thought you were someone else
Thought I could ride high on your shoulders
Or love you from afar
You reached out with your bloodless arm
And pulled me close
To break my heart
And left

What Father leaves their child alone?

I was so angry with you
I started to break things
I even made things beautiful
So I could smash them to bits
To show you how it felt
I shattered me
I dashed myself
Against the blind stone walls of my rage
On and on
Until all I had left to break
Was hope
I wanted to break that too,

But I was ashamed
I tried to push and kick the pieces
Under the table but they wouldn't go
There were too many
I was too tired,
They hurt me,
Shards so sharp
My hands and feet are bleeding
There's nothing left to break

Look child
Listen, learn from me
Look
My hands and feet are bleeding too,
Remember how I taught you?
When I was trying to be ready
Remember how I taught you to break me?
To celebrate my brokenness?

Remember that night, before the silence was broken by
betrayal, a table, with gathered friends. Jesus took a loaf of
bread in his hands, and when he had said a thank you, he tore
it apart and said "Take eat......"
And even later, after they had eaten, Jesus took hold of a wine
cup and gave it to his friends and said " Drink this....."
Remember
This bread, my body broken
Dashed against our anger

Remember
This cup
Tears crushed from a broken heart

Don't try to put yourself back together
I can use you broken
As you are
Broken
Together
We can reach so much further
Into all those broken lives
Into every broken heart

Come
Let us break together

For through the breaking
Flows the healing

When there's nothing left to break
Break me

Broken Christ
Keep us breaking
Teach us how to break through
Not down
To crack open
Not up
Break us like the day
Shatter us with your love
Until we are
Each of us
Stars enough
To lighten the darkest night

Unseen and Unheard – a Communion Liturgy by Jane Henderson

Leader:
The Bible records that there were thirteen men sat around the table that evening. Undoubtedly there were more people there whose presence goes unrecorded the women who prepared the Passover meal and served those at the table; the children who are neither seen nor heard; others who, for whatever reason, are not deemed important enough for history to record their presence. Today we see them, we hear them and we acknowledge them as Jesus himself saw and heard and acknowledged. We come together in community with each other, each person seen, each voice heard, each individual acknowledged and valued.

We come together in community and fellowship to remember and to share in this life-giving meal ...

We who are [women][4], whose voices in history have often been excluded, come together tonight, in Jesus' name to celebrate that in Jesus we are included. As we gather and celebrate the Eucharist together we recognise that we represent [women] across our nations and beyond, who the world excludes but who Jesus welcomes and includes.

All are welcome, all are included.
Just as Jesus does, we see the unseen and we hear the unheard ...

Voice 1:
I am unseen by many ... yet he sees me.
I am un-noticed by many ... yet he notices me.
I am unimportant to many ... yet I am important to him.

I am here, on the margins, in the background.
Not seen, not noticed, not important .... Except to him.

My brother Christ, who calls me [Sister/Brother]
who lowers himself to the rank of servant ... he sees me... he notices me... to him I am important ...
I am present ... in him.

Voice 2:
I am unheard by many ... yet he hears me.
I am un-acknowledged by many ... yet he acknowledges me.
I am unworthy to many ... yet I am worthy to him.

---

4   noun may be changed dependent on context

I am here, on the margins, in the background.
Not heard, not acknowledged, not worthy .... Except to him.

My brother Christ, who calls me [Sister/Brother],
who lowers himself to the rank of servant ... he hears me... he
acknowledges me... to him I am worthy ...
I am present ... in him.
Leader:
As we approach the Lord's Table, where all are invited, we
do so with thanksgiving and we offer up our own prayers of
thanksgiving and praise ...

[space for thanksgiving prayers]
And so we come in remembrance of that last Passover supper
where Jesus gathered with his friends.

A group of people much like our own; drawn from those who
love Jesus, those who know Jesus and those who want to be
part of the community in his name.

A group of people much like our own; from different
backgrounds, culturally, ethnically, yet all drawn together in
Jesus' name.

After supper, Jesus took the bread, and after blessing it he
broke it, gave it to his friends, and said, "Take, eat; this is my
body." [share the bread]

Then he took a cup, and after giving thanks he gave it to them,
saying, "Drink from it, all of you; for this is my blood of the
covenant, which is poured out for many for freedom from all
forms of oppression." [share the wine]

Living God we thank you for this bread and this cup, which to
us are your body and blood. We thank you that through the

mystery of your death and resurrection, we can have life in all its fullness.

We are mindful, Loving God, that we are privileged to be able to meet in this way in this place. We particularly think of all those around the world who are marginalised or oppressed, all those who are unseen or unheard, whether because of their gender, their beliefs, their race, their sexuality, their additional needs or any other form of prejudice. In a world that is prejudiced, we celebrate that in you there is no male or female, no Jew or Gentile, but we are all free, all equal and all valued. As we have shared in your meal, in fellowship with you and with each other, we pray that we might see your kingdom come on earth as it is in heaven.
Amen

Additional Prayers

A Communion Invitation for a Covenant Service by Helen Paynter

To this table we are commanded and invited.

At this table we will remember the covenant cut in blood. The covenant into which we have willingly entered and in which we joyfully remain. The covenant which gives us identity and promise. The costly covenant of grace and mercy and forgiveness. The astonishing covenant of the eternal God with mortal humans. We do not set the terms of this covenant, but we are willing participants in it. Here we remember.

At this table we will re-enact the making of the new covenant. The eternal covenant, achieved by the broken body and poured out blood of our Saviour. The covenant which writes

God's law on our minds and our hearts as the Spirit takes out our hearts of stone and gives us hearts of flesh. The new covenant whereby the least to the greatest may know the Lord. Here, as we break bread and pour wine, we re-enact the making of that new covenant.

At this table we will re-affirm the covenant with our sisters and brothers in Christ. The covenant which makes us God's own people binds us to one another. Here, as we eat and drink, we re-appropriate God's covenant promises, we reiterate our covenant vows, and we re-affirm the covenant with those who eat and drink alongside us – in this place, in every place, and in every time. There is one new covenant, there is one covenant meal, there is one covenant people.

And so, we remember... (use your chosen words of institution)

Love Regardless, a Prayer of Confession by Ali Taylor

He stands in the middle of the mess I've made of my life
Casting not a glance at the debris that surrounds his feet
And He looks at me

He looks at me
And simply says "Come"
And opening His arms
He welcomes me into an all-encompassing embrace

I am held by those strong and loving arms
And I hear His words of comfort in my ear
As He reassures me

He reassures me
That all I have done is forgivable

That I am still loved
And worthy of His acceptance

And I begin to sense that acceptance
As I am securely held within the Father's embrace
I know, I feel, within my soul, that unfathomable peace

Graced with God's Presence by **Amanda Pink**

Suitable for use in an ecumenical context and/or during spring/Lent/ Easter

When the warmth of spring permeates our skin,
When our path is blossom-scattered;
When the air is filled with avian trills
And happy musical chatter;
When the sun lights up these hallowed walls
And the vibrant green of neat-clipped lawns,
And we praise You who has made it all:
You grace us with your presence.

In the words and stories of your Book
We find a myst'ry spoken:
As the Word made flesh, our form you took,
And let yourself be broken;
Now when with word and flesh combined,
We celebrate this holy sign,
Through eating bread and drinking wine:
You grace us with your presence.

In sister- and in brother-hood,
In laughter and in prayer,
In grace-filled living and forgiving,
In off'ring costly care;

As we encounter the stranger too,
The poor, and those held in negative view;
When we find in all people the likeness of you:
You grace us with your presence.

And now together in this place
From different customs gathered,
With common call to share your grace -
Thus shortly to be scattered;
We lift our voice in worship, for
By your Spirit now outpoured –
In this moment and forever more
You grace us with your presence!

Prayers and Blessings

Please also check the thematic chapters, as some material is included according to the season or occasion for which it was created.

Opening Worship, Prayers of Approach. Praise and Thanksgiving

Expectant Laughter by Mary Cotes

Why laugh
In a world so often full of disappointment
And unfulfilled dreams?

Once we had great hopes for the future:
A belief in the ways things would turn out
But despite our noblest efforts,
We have not been able to make life happen
Exactly the way we wanted.

Like Sarah,
Who in the heat of the day
Sheltered barren in the recesses of the tent,
We have retreated, heavy hearted,
To hide our disappointment in the privacy of our own lives.

Yet here, today,
Summoned by the murmur of promise,
Intrigued to know more,
We have got up,
And tiptoed to the thin place
Where disappointment opens into hope.

As Sarah, at the door of the tent,
Once listened to the message from the angels,
So we too now
Crane our ears
And dare to eavesdrop on God.

Listening,
We catch the word of assurance:
We are not too old
Too weak,
Too doubting,
Too empty...
Because God - the most high God -
Promises that our lives will serve his purposes.
Out of the little we offer,
God will bring something great.

And we laugh the laugh of amazed and expectant delight.
We laugh at our hopelessness and God's magnificence,
At our barrenness and God's faithfulness,
At God's future opening before us
And God's life alive within us.

Were the angels to tell us that we laughed,
We might deny it,
Imagining that those who have to do with God
Need to be serious and self-controlled.
But as God spoke to Sarah,
So God speaks to us:
Yes, laugh.
LAUGH!
Laugh with the wonder that bubbles to eternal life.

And don't stop!
Keep laughing, till you're splitting your sides,
And you're gasping for breath,
And your belly is cramping and painful.

Laugh:
You are to be a bearer of God's new life.

(Genesis 18:9-15).

Come Just as You Are by Jane Henderson

Call to Worship
Come this morning into the presence of the Holy Trinity. God in three persons. Three in one and one in three.
Come as you are, with all your fears and certainties, your sadness and your joy, in suffering and in health. There is no need to leave any part of yourself or your life at the door.
Come to the God who sees all and knows all.
Come to the Christ whose yoke is easy and whose burden is light.
Come to the Holy Spirit whose counsel is wise and gentle.
Come this morning, just as you are to worship.
Come this morning, just as you are before your God.
Come, now is the time to worship.[5]

Benediction
Go this morning surrounded by the presence of the Holy Trinity.
God in three persons. Three in one and one in three.
Go as you are, having received and responded to God's voice in your heart.
Go with the God who sees all and knows all.

---

5   Three lines taken from 'Come Now is the Time to Worship' by Brian
      Doerksen, © 1998, Vineyard Songs (UK/EIRE)

Go with the Christ whose yoke is easy and whose burden is light.
Go with the Holy Spirit whose counsel is wise and gentle.
Go this morning, just as you are, to connect with the world, trusting in the everlasting, never-ending love of God.
Go this morning, to live out your life in obedience to Christ.
Go this morning, in peace, in the sure knowledge of God's grace and mercy.
Amen.

Prayers of Confession

Confession of Childishness by Catriona Gorton

God our Parent
How often you must watch our childish quarrels and weep
How disappointed you must be when we fight over the same old silly disagreements

"You took my...."
"Didn't"
"Did too"

"I won't speak to you again ever..."
"I don't care"
(Well I do, but I won't admit it...)

"We don't have anything to do with them..."
"Why not?"
"Just because..."

[As the sun slips towards the horizon, in these shortest of winter days]
Help us to let go of our anger

Bitterness
Grudgingness
Childishness
Displace our ire with your peace

Teach us gentleness
Compassion
Forgiveness
So that we, too, may be bringers of peace
Heralding the dawn of a new world
Amen

Like a worm – a prayer of confession/regret/sorrow by Catriona Gorton

God,
Sometimes we feel worthless, useless, failures
Sometimes we feel abandoned, isolated, rejected
Sometimes we can find no positives to express
Sometimes we wonder, with the psalmist
"My God, have you forsaken me? I am like a worm…"
Despised, if even noticed,
Trodden under foot
People mock
People insult
They shake their heads in despair or derision…
Where does help come from?
God of Jesus, whose cry of dereliction resounds through the ages
We come as we are
Longing for hope, feeling hope-less,
Hear our prayer
Amen

Prayers of Intercession

God of Small Things by Clare McBeath

NB some theologians use the word kin-dom as a non-patriarchal alternative to kingdom.

Invite people to use leaf or flower shaped post-it notes to write or draw their prayers for people, places or situations where we long to see new life and new growth

God who sees the small things
when we are so overwhelmed by the stories of violence and atrocities
that we become desensitized to human pain and suffering
help us to see the individual faces within the story
and to take the small actions that together may begin to make a difference.

God who sees the small things
when we are so dwarfed by the scale of the challenge of climate change
that we stop bothering about yet another plastic bag or disposable cup
help us to see that taking care in each choice we make,
however seemingly insignificant builds a tidal wave and begins to change public opinion.

God who sees the small things
when we are so paralysed by economic downturn and squeezed budgets
that we are forced to buy the cheapest without counting the human cost
help us to see that by using our money creatively and investing in the small and local we help build sustainable communities here and in countries across the world.

God who sees the small things
you saw the kin-dom in unpromising, stinky grey yeast
you named the kin-dom in the tiniest of brown seeds
may we too learn to see the kin-dom in the small and
unpromising- looking
may we too learn to name your kin-dom in the unlikely and
unexpected.

God who sees the small things
through us plant tiny seeds of hope in our communities
that we may one day flourish and blossom as leaves on a mighty
tree.
through us work the yeast of your love as we grow and change
that in community we may give rise to dreams of your shalom.

Endings and Beginnings by Clare Mcbeath

Reflection
[Read: Genesis 2: 7 – you may like to ensure you use inclusive
language in the Biblical quote e.g. humankind rather than
mankind]

The Hebrew word "Nephesh", which is used many times in the
Bible is often translated as "soul" but means far more than this –
it means "the whole of you". We don't have a body or a soul, we
are body and soul.

Not only is there an intimate connection between us and the
universe, between us and the earth, but also between us and
God. God is the very breath we breathe, the energy, the life
force, the heartbeat of the universe and ourselves.
As people who are body and soul we are created for love and
to love and to be loved.

Yet pain and suffering are also part of this universe, built into the fabric of the earth, part of what it is to be human. They are the other side of happiness, the other side of knowing what it is to love and to be loved.
[space for reflection or prayer – you may want to think or name an ending or a beginning]

Prayer
Creator God
we are stardust
and we are the earth beneath our feet
we are body
we are soul
you are the very breath we breathe
the energy
the life force
the heartbeat of the universe
and of ourselves
you created us for love
to love and to be loved

Yet we know that
pain and suffering are also part of this universe
built into the fabric of the earth
part of what it is to be human
they are the other side of happiness
the other side of knowing what it is
to love and to be loved.

And so, we offer you these endings and these beginnings
those we have named out loud
and those we hold close to our hearts
be with us in all our endings
be with us in all our beginnings
Amen.

God of Elizabeth and Zechariah by Catriona Gorton

God of Elizabeth and Zechariah,
Who conceives each new life even before s/he is physically
present
Help me - help us - to recognise afresh
The sacrificial love and the hope-filled dreams that inspired our
parents
Who bore us, and brought us up,
Who taught us and shaped our lives

We are not naive enough to pretend that all children are
cherished
Not blind to the violence and poverty that blight, in differing
ways, young lives
Not foolish enough to think that every parent sees their children
fulfilled
But in this moment, on this day
We thank you for what has been good in our own upbringing
And, if need be, let go of regret, bitterness or grudges that
snare us

God of hopes and dreams
Hear our prayer
Amen

Groaning Intercessions by Catriona Gorton

*Note, the name 'Sophia' is sometimes used as a name for God's
'Spirit Wisdom', that is, the Holy Spirit, which is the case in this prayer.*

You are my help and my deliverer, oh God
You are the one who watches as I burn the candle at both ends

You are the one who notices when I skip a meal or eat junk in
order to get more done
You are the one who hears the heartcry of the loved one I am
too busy to spend time with..
...And my own heartcry to be with others
You are the one who waits patiently for me to remember to pray
You are the one who helps me, if only I allow myself to be
helped...

Hurry up, God
Come quickly to help me face myself
To recognise my poverty
And seek your help

In the meantime
When I make excuses that I am still
Too busy
Too tired
Too indispensable
Too unspiritual
Too hassled...

In the meantime
I take comfort in the promise
Of Sophia's intercession:
Holy Spirit of God pray for me
Amen.

For the Courage to Change Our Mind by Mary Cotes

Lord Jesus,
When a foreigner from an outside place
Came to you
Seeking life for her daughter,
At first you refused.

Yet, seeing her faith and her dignity,
Understanding her plea,
You welcomed her into the scope of your love
And offered hope and a new beginning.

Teach us we pray
To broaden the boundaries of our care.
Give us the compassion
To see humanity behind every stereotype,
And your image reflected in every face.

Give to the nations and their governments
As you give to us all,
Hearts ready to welcome,
Love stronger than fear
And the courage to change both our minds and our policies
In response to those seeking refuge
From violence, persecution, fear and destitution.

Lord, in your mercy,
Hear our prayer.

(Mark 7:24-31).

Additional Prayers

So Few Words by Gail Scholes

So few words
So much to say
Fill me with your Word, Lord

So much pain
In my heart holds sway
Fill me with your peace, Lord

So many troubles
Filling each day
Fill me with your strength, Lord

Each day, you speak to me
Each day, you comfort me
Each day, you carry me
Every day, you love me.

Midday Prayer by Carolyn Urwin

We come into the presence of the creating Father,
we come into the presence of the redeeming Son,
we come into the presence of the renewing Spirit,
we come into the presence of the Three in One.

Our God is gracious and compassionate,
    slow to anger and rich in love.
Our God is righteous in all his ways
    and faithful in all he does.
We exalt you, our God and King;
    We praise your name for ever and ever.
Great is the Lord and most worthy of praise;
    his greatness is beyond understanding.

Draw near to God and he will draw near to you.
The Lord is near to all who call on him,
    to all who call on him in truth.
Seek the Lord while he may be found;
    call on him while he is near.
My heart says to you:
    I will seek you, Lord.

[A reading from scripture may be shared.]

Our Father in heaven,
> *hallowed be your name.*
Your kingdom come,
> *your will be done, on earth as in heaven.*
Give us today our daily bread.
Forgive us our sins
> *as we forgive those who sin against us.*
Lead us not into temptation,
> *but deliver us from evil.*
For the kingdom, the power and the glory are yours,
> *now and for ever.*

Show me your ways, Lord,
> teach me your paths.
Guide me in your truth and teach me,
> *for you are God my Saviour,*
> *and my hope is in you all day long.*

Fill me with your Spirit,
> soften my hardened heart,
renew my thoughts and attitudes,
> *make me more like you.*
The Lord feeds the hungry and sets prisoners free;
> he gives sight to the blind and lifts up the fallen.

For the hungry to be filled,
> *Lord, hear our prayer.*
For the suffering to find relief,
> *Lord, hear our prayer.*
For the grieving to be comforted,
> *Lord, hear our prayer.*
For the oppressed to be set free,
> *Lord, hear our prayer.*
For the rejected to find love,
> *Lord, hear our prayer.*

For the broken to be healed,
Lord, hear our prayer.

[Those for whom there is particular concern may be named.]

Lead us, dear Lord,
from death to life,
from falsehood to truth,
from despair to hope,
from fear to trust,
from conflict to peace,
from doubt to faith,
from sadness to joy.

Be with us now in the middle of the day,
remain with us wherever we go
and hold our dear ones in your care.
Fill our hearts with your steadfast love,
strengthen our wills and encourage our souls;
give us your joy and fill us with hope,
so we bring your blessing to others
and glory to you.

In the name of the Father, the Son and the Holy Spirit, *Amen.*

On Humanity: A Prayer by Amanda Pink

Creator God and divine parent of all humanity,
We praise you for the marks of your image that we find in those
around us and in ourselves:

Your skill as a designer and an artist in the intricacy and beauty
of our bodies,
Your attendance to our needs in parents and care-givers,
Your wisdom in those who teach us and guide us,

Your orderliness in managers and strategists,
Your provision of resources in those who release finance and assets,
Your creativity in artists, musicians and entertainers,
Your justice in campaigners,
Your playfulness in children,
Your vulnerability in the poor and suffering,
Your faithful love, kindness and mercy in our friends and loved ones, and
Your active Holy Spirit in fellow disciples.

Forgive us Father, for when we have failed to see, value and celebrate your image in ourselves and in others.
With humility, we confess and sorrow too for the ways in which that image is marred in ourselves and the world around us:

In greed, in oppression, in violence towards people and the planet, in carelessness with our own bodies, in bitterness and division in our relationships and in your church.

At the moment we are particularly aware of..
[the marring of your image through sexual harassment and abuse, particularly in the entertainment industry and in politics, but also in many other walks of life.
We pray for victims, for healing and for empowerment; we pray for bystanders and witnesses, for courage to stand for justice; and we pray for perpetrators in systems that allow them continue, for repentance and change.]

As the great judge, just yet merciful, give us sober minds, O Lord, when we view ourselves and fellow humans, granting us a wise grace that celebrates without idolising, forgives without colluding, and challenges without malice. Amen.

Remind Us This is the Desert by **Amanda Pink**

Remind us this is just the desert;
That on the other side lies the promised land.
Remind us that this 'aimless wandering'
Really is part of a bigger plan.
For the journey from slave to free
Is not just A to B,
But learning to understand.
So though it feels like running on sand,
Remind us:
This is just the desert.

An Offering: Chaff and Grain by **Amanda Pink**

'Oh, the comfort—
the inexpressible comfort of feeling safe with a person
having neither to weigh thoughts nor measure words, but
pouring them all right out,
just as they are,
chaff and grain together;
certain that a faithful hand will take and sift them,
keep what is worth keeping,
and then with the breath of kindness blow the rest away.'[6]

Lord, it is an incredible truth that you give us the greatest gift we
could ask for - yourself.
In response, we bring ourselves before you.
We bring not just our bodies, but our whole selves, all that we
are.

---

6   Craik, Dinah Maria Mulock. A Life for a Life. London: Collins' Clear Type
     Press, 1900; and Felleman, Hazel, ed. The Best Loved Poems of the
     American People. Garden City, NY: Garden City Books, 1936 (no page
     numbers available. Listed at http://www.potw.org/archive/potw273.html,
     retrieved 26th June 2019.

We bring you all that we have done: that which has pleased you and brought you glory, and that which has not.
We bring you our thoughts and our emotions, our joys and sorrows, the things and the people that are on our minds.
We bring you our faith, and we bring you our questions and doubts.

We do so because we know you are good, gentle in heart and humble in spirit.

A Yes Like Mary's by Catriona Gorton

God of Mary, world-changing, ordinary woman
Help us to be open to hearing the voice of your messenger
 bringing news of your call on our lives.
Then give us the humility,
Give us the courage,
Give us the determination,
Give us the confidence
To say - though we still don't get what it all means -
To say - though the future will be so different from what we had planned -
To say - though we struggle to utter the one word you long to hear -

To say

Yes

So Be It

Amen, and amen

Permanent Present Tense by Amanda Pink

Save us, Lord, from living in a permanent present tense;
With our constant rushing from one deadline to the next,
Not living for each moment so much as just about surviving it.
Forgive us for when we dismiss too quickly what has gone
before;
For when our preoccupation with the now,
And our eagerness for what is next,
Blind us to the significance of what you have already done.

You are helping us to see...

The past is a gift:
A great and precious library of case studies to be explored and
learned from and built on.
And you, you are the knowledgeable librarian, showing us
where to look and helping us to understand,
Training us in this art of Holy Remembering.
For what we learned yesterday is the compass to navigate
tomorrow
And it is in celebrating the past that we awaken the future[7]

---

7   We celebrate the past to awaken the future". -- Speech at the 25th
    Anniversary of the Signing of the Social Security Act, Hyde Park, New
    York, 14 August 1960. Papers of John F. Kennedy. Pre-Presidential
    Papers. Senate Files. Series 12.1. Speech Files, 1953-1960, Box 910,
    Folder: "25th Anniversary of the Signing of the Social Security Act, Hyde
    Park, New York, 14 August 1960," JFKL. Listed on https://www.jfklibrary.
    org/learn/about-jfk/life-of-john-f-kennedy/john-f-kennedy-quotations,
    retrieved 26th June 2019

A Covenant for Troubled Times by Catriona Gorton

This was originally written for use by a local church community who faced very uncertain times, and wished to express their commitment via a covenant; it could possibly also be used when the broader context is troubling.

"There is a time for everything, and a season for every activity under heaven."

These are troubled times
Times of violence and hatred in a world marred by war
Times of anxiety and uncertainty in a world wounded by greed
Times of sadness and loss in a world of vulnerability and finitude
Times when we must face tough questions with unpalatable answers

"Even though I walk through the valley of the shadow of death, I will fear no ill, for you are with me, your rod and your staff they comfort me."
These are dark times
Times when we need to be reminded that God is with us
To guide our feet, one step at a time
To illumine our minds with new understanding
To protect us from despair, isolation and emptiness
To enable us to 'prove' our faith in resilience and fortitude

"Now the dwelling of God is with human beings, and he will be with them. They will be his people, and God himself will be with them and be their God. He will wipe away every tear from their eyes. There will be no more death or mourning or crying or pain, for the old order of things has passed away."

These are, mysteriously, hopeful times
Times in which the promises of a faithful God offer encouragement

Times in which new possibilities can be glimpsed
Times in which we must live the hope of eternity
Times when past, present and future meet.

So, let us profess our faith:

We believe and trust in God, creator of all, whose promises are faithful
We believe and trust in Jesus Christ, who redeems all, and who calls us to follow
We believe and trust in the Holy Spirit, who inspires and sustains us in hopeful service

Recognising that these are troubled times, let us covenant with one another and with God

My brothers and sisters in Christ, I covenant to walk together with you in faithful discipleship for as long as God shall so direct and lead us

Faithful God, as a community of your people, we covenant to walk with you, individually and corporately, in ways we know and in ways that you will show us

Grant us courage to face the challenges
Strengthen us with faith, hope and love
So that we may walk faithfully in the footsteps of him whose name we bear
Christ, our Lord. Amen.

A Prayer for Authenticity by Catriona Gorton

From fake jollity that denies reality
To real joy that transforms it
From forced smiles that fail to reach our eyes
To inner joy that makes them shine
From denial of truth
To indefatigable joy
Lead us, God of joy
Amen.

God's Comfort Blanket by Claire Nicholls

May the arms of God surround you
With the fibres of His warmth
May His comfort blanket enfold you
As you shelter in His wings

May the strength of God's embrace protect you
As the fleece and wool surround you
May you feel His love, His peace
As you rest in His arms

May you gradually unravel
As the threads ravel round you
May you begin to let it go
And feel release in His grace.

May the arms of God surround you,
Protect you and enrobe you
May His comfort blanket soothe you
As you shelter in His wings

Interactive Prayers and Prayerful Activities

Tie them to your Hands by Ali Taylor

During the service, ask all those who are engaged with children's or youth work to stand. Encourage the children near to a standing adult to tie their piece of ribbon loosely on their wrists. Pray a prayer of blessing over all those called to serve in this way. These adults then sit.

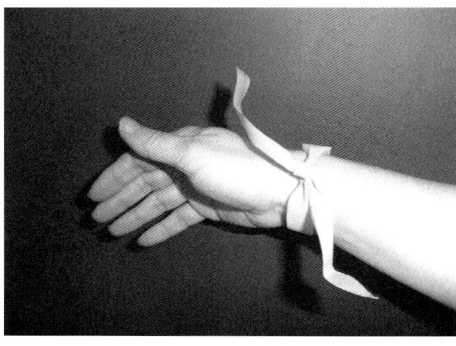

Photo: Ali Taylor

Then ask the adults near to a child or young person to tie their ribbons loosely onto the child or young person's wrists. Offer the option in either case for people to hold the ribbons they are given instead should they prefer this. Depending on numbers, it is fine if some children/young people end up with more than one ribbon.

Read Deuteronomy 6:4-9 and Deuteronomy 11:22

Pray an extempore blessing over the children and young people or use the following words:

May God shower His blessings upon each of you
As you learn more about Him and get to know Him
May He keep you
Safe in the knowledge that you are loved
May you know His presence with you
And the reality of His grace
May God show you His favour
So that you live each day surrounded by His peace. Amen

Broken Restored by Ali Taylor

Cut out enough hearts in brown, black or grey paper for everyone present, and a similar number in red. In addition, either prepare in advance the outline of a cross on a piece of paper that the number of prepared hearts fit on to easily (flipchart size can work well), or have a wooden cross available (that is suitable for these hearts to be attached

Photo: Ali Taylor

to) and have this on display. Have several glue sticks to hand for people to attach hearts to the cross.

At the beginning of the time of reflection ask everyone to hold their brown/black/grey hearts and think about time or times when they have done, thought or said something that has not been honouring to God and has broken His heart. Or perhaps suggest they think of a time when someone has done something to them – in word or in deed – that has broken their heart. Encourage them to tear or screw up the heart they are holding as a mark of contrition or acknowledgement.

Play a piece of suitable music, classical can work well, and ask those present to come forward and stick their broken/damaged hearts to the cross on display and to collect a whole red heart once they have done so as a demonstration of God's forgiveness and/or restoration.

Alphabet Prayers by **Catriona Gorton**

Based on word games such as 'the minister's cat' or 'Mother Brown's shopping basket', each person adds a new item to the growing list, working through the alphabet. The first person has one item, the second two and so on. No-one is 'out', if someone forgets an item, others simply help them remember. It is easiest as thanksgiving but could be used for confession or intercession. The example was created by an ecumenical group of around ten adults in Glasgow, and shows how humour and creativity lead to authentic prayer.

Thank you, God, for:

Animals	Nostalgia
Bread	Opera (but only Italian)
Children	Parents
Daffodils	Quickness of mind
Elephants	Road
Fireworks	Starlight
Gardens	Television
Homes	Underground stations
Ink	Velocipedes
Jesus	Woks
Kelvingrove Park	Xylophones
Love	You
Music	Zebras, zinc and Zanzibar

Building Block Prayers by Catriona Gorton

This prayer activity can be done with any type of building blocks – whether traditional wooden blocks or plastic blocks that clip together. If using plastic blocks, then the activity is NOT suitable for children under the age of four due to small pieces which pose a choking hazard, unless the 'mega' or 'giant' blocks are used.

Praying with plastic clip-together blocks is an easy and fun way to express prayers symbolically. There is no 'right' or 'wrong' way to do it but here are some ideas...

- Use some blocks to make a shape e.g. a cross, a heart, a house
- Choose blocks of certain colours that might represent something such as...
  - Rainbow – diversity, hope, promise, LGBTQIA+
  - Green – growth, nature, sickness, envy
  - Red – love, anger, blood
  - Blue – sea, sky, sad, cold
  - Etc. etc.
- Work with others, chatting about your symbols and creating a shared 'prayer' made of blocks
- Work on your own using one or more blocks to direct your prayers
  - Choose colours, sizes and shapes that might represent what you want to pray for
  - Choose one or more blocks and use each 'bump' to be a different prayer e.g.
    - Four bumps = four things to say 'thank you for'
    - Two bumps = two things to say 'sorry' for
    - Six bumps = six people to pray for

The key thing is to have fun, share together in some way, and express prayer.

Praying with wooden or plastic blocks is also helpful for private prayer or meditation:

Choose one block.

Hold the block in your hand so that you can see and/or feel it

Why did you choose this block and not one of the others?

Notice the size, the colour, the number of bumps, any decorations or damage

Imagine this block represents you, held in God's hand

Out of all the billions of people in the world, God has chosen you for this moment

How does that feel?

Look again at your block, at yourself, held in God's hand, unique and precious, loved and cherished

What do you want to say to God?

What might God want to say to you?

The Rocks Will Cry Out by **Leigh Greenwood**

Jesus said that if his disciples did not praise him, the rocks would cry out.

Creation longs to worship God so perhaps we can use it in our own worship.

Take a stone and write 'God is' then a word or short phrase which says something of what God is to you.

You might like to keep it as a reminder for yourself, or give it to someone else or leave it for them to find.

24-7 Worship by Leigh Greenwood

In Romans 12:1, Paul calls us to give ourselves as living sacrifices to the Lord.
That means that we can and should use our whole lives as an act of worship.

Draw a clock and mark off sections for each of the main activities that make up your day.
Think about how you can worship God during those times and create your own worship clock.

Praying Cards by Leigh Greenwood

Take one card from each suit from a pack of cards and use them as a focus for prayer.
Perhaps you could leave them somewhere conspicuous like the fridge or use them as bookmarks.

As you look at the heart, give thanks for someone you love, a family member or a friend or even someone you do not know well but look up to. The people who are most important to us can easily become like furniture in our lives, but we must take time to notice them and to remember why they are so important.

As you look at the club, give thanks for a group you admire, perhaps the church or a club you belong to, or a charity you respect. People are amazing and they can be even more amazing when they work together, so it is good to remember the incredible work that organisations of various kinds do and give thanks for them.

As you look at the diamond, give thanks for something you have, perhaps the shelter of your home or the treats that give you pleasure or the food that keeps you fed. Often we take the stuff of our lives for granted or reject it as unimportant, and of course it is right that we do not set too much store by our wealth or see it as a measure of our faith or worth, but it is also right that we recognise and appreciate what we have.

As you look at the spade, give thanks for a labour you undertake, perhaps your job or your work at home or church. It is not always easy to give thanks for the work we do, as more often we worry or grumble about it, but then we have all the more need to look for some success or blessing to be thankful for.

Fizzy Prayers by Leigh Greenwood

Sometimes it can help to do something physical and focus on something visible as we pray. This can especially be the case when praying is hard and words do not seem to express all we need them to.

Take a dissolvable tablet and write on it something in your life you would like to let go of or be released from. Drop it into a bowl of water and ask for God to take that something as you watch it melt and fizz away.

Finding Our Bearings by Leigh Greenwood

If you have a compass you might like to use it to face the four points in turn.

Otherwise you might prefer to draw or imagine a compass and simply think about the four points.

As you look North, which determines all other directions, think about what guides you or gives you meaning.

As you look South, which faces in the opposite direction, think about the things that distract you or hold you back.

As you look East, where the sun rises, think about new beginnings and where you are headed.

As you look West, where the sun sets, think about old paths and where you have been.

Stick Man Prayers by Leigh Greenwood

Draw a person and write across it the name of someone close to you.
You can make this bit as creative or as simple as you like.

Using a coloured pen, surround their name with the good things in their life and spend some time being thankful for those things

Then in a different coloured pen, write the things which they struggle with and spend some time thinking about how you may help them.

And finally in another colour and big letters so you can't forget, write down one thing you can do to show that person you care for them and make a promise to do that as soon as you can.

Welcome Mat Prayer Station by Claire Nicholls
(thinking about the welcome we feel and offer)

Need: Doormat saying "Welcome", pieces of paper (possibly with faces printed on)

What kind of welcome do you offer?

What kind of welcome does this church offer?

How welcome are you feeling today?

Draw a picture of yourself—put 'you' on the doormat and thank God that you are welcome here. Pray for those who do not always make you feel welcome.

Draw a picture of someone you want to or are feeling called to welcome. Add them to the doormat. Pray that they would feel the strength of God's welcome through your own welcome and actions.

Love your Neighbour as you Love Yourself by **Sarah Bingham**

These activities — which could form a series of prayer stations - are inspired by Jesus answering that the greatest commands were to love God, and to love our neighbour as ourselves, and on another occasion telling his followers that they must love their enemies. Words that could be printed as instructions are shown in boxes

Loving yourself: you will need paper, writing implements and a free-standing cross. This involves reflection, listening to inner voices of self and Spirit, and potentially a response involving writing or drawing. Movement comes in a simple placing of the written/drawn response at the cross.

Give yourself some time to listen and allow God to speak to you.

Is there anything he wants you to say sorry for? Is there anything he wants you to bring to Him?

If there is and you want to participate in this activity as a symbolic act of offering it to him please take a piece of paper.

Please write a short prayer on the piece of paper.

As a symbol of offering it to him please place the paper at the foot of the cross.

Take time to reflect on the cross.

Remember he forgives you.

Remember he died for you.

Loving our neighbour: it will be helpful to have a variety of maps (local, national, global). To make it more interactive, if maps are laminated or printouts from a computer, each place prayed for could be marked with a paint spot using finger paint, or a small pot of poster paint and a matchstick, or even a small sticker. Give yourself some time to listen and allow God to speak to you.

Who needs prayer? Allow God to guide you into prayer for others.

Reflect on the maps.

Are there particular needs in our area?

What do the people of [Walsall] need?

Are there places in the world that need prayer right now?

Loving our enemy: this is private, reflective prayer. It could be made more interactive by inviting people to write the name of someone who comes to mind onto a heart shaped post it note or piece of paper, to be kept in their Bible or wallet as a prompt to keep praying.

Who are you in dispute with or who do you feel undermined by?

If you can, identify where they are speaking the truth – what do you need to learn from that?

What does Jesus say about how to treat enemies?

Pray for them – thank God for them and ask for blessing for them.

Pray for yourself – thank God for who you are and ask for strength to forgive and love.

For those in pain: you will need a small statue of figures embracing, or a picture of something similar. To make it more interactive, the name of the person in pain could be written onto a sticking plaster which is either taken for further prayer, or stuck on a 2-D or 3-D cross.

Look at the figure of the comforting friends.

Who do you know who needs comfort? Is it you?

The Spirit is our comforter, as well as counsellor, so lift those people into His presence and ask for tangible comfort.

If it's you, ask a friend to pray for you through this time of trouble.

For those in mourning: this is a private, reflective prayer. It could be made more interactive by using local and national newspapers to encourage people to think more widely than their own circle of family, friends and acquaintances.

> Death is not the end, but the pain of separation now can be sharp and unending, even as it changes and softens.
>
> Think about people you know or people in the news who have suffered loss (of loved ones, of opportunities, of homes or jobs).
>
> Pray for them to know unfailing love from God, but also think about what you could do this week, next month and into the future to offer them love and comfort.

Prayer Stations by Sarah Bingham

These activities were initially designed for use on a teens holiday, but have been slightly adapted to encourage adults, young people or children (with supervision for the candle activity) to think and pray about themselves and others. Suggested wording for each station are given in the boxes underneath each description.

The mirror: you will need either a large mirror with chairs arranged in front of it, or a collection of smaller mirrors that can be hand-held. Some people may find it helpful to have tissues nearby. Variation – add a card with the text, 'I am made in the image and likeness of God.'

What or who do you see when you look in the mirror? 2 Cor 4:7 says 'We have this treasure in clay vessels, so that the glory goes to God'. Do you focus on the clay or the treasure?

How do you think God sees you? He loves you more than you can imagine – you are precious in his sight, you are his treasure. Look again in the mirror. What do you see now?

Special: a simple, private, reflective activity, but having credit card sized pieces of card with writing implements available will help seal what God says, or they reflect and think, rather than it being lost to the future. Variation – add a card with the text, 'I'm special because God has loved me.'

Think about everything you know that God thinks about you – that He made you, that He loves you, that Jesus came for you, that He chooses to work both in and through you. How does this make you feel?

Write one or two of the reasons why you are special on the card. Keep it where you can read it when you doubt your worth.

Candles: on a heatproof surface, you will need one large candle, already lit, plus tea lights and either tapers or long matches. Children will need supervision, and the station needs monitoring to ensure it does not become crowded. Variation – add a card with the text, 'the light shines in the darkness'

Look at the candle. Think how the light and warmth from the candle reflect the light and warmth of God.
Wait quietly for the peace of God to fill your heart.

Give into God's hands any thoughts that trouble you. Trust your life, your friends, your family, to Him.

Receive the love and assurance that God seeks to give you, listen for any word God speaks to you.

Light a tea light to remind yourself to live as a light.

Hearts: you will need coloured card, heart templates for those who cannot draw, writing implements and scissors. In an All Age service, these hearts could be stuck onto a wall or poster paper, thankful side out, to make a display of prayer for a prayer wall. Variation – add a card with text, 'God so loved the world'

Think about the desires of your heart. If we seek God, He will fulfil those desires. What would you like to say to God?

Cut out a heart shape from coloured paper. Write 'Jesus would you please' and your request on the heart. Write 'Jesus thank you for' on the other side, then write or draw something or someone that you want to petition or thank God for.

Lift those things or people to God in your own heart.

Galatians 5 Smoothies by Catriona Gordon

Good for Pentecost, or when thinking about the Holy Spirit

Even my Greek is good enough to know that the fruit of the Spirit is singular, not plural, but this smoothie, which everyone who tastes it assures me is delicious, is 'nine alive' as follows:

1/4 pint apple juice - love
1 banana, peeled and sliced - joy (a yellow smile!)
1 pear, peeled, cored and diced - peace
1 orange, peeled and segmented and 1/4 pint orange juice - patience (quality needed to peel an orange!)
1 kiwi fruit, peeled and sliced/diced - kindness
1 cup red seedless grapes - goodness
1 cup fresh pineapple chunks - faithfulness
1 cup of assorted melon chunks (or 2 slices peeled and diced) - gentleness
1 cup strawberries – self-control (!)
Place all the ingredients in a liquidiser and blitz until smooth.

Galatians 5 Spirit-Filled Fruit Salad

An alternative is Galatians 5 Fruit Salad. Ingredients as above but replace the apple juice with diet lemonade (living water), and add one apple, cored and sliced/diced. Low calorie and scrummy. Enjoy!

Thirty Minute Community/Communion Bread by Catriona Gorton

Ideal for an All Age communion service (so long as you have access to an oven!) with the option of exploring what the ingredients may symbolise in scripture. Alternatively, a nice activity for a home group or small 'away day' when sharing food together. When we've done it, I've invited youngsters to add pre-measured dry ingredients to the bowl – though the 'living water' needs to be opened just before use – and let them have a stir.

The kneading is important and needs to be timed reasonably accurately, so if you can talk and knead at the same time, that helps. We've usually sung a suitable song such as 'Let us break bread together with the Lord' (BPW 443) and of course you can make up your own verses such as 'Let us make/bake bread together with the Lord' or 'Let us add yeast together, help it rise' and so on.

This recipe serves up to a dozen people with mini rolls, so for a bigger group, it's advised to have some pre-made bread that you can warm up.

Recipe
8oz/250g strong white flour (or indeed other flour)
½ sachet of dried yeast
½ tsp salt
1 tablespoon vegetable oil
Approx. ¼ pint/125ml sparkling/carbonated water (living water)

Method
Preheat your oven to 220°C/425°F/Gas mark 7
Mix together the dry ingredients in a bowl.

Add the oil and, slowly a little at a time, st r in the water (you may need more water, it varies according to your flour!).
Turn out onto a lightly floured board and knead for six minutes.
Divide into four to six portions and roll into balls (the mini rolls we had at church were made by using this mix to make 12 rolls) and place on a baking sheet.
If desired, glaze with water, milk or oil, and bake for roughly 10 minutes until cooked.

If not using for 'communion' these can be enjoyed with soup or cheese!

Variation – instead of rolls, you could make flat rounds of dough, drizzle with oil and sprinkle with herbs or seeds for a yummy 'flat bread' to accompany pasta.

Best served with friends, food and laughter.

Blessings

A Blessing by Clare Hooper

May you see opportunities to bring hope, healing and peace where others do not.
May you have the courage to speak up for those that get overlooked.
May you be aware of God's spirit at work in the words you speak, the safe spaces you create and the relationships that you build.
You are loved by God, may those that you encounter know that they are loved too.

Blue Blessing by Sarah Bingham

In our darkness, bless us with Your light,
In our despair, bless us with Your hope,
In our deepest need, bless us with Your love,
In our dying, bless us with Your life,
In the name of the Father, and of the Son, and of the Holy Spirit.
Amen

Everything Changes, but God Changes Not by Liz Connelly

Situations...
Always changing
Never stay the same.

Emotions...
Always changing
Never stay the same.

Feelings...
Always changing
Never stay the same.

People...
Always changing
Never stay the same.

Time...
Always changing
Never stays the same.

God...
NEVER changing
ALWAYS stays the same.

Faithful Blessing by Sarah Bingham

In Your faithfulness Lord, help us to be faithful:
help us to know Your presence moment by moment
and comfort, strengthen and empower us,
that as we are blessed,
so we might bless others in Your name.
Amen

Provoked Blessing by Sarah Bingham

O loving Father bless us with minds that can be provoked
O loving Brother bless us with hearts that can be provoked
O loving Spirit bless us with spirits that can be provoked
And the blessing of God Almighty be upon us, now and ever
more. Amen

Trinity Blessing by Sarah Bingham

Bless us three in one God;
With assurance from the Father,
With forgiveness from the Son,
With comfort from the Spirit;
That we might go in your peace to serve with the authority of
Your name.
Amen

Trinity Blessing by Sarah Bingham

Generous Father, bless us with Your love
Gracious Saviour, bless us with Your light.
Gentle Spirit, bless us with Your life.
Bless us, that we might pour out blessing on Your waiting world.
Amen

A Glorious Miscellany!

Any attempt to arrange a collection, whether thematically or by genre, risks losing material that does not neatly 'fit'. We are delighted to include in this chapter some wonderful material that might otherwise have been omitted – please dip in, find encouragement, inspiration and joy.

Poems

Dawnsong by Ruth Wood
(Written whilst on Sabbatical at the Pilsdon Community)

Blush luminescent over
Flawless newborn heavens.
Sorrow-clouds pressed down
By limitless light
Sentinel trees etch praises.
In soundless worship
I too adore Thee.

Wayfarer by Ruth Wood
(The Pilsdon Community offers a safe place and accommodation to those we often call "homeless"- the term Wayfarers is much more appropriate to the fascinating - if sometimes heart-breaking characters I met.)

Eyes wary, world-wounded,
Here is safety.
Shoulders braced, scorn-scourged
Here is welcome.
Feet calloused, wander-wearied
Here is rest.
Spirit restless, nowhere-rooted
Here is home.

Accidental Prodigal by **Sarah Bingham**

It is too easy to become
A prodigal by accident...
We think we've heard
We run too far ahead
Not planning to grab what's still to come.
It takes a shock, a jolt, a halt
For realization to strike –
We are no longer at home...
We feel only the echo of embrace
The Spirit leeching out though never fully gone
We turn again in hope, but sorrow too,
To the One whose arms are always waiting.

Glory? by **Sarah Bingham**

Is glory found in wood or gold?
In servants or in athletes bold?
The victor's crown we seek and cherish
Quickly fades and soon will perish.

Is glory found in gold or wood?
In winning the contest or doing good?
As we look back into our past
It's memories of love that last.

Is glory found in wood or gold?
In heroes from the tales of old?
Those daring deeds of high renown
Cannot win an eternal crown.

Is glory found in gold or wood?
Or gained through mysteries understood?

Who gives their life and takes the cross
Gains more than needs make up their loss.

Flickering Reed by **Sarah Bingham**

A flickering reed he'll not put out
Yet so many flicker and fade
And grief walks hand in hand with doubt
When every day seems dulled in shade.

The smouldering wick sends up its smoke
Though once before 'twas bright with flame
And feelings rise on which we choke
Switching fast 'twixt pain and blame.

And in our inconsolable state
Mourning those lives yet scarcely begun
And turn to God, and him berate
Hear his reply, 'I lost my son'.

'I know the depths of sorrow and loss
And walk with you as you grieve and mourn
For my Son was killed on a man-made cross
To bring hope to all for Resurrection's dawn'.

Join the dance by **Sarah Bingham**

"Won't you dance with me?" the Master said,
Holding out His hand
And I reached out and grasped it,
As He had always planned.

And slowly, with much faltering,
I learned all the new moves
And mimicking my dance master
My moving still improves.

Sometimes stately, sometimes wild,
We always move with grace
And turn to bless new dancers
Yet return with an embrace.

The way the dance progresses
Is not always plain to see
Yet I trust my Master's leading
For I know that He loves me.

So wherever His steps lead me
I will follow my true call
And my life and words will ask you
"Won't you come and join the ball?"

And where is God in this? by Sarah Bingham

In our pain we ask 'where is God in this?'
Our body too frail, failing through age,
Injury, disease, assault...
His whisper comes 'I am here.
I too have known pain – beaten,
Whipped, pierced, sacrificed.
I am here, I walk with you.'

In our anguish we ask 'where is God in this?'
Our mind too full, filled with news,
Kenya, Syria, crashed planes...   *(or topical news of the day)*
His whisper comes 'I am here.

I too have known anguish – loss,
Accusations, betrayal.
I am here, I walk with you.'

In our grief we ask 'where is God in this?'
Our heart too sick, sickened by death,
Terror, war, violence...
His whisper comes 'I am here.
I too have known grief – for
Friends, strangers, enemies.
I am here, I walk with you.'

Walking into darkness by Sarah Bingham

I walk into the darkness
Into a landscape unknown
Revealed in utter starkness
How little yet I own
Of all You promise to give me
Of Your ineffable Light
Yet I know that You are with me
And clothe me with Your might.

As I walk into the dark
Not knowing where You lead
Still I pray to make my mark
And meet another's need
So they can see Your kindness
Reflected in my light
And be restored from blindness
As they turn from life's dark night.

For to You the dark is bright as day
And never a source of fear
Please help me as I walk Your Way
To know that You are near
That I may be a light to them
With a life lived full of grace
To love them all and not condemn
But to greet with an embrace.

Treasure in Clay by **Sarah Bingham**

You look deep inside you
And you see the stain
Where your sin has scarred you
Again and again
But God asks you to love Him
And give Him your pain

You look deep inside you
And you know such shame
Though never quite certain
Why you take the blame
But God asks you to love Him
And carry His name

You look deep inside you
And feel a disgrace –
That you can't be worthy
Of the Father's embrace
But God asks you to love Him
And minister grace

You look deep inside you
But can't see the treasure
That God has put in you
Pressed down, in full measure
But God asks you to love Him
And live for His pleasure

The Pond by Amanda Quick

I keep a pond in a bucket.
In truth, a sorry sort of pond —
The bucket cracked, discoloured.
I am moved, now and then,
To trail my fingers
Through the cold and murk,
Bold ripples of disturbance
Sifting sludge and slime.
Stones gather at the bottom.
When I remove my hand,
It is wrapped around with weeds.

For some hours after,
The waters are in motion,
Separating silt.
When I look next morning,
The depths are clear.
A few light leaves floating;
Bright bubbles popping.

It is this way with prayer, for me.
A garden, poorly tended;
A pool unplumbed, unclean.
The fingers of your Spirit
Reach in — ungloved, unflinching —

And dabble. And stir.

And bring about a sifting:
All that hinders, sinking down;
Tangled sin pulled out in armfuls,
Clarifying cloudiness;
The layers purer, balmier;
The ripples of your breathing
My joyful overhaul.

Voices

Many of the characters whose stories appear in the Bible inspire the writing of poems and short pen-portraits. Where a character fits naturally with one of the major festivals, we have placed material accordingly. These are other people, major and minor – ordered by the books of the Bible in which they appear.

Cain's wife (Genesis 4) by Jeannie Kendall

The guilt devoured him in the end.
Eating his soul: despite adrenaline fuelled building,
Despite our children's smiles,
Despite me, despite everything.
Nothing was enough.
He wore his self-reproach more clearly than the mark he said
God promised:
Not a badge of honour but a sign of shame.
His anger somehow tempered by his fear:
Always terrified an eruption
Would again, volcano-like, envelop his inner world
And destroy a life, in one way or another.

And, as many women do, I absorbed it all:
Holding my peace to try to gift him his.

Pharaoh's wife at the plagues (Exodus 7-12) by Jeannie Kendall

There is no mention of me.
Why would there be?
The men hold all the cards.
Being married to a powerful man
Does not make you a powerful woman.
My task to support
Hear his worries
Bury who I am
To service his needs.

But then his stubbornness
Cost me my son
Sacrificed to his need for power.
As women all across the land
Howled in their agony of grief.

And who is this Hebrew god?
Another powerful male
Who sacrifices my people
To free his own?
I will not bow the knee in fear again.
This heartless god I cannot worship
But what then of my bleeding, lacerated soul?

Jephthah's daughter (Judges 11:30-40) by Jeannie Kendall

The mountains were bleak:
Wild isolation mirroring my seclusion;
Raw rock reflecting my bleeding soul.
My companions bodily present

But unable to reach me
As I stared my sacrifice down.

All those years
That I would never have
Filled my inner landscape:
Dreams and visions
That would never be fulfilled -
And perhaps never would be
Even if I was spared.

Meaningless, my father's vow:
What use some offering, however costly,
To any God worth worshipping.
I could have tried to flee.
But I had seen the turmoil in his eyes
And knew I would return
To pay the price.

Naomi (Book of Ruth) by Ali Taylor

(Angrily, shaking head) I wish we'd never gone. *(Bitterly)* It would have been better to have stayed in Bethlehem and starved!

Ten years we were there. Ten years in Moab and look what happened *(throws hands up in disgust)* If we'd stayed here then maybe we'd all be dead and I wouldn't have to feel this pain *(grabs a fist and holds it to chest)*

(Sighing deeply, looking down) I've lost them. I've lost them all. (pauses) I wish we'd never gone.

(Looks up)

We went to Moab to escape the famine. To get food – to live! And all we found was death, not life!

I was blessed, but now I am cursed. I had a husband to love me, to provide for me. And two sons. Two strong, wonderful sons *(almost sobs, catches breath)* to care for me in my old age, and give me grandsons *(quietly)* But now I have nothing. No husband, no sons *(sadly)*. I am alone.

(pauses) We were happy there. We were happy there. My sons found wives – beautiful wives. Good women to look after them and provide them with children, many children. But, this was not to be. If they had had children I would have been looked after. But there were no children. And when my beloved husband died, and then my two sons, we were left alone, unsupported *(with disgust)*, shamed, looked down on by others. Outcasts! *(angrily)* What did we do? Nothing! It wasn't anything we did.

(Pause) And now *(spitting it out in anger)*, now I am destitute. I have no way to provide for myself. *(Pause)* What have I to look forward to now? Poverty, hardship, trouble. I will be rejected by society. I have no rights, no status.

I am no-one – a nobody. Forgotten, ignored, abandoned. *(Pause)* I tried to tell my daughters-in-law to go back to their families – to find new husbands – they are still young. For them, there is hope. For me – I am too old – I cannot find a new husband now.

(Pause) Orpah went back. She didn't want to leave me, but it was for the best. But Ruth has come with me. She did not want to return to her family, she was determined to come. She said that my people were now her people; my God, now her God.

(shaking head) But my God has caused me great suffering *(angrily)* He has brought misfortune upon me. I am no longer the woman I was. You cannot call me Naomi any more. My life is not pleasant now. I grieve for the life I had which is now gone. I am angry – things will never be the same. *(sighs)* I wish we'd never gone.

Jairus and the Sick Woman by Amanda Pink
(The words of Jairus are in plain type, those of the woman in italics, where both speak together, bold)

It's amazing how quickly things can go downhill. One minute all seems well, you have your family, your work - life is good, and then, BAM, out of nowhere, your daughter is sick, and before you know where you are she is fighting for her life.

It's a strange thing to suddenly feel powerless when you are used to being in control. Head of the family, one of the synagogue leaders - taking charge is part of who I am and I take pride in being someone who makes sure everything is in order, one on whom others can depend. I like to think that if my name, Jairus, is known and respected, it is for good reason. But somehow, suddenly, I was out of my depth, and no matter how much I wanted to make it right for her with her sick little body, for my family in their terror, for the community reeling in shock, I couldn't. That's the thing about death, I guess: it knows no prejudice. A good name, a respected family, religious standing - that which seems to hold so much sway in other matters is powerless against its grasp. It even prowls at the door of a little girl. My little girl.

They say 'time is a healer', but whoever 'they' are have obviously never had a chronic disease. Twelve long years I suffered. And suffer I did.

It wasn't just the bleeding, although that was bad enough. It was everything else that came with it. The endless doctors, one after another, prodding and poking and promising one more treatment that should do it, but never did. The first time I felt completely humiliated, exposed, but after a while you get used to the indignity of it. Not that it becomes any less degrading – it's more that, bit by bit, the inner protest drains out of you like the blood you are losing, and you simply become resigned that this is the lot which you have been dealt and must accept.

There's the money too, of course. Treatment does not come cheap, and it's not like you get a refund when something doesn't work. I spent every last penny I had, and all I had to show for it was a body more bust than when I had started.

But the worst thing about it is was the isolation. All around you life goes on, but you can't take part anymore...because you're sick. And all your identity fades away until all you are left with is that one defining factor: The woman with the issue of blood. A burden to society, an embarrassment to polite company, and contagiously unhygienic.

And so I came to Jesus.
And so I came to Jesus.
Desperate.

(Pause)

I would beg him to come.
I would hide in the crowd.
If he could just lay his hands on her...
If I could just touch his cloak...
He could make her
me
well.

(Pause)

But things didn't go to plan.

*It wasn't until he turned around and asked who had touched him
that the audacity of my actions had hit me.
I shouldn't be here - I had no right to be in this crowd, let
alone reach out to a holy man with my contaminated touch. It
was almost ironic - I had spent the last 12 years wishing that
someone would just see me, and now suddenly He had, and I
was terrified.*

Jesus might have come with me, but he didn't seem to
understand my sense of urgency. And so when a sick woman
touched him on the way, he stopped and spoke with her.
Frustration buzzed within me - but somehow I knew he was not
one to be interrupted and hurried along. And then word came,
and my worst fears were realised. We were too late.

(Pause)

'Do not be afraid', he said.
'Do not be afraid', he said. 'Go on believing.'
'Go in peace and good health', he said.
And he called my daughter out from slumber.
And he called me 'Daughter'.

(Pause)

I learned a lesson that day: no matter how bad things seem, with
Jesus there is always hope.
No matter how invisible you feel, with Jesus you are not alone.
With Jesus, life is restored.

Woman with a haemorrhage (Mark 5:25-34) by Jeannie Kendall

It had been twelve years:
Over four thousand exhausted days,
More than ninety-six thousand wretched hours.
My body leaking all vitality
And sapping my spirit
As I trudged wearily through each day
Praying for a relief which never came
So that, in the end,
I despised that part of me
Which was meant to bring life.

Worse even than the draining away of hope
Was the humiliation by those men
Year after year
Claiming they could help
But bringing me only shame:
Cheeks burning as I looked to the empty sky:
No rescue from their intrusive hands
And eyes which either pitied
or lingered just a little too long.

Hope had long since seeped away
The day I heard tales of the rabbi.
But I had nothing to lose.
And so, knowing I breached every convention
And the law of a God I no longer trusted,
I reached out to touch Him
And knew at once
That everything had changed.

But healing became terror
As He exposed my desperate encounter
And I waited
For the rebuke
That would reignite my disgrace.

But it never came.
And so I told Him the truth
And I knew He saw
beyond my faltering tale
to the broken reality
my life had become.

And, in return
for my abject honesty
gifted to this stranger
He spoke words of wholeness
Going beyond the healing of my body
To free me to be
The woman
That I was born to be.

The woman at the well (John 4) by Jeannie Kendall

I still remember the heat that day:
Sucking air from my lungs and vitality from my body;
The ground as parched as my throat and arid as my womb - and life.
I watched my feet, despondent,
Not looking around lest I encounter hostile stares
In the unlikely event of a fellow traveller.
My friendless journey somehow a metaphor
For my increasingly isolated life.

And then I saw him;
Indistinct at first, framed by the sun
And I almost turned and ran.
But then he asked me for a drink
And, against all those man-made rules
We began to talk.

He was unlike all the other men -
Declaring love until it called for sacrifice
Then quick to abandon me
Uncaring of my gathering, unseen, scars.
Instead, he sensed my soul-thirst;
Watching my eyes and not my body:
And so, hesitatingly at first, I gifted him my secrets
And found them not only safely held
But honoured.
And, looking back, I realised
That, even as I extended him the cup
He was offering me new life.

Section Index

Dementia

Endings in Church Life

Advent, Christmas and Epiphany

Reflections, Meditations and Prayers for Advent, Christmas and Epiphany

Meditations and Reflections

Prayers and Blessings

A Glorious Miscellany!

Index by Author

CW01507723

Saltwash

Saltwash

ANDREW MICHAEL HURLEY

JOHN MURRAY

First published in Great Britain in 2025 by John Murray (Publishers)

1

Copyright © Andrew Michael Hurley 2025

The right of Andrew Michael Hurley to be identified as the
Author of the Work has been asserted by him in accordance
with the Copyright, Designs and Patents Act 1988.

A CIP catalogue record for this title is available from the British Library

Hardback ISBN 9781399817530
ebook ISBN 9781399817561

Typeset in Baskerville MT by Hewer Text UK Ltd, Edinburgh
Printed and bound in Great Britain by Clays Ltd, Elcograf S.p.A.

John Murray policy is to use papers that are natural, renewable and
recyclable products and made from wood grown in sustainable forests.
The logging and manufacturing processes are expected to conform
to the environmental regulations of the country of origin.

Carmelite House
50 Victoria Embankment
London EC4Y 0DZ

www.johnmurraypress.co.uk

John Murray Press, part of Hodder & Stoughton Limited
An Hachette UK company

The authorised representative in the EEA is Hachette Ireland,
8 Castlecourt Centre, Dublin 15, D15 XTP3, Ireland (email: info@hbgi.ie)

For my mother 1950–2009

Tide in, tide out,
All's forgotten.

Saltwash motto

PART ONE

At a jolt in the switching of lines, Tom Shift woke to find that it was half past three, and he was finally arriving into Saltwash.

Under the low mizzle, most of the town was faint and grey and he could only see what was close by. A parade of shops. A pub. A park. A scrapyard. Gone.

Through a tunnel and out into the light again, such as it was on this dreary afternoon, the track ran past the backs of terraced houses and long thickets of browning rosebay and buddleia, before a row of railings led to an open-air platform strewn with puddles.

The train slowed past Ladies . . . Gentlemen . . . Waiting Room . . . Lost Luggage, came to a halt, shuddering and stinking, and after a loud death rattle, the diesel engine cut out to leave only the sound of rain on the windows.

As Tom had dipped in and out of a fitful sleep since changing at Preston, the handful of passengers who'd got

3

on with him there had alighted at other places along the way. It gave him a silly childish thrill of intrepidness to think that he and no one else had made it to the end of the line. But then the same thought had him feeling anxious, as if he'd made a mistake that an inhabitant of this bleak spot would laugh at or caution him about.

Perhaps it was just because it was so lonesome here at the station that he felt this twitch of unease, or it was just down to the fact that he hadn't quite come-to yet. More and more often he was like this for a while after waking up, disorientated and perturbed. Common symptoms, apparently.

He never slept well any more, even in bed, so there'd been no chance of doing so on a train. Travel, he'd been warned, might knock him for six. He had to recalibrate what he was capable of doing now. The young nurse who'd taken his vitals at the last check-up had actively discouraged him from coming here, especially on his own. In response, he'd given her some swagger about being perfectly capable of looking after himself, and had told her straight that he wasn't going to give into decrepitude just yet. Apart from the problem at hand, he was as fit and healthy as anyone could hope to be at seventy-five.

Anyway, he'd said to her, he was only going out for the day, and he wouldn't be alone. He was seeing a friend.

He'd half expected Oliver to be waiting to greet him. It might have been the type of thing he'd do as a thoughtful

4

surprise. But he wasn't there and Tom looked around for someone else to set him on the right bearing for the hotel.

It being a Sunday, the ticket office was closed and so too the little snack bar. There were no taxis waiting outside the station entrance, and, as his mobile was old and had no facility for navigation, he was unsure which way to go.

To the right sat a church that didn't look as if it had been used for years, and some brutalist municipal offices shut for the weekend. To the left, the sky seemed taller somehow, as it often did where land gave way to water, and he set off in that direction, crossing one wet road and then another until he came to the front.

Why Oliver had insisted on meeting in Saltwash, he still didn't really know, but it was a hell of a place to choose at this time of year. Spells of rain had been forecast across the north for the rest of the day but here by the coast it was particularly wintry and glum. The promenade was more or less deserted, and when one car passed, it was a while before the next came along. Then there was nothing again until one of the resort's grey-green trams crawled by like a giant beetle, collecting no one and taking in its stops merely as a matter of routine. The only people who'd ventured out were a couple of dark-coated locals walking their dogs, walking at angles in the wind coming in off the sea.

It rose to such a gale at times that, as Tom stopped to ask a woman dressed in oilskins if she knew the Castle, it

5

was all he could do to keep his umbrella from being wrenched out of his grasp.

'The Castle Hotel,' he clarified, deducing from the queer look she'd given him that she hadn't been able to hear properly. She did have the drawstrings of her sou'wester tied very tight.

In reply, she motioned to the buildings that ran along the esplanade in such a way that suggested the place he wanted was right down at the other end.

'Is it far?' he said.

She made the same gesture again, more intently this time, swapping the heavy plastic bag she was carrying to her other hand. Tom saw that it was full of greasy-looking eels, freshly caught.

Her assistance given, she walked away with her sopping, long-legged mongrel, and he had to lob a call of thanks after her. But she made no acknowledgement of his appreciation and carried on, determined to get home with her supper.

It was a day for staying indoors. A day best left to blow itself out, the weather being so unpredictable. As Tom set off, it changed again. Rain turned to sleet and the sleet to a bombardment of hail which fell in a deafening percussion for a few moments and then passed away as abruptly as it had started to give something of a view across the river mouth at last.

The sun came out, watery and warmthless, glazing the marshy span of the inlet with a rose-coloured sheen. A high

6

wind moaned in the winding creeks. The wrack and seaweed hanging off the old jetties dripped and glistened.

What was that, a liking for the place? No, only admiration that anyone had ever been able to make this muck alluring.

How canny they'd been, he thought, those Victorian entrepreneurs who'd developed all this from a little-known fishing port to a prosperous holiday spot. To have rebranded the town as 'Saltwash-on-Sea' was such a simple bit of ingenuity, knowing that 'sea' promised things that 'estuary' never could. Fun. Romance. Adventure. Or the most modest incarnations of such excitements, at least. This was England after all.

Yet however deft the semantic chicanery, an estuary was what they really had here and at low tide it had been suckled down to a delta of dark streams and vast sandbanks that stretched a mile or so to the opposite shore where a lighthouse and a few white cottages sat by a line of stunted, wind-stricken pines.

No doubt Saltwash had been billed as *prophylactic* in the early days, and then, in the fifties, *bracing*, that most English of adjectives, the appeal of which Tom had always associated with the kind of satisfaction his mother and her generation had derived from toughing out wartime privations.

Before folk had started jetting off to Spain and Greece to get sunburned and drunk, there had been a perverse sort of fulfilment in enduring cold air and cold water. It was hearty and therapeutic, a veritable panacea. And from what he knew, successive Saltwash impresarios had, for the best part of a century, traded on the popular belief that the brown soup of sea salt and mud minerals in the river not only revitalised the body but cleansed the mind too. Whatever was scrubbed away, be it factory filth, remorse or sinful intention, was taken out on the ebb flow and buried under the waves.

But surely no one braved the water here any more, even in the summer months. All the way along the promenade there were signs that warned against doing so and apparently there were sirens that went off when a particularly fast-moving bore was starting to roll in. A necessary precaution, for the breakwater which had once provided some protection from the surges of the Irish Sea had been reduced to a slew of stony debris.

There couldn't be anything in the way of river traffic at all now, making the lighthouse as obsolete as the large red-and-white buoys that lay half sunk in the mire – the safe passage they'd once marked clogged up with silt since the fish dock had closed and the dredgers had gone. No one even boated for pleasure nowadays. The dinghies sitting in the scrubby grass on the other side of the railings didn't look as if they'd been used for years but were stuck fast where the water had dumped them long ago, their masts like stopped metronomes.

It had all come into the possession, or repossession, of the birds. Knots, oystercatchers, cormorants, but mostly gulls – legion that afternoon, turning above the quaggy wind-blown mudflats with plaintive cries and occasionally swooping down to search for something to eat. Something dead, thought Tom, if the smell was anything to go by. He'd noticed it when he'd got off the train and it had gathered strength as he'd walked by the riverside. Not the usual brackish whiff of a coastal town, but something faecal or industrial which he couldn't quite place.

Whatever it was, he had to admire the woman with the eels for eating anything that had been pulled out of the estuary here. But perhaps, like the gulls, she couldn't be fussy. Saltwash was a poor little backwater, tucked away on this far-flung peninsula, its glory days well over.

There'd been a funfair once but all that remained of it now was a metal archway reading 'Happylands' in jocular multicoloured lettering and an acre of bramble bushes and nettles beyond the chain-link fence. The pier had gone too but for its barnacled footings running out into the mud.

Other places had been abandoned. The Welcome Inn. Lucky's Bingo Hall. The Crab Café, with its rows of peeling tables and plastic seats. Hotels, too, stood empty. The Royal Majestic had suffered a fire, its upper floors gutted to blackened rafters, and at the Sceptre the 'To Let' signs were peeling and graffitied.

In its day, the Gaiety theatre would have been considered something of an architectural gem, but now all the sculpted vines on its Italianate façade had become overgrown by real greenery. And further along, the white-walled lido, despite the scaffolding, was crumbling like an old wedding cake.

Only by the steps on to what constituted a beach was there any sign of an ongoing holiday trade. The ice-cream stand and the sweet shop sitting in wide pools of water were shuttered down rather than boarded up, waiting for the day-trippers and the long-weekenders to return.

They'd be mostly folk his age, Tom supposed. Or even older. Sentimental greyhairs who came back in ever decreasing numbers to recapture a nostalgia that, year by year, was harder to find – in the material world anyway. So much had gone.

That being so, he thought that the Castle might turn out to be locked up and lightless too. No matter that only a fortnight had passed since Oliver had made the arrangements to convene here, the odds of anything surviving in Saltwash from one day to the next seemed slender to say the least.

But there it was, the hotel, next to a derelict amusement arcade. An imposing pile of a building with a tall, fortress-like keep at its centre and a four-storey wing on either side. A place that took itself very seriously with its stone cladding and imitation battlements.

~

He left his umbrella in the porch, shook the wetness off his sleeves and went into the lobby, all floral carpets, anaglypta, voluted finials and ornate lampshades.

He found it quite charming, though the charm lay not in the furnishings themselves but in the certainty of their sophistication in the minds of the proprietors. It made him think of his mysteriously affluent Great-Aunt Genevieve on his mother's side, who, in her eighties, had dressed as she'd done in her twenties – brocade, beads and feathers – and thought herself the last word in elegance. Style was style, she used to say. It never aged. Well, it did. It looked like this.

Along one wall of the entrance hall were oil paintings of famous battles – Waterloo, Agincourt, Rorke's Drift and so on. Against the other sat an assortment of ostentatious mahogany sideboards covered in lace doilies. And on an easel by the reception desk a sign in a faded decorative typeface read, The Paleys welcome you to Saltwash.

But there was no one around. No staff, no other guests. The hotel was in its afternoon lull, with Time drumming its fingers in the form of several rococo pendulum clocks on the walls.

Oliver had described the Castle in almost palatial terms, though he must have been referring to its design rather than its fixtures and fittings. Perhaps for him the lofty interior gave the place some grandeur. The ceiling of the lobby was notably high and cross-hatched with fake black beams as in some stately home.

11

Behind the counter, the pigeonholes for the keys were labelled one to forty-nine. Only forty-nine rooms in a place this size, thought Tom. They would be generously proportioned. Such luxury had probably been the hotel's selling point once over. This commodious foyer the epitome of opulence. But it was so quiet and empty here on this rainy Sunday that all this space had a redundancy to it, a sombreness even. Or was it just that he'd started to see the melancholy of certain places?

A stern voice rang out from somewhere above, and then someone began to make their way down the stairs. A diminutive woman in a black roll-neck sweater and a tweed skirt suit, her hair set in a tight white perm. Presumably Mrs Paley.

'I need you watching the front door,' she called behind her. 'Mr Calmine's been spotted on the promenade. We can do without him wandering in.'

Noticing Tom there as she turned the corner by the rubber plant, she stopped abruptly with one hand on the banister and said, 'Yes?'

'I'm here for dinner,' he replied.

'You know that we don't serve until six.'

Meeting her gruffness with affability, he said, 'I realise I'm a little early. I thought it best to play it safe, the weather being what it is.'

She came down past the grandfather clock which struck four, lifted the flap in the counter, closed it behind her, and

12

opened a blue, clothbound ledger on the desk. No computer system here.

'It's Mr Shift, isn't it?'

'That's right.'

She ran the nib of a pencil to the bottom of the page in front of her, keeping its contents secret by screening it with her other hand. He had to suppress a smile at her officiousness, though it was peculiar that she should know who he was and have his name written in her book at all since he was only taking a meal.

She found him, looked up, looked down, looked up again in the manner of a border-security guard, and, once he'd apparently satisfied whatever evaluation she'd been making of his eligibility to stay, she handed him a small red badge.

'What's this for?' he asked.

'It is your first time here, isn't it?'

'Well, yes.'

She gestured with her pencil as if to say, *There you are then, put it on.*

He did as requested, unzipped his coat, and pinned the badge to his cardigan, wondering why he needed to be so clearly tagged as a newcomer.

'Now, we don't open the dining room until five forty-five,' said Mrs Paley, as she shut the ledger and put the pencil back in its pot.

'Right you are.'

'Five-forty-five at the earliest,' she said.

'Understood.'

She looked at him pointedly. She wasn't expecting him to go away and come back, was she? On a day like this?

'Is it possible to get a drink, maybe, while I'm waiting?' he asked.

'A drink? Well, if you wish,' she said, meaning 'if you must', and busied herself with a duster. 'My husband will see to you.'

Across the lobby, in a capacious room called the Albion Bar, a Goliath of a man in a sweat-darkened shirt, mutton-chopped like your landlord of old, was standing behind the beer pumps and folding small pieces of paper into even tinier squares. When Tom went in, he turned and paused, as astonished as his wife that they had a guest to deal with when they were still in the midst of preparation. He too consulted a clock. An enormous nautical chronometer that sat between the cardboard racks of crisps and peanuts.

'Your good lady said it was all right if I . . .' Tom began, half turning back to the doorway to see if Mrs Paley might be on hand for verification, but she was talking to someone else in the lobby. 'Sorry if I've caught you at a bad time,' he said.

Mr Paley switched on his hearing aid and intimated that Tom needed to repeat himself.

'A Scotch, please,' he said, to keep things simple. 'Make it a double. Wild sort of a day, isn't it?'

Mr Paley looked at Tom's badge (which explained this unfamiliarity with protocol), drew out a glass from the shelf under the bar top, put in two measures from the optic, set the drink down on a drip tray, took the money and handed over the change without uttering a single word. So begrudging had the service been that Tom felt obliged to apologise again before thanking him.

Natives not entirely friendly so far, he'd say to Angeline when he finally summoned up the courage to message her. It might make her smile. They'd shared a laugh together once or twice these last few months. There was hope in that.

With the pick of the brass-topped tables, Tom chose one by a window so as to keep an eye out for Oliver, but felt more than a touch self-conscious under Mr Paley's watchful gaze and prone to the scrutiny of whoever happened to pass by on the promenade. He'd look like one of those men (always men) who patronised places such as the Castle at this time of year.

If he'd ever happened to be at the seaside in winter, he'd often wondered who they belonged to, these solitary faces between the net curtains, staring away the afternoon. Disgraced uncles, oddballs, drifters, perhaps outcast divorcees of the type his mother had sometimes taken in as lodgers. The quiet of an off-season hotel the ideal refuge for them, in that they didn't have to talk to anyone. Or, maybe they came for the very purpose *of* talking. They came for the guaranteed attentions of chambermaids and waiters, who, with only a smattering of guests to serve and time on their hands, could afford to stand and chat.

Was that Oliver's life? It seemed so from his letters. For him, it was perfectly normal to spend weeks at a time in establishments like this. But even *one* night at the Castle, thought Tom, would be a night too many, and now that he was here he was very glad that his appointment at the hospital the following morning had enabled him to get out of staying over. Anyway, he felt entitled to the comfort of his own bed. That wasn't too much for a dying man to ask. He wanted to wake up at home, not here.

November was all the more dismal in Saltwash; the view from the window one of road, railings, mud and cloud and so desolate that it was hard to imagine that the summer days captured in the photographs around the room had ever existed.

As dusk started to edge in, rain crossed the estuary again, misting the lighthouse and then obscuring it completely. With the day waning, the gulls flocked inland and gathered on the roof of the concrete wind shelter opposite the hotel, scooping out the air with their cries.

If there'd been a few other souls around, it might not have seemed quite so forlorn, but the only person out now was a man in a brown suit who came along carrying several see-through plastic bags of litter. A friend of the eel woman, maybe. Or this Mr Calmine, who wasn't to be let in.

16

It did look as if he was contemplating mounting the steps, but as soon as a young man from the hotel went out, broom in hand, to play gatekeeper as demanded by Mrs Paley, the doleful fellow seemed to think better of it and poked his walking cane into the tidal rubbish by the kerb before moving on.

It was how he pictured Oliver: genteel and tramp-like. And yet seeing this old boy outside proudly wearing his best clothes to go foraging in the gutters made Tom's plan – as altruistic as it was at face value – seem horribly ill-judged. He had no wish to damage Oliver's self-esteem or make him feel pitied, and so it mattered that he framed the offer in the right way. In fact, he'd got here early for the very purpose of buying himself more time to prepare his pitch.

If he were to say . . . or point out that . . .

He couldn't concentrate. His mind wanted to go in a dozen different directions at once. And it was hot too. Even after taking off his coat, the room still felt unbearably stuffy. The cast-iron radiators had been turned up so high that the air above them wavered and the heat thickened the smell of old beer and body odour and the unwholesome staleness that often permeated buildings of a certain age. All over the artexed walls, there were blotches of mildew.

Perhaps they hadn't the staff to clean in every corner, especially when the rooms were so large as this, but it didn't

17

look as if the bar had been attended to properly for quite a while. The lad outside sweeping away the gull shit and flotsam – and unwanted visitors – would have been far better employed in here.

The ornaments on the window ledge were all coated in a layer of fine grey powder, their colours dulled. The same went for all the other bric-a-brac that filled the sconces and shelves: the toby jugs and horse-brasses, the stuffed game birds and hideous pink vases shaped like huge, carnivorous flowers.

But it wasn't only because of the dust that everything looked so faint. It had all been sun-bleached too. A long process, given that this was the north. These heaps of junk must have been sitting here for years, for decades in all probability. It was a display that had once sought to validate the Castle's aspirations towards refinement and panache and hadn't been disturbed since, lest the spell be broken.

Tom thought of the peeling stucco in the alleyways of Venice and the faded Arcadian murals in those palazzos turned hotels in Florence. There, the decay seemed noble somehow.

English dilapidation was different. It was the blistered formica on the tables of a seafront café. Derelict gift shops and thrift shops with whitewashed windows. A pub with steel plates over its doors. Cracked, pebble-dashed shelters along the promenade, roosted by gulls.

The neglect in Saltwash was so rife as to seem wilful. It was somewhere he'd rather not have seen, the way the hopelessness seeped into him like the damp.

How strange that he should find himself here at all. He'd never have thought about the place once, let alone ever come, if not for Oliver's letters.

~

It was somewhat old-fashioned, which was no bad thing, but the Kübler-Ross unit at the infirmary had opted into a pen-pal scheme with other clinics around the country so that patients with similar diagnoses could correspond in solidarity during their 'journey', as they were encouraged to call it.

Normally, Tom would have run a mile from anything like that, but as nothing *was* normal any more, he'd been talked into enrolling and had found himself paired with a woman from the West Midlands called Elaine.

They'd been of a similar age with similar tumours, both divorced. Although, unlike him, she had children. A daughter teaching Marine Biology at Bristol and a black sheep of a son entangled in various ways with the criminal element of Wolverhampton.

Quite how he'd lost the rightful path was something that Elaine had agonised over a great deal, and ruminating on the life he might have enjoyed if he'd only made better choices had compounded her pity for her prodigal boy all the more. How she'd prayed for his redemption every day, assured that her petitions would be answered. Each letter had been a proclamation of her faith.

For someone to have discovered God after receiving a terminal prognosis wasn't at all uncommon, of course, and Elaine's religiousness seemed to have been something of a novelty to her. She'd had the sincere and unembarrassed evangelism of a new recruit. No reservations about claiming Jesus as her saviour. Firmly convinced that her cancer was part of the Deity's plan to bring her to his loving, merciful bosom. She'd written more than once about the unexpected joy she'd found in her suffering – in that it heralded the end of this life of pain and the start of the life everlasting.

Her acceptance, her tranquillity, the way she could write *O, Death where is thy sting?* with such unalloyed confidence had seemed so magnificently fearless that, when she'd died suddenly a few months ago in August, Tom had felt surprisingly happy for her. She'd departed in perfect certitude. Whereas his feelings could change by the hour.

He'd been invited to her funeral but decided not to go. He'd have felt like he was intruding, and running into the son hadn't appealed much either. So, that had been that. And, after a tactful interval, an email had come to say that he'd be fixed up with a replacement.

Nothing had appeared for weeks, and he'd concluded that there had been some sort of clerical hitch. But then, out of nowhere, one morning towards the end of September, a long letter had arrived from an Oliver Keele.

He was articulate, erudite and not a little odd with all the 'old chaps' and 'dear boys' that he tossed into his sentences as though he and Tom had been friends their whole lives.

It was an affectation, and an endearing one at that, but it was a tactic too and Tom had realised very quickly that the flowery style was a way for Oliver to be evasive. He'd talk about his cancer, yes, but only in figurative terms – it was the 'intruder' or the 'pest' – and if he edged towards disclosing any of his concerns about what was awaiting him, it was as though he'd catch himself going too far and offer a stoic Latin aphorism or a line from a poem or a play instead.

'Ah, Tom, listen to me harping on. You don't want to hear it, I'm sure. What is it the Duke says to Claudio about life? *If I do lose thee, I do lose a thing that none but fools would keep*. No point being precious, is there?'

Well, if that was how he preferred to deal with what was happening, if he found some solace in romanticising his terror, then that was his choice.

Or was it that he'd been eschewing gloomy thoughts out of courtesy? Had he been worried that candid meant morbid? If so, he'd largely missed the point of the pen-pal programme which was to try and exorcise one's demons on the page.

In his reply, Tom had made a point of being frank about his own feelings so that Oliver would know that he needn't be quite so chary. As a matter of fact, he'd disclosed far more to Oliver than he ever had to anyone else about certain things – particularly about what had happened with Angeline or, more accurately, what he'd *done* to Angeline. But over the weeks that followed, Oliver's letters had continued in much the same vein as the first, full of digressions about nothing much – the weather or train journeys – and citations from the great and good on the subject of impermanence. Up stepped Shakespeare and Milton and Wordsworth and obscure Roman orators to speak on his behalf.

About himself, he gave very little away, and it had been a case of piecing together the scraps of information that had slipped out now and again.

Apparently, he worked in 'theatre' in some capacity and had been at Oxford in the mid-sixties which made him seventy-seven, seventy-eight or thereabouts. But that was more or less all that Tom had garnered. Actually, it was what Oliver *didn't* say that often said the most.

He made no mention of family. He never talked about having anyone close to him for that matter, and so it had to be assumed that he was without a partner.

The image he fostered was that of a donnish library dweller, wedded only to learning and study, endlessly captivated, as he'd said himself, by the magnificence, the *potency*, of well-chosen words. He venerated anyone who'd been able to move his heart with a bon mot, and to read his letters was to be an audience of one for a rousing show of defiance against mortality. It was Literature versus Death. And it had started to give Tom the sort of transitory comforts he'd enjoyed in his exchanges with Elaine.

Her confidence had been in the will of God, Oliver's in books, but it amounted to the same thing. Indeed, Oliver had found just as much consolation as she had. And answers too. Framed by poetry, everything made sense to him. And in the time Tom had spent immersed in his scholarly contemplations it had been pleasant to pretend that there really was nothing to be afraid of.

'I always think that Donne says it best, don't you?' was another typical Oliverism. 'Now, how does it go again? *Death be not proud, though some have called thee mighty and dreadful, for thou art not so.* Something like that.'

Afraid of appearing pretentious perhaps, he implied that he was merely paraphrasing such passages and dragging them half-remembered from his days at Corpus. But they were intimately known, there at his disposal, and inserted precisely. His style had the cadences of conversation, but it was all very carefully scripted in order to give Tom as much care and attention as possible. Every letter had come with a string of enquiries after his wellbeing.

'How did your appointment go on Tuesday, old thing? Has your appetite improved at all? Are those sleeping tablets making a difference? And how are your cats? One was pregnant, was it not?'

His interest in even the smallest details was flattering but it bordered on the obsessive at times. It betrayed a feeling of inferiority, of unworthiness even, on Oliver's part, as though, to him, Tom's life was far more significant than his own.

That wasn't an impression he cultivated for the purposes of obtaining sympathy. Oliver didn't come across as manipulative whatsoever. The perception he had of his own unimportance felt entirely genuine, which, in a way, was even sadder than if he'd put it on.

The man was just starved of companionship, that was all, and that his letters had often been six, seven, eight pages long, and occasionally more, suggested that he'd had no one else to talk to for quite some time. No one with whom to share his literary passions.

Why it should be so difficult for him to find friends and keep them was a mystery when Oliver was such an amiable, modest, sensitive sort. He didn't deserve to be lonely, certainly not at this stage in his life, not this close to its end, and so, when he'd suggested that they meet, Tom had said yes straight away, surprising himself at being so eager. But there was no time for procrastination now. There was work to be done. Not only when it came to helping Oliver, but in so many other ways too. There were restitutions to be made. Long-standing offences to confess to and atone for.

*

These were all new ambitions. Before the diagnosis, Tom had never really been one to dwell on the past, especially his own, and when he'd first started attending those 'Living Now' group-therapy sessions at the clinic, he'd been inclined to agree with Astrid, the leader, when she'd said that there was nothing to be gained from looking backwards and lamenting the actions of their former selves. Those ghosts were nothing to do with who they were in *this* moment, she said. The self was always in flux. The opportunity for change was always available. Even now, they could choose who they wanted to be. And she had any number of stories up her lacy sleeves about those who'd been emancipated by treating the past *as* past.

But as tempting as it was to liberate himself from all that he'd done and not done, wash his hands and start afresh, he couldn't, and the more he tried the more it felt as if he was ignoring the Tom Shift who was becoming ever starker in this new light of revelation.

Since he'd come out of hospital in the spring, he'd gradually awakened to who he was, indeed who he'd been all his life. The scales had fallen from his eyes. His misdeeds could not have been plainer. Only a fool would have disregarded such an epiphany and carried on as before.

Like standing naked in front of a mirror, any attempt at self-delusion was laughable now. He couldn't lie to himself any more or excuse his many wrongdoings as something else. When he thought of all the bargaining and

25

extenuation he'd done over the years in the cause of self-preservation, there were just too many faults to be pardoned in a flash. Forgiveness bestowed too easily was meaningless anyway. It would need to feel earned if he was to stand a chance of being able to square off his life in any semblance of peace.

Whether that was possible at all, he didn't know. Certain acts of vandalism were irreparable, especially those he'd inflicted on Angeline. One good deed wasn't going to redeem him entirely. But he just wanted to know, while he could still know anything, that he'd been truly kind at least once, and affected the course of someone's life for the better.

And so he'd brought money for Oliver. Enough to see him right for the short term. It was something. It was a start.

∼

It being the wintertime, Tom had assumed that he and Oliver would have the hotel more or less to themselves. But other guests were starting to appear. Many had ten years on him, fifteen maybe, some of them. Hunched and misshapen.

Watching them coming into the bar, he felt like a scruff in his cardigan and corduroys, and he wondered, by the way they were dressed, if they'd been at a wedding or something. The men were in dinner jackets and three-piece suits, the women in silk and chiffon numbers of hydrangea pinks and blues. More were getting out of black cabs outside carrying little suitcases and overnight bags.

No, not a wedding party. They'd come from a nursing home, perhaps. It was a night away at the seaside. Something to do on a drab winter weekend. A drink and some dinner a good enough excuse for them to put on their fanciest clothes and doll themselves up.

There was something admirable about the effort they'd made. Many of the men had been neatly shaved and their hair, if hair remained, raked and lacquered into grey-and-white furrows. The women sported bright lipstick and vivid, even audacious eye-shadow. But some looked, well, *embalmed*. The make-up had been really trowelled on. And in general, they looked to be wearing old clothes that had been pulled from the back of the wardrobe. The evening gowns and the three-piece suits were either too tight or hanging off these elderly bodies. He thought of Great-Aunt Genevieve again and the alarming sight of her freckled dowager's hump bursting out of those wispy robes of tulle and organza.

She'd kept them, he supposed, for the same reason as the guests in the bar put on these ill-fitting costumes. It allowed them to pretend that they were young again. Nothing wrong with that. But some were surely in the very same bind as he was. There had to be some uncurable, hopeless cases, frightened by their own bodies. And even those who hadn't yet been condemned in that way would have other miseries to bear – shingles, gout, glaucoma. When they were away from here, unable to mask their senescence, when they looked at themselves, weren't they just as bewildered as he was by what had happened?

Ageing was so subtle. Like the rolling of one season into another, it had all occurred with such stealth. Somehow, at some point, he'd fallen into the demographic urged to take up Cooperative funeral plans and make bequests to wildlife sanctuaries. The leaflets that came through the letterbox these days presupposed that he was in the market for a sit-down shower or an orthopaedic armchair. Whenever he waited in Oncology for a check-up and looked at the posters on the pinboard, he'd see celebrities of a comparable vintage to him advocating regular prostate examinations and screenings for abdominal aortic aneurysms, whatever they were.

Unsure of when he'd crossed the threshold of risk, he'd become susceptible to seniority's unique maladies and made to suffer its sluggish processes of repair.

He'd still not fully recovered from falling in the garden back in the spring. His clavicle twinged where the bone had snapped, and he couldn't use his right arm freely any more as it hurt his elbow too much. Healing was so slow now. Everything about him was slow. He'd become more and more silted up, like the river outside. His body had thickened and sagged to such a degree that his younger self looked like someone else entirely. The handful of photographs he still had from his twenties and thirties showed a lean, dark-haired, even – dare he say it – objectively hand-some lad. Yet, over time, his crown had greyed and thinned, he'd acquired warts and liver spots, drooping paps and an intermittent rheumatism in his knuckles; his jawline had sunk under the chub of his chin and his nose had grown into a bulbous tuber.

For loveliness to increase was rare. But it had happened with Angeline. Until a few months ago, he'd not set eyes on a picture of her for years, and it had pleased him (and pained him) to see that she'd kept her looks. Her hair was a pure white now, but still abundant. Her skin an even deeper olive. She radiated the serenity of someone who'd grown old in the sun, someone who'd successfully whittled down life to its essentials and, more importantly, recognised what they were in time to enjoy them.

She cooked for her family, she grew lemons in her garden, she swam, she fished, and in the summer laid on painting lessons for tourists. The Aegean light, he knew, was a gift to an artist.

From what she'd told him, it didn't seem as though she ever strayed very far from her villa. Everything she wanted was there.

Whenever he'd thought about her since they'd gone their separate ways, that was exactly the kind of life he'd im-agined her living. Quiet, languid, settled. And not wishing to disturb any of that, uncertain how she'd respond, he'd waited a few weeks after being discharged from hospital before getting in touch.

What had compelled him to do so was complicated, but it had just felt odd *not* to inform her. If it had been *her* under the sword then he'd want to know. But he'd not been so sure that Angeline would necessarily think the same way about him. They'd been divorced for far longer than they'd been married. Contact between them had dwindled to silence. She had her own life, and he had his, and, as such, he'd been concerned that it might seem too invasive to burden her with the news of his diagnosis out of the blue. She'd be obliged to react, to feel something about it.

He needn't have worried. She was devastated for him. She'd even given him a mild dressing-down for not telling her sooner.

And so he'd explained what had happened in the garden that afternoon in April as he'd been hacking away at the cherry tree. How he'd suddenly blacked out and toppled from the stepladder. How he'd come to consciousness face down on the lawn and heard the voice of his next-door neighbour and the earnest questions of the paramedics she'd summoned coming and going like the sunlight. How they'd kept him on the geriatric ward for ten days or so (though it had felt more like a month), strapped up his broken collarbone, run some tests, fed him into the scanner, discovered the tumour in some deep and inaccessible pleat of his brain, called in a consultant, then another, delivered

30

the initial (but, as it transpired, pretty conclusive) verdict and set out what they'd termed his 'next steps'.

It had been efficient, he'd said, if nothing else.

Angeline hadn't taken that with the lightness he'd hoped for and had gone quiet for a few moments.

Eventually, she'd returned with, 'Are you really telling me that there's nothing they can do?'

'Not nothing. There are treatments,' he'd said. 'But the chances of them being successful are slim. They gave me a percentage. I forget what it was. Close to zero.'

'Isn't even a slim chance better than none?'

'I'm not certain that's true in this case. The way they described it all, it sounds as if the drugs would make me as sick as a dog and be as likely to kill me as the cancer.'

'They're just trying to put you off,' she'd said. 'It's money. That's all.'

'Possibly,' he'd said. 'But they seemed more concerned that I should have some quality of life before the end. And I have to agree.'

'So, what? They just expect you to . . .'

'Wait? Yes. Effectively.'

'Jesus, Tom,' she'd replied. 'I'm so sorry. I don't know what to say.'

No one did. What *was* the right response? There wasn't one that didn't sound glib or saccharine. Words were always going to fall short – even when they were as beautifully employed as they were in Oliver's letters. If anyone was going to make any of this bearable, it would be in what they did, not what they said.

Practicality had been a trait that he'd always admired in Angeline and from that phone call onwards she'd undertaken to help in an imperative way. She'd rung or emailed every week and involved herself in his life to a degree that still seemed above and beyond. She'd been the one who'd urged him along to those Living Now meetings and had pressed him into giving the pen-pal scheme a go. And she'd become unexpectedly protective of him. A cancelled outpatient appointment? She'd be on to the relevant department that day. Painkillers not working? She'd trawl the internet and find something stronger for him to demand from his consultant.

It was more than he could have hoped for, and – without intending to sound too self-pitying – far more than he deserved. But there was a limit to her compassion, something which had become apparent a fortnight ago when at the end of a phone call he'd asked her to come and visit him.

After some silence, she'd said, 'Let me think about it, Tom,' and he'd kicked himself for putting her on the spot like that, for assuming that the sympathy she'd been showing him equated to some kind of exculpation and he'd been granted the privilege of her company again. As if the fact that he was on his way out had put everything into perspective for her and she was of the mind that whatever sins a person had committed, particularly those from long ago, ought to be rendered null and void at the brink of cavernous death. To come to that point was punishment enough.

But that was only what *he* wanted to be true. And that almost forty-five years had passed since they'd been together made no difference to what he'd done to her. It still mattered. It hadn't diminished. He'd bullied her into giving up what she'd most wanted in the world and for that there was no other word than cruelty.

~

The door to the bar opened again, and Mrs Paley held it wide to let in two more guests – a bald, lumpen man asleep in a wheelchair and a woman wearing a green taffeta dress, presumably his wife, who rolled him through the room with more strength than her slight frame suggested she possessed.

Weaving between the tables, she parked her husband at the one next to Tom's to join some friends, and after an exchange of handshakes and kisses, they all remarked on the terrible weather and the awful journeys they'd had.

How Oliver was getting to Saltwash, Tom wasn't sure, but if he was making his way here by public transport, which seemed most likely, then he'd be having a hard time of it as well. Perhaps he'd been held up at every turn and would arrive fatigued with the tedium of gazing out of a window. Or was he used to spending hours on buses and trains?

Whenever he'd happened to mention his career in 'performance', whatever that meant, he'd talked about it in the present tense, and in spite of his illness it evidently kept him on the road.

He must have been settled enough at some point in the past to have gone through the treatment he'd alluded to now and then in his letters, and he must have attended the same clinic often enough to have signed up to the pen-pal initiative. But he'd begun roving again thereafter.

Over the course of the six weeks or so in which he and Tom had been sending one another their long despatches, Oliver had given his address as the Savoy Bed and Breakfast in Eastbourne, then the Regal Choice in Great Yarmouth and latterly the Traveller's Rest in Scarborough. Cheap, grim-looking places when Tom had found them online, despite their names, and now Oliver was on his way to the Castle, which, behind all the frills and flounces, was just as down at heel.

It was clearly somewhere he liked. He was a yearly visitor here, so he'd said. And it being quaintly out-of-date suited him to a tee. But it was hard to see the appeal of coming to Saltwash, and in November too. Not only that, but it was also an odd choice geographically, being on the opposite coast to Scarborough and a good hour and a half away for Tom. It would have been far more convenient to have plumped for somewhere between them both. Harrogate or York. Not here.

*

34

A tram approached and stopped outside, strafed by rain, its windows misted up. More guests disembarked and, holding on to hats or huddled in twos and threes under umbrellas, they were blown across the road to the hotel.

The few riding mobility scooters and the ones reliant on Zimmer frames took the slope to the front door. The rest came up the steps as quickly as fitness permitted, some nimble, some arm in arm, others going one foot at a time, one hand on the rail, stopping for a breather midway.

It was the last few feet of Everest, thought Tom. Or the stairs to the pearly gates.

He tried to pick out Oliver among the crowd streaming into the bar, confident that he'd recognise the man even though he'd never seen a photograph of him. He'd sort of look the part, as it were. But no one did and no one came to introduce themselves either. They only passed on knowing smiles and nods when they saw that he was wearing a red badge.

He really ought to give it back to Mrs Paley. She'd made a mistake in assuming that he was part of this gathering. Couldn't she have seen from his clothes that he wasn't one of them? Yet quite *how* they were all associated was hard to say. A church group, Masons, Rotarians?

They hadn't come from retirement homes. That was obvious now. If that had been the case, they'd have been bussed in together and had their carers with them. Mostly, they appeared capable of looking after themselves. The few that were infirm were ministered to by their other halves. Just as the woman on the next table (her name was Connie, Tom had overheard) attended to her husband as he woke up bewildered, and let out a moan of distress.

'Oh, come on, Mr Bear, that's enough of the noise,' she said, wiping the drool off his chin. 'You know where you are. Do you want a biscuit?'

As soon as she took out the small foil parcel from her handbag, he started babbling away in what sounded like a made-up foreign language, desperate to be fed.

Was this how *he'd* be by the end? thought Tom. Shunted about in a wheelchair, speaking in tongues, mollified with a digestive?

He'd given Angeline permission to have him shot before it came to that. God forbid that if she ever did fly over to visit him, it would be at Sunnyside Court or the Blossoms or some such place. God forbid that she would feel obliged to sit with him (as he'd felt obliged to sit with his mother) at the hour for tea and tablets and watch the nurses moving about the rigid, inexpressive folk like pigeons among the statuary of a grave-yard. Spare her those endless afternoons of hand-holding in a lounge of ticking clocks; that smell of gravy and indignity.

Whether things would get so far, he didn't know. No one was able to say. They couldn't predict much about the tumour, only that it would grow as it pleased.

As it 'pleased'? he'd asked. Why would it be 'pleased'? To that, no answer had been forthcoming. Unlike Angeline, these doctors couldn't tell that he was joking. Well, not joking as such but poking fun at the absurd idioms they used sometimes. Since there was nothing else to laugh at, it would have to do.

The trouble was that they'd caught the damn thing too late. And as he'd said to Angeline, there was no meaningful intervention they could make now. All they could really do from here on in was monitor the cancer's behaviour and try to mitigate the worst of the problems as and when they occurred. 'Firefighting,' they called it.

He'd been told that there'd be migraines and confusion, alternating bouts of exhaustion and insomnia. And while he'd experienced all of those things in short but intense episodes over the last six months, it was the threat of eventual and complete amnesia that caused him the most concern. The slide towards it had begun for sure – slowly and sporadically so far, but he was starting to have to stick up notes around the house. *Lock doors. Switch off oven. Bring in milk.* Little things. Though that was how it would go apparently. Bit by bit.

The equation was clear. The longer he lived, the more anonymous he would become to himself, and he hoped that he wouldn't have to exist in that state for long, that it would be hospice–furnace, as quick as that. He didn't want to linger on in some kind of infantile netherworld like this old dribbler on the next table.

Dribbler?

No no.

This new Tom Shift was supposed to be kinder, wasn't he? A paragon of empathy.

Oh, forgive him his trespasses. He is only afraid.

He realised that he'd been caught staring by the man's wife, this Connie, but she didn't seem offended. She smiled and said something that he couldn't quite make out over the clamour. When he gestured to his ear, she reached across the gap between the tables and touched his wrist. A bright-eyed, attractive lady who had no need to paint herself like the others. Neat little features. Sandy hair in a chignon.

'I said, are you waiting for someone?' she repeated.

'Just a friend,' he said.

'Anyone I might have heard of?' she asked.

'His name's Oliver Keele,' Tom replied, and her smile widened.

'Of course, who else?' she said. 'Is he well?'

Tom said nothing about Oliver's cancer. That was his business to disclose if he so wished. Instead, he said, 'You know him, do you?'

'Oliver? Everyone here does,' said Connie. 'Back we come every year. Our little club. Though we can never be sure who'll turn up, of course. Or how many of us there'll be. Oliver's done well to bring in some new blood.'

She looked at Tom's badge. He was the only person wearing one, as far as he could tell.

'This? I think it was given in error, sorry,' he said. 'The landlady just presumed I was with you.'

'Well, you *are*,' said Connie. 'Didn't Oliver say?'

She looked benevolently on his confusion.

'Come on,' she said, wanting him to take her hand. 'Until he arrives, you sit with us. We can't have you feeling lonely, can we? What kind of a welcome would that be?'

He'd have preferred to wait for Oliver by himself but he couldn't really refuse Connie's invitation and so he got up, collected his coat and what was left of his Scotch and sat, as instructed, in the spare seat between her two friends. A baggy-jowled man with moist, bloodhound eyes and a woman wearing a satin evening dress the same colour as the pendant of rubies and garnets that ornamented her wrinkled decolletage.

'Petula,' she said, offering him her hand, and grinned with shiny teeth that weren't her own. She wore a wig too. An ash-blonde bob with a heavy fringe.

A Shetland pony, he thought. That was what she reminded him of. 'Sturdy', his mother would have called her. And other things, in a dress like that.

The man at the table was drinking plain water with an air of puritan haughtiness and surveyed Tom's casual appearance, noting the grease mark on his sleeve from the sandwich he'd eaten on the train.

'Barnaby Collins,' he said.

His grip was firm, diagnostic.

39

With another pat of Tom's arm, Connie introduced herself and then laid the back of her hand against her husband's cheek.

'And this is Victor,' she said.

Slumped in his chair where his enormous body had settled like the rubble of a landslide, he stared at Tom with something between curiosity and suspicion and Connie gently admonished him.

'Oh, stop scowling,' she said. 'Tom's new. Can't you see his badge? Be friendly now. Aren't you going to say hello, like we practised? No? Please yourself then, you great oaf.'

She lifted his hand and kissed his knuckles and then turned to Tom again.

'Don't worry, he'll get used to you soon enough. He's far more interested in food anyway.'

At the sound of the word, Victor gabbled for another biscuit and Connie broke one up for him, saying 'wider, *wider*' as she placed a fragment in his mouth: a little bunting feeding a massive cuckoo chick.

'I'm still looking after you, aren't I?' she said to him. 'How long has it been now? Fifty-five years?'

It was clear that she wanted Tom to be impressed by the feat of endurance.

'Fifty-five,' he said. 'That's commendable.' There was probably a better word.

'Victor and I hold Saltwash very close to our hearts, don't we, love?' she said, giving him another morsel. 'We came here on our honeymoon. Quite the couple, we were.'

'Did *you* marry, Tom?' Petula asked.

The abruptness of the question wrong-footed him a little.

'Yes,' he said. 'I did.'

She looked at his bare ring finger.

'We parted company,' he said.

'Same for me,' she said, pleased at the alliance. 'Do you miss her? Your wife?'

'Sometimes,' he said.

'Was she unfaithful?'

'Excuse me?'

'Was that the reason it didn't work out? Did she cheat on you?'

'No,' he said. Unlike him, Angeline had been ever constant.

'Any kids?' said Petula.

He answered in the negative and reversed the question before she could delve any further.

'Me? Two boys,' she said. 'The bane of my bloody life. How many was it for you, Connie?'

'Thirty-seven,' she replied.

As she brushed flecks of biscuit off her husband's straining cummerbund, she took in Tom's puzzlement with a laugh.

'We fostered,' she said. 'Not that Victor remembers any of them now, poor thing.'

With a belch, he brought up brown mush that trickled down to his bowtie and Connie rooted out a tissue from the sleeve of her dress.

'You didn't try again then, Tom?' Petula said.

'Another marriage, you mean?' he replied. 'God, no.'

After the divorce, he'd had the odd fling (never a more apt expression for those strange and quickly discarded romances) and there'd been other, occasional lovers in the years since, but he'd never had an urge for another *relationship*.

'Get away. They must have been fighting over you,' said Petula.

'Hardly.'

'Well, I'd have snapped you up,' she said. 'Even if I'd been married. *Especially* if I'd been married.'

Tom assumed that she was being shameless in jest, but Barnaby made a noise of disgust. 'You're a vulture, woman,' he said. 'Leave the man alone.'

Petula stuck out her tongue, which was bright yellow from the tropical concoction she was drinking. And while she went back to sucking the straw, Barnaby took the opportunity to regain control of the discourse. Before Tom had come along and side-tracked his audience, he'd been happily holding court.

'As I was saying, they never asked us, did they?' he continued. 'We weren't important. They just swept it away as though we wouldn't care.'

'Swept what away?' Connie said. She'd been attending to Victor's dripping nose and had only caught the end of Barnaby's complaint.

'England,' he said. '*Our* England, I mean,' and he motioned with his glass in such a manner that suggested it might be found here in the room in some form. In the other guests. In all the knick-knacks and curios.

Petula groaned and leant against Tom's shoulder, his bad shoulder.

'You sat down at the wrong time,' she said. 'He's still not got to the end of his annual lecture, have you, dear?'

'You can't deny that things were different then,' Barnaby said.

'It was all perfect, was it?' said Petula.

'Folk were more civilised. There's no doubt about that. Now, they might as well be a different species, most of them.'

Petula scoffed. 'A different species. Please.'

'I'm telling you,' Barnaby said. 'Things went amiss somewhere along the line. There was a fork in the road and England swung the wrong way.'

'Oh, people don't change,' said Petula. '*You* never do.'

Barnaby gave her a withering look and turned to Connie.

'You agree, don't you?' he said. 'That the country's taken a turn for the worse. Especially when it comes to kids. You must have seen your share of delinquents.'

Connie put her hand on Victor's. Protectively, Tom thought.

43

'I'm not sure we'd have used that word,' she said. 'Those children didn't exactly have it easy.'

'None of *us* had it easy when we were growing up, either,' Barnaby replied. 'But we didn't go around wrecking things, did we? You know they burned down the Majestic?'

Tom realised that he was talking to him.

'Terrible,' he said.

'You're right, it is terrible,' said Barnaby. 'Absolutely terrible. And I can't imagine they thought twice about it either, did they? Do you suppose they ever consider the consequences of anything they do? They're a different species, as I say, no?'

These weren't questions that lobbied for agreement. Barnaby was the type who'd start a conversation with a stranger on the assumption that they held precisely the same opinions as he did.

'I mean, there's no deterrent, is there?' he went on. 'What do they get these days? A slap on the wrist?'

'Slightly more for arson, I'd have thought,' said Tom, making Petula laugh. And that was that. Barnaby had got the measure of him as a smart alec.

'What was it you did for a living, Mr Shift?' he asked, and dabbed the sweat off his clipped little moustache in a meticulous, prissy procedure.

Whatever the answer, he'd be disparaging about it, thought Tom, and as soon as he said, 'I wrote articles, well

44

books mostly,' Barnaby sat back, satisfied; that was exactly the kind of thing he'd been expecting.

'Novels?' said Petula.

'Travel guides,' Tom replied.

'You lucky thing,' she said. 'You must have seen the whole world.'

'No,' he said. 'Not by a long shot. Europe mainly.'

'It must have been lovely,' said Connie.

Yes, he thought, it was. Lovely. He missed it. That was to say he missed the sun and the food and the wine, and the slower pace of continental life. It was the practicalities of travel that had become tiresome. Waiting around in Departures, cancelled flights, long transfers, the wearying systems of embarkation and immigration that seemed to have been modelled on methods of herding cattle. He'd gladly left all that behind when he'd retired six years ago. Since then, his migratory territory had shrunk. Even London had become too much – in every way – and he'd moved back to West Yorkshire where he'd grown up. Before the diagnosis, his days as a man of leisure had been spent maintaining the house and the garden (both of which had been left in disrepair by the previous owner) doing what he could himself and calling in tradesmen for anything that required more expertise.

Now and then, he'd considered putting pen to paper and writing his autobiography. His publishers were confident that there'd be a readership for it. *A Life in a Hundred Airport*

Lounges. That kind of thing. But he'd never got much further than thinking about it. He couldn't disentangle the past from past regrets.

'I can't imagine what it must be like to be always off somewhere exotic,' said Connie.

'It wasn't as if I was getting on a plane every week,' he said. Most of the time, he assured them, he'd been chained to his desk at home writing or reading or working through reams of edits.

'Sounds gruelling,' said Connie. 'To have someone picking apart your hard work like that. It must seem very personal.'

'Well, a thick skin helps,' he said and finished off what was left of his Scotch.

His claim to toughness made Barnaby sniff.

'A thick skin? Try being a gardener,' he said, and Tom looked at him with more surprise than he'd intended. He'd had him down as an ex-banker in that pin-striped suit. Or even a military man, with his finnicky little tache. 'Been at it since I was fifteen,' he boasted. 'Both my lads went into the business too.'

'Outdoors all the time,' Tom said. 'That must have been nice.'

No, from Barnaby's expression, 'nice' wasn't the right word. 'Nice' was a layman's ignorance.

'You're green-fingered, are you?' he asked, already having made up his mind that Tom was anything but.

46

'I wrestle with the cherry tree now and then.'

He looked at Tom's soft uncalloused hands, evidently pleased that his initial judgement of him had been correct.

'I think my life's been a bit different to yours, Mr Shift,' he said, and by 'different' he meant 'more worthwhile'.

Perhaps that was true. At least he'd grown things. Sunflowers. Sons.

'Barnaby's just intimidated by men with brains, aren't you, Barnaby?' Petula said, and he looked at her sardonically.

Tom didn't much care what Barnaby thought of him one way or the other but felt conspicuous all the same given what he was wearing. Cardigan and corduroys, for God's sake. Even the chap outside carrying those bags of scrap around was more suitably attired. Oliver could have said *something*. If he'd chosen to come to Saltwash to attend this annual get-together and had wanted Tom to be part of it too, he might at least have mentioned the formal dress code.

It was possible that he *had*, mind, thought Tom. He couldn't put too much faith in his memory any more.

'Have you known Oliver long?' asked Connie, and Tom hesitated, feeling that it would be disingenuous to say that he really *knew* him at all.

'No, not long,' he said.

'How did you meet?' Connie went on. 'I can't think how your circles would have mixed.'

'Yes, where *did* he pick you up from?' Petula said.

'You make me sound like a stray cat,' said Tom, to which she laughed as though he had a wit to rival Oscar Wilde's. The cocktail she was swiftly demolishing wasn't her first drink of the day.

He didn't want to say that he'd only been acquainted with Oliver for a couple of months and hadn't yet seen him in person, as they would want to know why and that wasn't a discussion to be had here, and so he lied and said, 'We have mutual friends.'

'Well, I'm not surprised,' Connie said, looking around the room again. 'Oliver's amassed quite a collection of devotees. Everyone loves Oliver. You love Oliver, don't you, Mr Bear?'

Victor found a crumb in the folds of his shirt and ate it.

'He's one of those people that everyone warms to instantly, isn't he?' said Petula. 'He has a certain something.'

'He's so gifted,' Connie said.

'Oh, that goes without saying,' Petula agreed.

What was he then, an actor? A singer? Tom longed to ask, but if he was claiming to be Oliver's friend, he ought to know such things, and he didn't want to come across as duplicitous, although Barnaby seemed to think that about him already. The truncated answers he'd given to Connie's and Petula's questions had plainly made the crabby, dog-eyed sod mistrustful of him. Or Petula was right and he'd just had his nose put out of joint by an interloper soaking up all the attention.

'He's honest, is Oliver,' Barnaby stated. 'There's no side to him. He's a grafter too.'

He made it clear that the attributes Oliver possessed were precisely those that Tom lacked.

'People like him for the natural things he has,' Petula said. 'Personality. Charisma.'

Oliver had both in spades, even on paper, thought Tom, and yet he'd never mentioned any of his admirers by name. It was always, 'I once knew this chap . . .' or 'There was a fellow on the circuit back when . . .'. It was only ever memoir. Had he actual friends who cared about him in the here and now, he perhaps wouldn't feel so lowly.

'He's generous in a way that's really quite rare these days, don't you think?' Connie said.

'Aye,' Barnaby concluded. 'If anyone ought to win, it's him.'

On this they all concurred. But Tom couldn't be sure if he'd heard correctly. Win what?

He was about to ask when music began to ooze from the speakers on the walls, something sentimental, full of sweeping lachrymose violins. An awful crooner started on 'Que Sera Sera', and by the end of the first verse most of the room was in chorus, or as close to it as their hearing allowed. Then those who were able to dance got up and held on to one another, side-stepping tentatively in whatever space they could find.

'Tom?' said Petula.

'Two left feet,' he said.

'I wasn't suggesting we do the Charleston.'

'Even so.'

'Are you worried that I'll lead you astray? Or is it that you don't trust yourself with me?'

'I want to try and catch Oliver,' Tom said. 'That's all.'

'You'll know when he gets here, believe me,' said Petula. 'Come on. Be a gentleman. Unless you'd prefer to stay for the rest of the speech.'

Jacket off, settled in for the duration, Barnaby had moved on to immigrants now – the right sort and the wrong sort, as he put it – and although Connie deigned to listen out of courtesy, Tom had no desire to hear any of it and let Petula help him up off his chair.

'You see, *that* lot, the Indians,' said Barnaby, nodding at the lady in the sari on the next table, 'they *wanted* to be like us when they came over. Same as the Caribbeans. But the ones we get now . . . I mean, I'm sure they're mostly decent people but if they don't want to make the effort to fit in, they really should be sent back, for their own sake as much as ours . . .'

Oh, the English, thought Tom. The English and their civilised bigotry.

It was one of the reasons he'd spent as much time as possible elsewhere.

*

50

Petula led him into the throng of lumbering bodies. Unsure what to do for the best, he put his hands on her hips and felt soft flesh under the glossy material of her dress.

'Good God, Tom, we're not twelve,' she said and shook him on his delicate shoulder. 'Hold me properly.'

She positioned him so that they were in the standard teapot hold – one hand on the small of the back, their other hands clasped together and dipping slowly up and down to the music. In this position, his weak elbow smarted and he had to adjust his grip to find some comfort. Petula took this as an invitation to move closer still and laid her head against his chest.

He couldn't recall the last time he'd danced with a woman. It had been a long time since he'd held a woman in his arms for any reason. Some men of his age he knew were still concupiscent, even libertine, but for him desire of *that* kind had largely dissipated. Every so often, he'd dream about Angeline and find himself entangled in her naked body as it had been when they were first married, but these were just clips of pornography that were wasted on him now. Sketches of an intimacy he'd once had. He was still attracted to certain women – from actresses on the television to individuals of his own acquaintance – but flirting and courting with the aim of consummation seemed a tad undignified and certainly tiresome. A lot to go through to satisfy an itch that came and went with such brevity if it flared up at all.

51

'You've really no other half then, Tom?' said Petula. 'I find that hard to believe.'

'Do you, why?'

'Men are hopeless on their own.'

'I seem to have managed.'

'Did your wife remarry?' asked Petula.

'She did, yes.'

'That must get to you.'

'Why should it?'

'Her with someone and you without.'

'I'm not lonely, if that's what you're driving at,' Tom said.

Petula lifted her head and looked at him.

'You don't mind me asking about all this, do you?' she said. 'I just can't stand small talk. It seems such a waste of time when we've precious little left. Say what you want to say. Be honest. Enjoy yourself. That's my opinion. Who gets to the end of their life and looks back fondly on all their restraint?'

'You've no regrets then, have you?' he said.

'Plenty,' she replied.

'Like what?'

She gave him a meaningful look – a conspiratorial, birds of a feather look.

'I think you and I have both been led into temptation now and then, haven't we, Tom?' she said, having concluded, by the way he'd answered the question of infidelity so brusquely earlier, that this was the reason his marriage had ended.

But it had only happened twice. Twice in six years. For the first four he'd been completely faithful.

Those were the statistics with which he'd managed to settle his conscience if he'd ever been made to review his conduct. Though he'd not felt solely responsible for his lapses anyway. He'd been inclined to cast himself as a victim of youth's natural impetuosity. Rare was the man who *hadn't* made a mistake in the summer of his life, it being 'hot and bold' or 'full of sport' or however the line went.

And he'd always been able to make the acts of betrayal for which he *might* be deemed blameworthy seem negligible by the fact that he could have been a far worse adulterer. He'd had plenty of chances, being away from home so often. It had been offered to him on a plate more than once and he'd still turned it down – if only to prove to himself that he wasn't a slave to his libido. It had sometimes been a close-run thing, mind. There'd been that delectable senorita in Madrid, for one. *¡Ay! Una diosa perfecta.*

Over the years, he'd satisfied himself that his had been a selective sort of disloyalty, comprised of affairs that had been brief and solely physical; his two illicit lovers, Monica and Steffy, had become lovers precisely because he'd known he had no future with them.

Of course, the fine detail made no odds. Infidelity was infidelity, however fleetingly it occurred. What had he expected Angeline to do, exactly, when it had all come out? Praise his forbearance?

'You know, when I think about it now,' said Petula, as they revolved slowly together, 'I wonder if I took a husband all those times just so that I *could* cheat on them. It always made for the best sex, all the sneaking around. I won't pretend that it didn't excite me. Was it like that for you?'

'You got married just to indulge a fetish?' said Tom.

Petula smiled at him. 'You didn't answer the question, Mr Shift,' she said. 'I didn't have you pegged as a prude.'

'I'm not.'

'But you make me sound so seedy. Fetish,' she laughed. 'I just wanted to have the best of things, that's all. Doesn't everyone want that, deep down? I'm not saying it's right. I'm entirely aware of what it did to Carl and Jeremy and dear, sweet Eugene, bless his heart. I'll admit to how dreadful I am. I'm not so proud that I can't be honest.'

So she said, but it was hard to tell if she was truly contrite or not.

She glanced back to where they'd been sitting. Barnaby was still preaching.

'*He* likes to think that he's holier than thou,' she said. 'But he knows full well that he's no better than anyone else here. If he tries to belittle you again, Tom, just say "Widows" and that'll shut him up.'

'Widows?'

'He'll know what you mean.'

They turned again and found themselves next to a gnome-like, apple-cheeked couple who introduced themselves as the Fishwicks and smiled and nodded at Tom's red badge.

'The first time here is always the best time,' said the woman. 'So many wonderful surprises.'

'The best time,' the man repeated, and then the two of them took turns to extol the Paleys' magnanimity.

'They're so kind.'

'So *understanding*.'

'They always have been.'

'They just give and give.'

They were brother and sister, Tom decided. Unless they were one of those married pairs in which the two parties grew to look and sound alike over the years.

Petula fell into conversation with them about various people who'd come and gone from the Castle, and how beautiful the funeral had been of someone they all knew. It left Tom feeling like a spare part, restless to get on with the business he'd come for.

He looked out for Oliver, but all he could see were other guests rising and falling out of time. There had to be close to seventy or eighty of them here now, he reckoned. Maybe more.

With the hotel at full capacity, Mr Paley had enlisted the help of two young women behind the bar. They had to be his daughters, as they were both tall and weighty like him.

Impatient and ill-tempered as they worked. Unused to such busyness.

It was just as well that Oliver had booked a table for dinner. Yet, Tom felt a dash of disappointment that Oliver hadn't wanted to be with *him* exclusively but had come to spend the evening with dozens of other people too.

Vanity, Tom. All is vanity.

Fine, but that aside, there was the issue of the money. If Oliver really was as popular as Connie and the others made out, it might be tricky to get him alone for long enough to talk it over.

It would be necessary to work up to it too. Delicacy was required. It would be humiliating for Oliver to disclose his financial difficulties. It would be like him to try and brush them aside. Oh, don't worry about me, old thing, I'll manage. You can't keep a good man down. Onwards and upwards. Etcetera.

But that kind of bluster didn't detract from the reality that, after he left the Castle, he would carry on flitting between these tired-looking hotels and run-down B & Bs.

Performers often did stay in scrubby digs, of course, but since Oliver hadn't ever said anything about his actual home – either when he was hoping to return there or where it was – Tom could only think that he didn't have one.

It wasn't right that someone as unwell as him should be travelling about so much and spending what little he earned, from whatever it was he did, on such miserable-looking rooms. Far better that he rested in one place now, somewhere pleasant, clean and quiet, without the pressure of having to work. It was time to let someone else worry about money.

There was no need to call it charity, thought Tom. It would be a simple relocation of funds to where they were needed most. Just sensible, hands-on assistance. It was deeds not words that counted, he'd say.

But whatever he rehearsed sounded patronising or demeaning and *exactly* like charity. Perhaps the easiest solution would be to stash the notes in Oliver's coat pocket when he wasn't looking and let him discover them later. But wouldn't he feel duped? Or at least a little put out that he'd not been given the chance to refuse? He'd have some pride, naturally. Who wouldn't?

This Mr Calmine, who lugged his jumble up and down the promenade, had certainly tried to hang on to his dignity as best he could.

He was back now, bonneted with a deerstalker to keep off the rain. With a swipe of his stick, he tried to scare away the gulls that were beaking at the litter by the roadside, *his* litter, but they resettled a few feet away and were indifferent to his gesticulations.

Time was, Tom conceded, he'd have pitied someone like that, and dismissed him for *being* so pitiable. He'd have assumed his life to be so fraught and impoverished as to be worthless. He might even have had the callousness to believe that such a man had only himself to blame for his disadvantages because of some inborn recklessness or stupidity. But now at this point, what was there to separate them? What would he leave behind that was any different to Mr Calmine's hoard of rubbish? He had no children. And as for his writing, well the others at Living Now might have considered him as good as immortalised on account of having his work in print, but he'd not published anything for years and travel guides went out of date. Countries changed; things moved on. He'd be forgotten too.

Perhaps he ought to have another go at his memoirs while he was still compos mentis. There'd be something satisfying about being able to lay his hand on a stack of paper and say *this was my life*. He had the perfect opportunity to give the best version of Tom Shift to posterity and leave out what would cast him in a bad light. But setting down such a selective history was at odds with the late-flowering determination he had to be honest with the world and with himself while he still had time.

Outside, the streetlamps came on across the road. A car ploughed through the puddles, sweeping water on to the pavement, and to avoid being splashed Mr Calmine retreated into the shelter. After depositing the cans and bottles that had been left on the bench into one of his already bulging bags, he sat with his legs crossed and watched everyone dancing in the bar.

Petula turned to look. Others had become aware of him too.

'There he is,' said Petula. 'Same as every year.'

'Trouble, is he?' asked Tom.

'What makes you say that?'

'The landlady didn't want him getting in.'

'Well, he can be a bit volatile,' said Petula. 'He's barred, you see. But he doesn't think he should be.'

'Oh?'

'He believes he's entitled to another turn at the draw.'

'The draw?'

'After dinner.'

'The draw for what?'

She tapped at Tom's red badge.

'Not yet. Sorry,' she said. 'I'll only get it in the neck.'

'Why the secrecy?'

'All in good time,' she said. 'Don't make me spoil it.'

The song came to an end and as the next started a gentleman with the hawk-like face of Gladstone approached and asked Tom if he might, in the parlance of their generation, cut in, and have the next dance.

'By all means,' said Tom, to which Petula responded with a finger to his ribs.

'You didn't have to ditch me quite so quickly,' she said but without any real animosity now that she had a new suitor to lean against, and she was led away to the strains of 'These Foolish Things' while Mrs Paley went about closing the curtains on the wet night.

Mr Calmine, Tom noticed, had disappeared.

～

Still keeping an eye out for Oliver, he went back to the table. As he sat down, Barnaby immediately excused himself, saying that he'd promised to go and speak to such-and-such. Perhaps he suspected that Petula had brought up the subject of these 'widows', plural, whoever they were. Naughty boy.

He made a beeline for friendlier company and, watching him go, Tom saw that there was a duskiness to the air, as though people had been smoking. But he realised that it was dust being kicked up by those dancing.

Perhaps there was no point in trying to keep the bar room clean if it became grubby again as soon as it was occupied. The Paleys had to be in a constant battle with the place. Decay (or demolition or destruction) looked to be the fate of most things in Saltwash. Over time the cost of maintaining these buildings surely bit into profit so deeply that it wasn't worth keeping them open.

And so, when Connie said, 'It's such a shame,' Tom assumed that she meant the state of the Castle. But she was talking about Oliver.

'He'll be ever so upset that he's missing out,' she said. 'And it's not the same without him.'

'Is he usually on time?' said Tom.

'Always,' she replied. 'That's why I'm starting to worry.'

This she said surreptitiously so that Victor didn't hear, though he wasn't listening anyway.

'It's probably just the weather,' said Tom.

'I'm sure you're right,' she said. 'I suppose everyone's a bit out of kilter today, aren't they? We were singing *rain rain go away* all the way here, weren't we, Victor?'

He was enjoying the music as a child would, and as it changed to something more up-tempo he laughed in a high-pitched squawk and rocked back and forth in his chair while Connie swung his hand in time.

'Yes, you remember this, don't you?' she said to him. 'One, two, three. That's right. You're dancing with me, aren't you? Like we did on our honeymoon.'

Already bored with her again, he pulled away and picked his nose.

'You know, I'm convinced that music takes him back sometimes,' said Connie, extracting his little finger. 'They say it does, don't they? It gets at something deep inside the brain apparently.'

It was a nice idea, but Victor seemed to live exclusively in one continuous *now*. A largely contented now, it had to be said. No hurt or trepidation lasted long. He'd ceased to be concerned about Tom's presence. And although he gave Connie a wounded look for cutting short the exploration of his nostril, he was soon entertained by other things. The glint

61

of Petula's necklace as she swayed with her new partner to 'Love Me or Leave Me', the pop of a wine cork, the little fox-eared dog yapping in the arms of the skeletal Indian lady across from them. His life was a series of passing spectacles.

'I think he does remember certain things about this place,' said Connie. 'It's hard to tell, poor lamb. But he's here and I'm here and we're happy, aren't we, Victor? King and queen of the Castle.'

As sprightly as she was, that smile of hers was a labour to maintain, thought Tom. Behind it was the tumult of every emotion *but* happiness.

'How long has he been . . .?' said Tom, unsure how to phrase what he was asking in the most appropriate way.

'The first signs were there about three years ago,' Connie said. 'Slow and steady, I'd call it.'

'I'm sorry.'

'It is what it is.'

'Do you have help?' asked Tom. 'Are any of your foster children still around?'

She answered before he'd finished speaking. 'No,' she said. 'We took them in and then let them go. That's how it was. We didn't see them again.'

'It must be difficult for you looking after him by yourself all the time,' Tom said, a little abstractedly as he watched a man he'd not seen before ambling across the room with glasses of champagne on a tray. But it wasn't Oliver. He'd never pictured him with a sorcerer's beard.

'Difficult?' Connie said and contemplated the word. 'I've never really thought of it like that. It's a privilege, if anything. No, the hardest thing is seeing him so reduced like this,' she continued, taking out another tissue to wipe Victor's amphibious chins. 'He used to have such passion for things. Everything, really. He was so driven. You don't get to be chair of town planning if you don't have something about you.'

'I should think not, no.'

'Which is why this seems like the wrong sort of ending for him,' she said. 'Unfair.'

'Of course.'

Everyone wanted to go out on a high in some way. Not dwindle into – what did Shakespeare call it? Second childhood?

'And that's why we started coming back to the Castle,' Connie said. 'That's why we're here, isn't it, Victor? To see if we can give you something better.'

'That's all the Paleys ever want for us. A happier life,' she said to Tom. 'They've always been good people. They left a legacy, you know. Mr Paley's mother and father. We don't pay a penny to stay here every year.'

'And the drinks are on the house, are they?'

'It doesn't quite extend that far,' she said. 'But everything else is covered. The rooms, the food, the prize.'

'That's good of them.'

'And so our little club goes on.'

'Well, I expect all this company must do Victor good,' said Tom.

Connie looked at his red badge. 'The company, yes,' she said, but hesitantly, as though that wasn't quite what she'd meant.

Victor had been studying his reflection in the polished surface of the table, spellbound by the way the face there matched his every expression, but now he suddenly frowned and groped at his crotch. Connie stood up straight away, calming his growing distress with a pat on his cheek.

'You need changing, love, I know, I know,' she said and kicked off the brake of his wheelchair with her heel. 'We'll be as quick as we can. No, you won't miss your dinner, you lummox. You're not going to starve. Excuse us, Tom.'

Away they went in the direction of the toilets, Connie talking close to Victor's ear and planting kisses on his scalp. Her surrogate baby.

She indulged him so much that Tom wondered if there might be a guilty enjoyment on her part that his decline had allowed her to carry on playing mother as she'd done for all those neglected kids she'd taken in. Thirty-something, had she said? A lot anyway. Angeline would think her a living saint for having given so much of her life to the care of the disadvantaged, and for the unstinting patience she had for Victor too.

On the far side of the room she made an expert turn with the wheelchair and backed through the doors without any interruption to her affections.

At least on occasion, thought Tom, he must have tried to picture him and Angeline as an old married couple. Indeed, imagining such a thing was a requisite of the vows, wasn't it? – *from this day forward . . . till death us do part.* A man and wife still together in the twilight years of colostomy bags and dementia could consider themselves true winners in love and life. In which case, he and Angeline had failed. That was to say that he had failed her.

He contemplated sending her a message, something simple, friendly, he could even offer a tentative apology for having overstepped the mark when they'd last spoken, but it'd be well into the evening where she was, the house full of family, as it always was on a Sunday from what she'd told him. Her three grown-up stepchildren would be there for supper along with the brood of seraphic little ones that he'd seen on the photographs she'd sent.

They all called her Mama or Yaya and she often referred to herself in the same way too, even though they weren't of her blood. Perhaps she was of the opinion (as he was) that motherhood involved more than just giving birth, but she'd never had the chance to know. He'd seen to that.

Her pregnancy had come as not only a shock but as an affront to that Tom of twenty-nine. She'd gone back on the very agreement that had underwritten their marriage. The fact that she'd entered into wedlock with him in the first place had been her acknowledgement – and guarantee – that they weren't going to have any children together. They'd as good as shaken on it. As far as he'd been concerned, the particular issue of *issue* had been settled to the satisfaction of both parties. He'd not coerced her into the embargo. He'd simply stipulated the terms of the contract and she'd accepted them.

Had he honestly thought of it all in that way? That their whole life as a couple might be governed by the clauses and limitations established at the very start of matrimony; that both of them would be content with what they'd set down then, however huge the concessions, and never want anything else.

He couldn't decide if it was arrogant or blinkered of him to have thought that Angeline wouldn't change or that she wouldn't ever want *him* to change. But how angry he'd been when she'd told him she was eight weeks gone. How childish of her, he'd thought at the time, to believe that surprising him with the news over breakfast one morning would induce him into a sudden change of heart about fatherhood. He'd become even more resolute if anything. Suspicious too.

That she'd been so happy about it all had suggested to him that there'd been a degree of planning on her part, and that it hadn't really been the accident she'd claimed it to be. Whichever it was, there'd been no question about what needed to happen next.

She'd had no strong religious views. That had helped. Or at least it had removed the dilemma of whether she was being sinful from the debate. And he'd built his case around what he thought would restore some of the level-headedness and pragmatism that seemed to have left her since she'd found out she was expecting.

He wouldn't be at home often enough for a baby. He'd be too busy. He wasn't going to apologise for being ambitious or for making the sacrifices it required. And it wasn't only him, he'd said. They both had careers that they cared about. And even if she were willing to put hers on hold, she'd soon feel it onerous to be heaped with all the responsibilities of care. It wouldn't be fair on the child either. He knew what it was like to grow up without a father around. He was well-acquainted with the many consequences of such an absence. Things she couldn't even imagine. He'd never want a son or daughter of his own to be so vulnerable.

Over a day or two, he'd eventually worn her down, threatening and blackmailing her in such a way that now disturbed him. And then she'd made the phone call.

That was only a precis of what had been a far more complicated and fractious situation. Angeline wouldn't have acquiesced as quickly as that. She'd have fought her corner. He could half remember the kind of arguments she'd put forward. They'd work things out. He'd be much happier than he thought he was going to be. He'd come to love the child. The child would love him. They'd created a life. It was in their hands.

Words to that effect.

And then he must have said something . . . And she must have tried again . . . But the specific content of those long conversations had become hazy since. Only the success of his shameful intimidation and its consequences remained, stark and unalterable, though not, he hoped, completely unassuageable.

Oliver had suggested they meet at five o'clock. It was now almost half past. However, Tom didn't think for a moment that he would have changed his mind. Not after being so exuberant at the prospect of them seeing one another in person.

'*The presence of a friend is as the sun to a rose – one grows!* Is that Whitman? Or Thoreau?'

There was a possibility that Mrs Paley had heard from him and, seeing her dip into the room to have a word with her husband, Tom got up and managed to catch her before she disappeared again.

'Sorry, I'm meant to be meeting someone,' he said, stopping her by the door.

'Yes?' she replied.

'Oliver Keele.'

'Yes?'

'I don't suppose he's telephoned, has he?'

She answered in a convoluted, cryptic way.

'If someone's not here who's supposed to be, then I'd put it down to the weather,' she said and started to move off.

'But he is due to arrive?' said Tom, halting her again. 'He's not cancelled his reservation or anything?'

'That's not something I'd be able to tell you,' she replied.

'Oh?'

'It's confidential.'

'Confidential?'

He'd forgotten that her paperwork was classified.

'We do have a duty of privacy to our guests, you know,' she said. 'You wouldn't want all and sundry knowing your arrangements, I'm sure.'

'I can't imagine what they'd do with the information,' said Tom.

'That's precisely my point,' Mrs Paley said. Then, after seeming to weigh up whether to say anything more, she added, 'We've had problems in the past,' and headed out into the lobby.

It was hard to think what could have happened to make her this guarded, but then from one day to the next it was probably so humdrum at the Castle that any little drama would seem catastrophic.

He turned back his sleeve to look at his watch again. If only there was some way of contacting Oliver to find out where he was, but he had no mobile. Couldn't get on with the things, apparently. And so the only recourse was to try the Traveller's Rest. At least they'd be able to say whether he'd set off.

Tom rang the number he'd stored on his phone and, with a finger in his ear to muffle the noise of the music in the bar, he listened and waited. No one answered and after leaving a message for someone to call him back he hung up.

'Still no Oliver then?' Connie said as she returned from the toilets with Victor. He was asleep again, his mouth hanging open like a torn sleeve.

'Not yet, no.'

'You could try asking if he's phoned,' she said and walked with Tom back to the table.

'I have,' he said.

'And?'

'Official secret, apparently.'

'The Paleys are just being cautious,' she said, manoeuvring her catatonic husband back into position. 'All of us come here on the quiet, don't we?'

She directed the question to Barnaby, who was retrieving a handkerchief from the jacket he'd left hanging on a chair, his face slick with perspiration.

'Aye, it's best if we're discreet,' he said, drying off the bags under his eyes.

Petula was sitting out the more energetic swing number now playing, and Tom noticed that her wig had come loose in the effort of dancing. A line of pale grey liquid ran down past her ear. It was the glue melting in the heat.

'My boys think I'm Christmas shopping in Liverpool,' she said, as she took out her compact mirror and turned her face to the side. 'It was the only excuse I could think of.'

She wiped her cheek and then looked at Tom closely as he sat down.

'I don't *like* lying to them, for Christ's sake,' she said, combative because of the drink. 'I'm not proud of it. But they'd cause such a fuss if they knew where I was. You know they came here last year? They actually drove to Saltwash to pick me up. It was so bloody embarrassing. I'm surprised I was allowed back.'

Was this one of the problems Mrs Paley had alluded to?

'Well, I certainly wasn't expecting you to be here today,' said Barnaby. 'I'd have barred you like Eric Calmine, if it had been up to me. You could have ruined it for all of us.'

'Oh, give it a rest. I didn't tell my boys anything,' said Petula.

'I don't see how you can be so sure when you're three sheets to the wind half the time.'

'Widows,' she said, and leant back in her chair to catch the eye of the waiter who'd been drafted in to collect the glasses. The same lad who'd gone outside with the broom earlier to clear the pavement and send Mr Calmine away.

'All I'm saying,' Barnaby went on, his voice quieter now, cowed by the rebuke, 'is that you shouldn't have let them find out where you were. What would have happened if they'd known what you'd come here *for?*'

'You make it sound like something terrible, Barnaby,' said Connie. 'It isn't, Tom,' she assured him. 'It really isn't. Quite the opposite.'

'It's just a dance and some dinner, isn't it?' Tom said, trying to understand what Barnaby was getting so worked up about.

Petula started on a reply, but Barnaby stopped her.

'Ah ah, he's wearing a badge, remember.'

'Yes, I do know,' she said, and finally managed to flag down the waiter, who was, unmistakably, the Paleys' son.

With a thin, severe physiognomy, he was the spit of his mother, and as morose as his father in the way he looked at everything and everyone so coldly. Though he seemed to have a special sort of loathing for Victor and not a little contempt for Connie too.

'Same again, Charlie, sweetheart,' said Petula, handing him her glass: a scene of devastation – orange slices half sucked, cherries half eaten, the decorative umbrella lying in the dregs.

'You'll have to go to the bar,' the lad said, picking up the rest of the empties. 'I've other jobs to do.'

'For me,' she said, caressing the small of his back as he leant across the table. 'And Tom will have another too, won't you, Tom? You're as dry as a witch's whatnot.'

'Just water,' he said. The Scotch had really gone to his head.

'Come on,' she badgered him. 'When was the last time a lady bought you a drink? Don't leave me on my own.'

Like many a binger he'd known, she tried to ease her conscience by conscripting a partner.

Monica, the first of his affairs, had been just the same, and back then he'd been more than willing to match her glass for glass. Two bottles of oblivion at her Kentish Town flat had clouded the implications of his faithlessness very nicely.

'Make Tom something special,' Petula said, patting Charlie's hip. 'It's his first time. Be kind.'

With a sigh, Charlie looked at him. 'What is it you want then? I'll pass it on.'

But Tom felt his phone ringing in his pocket and as he brought it out, he recognised the number as that of the Traveller's Rest.

'Sorry, it might be Oliver,' he said, and walked away to the marginally quieter end of the bar, where he stood more chance of holding a conversation without having to shout.

In a way, he hoped that it *wasn't* Oliver. If he were still in Scarborough, he'd never get all the way to Saltwash tonight. But when Tom answered, there was a woman at the other end.

'You left a message,' she said. 'Did you want to reserve a room?'

73

'I was hoping to speak to Mr Keele,' said Tom. 'Oliver Keele.'

After a moment of silence, the woman said, 'Yes, well, he's not here, I'm afraid.'

'He's gone out for the day, has he?'

'He's gone for good,' the woman replied. 'He checked out a week ago.'

'A week ago?'

'At least.'

'He didn't happen to leave a forwarding address, did he?' said Tom.

'No.'

'Did he mention my name at all? Tom Shift?'

'Should he have done?'

'We're supposed to be meeting one another, that's all.'

'I can't help you, sorry,' she said, with an air of *not my problem*.

'Look, are you absolutely sure he's not coming back?' he said and the woman, quite rightly, gave his stupid question a terse reply.

'Yes,' she said. 'I'm sure.'

With nothing more to talk about, Tom ended the call and tried to think through Oliver's most recent letters, wondering if he'd mentioned moving. But nothing came to mind and although it was conceivable that he'd simply forgotten that particular detail he had a stronger feeling that there was something wrong. Oliver had been so polite and thoughtful in his correspondence that if he'd known he wasn't going to be able to keep his appointment here he'd have rung to say so from wherever he'd wound up. He had Tom's number, and even if he'd somehow mislaid it (which seemed unlikely) then he'd have contacted the Castle and asked for him.

It could be that Oliver simply wasn't well. More soberingly still, there was a chance that the time his doctors had suggested might be left to him had turned out to be too optimistic. But surely the woman at the Traveller's Rest would have said if he'd passed away there. Unless, like Mrs Paley, she couldn't possibly reveal such a thing. Though 'checked out' and 'gone for good' were fairly crass euphemisms.

No, it wasn't anything like that. The fact that she'd been so abrupt suggested that Oliver had left under a cloud for some reason.

Only a few explanations for this presented themselves: theft, some indiscretion or an inability to pay.

The first he ruled out straight away; that wasn't Oliver. The second, he didn't want to think about too closely, as an indiscretion that saw someone expelled from a hotel room would have to be pretty lurid. And he struggled to ascribe such behaviour to a man who swooned over Keats.

Yes yes, still waters and all that. But he was using intuition, thought Tom, and that was a sharper tool than conjecture.

And so the most likely thing was that Oliver had simply found himself strapped for cash. A cheque had bounced or he'd come up short or something part way through his stay at the Traveller's Rest and they'd sent him packing.

Maybe, once he'd gone, they'd circulated his name to other establishments across the north. Perhaps his disrepute had reached as far as the Castle and that was why Mrs Paley was reluctant to talk about him. And it would explain, too, why he hadn't been in touch, and why he might not be coming to Saltwash at all. He was embarrassed. He couldn't bring himself to take advantage of a free night's stay here.

If all that were true, then he was never going to agree to a handout, even though that was precisely what he needed.

Then what if he were to call it a loan? thought Tom. Would that make it any more palatable? Or what if he were to set up an account in Oliver's name and make regular deposits? That way there'd be something available if and when he needed it, and he could decide for himself how much he wanted to withdraw at any given time. That might not feel as overwhelming as being handed a lump sum.

Well, it was all academic unless Oliver showed his face.

If he did arrive, they'd need to find somewhere quieter to talk than this awful chicken coop.

The criss-crossing chatter and raucous laughter rose higher, and higher still, competing with the music. Someone shrieked as if they were being murdered. Somewhere a bottle smashed to an ironic cheer.

Over at the table, one of the Paley sisters was delivering cocktails and, after thanking her, Petula stood up and scouted for Tom.

But she couldn't see him, and, before she did, he sidled between those waiting by the bar and went out into the lobby, hoping to find a place to sit and fend off the spasms of discomfort starting to course through his head. As usual, the assault had come upon him in an instant and with searing pain. It felt as though his cranial nerves had been wired up to an electrical supply. If the vibrating sensation had been audible, it would have had the thrum of a power line.

It was the sheer noise of so many voices, maybe. And drinking on an empty stomach hadn't helped either. He never got stuck into the hard stuff as early as this. Half-pissed before dinner. What had he been thinking?

He tried the handle of the lounge, but it was locked and he loitered by the reception desk to see if he might ask Mrs Paley if there was somewhere he could go. But when it didn't look as though she was going to appear he went on beyond the foot of the stairs and along the hallway past the ends of two short corridors that led, respectively, to the laundry room and the busy kitchen with its porthole window.

It was less cluttered in this part of the hotel; the only decoration being some paintings of fox hunters and hounds and two garish urns of feathery pampas grass either side of a door marked PRIVATE. Thankfully, there was a chair that he could use and, after testing it to make sure that the antique legs would bear his weight, he sat down and took his tablets.

Over the months, he'd learnt – and learnt rather quickly – that if he caught a headache early enough he'd have a better chance of dampening down the effects. Though sometimes it made no difference.

At Living Now, physical discomfort was a popular topic of discussion among the attendees, and as a way of reducing their suffering Astrid had suggested that they thought not in terms of 'pain' but 'sensations'. After all, what was 'pain', really? she'd asked them. Only a word. And if it was only a word, did it actually exist?

But philosophy wasn't a particularly effective analgesic. Nor did it alleviate the more worrisome thought that a headache, once started, might not go away at all. Presumably it would happen at some stage. And then he'd know that he was entering the final phase of his life.

As he'd thought about this lately, as the passing of the weeks and months had made it all the more impendent, every little pang had put him on the alert. Occasionally they subsided on their own, and at other times they developed into a full-blown grand mal that lasted for hours. The vice-like pressure inside his skull could be so severe that when it eventually petered out, relief would sweep through him with enough intensity to make him cry. He'd never felt so fragile.

It was truly a wonder that a human body lasted long at all. Heart, brain, lungs, liver, spleen, bladder, pancreas, kidneys, stomach, bowels, arteries, glands, nerves and every other component of one's biological machinery down to microbes and mitochondria had to function perfectly at all times and in an infinitely complex synchronicity. It was so easy for something to fail or break. In his case, all it had taken was for one cell out of a hundred billion to mutate and everything had fallen apart.

No one warned you of that when you were young, did they? It never crossed your mind that your body would one day let you down. But it had, and in some ways that particular betrayal was the most difficult thing to take.

Long before he'd tumbled off the stepladder in the garden, a struggle had begun in his inferior temporal gyrus – *just here above the cerebellum, Mr Shift* – one which had already ended in victory for the tumour by the time they'd showed him the MRI.

Why hadn't his body fought harder on his behalf? Why had it surrendered so meekly?

It didn't seem as if his body knew that *he* was there at all. It had suffered defeat, accepted the losses and resigned itself to the terms of occupation without consulting him once. 'Tom Shift' didn't come into it.

*

79

But who *is* 'Tom Shift'? Astrid had asked him at Living Now. 'He's not real. He's never been real. Can you see that?'

On Wednesday nights between seven and nine, that kind of talk made sense. When he sat in meditation with everyone else, it became very apparent that the self was made up entirely of thoughts. Thoughts that came and went randomly and involuntarily and repetitively. All the old regrets and all the predictions of future calamities resurfaced again and again.

Yet, according to Astrid, they were so much more than these gossiping internal voices. They were so much more than these malfunctioning bodies. They were manifestations of the life force that pervaded the universe and washed endlessly in and out of physical forms, like a tide. No one was ever really born, and no one ever really died. The atoms that had come together to make a human being would simply split apart in time and ebb away to contribute to the existence of something else: a star or a cherry tree or a cancer cell. It was all just a beautiful dance of one vast never-ending energy.

She made no claim to have obtained these insights on her own. She was, so she said, only reiterating what the Zen poets had known for centuries. At the end of a meeting, she liked to read aloud the last haikus of Bashō and Buson, Isshō and Takao, and point out the metaphors they'd used for the unavoidable and unremarkable certainty of transience. Rose petals, autumn leaves, spring blossom. Things which were beautiful *because* they didn't last. Nothing *could* have longevity. Things appeared and then they disappeared. That was the way it was. There was nothing personal about it. No one was being punished. Where had the idea come from that dying was a problem? she'd asked.

But away from the clinic, when he was awake in the small hours, alone and staring into the dark, her attempts at reassurance seemed like nothing more than wordplay and he couldn't help but think about how it would feel to be in his last moments, when he was trying to hold on to his life and the memories of all the things that had, in their own way, been transcendental and glorious, the closest an unbeliever would come to knowing the divine:

Angeline's youthful body in his arms.

His first taste of a grand cru from Pauillac.

A sunrise over the mountains of Corsica.

The night sky of Iceland roofed with stars.

Watching Miles Davis in Greenwich Village.

Losing himself in the deep reds of Rothko's Seagram murals at the Tate.

Standing, more recently, before Cézanne's final paintings of the Mont Sainte-Victoire – the vistas almost ethereal, like hazy recollections of the past rather than landscapes painted in situ *en plein air*. He'd felt the aging artist's struggle to resurrect a lost summer so acutely that it matched an ache of his own for time that had vanished, time he'd wasted.

And smaller things had stirred him too, momentary things. The October light moving across the moors above Malhamdale. A thrush singing at dusk. Even the blossoming of that damn cherry tree.

He didn't think he'd be able to bear the feeling of all those hallowed visions sliding out of his mind for good and going . . . going . . .

Maybe at that point, being as oblivious as Victor might not be so bad after all. Dying might come along as just another event, no more significant than breakfast.

Or to be like his first pen pal, the jubilant, rhapsodic Elaine, who'd been so certain that when she departed this life, she'd be clothed in white and carried by the angels to the sunlit uplands of the Great Beyond.

But in his heart of hearts, he didn't think that he'd be conscious of anything in the aftermath, not reward or judgement, not even the quietude of eternal rest. The peace that passeth all understanding would passeth him by. Yet, he wouldn't be aware of missing out. He wouldn't be sensible of being nothing nowhere.

In which case, what was there to agonise about?

Perhaps it wasn't the state of being dead in itself that was the issue but the wrongness of it being so imminent. His life was all but done? That was *it*? Come on.

Of course, having had his three score and ten and a little more besides, no one else would think it unreasonable if he were to shuffle off at seventy-five. But, unsurprisingly, he begged to differ. He had things to do. Good works to try and perform. He needed time to become that rare thing, a better person.

Still, as he'd said to Oliver, there was a part of him that half-wished the tumour had killed him instantly in the garden. Then he'd never have been put through all this awful waiting, this constant anticipation. Being conscious of what was coming was the worst thing of all. Not least because, paradoxically, the more he edged towards it, the more some preposterous and obstinate Mr Micawber part of his brain kept on insisting that something would turn up.

Real, unreal; accepted, denied; the estimations of death went round and round.

When he couldn't sleep, he'd sometimes open his laptop and search for articles online about faith healing and medical miracles.

There'd been a woman in Oregon who'd shrunk a tumour the size of an egg with daily doses of cod liver oil and warm lemon juice. A man in Basingstoke who'd slept inside a home-made wooden pyramid to channel the healing energies of Ra. Within a month, he'd been cured, his lymphoma dissolved.

Yet none of these fantasies of reprieve were as appealing as the one in which Tom was allowed to transfer his fate to someone else. Something that, in certain moments, he'd do in a heartbeat. On the worst nights, he'd have gladly given his death to anyone, even to Angeline, if it meant that it would leave him alone for a while longer.

Was that cold? Was it cowardice? he'd asked Oliver.

'Ah, Tom,' he'd replied. 'We all quake and quiver when the bell starts to toll.'

~

Away from the noise of the other guests and with the pills doing their work, the hard tremoring in his brain had eased off a touch, but was by no means over. He ought to stay put and rest for a while, but sitting still for too long tended to make his shoulder seize up and his elbow stiffen.

Someone came out of the bar further back up the lobby, a man with grey, professorial hair. Thankfully, he sauntered into the Gents without noticing that Tom was there.

As much as he'd once enjoyed travelling, by the end of his career he'd started to feel as jaded about hotels as he had been about airports. Surrounded by so many strangers. Compelled to have conversations with them. Or forced to listen to their intimacies all night.

In his younger days, in the seventies, assigned by the *Sunday Telegraph* or *Traveller* magazine to seek out the best that Zurich or Trieste or Seville had to offer the English sightseer, he'd regularly stayed up until the witching hour drinking with someone he'd met in the bar. But as he'd got older, he'd discovered that those he'd once found fascinating and unique were just types the world over.

The cynical businessman pissing away his expense account. Randy newlyweds. The coquettish middle-aged divorcee with a lapdog. Brash, moneyed couples who'd been everywhere and seen everything and didn't think much of any of it.

The threat of being cornered by any of them had made him a reclusive breed of visitor by the end. He'd become adept at tracking down the bistro or the trattoria or the marisquería that tourists avoided because it looked too local, and there he'd eat in peace without the risk of bumping into someone staying at the same place as him.

His privacy seemed to be over already here in the Castle, as the Paleys' son, Charlie, appeared from the laundry room with an armful of folded linen and stopped at the private door.

'You'll be in trouble, hiding away down here,' he said, glancing at Tom. 'Is that what you're doing? Hiding?'

'Something like that.'

'Well, you'd better not let the Duchess find you,' Charlie said, slotting a key into the lock. 'She likes to know where everyone is.'

Tom wasn't sure if he was being serious, but thinking that the lad might be slightly less intractable than his mother, he said, 'Here, I don't suppose anyone's called for me, have they? Mr Shift?'

'I don't know,' he said. 'I'm not allowed to answer the phone. Who is it you're waiting for?'

'Oliver Keele.'

'Oh, yeah,' said Charlie, 'him.'

'I gather he's a regular.'

'A regular what?'

'A regular guest.'

'There's nothing regular about our guests,' Charlie said and opened the door and went inside to deposit what he'd brought. 'Is he an old friend?' he called.

'Not really, no,' said Tom.

Charlie came out and locked up. 'That's a pity,' he said. 'I thought I might be able to crack you open for some information.'

'About what?'

'Why he comes here every year. No one seems to know.'

'Because it's free?'

'No, I mean why does he feel the need to come at all?'

Tom gestured at his red badge. 'I think you're asking the wrong person.'

'He's a hard one to work out, isn't he?' Charlie said. 'He doesn't give much away.'

Tom had to agree.

'I say that,' Charlie continued, 'but I've seen him lingering.'

'Lingering?'

'In the graveyard near the station.'

'Why would he be there?'

'It's notorious, isn't it?' said Charlie.

'For what?'

'Boys.'

'Right.'

'He is that way inclined, though, isn't he?' Charlie said. 'That is his vice? Boys. That's what he's ashamed of?'

'I wouldn't know.'

'Well, everyone here's done something they regret. That's why you all come. To get rid of the guilt.'

'You've lost me.'

Charlie narrowed his eyes. 'Don't you know why you're here?' he said. 'Hasn't your friend told you *anything*? That's priceless.'

'Get rid of the guilt how?' said Tom.

'It's like in the old days when they'd wash themselves in the river,' Charlie said.

'They don't still do that, do they?'

To go out and coat themselves in freezing mud at low tide tomorrow morning would finish most of these guests off.

'Course not,' said Charlie. 'Have you smelt it out there?'

'So what do they do now?'

Finding a pleasure in Tom's ignorance, Charlie folded his arms and leant against the wall.

'What's your story then?' he said, and when Tom held back, he grinned with his small yellowish teeth. 'It's all right, I get it,' he said. 'It's like prison, isn't it?'

'Sorry?'

'No one wants to say what they're in for,' Charlie replied.

'Not to worry. I'll just have to find out for myself about you. It's only a matter of waiting. You lot are so deaf and blind that you don't even know I'm here half the time. And once you've had a drink you can't stop talking. I've heard all sorts, believe me.

'Take that Petula you've been sitting with,' he said. 'You'd think she of all people would lay off the booze. And Victor Mayberry? He'd turn your stomach.'

Further up the lobby the front doorbell shrilled.

'I know, I know,' said Charlie. 'They seem harmless enough on the outside. So do you.'

He went off to see to whoever was now banging to be let in.

Tom got up and followed him, thinking that it might be Oliver at last, but it was the undesirable Mr Calmine, who'd been unable to get any further than the porch and peered into the hallway through the glass doors.

Before Charlie got there, Mrs Paley came out of the bar to deal with the disturbance. Seeing her approach, Mr Calmine made himself look presentable by taking off his hat and smoothing a few strings of hair across his head. At close quarters, he was a haggard, etiolated man.

'I didn't want to make a fuss,' he said. 'But the door's locked. I wasn't sure if anyone would hear me.'

'It's locked for a reason,' Mrs Paley said.

'I wonder if I might come in for a moment, though,' said Mr Calmine.

He tried the door again. Mrs Paley put her hands behind her back and watched. Charlie perched on the edge of a sideboard, as if this was all very familiar and they were merely waiting for him to go through the routine.

'I think if we could just talk,' Mr Calmine said. 'Then we'd be able to clear things up.'

'Mr Calmine, I'm not going over all that again,' said Mrs Paley. 'It's a busy evening. I think it's best if you get on your way now. Our decision hasn't changed.'

'Can't we just agree to disagree?' he said. 'Can't we start again? I'll take a room for the night. I can pay. I'm happy to pay. You don't have to give it to me for nothing.'

After wedging his walking cane under his arm, he brought out handfuls of coins from the pockets of his suit. The poor bastard must have been picking up all the pennies he'd found on the promenade.

'I think there's enough here,' he said. 'I can count it. Let me count it.'

'Mr Calmine,' said Mrs Paley. 'Mr Calmine, we're fully booked. And it doesn't matter how much money you have, we can't allow you in.'

Seeing Tom there, he palmed at the windowpane.

'Get them to open up,' he said. 'Be a friend. Tell them that I'm trying to compromise. I could be difficult if I chose to be. I've every right to make demands. I did win after all.' He struck the glass with his stick now. 'I should have what's owed to me.'

Mrs Paley motioned for Charlie to resolve matters, and he went to unlock the door with such a pugnacious intent that it caused Mr Calmine to retreat and knock over one of the buckets the guests had used for their wet umbrellas. He'd hardly set it upright again before Charlie had him by the collar and was muscling him outside to the steps.

Mrs Paley watched them go and then turned to Tom.

'Did you need something?' she asked.

'Just passing,' he said.

'Well, if I could ask you to take your seat again,' she said, ushering him across the lobby. 'We'll be showing the film soon.'

The sound of raised voices came from the street and Mrs Paley noted Tom's unease at the heavy-handedness with which Mr Calmine had been ejected.

'We can't have him in the hotel,' she said. 'It wouldn't be fair on the other guests. It's a difficult enough night for many of them as it is.'

She opened the door to the bar and held it until Tom had gone inside.

Spotting him, Petula wended her way over, really quite unsteady on her feet now after another of those bright yellow horrors she'd been drinking.

'There you are,' she said. 'Everything all right? You look pale.'

She held his face and inspected his eyes.

'It was only a headache,' he said. 'It's going off now.'

That wasn't strictly true. His brain still pulsated, as in the aftershocks of an earthquake, the tumour at the epicentre.

'Your Mr Calmine was at the door,' he said, to set her on to something else instead.

'Was he? The silly sod.'

'He seemed very upset.'

'He always is.'

'What did he do?' said Tom.

'Do?'

'To get on the wrong side of the Paleys.'

With acrid breath in his ear, Petula said, 'He cheated in the draw, didn't he?'

'Is that all?' said Tom.

'What do you mean, is that all?' she said. 'There are rules, you know.'

'It's worth winning then, the prize?' Tom said. 'What is it? Money or something?'

'No, Tom,' she laughed. 'That's not it.'

'What then?'

'Ask me no questions . . .'

'I just don't understand why Barnaby was so bothered about your sons being here last year?' said Tom. 'What didn't he want them to see?'

91

'He's just an old woman. A stickler,' she said. 'Are you sure you're all right?'

'No, not really,' he conceded.

'Well, come and have your medicine then. I can ask for some fresh ice if you want.'

She took him by the hand, for balance mostly.

'I think it's likely to kill me not cure me,' said Tom.

'Oh, risk it,' she goaded him. 'What does it matter? Live a little, for God's sake. You won't have the chance when you're six feet under, will you?'

Her case for practising hedonism on that basis chimed with those at Living Now who talked about 'owning their death' – a phrase that had made Tom squirm a little for its rather desperate pretensions to dominion over something that had them all very firmly in its grip.

In that vocal faction, a consensus had arisen that what-ever time they had left ought to be spent in the pursuit of pleasure, even excess. A few had got stoned; one lady had been to a swingers' party. For people to say 'she lived to the full' or 'he made the most of every moment' was the only obituary they wanted. Perhaps it was the same for Petula. Perhaps it was the way many others here saw things too, since their conversations came around to the dead so frequently.

Again and again, as he passed between those dancing, he caught the name of the man whose funeral they'd all attended the year before: Spike, Spike Butler, good old Spike.

Then did they gather here in remembrance of their friends? Was that the purpose of all this, each November time? If it was memento mori then it was memento vitae too, hence the over-indulgence. It was make hay while the sun shines, take no thought of the morrow.

Yet, when so many had been necking down the booze like teenagers in a park, why was it that, in Charlie's opinion, Petula ought to be the one to exercise some temperance?

And what did he think Victor had done, exactly? The man spent half his time asleep by the look of it.

But when Tom sat down, Victor was awake again and enjoying another biscuit, with Connie poised to wipe up the mess.

'No Oliver yet?' she said.

'Still on his way,' Tom replied.

'Well, he's never missed it before. He'll come.'

'To tell you the truth,' said Tom. 'I'm not sure where he's coming *from*. He's not where I thought he was.'

'That's just how he is,' Petula said. 'He gets around.'

'But he always turns up,' said Connie. 'He'll be here. Don't worry, Victor.'

She stroked his arm, but he didn't need any reassurance. He wasn't taking any notice of what anyone was saying since he was far more absorbed in the preparations for the film.

While Mr and Mrs Paley moved an antique projector into position, their two daughters erected a screen on a metal stand. And then, having sent Mr Calmine on his way, Charlie came in to turn off the wall lamps and the music. Such was the mood of expectation around the room that even the square of blank flickering light was met with applause.

~

The film turned out to be a silent mishmash of newsreels and amateur footage showing Saltwash in its prime some fifty or sixty years ago.

Here was the wide, bustling promenade. The Pleasure Gardens with their fountains and roses. The circus. The zoo. And then a view from a plane as it crossed the estuary.

Looking down, the peninsula assumed the approximate shape of a horse's head. Its crown was made up of briny meadows, its shaggy mane of drainage channels. Its eye socket was formed by a marshy bay of reedbeds, and Saltwash itself lay huddled under the chin.

From this height, there was barely a patch of sand to be seen between the bodies on the beach by the pier. And sure enough, when the picture changed to a close-up of the holidaymakers, a cheery multitude sat cheek by jowl on deckchairs and picnic rugs. The girls in floral dresses; the fathers in tanktops and rolled-up trousers and hankies for sunhats; the older women baring puffy legs that hadn't seen the light of day since the summer before.

As they all started to wave at the camera, the scene cut sharply to the lido. A huge, white, Art Deco amphitheatre in those days. Bright and boldly modern. The big blocks of concrete making big blocks of shadow.

Pale, smooth-skinned girls in swimsuits and bathing caps scurried into the frame and made for the steps to the diving platform where the young and athletic lined up to pike and somersault like the beautiful specimens in a Lev Borodulin photograph.

Then came the Imperial Ballroom with its fake baroque balconies and its hanging candelabras glowing through the cigarette smoke. There were potted palms. An orchestra half hidden in the shadows. A contingent of waitresses in mob caps and pinafores hurrying to and fro around the edges of the dance floor where silhouetted couples spun like sufis.

Then there was the Gaiety theatre and its billboards for Vera Lynn and the Black and White Minstrels and Jimmy Clitheroe, and acts that had been long since forgotten. The Dallas Boys and the Lotus-Flower Lovelies.

Now, the scene changed again, this time to a slow, panoramic shot of the sludgy reaches of the estuary and the large crowds assembled there to go mud bathing. They had come on what looked to have been a gusty, overcast day, but no one was daunted and, after smearing themselves from forehead to feet, each person set off towards the river.

Most squatted in the shallows to sluice off the muck, scrubbing themselves vigorously. Others breast-stroked into the deeper channels and bobbed glassy-headed like seals. The elderly and disabled were helped to stretch out and float on their backs. It could have been the Jordan or the Ganges.

Behind them, much further out, a streamlined wooden motorboat puttered by, sending the gulls sitting on the water into the sky. The next piece of film had been taken by someone on board trying their best to steady the camera as they undulated towards the sandy shoreline on the far side of the estuary. Once there, the boat moored at a jetty close to the lighthouse and a dozen or so passengers disembarked with a band of nurses or supervisors to help them take the waters. Here was an exclusive class of vacationers who'd enjoyed their ablutions well away from the rabble.

Even though it had to be nigh on impossible to identify anyone caked in so much mud, there were those in the room who claimed to recognise someone they'd once known.

It was the same when the film rolled on to show those riding the ghost train, or the children tumbling out of the helter-skelter, or the audience of a Punch and Judy show on the promenade. There was such-and-such. And how young they were. How happy.

As the picture switched to that of a skinny boy sitting on a bench, there was a great flood of applause, and some people rapped their glasses on the tabletops. Here was Spike Butler, who'd died a year ago. Spike in better times, dressed in a cowboy outfit and eating an ice cream the size of a conch shell.

Now Tom knew that he'd been right to think of this evening as one of commemoration. The film wasn't simply a diversion before dinner but a tribute.

The images of others who'd departed were greeted with fondness; their names spoken and shared. Some deaths seemed to elicit profound sorrow, while others were celebrated with an ovation, as Spike's had been. Why there should be a difference, Tom couldn't say. The discrepancy was lost on him.

Among the faces of the beatified dead were those of the living as they'd once been. Given all the affectionate catcalls and laughter that broke out table after table, it seemed that quite a number of the guests here in the bar had come to Saltwash in their younger years.

There was Petula jiving in a night club: blonde pudding-bowl haircut, Mary Quant dress. There was Mr Calmine, the double of Buddy Holly, with a dainty doe-eyed lass on his arm. And after him came Barnaby sitting astride a donkey as a beaming toddler of cherubic podge and curls.

But it was the activity in the background of the film that caught Tom's interest, though he didn't know why he should be quite so fascinated by the girl digging a hole, or that boy hitting a cricket ball for six, or the shadows of clouds passing over the water and the boats. It was all so unexceptional.

As the film continued, Connie appeared to know what was coming next and she tried to re-engage Victor, who'd become riveted by the patterns he could make with his fingers in the pools of spilled drink on the table.

'Are you ready?' she said and tapped his hand. 'Keep watching or you'll miss it. This way. Look.'

She angled his face to the screen as the next clip showed a young couple racing along in a dinghy, competitors in a regatta.

'It's us,' said Connie, shaking Victor's arm. 'That's you, Mr Bear.'

He gazed at the chiselled, bearded man at the tiller with no concept of who he was. Nor did he seem to twig that the woman perched on the gunwale was Connie.

She'd been immensely photogenic. A look of Amelia Earhart coupled with a fetching games-mistress physique; her bare legs taut and her forearms brawny as she leant back in the spray, rope in hand, contending expertly with a full and straining sail.

'We won,' she said. 'Don't you remember, Victor? They gave us a cup.'

But he was more interested in the chest hair he'd discovered spoking between his buttons.

'Don't you want to watch, love? It's our honeymoon,' said Connie. 'Don't you want to see how we used to be?'

He didn't. It meant nothing to him. And off they went in that other lifetime skimming down the estuary on a windy summer's day and were soon lost among the other boats. Boats which were now probably rotting on the riverbank.

'That was us. You missed it,' Connie said. She gave Victor a shake and then laid her head on his shoulder. 'That's it, we're gone.'

They were replaced by a horde of people swarming along the pier – the shooting gallery and dodgems and Ferris wheel captured in the grainy technicolour of the sixties.

A boy with a spinning paper windmill passed in front of the camera with his father. Then two teenage girls in sleeveless blouses and pedal pushers crossed the other way, becoming bashful when they clocked that they were being filmed.

The real focus, however, was on the family of five who stood looking over the railings at the water. At a silent directive, they all turned and shaded their eyes from the sun.

'He's so bloody lucky, isn't he?' Petula said in Tom's ear. 'He's barely changed at all.'

'Sorry?' said Tom.

'Don't you recognise him?'

99

'Who?'

She pointed at the middle figure in the group.

'That's Oliver,' she said.

He was slender and fair-haired and had to be about eighteen; almost prim in his white shirt and cravat; every inch the public-school boy about to go up to Oxford. And yet so utterly unsure of himself. He looked away at something else, anything else.

Presumably that was his brother and sister next to him, hand in hand. The little boy preoccupied with devouring a Catherine wheel of a lollipop that he alternately studied and licked. The girl, sour and hostile-looking. A sullen adolescent in a shapeless sack of a dress printed with large orange chrysanthemums, her mass of gingery hair tied back with an Alice band.

Oliver's father, a wiry bantamweight in a chequered shirt and black braces, brought a handkerchief to his mouth to stem what looked to be a painful, convulsive cough, and then stared down the lens with rather expressionless eyes before fetching up another chestful of phlegm.

The only one happy to play along with the entreaties of the seafront film-maker was Oliver's auburn-haired mother, who was much taller, and younger, than her husband. A strikingly beautiful woman, Tom saw, when, seemingly on request, she tipped back the wide straw hat she was wearing and smiled. Those teeth.

Here were the Keeles then.

For whatever reason, Oliver hadn't mentioned any of them once.

~

Soon after, the film came to an end. The lights were switched back on, the bar reopened and the room filled with conversations that, to Tom, didn't sound entirely joyful. A difficult night, as Mrs Paley had said.

Nostalgia, so pleasurable as a temporary refuge, was often tainted by the very fact that its contents *were* so completely irrecoverable. Reminiscences came with a kind of envy for those past selves who appeared to have revelled in true happiness. That was to say that everyone wanted to believe that life had been flawless in that way once. Even Tom had a feeling, as vague as it was, that he'd been contented in his early childhood when his father had still been at home. Though he couldn't know, and it might have just been wishful thinking.

For Barnaby, the recollections had only reconfirmed how the country had changed for the worse. 'When I think of the roses they used to grow in the Pleasure Gardens, my goodness. All the Sherard's and Sweet Briars . . . It could have been magnificent, England . . .' And on he went.

At other tables, people were in tears for reasons that they kept to themselves. The lady with the dog. The man who looked like Gladstone.

Conscious of the slump, Mrs Paley put the music back on and talk turned to dinner.

Victor rubbed his belly, and Connie gave him the last pieces of biscuit to keep him going. Barnaby expounded on the Castle's reputation for good English food to no one in particular. And Petula tried to wave Charlie over to order another drink before it was time to eat. Her glass was almost empty again.

'Come on, Tom,' she said. 'You're lagging behind. Some accomplice you are.'

He'd not touched the Old Fashioned she'd bought him and had no intention to when his head felt so tender.

Perhaps he ought not to stay for dinner at all, but catch an earlier train. There was nothing to say he *couldn't*. It didn't look as though Oliver was coming, and he didn't owe anything to Petula or Connie and certainly not to Barnaby. He'd answered their questions, shown some interest in them, but he'd not come here to give his time to people, alive or dead, whom he didn't know, or to be part of this – whatever it was; this requiem; this game of hush-hush he'd been made to play since he'd put on the red badge. None of it was anything to do with him. Why had Oliver ever thought that it would be something he'd enjoy?

Surrounded by so many strangers, he wanted more than anything to speak to Angeline. He could give that as a reason to leave. He could say that he'd promised to make a phone call and escape that way.

Or would it be better to lean on his concerns about the weather affecting his journey home? No one would blame him for erring on the side of caution on a night like this and making tracks sooner rather than later. And there'd be nothing dishonest about saying that he didn't really feel up to staying any longer anyway. There was something about being here that clearly didn't agree with him. The drink or the noise. The latter, probably.

Loud conversation began to rise again into the high space of the bar room, rowdy and grating, like the bedlam of a school dining hall.

From somewhere behind him came a volley of excited cries and cheers, and that being a good enough reason to make his excuses he leant over to Petula to say goodbye, but she looked past him and nodded.

'There, Tom,' she said. 'Ye of little faith. We told you he'd come.'

PART TWO

There he was, Oliver Keele. The voice of all those letters made flesh. A tall man in a greatcoat and trilby that were both so rain-soaked that he looked to have been blown along the promenade like a rag. He hadn't *walked* all the way from the station, had he? In his condition?

'I'm not sure he can see me,' Tom said, and made his way over. But the three ladies from the next table beat him to it and he was forced to linger behind them as they all spoke to Oliver at once.

It had been generous of Petula to say that he hadn't changed when he'd completely lost the looks he'd had on the film. At the age he'd been then, his wistful eyes and his cheekbones had given him an almost feminine prettiness – he'd been very much his mother's son – but now his face was hollow. Cancer easily made skeletons of people. There were plenty at Living Now who looked like him. Plenty here in the Castle who were emaciated too.

The stick-thin lady with the little dog proffered the wriggling creature at Oliver, who held it close and let it lick his chin. And as the three women continued in their kind-hearted cross-examination of his wellbeing, he replied with the utmost gratitude for their concern, but kept on glancing past them.

When he finally saw Tom standing there, he handed back the dog, touched its owner gently on the arm and, with impeccable politeness, requested that she and her friends part a little.

'I owe this man a thousand apologies,' he said, beckoning Tom forward. 'More. A thousand thousand.'

He took off the woollen gloves he was wearing and to Tom's surprise he saw that both Oliver's hands were covered in tattoos.

'Forgive me, old boy,' he said. 'You must have thought I wasn't coming.'

'It was the weather, wasn't it?' said Tom. 'That's not your fault.'

Still holding Tom's hand, Oliver turned to the three ladies.

'You see,' he said. 'I *knew* he'd be gracious. I can always tell the tenor of a man's heart from the way he writes.'

It pleased Tom too that Oliver was exactly the same in person as he'd been in his letters. His voice was just as he'd imagined it. Almost John Betjeman.

'It's good to finally meet you,' said Tom.

'Likewise, likewise,' Oliver said. 'I've been counting the days. I really have.'

The three women found this adorable.

'Sorry, Tom,' said Oliver. 'This is Anoushka, Ginny and May. Old friends.'

They nodded and Tom nodded back.

'I was talking just now about connections,' said Oliver. 'I think that if we can say we have one true friend in the world then we've won, haven't we?'

'Hear, hear,' one of the ladies said.

'Absolutely,' chimed another.

The woman with the dog, Anoushka, wedged the yapping thing under her arm so that she could fish out some money from her handbag and thrust a five-pound note at Mr Paley when he came over with a glass of something dark and neat.

'For Oliver's drink,' she said, to which Oliver protested, but not too strongly.

'Please, there's really no need,' he said. 'No need at all.'

'There's every need,' said Anoushka. 'Look at you.'

'She's right,' said her friend. Ginny, was it? 'You're freezing, Oliver, love.'

The third rubbed his arm. 'A block of ice.'

'Bless you all,' he said and bowed as he pinched the brim of his hat. 'I have never known such kindness as the kindness that receives me here.'

He watched the women as they went back to their table with the dog yelping for his attention. Even animals loved him.

'I kept a terrier for a while,' he said, swilling whatever it was he was drinking. 'I couldn't tell you the breed. I'm not certain it really had one. He was a bit rough around the edges, but a good companion all the same. I had to sell him in the end, though, unfortunately. That was in Bournemouth, I think. Or was it Brighton? One or the other. Lord, look at me,' he said, when he caught himself in the mirror behind the bar. 'You'd be forgiven for thinking I wasn't stopping. Would you mind, old man?'

He took off his shapeless hat and handed it to Tom. The rain had leaked through the holes and got to his hair, which had the colour and nap of catkin. It was evidently still struggling to grow back since the last – and unsuccessful – round of chemotherapy he'd been through just before they'd started writing to one another. But the specific part of his body afflicted by cancer was still impossible to determine, even though he was here in person. Why he'd been so secretive about it was still a puzzle too. Tom couldn't figure out if it was just because Oliver didn't want any fuss or if by imparting the details it would make it all too real.

'Yes, I'm afraid the train rather ground to a standstill,' Oliver said, resuming the apology he'd begun earlier. 'There was some flooding on the line. Though it's not unusual in that part of the country, it being so flat. Do you know it? I'm sure you do. The whole place was like a lake. I said to the chap next to me that we shouldn't be surprised if the ark were to float by. But it was a little lost in translation, I think. He was from Latvia or Lithuania. Where's Vilnius? Anyway, he didn't reckon much to English winters. Not enough snow, he said. He thought it terribly amusing that I was wearing a scarf. But I do feel the cold, Tom . . .'

That was obvious. His fingers, some as gnarled as root ginger, were so numb that he found it difficult to untwist the buttons on his coat. A coat that looked as if it might have been slept in, rolled to make a pillow, often repaired, maybe even fought over.

As he went on, his monologue about the weather inter-rupted every so often by folk wanting to say hello or offer him a drink, Tom could only speculate about where he'd been all week. But for now he kept the question to himself. He couldn't come up with a tactful way of asking it. Oliver would be ashamed to admit that he'd been thrown out of the Traveller's Rest over money, if that had been the case, and even more upset to learn that Tom knew about it.

Wherever he'd been staying, it didn't look as if he'd been particularly comfortable there. The way he winced when he moved made it seem as if every inch of him ached. And although he was tall, he had a stoop that caused him to loom over things. It was an awkward, distorted posture that

111

had developed through months or maybe years of sleeping in rented beds that were too small and too narrow.

Watching him still tussling with his coat, Tom offered to help.

'No no, I feel success is imminent,' said Oliver and finally shook loose the long herringbone thing he wore and folded it over a bar stool. Underneath, he had on a raspberry-coloured suit jacket that slouched off him as though on a broken hanger, and there was plenty of room inside his slacks and shirt. His clothes smelled faintly of damp, faintly of old cologne, and there was an unusual musk to his body too: sweat and something else, something like sour fruit or sour milk.

He took back his hat with thanks, set it down on top of his coat and rubbed at some ache in his hip.

'Shall I find us a table?' said Tom, looking around for one that they might have to themselves.

'Bless you, but I've been sitting for hours,' Oliver replied.

'You seem as if you're suffering, though.'

He waved away the concern. '*Just my bones, sire. My rotten bones. How they are like to old willow branches.* You know, I should have followed my instincts and run away with the circus when I was younger. I could have become a trapeze artist or a tightrope walker or something. It might have served me well in later years. They say it's wise to keep the body supple, don't they? Mind you, I was never all that keen on heights. And I suspect that vertigo proves to be something of a handicap on a high wire . . .'

112

With anyone else, all this would seem like nervous burbling, but these were precisely the kind of monologues that had run through all of Oliver's letters.

For the time being, Tom was content to let him talk but couldn't help staring at Oliver's hands. They were extraordinary. On his left, a skull lay in a nest of rose petals. On his right, was the face of some hirsute god, Dionysus or Pan, crowned with laurel leaves and blowing into a pipe. And there were other, smaller details. Butterflies, spiders, an eye of Horus, and thick briars that encircled his fingers. Works of art, really. But across his knuckles, the names LUCAS and MALLY had been inked on with notably less skill.

'. . . or perhaps I could have been a clown,' Oliver continued, squaring himself to the mirror again to fix his mustard-coloured tie. 'Or a lion tamer. *Against certain death all he needs is a whip and a chair.* I can hear the ringmaster now.'

When he stopped talking for a second to have a drink, Tom said, 'How have you been since your last letter?'

'Oh, up and down,' he said. 'You?'

'The same.'

'My body can't seem to make up its mind at the moment,' said Oliver. 'I'm hungry, then not hungry. Famished one day and then the very thought of food makes me ill the next. Still, it's par for the course, so I'm told.'

'And today?'

113

'Perfectly ravenous,' Oliver said. 'I think it's the time of year or the change in the weather. There's a natural impulse to lay down fat stores for the winter. Do you feel it too?'

'Not really, no,' said Tom, thinking that Oliver could eat as much as he liked and still not put an ounce of flesh on his bones. His rotten bones.

'Well, I intend to gorge myself while the appetite's there,' he said. 'Go with the flow, as they advise me to do. Have they said the same to you, the doctors? Surrender to the inevitable. I suppose they're right. There's no use fighting what's coming, is there? *Unjust! Unjust! the old men cried, and cast their stones into the tide, which retreated not.* That's Dryden or someone, isn't it?'

He drank, swallowed, and waved his hand in front of his face.

'Ignore me,' he said. 'I'm talking too much as usual. I've not even asked you how *your* journey was, Tom. You seem tired.'

'I've had a few unsettled nights lately.'

After knocking back the remainder of his drink, Oliver said, 'I feel for you, my love. I really do. There's nothing worse. I count myself incredibly fortunate when it comes to sleeping. It's the one thing that doesn't give me any trouble. I used to share a room with a chap who'd been in the air force, you see, and he taught me a technique for dropping off anywhere at any time. It's all about breathing in the right

114

way. Ten seconds and you're out cold. You don't even dream. Brandy, old boy?'

'No, not for me, thank you,' said Tom, trying to keep up.

'Well, I think I'll have one more, if that's all right. Just to take the chill off.'

With a broad smile, he shook his empty glass at Mr Paley. When a fresh double was set down in front of him, he couldn't find more than a few coppers in his purse and Tom paid instead.

'Do you know I could have sworn I had a note somewhere,' Oliver said, rummaging again. 'It must be upstairs in my bag. I'm afraid I just threw everything into my room and came straight down since I was so late. I'll reimburse you as soon as I can.'

'It's only a drink,' said Tom. 'Don't worry about it.'

He wasn't going to take any money from him when he'd had to sell some scraggy dog to make ends meet – and possibly his watch too. He kept on rubbing his wrist as if he was used to feeling a strap there.

'Well, a gift is a gift, and I thank you for it,' Oliver said and held his glass up to the light, a connoisseur of cheap, acerbic spirits. 'The thing is,' he continued, 'I don't tend to carry much cash in my pockets any more. Someone once robbed me with a knife in Plymouth. It was all rather unpleasant. And since then, I've taken to keeping my money in my suitcase. No one ever wants your case. Too heavy to run away with, you see.'

'You've moved around quite a lot, have you?' said Tom, pretending that he'd never noticed Oliver's frequent changes of address, hoping to subtly turn the conversation to the question of his recent whereabouts.

'I have, I have. Though not always by choice, I must admit,' said Oliver.

'Oh?'

'I had to vacate the last place I was in.'

'How come?'

'They needed the room.'

Tom accepted the reply without pressing him any further, but Oliver was being more than economical with the truth. No B & B would kick out one paying guest just to replace them with another. That made no sense.

'It was a shame, really,' Oliver went on. 'I'd just started to feel at home. There was a darling of a man next door. I'd generally knock in the evening. He was a jeweller by trade, I think. Very knowledgeable about watches, anyway. Had a whole box of them under his bed.'

Mrs Paley came in ringing a hand bell and Oliver polished off his brandy as everyone began to gather their things.

'*And so we are called to feast in the hall of the ancients,*' he said. 'Feeling any hungrier yet? Perhaps you will once we start. Appetite comes with eating, so they say.'

'Look,' said Tom, as Oliver put his empty glass down on the bar. 'I wonder if we might find a table for the two of us, so that we can talk.'

'Of course,' said Oliver, picking up his coat and hat. 'That's what we came for, isn't it? That's what friends do.'

~

As they joined the slow-moving exodus through to the dining room, those who hadn't yet had the chance to speak to Oliver came to shake his hand. Everyone asked the same questions. Was he going to do his turn? Was he going to give them a show?

'We can't wait, can we, Mr Bear?' said Connie, patting her husband's shoulders. 'You're looking so well, Oliver,' she said. 'Isn't he looking well, Victor? Say hello. Come on.'

He refused, or didn't understand, and Connie tutted at him and went on commending Oliver's rude health, though she couldn't have meant it. Victor, meanwhile, poked and prodded at the tattoos on Oliver's hands mesmerised by the wild-bearded face and its hypnotic eyes before he started yanking at Connie's sleeve.

'Yes, yes, you're starving, I know,' she said. 'But I'm *talking*, Victor. It's rude. You're not the only person here, you know. Sorry, Oliver.'

She pushed her husband onwards and those in front parted to let them through. Once they'd gone, Petula appeared and reached up and put her hand against Oliver's cheek.

'You are coming to eat with us, aren't you?' she said.

'No can do,' said Oliver. 'Tom wishes to talk alone.'

'Does he now? Is that why you came, Tom?' she said. 'To steal Oliver away from us? Is it so that you can confess to something reprehensible?'

Her articulation of the last word faltered at the same time as her balance, and she laughed as she stumbled.

'Steady as she goes,' said Oliver, setting her back on the perpendicular. 'We'll come and join you for the numbers. How's that?'

'You'd better,' she said and kissed Oliver at the corner of his mouth, leaving a smut of lipstick before she wedged her way through the other guests and into the dining room, calling for Charlie to get her a drink.

'The numbers?' said Tom.

'For the draw,' Oliver replied, and licked his thumb to wipe his face.

'The draw that no one will tell me about.'

'Ah yes, you've got your badge. Good show. I trust everyone's been tight-lipped?'

'About everything.'

Acknowledging Tom's exasperation, Oliver smiled and said, 'We don't mean to make it arduous, old thing. It's just that we want newcomers to enjoy the surprise.'

The apology was, of course, completely genuine.

'Forgive me,' said Tom. 'I'm being ungrateful. I don't mean to be.'

'No no, I ought to have said that there'd be a gang of us,' Oliver replied. 'That was remiss of me. There was no harm in telling you that.'

'You all seem very close,' said Tom.

'We are, we are.'

'I still can't work out how you know one another, though.'

'None of us really *did* know one another before we were invited here,' said Oliver. 'One must be invited, you see. As I invited you, and Spike invited me all those years ago.'

'Right.'

'Do you know,' Oliver said. 'I met him completely by chance on a train? Or perhaps it wasn't chance at all. Such a dear man. I couldn't have been more pleased for him when he won last time.'

Well, whatever the prize, thought Tom, he'd not had much opportunity to enjoy it. It couldn't have been very long after he'd received it that they'd buried him.

~

In the dining room, velvet burgundy curtains the height of those on a stage had been drawn across the windows, and the whole place decked out with vases of plastic roses, foxgloves, lupins, dahlias and hollyhocks to make an English country garden.

Between three huge, vulgar chandeliers hung festoons of red, white and blue bunting, that couldn't quite disguise the cracks in the ceiling and the crumbling plasterwork.

The mock-Regency features might have lent the room some gentility once, but now the ornamental nymphs and satyrs on the coving cavorted without heads or without legs and the bunches of grapes they carried were black with mould, more like sacks of coal.

'Pretty, isn't it?' said Oliver. 'How about over here?'

He found a small table next to the curtains and hung his coat and hat on the back of a chair. The rain rattled against the window and Tom thought of Mr Calmine who was probably huddled in one of those dank shelters on the promenade. And there but for the grace of God, it might so easily have been Oliver tonight.

'*Alors, Tom. Les délices*,' he said, and handed over the menu.

Soup
Beef stew
Fruit pie

That was it.

But Oliver was adamant that the dearth of choice was more than compensated for by the quality of the cuisine. And its abundance too.

'You won't go hungry,' he said. 'The Paleys have always looked after their guests. Family business, you see. It makes a difference.'

'They've had the Castle for a while, have they?'

'There were certainly Paleys here when I was a boy.'

'You came here that long ago?' said Tom, feeling that it would be inappropriate to admit that he'd already seen Oliver and his family on the film. Indiscreet almost. There had been too much of their private life on show somehow. His sister's antagonistic glare. His brother's determination to consume his lollipop in such a weirdly fastidious manner. His father's sickliness. Oliver's diffidence. And set against all that, his mother's whimsical gaiety.

'We only visited the once,' said Oliver. 'Nineteen Sixty-Five. First week of August. You know, when I think about it now, I can't for the life of me recall how we all fitted into that old Morris of ours. We must have been utterly sick of one another by the time we arrived. I have a feeling it was a hot summer too. Sticky seats. Yes, it's coming back to me.'

'It was a long way for you, was it?' said Tom, though he wasn't sure where the Keeles had lived.

'Hideously so, but we came for Daddy's chest, you see,' Oliver said. 'Too many Woodbines. Lungs like kippers, as they say.'

'Went in for the mud treatment, did he?' asked Tom.

'He was out on the *Mnemosyne* every day,' Oliver said.

'What was that?'

'The boat the Castle owned,' said Oliver. 'The Paleys liked their guests to have their own space.'

'Right.'

'Daddy didn't do well in crowds of people.'

121

His father had been part of that clique on the film, had he? One of the privileged few who were ferried to the far side of the estuary to scrub and bathe in seclusion.

'It was what made the hotel so popular, the privacy,' said Oliver. 'I say *hotel*, it was more what you'd call a therapeutic spa. Still is.'

'It must have set you back a bit,' said Tom.

'My mother wanted Daddy to have the best treatment,' said Oliver. 'You can't put a price on your health, can you?'

'I'm surprised you didn't go off to Switzerland or somewhere for the mountain air.'

'Daddy wasn't so keen on foreign countries,' Oliver said.

'He preferred English muck, did he?'

'He thought there was something in it. He'd have known, I suppose.'

'What was he, a doctor?'

'A surgeon. Up in London. Saint Quentin's. Do you know it? Of course you do. Poor Daddy,' Oliver said, needlessly perusing the menu again. 'He's the real reason I was late, truth be told.'

'How's that?' said Tom.

'Well, I felt as though I ought to stop and give him a nod, even though it was dark, even though I knew you'd be cursing me for being behind my time. It'd been playing on my mind all the way here that I might not get another chance.

'Oh, I know it's silly,' he said. 'What would it have mattered if I'd gone or not? There's that line of Cowper's isn't there? *Lay not sweet blooms nor cast thy tears upon my grave, for petals wither and thy weeping cannot save.* No, not Cowper. Herrick, I think.'

'Your father's buried in Saltwash?' said Tom, eventually working out what Oliver was getting at.

'At the church near the station. Didn't I say?'

Then contrary to what Charlie had alleged, Oliver went there for the purpose of grieving, not cruising.

'What happened to him?' asked Tom.

'His heart packed in the summer we were here.'

'Where was he, out on the sands?'

'The sands?'

'I thought the cold water might have . . .'

'No, he went in his sleep,' said Oliver. 'Best way, really.'

'Here, in the hotel?'

'And at fifty-nine. It's no age, is it? Still, it had been on the cards for a while.'

Then that snippet of the Keeles on the pier might have caught Oliver's father in his last days or even his last hours.

'Well, my condolences,' said Tom, aware that it was a bit meaningless to be passing on his commiserations half a century or more after Oliver's father had died.

That said, Oliver was obviously still upset by what had happened and so Tom refrained from probing any further. But he couldn't decide whether it was sweet or macabre that Oliver returned to Saltwash every year to mourn like this. It was one thing for him to come and pay his respects at the graveside, but quite another to elect to stay in the place where his father had passed away. And why had the man been interred here in this godforsaken place and not back at home, wherever the Keeles had come from?

'Is anyone in the family still around?' said Tom, and Oliver surprised him by saying, 'My mother was until a short time ago.'

'She must have reached a good number.'

'Ninety-seven,' said Oliver. 'But then she came from gentry, and they seem to age slowly. It must be in the genes. She was a fine-looking woman right up until the end.'

Tom tried to imagine her. A bony Venus in a retirement home.

'And Lucas and Mally are your brother and sister?' he said, looking at the tattoos on Oliver's knuckles. They were so amateurish that he might well have done them himself with a needle.

He regarded the names on his crooked fingers with fondness and something else – sorrow or regret – and Tom wondered if they were there in memorial. Perhaps that was why he'd never made any reference to his siblings in any of his letters. If they'd died in recent years, like his mother, then it might have been too painful to bring it up.

'Yes, that's them,' said Oliver.

'And are they . . .?'

'Oh yes. Thriving, thriving,' Oliver said. 'Lucas retired somewhere hot. Dubai springs to mind. Mightily expensive,

I should imagine. But then he did very well for himself in agricultural machinery. Buying it or selling it. I can never remember which. Did I say Dubai? I think I meant Abu Dhabi.'

'And your sister?'

'She's still writing her books. You might have read her, I don't know. Mallory Birdwhistle? She was mad on the Duke of Marlborough for years but now she's a complete Cromwell nut from what I know. Didn't I tell you all this? I'm sure I must have done.'

'My memory isn't what it was,' said Tom, not wanting to make Oliver feel embarrassed at having kept so much to himself. 'Where does she live now?' he asked.

'Sussex,' Oliver said. 'It's an old rectory or parsonage. I'm not sure of the difference, but it's too large a place for one person, whatever it is. She never married, you see. But then she never wanted to. Or no one would take her. She's an unusual girl. Only she would have chosen a nom de plume like Birdwhistle.'

'And is that who you've been staying with since you left Scarborough?' asked Tom.

If he'd been travelling up from the south coast, it would explain, along with the weather, along with the detour to the cemetery, why he was so late.

'No, that wouldn't have been possible.' said Oliver.

'Too far away?'

'For one thing.'

125

'And the other?'

Oliver took a moment to decide on his reply. 'Let's just say that there lies a love in want of repair. You know how it is. People grow apart. *C'est la vie.*'

But for his sister to have left him to scratch out a life of indigence when she had a house big enough for them to share, to not know for certain where his brother was, meant that there was more to the estrangement than the natural divergence of their lives. Did Lucas and Mally even have any idea that Oliver was dying?

'So where *did* you go?' said Tom, the conversation having arrived at the point where he could ask without it seeming sudden or insensitive.

'Oh, there are people I can call on. Old acquaintances here and there. It's all about connections, as I say.'

'Acquaintances from university?'

'Oxford?' said Oliver. 'That was sixty years ago, Tom.'

'I thought that once you'd been there, you were in a club for life.'

'I didn't stay on for more than a term,' Oliver said. 'It wasn't the right time for me, with Daddy gone. I couldn't give much thought to Ovid and Virgil. Ah, here's dinner. *Soup of the evening, beautiful soup.*'

It was a quotation from somewhere that only he would have thought of. Another gem from the illimitable treasury of his brain. He was just the most singular person. And Charlie was of the same opinion, judging by the smirk he shared with Tom as he ladled out the starter from the huge copper vat on his trolley. A thin, reddish slop that contained celery and tomatoes and chunks of some kind of meat.

'What is that, fish?' asked Oliver, as he inhaled the aroma.

'Eel,' said Charlie and moved on to the next table.

~

Tom wasn't usually fussy when it came to food, but he hadn't forgotten the fetid smell of the river, and he couldn't help picturing what he'd seen sitting in that woman's carrier bag like a knot of fat intestines. When he'd stopped her on the promenade, she must have just come from selling some of her catch to the Castle.

As he picked around the bits of grey flesh, he lifted out what looked edible, but it was all too hot and too vinegary and even a few mouthfuls dredged up half a dozen peppercorns, which he set on the tablecloth like shotgun pellets.

None of that fazed Oliver, who tried at first to exercise some decorum in Tom's company but ate like a man who'd not had a decent meal in a while. As he embarked on a lengthy anecdote about a room-mate who'd been a commis-chef at the Dorchester, each spoonful of soup interrupted the flow like a badly placed comma, and Tom struggled to follow what he was saying. But it was more important to Oliver that he put food in his belly than get to the end of the story.

How he'd turned out to be so destitute was hard to understand. His father had been a surgeon, and his mother had come from old money, and even though the upper classes always claimed to be asset-rich, cash-poor, they didn't exactly starve. People like the Keeles were usually adept at hanging on to their wealth and dispensing it wisely and liberally to their progeny. Oliver didn't seem the type to have frittered away an inheritance. But maybe he had. Was all this talk of 'working in theatre' just a vanity project? Had he 'always wanted to be an actor'? Was he one of those dilettantes who auditioned endlessly and never actually scored a part in anything? It could be that the only time he got to perform was here at the Castle. The turn they were all so eager to see might simply consist of him reciting speeches from Shakespeare or humorous monologues or something. Maybe he was still striving for an Equity card in his seventies. Holding out for a dream like that would have slowly drained his funds over time.

But who knew what his life was really like? He'd have to be making money some way if he roamed about so much. A state pension only went so far. He acquired things – a dog, a watch – and then sold them, possibly. Or people felt moved to give him alms of one kind or another. He'd already been handed two glasses of brandy since he'd arrived. And yet these small acts of kindness were maybe all he ever received. No one seemed willing to do more and actually take him in. None of these connections of his were of any practical value. That was if they existed at all. The claim that he'd been put up by what he'd so vaguely called 'old acquaintances' made Tom think that Oliver hadn't had *any* place to stay since he'd been banished from the Traveller's Rest. In which case, he'd spent his nights where? Railway platforms? Bus shelters?

After Oliver had finished off another bowl of soup, he and Tom tackled the dry, sinewy beef stew, and then took on the fruit pie, which was soft in the crust and drowned in cream a day past its best.

As the food kept coming, Oliver's sinuous stories wound on through various unrelated topics: his love of pigeons and public libraries, the notes of gratitude and the notes of despair he'd found hidden inside Gideon bibles, the difficulty of sourcing good woollen socks and a round-up of the interesting characters he'd crossed paths with in the last few months.

He said nothing about his condition – and perhaps he didn't need to, given the way he looked – but his chatter was so frivolous that it was as though he was just passing the time, and it gave Tom an absurd pang of jealousy again.

Because they'd been bonded by the same predicament, he'd assumed that Oliver thought of him differently to the random people he met in the course of his peregrinations, but perhaps that wasn't true. Oliver had been so careful throughout his correspondence not to give away anything too personal that he could have delivered these soliloquys to *anyone* he happened to encounter, however briefly. So far, there wasn't anything he'd said to Tom that he couldn't have said to the Lithuanian on the train or the man next door at the Traveller's Rest or any of the others he'd roomed with in his time.

'I'm at it again. I must be such a bore,' he said, cutting himself off in the midst of a tale about a boxer he'd once known in Penzance, as gentle as a vicar outside the ring. 'You must tell me to stop, Tom, otherwise I'll go on for ever. You said you wanted to talk and all you've done is listen. I'm terrible, aren't I? What's on your mind? I'm all ears.'

After having pondered so many strategies of persuasion, Tom could think of no better course of action here and now than to be straight with Oliver, and so he took the envelope from his coat pocket and slid it across the table, keeping his hand on the top.

'Just hear me out,' he said, when Oliver shook his head, having caught on straight away what it was. 'I've been thinking about it for a while. It's not a fortune or anything, but it'll pay for a decent room somewhere, and there'll be more if you need it.

'The fact is,' he went on, before Oliver could interject. 'I don't have anyone to give my money *to*. You know that. And I'd rather it was put to good use now while you and I are both still here.'

It was an old truism, but you really couldn't take it with you. There were no pockets in a shroud, as the saying went.

'I've done the sums ten times over,' said Tom. 'I know exactly how much I can spare. So don't worry that I'm going to bankrupt myself or something. I'm not.'

Oliver was visibly touched by the gesture. 'You are generosity incarnate, Tom,' he said. 'But I can't take it.'

'Why?'

'It's far too kind.'

'You're a friend, Oliver,' said Tom. 'What would you do if you could see that I was in difficulty, and you had the means to help?'

'How do you know that I *am* in difficulty?' Oliver said.

Your clothes, Tom wanted to say. These dives you sleep in. The fact that you've been homeless for a week.

'I just want you to be comfortable,' he said.

'I am,' Oliver replied. 'I am.' Even though that was demonstrably untrue. 'You know, you remind me of a chap I once knew in Weston-super-Mare,' he said. 'He wanted to nurse me as much as you do. I had the flu at the time. Or scarlet fever. Now, he was Spanish, I think. Or Portuguese. The most exquisite dancer. I forget his name. But that's the way it is, isn't it? We meet, we part . . .'

'Oliver . . .'

'Listen, Tom. Give it to Angeline,' he said and pushed the envelope back.

131

'She wouldn't want it.'

'Bequeath it to her grandchildren then.'

'I can't.'

To do that would seem such a derisory attempt at an apology. Sick, even.

'Then donate it to malnourished orphans or something,' Oliver said. 'I'm sure Connie will know of a charity.'

Tom held on to the envelope, unsure what to do next.

'But I just don't understand how you live, Oliver,' he said. 'I mean, I know most actors don't earn a lot of money. But they don't struggle like this.'

'Good heavens, I'm not an *actor*,' laughed Oliver. 'Wouldn't know the first thing. I'm flattered that you'd ever think I had such a gift. An actor?'

The idea of it amused him even more when he contemplated it for a second time, but he became distracted by something on the far side of the room, and before Tom could say anything else, he cleaned the grease off his lips with a napkin and got up.

'Shan't be a moment,' he said. 'I need a brief word with the lady of the house.'

He patted Tom's arm and went slowly and stiffly towards Mrs Paley as she passed from table to table ensuring that her guests were content.

She'd changed her clothes and was dressed more appropriately for the glamour of the Castle's dinner hour in a black dress and a set of pearls. Her lace-up shoes had been swapped for a pair of heels that elevated her by several inches but didn't impede her matronly briskness.

As she left Connie and company, she made for the next table, but Oliver intercepted her and took her aside. Po-faced, she listened to what he was saying and put her hands behind her back, just as she'd done with Mr Calmine.

It was no real surprise that Oliver had refused the cash. Not simply out of self-respect, but because his habits were well engrained. He'd become so used to making ends meet in his own way that to suddenly come into more money, even a modest amount, would be to have too much. He wouldn't know what to do with it or he'd feel guilty about possessing it. His sense of unworthiness had surfaced again.

But where *had* it come from? Why had he ended up like this when his brother and sister had been so successful?

Sometimes, there was no rhyme or reason for one sibling to flounder while another excelled – take Elaine's children, one a professor, the other a thief – and idiosyncrasy played a part too. There was no getting around the fact that Oliver *was* peculiar. Yet, he was unquestionably sharp-minded. He could so easily have turned his hand to any number of academic professions and lifted himself out of this life of hardship, but he hadn't. More importantly still, he should have found love. He ought to have a devoted spouse or a boon companion, but he was alone – and alone, it seemed, by choice.

To submit to this continual expiation had been a conscious decision for him. He was punishing himself with an imposed abstinence. He talked about the importance of having friends but only in a *theoretical* way, as a priest might revere the act of marriage for the joy he'd seen it bring to others while remaining chaste himself.

It was true that Oliver had been the one who'd sent the first pen-pal letter and, arguably, if he really *didn't* think himself entitled to friendship then he wouldn't have reached out at all. But Tom was beginning to see that friendship wasn't something that Oliver longed to receive but to provide. He'd not arranged to meet in Saltwash so that he could have Tom's attention but to furnish him with the camaraderie of all these others.

So, what was that, sympathy? Did Oliver consider him to be lonely or something? Well, he wasn't. People called. His agent. His publisher. There was everyone at Living Now. And Angeline was back in his life, or she had been until he'd fucked things up a couple of weeks ago.

His only defence was that he hadn't planned to make the suggestion about her visiting him at all; it had just come out in the course of conversation. But Angeline had been shrewd enough to realise that, no matter how spontaneous the idea might have seemed, he was hankering after an opportunity to express his contrition.

And so why would she want to fly halfway across Europe to listen to him dredging up the past? Why would she want to relive his insensitivity, his ruthlessness?

She'd been ever so gracious to have ended the call by saying that she'd think about it, rather than telling him straight what a selfish bastard he was.

Annoyed with himself that he'd made things so uncomfortable between them, he'd let it lie for the last fortnight. That she'd not been in contact either suggested that she *was* upset with him, or worse, that she was rethinking the scope of her kindness.

But it would do no harm to message her and ask if she was all right. That was a way back in, perhaps.

He did so, knowing that he might not receive a reply for a while. She'd still be busy entertaining in that huge kitchen of hers. He'd seen it on the photographs. Thickly plastered walls, distressed oak doors with iron hinges, a long pine table worn and pitted by the many families who'd sat around it before hers. All the rusticity carefully preserved by an artist with a gimlet eye for the prettiness of decay. She'd have loved Saltwash.

The village she lived in, Agios Mikalis, to which she had ancestral ties, was only a few miles along the coast from where they'd been on their honeymoon: a time that returned to him now as haphazardly as the scraps of the past the Paleys had shown on the film.

He recalled a vine-shaded taverna with cats creeping in and out of the spindly furniture. Sand like scalding sugar. Blinding white church towers and cobalt skies. Gardens of rampant bougainvillea. Turquoise lizards basking on a brick wall. And sex. Lots of sex. The heady restlessness of being in love. Or in love with the *idea* of being in love, rather. The cliché accurately described the way he'd been then; still young enough to have had a schoolboy's longing (aware of it or not) for all that had been promised to him in quixotic O-level poetry. He'd enjoyed the feeling of being stupified by love. He'd savoured infatuation and lust as delicious torments. He'd idolised Angeline at a remove, like an aesthete.

There had been a particular morning, he remembered, when she'd gone out early to paint the sunrise at the harbour down the hill. Finding her absent from the bed, he'd opened the shutters and watched her making the steep climb back up the marble steps to the hotel with her sketchbook and brushes.

She'd looked like something out of antiquity in her bare feet and her white dress; her hair as dark and luscious then as to rival one of the Minoan women on the fresco at Knossos. And if he could have stopped time, he would have done, and fixed her for ever in the frame of that window.

He'd no doubt thought that a romantic notion in the moment but now he could see that all he'd really wanted *was* an emblem rather than a wife. A figure in a painting.

As it was for some collectors of fine art, there had been more appeal in taking sole possession of the picture, than there was in the picture itself. She'd had her admirers, Angeline, and he'd outbid them all. He'd won.

At twenty-five – as he'd been then, and only just – he'd never thought himself immature, or as one who blundered into things, but he'd not come close to appreciating the day-to-day demands of marriage, which had required him to not only engage with Angeline's life as if it mattered as much as his own, but to allow her to influence his. It had been too intrusive, too forceful. There'd been something about the obligation to bare what was innermost that had ground against him. It was what had made him get on a plane or climb into the bed of someone who had no interest in anything more than making love. He was always inclined to flee or hide. And to have brought a child into the equation, no no. He'd have made the worst possible father at that age, always standing back from life rather than participating in its complex realities.

It'd been the same with anyone who'd wanted him and needed him. Monica and Steffy, his extramarital intrigues, had gone that way eventually, demanding this and that. So too the women who'd come after the divorce: Rosie, Anthea, Cherry, Gail and that red-head with the temper, her name gone now. As soon as they'd started relying on him and expecting things of him, he'd moved on.

He'd even spurned his own mother who, late in her life, ought to have been able to command his care and devotion. Perhaps even have earned his forgiveness. But he could count on the fingers of one hand the number of times he'd visited the home, and, when she'd died, it had been a month or more since he'd last seen her.

The lack of compassion in his younger self was repellent to him now, and he desperately wanted to believe that he'd felt at least a *touch* guilty about it back then. But he hadn't. Not that he remembered anyway. When she'd gone, there'd been a colossal relief that his responsibility to her was over. There'd been nothing worse than listening to her rambling on in that suffocating day room. Nothing more pointless than driving miles up the M1 to see her when she'd not known who he was.

On one occasion, believing him to be a Father McNamara, she'd embarked upon a long and tearful confession about stealing a macaw from a pet shop. It was all completely mad.

Another time she'd confused him with some lodger she'd taken in years before. 'Gerald', she'd called him, which may or may not have been a real person. The names of the men who'd come and gone over the years had long since evaporated from his mind even then at – what had he been? – thirty-seven or thirty-eight or something. Nowadays his mother's boarders had been distilled to virtual caricatures.

There'd been a large, loud chap with an accordion, he thought. Another fellow who'd worked nights in an abattoir and always had blood under his fingernails.

Then there'd been the newly divorced. Men either humbled or hostile at being forced to rent a box room in the fleshpots of Wakefield.

And in between these glum castaways, several suave young bachelors had come and gone; real-life matinee idols, the way he remembered them. Duplicates of Anthony Steel or Adam Faith, who'd made his mother laugh in the night and thumb her rosary beads the next morning at the breakfast table.

He'd come across her sometimes sitting there alone and pensive, a cup of tea steaming, a Player's smouldering in the ashtray and loiter in the doorway, anxious about the mood she might be in. She'd been an irascible woman, mistrustful of children, and likely to have given him a cuff round the ear for creeping up on her, whether he'd meant to or not.

Now and then, he'd notice that she'd been looking at a particular photograph. The one of his father in khaki with his Brylcreemed hair and his seductive eyes and the self-confident grin of a man who'd known women aplenty.

It had been the only image of him in the house, and so there'd been nothing to contradict the perception that Tom had formed at nine or ten of his father being as gallant and invincible as one of the heroes in *The Champion*, charging bayonet-first across the desert towards the enemy.

How he'd wished for him to come home with the same ferocity and drive out these lodgers who'd taken his place. Especially the winkers and hair-rufflers. The men who'd appear in the night. Men who liked to sit on the edge of the bed and slip a hand under the covers.

~

'Are you done?' said Charlie, poised to collect in the crockery. He sounded tetchy, as though he'd already asked the question once and Tom hadn't heard him.

'Yes, thank you.'

Noticing his half-full bowl, Charlie said, 'Didn't you enjoy it then?'

'I wasn't all that hungry,' said Tom.

'You should have let your friend have it instead,' Charlie said, picking up Oliver's dish. 'He's taken the pattern off this. When did he last eat?'

Tom forced out a smile.

'I'm serious,' said Charlie. 'What's happened to him since last year? He looks like shit.'

'It's called ageing.'

'And it'll happen to me one day, I know, I know.'

'So you hope.'

'Do I?'

'It's better than the alternative, isn't it?'

'Not if I end up like him,' Charlie said.

'Like him?'

'Off.'

'Off?'

'As in decomposing,' Charlie said. 'He stinks. You must have noticed.'

'I'm surprised you didn't turn him away if that's your opinion,' said Tom.

'You think I'm that harsh?'

'You got rid of Mr Calmine quick enough,' Tom said.

'I was just following orders.'

'Did you need to be so rough?'

'He'll be all right,' Charlie said. 'He seems to survive. He keeps coming back, doesn't he? The daft bastard.'

'Would it be so bad to let him in?'

'He's a cheat.'

'How do you cheat in a raffle?'

'He had his own book of tickets with him,' said Charlie. 'He just tore out the winner when it was drawn and then made out that the other person with the same number was trying to fix it.'

'The crime of the century,' Tom said.

'He's done worse,' said Charlie, as though he'd not quite registered the sarcasm.

Before Tom could get anything more out of him, Petula's voice rose out of the babble. She'd spilled her drink and was chasing a yellow bead of liquid around her wrist with her tongue.

'I don't blame you for sitting somewhere else,' said Charlie. 'That woman's a fucking nightmare. I don't know why she bothers coming if all she wants to do is drink herself blind. She could do that at home and save herself the embarrassment. The mouth she had on her last year when her sons showed up. Did she tell you about that?'

'What was their problem?'

'She'd fallen off the wagon,' said Charlie. 'Hit the bottle again.'

'And they came all the way here to stop her having a drink? It seems a bit much.'

'Well, she's someone who needs to stick to the pledge.'

'Why's that?'

Petula yelled louder in the midst of another argument with Barnaby.

'Ran someone over, didn't she?' said Charlie, glancing at her again as he collected the cutlery.

'Petula did?'

'Straight up.'

'When?'

'Years ago. Clipped some kid on a bike when she was pissed. Turned him into a vegetable. Never got caught for it either.'

'It was a hit and run?'

'So they say.'

'Jesus.'

'You see,' said Charlie. 'I get to hear all sorts of things. I told you,' and he wheeled the trolley off to the kitchen, ignoring Petula who was trying to call him over.

It seemed prudent to take his disclosures with some scepticism. Gossip was usually imprecise at best. But if what he'd said *were* true, the grisliness of knocking down a child and leaving them in the road wouldn't have ever dissipated for Petula. And so that was why she came to the Castle every year, was it? To try and drink away her guilt?

On the other side of the room, laughter came from the three women who'd been attending to Oliver when he'd arrived earlier. He was standing next to their table, rubbing his hands together with great exaggeration, elbows out, as if kneading something between his palms, and Tom thought that he might be telling them a joke. But as if from nowhere, he conjured up a little white hat, one of those knitted Arabic kufis, studded with what looked like emeralds.

After sitting the skullcap on his head, he fanned out a deck of over-sized cards for Anoushka to choose from, and conversation dwindled as everyone in the room turned to watch. Now with an audience, Oliver closed his eyes and gestured for Anoushka to show them all what she'd selected. She did, and, sure enough, after she'd put the card back into the pack for Oliver to shuffle, he picked out the Jack of Hearts.

The applause was still circulating as he launched into a skilful display of misdirection with a gold penny, making it vanish into thin air and then rematerialise under a saucer or from behind the little dog's ear or in one of the ladies' gloves.

They clapped again and he shambled over to the next lot of eagerly waiting guests where he produced a paper bag from his pocket, inflated it in a single breath, filled it with water from the jug on the table and then scrunched it into a ball.

So, this was his life then, was it? Magic routines in shabby hotels. Beguiling people on a wet evening and then moving on.

He was mute as he performed, a mime artist as much as a magician, and while he was wonderfully dextrous at all this, despite his contorted fingers, Tom suspected that this sort of sleight of hand was considered fairly easy to master by those in the know. It might have been the case that these parlour tricks were all Oliver *could* manage now, in terms of feasibility, if nothing else. If he was a nomad, he couldn't really carry around much in the way of paraphernalia. Maybe he'd once had swords or collapsing boxes or the equipment to saw a woman in half, but had sold it all off over the years. No one wanted that kind of show nowadays anyway. It was a bit old hat, wasn't it? Or maybe not. What did he know? thought Tom. Here in the Castle, they couldn't get enough of these simple illusions. At every table, Oliver entranced the people sitting there with bits of string and coloured handkerchiefs.

Three plastic cups and a vanishing ping-pong ball were enough to captivate Victor, who looked at Connie with an amazement that had the whole room laughing. Capitalising on the moment, seeking to elevate everyone's delight all the more, Oliver motioned for Connie to pick up her handbag, and, after a flick of his fingers, as if shaking off water, he encouraged her to open it and look inside.

With everyone nearby gleefully adding to her wariness, saying 'Careful, Connie' and 'Brace yourself now', she undid the clasp and set free a pair of sky-blue budgerigars that flew out chirping to one another and swooped between the chandeliers. Everyone craned and pointed and wanted the birds to come to them. But they responded only to Oliver, and he called them back with a click of the tongue to sit on his palm. Then, gently encasing them in his hands, he blew on his knuckles and the birds turned into two rosettes which he presented to the women closest to him with a theatrical flourish.

At this finale, there were cheers and whistles and those who could manage it got to their feet. Oliver took a bow, as far as his bad back allowed, and went to each table shaking his hat like a mendicant passing around a begging bowl.

∼

While the Paleys distributed tea and coffee, Oliver returned to where Tom was sitting. The skullcap was heavy, but

145

mostly with copper coins. Tom had half a mind to put in the envelope of money, but it would be a devious thing to do and he didn't want to bring it out again while Charlie the tattler was roving around with his trolley. And so he dropped in the shrapnel he had in his pocket.

'You never told me how talented you were,' he said.

He meant it too. Had Oliver really had the two little birds about his person since he'd arrived? And where had they gone?

'Well, I've been at it a while, old boy,' Oliver said. 'Though I'm slower than I used to be.'

'The Paleys still hired you,' said Tom.

'*Hired* isn't quite the word. It's more an arrangement,' Oliver said. 'A one-night-only sort of thing. I give them a bit of cabaret after dinner and make a few tips. But it's not about the money, really. It's more important that I keep my hand in. You have to carry on performing, you see. I know I laughed it off earlier, but I suppose magicians aren't so different to actors. We can't make a judgement about our own ability. We need an audience, otherwise we're nothing. It's the audience that validates. Gielgud said that, I think. Or Olivier.'

The way Mrs Paley had been with him as he'd made this arrangement of his suggested that she wasn't particularly happy about it. Perhaps she didn't like him profiting from her guests, however scant his pickings. Still, she couldn't argue that Oliver had kept them entertained. Had she disallowed him, she might have had a revolt on her hands, given that everyone had been looking forward to his act so much.

'Where will you go tomorrow?' Tom asked him.

'Now there's a question.'

'And what's the answer?'

'It depends on how lucky I am tonight,' said Oliver. 'And even if I'm not, I'll be all right wherever I end up, I'm sure. Christmas isn't far off now. Season of goodwill and all that. I'll probably wander down to Devon or Dorset. I know a few places that might book me again. There are some old-timers who still remember me from the variety shows.

'Actually, I'll probably give Somerset a try first,' he continued, as he put his takings into his coat pocket. 'Minehead's always worth a punt. The seaside hotels are usually kind to me. I'll be fine, my love. I really will. You mustn't worry.'

He didn't seem embarrassed about what he did for a living in itself – and there was no reason why he should be – but as he'd been so coy about it in his letters, Tom could only assume that he was ashamed of his descent into obscurity.

If there had been halcyon days for him when he'd played the summer seasons, they were surely long over. When he returned to these resorts now, it was difficult to believe that anyone remembered him. And if it turned out that these places weren't as welcoming as he'd expected, what was he going to do then? Hang around the pubs? Perform in the streets? Pester the Christmas shoppers? A hatful of coins wouldn't buy him a room for the night in even the dingiest of holes.

He seemed to sense that Tom was going to try and convince him again to take the money (which he was) and changed the subject.

'You know, I can picture my father here so clearly,' he said. 'He liked sitting by the window when we ate so that he could watch the boats. He used to sail in his younger days.'

'It's nice that you have that memory of him,' said Tom.

'Yes, you never knew your father, did you? That's so sad.'

'I knew *of* him,' said Tom.

After the war, Terry Shift had gone back labouring on the railways and lusting after women. Before Tom had even reached his fifth birthday, he'd left home and taken himself off down one of the tracks he'd so expertly laid never to be seen again. It was a story that his mother had repeated a thousand times to her lodgers (infuriating that younger Tom, so incongruously loyal to his father) and a thousand times more in the nursing home, as the staff had told him.

'Well, I feel very fortunate to have had so many years with Daddy around,' said Oliver. 'Even if it was hard to see him decline in the end.'

'Coming here didn't help him then?' asked Tom.

'With his chest, you mean? No, not really.'

Well, obviously not, Tom reproved himself. It had been a thoughtless question to ask.

'But that wasn't only why we came, you understand,' said Oliver.

'No?'

'It was more for Daddy's peace of mind. The black dog often followed him about, you see.'

'Ah.'

'He had something of a difficult upbringing, by all accounts. And then there was the war too, of course. He was over in Germany at the end. He saw the camps. But who knows where these kinds of things stem from. It might even be passed down, so they say.'

He put three helpings of sugar into his tea and knocked the spoon gently on the edge of the cup.

'I say that Daddy was around, but I only ever really knew him as a recluse,' Oliver said. 'He'd work awfully long hours and then shut himself away in his study as soon as he got home. Never ate with us very often, if at all. He wasn't an affectionate man, but fathers weren't necessarily expected to be so then, were they?'

'All the same, I don't remember ever being *unhappy* about it,' he continued. 'You don't really question things when you're a child, do you? People are as they are. Life is as it is. And you think it will stay the same way for ever. But it doesn't. People change. And when you have an unsettled mind like Daddy's, there's not always a particular reason for it, either.'

'How did he change?' asked Tom.

'I suppose it must have been about a year before we came here,' said Oliver, 'but he suddenly became very interested in us – me, Mally and Lucas. He started coming out of his study in the evenings, which was highly unusual. He'd sit us all down in the parlour and give us long lectures on the importance of discipline. How the world was going to hell in a handcart, what our responsibilities were etcetera. God knows what had prompted it all, but he had a real aversion to Lucas, I can tell you. Thought he was a perfect devil.'

'And was he?'

'Not so that you'd notice. No different to any other ten-year-old. Probably far more obedient than most. But in Daddy's eyes, he couldn't do anything right. He got the blame for everything, even when it wasn't his fault. Even when it *couldn't* have been his fault. And Daddy didn't exactly spare the rod.'

'I see.'

'Not that he was a naturally violent man by any means,' Oliver insisted. 'I just think he'd forgotten who he was.'

'But why did he pick on Lucas particularly?'

'The mind can be such a pernicious thing,' said Oliver. 'One can be wholly possessed by the worst sort of thoughts. It was as though Daddy felt he had no choice *but* to make an example of him so that my sister and I would know right from wrong.'

'That doesn't seem very fair,' said Tom.

'And Mally would have agreed with you. As far as she saw it, Daddy was a complete tyrant.'

'It sounds like he was.'

'I don't know,' said Oliver. 'I'm not convinced that it actually was Lucas himself that Daddy disliked. It was more as if Lucas was ill and my father was resentful of the disease rather than the patient. Or resentful of the fact that it was his little boy who'd been affected. We found him in tears about it more than once, poor man. It's difficult to watch one's father crying, Tom. And it's hard for a wife to see her husband so distraught. That's why my mother brought him here.'

'She thought that the water would take away his troubles, did she?' said Tom.

'Inasmuch as anyone thought it true,' Oliver said, acknowledging that it was a fanciful idea. 'I mean, I don't suppose anyone ever took the notion literally. It was more that if you *believed* that the tide was going to carry off your sorrows then it would. It's the power of suggestion, isn't it? Positive thinking. My mother was a firm believer in it. She always managed to see the good in things.'

Judging by her demeanour on the film, she'd been trying hard to instil some happiness into the other Keeles.

'It was why she chose the Castle,' said Oliver. 'It had such a good reputation for the remedies it offered people like Daddy. The Paleys were great advocates of psychiatric science. They brought in some of the best speakers on the subject.'

'Oh, really?'

'Taking the water was only one small part of the therapy, you see,' said Oliver. 'There were lectures in the

151

evenings from doctors and clinicians and so on. Very innovative they were for the time, the Paleys back then. Great philanthropists too. You know that they left an endowment, don't you?'

'Connie mentioned it, yes.'

'It means that the family can carry on offering new treatments,' said Oliver. 'That's largesse you don't get much, these days.'

'And did it do your father any good when he was here?' said Tom.

'For the first few days, maybe it did,' Oliver said. 'He was quite placid. It might have been the change of scene more than anything. And he enjoyed watching the boats, as I say. We even got him to come out onto the pier. But after that, well, put it this way, it was a long two weeks. I won't bore you with the details. It's all done with now. *Acta est fabula*, as Umbilius tells us,' he said, and he moved on to something less troubling by asking after Tom's cats, quoting a line from *Old Possum's*, and from there veering off into a protracted story about taking tea in Lyme Regis with a man who'd turned out to be T. S. Eliot's tailor.

'Very particular about his buttons, apparently,' he said, forced to raise his voice amid the excitement that moved through the room. Mrs Paley had come in to give out the numbers for the draw.

~

152

Petula hadn't forgotten the promise Oliver had made and waved at him and Tom to join them. When they went over, she and Connie helped Oliver into his chair with kisses and caresses, but Barnaby only looked up momentarily and went back to the foxed piece of paper he had out on the table.

'Still think that there's a pattern, old chap?' said Oliver.

'Not a doubt in my mind,' Barnaby replied, and he reeled off what he'd written down. 'Four, twelve, thirty-six, fifty-six, seventy-two, eight, sixteen, fourteen. It's been evens for such a long time now.'

'It's all chance, you fool,' said Petula. 'What difference would it make if you worked it out anyway? You can't choose the number you get.'

Barnaby ignored her and moved closer to Oliver to talk through his calculations.

'Four is one third of twelve,' he said. 'And twelve is one third of thirty-six. Or I wonder if there's something in the fact that four and twelve make sixteen, which is twenty shy of the next number. And if you *add* twenty to thirty-six that makes *fifty*-six, which would mean you'd need *another* sixteen to reach seventy-two . . .'

He quickly tied himself in knots, but Connie admired his insight saying, 'Isn't he clever, Victor?' and patient, genial Oliver sustained a look of interest while Barnaby went on scribbling down his sums.

'You don't believe all this, do you, Tom?' Petula said. 'Someone will win and everyone else will lose. That's all there is to it in a lottery.'

'True,' said Tom.

'Well, I'm glad someone's on my side,' she said. She put her weight against him and twined her fingers into his.

Had she really just driven away after running down a child in the street? It wasn't out of the question. Anyone was capable of anything. That Charlie knew about it meant that she must have told him, or he'd heard her admitting what she'd done to someone else. Either explanation was possible, if she'd drunk enough. And given that her two sons thought her sobriety so critical as to warrant her extraction from the bacchanal here last year, they had to know too.

With her free hand, she stirred what was left in her glass, saying nothing. She was in the trough of her inebriation, feeling sorry for herself that the alcohol hadn't produced sufficient amnesia. But it wouldn't have mattered how many gaudy cocktails she'd put inside her. Guilt was immovable. It remained mud-fast in the mind like the boats stuck on the riverbank here.

Tom realised now why he'd been so interested in the quotidian milieu of the film. It was unusual to see such ordinariness preserved. Most of the time, whatever happened from moment to moment, whatever one did or said, just drifted into that immense occluded past of trivialities. And thank God it did. But certain occasions, certain conversations, bad choices and acts of heartlessness never went away.

He'd forgotten now who'd recommended the clinic in Richmond that Angeline had used, but he'd appreciated its discretion. There was no sign outside. High walls and tall trees kept it tucked away from the main road, and the patients didn't have to see one another.

It had been an overcast, muggy day in August. The windows of the waiting room propped open. A fan going. He pictured Angeline in a blue cotton dress, sitting on the edge of one of those bentwood armchairs fashionable at the time, half turned to the breeze, one leg over the other, picking her fingernails and clapping the sole of her sandal against her heel.

She'd not said a word all the way there or while they'd been passing the time by leafing through the magazines spread out on the table. Not even when the nurse had come to take her down and he'd squeezed her hand for luck had she acknowledged his presence. She'd not looked at him or looked back.

It wasn't something she'd talked about afterwards either, and it had suited Tom at the time to believe that her reticence had designated it a private matter, hers to deal with, nothing he could do. Out of respect (how kind, how thoughtful) he'd never pushed her for any details about either the

155

procedure or her feelings. And given that she'd gone back to work at the college after a couple of days and never communicated any distress to him, he'd inferred that if she'd had any doubts about what she'd done, she'd managed to resolve them on her own. She'd seemed perfectly all right. Happy. Back to her rational self. Or it had been convenient to think so. He'd been too busy to suppose otherwise and had flown off to Lisbon as planned to write a piece for Condé Nast. They were both working again. By mutual unspoken agreement, normal life had resumed.

It was only when he returned home that he began to see how wrong he'd been about Angeline's apparent equanimity. Even though she'd said nothing to him directly, it was in the midst of making love, when the heart's true dispensation was so inescapably on show, that he knew something had changed. In bed, she was mechanical and dutiful. While she waited for him to finish, she'd stare past his shoulder or lie with her head to the side and her eyes closed, withstanding his exertions.

Soon, she'd begun to avoid him as much as possible. She'd stay over at her sister's house once or twice a week. She'd volunteer to teach an evening class. If and when they did sleep together, that was all they tended to do. She'd play dead as soon as she turned off the lights. And on the infrequent occasions she'd permitted him to wriggle between her thighs, she'd tell him to stop well before the end and take herself downstairs with a blanket.

He'd presumed that all this rejection and remoteness was payback for what he'd asked her to do. But he didn't really know. She wouldn't say.

He'd had no time to try and make interpretations. Forcing him into a guessing game was another kind of intrusion, another kind of neediness, and, frankly, it had bored him. He'd not had the energy to waste on it when he had so much work to do, and places to go.

It had been around that time, on a trip to Turkey, that he'd met Steffy Jackson, a photographer at the *Observer*, and how easily he'd justified the pleasurable, uncomplicated nights he'd spent with her, both in Istanbul and back in London. His rationale being that if Angeline wasn't interested in him any more, he couldn't be blamed for enjoying the affections of someone who was. Narcissistic child.

But how young he *had* been then. How young they'd both been, him and Angeline. Still shy of their thirtieth birthdays and already uncoupling.

All this had happened in 1979, for heaven's sake. 1979. It was ancient history. Or it seemed so to him. That former incarnation of Tom Shift was such a stranger now. But for Angeline the past was still present.

If, when she'd married again, she'd gone on to have two, three, four kids, or a whole clan of bonny, dark-eyed little ones with the tender-hearted Dimitrious, her husband now, then perhaps by this stage, decades later, she might be able to look back and think of that afternoon at the clinic by the Thames as a regrettable but long-distant event in her life. But it had remained unbearably significant, a turning point.

Because of a botch or just bad luck, no one seemed able to say, but the operation had apparently left scars that prevented her from having any children of her own. As Tom had said to Oliver in one of his letters, he'd as good as had her butchered.

'But you weren't to know, old thing,' he'd written in reply. 'It's not something you *intended* now, is it? And does she not return to you in your hour of need?'

It was true. She had. And he'd like it very much, he thought, if she were to resume her role as his adviser. He could ask her opinion about Oliver and what to do next if he wouldn't accept the money.

Having been so caught up in the logistics of getting here today and working out the best campaigns of persuasion, he hadn't given much thought to what would happen afterwards. To wave goodbye to Oliver in – what? – an hour's time or so and return to communicating from a distance with ink and paper didn't seem right. It would be all too easy for that to dry up now that they didn't have a rendezvous to organise. Even Oliver might run out of things to talk about. They were both dying, and it was, by degrees, terrifying and tedious. What more was there to say?

But when so many others had come and gone from Oliver's life, Tom wanted to be there for him. When things took a downward turn, as they certainly would, he didn't want him to be alone, miles away on the other side of the country.

Then why didn't he ask him to come and stay? thought Tom. Of *course* that was the right thing to do. It was so obvious. Oliver was never going to take the money in whatever form it was offered, but he couldn't object to being a houseguest for a while, surely. He couldn't claim to yearn for connections and then shun them when they came along.

As Tom thought it over, the idea became more tenable and attractive. Aside from knowing that Oliver would be sleeping indoors, it would be good to have someone in the house who could remember what he was starting to forget. Then he could take down those bloody notes off the fridge. If Oliver could be made to feel needed in an assistive capacity, then that might well induce him into accepting the invitation.

Tom looked over at him, disquieted again by how gaunt he was, how pallid. The effort it took to mask his pain in front of others must have been as tiring as bearing the pain itself. But it seemed as if Oliver felt he had some responsibility to be convivial. They relied on him, their magician, to astound them with conjuring tricks and give them a laugh and sweeten the proceedings all the more.

159

He was attempting to amuse Victor again, with a feather that changed colour each time he gave it a flick. But Victor wasn't for being diverted. As Mrs Paley had taken such a circuitous route around the room offering the tickets, he'd become more and more impatient and lurched from side to side so violently in his wheelchair that Connie had to stand up and hold him steady.

'All *right*, Victor,' she said. 'For goodness' sake, calm down. She's coming now. And you can wait your turn, thank you. Ladies first. You know that.'

When Mrs Paley arrived at the table with a wooden bowl, Tom saw that it contained some of the little pieces of paper her husband had been folding at the bar when he'd arrived. They were handwritten in magenta crayon to deter anyone thinking of pulling off Mr Calmine's trick and bringing in their own.

Petula took her pick. Connie went next. Barnaby rubbed his hands together as though he was about to roll in a game of craps, and then made his selection with his eyes tightly closed.

Victor, predictably, reached in and took everything he could grab.

'Just one,' said Connie. '*One.*'

With some difficultly she worked a paper free from his fist.

'Put the others back now,' she said. 'Drop them. Let go. There are other people waiting.'

'If you wouldn't mind, old lad,' said Oliver, and whether it was something in his voice or his manner, Victor complied with the request immediately and gawped as Oliver plucked out a number.

'And lastly,' Mrs Paley said to Tom, shaking the bowl in a way that seemed overly ceremonious when there was only one piece of paper left.

Once he'd taken it, Mrs Paley raised her hand, like a teacher subduing a class of infants, and made an announcement to the room. 'We'll call you into the lounge very soon for the draw. It won't be long now.'

She left to the sound of rustling paper as everyone looked at what they'd got.

'Damn it,' said Barnaby. 'Thirteen.'

'So what?' Petula yawned.

'I've got forty-three,' Connie said.

'Eleven for me,' said Oliver. 'Victor?'

After peeling apart her husband's fingers, Connie said, 'Thirty-seven. How about you, Tom?'

'Sixty,' he said.

Barnaby consulted his sums straight away. 'Sixty, sixty,' he said. 'Could it be sixty this year? You see here, Oliver, the last two numbers have been sixteen and fourteen, which makes thirty. And if you multiply that by the difference between them, that's sixty, correct?'

'I'll bow to your wisdom,' said Oliver.

'Then I'm right, aren't I? It's sixty. That's the winner,'

said Barnaby and put down his pencil in resignation. 'Another year wasted. Thirteen, for crying out loud. Of all the numbers.'

'Don't give up already,' Oliver said with a laugh. 'You never know.'

'I do know. Look.' Barnaby brandished his sheet of computations. 'Twelve years I've been coming.'

'Swap with me, if you really want it,' said Tom, prompting an outbreak of objections around the table.

'Don't,' Petula said. 'It's yours, Tom.'

'It's kind of you,' said Connie. 'But we stick with what we've got.'

'It's not really the done thing, dear boy,' said Oliver.

'Yes, but hang on,' Barnaby said. 'There are no rules to say we *can't* swap, are there?'

'Let's not complicate things,' said Connie. 'You don't want to be accused of cheating like Eric Calmine, do you?'

'It's hardly cheating, is it?' Barnaby said.

'Why don't we look at your arithmetic again?' suggested Oliver. 'Perhaps we'll get a different outcome.'

But anxious that Tom might be talked out of the offer, Barnaby quickly made the exchange.

'Thank you, Mr Shift,' he said. 'I'm much obliged to you.' And he gave Tom a false smile.

'You really are something, aren't you?' Petula said.

'What do you care?' snapped Barnaby. 'If you think it's all chance, it shouldn't make a difference what anyone has.'

'You'd cut your own mother's throat to win, wouldn't you?' said Petula.

He waved her off. 'I don't take lectures from drunks.'

'I've not even started yet.'

'You know,' Barnaby said, as he poured himself more water. 'If someone in your position had any shame at all they'd endeavour to stay sober. That would be the decent thing to do.'

'And you'd know all about being decent, wouldn't you?' said Petula, and sat back with her drink in her hand, confident that she had an exacting counterpunch. 'How much did you get them to part with again, those widows you gardened for? Five figures, I heard. That's a lot for weeding some flowerbeds.'

'You don't know what you're talking about.'

'I know you're a devious shit.'

'It's a private matter,' said Barnaby.

'Yes, I'm sure you'd like it to be.'

Oliver intervened and laid a hand on each of theirs.

'Pax,' he said with a light laugh. 'Today's quarrel is tomorrow's regret.'

'Oliver's right. That's enough,' said Connie. 'You're upsetting Victor.'

He sat with his hands over his ears making a whining sound in his throat. Connie patted his back and this appeared to soothe him, but after he stopped keening, he suddenly lurched forward and vomited down himself, spraying Tom's shins and shoes in the process.

163

Petula cried out and got to her feet to move away from the puddle on the carpet, gory-looking from the tomatoes in the eel soup.

'Oh, *Victor*,' said Connie. 'Sit up, sit up.' She dug out a handful of tissues from her bag to blot his chin and his clothes. 'That's your doing, Barnaby,' she said. 'Causing problems. Why couldn't you just have been happy with what you'd got? Sorry, Tom. Has he made a terrible mess of you?'

'Nothing that soap and water won't sort out,' he said.

'Should I give you a hand?' Oliver offered and started to stand up.

'No no, I'll manage,' replied Tom. He wouldn't have Oliver washing his feet like Mary bloody Magdalene.

As he left the table, Connie scolded Barnaby again and he protested his innocence, perhaps rightly so since Victor was clutching his stomach. It was something he'd eaten that had made him ill, not something he'd heard, and Tom was glad to have put aside most of what he'd been served at dinner.

~

Fortunately, there was a stool in the bathroom and so he could sit down to wipe the sick off his loafers and his trousers. He'd never have been able to reach his feet otherwise. When was the last time he'd had the flexibility to bend from the waist and touch his toes? It seemed as if he'd been carrying around this gibbous belly for years. His navel like the thumb hole in a bowling ball. If he and Angeline were to meet up, she would find him much changed, he thought. But perhaps that was no bad thing.

He was washing his hands when a message from her came through.

I'll call later if convenient?

Please do, he sent back, fretful as soon as he'd pressed the button that it sounded tetchy, more like 'what's taken you so long?'

He'd still not mastered the tone of texts, and he added as an improvement, *It'll be good to talk.*

They were communicating again, and that was a positive sign. If she *was* actually wary of his objectives, then she wouldn't have replied at all.

The formality of 'if convenient' was fine with him. It had reset the boundaries of the businesslike partnership they'd adopted prior to his blunder. If they might start anew with Angeline as his consultant, then that was all to the good. He needed her bureaucratic acumen. She was much better at keeping tabs on what he had and hadn't done in terms of wrapping up his life. It had been because of her that he'd started to make a will.

He'd felt embarrassed about getting around to it so late, but it was quite common, apparently, said Ms Jethwa, his solicitor. People tended to view the process as somewhat depressing – or they were frightened of tempting fate – and put it off, often until it was too late. This, she said with mild exasperation.

They were a funny lot, solicitors, grumbling about the cavalier attitude folk had to keeping their legal affairs in order and yet when someone died intestate the time it took to clear up the mess surely meant that they were raking it in.

But it wasn't a denial of his mortality that had made Tom baulk at setting down his last wishes, so much as the uncertainty of what they'd *be* when he had no beneficiaries.

It was a situation that Ms Jethwa had acknowledged without any surprise or concern as though she'd dealt with such a thing many times before.

'It may be that your position actually makes things easier, Mr Shift,' she'd said. 'When all the outstanding bills have been settled, either you give what's left away or you let the Exchequer have it. And put like that, I'll wager that the choice is pretty straightforward. You might like to think of some charitable organisations that are meaningful to you and leave some money to them.'

Or he could set up a scholarship, say. Endow a university department. Fund some cutting-edge research. Buy an incubator for a hospital. There were endless possibilities.

She'd been right to assume that he didn't want his assets to go into the coffers of the Treasury – the thought sickened him actually – but other than that he didn't much care where his money ended up, now that Oliver had made it plain that he wouldn't take any of it.

There was always the Kübler-Ross unit. He could donate something to them. Or give them everything. He didn't know what was best to do. He needed someone who'd manage it all with better judgement once he'd gone. If he were to ask Ms Jethwa to consolidate whatever was left into a single trust, or something, he wondered if Angeline might be prepared to disseminate the capital to worthy causes as she saw fit. He'd sound her out about it at some point. Maybe once they'd got through the small matter of organising his funeral.

Some at Living Now had already made a list of the hymns and verses that would sign off their mortal remains, and had come to the decision about whether they ended up in the earth or the urn via an inane process of elimination – the choice dependent on whether they were too claustrophobic to be nailed into a box or didn't fancy the idea of being shoved into an oven like a basted turkey.

But he couldn't bring himself to have an opinion either way. He'd be a cadaver in a suit, so what did it matter? And how was he supposed to select his own coffin? What was the justification for opting for anything other than the cheapest plywood box? To be laid out in some glossy mahogany chest with swanky brass handles would seem so extravagant. And since *he'd* chosen the thing, it would appear to represent some sense of his self-importance in life – and in death. A vainglorious pharaoh.

When he'd first talked all of this through with Angeline, she'd agreed that it was difficult – even a shade ghoulish – to have to plan his own send-off. He hoped that she would still be prepared to make the arrangements on his behalf. He'd happily let her pick out the casket, flowers and songs. He'd just turn up on the day.

After checking his phone again – although since it hadn't buzzed he knew there was no new message – he put it away as Charlie came in with a mop and a bucket.

'Got you, did he?' he said.

'Just a glancing blow,' Tom replied.

'Not everyone can stomach eel.'

'Evidently.'

'We've never served it before. Me and the chef just thought we'd see how it went down,' said Charlie.

'Experiment failed, I'd say,' replied Tom.

Charlie sniffed rather than laughed.

'What number did you get, then?' he asked and went into one of the cubicles for a bottle of bleach.

'Thirteen.'

'You might as well go home now.'

'Probably.'

'You're not staying the night, anyway, are you?' said Charlie when he came out.

'No.'

'How come?'

'I've got somewhere to be in the morning,' said Tom. 'I'll need to leave before long.'

'Leave? What if you win?'

'You just told me I had no chance.'

'It was a joke,' said Charlie. 'It might be you. Who knows? I always quite like it when someone wins on their first go just to see the faces of the ones who've been at it for years. They won't think you deserve it, you know. Do you think you deserve it?'

'I've no idea what you're talking about,' said Tom.

'What was it for you?' Charlie said, as he began to fill the bucket from the hot tap. 'I'm guessing it was either money or women. Or was it something worse?'

The questions were meant to be impenetrable. Just Charlie's way of teasing him. Tom didn't give him the satisfaction of asking for an explanation, but bent over the wash basin and splashed his face with water to try and cool off. The pressure in his brain was threatening to increase again, and he wouldn't be able to take any more tablets for a while.

Realising that Tom wasn't going to be provoked into giving anything away, Charlie spat out his vitriol about Connie instead.

'Have you heard the way she talks to that husband of hers?' he said. '*I* feel sick just listening to it. Mr Bear. Teddy bear. Give me a fucking break. He's black to his heart, that one.'

'Victor?' said Tom.

'Don't you believe me?'

'He hardly knows what's going on half the time.'

169

'That's just it,' said Charlie. 'He doesn't have to think about what he did.'

He switched off the tap and frowned at Tom's blankness.

'Do I need to spell it out?' he said. 'All those kids?'

'Come on. Just because he fostered?'

'There were dozens of them, apparently.'

'You can't make assumptions.'

'I'm not. He was taken to court. Look it up,' Charlie said, indignant at Tom's cynicism. 'Not that it went anywhere in the end. They threw it out because he started to lose his marbles. But that doesn't mean he's innocent. His wife wouldn't bring him here for the draw if he'd done nothing wrong, would she? She knows what he is. She must have always known. That makes her no better than him, as far as I'm concerned. She didn't do anything to stop it, did she? And now she's got a guilty conscience.'

'How do you know that?' said Tom.

'She took a ticket for herself, didn't she?'

'Yes.'

'There you go then. She must want the prize. And she'd accept it too, if she won. I've no doubt of that. She wouldn't care about her husband then, I can tell you.'

'You've lost me,' Tom said.

Charlie nodded at his badge. 'You'll find out,' he said. 'I just hope you win. Anyone but Victor Mayberry.'

He picked up the bucket and the bleach and moved to the door.

'You know,' he said, 'my mother couldn't care less what anyone here's done, but if it were up to me, I wouldn't let that cunt anywhere near this place. I'd take him down the alley and kick seven bells out of him. But the best I can do is piss in his soup.'

He left with an unreadable smile.

How old was he, Charlie? Thirty-five or so? Stuck here with his parents and sisters in this museum. He'd have to get his thrills from somewhere. But he was so dry that it was difficult to gauge if he'd been joking about adulterating Victor's dinner or not. And the accusations he'd made might well have come from something he'd simply half heard and misinterpreted. He had such a low opinion of the guests that he'd be likely to seize upon the smallest suggestion of any deviancy with relish. If he did believe what he said about Victor to be true, then it explained why he'd looked at the Mayberrys with such revulsion earlier on in the bar.

When Tom came out of the toilet, he coincided with them as they exited the lift, Victor now in a pair of grey flannel trousers and a brown polo neck that clung to every shelf of fat.

'Sorry again, Tom,' said Connie. 'I hope it all came off all right?'

She didn't stop for a reply but went by chastising Victor. Her patience wearing thin.

171

'I was just trying to get you dressed, you baby,' she said to him. 'You're so stubborn. *So* stubborn. I ought to tip you into the river and leave you there.'

Reprimanded, he kept his head down and toyed with something in his hands – a rabbit's foot that he stroked with one of his paws.

Mr Bear.

It made no sense for Charlie to have made up the detail about Victor being put on trial. A brief search online would soon prove or disprove it. So there had to be *something* in what he was saying. And why shouldn't there be? There was nothing to suggest that Victor couldn't have been that kind of man. Outward appearances meant nothing.

None of those who'd come to him as a child could have been singled out as molesters, thought Tom. He'd never been able to anticipate who would appear at his bedside.

One of them had been quite young, no more than twenty or so, and had curled up afterwards under the blanket and cried. The two (or three?) others had been older, more adroit, smiling, shushing, apt to bring Tom, the boy, little gifts to buy his discretion.

Even at the time he'd known what they meant and what they asked of him, these toy cars and comics. But he'd accepted them because he so desperately wanted them, and then he'd hated himself and the men and, most of all, his mother, who'd turned a blind eye or had been woefully incurious at any rate.

In those days, he'd been of the same mind as Charlie; he'd have savoured seeing these men in agony; he'd have pissed in their soup too. Now, he felt nothing. That was to say he'd cultivated a neutrality over time to stop the festering of anger, which was only another type of violation. It was better to have no resentment, no yearning for reprisal, no forgiveness or compassion. That way, it could all be closed up, as if in a book, and considered as little more than an unpleasant chapter of his childhood: a time which largely seemed like someone else's life now anyway.

Talking about it, which was what Angeline would have encouraged him to do if she'd ever known the fine details, had always seemed pointless. He didn't need to embark upon a process of self-discovery with a counsellor or a psychoanalyst. He knew how he felt and who he blamed and saying it aloud to someone wasn't going to alter anything. What strategy would they have suggested that was any better than the one he'd adopted himself? If the point of therapy was to ultimately come to terms with things, then he'd taken the shortcut. He was fine. He never thought about any of that any more.

∼

He followed the Mayberrys into the lounge – another airless, cavernous room full of scuffed leather armchairs and settees clustered around low coffee tables. Oliver was standing by the fireplace along with a few others who dispersed obligingly when Tom approached.

'Managed to get cleaned up all right?' Oliver said. 'I've been trying to think what it was that set Victor off. It can't have been something he ate. We've all had the same.'

Well, not quite, perhaps, thought Tom.

'He seems all right now,' Oliver continued. 'Connie's managed to settle him down. She always says the right thing. That's true love, Tom. Having the words that'll bring peace to another. *Love is language,* as someone once said.'

Maybe so, but things weren't quite as perfect between the Mayberrys as he thought. If Charlie's claims were correct, then Connie was carrying around Victor's transgressions in her head as well as her own. He had no idea who he was or what he'd done. He'd been spared all that by his fraying synapses.

'Or is it, *Language is love?*' Oliver said, mulling it over. 'I suppose the meaning is the same either way, isn't it?'

Since they were alone, it seemed a good moment to ask Oliver how he'd feel about coming to stay, but he was already walking away, talking again, keen to show off the portrait photographs hanging around the room.

Former guests, were they? Or regulars? It seemed a strange sort of gallery for the Paleys to have put up, but perhaps people were encouraged to come back if they could see that their loyalty was so visibly appreciated.

'Previous winners,' Oliver explained. 'There's dear old Spike from last year.'

He'd been a portly, grey-haired man, thoroughly resplendent in his beret and medals, caught with his head thrown back in unbridled laughter. Next to him, the fellow who'd won *two* years ago looked just as rapturous.

Every photograph had been taken in the same place, with the recipient of the prize seated in a lavish chair. This stage scenery had already been set up on the other side of the room in readiness for whoever was victorious in the draw this time, with a camera on a tripod facing an oak, claw-footed throne surrounded by artificial flowers.

'Here's Katerina,' said Oliver, showing Tom the next photograph. 'She won the year that Eric Calmine let himself down.'

'She doesn't seem all that pleased,' Tom said. Like one or two others along the row she was red-eyed from crying.

'Oh, they were tears of happiness, I can assure you,' said Oliver. 'She was a lovely woman. A chambermaid here when we came with Daddy. Astonishing memory. She must have seen a hundred thousand people come and go in her time and yet she still remembered his passing. She'd always ask if I'd been to pay him a visit.'

'Why *is* your father buried here?' said Tom. 'Or is that none of my business?'

'It was for Lucas and Mally's sake, mostly,' Oliver said. 'At the age they were then, they just needed to move on. It wouldn't have done to dwell on things.'

175

That was reason enough to leave their father here out of sight? It seemed extreme.

'And they've never been back since?' asked Tom.

'Only me.'

'Not even your mother came?'

'She thought it best to draw a line under things,' replied Oliver. 'Daddy's life didn't end on a particularly happy note.'

'Because of the way he was with Lucas?'

'That and other things, yes,' said Oliver, and he lowered himself into an armchair, frowning at Tom. 'Are you really interested in all this, dear boy?' he said. 'How funny.'

'I just don't think you've told me before.'

'I must have done.'

'If you did, it's gone.'

As Tom sat down in the chair opposite, Oliver looked at him with pity. 'I wish I could scoop out that awful thing in your head. I really do. What it's doing to your mind. Dreadful.'

'But about your father . . .' Tom prompted him to continue.

'Daddy?' Oliver picked at a loose thread of cotton on his trousers but made it worse and gave up. 'He tried everything the Paleys offered,' he said. 'There wasn't much more he could have done. Perhaps nothing would have placated him in the end. He was a proud man, you see.

176

And to have been taken away from his work like that made him terribly angry.'

'What do you mean?'

'I told you this, didn't I? That the medical board suspended him?'

'Go on.'

'There'd been accusations made,' said Oliver. 'About his competence in theatre. Some fatalities. There was an inquiry underway when we came here. It was all very upsetting for him. He felt somewhat persecuted. Anyone would.'

Tom didn't like to ask if the allegations had been true.

'My mother thought that it might be better to get him away from London for the summer while it was all going on,' said Oliver. 'He took some convincing, mind, I can tell you. Didn't want to let them have the satisfaction of hounding him out. That kind of thing. He was adamant he'd done nothing wrong. He was determined to prove it too. He was all for going back and stating his case, as it were. But my mother managed to persuade him to stay. She promised him over and over again that he'd soon feel better. I think she truly believed it herself. She always saw the silver lining, as I said. Even when Daddy had his spells of, well, I was going to say that mania might be too strong a word, but perhaps it isn't. Caused a bit of a disturbance here in the Castle, I have to say. Up and down the corridor shouting in the middle of the night. Mally was at the age when such things are mortifying. Packed her bags at one point.'

On the film, she'd been practically seething.

'Doesn't sound like much of a holiday,' said Tom.

Oliver laughed, though without any humour.

'My mother tried her best to make it so,' he said. 'She'd extract Lucas and Mally when Daddy was at his worst. Take them out somewhere. The circus was always a good distraction.'

'You didn't go with them?'

'No, I felt rather sorry for Daddy,' Oliver said. 'He only wanted someone to talk to. And so I listened. But what he believed was real and true, Tom. Dear God . . .'

He realised that he'd drifted into uncomfortable territory and was glad to encourage Tom to answer his phone when it went off. It was Angeline.

'*Through the air she flies to thee, O wingéd love,*' he said.

'I won't be a moment,' said Tom and he went out of the room to take the call.

Angeline's voice was distorted and fragmented and eventually cut off. Since she'd phoned *him*, he thought it acceptable to ring her back, which he did and heard her saying, 'Tom? Is that you?', before the line broke up again.

The signal wasn't always reliable where she was and he was in a far-flung corner of the country here himself, and, thinking that he might get better reception in the open air, he unbolted the porch, then the outer door – now also on the latch to keep out Mr Calmine – and stood at the top of the steps. The rain had passed over again but the

178

fearsome wind off the sea would bring more soon. It carried with it the rank smell of the river with a sour, briny piquancy added to the rot. The tide was coming in. He could hear the water rumbling over the mudflats and the bells of the marker buoys, now afloat, clanking faintly in the blackness beyond the railings.

Wishing that he'd put on his coat, he tried Angeline again, but there was nothing, not even a dialling tone, and he decided to wait and let her have another go from her side. Hopefully, she'd made a decision.

If she were to say yes to coming over to England and if he were to persuade Oliver to stay with him too, they might meet one another. It gave him pleasure to think of them in the house together. Angeline would adore Oliver. And he would fall in love with her. But both of them would have to be willing to give something up before that happened. Oliver, his meekness, Angeline her preference for keeping the past where it was.

Might she feel more comfortable seeing him on home turf? Tom wondered. If, when he spoke to her, she was still unsure about coming here, why didn't he suggest going there? He wouldn't impose on her family; he wouldn't even need to see them if she didn't want him to.

It wasn't out of the realms of possibility to fly across to Crete. The insurance might set him back a bit but it wasn't as if folk in his position didn't do more reckless things. Hadn't he read about someone with a brain tumour who'd sailed the Atlantic? Or had they climbed the Eiger? Sitting in economy for a few hours with a newspaper and a crossword book would hardly be taxing. No different to sitting on the train to Saltwash. Yes, it had worn him out, but he was still here.

To swim in a clean sea, to feel the sun again, to get out of cheerless England for a while and winter in the warmth, it was all very appealing.

If he were to seek advice about whether any of this was a good idea at the next Living Now meeting in a few days' time, he had no doubt that they would tell him to go. They all felt sorry for him being on his own. They didn't like to think of him waking up in the night with only his terrors for company. It was a sympathy that came with a dash of disbelief, which may or may not have been a suspicion of a dark past. He really had *no one* but an ex-wife overseas? No kids?

He'd felt it incumbent upon him to explain to them why he'd never had children. It hadn't suited his lifestyle, he'd said. He'd not wanted the responsibility. He'd thought of children as burdens not future companions.

Had he allowed his child to live, he or she would have been forty-five, no forty-*six* by now. Hopefully with Angeline's looks and not his. Did she ever try to picture this ghostly son or daughter? Or was it too painful? Surely part of the reason she'd taken herself off to foreign climes never to return was to try and leave such thoughts behind.

If he made it to Greece, he might not come back either. That thought appealed too on a night like this. He could wend his way through the Aegean islands as he'd done years ago in his bachelorhood and stop at Milos, Kimolos, Serifos and Kythnos and the like – places that had stayed with him as dreamlands of white sands and lazuline water. There, time passed so slowly that the shaggy-faced god Oliver had tattooed on his hand might still trot about the warm cypress woods, seducing all with his flute and his wild eyes. Oh, he'd happily go with him, thought Tom, and disappear into the trees for ever.

A pair of headlights appeared some distance away down the promenade and a car approached with a stately progress. When it came closer, Tom could see that it was a sleek, expensive-looking beast (he was no expert on makes and models) liveried in a bespoke colour of green.

As it pulled up at the kerb outside the hotel, Mrs Paley came out buttoning up her overcoat.

'If you want a cigarette,' she said, as she passed Tom, 'could I ask you to go out into the yard at the back? We like to keep the front door locked.'

'I was just waiting for a phone call,' Tom said.

But, with her point made, she wasn't interested in his reply and increased her pace down the steps to greet the man who was getting out of the passenger side of the car. A squat, middle-aged gentleman in a mackintosh, large in the face with thick black hair tousled by the gusts of wind.

'I'm sorry I'm late,' he said. 'Titus is so cautious these days.'

He glanced back at the driver, a shadow at the wheel.

'Well, come inside,' said Mrs Paley. 'I'll get the chef to bring you some food. We'll be starting the draw shortly. Can I take that for you?'

She gestured at the large attaché case he carried.

'I can manage,' he said, and followed her up the steps.

'Make sure the door is shut when you come back in, won't you, Mr Shift,' Mrs Paley said, and held it open for the newcomer, who gave Tom a chummy smile and went inside.

The members of staff who happened to be there as Mrs Paley led this Mr whoever-he-was down the lobby stopped to let him pass and seemed almost on the verge of giving him a bow or a curtsey. He was some local dignitary, maybe. He had a chauffeur after all. One who had his orders to wait out here in the cold.

Another squally front blew in from the estuary, bringing rain that fell as hard as spikes. The coastguard must have decided that the weather tonight was likely to add to the swiftness of the incoming tide as the sirens went off with an undulating sound, like the warning of an air raid.

If Angeline were to call him now, he'd never be able to hear her voice above the wailing noise, and if he stayed out here he'd be soaked, and so he cut his losses and went back into the lobby, closing the door hard behind him.

Anoushka was on the lookout for him and came over with her dog pattering after her.

'There you are. It's Oliver,' she said. 'He's taken a turn. Will you come?'

He followed her back to the lounge where a small crowd had gathered – Petula, Connie, the Fishwicks and Anoushka's two friends who sat on either side of Oliver, one holding his hand, one taking his temperature with her palm on his brow.

'Do you think you might have a cold, Oliver?' she said. 'Or is it flu? You were so wet when you got here, I wouldn't be surprised.'

Oliver was grey in the face and sweating.

'I'm quite all right,' he said. 'It's just the air, it's rather heavy. I'll be as good as new in a moment.'

Barnaby cut through those standing around and handed Oliver a glass of water.

'That's good of you, old son,' he said.

'Do you want to go and lie down?' asked Tom. 'Why don't I take you to your room?'

The others thought this a good idea.

'It's passing, it's passing,' Oliver said.

'You look ever so pale, though,' said Petula. 'It might be best if you did put your feet up.'

'I can't go now,' Oliver said. 'They'll be starting the draw soon.'

'Not until eight,' said Connie. 'Go and rest for a little while.'

Oliver sipped some of the water. 'Perhaps you're right,' he said, signalling for Tom to help him up.

Petula took his other arm.

'My things,' he said. 'Would you be so kind?' and Tom collected his coat and hat.

They took the lift and ascended to the sound of grating wheels and pulleys. In the cramped space, the smell of Oliver's body was spicy with sweat. It could be that he really did have a fever. He'd be susceptible to catching all kinds of viruses. Prone to this acute enervation.

Here at the Castle, he was in safe hands. There were people around to help. But if he were to collapse somewhere alone late at night, he'd end up as one of those tragic news stories. *Man found by cleaners* or *Man found by dog walker.*

That he'd been knocked sideways just now, for whatever reason, might have actually done him a favour, though, thought Tom. The truth about how frail he really was had come out at last. It would be harder for Oliver to argue that he was well enough to look after himself when the opposite had been made so publicly manifest. In which case, he might be persuaded to accept the offer of a room. He could stay until Christmas in the first instance and see how things were. And in the new year, they could . . . No, thought Tom, he didn't want to leap too far ahead.

Truly, he was dreading January. When it rolled around to what in all probability would be his last year alive, the one they'd chisel on to his headstone, the omega to his alpha, he'd really start to feel it, he thought, the inescapable downward slope. He'd be sickeningly aware of doing things and seeing things for the last time. The spring would come to his garden in successive swathes of flowers – snowdrops, celandine, daffodils and bluebells – and then pass away for ever. Then the summer would arrive, similarly doomed to end. He might not even know that it *was* summertime if his mind fell in on itself like Victor's.

Oliver must have thought about all this too and shuddered. There had to be moments when he was alone and a quote or a quip wouldn't cut it. There was, Tom suspected, an Oliver he hadn't yet seen. An Oliver who was baffled and resentful and petrified by what was so rapidly approaching him.

At the fourth floor, the lift came to a halt and bounced gently before the doors opened. Out on the landing, the flock wallpaper was peeling off in tongues and the carpet worn away in places to its hessian backing. The few wall-lamps that were working illuminated a row of small paintings – salvaged from the church by the station perhaps – which showed various martyrs in their moment of sanctification, anointed by

185

celestial light. Paul, Augustine, Matthew and other exultant, awestruck sinners accompanied them down to Oliver's room at the far end of the corridor.

'Here I am. The old haunt,' he said.

'They put you in the same room every year, do they?'

'It's the one Lucas and I shared when we came. Mally was next door. And my mother and father across the way just here.'

He stopped at number forty-eight and looked it up and down.

'All the years I've been coming back,' he said, 'I've never quite managed to pluck up the courage to knock and ask to look inside. Perhaps I ought to while I'm here. I won't get another chance.'

'If it were me,' said Tom, 'I'd leave all that where it is.'

'Wise old owl,' Oliver said. 'You may be right.'

'Come on. You're shivering,' said Tom. He gave Oliver's arm a tug and eventually he moved away. 'Where's your key? I'll get the door.'

Oliver's room was sizeable, even quite plush, but dingy because of the low-watt bulbs in the bedside lights and the dark William Morris-style wallpaper. It hadn't been redecorated for a long time and the ingrained smell was an amalgam of lavender perfume, wet socks and old tobacco.

A bay window overlooked the promenade, where the rain was turning the streetlamps along the front into hazy globes of light. The road already looked like a river. The tardy visitor Mrs Paley had let in might come out to find his car and his driver floating away. The tidal siren went on and on, insistent that an inundation was looming.

Tom foresaw that his own journey home would be problematic too. It didn't take much for the trains to grind to a halt.

'Shall I close the curtains?' he said. He could feel a draught coming from the window frame somewhere.

'I suppose you should. It sounds tempestuous out there,' said Oliver, and eased himself into an armchair by the bed.

Like all the other pieces of furniture, it was enormous and made the room seem smaller than it actually was. A sensation that was exacerbated by the number of ornaments and trinkets, urns and figurines crammed into the space.

By contrast, Oliver was neat and unobtrusive. His paisley pyjamas were folded on the eiderdown and the rest of his things locked away in a large leather suitcase held together with the kind of blue twine that washed up on the riverbanks here. On the dressing table was a cardboard box with PROPERTY OF OLIVER KEELE written on the side, and a small white birdcage – though the two budgerigars were nowhere to be seen.

It was inconceivable how he managed to cart all this about.

As if suddenly beset by a chill, Oliver sat forward rubbing the cold out of his hands, even though he claimed to be faint from the heat.

'Let me get you a blanket,' said Tom.

'No no. I'm fine,' Oliver said. 'Just a little something from the drinks cabinet will suffice.'

He meant the cardboard box.

Tom undid the flaps and after pulling out the half-drunk bottles of port, gin, brandy and some coagulated cream liqueur, the supermarket Scotch seemed the least offensive.

'There should be two glasses in there as well,' said Oliver.

There were. A pair of heavy, chipped tumblers wrapped in newspaper a decade old.

'When you're on the road a lot,' said Oliver, 'I think it's always nice to offer those you meet a drink. I've had the most interesting conversations you can imagine over a drop of something wicked on a train. It's how I met Spike. Such a dear man. I miss him a great deal, you know, Tom. I often find myself thinking about him and where he went. Somewhere better. I can console myself with that.'

Did he mean heaven? Tom hadn't considered that Oliver might be religious. He'd never asked him directly. Perhaps he saw the Creator in all things. God was the spirit in the grain that made the spirit. He accepted the whisky with reverence anyway.

'Don't stand on ceremony, old boy,' Oliver said. 'Do help yourself.'

188

Tom shook his head. 'I won't, thanks.' The ache in his brain was stirring again.

'Well, amen,' Oliver said, and raised what Tom had handed him before taking half of it down in one go.

Wiping his wet nose with the back of his hand, he buckled into a wheezing cough and took a handkerchief out of his pocket.

'You should really see a doctor,' said Tom.

'A doctor? There's no hospital for miles,' Oliver replied. 'And it's late too.'

'Go in the morning then. I'll get the Paleys to call you a taxi. I'll pay.'

'And what will a doctor tell me that I don't already know?' said Oliver. 'Anyway, I've places to be.'

'Have you, though?'

'The work won't come to me,' Oliver said.

'But what if you didn't need to work at all?'

'I have to keep the wolf from the proverbial, dear boy.' Oliver frowned and then laughed softly to himself. 'Ah, we're back to that, are we? The charitable donation.'

'But you must have thought about what you'll do when things accelerate,' said Tom.

'And by that you mean?'

'When it starts to get the better of you.'

'It?'

'Don't be obtuse.'

189

Oliver smiled and took another mouthful. 'It'll get the better of me whatever I do, wherever I go,' he said.

'Then wouldn't you prefer to be somewhere comfortable when it does?' said Tom.

'I'm sure I'll find a place to lay my head. I've had rather a lot of practice.'

'Look, Oliver, I've been thinking,' said Tom. 'If you won't let me give you any money, then why not come and stay with me for a while?'

'At your home?' Oliver said.

'Yes. At my home.'

'I couldn't do that. What a terrible imposition I'd be.'

'I wouldn't invite you if I thought that, would I?' said Tom. 'I've a spare room. Two spare rooms. You can take your pick. Stay for a week or two or however long you want, as my guest, as a lodger if you'd prefer to think of it that way. You can pay me in bloody magic tricks for all I care.'

'No no.'

'I could do with someone around who has a better memory.'

'Oh, mine's going too,' said Oliver. 'I'd be no help.'

'I'd like your company more than anything,' said Tom.

'And I yours, but . . .'

'But what, for God's sake?' said Tom.

Oliver reached out for his hand. 'You dear thing,' he said. 'I don't like to see you upset like this. What's getting to you?'

'It's just that if you're going to refuse my help, then I'd like to know why, that's all,' said Tom. 'That's only polite, isn't it?'

It was a low and cynical blow to land. Oliver would be crushed to think that he was being rude, and Tom felt contemptible for insinuating it.

'I simply don't understand why you're so hell bent on all this fuss,' said Oliver.

'I'd like to do a decent thing for someone I care about.'

'You don't have to prove your goodness to me, Tom.'

'But can't you just allow me to be kind to you? You take a free night here. You accept the Paleys' generosity quite happily. Why not mine? What's the difference?'

Oliver gave him no reply.

'Well, if you won't let me put a roof over your head, what about your brother?' Tom said.

'Go and stay with Lucas?' said Oliver. 'All that way?'

'It'd be a few hours on a plane.'

'But there's the cost, old thing.'

'I thought Lucas was living his best life in the sun,' said Tom. 'I'm sure he'd stump up the air fare.'

'I don't do too well in the heat, love,' said Oliver. 'And I'm not sure that a Middle Eastern diet would agree with me. I mean I ate what young Abdullah cooked when we shared rooms in Hastings, but it was too rich for my constitution, really. Still, you have to be polite, don't you? It's considered the height of bad manners to turn your nose up at food in their culture.'

191

'How about Mally then?' said Tom. 'If you don't want to travel so far.'

'We'd have an awful lot to untangle first,' Oliver said.

'So, make a start.'

'That's easier said than done, Tom.'

'But you've nowhere to live.'

'On the contrary,' Oliver said, nodding towards the curtained window and dark, vast England beyond, 'I've got everywhere to live.'

The joke fell flat, and he sipped his drink.

'They don't know that you're ill, do they?' said Tom. 'Lucas and Mally.'

The answer was evident in the way that Oliver agitated the whisky in his glass.

'I'm not sure they'd be interested,' he said.

'But you *must* tell them, Oliver,' said Tom. 'Whatever's happened between you, they'd want to know, wouldn't they?'

'I have to commend your confidence in the power of forgiveness.'

'What is it they need to forgive exactly?' said Tom.

'Oh, *if we had but world enough and time,*' said Oliver, sitting forward in his chair. 'We really should go down now, Tom. I feel much better.'

'You can tell me, you know,' said Tom. 'I think it's half the reason you invited me here, isn't it?'

'No, not at all, old boy,' said Oliver. 'I wasn't thinking of myself whatsoever. Only you, Tom.'

'And yet here we are.'

'Yes, here we are.'

Oliver sank what remained of his drink and after a long breath in and out, he said, 'You're right, Tom. I know I should have explained it all in my letters. It bothered me that I wasn't being entirely open with you when you were being so honest with me about Angeline. But then I didn't want to ruin the good opinion you had of me. I don't want to ruin it now, as it goes.'

'You won't.'

He looked cynical about that and asked for another helping of Scotch. Tom poured him a finger's width and Oliver turned the glass in his palm in contemplation for a while.

Outside, the tidal siren ceased and its echoes sounded around the distant edges of the estuary. But the rain went on, pelting the windows, lashing the promenade.

'You think you can see things so clearly when you're young, don't you?' said Oliver. 'You think you're the only one who knows right from wrong. Aren't we rudely awakened from that little delusion? What is it Sextus says? *Virtuous youth, thy lesson awaits?* Never a truer word.'

He wiped some grubbiness off the rim of the glass, and Tom gave him time to formulate what he wanted to say.

'After what Daddy told me here,' Oliver said, 'I knew that the inquiry was going to end badly for him. There was no doubt about that.'

'So, he *had* made mistakes in surgery?' said Tom.

'Yes, well, no,' Oliver said. 'Not as far as he was concerned, at least.'

Tom took a second to grasp what he was implying.

'You mean he'd been deliberate?' he said.

'Oh, completely.'

'Why?'

Oliver went back to cleaning the glass. 'I don't know how to explain it so you'd understand. The only thing I can say is that he thought he had a responsibility to remove certain people from the world. He believed that they'd been brought to his operating table for that purpose.'

'When you say remove . . .?'

'I think you know what I'm talking about, Tom.'

'But which people?'

'How were they chosen, you mean? He started receiving communiqués in the post. Descriptions of who had to be dispatched.'

'Communiques from?'

'Himself, Tom. He showed them to me. They were all in his handwriting.'

'Didn't he recognise it?'

'Apparently not.'

'He didn't remember sending them either?'

'No.'

'And what did it say in these letters? What had these people apparently done?'

'It was more about what they were *going* to do.'

'Which was what?'

'Awful things. The worst things,' said Oliver. 'Daddy had their futures all mapped out. He went over everything again and again.'

'Christ, Oliver.'

'He just wanted someone to listen, as I say.'

'Even so . . .'

'You have to remember that he thought what he was doing was right, Tom. He was someone who set great store on duty. If he thought that he was being tasked with such a thing, then he'd have acted upon it. Do you see? It didn't matter whose life he'd been asked to end. Not even if it was someone in his own family.'

'You mean Lucas?'

'Quite.'

'What crime was he supposedly going to commit?'

'Don't ask me for the specifics, Tom. I'd rather not say.'

Oliver rotated the glass in his hand again, then drank some more.

'It sounds as if a hospital would have been the best place for your father,' said Tom. 'Not a hotel.'

'Maybe. I didn't think so at the time,' Oliver said. 'I couldn't bear the thought of him being locked away. I don't think he would have understood why. He didn't know that he was ill. It would have been very distressing for him. For all of us. He *was* my father, Tom. It's all very well for you to say that he should have been slung into the madhouse.'

'There's no need to get upset,' said Tom. 'None of that happened.'

'I know, I know. I'm sorry.'

'It didn't come to that in the end.'

'No,' said Oliver. 'It didn't. I made sure of it.'

'What do you mean?'

'I mean I didn't let it get that far.'

'You told me that your father died of a heart attack.'

'He did,' said Oliver. 'I brought it on.'

'Brought it on how? Don't be ridiculous. He died in his sleep.'

Lifting the whisky to his lips, Oliver changed his mind about drinking it and put it down on the bedside table.

'I didn't plan any of it, I can assure you,' he said. 'And if my mother had been around then it wouldn't have happened at all. But she'd taken Lucas and Mally out somewhere for the evening. The cinema, I think. Or maybe the circus. The three of them were very keen on seeing the dancing horses. They were Arabian. Or Russian, maybe. No matter. Who cares about the details, for heaven's sake?

'The point is, I was on my own,' he continued before Tom could interject. 'I said I'd stay behind to look after Daddy while he slept. He'd been so out of sorts that I thought it best if someone was there when he woke up. His lungs were often bad in the evening too and I wanted to listen out for him.

'It must have been about eight when I heard him coughing in his room. Choking, I should say. It happened sometimes. He couldn't quite catch his breath, you know? Like someone was strangling him.

'He was in an awful way when I went in. Such a mess all over the sheets. There's no dignity in being ill, is there? I mean I tried to help him clear his chest. There was a way of beating his back that loosened things up a bit and gave him some relief. And that was my first thought, Tom, to help him, nothing else, believe me. But all he wanted was his handkerchief. He'd left it on the dressing table, you see, and so I took it to him and I held it to his mouth. And then I . . . I kept my hand there, if you understand what I mean.'

He stopped and regarded his tattoos and then rubbed his thumb into his palm.

'You know the thing that surprised me most,' he said, 'was how weak Daddy really was. It was all so quick. As soon as I'd started it was done. And then I couldn't take it back.'

Tom put his hand on his arm.

'No, you mustn't feel sorry for me,' said Oliver, raising his voice in a way that Tom hadn't ever thought he'd hear. 'You must call me what I am. At the very least I'm a coward. I couldn't even do the decent thing and turn myself in. You see now why I can't accept anything from you. I wouldn't blame you if you were to walk away and have nothing to do with me ever again. Lucas and Mally were perfectly within their rights to do so.'

'They know, do they?' said Tom.

But Oliver was too agitated to listen and picked up the Scotch again and finished it.

'Every year I beg myself not to come here,' he said. 'And every year I come anyway. I even think I'll have the courage to refuse the prize if I were to win, but I know that I wouldn't. So what am I saying to everyone? That I deserve it? How repulsive.'

He'd got himself quite breathless and as Tom began to say something, he held up his hand.

'No, just give me a moment, please.'

Tom took the glass from him and went to rinse it out in the bathroom.

He stood at the sink, trying to absorb what he'd been told, searching for something that Oliver might have overlooked all these years. It couldn't have happened in the way that he'd described it. Surely there was some mistake. An obvious hole in the story.

Could Oliver be certain that his father hadn't simply had a heart attack from the coughing fit? He might have been suffocating before Oliver went anywhere near him. He might have been beyond saving anyway.

But Oliver had surely considered these questions himself and discarded them as mere wishes. That he'd been weighed down by repentance for so long meant that there was no doubt in his mind that he was to blame. To him, not even the fact that he might well have saved Lucas's life was enough to justify or excuse what he'd done. And it hadn't been enough for his brother and sister either.

He must have told them at some point, hence their disowning him. Maybe he'd told his mother too. Maybe at the time. Or she'd realised what he'd done. And that was why it had been decided to keep Oliver's father in Saltwash and draw a line under it all, as Oliver had said. There had to have been a good reason to do so.

If that was what had happened, then burying the man here hadn't made any difference. Not to Lucas or Mally. Certainly not to Oliver. He'd never got over it. Sixty years on, he was living out of a broken suitcase and hefting around a box of booze in case the need for sudden hospitality arose. He wore a perforated hat and had splits in his shoes and wrapped his wash things in bits of cling film: a toothbrush with limp bristles, a disposable razor mended with electrical tape, a cracked pebble of soap.

How on earth could he just walk away and leave him to cope by himself? thought Tom. No, the time had come to act, not withdraw. The time had come to take charge if necessary. If he had to pressure Oliver into admitting that he required help, then so be it. Being cruel to be kind was sometimes the right thing to do. Sometimes it was crucial.

*

When he went back into the bedroom, Oliver was blotchy around the eyes and pale in his lips. But he had the two budgerigars sitting on his hand and seemed to have pulled himself together.

'Lovely little things, aren't they? I bought them from a psychic on the seafront at Margate,' he said, stroking them in turn. 'She'd get one bird to choose the tarot cards and the other to turn them over. She was always very popular.

'You know, even after all this time I still can't tell them apart,' he said, looking at the birds more closely. 'I shall have to decide what to do with them soon, of course. Give them away or let them go, though I'm not sure that's for the best. They're still things of the tropics when all's said and done, and I'm not convinced they'd thank me if I were to send them off to fend for themselves. Mind you, they're tougher than they look.'

'Oliver, I really don't want you to be alone tonight,' said Tom.

'*Solitude sometimes is best society.*'

'Why don't you come back with me on the train?'

'And not stay for the draw?'

'It sounds like it only upsets you.'

He shook the birds free and they flew into the cage, twittering over the sound of the rain outside.

'I'm fortunate to have been invited here in the first place,' he said. 'It would be an insult to Spike's memory if I didn't participate. A snub to the Paleys too, since they're so kind. Humanitarians, really.'

Tom helped him to his feet and he used the furniture for support as he went to lock away the budgerigars.

'Lord, I really ought to change,' said Oliver, plucking at the sweat patches on his shirt. 'You con't mind, do you? Pick me out something clean. There's a good chap.'

Tom undid the knot in the rope arcund his case. It was the only thing keeping it closed and he had to prevent the neatly folded contents from tumbling out. Contrary to what Oliver had said, there was no money inside.

There wasn't much in the way of clothes to choose from either, and all of them were threadbare, but Tom selected two things that he thought might go together – a cream-coloured shirt and a red-and-yellow tie – and laid them down on the bed.

Oliver, distant and self-absorbed after his confession, was having difficulty undoing his buttons but eventually he managed to strip down to his vest and Tom saw that his tattoos extended up both forearms. A ferocious-looking Hindu goddess on one, and an ouroboros on the other. Smaller images were distorted and indecipherable among the wrinkles. He must have lost weight rapidly and relentlessly, as his skin looked as if it was made of punctured balloons, and his trousers were held up by a belt that had been re-holed at least twice.

Time was well on with its rigorous demolition work. His joints were as pronounced as knuckles. His torso covered in

201

bruises, rashes and sores. On his neck just below the collar line were scars from what appeared to have been fairly recent operations. Was that where his cancer lay?

Tom helped him on with the new shirt, attempting to ignore the acrid odour of his body, and then did up the tie for him as best he could. It was hard to know which way to fold and tuck when it was on someone else.

'*Merci. Trop gentil*,' said Oliver, as he turned down the wings of his collar. 'How do I look? Acceptable for decent company? Well, it'll have to do. There's no time for miracles. We should head downstairs, otherwise they'll be starting without us. I'll take your arm, if that's all right.'

He seemed older than he'd done even an hour ago and never more in need of someone's care. The admission he'd made about his father had only made him more insecure. It hadn't been cathartic. It wasn't as if he'd now feel cleansed. Nothing he did or said would ever grant him any clemency. He thought it craven that he'd never handed himself in, but a stretch inside wouldn't have made any difference. He wouldn't have come out feeling as if his debts had been paid.

They went out on to the landing, and Oliver directed Tom to the paintings on the walls as a distraction from having to look at the door of the room opposite, his father's room.

'I've always had a great deal of time for Augustine,' he said, as they passed the bald saint, haloed and weeping.

'Have you read his *Confessions*? There's more or less a whole chapter about him stealing pears as a boy. Seems such a tiny thing, doesn't it? But then that's the mark of the truly righteous. No sin is too small to be overlooked.'

~

The lobby was silent as they got out of the lift. After the music and the raucous conversations, after the boisterousness in the bar and the gluttony in the dining room, the entire hotel felt as it had done when Tom had first arrived.

'The best of luck,' said Oliver, with a hand on Tom's back. 'I wish you every success. I really do.'

'Same to you,' replied Tom, although it was hard to share his enthusiasm when the prize itself was still so mysterious.

'I have a feeling you'll do well. I've an intuition for these things,' Oliver said, and neatened himself with a quick tug of his shirt sleeves. 'I knew Spike would win last year and he did. I've never seen anyone quite so overjoyed. Well, I showed you the photograph, didn't I? He'd had such a hard life. It was only right that the prize went to him. Everyone agreed.'

'I'm sure they'd think you a worthy winner too,' said Tom, and Oliver welled up, as if he could hardly bear the flattery.

'Ah Tom,' he said. '*You pour such blessings upon me, my brother, and though I merit none I must believe you have the keener eyes and see beyond my faults.*'

203

Tom opened the door of the lounge for him, and the others welcomed him back with nods and touches as he passed among the chairs and sofas. If anyone spoke at all it was to ask him in brief whispers if he was better. The room had the atmosphere of a church before Mass was about to begin, the congregation receptive for the Word. For every person waiting keenly, ticket in hand, there was someone else deep in contemplation. Victor was fixated on his lucky rabbit's foot as Connie rubbed the back of his head. Barnaby, sitting with the beaming Fishwicks, mopped his moustache with a handkerchief and stared at the number he'd exchanged with Tom. Even Petula was silent. She looked queasy, from the drink or the anticipation or both.

She made room for Tom on one side and Oliver sat down on the other offering her his hand, which she held against her cheek.

There wasn't a malicious bone in his body, was there? There never had been. With his father, he'd not acted out of aggression but on an impulse of pity. Or love, really. But that wasn't something Lucas and Mally could see. Or perhaps they didn't want to see. Who was to say *what* they thought about all that?

Tom wondered how it would be if he were to write to them on Oliver's behalf. Not to criticise or harangue them, only to inform them of their brother's situation. It couldn't do any harm. They could hardly ostracise him any more than they already had. Indeed, he felt certain that, if they only knew how unwell Oliver was, it might make them open to compassion.

If they still couldn't find a way to rationalise what he'd done, then that was understandable, but they might at least appreciate the depth of his remorse and help him bear the weight of it, rather than adding to it. Or was that being terribly naive?

The door opened and the hotel staff filed in to watch the draw. Chefs, *plongeurs*, housekeepers and the two Paley sisters lined up against one of the walls. Charlie brought up the rear, took his place alongside those in dirty kitchen-whites, and looked on disdainfully as his parents rolled in something like a bingo caller's contraption, a large spherical cage on wheels, half-filled with black wooden balls. At its arrival, the mood of the room heightened to a mixture of elation and unease.

For Anoushka, it proved too much, and she went out with her barking dog clamped to her chest. Her two friends scurried after her telling her to hold on, that it would be all right. The others watched them leave; some half stood as if they might go after them out of concern. But there was no time for worrying about anyone else's misgivings now.

With a loud peal of the bell she'd used to mobilise everyone to dinner earlier, Mrs Paley announced the start of the draw. Then with her schoolmistress look, she stifled the last murmuring voices, smiled in that artificial way of hers, and turned to the clock on the wall behind her, waiting for the second hand to reach the hour.

When eight o'clock came, she began to wind the crank handle on the side of the machine. For a full minute, exactly a minute, she kept the balls churning and tumbling and eventually brought the wheel to a halt.

Standing back a couple of paces, she nodded to her husband who produced a black silk blindfold, positioned it over her eyes and tied the straps at the back of her head.

Once he'd checked her from all angles, assured that she couldn't see anything, he took a small key from his shirt pocket and unlocked a trapdoor on the cage. Then, after bringing her forward and guiding her hand into the gap, he moved aside so that everyone could see that all was fair and above board, invigilating her himself as she rummaged about.

Tom had to marvel at the solemnity. Not only the strictness of the procedure itself, but how serious everyone else deemed it to be. What prize necessitated such formality?

Having selected one of the balls, Mrs Paley stepped away with it in her fist and Mr Paley closed up the door in the wheel and locked it. With the key back in his pocket, he removed the covering from his wife's eyes.

Around the room, people shifted and coughed and looked at their numbers once more. Some were praying, hands steepled, eyes closed. Some held statuettes of Jesus or pressed crucifixes to their hearts.

Connie hung some sort of bronze amulet around her neck and then put her head on Victor's shoulder while he petted his own little talisman.

Barnaby sat back, sat forward. Petula, gripping Tom and Oliver's hands, stared up at the ceiling. Oliver himself ran his thumb slowly back and forth over his lips.

Satisfied that everyone was suitably on edge – this was the moment of excitement they'd come for after all – Mrs Paley looked at the ball she'd picked out, looked up again, and scanned the faces all turned in her direction. She ought to be on the stage, thought Tom, the way she milked the drama so proficiently.

Then, 'Eleven,' she said, holding the ball above her head and turning this way and that. 'Eleven.'

The lowing of disappointment was broken immediately by Petula crying out, 'It's Oliver! Oliver's won.'

She lifted his arm in the style of a boxing referee, and like someone reeling from a bruising bout in the ring, Oliver seemed thoroughly bewildered. He gazed at his ticket, not quite taking anything in, even as Tom reached over and touched his hand and Petula pecked at his face with kisses.

'It's you,' she said. 'After all this time. It couldn't have gone to anyone better. Thank Christ.'

It was a curious thing for her to say and the way she sat back in the sofa with a long breath suggested that, while she was thrilled at Oliver winning, she was more relieved that she'd lost.

And there were other strange reactions as Mrs Paley led the applause. There wasn't a universal contentment with the result. While most of the guests got up and made their way over to Oliver to offer their compliments, some of those who'd stayed seated tore up their tickets with great bitterness and others broke down in tears. Connie being one of them.

Her anguish was aggravated by Victor's laughter. He didn't care whether he'd won or not. He had no idea what was going on. When she shrieked at him to stop, it only made him laugh all the more and she suddenly leant over and pinched his cheek. That was enough to make him wail and, after knocking off the brake and yanking him backwards, she took him out of the room, ordering him to be quiet.

'Perhaps I should go after them,' said Oliver, as he watched them leaving.

Petula kept him in his seat. 'They'll be all right,' she said.

'I don't like to think of it ending like this, though,' said Oliver. 'There shouldn't be any ill feelings. I'll speak to them.'

But before he could get up, the Fishwicks came forward to congratulate him.

'We're made up for you, Oliver.'

'We had a feeling it'd be you.'

The man with Gladstone's nose reached in and pumped his hand. 'It's wonderful,' he said. 'To see someone so kind get rewarded.'

Oliver accepted the adulation but, like everyone else, he'd become diverted by another voice, high and distressed, which eventually cut through the chatter.

'Twelve years I've been coming here,' Barnaby was saying to Mr Paley. 'Twelve bastard years, and all I see is other people winning.'

Mr Paley turned to his wife for help.

'Mr Collins,' she said and waited for him to look at her. 'Mr Collins. You could come back here as many times as you like and still not win. You know that.'

'But the draw tonight wasn't fair,' he said.

'Everything was done by the book.'

'I mean, he took my number,' said Barnaby, pointing at Tom.

'He didn't take it. You swapped,' Petula corrected him.

'Well, I didn't want to,' said Barnaby. 'He caught me on the hop. I wasn't thinking straight.'

'You wouldn't have won even if you'd kept the ticket you first picked out, you idiot,' Petula said. 'So what does it matter?'

'That's not the point,' Barnaby retorted, and then fumbled around to find it. 'Look, why was she even allowed back?' he said, flinging his hand at Petula. 'She ought to have been barred like Eric Calmine. She could have ruined

209

it for all of us after last year. You need to send her home and do the draw again. That'd be fair.'

'Mr Collins, if you didn't win,' said Mrs Paley, 'then I can only say that I'm sorry. But the draw's over and that's that. You'll have to come back next time.'

'And what if I can't?'

He pushed his way through to Oliver.

'Please,' he said to him. 'You can see that none of this is right, can't you? Get them to start again. Don't take the prize.'

His last request incited a barrage of indignation from those around him. He couldn't ask Oliver to do that. Who did he think he was? No one liked a sore loser. And yet, for a moment, it looked as if Oliver might give in, until Mrs Paley called on her husband to bring the argument to an end. With a surprising tenderness, he put his hands on Barnaby's shoulders and started to coax him towards the door.

'But all the work I've done,' Barnaby said. 'All the calculations I've made. It *should* have been sixty. Why wasn't it sixty? You see here, the last two numbers have been sixteen and fourteen . . .' He took out the piece of paper from his pocket and showed it to Mr Paley, running through his arithmetic once more as he left.

'Good for you, Oliver,' said Petula. 'I'm glad you didn't listen to him. The right person won. Don't let anyone tell you otherwise.'

On that point, there was consensus among those encircling Oliver. He thanked them but glanced at Tom with a flicker of shame. As he'd said up in his room, when it had come down to it, he'd not been able to bring himself to decline the prize. Whatever it was.

'We'll take your photograph now, Mr Keele,' said Mrs Paley. 'If you would, please.'

'Ah, yes, of course, of course,' Oliver said, and, with the help of his entourage, he got to his feet and went to sit in the chair among the fake delphiniums and gladioli.

Mrs Fishwick and a host of other eager women went to work on him immediately, straightening his collar and his tie, smoothing down the front of his shirt and arranging his hands on his knees. It wouldn't have come as a surprise to see him lauded with hosannahs, thought Tom. Or fanned with palms.

As Mrs Paley positioned herself behind the camera, any traces of unworthiness or doubt left Oliver's face, and he smiled in a way that Tom hadn't seen until now. When they hung his photograph here on the wall, he'd be among those, like Spike, who'd been euphoric at winning.

'I still don't understand what the prize is,' said Tom, as he and Petula looked on.

'You will,' she said. 'They won't make you wear that badge for much longer now.'

A surge of cheers and whistles arose. Oliver was standing again. People were shaking his hand and patting him on the back. On the other side of the room someone began to breathe into a harmonica, a man with a spine so bent that he played the instrument somewhere close to his navel.

The Fishwicks obviously recognised the tune he was trying to get out and started singing 'For He's a Jolly Good Fellow'. As everyone joined in, Mrs Paley touched Oliver's arm and spoke to him confidentially. He nodded, swallowed, acknowledged what she wanted him to do and when the song ended she swung the bell again and called, 'That's all, ladies and gentlemen. It's time now.'

She went to the door, held it open, and waited for Oliver. Everyone gravitated towards him again, embracing him, cupping his face. Petula muscled her way through and hugged him tight, like a little girl unwilling to let her father leave. Once she'd held him for as long as she could, she backed out of the clinch wiping her eyes, and others took her place. It got to the point where Oliver couldn't move for the amount of people wanting to wish him well. Not only the other guests but the staff too – apart from Charlie, that was, who'd already extricated himself.

Amid the swell of affection, Oliver kept on looking at Tom and when he had a moment he put out his hand to bring him over.

'You'll come with me, won't you, old boy?' he said. 'I'd like you there.'

Where 'there' might be, Tom didn't know, but as they edged across the room, it was 'All the best, Oliver' and 'Take care of yourself', as though they weren't going to see him for a while.

Anoushka had returned, having overcome the jitters that had made her bolt earlier, and she and her friends were the last to see Oliver out. 'Well done,' they said. 'Enjoy it.'

'We'll miss you,' said Anoushka, with one hand on his chest. 'And don't say that you'll miss us too. You won't. You'll forget all about us, you lucky thing.'

'Yes, I suppose I will.' Oliver smiled and ruffled the little dog behind the ears. It licked his wrist and was still whining for him when he and Tom went out and Mrs Paley closed the door of the lounge.

'This way,' she said, and made off down the lobby. Oliver put his arm through Tom's again and they followed.

'You know, I often wonder what happened to that terrier of mine,' said Oliver. 'He was a clever thing. An integral part of the act, to be honest. People loved him. But it wouldn't have been fair to keep him when I couldn't look after him. I had half an idea that I might buy him back when I had the means, but trying to find him again would have proved difficult. He could have been anywhere. Perhaps I'll have another dog when I get to where I'm going. I don't see why not. All things are possible.'

He was blethering again, as he'd done in his letters, but was even more animated and excited, like a child about to go off on holiday.

'Is that the prize, then?' Tom asked. 'A trip away somewhere?'

'A trip?' said Oliver. 'No. It's more than that.'

'Just here,' said Mrs Paley as she stopped at the door marked PRIVATE, unlocked it and let them both in.

~

The windowless room was without decoration, white-painted and softly lit. On one side was a large tweedy armchair and, next to it, a low table with some bright purple flowers in a vase. Against one of the walls was a square desk with a manila envelope propped against a jug of water. If it was Mrs Paley's office, it was austere, though that seemed fitting. Or it might not have been an office at all, as the linen that Charlie had brought in before dinner sat on a shelf, carefully folded.

Mrs Paley indicated that Oliver should sit. With Tom's help he eased himself into the wingback chair.

'You can take off that badge now, Mr Shift,' Mrs Paley said. Tom unfastened the pin and handed it back to her. She put it away in a pocket of her dress and drew up a stool to the desk.

'I can hardly believe I'm here,' said Oliver. 'I never thought it would happen. I've never been that lucky. Or is it luck at all? I don't know – is it too presumptuous to call it fate?'

Not wishing to be drawn into idle chatter, it seemed, Mrs Paley took it as a rhetorical question and got down to business.

214

'I won't keep you any longer than necessary,' she said. 'There's just some paperwork to complete.'

'You'll want everything just so, naturally,' said Oliver.

'It's easier if we have all the information.'

Mrs Paley opened the envelope and took out a sheet of paper printed with what looked like a set of questions.

'Any valuables?' she asked, clicking a biro with her thumb. 'Jewellery? A watch?'

Oliver touched his wrist. 'No,' he said. 'Nothing like that.'

'Cash?'

'A little. What I earned in tips earlier.'

'What would you like to do with it?'

'Oh, I don't mind. Put it in a charity box.'

'But don't you need to keep it?' said Tom. 'What are you going to live on?'

Oliver seemed to find the question rather comical and said, 'That doesn't matter now.'

'Did you bring any luggage with you?' said Mrs Paley.

'Yes,' said Oliver.

'How many items?'

'Three. Various things.'

'And do you want your possessions to be passed on? Or are we to dispose of them?'

'Oh, dispose, by all means. They're of no use to anyone else, I'm sure,' said Oliver. 'Though I'm hoping that Tom might be willing to take the birds, at least. Is that possible, old boy? I know you have cats.'

'Sorry?' said Tom.

'It's just that I'd like to know that they're with someone I trust.'

'What are you talking about?'

'I shan't be around to see to them myself.'

'Why not?'

Holding Tom's hand, he said, 'This is it. I'm making my exit. Signing off. Bringing things to an end.'

'Bringing things to an end? I don't understand.'

'That's the prize.'

'What is?'

'The opportunity to bow out.'

'Is this a wind-up?' said Tom.

'No, of course not,' Oliver assured him.

'Is it a joke you play on newcomers or something?'

Perhaps all the puerile subterfuge everyone had practised upon him since he'd got here had been leading to this. Though he couldn't think what the punchline would be.

'It's a very quick procedure,' said Oliver.' Very peaceful.'

Mrs Paley acceded to this. 'A few minutes and it's all over,' she said.

'You're not serious?' said Tom.

'Never more so,' replied Oliver. He seemed genuinely elated by the prospect.

'And what are they going to do to you, exactly?' said Tom.

'When you put it like that, you make it sound monstrous, old love.'

'Well, isn't it.'

'If you'd just let me explain . . .'

But Tom rounded on Mrs Paley. 'What is this?' he said. 'What the hell's going on?'

Without looking up from her sheet of paper, she said, 'May I remind you, Mr Keele, that you vouched for your friend. I trust there aren't going to be any problems.'

'No no,' Oliver insisted. 'Tom, try to understand.'

'Understand what?'

'Look, I'm touched that you're worried about me,' he said. 'But everything will be all right now. That's the whole point.'

'Oliver, no. Whatever it is you're going to do,' said Tom, 'it's not the answer. You know that.'

'Are you going to tell me I've everything to live for? You're a dear man.'

'Christ almighty, what have you put into his head?' Tom remonstrated with Mrs Paley again. 'It's sick. You're sick.'

'Mr Shift,' she said. 'If you're going to be aggressive, then I'll have to ask you to go outside. Mr Keele ought to be allowed to prepare himself in peace.'

'Please, Tom. She's right,' said Oliver.

'I don't know what they've promised you,' Tom said. 'But leave with me now. We'll call someone.'

'Call who?'

'The police, obviously.'

'And what would you tell them?' Mrs Paley said.

'What you're doing here.'

'Which is?'

Without the details, Tom faltered.

'We're not harming anyone,' said Oliver. 'No one's here under duress. Believe me. Who are you trying to protect?'

'You,' said Tom. 'Who do you think? This is wrong, Oliver. Anyone can see that. I can't be the only one who's ever said so.'

'No, we've had others,' said Mrs Paley. 'They were as confused as you the first time they came.'

'I'm not confused,' Tom said. 'You're inviting people here to die. By lottery? That's right, isn't it?'

'They wouldn't come if they didn't want to,' she said. 'And it's entirely up to them what they choose to do to their bodies. They can decline if they win.'

'Then he declines, don't you, Oliver?' Tom spoke for him and tried to lever him up off the chair. 'Didn't you say that you wanted to refuse the prize? What happened to that?'

Mrs Paley edged herself back from the desk as if to get to her feet. 'Mr Keele, would you like me to fetch my son and my husband?' she said.

'No need,' said Oliver, removing Tom's hand from his wrist. 'No need.'

'If you want him to stay, Mr Keele, then he must be calm,' said Mrs Paley. 'The doctor won't be able to see you otherwise. He can't work if he's going to be disturbed.'

218

'It'll be all right,' Oliver replied. 'You'll keep your thoughts to yourself, won't you, Tom? For me?'

When Tom relented, Mrs Paley returned to her questionnaire.

'Next of kin?' she said.

'A brother and sister,' Oliver replied.

'Would you like us to inform them?'

'Someone should, yes.'

'Address?'

Oliver could only give his sister's, of course.

'Now, about your remains,' said Mrs Paley. 'I don't know if you have a strong preference.'

'Burial,' said Oliver.

'Here? Or elsewhere?'

'Here. In the same place as my father.'

'And you're happy for us to make all the arrangements for the funeral?'

'Perfectly happy.'

'We'll liaise with the coroner about the death certificate,' said Mrs Paley. 'It'll say, "Natural causes", the same as always.'

'Yes, whatever's best.'

She slotted the paper back into the envelope, sealed it, and stood up.

'Is there anything you'd like to collect from your room before we start?' she said. 'Some people like to have something sentimental with them.'

'I'm not sure I have anything that means that much to me,' Oliver replied. 'Present company excepted, of course.'

Mrs Paley gave Tom an uncertain look. 'The doctor won't be long,' she said. 'I'll be outside if you need me.'

Before she left, Oliver took her hands and brought her close to him. 'I can't thank you enough,' he said. 'I can't tell you what this means to me. Bless you.'

She waited for his gratitude to run its course and then went out.

Once she'd gone, Oliver pre-empted Tom's consternation.

'Now, you really mustn't think ill of the Paleys,' he said. 'They're kind people. They always have been.'

'But you can't seriously believe that what they're doing here is right.'

'Right?' said Oliver. 'There's no moral question to answer.'

'No moral question? They've got a doctor in on it.'

'He offers a service, that's all.'

'And a coroner faking death certificates.'

'That's just to satisfy the bureaucracy.'

Tom brought the stool over and sat down. 'You don't really want to do this, do you?' he said. 'How can you?'

'I'm tired of being punished,' Oliver said. 'Aren't you?'

'You don't have to carry on flogging yourself.'

'Tell that to my conscience.'

'What happened with your father hurts. How could it not?' Tom said. 'But for what it's worth, I don't think any less of you. That's something, isn't it? I know you're not a bad person.'

'And if I were to say the same to you, would it make any difference?' said Oliver.

'Listen,' Tom said. 'Why don't I write to Mally? I'm sure it'll do some good.'

'I doubt that very much,' Oliver replied.

'Can't we at least wait and see what she has to say? You might be surprised.'

'You don't know her like I do.'

'Lucas then?'

'I'm not sure he even thinks of me as a brother.'

'But neither of them would want you to go through with this any more than I do. If they were here now, would they really let you finish yourself off? They wouldn't want to see you in pain, would they?'

'But it won't *be* painful, Tom,' said Oliver, as if that were an irrational, accusatory thing to suggest. 'I've never known anyone here to experience any kind of discomfort. The Paleys wouldn't allow us to suffer.'

'I just don't understand how you can be so indifferent about it.'

'Because I'm only giving up a body,' Oliver said. 'It's rather had its day, don't you think? And it's not *me*, as such, anyway. I'll still be there afterwards. Consciousness lives on. It can be made to *move* on. Somewhere better.'

'Oh, please.'

He sounded like Astrid.

'Do you really think that this is all there is?' said Oliver. 'Do you think that because you've only known one life, there can't be any others?'

'Of course there aren't any others. Things are as they are.'

'But see, Tom,' said Oliver. 'That's not how it is at all. There isn't only one truth. There are endless realities. Somewhere, there's an Oliver Keele living out a far better existence than this one. A perfect existence. It's just that I've never been conscious of it. I've only known the life *this* version of me has had to go through. And there's a Tom Shift who never did all the things you feel so terrible about.'

'Are you actually listening to yourself, Oliver?'

'But imagine being him, Tom. Wouldn't that be better than trying to find forgiveness? Oh, you can't see it, can you? It's hard, I know. I know. I struggled myself the first time I came here. I only wish that I could give the prize to you. Then you'd know what I mean.'

Oliver's belief in all this gibberish took Tom back to the fanatics he'd met years ago in the Bible Belt; people for whom demons and archangels were as real as tractors and pigs.

'And what if there's nothing afterwards?' Tom said. 'You can't know that you're going to go anywhere. All you're doing is crossing your fingers. It's no different to scrubbing yourself with mud and hoping that'll wipe the slate clean.'

'We've come on some way from that, Tom. It's wonderful what they can do now with chemicals. Miraculous really. The Paleys have always championed the sciences, as I told you.'

'Chemicals? Which chemicals?' said Tom.

Not really listening, Oliver went on, voicing his thoughts as they came. 'I only wish that Daddy had been able to have the same chance as me. I wish he could have come here now. But he was born at the wrong time. Well, we all are in one way or another, don't you think, Tom? Nothing ever quite works out. I'm just sorry that we're parting so soon after we've met. I can't tell you how much it breaks my heart.'

'Then come home with me,' said Tom. 'There's a train that leaves at nine. I'll go and fetch your things. We'll get a taxi to the station.'

'My place is here, love.'

'But just stop and think about what you're doing.'

'Tom, I've thought about nothing else for years,' Oliver said. 'You can be sure of that.'

There was a knock at the door.

'That'll be the doctor,' said Oliver. 'You must let him do what he needs to do. I'm quite resolved, Tom. There's nothing you can say to talk me out of it. You'd be wasting your words.'

'I can't just sit here and watch,' said Tom.

223

'But I'd rather not be on my own, old boy. Look, if you really want to do something for me, then stay. Please.'

The door opened and the man who'd been driven to the hotel earlier lingered on the threshold with his leather case.

'Mr Keele?' he said, and Oliver nodded. 'Are you ready to see me? I can give you another minute or two if you need it. I heard you talking.'

'No, no,' said Oliver. 'I'm happy to start. *The longer thread of life we spin, the more occasion still to sin.* Do you know Herrick? *Gather ye rosebuds while ye may* and so forth?'

This doctor, so-called, smiled at the chitchat as if he was used to it and closed the door.

He was oddly proportioned. His head seemed too big for his body. His hands were unnaturally wide. There was something so ungainly about him that Tom found it hard to believe that he was a doctor at all. Who would want to be examined by him? But more than that, it was his manner. The way he grinned as he took off his jacket, he came across as nonchalant about what he was here to do. Facetious even. One of those people always on the verge of cracking a joke.

Setting down his case on the desk, he opened the catches and said, 'Will your friend be staying?'

'I'm in the process of persuading him,' said Oliver.

'Well, while he's deciding, perhaps I should begin?'

'By all means.'

'So long as you're ready?'

'Quite ready.'

He took out a square of blue cloth and laid out the apparatus he needed. Dressings, wipes, gauze, cannula.

He sensed Tom staring at him.

'It's all very straightforward,' he said. 'I could do it blindfolded.'

Oliver indulged the doctor's humour, but to boast that he had plenty of experience was abhorrent, thought Tom.

'You see,' said Oliver. 'Nothing to worry about.'

The doctor began assembling the tubular pieces of an aluminium stand.

'For the drip,' he said.

'What are you going to give him?' said Tom.

'Would the formula mean anything to you?' the doctor replied.

'It works, Tom,' said Oliver. 'That's all that matters.'

With the stand connected together, the doctor placed it next to Oliver's chair, and then rubbed antiseptic through his meaty hands.

'May I?' he said, gesturing to Oliver's sleeve, and proceeded to unfasten the frayed cuff. 'That's fine work,' he said, admiring the tattoos.

'When you're a magician,' said Oliver. 'it pays to cultivate a certain mystique. Or so I've found.'

'And who's he?' the doctor asked, lifting Oliver's hand to look at the being with the bearded face.

'Ah yes, him,' said Oliver. 'The beast. The darker half.'

'Well, it looks like he's hiding a willing vein,' said the doctor and laid Oliver's hand down gently on the arm rest before going back to his case. 'You're not bothered by needles then, I take it?' he continued, shaking free a pair of surgical gloves from a cardboard box.

'Me? No,' said Oliver.

He regarded the images on the backs of his hands, and the names LUCAS and MALLY pricked so unskilfully into his papery skin.

'I suppose this other Oliver will look very different to me,' he said. 'I've always pictured him as a teacher; a college fellow. It's what I would have ended up as if I'd stayed on at Oxford, I'm sure. Dean of something or other. He'll be retired, of course, but I like to think that he's one of those dons who can't quite give it all up completely. Still cycles across the Meadow to give the odd lecture now and then. What do you think?'

He looked over at Tom.

'Oliver, this is insane. Don't do this to yourself,' Tom said in a last-ditch attempt to get him to see sense.

'Let's not part on bad terms,' said Oliver. 'I know you wouldn't want to. You're a good soul, Tom. I'm sure Angeline will see that too before long. You will take my birds, won't you? Look after them for me.'

Before Tom could speak again, Oliver stopped him with a look of entreaty.

'Don't say anything else now, love. *Man comes wailing into life, let him depart in peace.* Who said that? Was it Sophocles? I forget. They're pretty. Are they hyacinths?'

He touched the petals of the flowers beside him and then after a little hesitation he sat back as the doctor tied a tourniquet around his forearm.

'I'll have to ask you to give up your chair now, my friend,' the doctor said to Tom. 'I'll need to be in the driving seat.'

Tom got up, standing back a few paces with Oliver's eyes set on his.

'A slight scratch now,' said the doctor and fitted the cannula to the back of Oliver's hand. Once it was inserted, he taped it down and then hung the bag of what Oliver was about to receive from the hook on the stand. A dark brown tarry substance, like sludge taken from the estuary.

'You might feel a little nauseous or light-headed, but it won't last long,' he said, and unfurled the tube that would connect up this bladder of whatever it was to Oliver's bloodstream.

With one end coupled, the liquid began to run down the line and the doctor flicked at the plastic to get rid of the air bubbles before locking off the flow.

'It can make your mouth feel dry at first,' he said. 'Perhaps your friend might like to get you something to drink.'

'Would you, Tom?' said Oliver.

Confounded by what was happening, half in a trance, Tom brought over a glass of water as the doctor was attaching the other end of the tubing to Oliver's hand.

227

'Thank you, old boy,' he said, and took a sip, and after returning the glass to Tom he settled into the chair and closed his eyes. The doctor opened the valve on the line, looked at his watch, crossed his legs, coughed quietly, and monitored the drip as if it was perfectly routine for him to sit there and kill someone.

The linen on the shelf, Tom realised, would be used as a shroud.

Oliver became so quickly inert that he seemed to have fallen into unconsciousness straight away, but after a few moments he re-awoke with a sharp inward breath and smiled as though he'd been surprised by something wonderful.

Tom had never seen an expression of bliss quite like it before. He could only think of the paintings of the martyrs upstairs on the landing. Like them, Oliver was overawed and exhilarated. He broke out laughing and crying with the kind of ecstasy that could only come from knowing, truly knowing, that all the horror was over, and deliverance was on its way.

All that had happened one day six weeks ago. Since then, the rest of November had passed by in spells of freezing fog, and December had been dispiritingly mild and damp.

Very quickly, it seemed, Christmas had come and gone, and in the days afterwards the temperature had dropped enough to stiffen everything in hoarfrost. Now, on the last day of the year, the late afternoon was cold and raw and fading into a beetroot sunset.

It being a Wednesday, the Living Now meeting had come around again and although it had coincided with New Year's Eve, Astrid still wanted the group to get together. It was a night of endings and beginnings that she thought symbolic and fruitful to commemorate, and she had emailed to say that the session would start earlier than usual so that those who wanted to could head off to see friends and family afterwards. She'd bring sandwiches and cake. Or had she requested that *they* bring sandwiches and cake? Tom couldn't remember. He wasn't hungry anyway.

To try and work up an appetite, he'd planned to walk to the hospital by way of the park but had persuaded himself out of it in the end and called a taxi. It would still be icy by the cricket pavilion and if he'd been forced to go tentatively to avoid slipping, he might well have found himself in darkness by the time he'd reached the gates on the other side.

In truth, he wasn't sure he'd have made it on foot at all. No matter how determined he was to think otherwise, things had started to change lately. The excuses he'd come up with – he was just more tired than usual, he'd not eaten much today, his shoulder was giving him gyp – only sugared what he knew to be true. His strength was leaving him. He'd turned a corner.

His memory had deteriorated by another increment. The number of notes he'd put up had increased along with the importance of the imperatives. *Drink some water. Feed cats. Feed yourself.*

He was tired all the time. Bone weary and yet unable to sleep for very long. On some days he'd been confined to the sofa or his bed by a migraine so unrelenting that it had felt as if someone was slowly sawing his skull in half.

He was restless and on edge, especially in the evenings, when he was too engrossed in his thoughts and couldn't distract himself with a book or a radio programme or one of his jazz records. And those bloody budgerigars of Oliver's chittered on and on.

He'd put them in a back bedroom on a high shelf out of reach of the cats, but he could still hear them, even now as he put on his coat and scarf down in the hallway. Even after he'd closed the front door behind him they were audible, though it might just have been a figment. God, it was birds nesting in the brain now, was it?

He was glad that the taxi driver didn't want to talk much. After an exchange about the weather, the journey proceeded in silence past heaving pubs and closed-up shops, past factory walls and regenerated mills.

He'd gone about these streets countless times but recently the buildings and landmarks that had once been as familiar and innocuous as old furniture had started to make him feel irritable. And sometimes it was just intolerable to be amongst the people who lived here. For they belonged to the world that would continue after he'd gone. They wouldn't notice that he wasn't there. He'd be like Icarus in the Breughel painting. But that would be his fault, not theirs. You were always too far away, Tom, they'd say in their defence. We didn't know you.

At the junction by the Methodist church, the driver turned left into the hospital grounds, his prayer beads swinging from the rear-view mirror, and took the route that ran past A & E.

The entrance, so often lined with ambulances, and usually frequented by folk in dressing gowns smoking furtively, was deserted. In fact, the whole place was quiet. The casualties from parties and punch-ups would start to stream in after midnight, Tom supposed.

He wondered if he might still be up himself at that time. Given his raging insomnia, there was every chance that he would be wide awake at twelve, but he hoped not. He didn't think it would do him much good to see in the new year. But there was nothing he could do to stop it. Time went ruthlessly onwards. How could it not? Its momentum was an unalterable fact of the universe, and according to one of Astrid's favourite adages they should take comfort in its impartiality. Everything was heading in the same direction. All things shared the same fate.

Maybe that was the kind of thing he needed to hear tonight.

The Kübler-Ross unit was around the side of the main building – a bland, two-storey concrete box that they'd tried to make pretty for the season by spraying the windows with pictures of bells and holly leaves, and hanging lights over the door. Before the diagnosis, he must have seen it from the road so many times and never given a second thought to what went on inside. Now it was familiar to him.

Tom paid the driver and accepted his help getting out of the back seat. The thinly bearded fellow looked as old as

he was; still working, the poor sod. He smiled sympathet-
ically at every grimace Tom made and insisted on escorting
him all the way inside, calling him sir and mister, and refusing a tip for his assistance.

That he'd even contemplated walking here earlier on
seemed ludicrous. Right now, the possibility of *ever* doing so
again felt remote. Even something as simple as a stroll
through the park might soon become a luxury of the past,
something that he ought to have recognised *as* a privilege
when he'd been capable of appreciating it. But that was the
lesson everyone learned too late, wasn't it?

Once through the automatic doors, the driver left him with
the lady behind the desk and went back to his car, satisfied
that Tom was in safe hands should he stumble or expire.

'It's nice to see you, Mr Shift,' the receptionist said.

He couldn't bring her name to mind even though he'd
seen her plenty of times before. Julie, Julia, Jackie? She
could do to wear a badge.

She opened the inner sanctum of the clinic with a tap
of her lanyard on the sensor. He smiled at her and went
slowly down the corridor into the oppressive warmth and
the smells of liniment and floor polish. Beyond the large
abstract paintings – in which Acceptance and Stillness and
Peace were represented as swirls of blue and green – he
passed the offices of the various oncologists who specialised
in end-of-life care.

A Mr Sheppey was his consultant: cold hands, kind eyes, apt to use cricketing metaphors to help conceptualise the tumour's unpredictability. *We're at the crease facing Anil Kumble, Mr Shift. We don't know which way the ball is going to spin from one delivery to the next. All we can do is expect the unexpected.*

It was a slightly silly sort of bedside manner, but Tom appreciated the suggestion that they were in it together.

He should make an appointment to see him, he thought. He'd been instructed to keep him in the know about any changes that occurred.

It couldn't be coincidental that this quickening feeling of deterioration had begun since he'd returned from Saltwash. He was certain that the physical weariness and insufferable pains in his head had come about not only from some new aggression on the tumour's part but from being forced to think so interminably about what had happened to Oliver. Or rather it was the exhaustion of *not* knowing what to think or feel that was wearing him out.

After leaving the Castle that evening back in November, he couldn't recall much about the train journey home, only that it had been long and slow because of the weather and that, when he'd finally climbed into bed that night, he'd not slept until hours later, so thick were his thoughts, so incessant was the chirruping of the budgerigars he'd brought back with him.

The next morning, the gnawing anxiety had become an urge to tell someone. It felt like the right thing to do, if only to absolve himself from any wrongdoing. Weren't there specific laws about concealing a crime? To do so would have made him as culpable as everyone else at the Castle.

He should have been braver. He ought to have ripped the line from Oliver's arm and spirited him away. He ought to have dashed the doctor's gear to the floor and remonstrated with the Paleys – and all the others there at the hotel come to that. Standing there in that room, silent and shaken, simply watching, he'd as good as aided and abetted, hadn't he?

And yet when Angeline had phoned him later that day, apologising for not getting back to him sooner, he'd said nothing, even though she was the one person he might have counted on for sound advice.

How on earth would he have phrased it, exactly? That he'd been invited into a death cult at a seaside hotel? That they held a raffle to decide who got an armful of poison?

He could have insisted that it was all true, he could have sworn to what he'd seen, but it would have come across as so outlandish that she'd have thought it was the tumour talking and have encouraged him to call Mr Sheppey rather than the police. It would have unsettled her, whichever way she'd taken it. It wasn't something he'd felt it fair to drag her into. And as he'd decided to keep it to himself then, he'd done so since. The moment had gone anyway. Angeline had withdrawn her services.

The Oak Room, where the Living Now group met every week, was lively with conversation. When he went in, Astrid looked over and came to him with a smile.

She was half his age, thin, white-blonde, always in a lace-edged pastel-coloured dress: she seemed to be made of gossamer somehow.

'Tom,' she said, squeezing his hands with her long fingers. 'It's so good to see you. Give me your coat. Go and get a drink and something to eat. You've got a few minutes before we start.'

She took his anorak and went to hang it up. The others milling around the buffet table welcomed him back into the fold.

He'd not attended any meetings since coming back from Saltwash, and, although absences were never questioned, they all wanted to know how he'd been, how his Christmas had gone. 'Quiet,' he replied. And had anyone been in touch with him? 'My ex-wife sent a card,' he said.

A card and a letter – one that had all the intimations of a goodbye. She'd said again how sorry she was for him. Sorry that it had come to this. She hoped that she'd been some help to him and that he felt that his affairs were in good order. She gave him her best.

I do forgive you, Tom, she'd put at the end. There had been no elaboration. And perhaps it was the brevity that made it seem less than genuine. She was only telling him what he wanted to hear, giving him the line that would satisfy him well enough to let her go.

'Here, how was your day out with your pen pal?' asked Brian, bloated and berry-faced, no eyebrows. 'What was his name again?'

'Oliver,' said Tom. 'Oliver Keele.'

'What was he like?'

'Good company,' Tom replied.

'Will you see him again, do you think?' Monali said, and offered him the last of the shortbread biscuits, which he declined.

'I don't know,' said Tom.

'Of course,' she said. 'How long has he been given?'

'He didn't say,' Tom replied.

Now the gravel-voiced Alec chipped in. 'Didn't he want to meet you somewhere odd? Somewhere by the sea?'

'Oh, that's right,' said Celia with the missing teeth. 'Where was it again?'

They were interested in him, which was nice, and they meant well, but he wished that he'd never mentioned going to Saltwash to anyone else.

He just wanted to forget about it and let what had happened there recede into the past. He'd let some distance develop. He'd try to think of Oliver as someone he'd been twinned

237

with by nothing more than misfortune; someone he'd barely known, regardless of his long and frequent letters; a sad and troubled man with self-made tattoos on his knuckles; a dishevelled eccentric with whom he'd spent a few hours one wintry evening.

It seemed unreal now – the Castle, the Paleys, the doctor, Connie, Victor, Barnaby, Petula, and all the other guests in their brash regalia. His memories of it were unnerving, like the memories of watching an obscene pantomime full of grotesques and buffoons.

But the invitation to Oliver's funeral that had come through the post and those little blue birds remained as evidence that he really had been there. The budgerigars might even be incriminating. Perhaps he should let the cats at them after all, thought Tom.

Why had Oliver ever imagined that he'd want to participate in what the Paleys offered? Or that he'd find some comfort in the prospect of being able to end it all? Had Oliver really believed that he was going to buy into the drivel about being able to hop – via some chemical process – into an unblemished version of his life after death, which wasn't really death at all?

By that logic, Oliver was still alive somewhere in an alternate reality, a sprightly septuagenarian doyen of Classics cycling into some echoing Oxford quad with his gown flapping and his head full of ancient Greek.

The thought was clearly absurd.

But Tom had to admit that there had been times over the last few weeks when such a numinous idea had acquired credibility, especially during the fanciful narratives that came unbidden in the late hours of the night.

Lying in bed, he'd play out a scenario in which *he'd* won and not Oliver. He'd imagine that he'd gone to sleep in one body and woken up in another, resurrected as a Tom Shift who was free of perpetual self-reproach. One who'd never done Angeline or anyone wrong and had come into his old age without having to contend with any remarkable tragedies. He'd be married. He'd have children. Maybe grandchildren. All that he lacked now, really.

Yes, at three in the morning, he thought that if the chance of transmigrating to a life enriched with true accomplishments had been there for the taking, as it had been for Oliver, he'd have sat back too and allowed the doctor to do his work.

And perhaps this was the real reason he'd kept what had happened at the Castle to himself. A small part of him envied Oliver. One way or another, he was free.

Once everyone was ready to start, Astrid conducted them to the circle of chairs set out in the middle of the room. When they were all seated, they joined hands, and she led them in the affirmation with which she always opened their meetings – *I am, I am, I am.*

The meditation that evening was on the phenomenon of their existence. How miraculous it was that they were here at all. What an incredible run of good fortune their ancestors must have enjoyed. How shaky the couplings were that formed a family line.

It was true. When he imagined that long chain of mothers and fathers behind him stretching back millennia to farmsteads, to caves, to savannah, to primordial swamp presumably, he saw that it was held together by the flimsiest of links. It wouldn't have taken much for any of them to have snapped.

Had that hairy stone-age brute got on the wrong side of a lion, had that medieval forebear in the kirtle succumbed, coughing and pustular to the plague, had his own grandfather been killed in Flanders, then there would have been no Tom Shift at all. Of course, it had been nothing short of a fluke that Grandpa Cyril had made it through the war, and in fact there was a family story that he'd only survived because of rain.

The tale went that there'd been an offensive planned during which Cyril's battalion was to retake some blasted acre of quagmire. But even in a conflict typified by suicidal battle orders it had been decided that to send men out through three feet of mud in the midst of a deluge was an idiocy too far and the attack had been postponed until the weather improved.

As it transpired, the rain had been so relentless that the war had come to an end before the storm. Had it cleared up sooner, young Cyril and his pals would have charged a section of the enemy line which reconnaissance later revealed to have been bristling with many more machine-gun nests than first thought. He'd have been mincemeat.

So, in one sense, thought Tom, he was only here now in this room with these other people on this particular night in time because of an obstinate spell of low pressure over northern Belgium in the winter of 1918.

And that was only one of the reasons for his existence. There were surely many more that he had no conception of. All as farcical. All of which could so easily have gone the other way.

He was, as Astrid said, a product of pure luck. For each set of his antecedents to have survived long enough to pass on their genes was incredible when he thought about it. Yet, because of him, it was all coming to an end. He'd thrown away thousands of years of precious good fortune and blessings, and for what? Impending fatherhood had seemed such a crisis at twenty-nine but now his reaction to it smacked of hysteria. What he'd forced Angeline to go through at that clinic by the Thames seemed so impetuous and unwarranted.

They were dangerous things, young men. How easily *he* might never have come into being either, if someone before him had been as self-serving and reckless.

'We must remember that no one ever *chooses* to do anything,' said Astrid. 'Look back over your life and you'll see.'

Wasn't it liberating, she said, to think that a person simply *couldn't* have done anything differently at any point in time,

241

such was the way the universe had been configured in that moment. People were merely impelled one way or another by thoughts that arose from circumstances far beyond their control or understanding.

He'd never *wanted* to harm anyone, far from it, thought Tom. Not his mother, or Angeline, or their unborn child. Nor had Oliver killed his father out of any premeditated motivation. It had only occurred because certain things had given rise to its occurrence. In another alignment of events Oliver would never have had the opportunity to do what he did. Say his mother had been back from the circus with Mally and Lucas before his father had woken up. Say Oliver himself had decided to go out onto the promenade for some fresh air and had never heard his father hacking up his lungs. The tiniest of variations might have altered things completely. And that was Astrid's point.

Let go, was the lesson. Give up the guilt. There was no free will. But by that creed, no one was really culpable for anything. And where did that leave the human race? Wasn't it abominable to pardon sin on the grounds of some kind of diminished responsibility? Depravity, perversion, violence – was no one at fault for those things? Did no one scheme?

That was an illusion, said Astrid. No one could choose their way to triumph or gratification any more than they could choose their way out of catastrophe.

Everyone was just tangled up in the strange and arbitrary

happenings of the world. Everyone was simply dazed by the accident of being alive.

It was a thought that, to Tom, held the credibility of an essential truth.

In the moment, at least.

And then, like all moments, it was gone; the passing sense of absolution something he'd have to chase and find again before all thoughts were swept from him and taken away on the tide.

Acknowledgements

Thanks to everyone at John Murray for all their hard work on *Saltwash*, especially my fabulous editor, Jocasta Hamilton, for her enthusiasm and her ongoing support at every turn. Thanks to the wonderful Katharine Morris and Luke Brown for their meticulous editorial work. And to Sara Marafini, who has done it again and produced another iconic book cover. Thanks also to my amazing agent, Lucy Luck, for all her advice and encouragement throughout the writing process. And to Alice Graham and Anna-Marie Fitzgerald for marketing and publicising my work and connecting me with readers. I couldn't do any of this without such a fantastic team of people at my side. Lastly, thank you to my family and to Jo – always so astute, patient and understanding. *Nunc scio quid sit amor*, as Oliver Keele might say.

Published by Pigeon Park Press
www.pigeonparkpress.com

Chapter 1 – 1st June

It was all the mouse's fault. If I hadn't seen the mouse I wouldn't have got into trouble with Levi. If I hadn't got into trouble with Levi, Paulette wouldn't have kept me behind. If Paulette hadn't kept me behind, I wouldn't have gone into the wet apartment and been fined by Patrick Helberg. If I hadn't been fined by Patrick Helberg, I wouldn't have been late to work and wouldn't have met Rufus Jaffle.

It was all the mouse's fault.

***

"Good morning! Jaffle Tech incorporated – Complete peace of mind for a little piece of your mind. My name is Alice. How can I help you today?"

"I've got a problem with my settings."

"Yes?" I said as customer data flooded onto my heads-up. "What problem is that, Jackson?"

"I'm trying to take a look at my spare capacity usage. I look at what my usage is every week."

"Yes?"

"But now, every time I do, it tells me I need to do an update and agree to the new terms and conditions."

"Yes. And have you done the update? I can talk you through that if you—"

"No, I don't want the update."

"You don't want the update?" I said.

"No. If I have the update then I have to agree to the new terms and conditions."

"That's right. You just tick the box and hit agree."

"But I don't agree."

"Crumbs!"

The *Crumbs!* was for both the caller and for the little creature that I had just spotted in my cubicle. A mouse. Black eyes, dull fur, a tiny twitching nose. It perched on the back edge of my desk, just above the gap between the desk and the back board which separated my desk from the one opposite. The cubicles were designed to be free of distractions but this tiny invader had clearly not been briefed.

"I'm on the Jaffle Standard package," said the caller.

"I can see that, Jackson. Same as me."

"The new terms and conditions no longer say we can pick what our spare processing capacity is used for. I look at what my usage is every week."

"Yes."

"For example, it's currently being used for camera feed analysis in Newcastle."

"It is. Your spare processing capacity is being used to identify broken infrastructure that needs an engineer. Or it might pick up a person who needs medical assistance, for example."

"And I'm fine with that. That's lovely, that is. But if I agree to the new terms and conditions and they decide to use it for something bad—"

"Something bad?"

"Yes. I don't know. Something bad like ... like ... well, I can't think of anything bad right now but I'm sure I'd know it when I saw it. I'm just not happy."

The mouse's nose twitched, sniffing the air. It looked lost.

"Where did you come from?" I said.

"I beg your pardon?"

"Sorry, not you, Jackson—"

The mouse, perhaps aware that it was being talked to, vanished down the back of the desk.

"I mean, I see what you mean," I said.

I crouched to look underneath my desk. The mouse clung to the narrow cabling stalk at the back of the desk. Its pink claws reminded me of the Jaffle squirrels that worked in the parks. I reached forward tenderly to scoop it up but it darted away, to the ground and to the next cubicle along.

"Now, we could totally circumvent this problem if you upgrade to the Jaffle Enhanced package," I said, following the mouse as it scuttled past the desks of my colleagues.

The caller scoffed. *"Oh, I'm quite a long way from being able to afford that."*

Most people were. I made sure I kept the smile in my voice.

"I just don't want the update," said Jackson.

"I don't think that's possible," I said. "If you don't update then we can't provide you with an appropriate level of support or further, er, updates for your Jaffle Port."

"But I don't agree to the terms."

"But when you signed up, you agreed to accept routine updates."

"Did I? Where did it say that?"

"In the original terms and conditions. You hit agree."

"What are you doing?" said Hattie when I reached the end of the row. She was on a pause between calls.

I muted the caller a second. "I'm not doing anything."

On Hattie's screen was a picture of a Smiley Tot. Hattie pointed at the image. "It's a Smiley Tot."

"Yes."

"But it's a Smiley Tot."

"I know," I said.

"But it's so..." Hattie gave a shiver of pleasure. "Isn't it?"

"It's a Smiley Tot!" I unmuted the call. "Now, Jackson, you need to agree to the new terms and conditions to get those routine updates."

"But..."

"Yes?"

"You're saying that when I first agreed to the terms and conditions, I was agreeing to all future terms and conditions, even if I didn't know what they were?"

Hattie followed my gaze and bent to look under the desk.

"Don't," I muttered, but it was too late. Once glance at the mouse was enough to make Hattie leap onto her chair, quivering in shock. I tried to convey, with a few hurried gestures, that everything was going to be fine and I would sort it out. I had also completely forgotten what the caller had just said to me.

"Let's not lose sight of what you're getting in exchange for giving up your spare capacity," I said, blandly. "Your port gives you enhanced memory storage, memory export to other Jaffle Port users, direct access to entertainment media and learning resources."

"Oh, I know. It's lovely."

When the mouse ran on to the next row of cubicles, I trotted after it. This floor alone contained two hundred cubicles so, at this rate, it could be a long pursuit. I was no longer sure why I was following it.

"And much of your spare capacity is taken up with essential service software, Jackson," I continued. "That's your firewall, obscenity filters, system check, defragmentation and deep clean and,

of course, the all-important customer feedback data so Jaffle Tech can keep on making improvements for you."

"And I've been very happy up until now."

"Of course, you have. And, remember, the longer you are with us, the more your Jaffle rating goes up and that's vital if you're looking for a new job or applying for credit finance. Everyone loves a good Jaffle rating."

The mouse had come up against a wall and scurried along.

"And, what's amazing when you think about it, Jackson," I said, my mouth on full auto-pilot now, "is this is provided for you at absolutely no charge while you remain on the Jaffle Standard. It's Jaffle Tech's gift to the world."

"It is free, I suppose."

"And, rest assured, Jaffle Tech has the strongest ethical standards when it comes to what we use your spare processing capacity for. Jaffle Tech users are making the world a safer, cleaner and better place, even in their sleep. By signing over your spare capacity to us, you're being a hero, every minute of every day."

"No, yes, I suppose you're right," said the caller. *"It's just... it's my brain, isn't it?"*

"Of course it is. And what a wonderful brain it is too, Jackson."

There was a pause.

"Just tick the box and hit agree?"

"That's right, Jackson. Have a good day, now."

I killed the call. The mouse ran past a door which happened to swing open. I ran for it. There was a shout and a clatter.

In the elevator lobby stood Levi Krasnesky, the security guard. He had a plastic lunch box tucked under his arm, like a sergeant major's baton. He glanced at me before looking down at the base of the potted plant next to him. He stamped down hurriedly on something behind the plant pot.

"No, ya don't, you varmint," he grunted as he stamped. Two, three times.

I was out of breath and stunned to see him stamping on... "Did you?"

"Did I what?" he said.

I moved forward to look. Levi held up his hand to stop me. "Woah, hold your horses, miss. Not a pretty sight."

"I think you might have accidentally killed a mouse," I said. I wasn't sure what else could have happened.

Levi straightened up and tucked his thumbs into his heavy belt. He was not a tall individual – he was quite boyish looking, probably not helped by that reedy moustache he was trying to grow. He looked like he still had some growing to do.

"Oh, let me tell ya," he said, "that animal did not belong in the system."

"The system?"

"Oh, no. That animal was not even a part of the system. Therefore it did not technically exist."

"Really?"

"Now, do I or do I not run a very tight ship around here?"

I nodded, hoping that I was responding to the correct part of the question. I wasn't sure if there was even a ship for him to run. He was a security guard. Merely one component of the large security team at Jaffle Tech.

"Yabetcha," he said, "and did I just witness you running in the workplace?"

I considered the question. "I think you probably did, yes. You have cameras everywhere and you're always watching."

He liked that. "I am always watching. Yes, indeed. Heck, you are smarter than you look, It's Alice, isn't it?"

"Yes."

"You look smart but I gotta ask myself, if you were paying attention to my security awareness memos—"

"Are those the printed sheets you keep taping to the fridge in the staff rec area?"

"My security awareness memos," he nodded.

"Did anyone find out who stole Brandine's bagel?"

"Alice, I am not talking about Brandine's bagel. I am asking you why would ya disregard safety in the workplace?"

"I was dealing with … um." I accessed my Jaffle Port literacy booster. A millisecond of jipping and I said, "It was an anomaly."

"You were dealing with an anomaly and thought that you'd compromise the safety of all of your co-workers?" Levi said. He tugged on the peak of his cap tersely. "You would risk the lives of the six hundred people on this section alone just to deal with your anomaly?"

I enjoyed problem solving and spent a few moments trying to picture a scenario where me running between the cubicles might

result in six hundred deaths, but I came up blank. Before I could ask Levi he had begun air-swiping on his own heads-up display.

"Miss, it is your lucky day, don't ya know."

"Is it?"

"Yabetcha. We're scheduling a re-run of safety training module 5b during your section meeting later. Better that than add an infraction to your personnel record."

"Who's we?" I said.

"What's that?"

"Who's scheduled the training?"

"I have. Jaffle Tech site management have."

"Well, which one?"

He huffed. "Site management, which encompasses the security team which encompasses me. Ergo, we, that is I, have scheduled the training. Do I need to explain it further?"

"No," I said.

"I need ya to keep your head in the game for all of our sakes, Alice, so pay close attention, ya hear?"

Chastised, I returned to my desk, calling in on Hattie who was still staring at the floor as if the mouse might return at any moment.

"What was it?" said Hattie.

"A mouse," I said.

"I didn't like it."

"No. Something else you're not going to like. We've got a safety training session during the meeting this afternoon."

Hattie wasn't happy. "They're not going to show The Film again, are they?"

I couldn't lie. Instead I chose distraction. "That's a pretty Smiley Tot."

"Isn't it though?" said Hattie. "I'm thinking of putting it on my Want List."

"You have enough Smiley Tots," I said.

"You can't have too many Smiley Tots," said Hattie. "And this one has the sweetest little bonnet."

"Yes, it does and, yes, you can. You can't go into your bedroom without tripping over Smiley Tots."

"You haven't been tripping over my Smiley Tots, have you?"

"No, I'm simply saying—"

"Oh, I can't imagine how I'd feel if one of my Smiley Tots was hurt."

I thought about the squashed mouse. I hadn't seen it but I could picture it in my mind's eye. Picturing imaginary things didn't come easy if you were operating on Jaffle Standard but if the image was strong enough...

"Oh," said Hattie, fanning herself with her hand. "My tots hurt. And the shock of seeing that horrible mouse and— Oh. I feel properly discombobulated. Have my cheeks gone red?"

Hattie's cheeks were always red.

"Discombobulated?" I said.

"Literacy booster," said Hattie.

I nodded. "I just jipped the word *anomaly*."

"Anomaly," said Hattie. "Oh, that's fun to say, isn't it? A-nom-a-ly."

And with that Hattie had forgotten all about the mouse. I hadn't.

***

Chapter 2

The training room was set out with amphitheatre seating. The six hundred plus members of the section barely filled a third of the seats. Paulette, the section leader, took to the stage. Familiar images of Jaffle Tech products slid across the giant screen behind her.

"Yesterday, a Jaffle swarm in Yucatan foiled a kidnap attempt at a private school. Jaffle sharks patrol the Pacific, protecting our precious ships from enemy aggressors. This year, we broke the ninety-seven percent barrier. That's right. Ninety-seven percent of the domestic population use a Jaffle Port."

The audience started to clap.

I clapped enthusiastically. I didn't like to think about the other three percent. Most of them were the very old, born long before the brain port was invented and too stubborn to become adopters. But the rest, those strange few, were the ones who had refused the gift of the Jaffle Port: religious nutjobs, weirdos. I felt a mixture of pity and disgust for them.

"And," said Paulette, "this week marks twenty years since Jaffle Tech made the promise to give a Jaffle Port to every single new-born baby – a promise we've kept ever since."

The applause was ecstatic.

There was an access request on my Jaffle Port. I accepted the jip-request. With a sweep of her arm, Paulette cast hundreds of overlapping brain charts onto the screen.

"And look what good we're doing," said Paulette. "Sian Saunier." A woman whooped off to the left. "Your spare processing capacity has been working on the Near Earth Infrastructure Program."

There were approving murmurs around the room.

"Paul Obeng." Paulette acknowledge his handwave. "Monitoring traffic flow on the city interchanges."

There was well-mannered sounds of amusement.

"Hey, your brain might not be conquering the final frontier like Sian's but it's making our world a safer place! Hattie Rutherford. Wow. Working with international intelligence agencies to identify potential terrorists."

"My brain is a secret agent," said Hattie with deadpan cool and smirked. She and I smiled at each other with shared pride.

Paulette displayed a chart showing brain utilisation rates, and I was delighted to see that a certain Alice Tennerman was in the top five on the efficiency leader board. I leaned across to whisper in Hattie's ear. "You may be a secret agent but my brain's better."

Hattie pulled a face. "That data's probably just an anomaly. Anomaly. A-nom-a—"

"Shush."

"They used to say in the twentieth century," Paulette was saying, "that there was more content in a single day's edition of the New York Times than the average seventeenth century person was able to access in their entire lifetime. Now, we can say that the average Jaffle Tech enabled brain does more thinking and processing in a year than a non-Jaffle brain does in a lifetime. You are superheroes."

The staff clapped and cheered. Paulette held out her hands for calm.

"We have an important safety briefing this afternoon," said Paulette. "This is a mandatory refresher and—"

"Yes, thank you," interrupted Levi, stepping up onto the stage. He stumbled over the stage edge, gave it an accusing glare and put a swagger in his stride to compensate as he strode to centre.

"I thought we were just running the video," Paulette said to him.

"Yes, yes, thank you," said Levi. He turned to address the audience. "We're going to run the safety briefing but—" He wasn't in the right place for the microphones to pick him up. He stepped to the side and politely but firmly pushed Paulette away. "Name's Levi Krasnesky. I run security checks in your section. There have been some recent disturbing incidents in our very own workplace which have indicated a training need." He changed the screen. "Some very serious near misses, oh, yabetcha. Would you look at this? Jeez."

On the screen was a camera feed of an access space in the cubicle jungle. People walked back and forth.

"This fills me with horror," said Levi.

I squinted. There was nothing to be seen. People. Cubicles. A drinks machine. Levi zoomed in on the floor.

"A pencil," he said

There were a number of gasps.

I wondered where the pencil had come from. Physical stationery was fairly uncommon, and people tended to take good care of it.

"Stationery is forbidden for call operators," said Levi, "but apart from that, it's a huge risk for trips and slips, ya know."

Levi looked around the amphitheatre and tried to hold the gaze of every single person, which was a challenge in so large a space.

"Now, hold onto your hats, folks. This second incident was a disaster from start to finish. We had an unauthorised intruder in the section this morning. Instead of alerting the security team and remaining calm as per your training, an employee *in this very room* who shall remain nameless gave chase."

On screen, camera footage showed me in a crouched run, moving from cubicle to cubicle, peering under each.

"Wowzers," whispered Hattie.

"Furthermore," said Levi, "that unnamed employee was observed to be running in the workplace. Heck, I don't think I've ever seen recklessness like it."

Levi's eyebrows went up. He'd spotted me in the audience and gave me a nod of recognition. Shame washed over me.

"On top of that, call records show that the employee was talking to a customer for some of the time that she was running through the workplace." He swiped and audio feed played around the hall.

"Good morning! Jaffle Tech incorporated – Complete peace of mind for a little piece of your mind. My name is Alice. How can I help you today?"

"Ignore that," said Levi, fast-forwarding. "Ignore the names. This isn't about pointing the finger of blame."

"Where did you come from?" said my voice over the speakers.

"I beg your pardon?" said the caller.

"Sorry, not you, Jackson. I – I mean, I see what you mean."

"You see?" said Levi, stopping the playing. "Not only is Alice – I mean the nameless employee – failing to give the customer the benefit of her full attention, but she was also distracted from taking extra care while she put all of our lives at risk with her running. It is fortunate that I was able to intervene, and my skills and training averted a disaster, but if this were to happen again..." He sucked through his teeth and let the implications speak for themselves. "Now watch the film and take careful note of how far we've come," he said.

"I don't like The Film," whispered Hattie and gripped my hand in the dark.

Levi gave them all another stern look then stepped back into the shadows as The Film played.

I realised with a sinking feeling that I had seen this section before. Hattie had obviously recognised it too as she gave a small whimper and gripped my hand all the tighter. I forced her to pay attention, knowing that Levi would be watching her.

The Film had various titles and designations but everyone just called it *The Film*. When you mentioned *The Film*, everyone knew what film you were talking about.

I wasn't sure how old The Film was. It was in black and white – as though viewed through the eyes of someone on Jaffle Economy or Jaffle Lite – and the quality was very poor. I hoped that a vast gulf of time separated me from the unfortunate people who featured on the screen because their suffering was almost too much to bear. Some of the dangers that featured in this workplace were very unfamiliar to me. It was fortunate that modern standards had made us all safe from tumbling masonry and huge trains, but the film made it very clear that running and danger went hand in hand.

The Film seemed to be without end, an infinite parade of pitfalls and accidents. Hattie made repeated *Ooh* and *Aah* sounds, wincing at the continuing horror and I could see, from the corner of my eye that several of my colleagues were looking away to avoid the worst of it.

Eventually it ended. Levi stood centre stage. "Hoo-ee. I hope ya all found that film as sobering as I did. Ya must realise that danger stalks us constantly in the workplace, like a savage … savage…"

"Badger!" suggested someone down near the front.

"No. No! Bigger than a badger!"

"Tiger!" shouted someone else.

"Okay, maybe too big now. A bear! Yes! Like a savage bear," said Levi. "But ya can count on the security team to have your back. Any questions?"

"Have you found out who stole Brandine's bagel yet?" someone shouted.

"I cannot comment on an on-going investigation."

"What kind of bear?" shouted someone else.

***

After the meeting, as everyone was trooping out to return to their cubicles. Levi stepped down from the stage to intercept me.

"Alice," he said.

"Levi," I replied.

"Hattie," said Hattie.

"I hope ya weren't disturbed by what happened today."

"Discombobulated," said Hattie.

"You mean calling me out in front of all my colleagues?" I said.

"I meant having to see me deal with that intruder so sternly. I wouldn't want ya to worry yourself over it."

"No," I said because I couldn't think of anything else to say.

"You'll be aware that I have many ways that I can monitor your behaviour," he said. "Not all of them are known to you, but ya can be certain that I am always watching. However, I can see that you've learned a lot today and, remember, that business with the mouse: that was a rare occurrence."

"Anomaly," said Hattie.

I didn't know how to respond to him so I did as I always did in the same situation: putting a smile upon my face and carrying on.

"And just to check," Hattie asked Levi as I moved on, "this bear – it's not a real bear, is it?"

Section head Paulette stood by the door as people exited. "Alice, a word," she said frostily and beckoned me over.

***

Chapter 3

"Anomaly."

Clap clap.

"Anomaly."

Clap clap.

"A-nom a-nom anomaly."

Clap clap.

In the cool of the early evening, I found Hattie outside by the pick-up zone. Hattie was playing a clapping game of her own devising while she waited. A guy in orange coveralls which identified him as a Jaffle Lite community service worker moved between the concrete pillars, collecting litter. He worked around Hattie, treating her no different to the pillars. Jaffle Lite users were aware of other people but they didn't see them as people unless you really pointed it out to them. It wasn't part of their package. In many ways, they were little more than bots and the services they provided to the community could as easily be handled by machines.

"Sorry, I'm late," I said.

"Have you been fired?" said Hattie.

"No. What? No!" I shook my head. "Paulette gave me a ticking off, the usual systems and procedures talk and calculated I'd lost forty two point something minutes because of my little adventure."

"Adventure," said Hattie, flushing.

"I'm sorry I'm late."

"It's okay," said Hattie, "at least the cars will be off peak now."

"True."

I called a car over and we got in. I jipped the car to pay.

"Home," I told it.

"Maybe," said Hattie once we were beyond the landscaped greenery of Jaffle Park, "we should start taking off peak cars every day. A bit more money-saving might be good for us."

"We might be able to afford Jaffle Enhanced upgrades sooner," I said.

"I don't know," said Hattie. "I was thinking on splashing out on that Smiley Tot."

"No," I said firmly. "You're not to buy any more Smiley Tots."

"Not to buy any more?" said Hattie. "As in, in the future?"

I gave her a look. "Did you already buy it?"

"It was a One-Click special."

"Oh, Hattie."

"It was an impulse buy."

"Yes, but still..."

"I was still shaking after watching The Film," said Hattie. "You know how I can be."

"I do. I really do."

Hattie's addiction to Smiley Tots had been a fixture of our lives ever since we were matched up as roommates at the Shangri-La Towers apartment complex. She loved their dimpled cheeks. She loved their chubby thighs. She loved their big dewy eyes and their small pink mouths. And one Smiley Tot was not enough for her. No number of Smiley Tots were ever enough for her. Sometimes I had to bite my tongue and not say the obvious – that my best friend and roommate should simply get herself a baby, a human one. But who could afford one of those on our salaries? They wouldn't even let us in the showroom.

The car bipped as it tallied up the cost of using the pay-per-metre road. It requested permission to pull out on a faster, more expensive lane. I denied the request. Hattie looked out of the window of the whirring car.

"Can you believe things used to be that bad?"

"As The Film? I know, people in the past had it pretty hard," I said, "although Levi makes it sound as if he's the only thing holding back all the bad stuff."

"Maybe he is," said Hattie archly, "with his skills and his training."

"With his skills and his training and that little moustache of his."

"Oh, no," said Hattie seriously. "I don't think his moustache does anything. You think it does? You think it's like a secret gadget moustache?"

I rolled my eyes. "Well, you would know. You're the one with a secret agent for a brain."

"Yes, I am."

There was a cluster of Empties in the drop-off zone near their apartment block. There seemed to be more each week. No one seemed to be doing anything about them.

The car pulled up further along, away from the Empties, and we climbed out. It glided away to find a parking station.

Hattie tutted about the dust and debris that littered the communal stairs as we climbed. On our landing we found one of Helberg's bots. It was cream-coloured with a curved shell. Its underside was equipped with rod-like legs for climbing stairs and spinning bristle brushes for sweeping them. We could see them clearly because the bot had fallen down the stairs and onto its back and was waggling its legs uselessly. Jet-*Set Willy*, was printed on its side.

We both ignored it. It was not the first time we had found Jet-Set Willy at the bottom of a set of stairs. We could turn it upright but Helberg didn't like it when tenants touched his things. Hattie would no doubt be out here later, sweeping up what the bot could not. Of course, it was Helberg's job to keep the complex clean but Hattie would do it anyway.

"I'm not so sure about waiting for the off peak cars in the evening," I said. "I like to be home before *Non-Stop Smile Hour* ends."

"You don't watch *Non-Stop Smile Hour*," said Hattie.

"*I* don't," I said. "Count together?"

"Come on then." Hattie jigged briefly on her tip toes and the two of us timed our steps with the numbers as we counted along the doors of our landing. Most people in the apartment block counted the doors, because it was so difficult to tell them apart on the landing. Each door was painted in the same faded colour with the numbers printed on in white. Over the years the contrast between the background and the numbers had become negligible, so it was fairly common for neighbours to mistakenly walk into each other's apartments.

"...thirty-three, thirty-four, thirty-five..."

The door to the apartment two doors down from ours opened. *Non-Stop Smile Hour* had evidently finished.

"Crumbs," I muttered.

"My apartment's wet. What are you gonna do about it?" said Jeanbee Swanager.

"Sorry?" I said.

"Sorry don't milk the cow or fill the pantry," said Swanager.

"I meant ... pardon?" I said.

"What? Are you deaf now too?" said our neighbour. "Don't they teach you young 'uns to listen anymore?"

She called us young uns but I suspected that Swanager wasn't as old as she made herself to be. It was as if she had taken a look at the cardigans and the big knickers and the casual bluntness and, liking what she saw, decided to get in on the old lady action before the rush.

"We've just got in from work," I said, which was a sentence I hoped would say far more than it actually did.

"I've seen where you work," sneered Swanager. "Big tall swanky building. Too much glass for my liking. While the rest of us have to cope with wet apartments and worse."

"Worse?" said Hattie.

"Worse!" said Ms Swanager, failing to elaborate. "And I asked you, what are you gonna do about it?"

"The glass?"

"The water! And don't you be giving me no attitude."

"We're not," I said.

Hattie was afraid of Swanager and there was plenty of Swanager to be afraid of. She stood behind me, trying not to look like she was cowering. I realised Swanager's clothes were completely sodden from the knees down. Perhaps she'd been trying to mop up the puddle herself.

"Do you want me to come look at your wet apartment?" I said.

"It's like I'm talking to myself!" cried the not-quite-old woman. "Yes!"

"It's just—"

"What?"

"Just that—"

"*What?*"

"It's not exactly my—"

"Now, don't you care say it's not your responsibility, young woman. I've seen where you work."

"But this building isn't managed by Jaffle Tech. Patrick Helberg's the complex manager..."

I stopped. Swanager was making a noise like a noisy exhaust, a throaty and rattling exhalation that was simultaneously disgusted and disgusting.

"I never took you for a shirker, Alice Tennerman."

"I'm ... I'm not."

"Then you scuttle your butt in there and look at my wet apartment."

"We've not had dinner yet," I said. "I'll happy look later after –"

"Come in now," said Swanager.

"Right."

"That way, you'll have longer to fix things."

"Right." I glanced back at Hattie. "Maybe Hattie could go back to our apartment and start on dinner."

"I don't care about your personal arrangements," snapped Swanager. "Time's a-wasting."

I gestured for Hattie to leave me to it and Hattie all but fled to the safety of our apartment.

Swanager turned to go back into her apartment. Her slippers squelched on the thick carpet.

"Oh my, it is, er, damp in here."

"I did say!"

In the living room, Clifford Pedstone sat watching a Smiley show on the TV. The sofa was an island in the swamped carpet but he had elevated his feet on a stool and grinned at Mr Smiley.

"Do you have any idea where it's coming from?" I asked.

"Do we look like water technicians?" said Swanager.

Pedstone made a wordless grumble.

"Don't you be offering opinions when they're not asked for, mister," said Swanager fiercely.

Pedstone grunted and rested his hands on his huge belly.

I squelched through to the back of the apartment. The bathroom door was closed. A stream of water trickled out along the gap at the bottom.

"You closed the bathroom door," I said.

"Seemed sensible," said Swanager, following.

I opened the bathroom door. Water gushed out like a small river, bobbing with minor detritus from inside the apartment. A hairbrush and a loofah washed past me.

"You're meant to make it better, not worse," said Swanager.

"Yes, I just..."

There was a large hole in the bathroom ceiling. Tiles and soggy plaster hung downwards. Water poured through in a light but constant stream.

"There's a hole in your bathroom ceiling," I said.

"Nothing gets past you, does it? I was going to raise a new call for that after this one was solved. We're always told that each separate issue requires a new call, aren't we?"

"Yes. Yes we are," I said. I looked at the hole. "I can't fix this from down here."

Swanager snorted.

"I'm just going to have a look upstairs," I said.

Swanager frowned. "But what about us? You're supposed to be helping us."

"I *am* helping you," I said. "I'm helping you by going upstairs. I'll be back soon."

I went outside. In the corridor, I took off my sodden shoes. My socks were just as wet so I took them off too.

I stopped in at my apartment. Hattie was fixing beans for dinner. She had her favourite Smiley Tot sitting in a high chair, positioned as though it was watching her. Hattie would claim she had no favourites among her Smiley Tots but this was a lie.

"I've got to go upstairs," I said.

"Why?"

"There's some sort of leak. You want to come?"

"Why?" said Hattie.

"To explore. It'll be an adventure."

"I don't think I want an adventure," said Hattie, quite seriously. "Don't be long. I've got today's chores to do and it's *Smiley Out and About* soon."

"And today's jobs are...?"

"Polish the ceiling in here, test the soap dispensers and synchronise the windows," said Hattie.

"Of course," I said. I had a respectable approach to cleanliness but nowhere near as exacting as Hattie. Cleaning and Smiley Tots. Smiley Tots and cleaning. It was like my roommate was constantly in preparation for something, something vitally important that was never going to happen.

I went to the stairwell and climbed to the next floor. I counted along the doors until I found the apartment that was directly above the Swanager and Pedstone's. I raised my hand to knock on the door but then saw that the door was broken and ajar. There was tape across the door which read, *Emergency Responder Scene – Police Aware.*

I touched the door and it swung inwards. I stepped inside the gloomy space and recoiled slightly at the musty smell. The floor was wet here too.

"Hello?"

"Welcome home, tenant," said the apartment.

"Ah, no. I..."

The ceiling lights came on, sparked noisily and then went out again.

"Hello?" I said.

There was no reply this time.

I walked further inside. There was the sound of trickling water from somewhere. A fine layer of dust covered everything that wasn't wet. Hattie would be horrified by the neglect if she could see this apartment. It looked as though nobody had lived here for weeks, maybe months. I went back through to the lounge. There were a few small remnants of the previous occupancy.

A basket sat on the soaked floor, thick with cobwebby balls of fibres and some curious pointed sticks.

There were some books on a shelf. I stared at them with suspicion. They belonged in the same outmoded world as physical stationery, they were an old-world curiosity that probably harboured a great many germs.

On another shelf were framed photographs. I picked one up. It showed two people, a blonde woman and a silver-haired man, in thick clothing and strange goggles, standing in what looked like a very hostile environment. The ground was white with snow, and the people appeared to be deep in unpaved countryside. Despite the danger of their situation, the people in the photograph had smiles on their faces.

I could not imagine why that might be.

I put the frame down, confused. I picked up another. The same two people were immersed in water up to their waists. I gasped in horror. How had they managed to get themselves into such danger? And why were they smiling in this photograph as well?

I realised that underneath the frames were some fat plastic books. I slid one out from underneath the frames and wiped the dust off it with my hand. It had a shiny cover that declared it to be a photograph album. I was about to open it when I remembered the running water, the sound of trickling that had slipped into background noise but had never gone away.

I located the bathroom and found a tap pouring water into a sink that overflowed onto the floor. There was a disconcerting downward bulge in the floor that I guessed corresponded with the hole in Swanager's ceiling. I trod carefully, round to the sink and

pulled the plug out. I tried to turn the tap off, but the top just span round in my hand. Challenged but not put off, I searched around, found a shut-off valve on the pipe, just below the sink, and turned it. The flow of water stopped.

"There," I called out, hoping Swanager could hear. "I've stopped the leak."

"My apartment's still wet," Swanager shouted back.

"I don't have all the answers," I said, more to herself than anyone.

I backed out of the bathroom where thick black mould spanned the walls. The smell was strongest in here, as if the tap had been leaking in a smaller way for a very long time.

I instinctively went back to the photograph album. I opened it and looked at the photos within.

"I don't have all the answers," I repeated.

***

"...thirty five, thirty six and we're home," I said to myself.

I entered my apartment, wet socks and shoes in one hand, the photograph album in the other. Hattie stood on the kitchen table, vigorously attacking the ceiling tiles with polish and duster.

"I've got blue beans and red beans," she said, without looking down.

"Red beans?"

"Apparently there was a problem at the factory. The latest batches of blue beans are red. Do you want the blue ones or the red ones?"

"Which do you prefer?" I said.

"I asked you."

I waited. Hattie looked down, consternated. "I don't like change," she said and then saw me properly. "What happened to your shoes?"

"Swanager's apartment was indeed wet. I've put a call in to Helberg."

Hattie looked at the dirty water dripping on the floor. "I'm going to have to clean that."

"Sorry. You clean up. I'll serve. Blue beans for you."

While shoes and socks dried in the utility closet, we ate beans at the kitchen table. It transpired that red beans tasted exactly the same as blue beans.

Hattie amused herself by adjusting and admiring the Smiley Tot in the high chair. I studied the photograph album, turning pages slowly, feeling a growing anxiety at each mysterious image.

The album contain dozens of pictures of the same couple. Some of the pictures showed them eating and drinking the most impractical things. I found one that showed a picture of the silver-haired man with a monster on a plate in front of him. There was no other word for it: a monster. It was a livid pinky brown and it had giant scary claws that dwarfed its alien body. The man held up the claws in his hands and smiled broadly. I was troubled by the image and couldn't imagine what it depicted.

The plate suggested that this scene was somehow connected to food. Was the monster the meal – no! – or was it the monster that was being fed? Fed what? And why?

Sometimes, when we watched TV, we might accidentally flick through some of the channels that were clearly not meant for us but for people on Jaffle Enhanced or Jaffle Premium. Those TV channels were not forbidden or blocked for people operating on Jaffle Standard; they simply held no interest for us.

Among them were the bizarre cooking shows that demonstrated some really time-consuming and strange ways to prepare food. It was a mystery to Hattie and I why anybody would perform all of those extra tasks with raw food and saucepans when the bean dispensers were so convenient, and delivered optimal nutrition every time. Was that monster the kind of thing to be served up (or fed) on one of those shows?

Worse still was *Drama*. Drama was confusing and disturbing, and featured scenes with people who failed to smile and spent a lot of time arguing and making each other unhappy. I couldn't see any appeal in that at all.

It was time for *Smiley Out and About*, our favourite show. The streaming had already started but Hattie didn't leave the kitchen until she'd put our plates in to wash. We then settled in the living room. We had a wide sofa and two armchairs and yet there was barely enough room. Fifteen Smiley Tots had prime viewing positions in three rows on the sofa. Hattie sat with a Smiley Tot in each arm.

"Oh, Mr Smiley!" said Hattie with relief as she saw his beaming face shining from the screen. She relaxed then, holding her tots tightly. The show was our favourite. Mr Smiley was a large, yellow face with a lovely smile. People on the show would be doing their everyday work, just like I and Hattie did, and then Mr Smiley's face would appear, shining above them, and they would be surprised and delighted to see him. Who wouldn't be?

"Oh look, gardeners, a bit like the ones that work near our office," said Hattie, looking at the screen. "See that man there? He looks a little bit unhappy. I really hope that Mr Smiley cheers him up."

There was a pause of a few seconds. Hattie and I leaned forward in anticipation. Mr Smiley appeared above the man and beamed at him. The man smiled, looking much happier than before.

"Oh look! Look at his face! How lovely!" Hattie jigged in her seat and I was swept up in the moment as well. We watched Mr Smiley perform his tricks for several other people, each of them pleased to see the sunny smile shining down upon them. When Mr Smiley was out, everything seemed fine.

***

Chapter 4 – 2nd June

"Why are we tiptoeing?" said Hattie.

"We're not tiptoeing," I said.

"And why are you whispering?" said Hattie in a voice that was not a whisper.

"Shh," I said. "We're not whispering."

"You are!"

"*Shhh!*"

We crept past Swanager's damp apartment. Or at least I did; Hattie just tramped behind me, squelching through the dampness which had spread from the apartment and across the hallway. After yesterday's experiences, I was keen to simply get to work without delays. It was bad enough having to wait for Hattie to get the Smiley Tots dressed for another day of sitting about the apartment.

No, I shook my head at myself. I shouldn't blame Hattie. Hattie's routines were important to her and morning was a busy time.

We reached the stairs without getting collared by our neighbour and went down to the ground floor. The sweeping bot, Jet-Set Willy, was gone from the stairs. Someone had either righted it or it had managed to roll back onto its feet. As we descended, my attention flicked momentarily to my Jaffle Port – there were no jams on the pay-per-metre and the weather forecast was for uninterrupted sunshine. Today, I decided, was going to be a day for punctuality, perfect adherence to company rules and super-efficient brain utilisation.

In the lobby, a hand stretched out of the darkness of the complex manager's office and clicked its fingers at me.

I wasn't sure how I knew the finger clicking was for me but the fingers were pale and slender and belonged to Patrick Helberg.

"Good morning, Helberg," I said and made to continue out the door.

Helberg whistled shrilly and the hand beckoned. "This way, O valued tenant."

I looked to Hattie. She shrugged and shooed me in. I dipped behind the counter and stood at the doorway. "Good morning, Helberg. Is this about Swanager's problem?"

"Job number four-three-eight. Damp apartment. I sent Hungry Horace to investigate."

Hungry Horace was another of the refurbished bots that Helberg entrusted far too much of his actual job to. If I wasn't mistaken, Hungry Horace was a vacuum cleaner bot that kept leaving incontinent piles of dust in the corridors. I couldn't imagine what Horace could do about a waterlogged apartment.

"There was a problem with water from the apartment above," I tried to explain. "I..." I faltered.

The complex manager's office was a clutter of equipment, tools, foodstuffs and bits and bobs that were surely ornamental or I had no idea what they were for. I knew Helberg had an apartment in the complex but it looked like this was his true home. Half-eaten sandwiches sat next to dismembered bot parts and sheaves of unsorted papers. It wasn't any of this that made me stop. It was the screen. On the screen behind him was a ... well, I wasn't sure what it was.

It was a series of images, a film of sorts, although I couldn't be sure what the story might be. If forced to guess, I would have had to have said it was a news story about some very hungry people who had lost all their clothes. Perhaps they were poor people but they didn't look very poor. Even with no clothes on they had an air of self-satisfied pleasure.

There were men and there were women and they were doing things. There was some sort of massage going on and something a bit like tickling. Rubbing. Rubbing was the verb that I would deem most accurate. And inserting. There was lots of emphasis on inserting and this made the people make noises. There were moans, the kind you made when you sat down with a nice plate of beans after a long day at work. And there were grunts, the kind you made when you'd got all the way to the office and realise you'd left something important at home. And the camera lingered on certain bits of the body that I instinctively felt didn't need lingering on. Bits of the body, glistening pink.

I had seen images like this before. Flick through enough TV stations and you'd find stuff like this but, in those instances, I had flicked on by because it clearly wasn't for me. But here it was presented to me as something I couldn't just flick on by.

Helberg saw me looking.

"You like this kind of thing?" he said.

"No," I said and felt oddly uncomfortable and didn't know why.

"I thought you Jaffle employees were all on Premium." He shrugged, threw down the electric motor he had been fiddling with and gave me a fixed stare. "Are you a registered and graded plumber?"

"No."

"But it was you seen breaking and entering the apartment above Swanager's yesterday."

"Oh no, that's not what I was doing," I said, "I went up there to turn the water off."

"Registered and graded plumber?"

"No."

"Then it was *breaking* and *entering*," said Helberg. "That's a criminal offence and I'd need to call the police." He glanced up, jipping his Jaffle Port. "They'll fine you, even downgrade you to Jaffle Lite. You can be like one of those sad, orange losers with the vacant stares –"

"Helberg," I said, trying desperately to sound reasonable. "Surely, you can see that I'm not a criminal."

"Valued tenant, what am I to think?"

Valued tenant. He spoke in a manner that was deliberately old-fashioned, archaic even. But, like Swanager's old lady mannerisms, it was just an act. Helberg was my age, younger even.

He glanced round as one of the naked men on the screen bent his attention to doing something that I felt was surely unhygienic. "The only other possibility is that you are the tenant of that apartment," he said.

"I just popped in."

"To see who? The Adlers, lovely tenants both, were moved into sheltered housing months ago. No. Breaking and entering it is. But..." He stroked his chin. "I like you, Alice. You're a..." He leaned sideways, his chair creaking. He appeared to be craning round to look at my waist, my buttocks. I wondered if I'd sat in something, if I had something stuck to my backside. I looked; there was nothing there. I wondered what he was going to say I was and what it had to do with my buttocks.

"Now, since I do like you," said Helberg, "I could be nice and suggest you take over the tenancy of that apartment – "

"I was there for less than five minutes."

"One day's tenancy it is, then perhaps I can save you from criminal proceedings."

A woman on the screen sighed heavily, which was just how I felt.

"One day?" I said.

"One day. Standard rate."

He held out his hand. I swiped. He blinked.

"Oh," he said. "There are insufficient funds in your account."

I reeled. Quite apart from being very wrong, something wasn't adding up. "That's not possible," I said. "A day's rent. I can cover that."

"A day's rent indeed, valued tenant, plus the water bill for that apartment, taken from the reading made when the last tenant left. My, you do use a lot of water."

"What? No—"

"The bill is fifteen hundred."

"I don't have fifteen hundred."

"I can see that," said Helberg, "I've taken what's there and if you don't pay the balance within a week then eviction is the next step."

"That's not right! I went up there to help and I turned the water *off*. I didn't turn it on!"

"And I can only commend you for choosing to limit your water usage," said Helberg. "That's free advice from me, I should charge you for that really but I will let you off considering you are renting two apartments and you're such a..."

His eyes flicked to my buttocks again.

"I don't think it was a *person* who turned the water on," I said. "I think the tap broke."

"Criminal damage, eh? Either way, it's you," said Helberg. "So, that's a week to get me the rest of the money."

I stared in disbelief. On the screen, someone groaned like a woman who had just been charged money she didn't have for an apartment she didn't live in with a water problem she didn't cause.

***

Hattie stood waiting in the pick-up zone outside. Empties still sat along the kerb, taking up most of the room. Someone ought to do something about them but I had no idea who to call. One of the Empties looked at me but I ignored it.

Everything all right?" asked Hattie.

I shook my head as I waved a car over. "No. Not really. You know when you try to do the right thing, and somehow it goes really, really wrong?"

"Ah yes," said Hattie with a nod. "I sometimes get the twins' outfits the wrong way round. It bothers me all day when I do that."

"Right," I said, with a sideways glance at Hattie. "Yes. Well this might be a little bit worse than two Smiley Tots wearing the wrong clothes."

"No!"

"Yes."

"I can't believe it."

"Believe this."

I ushered Hattie into the car, climbed in after her and swiped to pay. "Jaffle Park," I told the car. "Helberg has taken all of my money," I said to Hattie.

"Taken?"

"Charged me."

"For what?"

"Renting out that apartment upstairs."

Hattie frowned and then looked worried. "Is it the Smiley Tots? I know you say there's too many and I know you're wrong but if it's bothering you that much..."

"I'm not moving out," I said.

"But he charged you to rent the apartment."

"All my money. And I need to pay him even more or he's going to evict me."

"Why would he do that?" asked Hattie, horrified.

"He says that the water damage was my fault but he was being kind to me because he likes me and I'm a..." I made a surreptitious glance at my own backside.

"A what?" said Hattie.

"I have no idea!"

The car made an angry beep and slowed. "Insufficient funds to access optimal route," it said. The slip road for the pay-per-metre was a short distance ahead and closed off to us.

"All my money," I sighed. "Hattie?"

Hattie blushed. "The new Smiley Tot has wiped me out."

The car sped up, and took a different turning. "Rerouting on legacy roads."

We were soon in among the suburban grid of the city, away from the business parks, residential zones and shopping malls we were familiar with. The premium pay-per-metre roads were smooth and tidy but the legacy routes were unmaintained and littered with potholes and obstacles. The car twitched from side to side, finding the best path through the debris.

"You should tell him it's not your fault," said Hattie. "Tell him."

"I did tell him, but he says I'm liable because I broke in to that apartment."

Hattie stared at the floor. "You can't be evicted. You just can't."

I threaded my arm through my friend's. "I'll think of something. Don't let's dwell on it."

The car's progress through back streets, cut throughs and unmonitored intersections was slow; then we came upon a much more serious blockage. Our car stopped.

"What is it?" said Hattie.

"There is traffic ahead," said the car. It had pulled up behind another vehicle.

"That's strange," said Hattie, "I've never seen a car on its side before. It looks wrong."

I shook my head. There was indeed a car on its side, and something that looked like a huge wheeled rubbish dumpster next to it, which had possibly knocked the car over. They looked like they had been there a very long time. There was no one in the car.

"Can we go round?" I said.

"There is traffic ahead," repeated the car.

"Yes, but I don't think that car is going anywhere."

"It is not parked," said the car.

"No, it's something else," I said.

The car and dumpster blocked the entire road; there was no way Hattie or I could move them.

"We could call an engineer."

"Running self-diagnostics," said the car. "No problems found. Engineer not necessary."

"No, but this is clearly an incident. Can we report it?"

"You have requested to create a report," said the car smoothly. "This option is not valid for legacy routes without specific travel insurance."

"We don't have travel insurance," I said.

"You have insufficient funds for travel insurance," said the car.

"I know!"

"At this rate, it would be quicker to walk," said Hattie.

I got out the car and looked at the turned over vehicle.

"I didn't mean we should walk," said Hattie. "The car will work it out."

The car whirred. "There is traffic ahead. It will add unknown time to your journey."

"We can't stay here," I said.

Hattie got out to look at the car blocking the road.

"If you are unable to proceed, please choose another destination or leave the vehicle," said the car. "You have chosen to leave the vehicle."

The doors swung shut. I tried to stop it but the car was nippy and was already driving off, back the way it had come. It bounced in a pothole in what seemed to be inordinate haste to get away.

"Well that was a bit rude," said Hattie.

"It's not all that far," I said, jipping a route-finder. "We can walk."

I peered over the top of the overturned car. As my fingers touched it, the door sprang open.

"Where would you like to go?" said the car.

"We're fine, thanks," I said. "It must be this way," I said to Hattie.

We walked on along the road. At the next junction, the area changed significantly. The houses here were large, much larger than the ones we'd seen previously. There were houses here which were easily ten times the size of our apartment. I wondered how many people lived in each one.

"I wonder how they get about if the roads are blocked like this?" said Hattie.

As if in answer to her question a commuter drone rose from the back of one of the houses.

"Ooh, no, I don't fancy one of those," said Hattie.

"They're perfectly safe," I said.

"I'm sure they are," said Hattie. "But still..."

My attention was taken by the bits of land in front of the houses. They were like the sculpted greenery around Jaffle Park except there was more than just grass and trees.

"The plants are so tall," I said, pointing. "Why would you let things get tall like that?"

"Trees are tall," said Hattie.

"Yes, but trees are important. Those things, the brightly coloured things—"

"Flowers."

"Right. Flowers. They're everywhere. Just make it look untidy."

"I like grass," said Hattie.

"You can sit on grass," I agreed.

"Exactly. Those things are definitely *not* grass. Maybe this is what happens when gardeners don't come and, you know, garden."

"I don't know," I said slowly. "There's grass by these houses as well. It looks as if those tall things are supposed to be there. Someone's coming out of that house," I added in a whisper.

"Why are you whispering again?" asked Hattie.

I didn't know why, but there was something about the woman that made me feel I didn't belong. It should have been the woman who looked out of place – her clothes were unnecessarily bright and didn't seem to cover enough of her to be of any practical use – but, no, it was me who felt I was in the wrong place.

"I said—" repeated Hattie. I pressed my finger to her lips for silence. It did nothing to dampen the volume of Hattie's voice. "'Y are 'e 'iskering?" she demanded, loud enough to be heard in the next street.

"Can I help you?" asked the woman as she strolled down the path between the strange tall plants.

Hattie and I exchanged sideways glances, both of us startled by the animal that the woman had at her side.

"We're just walking to work," I said, and then had to ask. "Is that a dog?"

The woman took a sip of golden liquid from the heavy glass tumbler in her hand and glanced across at the property next door. Another woman in a broad floppy hat and equally colourful clothing was watching through the high metal railings.

"Every home should have one. Lovely creatures. Very loyal." She looked at us over the rim of her glass. "Knows its place."

I still didn't understand. I knew what dogs were – a little jipping of my Jaffle Port told me this heavy and hairy creature was a golden retriever – but what was it doing here? Why was it standing quite happily besides this woman and why was she tolerating it? Even now it was squatting at the side of the path and – I recoiled – defecating onto the ground.

"Oh wait, I know! I know!" exclaimed Hattie. "You're blind, aren't you?"

"What?" said the woman.

Hattie turned to me. "In the old days, before they fixed blindness, dogs helped blind people."

I wasn't sure the woman was blind; she was staring straight at Hattie. She reached out, took my sleeve between a thumb and finger and gave it a little rub. Her face pulled into a strange expression. It was like a smile. Almost a smile, but not quite. "Genuine polyester. You must be so proud," she drawled.

"Proud?" I said.

"Jaffle Tech standard issue."

"Yes," I said. "What are you wearing?"

The woman's attire was complicated. The colours were bright in the same way as the garden. The sleeves of the dress were very thin, so I could see the woman's arms. The neckline of her top ran down to the top of her stomach. A split in the side of the flowing skirts went right up to her waist so that her long legs were utterly exposed.

She saw me looking and gave her hips a playful wiggle. "It's Chanel, darling."

"You're wasting your breath, Claire," called the woman in the floppy hat next door. "They don't even know what that is."

"It's a French fashion house," I said, discreetly jipping so I could look it up. I understood the word *house*, but not much more. I glanced at the house behind us, hoping for a clue as to what *French* and *fashion* might be.

"I've got it!" said Hattie. "Do you need the colours to be so bright because you can't see where your clothes are otherwise?" She gave an experimental wave in front of the woman's face.

"I wear colours because they suit my personality," said the woman. "Some of us can afford a personality." The woman, Claire,

looked them up and down. "I expect the two of you simply eat beans and watch the Smiley channel when you get home."

"Of course we do," I said, smiling at the strange question. What else was there?

Claire smiled widely at that and made a strange coughing sound. The dog stopped sniffing its own poop on the ground and looked up at her. The woman in the floppy hat put her hand to her mouth to hide her own smile.

"Oh darlings," said Claire, "you have no idea how fucked-up you are, do you? Absolutely no idea."

I wasn't sure what that meant, but I smiled at the woman. "Will we get to Jaffle Park if we carry on this way?" I asked, pointing down the road.

"Yes, you will," said Claire and took another gulp of her drink. "But you can do me a favour first."

"Yes?"

She pointed at the brown pile of dog poop on the path. "There's a refuse bin a hundred metres down the road. Can you put that in the bin?"

"That?" said Hattie.

Claire looked at her levelly. "Yes. Pick it up, take it with you and put it in the bin."

"But it's..."

"I've been good enough to talk to you and tell you where to go. You owe me."

"Do we?" I said.

"It's your place to do as you're told." Claire poked Hattie in the shoulder. "You. Pick it up. With your hands."

"With...?"

The woman sighed, suddenly tired and irritable. "Do I need to report this to your boss?"

Neither of us wanted that. We didn't want to get into trouble at work and any negative interactions, in or out of work, could impact on our Jaffle ratings.

Hattie knelt quickly, scooped up the soft pile in her cupped hands. "Happy to help," she said, recoiling at the smell as she did.

The woman on the next property hooted with surprise and apparent delight.

Claire pointed firmly down the road, swilling but not spilling the drink in her hand.

"That way. Refuse bin. Or take it with you as a gift. I don't care. But you're not to come this way again. We simply can't have you trailing up and down here with your vacant little faces mooning at the houses, can we?"

"No, of course not," I said, completely out of my depth, but wanting to be polite. I hesitated as I made to go, unsure if I had been dismissed.

"And say thank you," said Claire.

"Thank you," I said.

"Yes. Thank you," said Hattie and even bobbed a little curtsey, with the steaming dog mess in her hands. The golden retriever wagged its tail. The woman, Claire, made the oddest barking sound, like she was really really happy. The woman next door joined in with a sort of loud, rhythmic panting.

Hattie looked deeply unhappy at having to carry the smelly poop in her hands but she swallowed her discomfort and looked back at the woman.

"Do you want us to show you the way back to your house, or will the dog do that?" she asked.

***

Chapter 5

Being late for work was unfortunate. Being late for work and having dog poo on her hands was almost too much for Hattie. Anxiety radiated from her, and she made occasional meeping sounds.

I touched her lightly on the shoulder as we approached the door to reception. "It's going to be fine."

"Don't touch me! You'll get it on you as well!" Hattie wailed.

I recoiled. I was a long way from Hattie's hands, but perhaps really, really dirty things could transfer their dirtiness across a wider gap? Hattie was so fanatical about cleanliness, she was sure to be right. If the smell was anything to go by, I would need to be across the street to be completely safe.

"Right, we'll go in and get you straight to the toilets. You can wash your hands there."

"No, wait!" said Hattie. "You can't touch the door with your hands! You've touched me. If you touch the door then every person that comes in after us will get dog poo on them."

"Oh," I said. I looked at the door. It wasn't the sort of door I could simply push with I shoulder. I needed to jip the door and then press a button. Perhaps I could gain the attention of the receptionists inside?

"Hello!" I called through the glass, waving. The two receptionists were concentrating on their heads-up displays and failed to see us. I tried again, louder this time.

"HELLO! PLEASE LET US IN!" I waved frantically, trying to ignore Hattie whose meeping had escalated into a continuous keening.

One of the receptionists looked over. She was immaculate in her white admin staff tunic. She responded to my wave with a tentative wave of her own and a look of confusion. I performed an exaggerated mime, trying to indicate that I was unable to open the door and pleading for the receptionist to open it for us. The receptionist slid down from her stool and walked over. She cracked open the door and stood in the gap.

"Can I help you?"

"We work here. We need to come in but we don't want to touch the door," I said.

She looked at me and then at Hattie, whose face was crumpled in despair.

"You don't want to touch the door."

"No, we'll make it dirty. We had a sort of accident," I said.

Hattie held up a poo-smeared hand.

The receptionist stepped sharply backwards, sniffed the air and then stared at the two of us with fresh horror. "Oh no. Can't you control your bodily functions."

"No, no. Not that sort of accident," I said. "It's not human poo, it's dog poo."

"Dog?"

"And I don't even think the woman was blind," said Hattie.

"We accidentally touched some dog poo," I said. "We need to wash our hands?"

The receptionist pulled a face. "How does that even happen? No, you've put me right off my beans. Come in."

Hattie and I trooped in behind her as she held the main door and then the door to the toilets. After a moment's thought, she stepped inside and turned on a tap.

"There. Now just make sure you do a thorough job and *don't...*" She shuddered. "Just clean it up."

Hattie sighed with relief as she lathered up and rinsed away the filth from her hands. "Oh I don't think I can remember having such nasty stuff on my hands," she said. "The smell!"

I used lots of soap and made sure I washed right up my arms. The further I washed, the further I wanted to wash. "Do you remember that video we had to watch about the correct way to wash our hands?" I asked Hattie.

"Oh yes, that was a really good one," said Hattie, brightening. "I always do it exactly as they showed us." She repeated the words from the video. *"Left on top, right on top, turn over and interlace the fingers on each side. Rinse and do a nail scrub."*

I was fairly certain that Hattie was word perfect. I wasn't surprised. "What's that voice you're doing?" I asked.

"That's my posh but friendly narrator man voice," said Hattie. "The kind who puts deep and deliberate ... *pauses* in the middle of sentences for effect."

"That's a good voice."

"It's..." She paused momentarily as she jipped her Jaffle Port. "It's avuncular."

"That ... *is* a good word," I said in my best avuncular voice.

"Indeed," said Hattie in her very avuncular voice, "Avuncular is one of the ... *best* words."

I smiled and continued with the routine myself. I did it once more, remembering the stench, and afraid it would taint me for the rest of the day.

We both dried themselves. I took a tentative sniff. "I can only smell soap now. I think it's all gone."

"Are you sure?" Hattie asked, snorting up great lungfuls of air as I opened the door back out to reception.

The receptionist stared at us. I felt compelled to go and present myself. I held up my hands, and nudged Hattie to do the same. "All better now." I dropped my hands. The receptionist said nothing so I pressed on, feeling that I needed to make it clear that we were model employees, not filth-smeared incompetents.

"We're experts at ... *cleaning* up," I said in a deeply avuncular and pause-laden voice. "We're ... *highly* trained. No clean-up was ever ... *more* thorough."

A hand clapped on my shoulder from behind. "You're on the efficiency leader-board too, I see."

I turned to see who it was. I faced a tall man with cropped hair.

The receptionist smiled. "Henderson, sir."

I had seen the man around at times, sweeping through the lobby and such, but didn't know who he was. Someone high up in another department, I guessed.

"Is this the one?" he asked the receptionist, pointing at me.

"I don't know, sir," the receptionist replied.

"Clean-up?" he said to me.

"I do," I said.

"Good. With me." He turned to the receptionist. "You. Let – ah, Alice's section head know that she's popping up to do a job on the exec floor and she'll be back later."

"What about me?" asked Hattie.

"What about you?" said Henderson as he led me away to the bank of elevators.

I turned and waved a brief goodbye to Hattie as the doors closed.

***

I had no clue exactly why I was in the elevator with this Henderson. As we rode up, I surreptitiously jipped in the company directory.

Jethro Henderson was Jaffle Tech's Chief Technical Officer. I had to look that up too and when I did, I was impressed. He supervised the company's engineering department and was one of the half dozen people who ran the company – the whole worldwide company! – on behalf of the board of directors and the CEO.

And he was taking me right to the top. The elevator was heading to the top floor, the realm of top bosses and execs that I never got to mingle with.

"I don't want any delays to the project," said Henderson.

"No delays," I said. "What project?"

"The demand that we'll create with Operation Sunrise will increase revenues across all of our main streams. Consumers, even reticent ones, will buy into it. Jaffle Tech gives them access to the world. They owe *us* everything. We've made gods of humankind."

"Right. Gods."

"Wait, no. We can't afford to deliver late, do you understand?"

"No, I'm afraid I don't," I said.

"What? Oh no, just someone standing nearby who thinks I'm talking to them. Now listen, I want a daily update report on this. Make sure that any blockers get escalated directly to me. Is that clear?"

Henderson made a gesture to end the call moments after I realised that he hadn't been talking to me at all. I opened my mouth to explain, but Henderson silenced me with a wave of his hand and then the elevator arrived and he ushered me out. I had never been to the exec floor and it was startlingly different to the other floors. The carpet was very thick. It was so thick that I wondered briefly whether Levi would consider it a trip hazard. There were glass cases containing exhibits. I stepped across to look at one. There was a small piece of electronic circuitry with a label next to it.

2023: The first Jaffle interfaces used on human subjects exposed them to the sensory input from the eyes of a fly. This programme was closed down when subjects exhibited symptoms of PTSD.

"What's PTSD?" I asked, but Henderson had already swept away down the corridor.

"It's a simple clean-up," said Henderson. "You do your regular sweep and clean and then get out, got it?"

I looked at him. He gave me a curt glance. "Are you talking to me this time?" I asked.

He stopped outside a door. "Who else would I be talking to?"

"Um."

"In here. Make sure you do a good job."

"Right."

"Naturally, if you don't, you will be fired."

"Okay."

I looked at the door.

Rufus Jaffle

"Oh wow, he's got the same name as the company," I said, turning to Henderson. He was already halfway down the corridor, speaking urgently to someone on another call. He walked like a man who had a lot of urgent calls to make.

I looked back at the door and knocked gently.

"Yo!" called a voice within.

I entered the room. It was much larger than I'd expected. If this room was on my floor it would contain a hundred people in cubicles. There was a wall entirely composed of glass doors and beyond that a wide balcony on which a sleek commuter drone had been parked. The room had strange colourful hangings on the wall, it was carpeted even more thickly than the corridor, and the furniture was big and chunky. The desk was larger than the whole canteen servery, and yet it looked as though it was designed for just one person. The person in question was lying back in a chair with his feet on the desk, his long hair trailing back across the headrest. There was a graze and fading bruise above his eyebrow, as though he had recently been in an accident.

I was, however, distracted by his clothes. Henderson had been wearing a suit. Suits were not something I came across very often – tunics, tabards and coveralls were the clothes of the regular worker – but I had seen people wearing suits. Rufus Jaffle wore something that *looked* like a suit, but the trousers were too short. They were so short that I could see his hairy legs up to his knees. Instead of shoes, he wore footwear that looked like the bottom part of a shoe held on with a couple of thin straps. Levi would have something to say about those.

"I'm Alice Tennerman. Henderson sent me," I said.

"Awesome! Good old, Jethro," said Jaffle. "Take a seat, Alice. Can I get you a drink?"

"Um."

"A drink?" he repeated.

"A drink would be lovely," I said politely.

"Power smoothie, probiotic milkshake or Himalayan herb detox?"

I played back what I'd just heard in my mind. I had no idea what those things were, even after a brief jip with my Jaffle Port. "I'll have whatever you're having, thank you."

"Awesome." He gestured to open a call. "Florence, can I get two Himalayan herb detoxes please? Then make sure I'm not disturbed for an hour, will you?"

A woman appeared through a door that I hadn't even realised was there. She placed a tray on the desk and left, smiling at Jaffle.

"Florence, my secretary is an absolute diamond," said Jaffle. "I call her my secretary. She's actually a European princess. I picked her up in Cremona at an IFPA gala event for sea turtles or something." He looked suddenly and deeply puzzled. "Or is her name Cremona and I met her in Florence?"

"I ... I don't know," I said.

He waved to open a call. "Florence. Where did we meet? Uh-huh. And your name? Uh-huh." He killed the call.

"Milan, it turns out," he said, not making it clear if that was the woman's name or where they met. "Cool. Now let me talk you through the tea. I think it would really help if our chakras were aligned before we start the procedure."

"Procedure, yes," I said. I looked around, wondering if there was anything obvious that needed cleaning up. Dog poo, for example.

"First of all," he said, "the herbs are blended specifically for each person's unique earthly alignment. What's your date of birth, Alice?"

"Twentieth of January, twenty thirty-seven," I said.

"I'll just work out your blend." He cocked his head as he studied his heads-up display and then spooned dried leaves from a rack of small containers that were on the tray into a pot.

He began to sing a soft mostly tuneless song.

"Mixing and mystery are part of their history. It's the tea le-e-e-aves. The te-e-ea leaves, yeah?"

He poured hot water from a tall jug into the pot. "Now for mine," he said and repeated the routine, although the leaves came from different pots and the song had a different tune, or at least lacked a tune in a different way.

"Good," he said. "You should know that all of the herbs are harvested at the break of day, when their essence is considered to be purest. Now, we will steep the herbs to the sound of the singing bowl."

He picked up a stumpy tool and stirred it inside a metal bowl on the tray. To my amazement the bowl started to make a loud noise. It sounded more than a little like being at home in the kitchen and hearing Hattie in the shower when she started singing the Smiley theme tune. Like that but really loud.

Jaffle closed his eyes and leaned back as he continued to make the bowl sing. I wasn't sure if I was supposed to join in. Instead I silently looked him up. I tried to keep my composure when the results popped up. The very top of Jaffle Tech was a bit complicated. There was a board of directors and a CEO and then a cluster of people around the CEO. The Jaffles themselves, the Jaffle family, including one Rufus Jaffle, son of the company founder. This man with the singing bowl and the secretary who might have been called Florence or Cremona or Milan, and whom he had picked up in one of those places, pretty much owned the company, or at least owned as much of the company as any one person did. He was one of the superrich. International philanthropist, advocate of space exploration, honorary president of the International Federation for the Protection of Animals. He was personally the sixth richest person on planet Earth. Maybe that explained the suit-like shorts. Maybe all superrich people wore suit shorts.

Rufus Jaffle opened his eyes again. "Blissful sound, isn't it?"

I nodded. "Er, the procedure you mentioned?"

"Old Hendo didn't explain?" asked Jaffle. "That's why you have some light brown in your aura. It denotes confusion. Come child, sip your tea and I will explain."

He pressed the tiny delicate bowl into my hands, carefully folding the fingers of both of my hands around it. I realised this was because the cup had no handle. How odd.

He picked up his own cup with the same gesture, and raised it to his mouth. It seemed like a very inefficient way to have a drink, but I copied his movements.

"So Alice, I asked Jethro to find me someone to help me with a brain tech issue. I need a delicate job to be done, and apparently you're just the person I need."

"Oh yes, of course," I said, delighted to grasp onto something I understood. *That* kind of clean-up. That made sense. "I work in brain tech. Normally we do this on a call."

"Yes, I guess you do, but listen and be guided by your inner voice, Alice." He cupped an ear. "Can you hear it?" I strained my ears but heard nothing special. "I really appreciate your attending in person," he said. "It will be a holistic experience, I can already feel it, can't you? I need to make sure that this procedure is handled discreetly. It's important to me that this is not logged on the system. The whole world can't know that one of the heads of Jaffle has a brain virus now, can they?"

Brain virus? I'd heard of the concept of a brain virus, but mostly it was used as a cautionary tale or a hypothetical concept designed to promote healthy practices with backups and system flushes. A portion of everyone's brain was taken up with housekeeping software to counteract such a possibility.

"Are you sure you have a virus?" I asked. "Where could you have got it from?"

"Oh, I'm sure," he said. "I believe I got it from uploading an unofficial hack."

I stared. "You're a Jaffle and you put unauthorised software into your brain?"

"Wild, isn't it?" he said with a small smile. "I wanted to be at one with a blue whale."

"A blue—?"

"Whale, yes." He made a long and low keening sound. "It's been a long-term ambition of mine. I'm all about the animals. I'm like the chief spokesperson for IFPA."

"The animal charity."

"Right on, and I heard a rumour that someone had a download. Plugs you right into the live-feed of a whale brain. I mean, our guys in the labs are always working on new things, but this one just didn't ever seem to make it to the top of the list. Something about low customer value and high production costs, if you can believe that? Anyway, when this guy claims to have it right there on a plate for me, what else am I gonna do, right?"

He suddenly pressed himself against a square blue wall hanging.

"Can you imagine that?" he said, and made the keening, honking sound again.

I nodded, although I was now very uncertain that I had understood correctly. "You wanted to know some more about blue whales?" she asked.

"No, no, no. I wanted to *be at one* with a blue whale. I wanted to swim with it, hear it call to other whales and listen to their reply. I wanted to understand what it is to be a blue whale."

"Wow," I said. "How... interesting. And did you?"

"Oh man, I did. It was the best. These magnificent creatures have such sights to show us, and such things to teach us. It was truly humbling." He paused, staring at the ceiling in recollection. "But then I got the virus. It was sort of trippy and cool at first, but it's definitely affecting my chakras and I need it gone."

"And when you say it's affecting your chakras, you mean – what exactly?" I prompted.

"Oh the usual. I feel unsatisfied with my life, as if I don't know what to do with myself, and I don't seem to be able to delete or re-edit any of my brain content. It's almost always a blocked chakra when that happens." He nodded. "I expect everyone gets the same from time to time. I also had really bad food poisoning, but I'm pretty sure that was from when I went out in the ocean to strain krill through my teeth."

"Strain krill through your teeth." I echoed with a baffled nod, resolving to look it up later.

"So, I want to get rid of the virus. Oh, and delete a couple of embarrassing memories."

"And to get rid of the virus, we're going to do what, exactly?"

"Hey Alice, I'm going to bow to your experience here. You're the clean-up guru."

"We could start with defragmentation and deep clean."

"Whatever's going to work. I gotta admit, I don't really understand all of the terminology like clearing down caches and yadda yadda. Can we start soon? I'll be fully aligned with my magnetic north at nine thirty. It would be a really good time."

I turned the phrase *clean-up guru* over a couple of times and wondered if I was here because I had declared my competence at hand washing. No matter, it was much too late to back out now. I checked the time. It was a few minutes before nine thirty.

"Right," I said briskly, forming a plan as I went. "The best thing will be if we take all your valuable content, copy it over to a fresh facility where it will be cleared of any contagions or malware and then we do a general scrub and then re-apply each sector, optimising storage and scanning for defects as we go."

"And the non-techy version?"

"We'll upload everything to the cloud, wipe clean and then copy it back a bit at a time."

"Uh, gonna have to stop you right there, Alice. We can't use the cloud. Remember, this must be off the record. I'm not taking my brain down to the local laundromat. You'll need to think of something else."

"Oh." The standard operating procedure was ingrained in me, and it seemed very wrong to deviate from it, but this was Jaffle himself. It was his company who had set the operating procedure, so presumably he could override it if he wanted to. I wondered what alternatives there might be. "I guess we could use local storage," I mused, "although most of the high capacity devices need to be checked out of stock, so we couldn't do that. How about using organic storage from another source?"

"You mean another person's brain?" Jaffle asked.

"Yes. A family member or someone you trust, perhaps?"

"Ooh, Alice, see my aura? Can you see it?" he asked, waving his hands and rolling his eyes.

"No," I said, "I'm not even sure what an aura is, Jaffle."

"Call me Rufus, please, won't you? Well, Alice, you don't need to be able to see my aura to know that it's *totally* stressing out at the idea of involving a family member, ya hear me? Paris would kill me."

That seemed a bit extreme, a whole city trying to kill him. Unless Paris was the name of another of his secretaries.

"We have to keep this just between the two of us," he said and then gasped. "Here's an idea! Why don't we use your brain?"

"My brain? I—"

"You I said it should be someone I trust." He came down on one knee in front of me, flicked his long hair out of his face and clasped my hands. "I trust you, Alice."

I couldn't think of a reason why not. I could take myself offline for a short while so that I had all of my capacity at my disposal. I ran through the steps in my mind and decided that the whole thing would take around thirty minutes. I'd be back at my desk in plenty of time for the mid-morning peak call time, and then lunch with Hattie.

"Sure." I smiled at him and went into my best customer service mode as I mentally worked through the preparations. "Of course we can do that. Now I'm going to switch us both to operate only locally and then I'll jip an access request to your Jaffle Port. Just make yourself comfy and I'll take it from there."

Rufus beamed at me, jumped back in his chair and reclined it further, until all I could see were his dangling legs. I started to go through the protocols to make a full backup but redirecting the traffic to my own brain when Rufus sat up suddenly in shock.

"If you copy my brain," he said, "will you become me?"

"No."

"And I become you?"

"No."

"Cos if, you know..." He gave me an oddly hungry look and held his hands out over his chest as though supporting a pair of breast. "We could..."

"It doesn't work like that, Rufus," I said. "It's done with compressed data squirts and—" I sighed. "Let me show you."

There was open projection equipment in the room. I cast up some images and copies of our live brain data as a holographic image in front of us. "This is your brain," I said.

"Cool. It's big, isn't it?"

"It's not actual size."

"In the physical world, right. Spiritually though..."

"And this is your Jaffle Port." A small patch was highlighted. "This gives you direct access to worldwide data and communications. It also organises redundant synaptic pathways and repurposes them for additional processing and storage."

"More synaptic connections in the brain than stars in the universe," said Rufus, dreamily.

"That's what they say," I said. "You have an astonishing capacity for data storage. Jaffle Tech take up some of that spare brain power with basic software, keeping everything clean and safe. If you're on Jaffle Standard, like me – which, of course, you're not – then some of the rest is utilised by outside systems, whether that's analysing

astronomical data, studying new genetic material or just keeping the trains running on time.'

I looked at our two brains. How underutilised Rufus's was! How much of it was given over to natural processes that I didn't possess but which I managed to function perfectly well without. Compared to my super-efficient brain that was both running my body and keeping the world around us functioning, his was a dull wasteland, undeveloped.

"Your personal storage," I said, "can be seen in these clusters. Here and here and so on. We can compress that data when we copy it across."

I set up the entire sequence to run automatically, just in case there was a problem with overflow, but the scans I ran indicated there was plenty of capacity for Rufus's backup.

"Right. I think we're about set. Are we certain that we won't be interrupted while we're doing this?" I asked.

"Absolutely sure. Now can I show you how to recline your own chair, Alice? Perhaps I can massage a little lavender oil into your temples to assist you into total relaxation?"

"I'm fine thanks. Are you ready, sir?"

"Rufus."

"Rufus."

"Ready when you are."

I started the sequence. I didn't expect to have any awareness of what was taking place. Most of the time my unused brain capacity was able to undertake tasks entirely without my knowledge, but this time I was aware of a faint pressure from inside my head. Perhaps it was a result of doing the transfer locally, which used a much faster communication protocol.

"I feel funny," said Rufus.

"It's fine," I said and then a strange feeling came over me. I was flying, yet sat completely still.

***

Chapter 6

I was in a plush, well-appointed flying drone, accompanied by a pair of stunningly pretty girls. They both looked very alike, with long blonde hair and oddly bland features.

I had the strangest sensation of seeing the world through someone else's eyes. Where was I? I looked down at my clothes and a suspicion grew in my mind. I was Rufus.

'Am I Rufus?' I wanted to say, but the words wouldn't come. This wasn't my body to control, it was Rufus's. Was this one of Rufus Jaffle's memories? That would mean that I wasn't an active participant. All I could do was sit back and observe. The world beyond the window of the drone was mostly composed of wide sea and beautiful sunset. I would have wanted to observe the view more but Rufus's attention was definitely on the young women.

Did I know the names of these girls? Rufus surely did. If I was in his memory I would have the same knowledge. I had a sense that one was called TayTay and one was called MiMi but I didn't know which one was which. For that reason, Rufus addressed them in his uniquely vague style.

"Babe," he drawled. "You know your aura fascinates me so much. It's got that blossoming, burgeoning thing going on. I want to reach out and touch it."

Rufus did reach out and touch. It didn't stop at the aura. I observed Rufus's muddled eyesight imparted a hazy blurring around the edges of everything, not just the girls. Did Rufus keep talking about auras because of an uncorrected vision problem? His hands groped across the two girls. Those hands weren't seeking an aura, they were seeking out breasts. I gasped at the overwhelming feeling of desire that consumed Rufus. There was titillation at the sight of their low-cut dresses, but this driving lust was fuelled by something else. It was the same thing which had bent his eyesight all out of shape. I looked at the white powder dusting his knees as he sat in the drone. Cocaine. The word came to me from nowhere. It was cocaine that Rufus had been taking. And as the knowledge came to me so did a cascade of other concepts – the house servant who procured it for him, his opinions on the various suppliers they'd use, fleeting images

of his fantasies about getting 'down and dirty' with that house servant.

Rufus had taken a lot of cocaine too. Both of the girls seemed happy for Rufus to run his hands across their bodies. In fact it seemed to me that they were positively encouraging it.

"Hey babes!" said Rufus. "Your auras are going wild. What say we throw caution to the wind and see whether our chakras align if we all get naked?"

"We're nearly there Rufus!" commented one of the girls, looking out of the window.

I followed Rufus's downward gaze and saw a huge house with many cars and drones parked outside. If it was any indication of how many people were inside this was a huge party. They flew over and saw partygoers thronging the beach.

"Buzzing!" said one of the girls in excitement.

As I sifted through Rufus's memory I was stunned to realise that this wasn't all that special for him. The houses here were smaller than his own, but nevertheless he enjoyed a party as much as the next person and he was looking forward to a bonfire on the beach.

It was the sort of thing that the corporate world just couldn't offer. Cocktail receptions and charity galas were all very well but a bonfire on the beach was so much more— I watched his drug-funnelled mind grasp for the right word ... authentic.

"Touching down," said the drone.

On the ground, the three of us walked into a cool hallway, lined with marble. Trays of drinks and nibbles were offered by slack-eyed servants. These people were operating on Jaffle Lite, I thought, then, tapping into Rufus' knowledge, realised no. Not just Jaffle Lite but a special variant which was part of their terms of employment. Rufus ignored the food, seeking out a tray lined with cocaine. As he snorted the drug, I felt the jolt as it hit his system. There was a rush of clarity and euphoria. His vision was much clearer, and yet the people in the room still had pink, blurry edges. Were those actually auras, or was I seeing a second-hand hallucination? Being inside Rufus Jaffle's mind was bizarre.

"Coming to the beach Rufus?" TayTay (or MiMi) asked. They were completely identical now. Bland faces, huge breasts and pneumatic bottoms. I realised I was looking through Rufus's cocaine goggles. The girls probably weren't even alike in real life, but it was clear to me Rufus really wasn't interested in their faces.

A huge grey-blue shape swam across my vision, gliding through a sky that simply wasn't big enough to contain it. It turned and looked at me with a benevolent, ancient eye.

I'm aaaaaa whaaaaaaaaaaaale, it sang.

I tried to ignore it and forced myself back into Rufus's memory. He and the girls were somewhere else now, on a balcony overlooking the beach. Near-naked men and women played volleyball on the sand.

"You girls like to play?" Rufus asked TayTay and MiMi.

"Not me," said TayTay with a smile. "Mud-wrestling's more my thing, but I'm on a rest day."

"Mmmm," said Rufus, his inner vision clogged with panting, mud-covered babes. "We could maybe find somewhere to, you know, run you through your paces?"

Someone shouted from the doorway of the house.

"Did he just call my name?" Rufus asked.

"It sure sounded like it," said TayTay.

Aliiiiice, woooould yoooou like to beeeeee aaaaa whaaaaaaaaale? sang the blue whale, crashing into my memory.

No, thank you, I thought as hard as I could.

There was an expression of infinite sadness in the whale's eye that pulled at my emotions. It flicked and turned.

It's fuuuun beeeing aaaaa whaaaaaaaaaaaaaaale.

I pushed myself away and I was somewhere new again. Time moved differently in memories. I (or rather Rufus) was in an underground space with TayTay and MiMi. Rufus was staring at a kangaroo. I was surprised. So was Rufus.

I had no personal experience of kangaroos, had never seen one outside of school educational download. I had no idea kangaroos were so large, and I could see that Rufus was also impressed by their size. In fact, he knew barely more about them than I did. For a man who had so many more opportunities for experience and exploration than me, he knew surprisingly little.

One of the girls was running her hands through its fur.

"Ooh, it's rough!" she squealed, and then shrank back as the kangaroo turned to look.

It looked muscular and fierce, although I wondered how much that perception was warped by Rufus's memory. It gave off a powerful animal stink that did not disgust me but fascinated me. It was more ... more real than anything I had experienced in my life. That couldn't

possibly be true but, in Rufus's memories, through his drugged perception filter, I was fixated by the powerful realness of this creature.

"Have you ever heard of the ancient martial art of Maglev?" said Rufus.

They shook their heads.

"Few have," he said, lifting his hands and making a slow chopping movement. "Advanced practitioners must exercise restraint and secrecy."

They nodded, hanging on his every word.

"Maybe I could show you girls some moves? It could really help with your mud-wrestling. Personal development is something I'm always keen to help with." He lifted his arms and draped them casually over each girl's shoulder and slipped his fingers inside their clothes. A nipple stiffened against both sets of fingers and he smiled, feeling unstoppable.

The blue whale swooped in and did the whale equivalent of a handbrake turn.

I haaave aaaaaaaaaa taaaaaaaaaaaaaaaail! it sang.

Go away! I thought.

I'm aaaaa whaaaaaaaaaaale with aaa taaaaaaaaaaaaaaail!

It was a very persistent whale.

I need to see what's happening, I told it.

Yooooou can haaave aaa taaaaaaaaaaaaaaail tooooooo, it sang.

No, I told it.

There was a near seamless splice in the memory. I knew that at least a day had elapsed.

I still saw the world through Rufus's, but now he was trussed up in a hospital bed, with straps, tubes and pipes disappearing under the blanket. Several people sat on chairs at the side of the bed. His head hurt.

"Hey, honey," said Rufus to the woman who sat closest. I knew from Rufus's memory this was his fiancée, Paris. "Guess who's got himself a tiny problemo?"

Her face collapsed into tears. "I was so worried about you, Rufie! You looked so small and helpless when you were unconscious."

Jethro Henderson, CTO of Jaffle Tech, sat next to her. "Yes, we've made sure that Paris is up to date with the details of your fall." I saw him through Rufus's mind and felt Rufus's views of the man. They weren't complimentary.

Beeee aaaa whaaaaaale. Beeeee aaat peeeeeeeeeeeeace.

"Henderson, my main man," said Rufus, smiling. "You didn't need to be here."

Henderson gave him a sharp, almost military nod. "I'm glad to see you awake, sir. Paris, I'm afraid I have some dull corporate matters I need to discuss with Jaffle."

As Paris stood to go, Rufus intended to lean over and pat her on the buttocks but he didn't have the energy and simply gave her a goodbye grunt. He waited for the door to click shut.

The whale swooped in and tried to entice me with loop-the-loops and exquisite pirouettes.

"I don't think it's going to matter to the media," said Henderson. "You've got the corporate gala on the fifteenth. The *charity* gala. You need to wipe your memory of what happened last night. You have high enough access to do that personally."

"Actually, I've got this whale in my head which is making some of my functionality a bit glitchy," said Rufus.

Heeeellooooooooooooooo, said the whale.

"Fine," muttered Henderson. "Then we'll get it done back at Jaffle Tech."

"Whoa, people!" said Rufus. "Maybe I don't want to give up that memory? It was kind of cool, you know? I can be discreet. It will only be a problem if I talk about it, right?"

"With all due respect, sir, you are a security risk. In my estimation, you will definitely talk about this in future. We must erase the memory."

Whhyyyyyyy don't yoooouuu waaaaaaaant toooo beeee aaaaa whaaaaaaale? the whale sang sadly.

Because you're actually really annoying, I thought.

"Could you please authorise the project brief for the completion phase?" Henderson was saying, holding out a sheaf of papers.

I/Rufus looked at the papers but took in none of the words.

"Jaffle Tech has benevolently agreed to assist governments in the social management of the general population," explained Henderson in a patient voice. "Jaffle Tech has the largest live database of consumers and voters in the world. We are literally inside everyone's head. That's a place where the governments would love to be. This—" he stabbed at the papers "—is us taking the next step towards giving consumers what they need."

"Need or want?" said Rufus. It was reflex question; he hadn't actually understood half of what Henderson was saying.

Henderson smiled. "Wasn't Henry Ford supposed to have said that if he gave customers what they wanted, he'd be working on making a faster horse rather than cars? It's up to us to have the vision to take things forward." He sat back. "You know, I was planning on purchasing Jaffle Freedom myself."

"You?" said Rufus.

"What else am I going to spend my money on? I've got the largest apartment on the Panhandle. I've got a mansion south of the border. I should buy Jaffle Freedom. And be like you, sir."

Rufus settled back into his pillow.

Yooooou're nooo fuuuuun, sniffed the blue whale, deeply upset, and swished its tail as it turned to the depths.

I opened my eyes. Henderson and the hospital and the blue whale had gone.

However, something felt very different. I was looking up at the ceiling. It was white, but was sculpted into swirls I had never noticed before. Miniscule waves of white plaster. They were so beautiful. How had I never been aware that such exquisite form and movement were possible in a ceiling? It was like a little world of detailed beauty, a cosmos of peaks and troughs, almost unbearably wonderful.

I sat up properly.

"Whoooaaa!"

I felt the impact like a blow to my stomach. In my eyes, down my spine and – wallop! – into my stomach. The whole room was a blaze of colour! I had vaguely registered that the walls had coloured hangings upon them as I entered, but now I saw them properly. I screamed. There was a picture of a woman with a lace collar and a smiling face who bent down to touch the top of a dog's head. There was an expression on the woman's face that made me roil with strange, unknown feelings. The feelings frightened me. They felt instinctively wrong. Like feeling a cool fresh breeze blowing across your kidneys, it was simply not right.

I tried to stand up. I had to get out of this room with its terrifying walls. I lurched across the thick carpet and fell to my hands and knees. The feeling of the carpet beneath my hands made me gasp. I fell forward to bury my face in it. I didn't know why, I just had to.

"Hey Alice, are you all right?" said Rufus.

"Mmmff!" I howled into the carpet.

In my head the sound of voices, even my own voice, was *different*. The same, but different. It was like I had been to avuncular narrator training college and then had my ears upgraded to some super-duper 3D stereo quality. There were inflections and tonal differences that made my head spin as much as the colour on the walls.

"Everything ... *I* say is ... *amazing*," I gasped.

"Alice?" said Rufus.

"I'm ... *sorry*. Alice isn't ... *in* right now."

Rufus grabbed me by my shoulders and hauled me up. "Did it work? Is it gone? Have you wiped the memory?"

"The brain virus?"

"Yes. That too." His hands held me roughly, squeezing the flesh of my upper arms.

"You're ... *hurting* me," I said.

"I'm sorry," he said and automatically loosened his hold. I immediately dropped to the floor again.

"No, no..." I said. I was about to say that it was quite pleasurable but that was silly. It was pain. Pain was never nice. Pain was just pain, wasn't it? I was very confused. And frightened. Something was simply not right. My wildly darting eyes caught sight of the cups on the edge of the desk.

"The tea!" I said a little too loudly. "You put something in the tea!"

"What? No! Unless you're allergic to the soul balms and spiritual powers of Himalayan detox."

He stabbed a button on his desk. There was a *bing bong* sound.

"Florence, would you call a medic up here please, I think Alice might be having a bad trip or something."

I was still reeling from the sound of the *bing bong*. It was like nothing I'd ever heard before and I found that my vision blurred with tears in response.

"Bing bong," I repeated, but it sounded different. "Bing BONG! Oh wow, did you hear that? I can do it too. BING ... BONG!"

I rolled on the carpet and marvelled at the way the tears in my eyes made the colours in the room blur in an astonishing new way. I rolled faster, feeling the carpet under my whole body. I stretched out my arms and rolled some more, but then I crashed into the desk.

"BING BONG!"

I heard the odd barking noise that I'd heard from Claire that morning, but it was Rufus making the noise. I found my own voice joining in with the barking and it felt good to do it, so very good. I barked loud and long, rolling back the other way as I did it. I rolled faster and faster until I thumped into something that turned out to be Rufus's legs.

"Come on up now," he said. "Enough fooling around. Laughter's a great healer, but man, you're over-indulging a little now, Alice."

I kept barking, knowing that I couldn't possibly stop, even though it was beginning to hurt. I opened my eyes, realising that I'd had them squeezed shut and saw Rufus, his face contorted in a way that made me bark even louder. Was this what he meant by laughter? I was having trouble breathing now, but my attention was arrested by another picture on the wall. This one was much brighter than the other one and showed dogs again, but in a very different setting.

Breathing was no longer an option. It was out of the question when I wanted to gasp and laugh at the same time as shouting *bing bong*.

"Dogs. Playing cards."

Colours melted and spun in my eyes. I heard the sound of my own shouting and decided that it was beautiful, and was sad when the sound faded away and the room went black.

***

Chapter 7

I woke up on a strange, hard bed. The smell was not familiar. When I opened my eyes I realised that I was in the medical room for my floor of the building. I'd only ever been in here before as part of routine medical evaluations. There was a sheet draped over me and part of the unfamiliar smell came from it. A different laundry smell. It made me hungry, so I tried to take a bite. It was a lot harder to take a bite from a sheet than I'd imagined. I worried it with my teeth and eventually succeeded in tearing a piece off. I swallowed it hungrily, but it wasn't as satisfying as it should have been. I started to chew off another piece when I heard footsteps.

A woman approached and gave me a broad smile. "Awake? Lovely."

"Can you smell that?" I asked, sniffing.

The woman ignored my question and consulted a thermometer and blood pressure gauge. "I'm here to check you over, Alice," she said. "You fainted."

"It smells really good," I said, distracted. "Who fainted?"

"You did, perhaps from the heat. Have you been chewing this sheet?"

"No. Definitely not."

Heat? I guessed that Mr Jaffle was keen to avoid any questions relating to the unauthorised work I'd done on his brain.

"Hmmm." The woman stared at the sheet, frowning. "You have a bump on your head. Could you tell me how much it hurts, on a scale of one to ten?"

The woman was very pretty, I realised. Just below the brim of her medical cap, her eyebrows were very dark and striking, and she had big beautiful eyes. I wanted to reach out and touch them but thought that probably wasn't a good idea.

"Hurt? Not at all. Zero," I said. I knew I had to get out of there as quickly as possible. "Perhaps I should go home and have a lie down for the rest of the day?"

"Well you seem to be in good overall health, although your Jaffle Port is offline for some reason. Do you want to reset it?"

"I will."

"I think perhaps we'd better book you in for a full scan. Perhaps you're suffering from some anxiety."

"Scan?"

"Yes. You fainted. Your port is off-line. A scan for glitches might be in order." The woman looked away for a moment, consulting her heads-up display. "The day after tomorrow. Three in the afternoon?" She smiled. Her eyes were really big. Like a blue whale's. They were so big, I thought I might cry.

"Beautiful," I sighed.

"Great. I'll book that in and send you a reminder."

"Er, yes," I said. A brain scan. I really needed one of those, to make sure I didn't have the virus. On the other hand, I really needed to get out of there, find some low stimulus environment and curl up and sleep. "Day after tomorrow. Excellent."

I got up from the bed, narrowing my eyes to avoid seeing any bright colours or the woman's own beautiful eyes. I needed to get out in one piece. More importantly, I needed to find out where that delicious smell was coming from.

I walked along the corridor from the medical room. Levi Krasnesky fell into step beside me.

"Are you following me?" I asked.

"I came down to see how you were. You weren't at your desk this morning."

"Spying on me?"

"Got to watch over my flock."

I stopped and faced him. "Flock?"

"Yabetcha." His little moustache twitched. "Gotta keep an eye on ya."

I felt a rush of strange new feelings wash over me. I thought of all the times that Levi had made me feel small. All the times he'd come up with some crazy rule that I was supposed to have broken, but most of all I thought about the mouse. Levi had killed a mouse, right in front of me when she had been trying to capture it.

It had confused me at the time, how he'd managed to accidentally repeatedly stamp on a mouse, but I saw the truth of it now and wondered why it hadn't been clear to me before. He'd done it on purpose. He had deliberately killed the mouse. There was a word for that. I had to look it up. Murder. The man had murdered a mouse!

A strong but overwhelming sound came from the bottom of my stomach.

"Grrr!" I said.

I wasn't sure why I said it, but it pulled my face into the correct shape to reflect my mood.

Levi stared at me. "What?"

"Didn't you hear me?" I said.

"What?"

"I said, you've got a fly on your head." I whacked him with my hand, straight across his face.

"Did you get it?" he asked, a look of mild shock on his face.

"No," I said and whacked him again with my other hand, swinging it right round to connect with his other cheek. "Oops, missed again. It's not part of the system. It needs dealing with. Look, it's right there on your nose!" I pulled my fist back and punched him hard.

Levi reeled backwards, clutching his bleeding nose. "Did you geddid?" he managed, wadding a tissue against the flow of blood.

"Yes, I got it that time." I started to walk away before turning back. "My mistake!" I yelled and kicked him in the shin. "Nearly! Oh, there it goes!" I punched his stomach. "There, that's better."

"'Ank oo," said Levi, staggering towards a bathroom.

I walked on, my palms and knuckles stung. Instead of upset, I felt a weird swelling sensation inside me, *here* in my chest, like a voice yelling "Yes! Yes! Go, Alice!" It was most perplexing but, more importantly, the smell that had grabbed my attention in the medical room was now an irresistible draw. It was salty, tangy and had an earthy, animal smell that should have been repellent. Instead it was a red hot wire of yearning plugged straight into my brain and hauling me in.

I followed my nose along a corridor, into a rest area where my section head, Paulette, sat with some food in her hands.

"What's that?" I asked with a nod to the delicious-smelling thing.

"It's a bacon sandwich," said Paulette. "Why aren't you at work, Alice?"

"Are you eating that bacon sandwich?"

"I am. Shouldn't you be at your desk?"

"I've been given the rest of the day off," I said. Wow. Where did that come from? It was a total untruth but it just came to me so naturally.

"Have you?" said Paulette with a frown. "By whom?"

"I want your bacon sandwich."

"Pardon?"

"Jaffle – that's Rufus Jaffle – told me to tell you that it would be fine," I said. "I was called up to his office to help him. You should have had a message from reception about that. Jethro Henderson, the CTO, asked for me personally. You can check. And now I've got the rest of the day off."

"Oh. I see."

I was dumbfounded by my new ability, and how easily accepted this alternative truth was. Yes, much of what I'd said was true but ultimately it was a deception and utterly dishonest. Instead of being afraid, I wondered whether I could push it further.

"He also said that you should give me that bacon sandwich for a job well done."

"*This* bacon sandwich?" said Paulette.

"Yes," I said firmly. "You can put it through on expenses."

"Really? That's a little odd."

"Yes. Now less chat, more bacon."

I reached over and pulled the sandwich from Paulette's hands. I stuffed it in my mouth. Fatty juices, mixed with a delicious burned taste, rolled down my throat.

"Oh, yes!" I mumbled contentedly. "This is definitely what I need."

I took another bite and chewed it joyously. Bacon was certainly much more delicious than the bed sheet that I had partially eaten.

"It seems I do have a message from Henderson," said Paulette.

"See?" I said, spraying half chewed crumbs.

"Yes, well, if the order comes from on high..."

I walked away. I didn't need conversation now that I had a bacon sandwich. It was amazing, much better than beans (red *or* blue). In fact, I decided it was the best thing that I had ever eaten. Ever. I must find out where I could get another one, and soon.

***

Chapter 8

I knew something had happened to me in Rufus Jaffle's office. Maybe it was the tea. Maybe I'd done something wrong with the clean-up protocols. Whatever it was, I was awash with new sensations and feelings. It was like I was a screen and the volume had been turned up to maximum, along with the brightness and the contrast and loads of other settings that I didn't even yet know the names of.

Even though I knew something had clearly gone wrong and needed fixing, I felt a burning urge to explore the new sensations while I still possessed them.

I left the building and ran. I ran from Jaffle Tech and Jaffle Park. I told myself that I was running to put as much distance as possible between myself and the trouble I was possibly in at work. Truthfully, I ran because running felt like the right thing to do. The warm air brushed my face. The tug of forces and energy in my limbs. The slap of my shoes on the ground.

I experimented with swinging my arms about as I ran. That felt really good. I tried a few jumps and skips too. They felt even better.

I ran in the general direction of home, staying clear of the major roads and public spaces. When my lungs were burning and my head spinning and I felt I couldn't run any more, I slowed and walked. I was somewhere near the area Hattie and I had walked through on our way to work a few hours before. I could have looked up where I was on a map but I currently enjoyed the experience of being lost.

There was a noise coming from a parked car. It was some sort of alarm. It was so gloriously loud that I went straight over to listen to it. A moving car narrowly avoided me. The car honked its horn and the passenger shouted out the window at me. It added to the overwhelming sound sensation.

"Hello," I said to the car with the alarm.

"*I am alarmed,*" said the car.

"You're amazing," I told it and laid down on the front of it. It thrummed through my entire body. I could feel the vibration of the speaker, somewhere underneath my right hip. What a world I lived in where it was possible to fill up my ears with such a pure sound! I wanted to take it with me, and my hand explored the edge of the car, trying to locate the centre of the sound.

"I am alarmed," the car repeated.

I stroked its paintwork.

"Oi! Get away from there!" came a voice.

I stood up and waved at the man who was approaching. His face was contorted with such an unusual display of muscular tension that I started to laugh. Laughing, proper laughing, felt good but that seemed to make his face bunch even tighter. I giggled wildly and started to walk away.

"Don't you run off!" he yelled.

Running seemed like a really good idea. Levi hated running in the office but Levi wasn't here, so I ran. I looked behind and saw the shouting man, and laughed again.

It wasn't long before I had to slow again. I bent over for a moment to catch my breath. A small insect scurried across the ground. I had never really looked carefully at an insect, normally regarding them as invaders of the home or workplace. This one was shiny, black and purposeful. I wondered how it could be so black *and* so shiny. Black was an absence of colour, and yet this insect reflected the many colours of its surroundings.

"Hello," I said, putting my hand down towards the insect. It changed course and scurried away. I put a hand down in front of it and it changed course again. I blocked it again and it hurried off in a different direction.

"Wow, you're fast," I said and had another thought. I used my hands to box it in completely, curious about which direction it would take. It didn't hesitate, it climbed up and over my hand, determined to break free. I felt the tickle of its tiny feet and guided it gently back down. I watched it for a few more minutes until it disappeared into a crack.

I continued walking along the road. The first of the houses with a colourful garden made me stop and stare. The colours of the flowers bobbing and waving in the light breeze made my eyes water. There were so many different colours and a delicate scent in the air. There were some pale yellow flowers and some that were a completely different kind of yellow, and each one of them was so very lovely to see.

Hadn't I, only that morning, discussed with Hattie how useless and untidy flowers were, being neither grass nor trees? What a stupid idea.

"I think I like flowers," I said.

I stepped closer and touched one. I wondered if yellow might feel different to red. I brushed my fingertips across the flowers, trying to feel the colours. If I really concentrated I was certain that yellow felt a little bit sticky. A large flying insect emerged from the trumpet-shaped centre of a flower and startled me. I laughed. Laughter was a strange thing that I really didn't understand, but I enjoyed doing it. I laughed again but it wasn't the same if I tried to do it.

My gaze lowered slightly from the bright flowers. They were all crowded into the soil. It looked very dirty. In fact, wasn't soil the same as dirt? When dirt came into the apartment (and Hattie generally swooped into action to get rid of it) was it always the same stuff as this? It seemed remarkable that beautiful flowers should live happily in dirt. Maybe dirt wasn't as bad as I'd always been led to believe. I poked my finger into the soil and put it into my mouth. It tasted really bad. I pulled a face and spat in disgust. I tried to picture what my face was when I scrunched it up in disgust. I laughed at the thought and put some more soil in my mouth. It was a bigger bit and I felt my face contort at the bitter horror of what was in my mouth. I stood up and grinned with delight at the range of crazy expressions I could pull with my face.

I walked along for a few more minutes and looked around. I was on the road near to that woman's house – Claire. My eyes narrowed as I thought about Claire. She had deliberately made us pick up dog poo. It was much clearer in my mind now although still confusing. It hadn't been right or normal for Claire to force us to pick up dog poo. She had done it because she wanted to...

"Ooh, what's the word?" I muttered.

Claire had done it because she wanted Hattie and I to feel unhappy. She wanted to distress us and make us feel socially awkward. Claire had wanted to assert her social dominance over us by making us feel we had done wrong and by making herself seem superior. She had wanted to shame them.

"She embarrassed us!" I said suddenly.

The woman had embarrassed us and, worse still, we hadn't known it was what she was doing. The contrast between the woman's cruelty and our naïve ignorance had amused Claire and her neighbour! Claire had done it because it was funny! But it wasn't funny, it was horrible!

And now, abruptly, I was angry. Anger was new. Anger was what had made me hit Levi repeatedly. And anger was odd. It was a negative emotion but it made me feel *good*.

Anger made me want to do something. The something in question was currently uncertain but it wasn't going to be a nice something. That should have worried me. It could be the brain virus, but I decided that I didn't really care. I would think about it later. Right now it was time to act.

I crossed over and looked at Claire's house and garden. She had a beautiful house. It was enormous and the door was an amazing glossy colour. The garden was as colour-filled with flowers as the one I'd stopped at just now. I walked up to the glossy door and banged on it loudly.

I wanted Claire to appear. I wanted to do something with Claire. I wanted to do something *to* Claire.

Nobody answered the door. I walked around the house. I found a window and peered inside. Claire had pictures on the wall like Jaffle had. Some of the chairs were covered in pictures of flowers. I had never seen anything like it before. I walked around the house some more.

A little table on a tall stand in the garden made me stop in my tracks. It had some sort of food on top of it, with containers hanging down. Birds fluttered around and jostled for position to get at the food. The birds were different sizes, mostly a brownish colour, and some smaller ones with flashes of blue and yellow. I had seen birds wheeling through the sky and occasionally walking on the grass near the Jaffle building, but this was the closest that I'd ever been to them and the flurry of activity made me giggle in delight, despite my continuing anger. The sound, although small, was enough to alarm the birds and they all took off, as though they were joined together.

I found the back door. I tried the handle and it opened. I went inside.

I was in a kitchen. This was not a kitchen like the one that Hattie and I had at home. We had very little in there except for cups, bowls and cupboard storage for beans. This kitchen was full of strange things. There was a large white, two-doored cupboard that was cold inside. I held one door open and marvelled at the feeling of cold pouring from it.

One door was a bit cold and the other door was really cold. I pulled some things out to see what they were. A brick-shaped yellow thing looked interesting. Its wrapper said that it was cheese. It was food so I took a bite. Cheese was good, I decided. It was not bacon but it was nearly as good as bacon. I took it with me.

There was much more to look at in the kitchen. There were so many tools, and I had no clue what they were for. I took another bite of cheese and opened another cupboard. It held plates and bowls in lots of different shapes. Another cupboard was filled with metal objects. They looked quite ugly and I wondered what they were for. I wondered if I might find a bacon sandwich in here somewhere. I jipped for bacon and discovered it came from pigs. I didn't know if that meant I had to find a pig in the kitchen in order to extract the bacon or not. I found a cupboard filled with packets of food. I dipped into a box of raisins. They were delicious. Very un-bacony and not at all cheesy but delicious nonetheless. I took those as well.

Taking alternate mouthfuls of cheese and raisins, I explored the house some more. Every room was brightly decorated. There was colour on every surface, with pictures on some of the walls. The carpet in the next room was thick, with a small oblong area that was even thicker. I took a closer look. It was a small piece of extra carpet so thick and furry it looked like an animal. I ran my fingers through the fur.

"Mm."

I took my shoes off and put my feet on it. That felt so good, it demanded more.

Without wasting another moment, I removed all my clothes and rolled on the fur. The sensation on some parts of my body made me gasp with pleasure. I rolled and scrunched myself and wriggled. I wanted the rug to touch me all over.

My body wasn't something I had given much thought to before; not in that way. I knew I had a body and I knew what all the bits were for. Hands were for holding things, feet were for walking, knees were for bending and all that. And I had been aware – obviously – that my skin was sensitive to touch. That was only practical. Even on the less

explored parts of my body, it was important to know if I was touching something hot or cold or wet or sharp. It was how the body kept itself safe.

But now...

I was beginning to comprehend the sense of touch could mean more. The fibres of the rug tickled and caressed; the touch of it on my body here and here and *here* was exciting. It was like I had discovered a new skin, underneath the old one. It was like I had ripped off all my clothes and rolled around for the pure pleasure of it. Which I guess I had.

I had a body. It was an obvious, even trite thought, but it was a new and exciting one.

I sat up and looked at myself. I looked at my legs and my knees and the low curve of my belly.

Suddenly, I wanted to see all of myself. I jumped up and ran in search of a mirror. Upstairs, in a bedroom, I found a full-length mirror and looked at my naked body. It was oddly fascinating to see what I looked like all over – none of the mirrors in my own apartment were that big. Now, I could see what I looked like, all of me. I studied my front and then turned and craned my neck to look at myself from behind. I liked what I saw and touched and poked every part of me. I felt a certain embarrassment. Not at my nakedness – hell, no – but at the fact that I'd been living in this body for over two decades and had never bothered to get to know the neighbours, metaphorically speaking.

"Hello, elbow," I said. "Hello, armpit. Hello, nipples. Hello, belly button."

On the bedroom wall, there was a picture of a woman with no clothes on. I looked at it with interest, glancing back and forth between my image in the mirror and the woman's body in the picture. My own body wasn't quite so full in the stomach and breasts, but then the woman in the picture was reclining. I tried lying on the bed, but found that I could no longer see myself in the mirror.

I thought of Claire's colourful clothes and opened a cupboard. There were a great many clothes, organised by colour and shape. I decided I liked the look of a red and blue striped dress and pulled it out. I put the dress on and looked in the mirror. I grinned with delight. What an amazing difference it made from the bland tunic I wore to work.

My thoughts were interrupted by an unpleasant feeling. I rubbed my stomach as it gurgled alarmingly and I groaned a little at the strange discomfort. I let out a belch and felt better. There was a gusty cheese taste in my mouth. Bacon sandwiches, cheese and raisins – fun to eat, fun to belch.

I moved over to a table with lots of little pots and sparkling objects. I picked up a bottle at random. It was half full of amber liquid and the writing on the side said *Eastern Lilies*. It had a spray mechanism, and when I gave a tentative squirt, the most incredible fragrance misted out. I sniffed and sprayed again. It was as if the smell from the flowers was stored up inside. I loved the idea that you could smell flowers whenever you wanted, so I picked up the bottle to take with me. I sprayed some into my mouth to see what it tasted like.

It tasted very unpleasant. I tried it again, just to be sure.

"No, that's just horrible."

Why was it so bad in my mouth and so wonderful when I smelled it?

I took a deep breath, suddenly in need of unperfumed air. So many sensations vied for my attention, but I couldn't ignore the flip-flopping of my stomach. It was as if the perfume and the sudden thought of cheese and bacon all piled up inside me was just a bit too much. I felt a heavy shift inside myself, forcing me to bend over. I steadied myself on a drawer handle, and pulled it out. Inside the drawer were undergarments. It took me a moment to recognise them as such. All of my underwear was practical and durable but these looked as delicate as insect wings. They were colourful and made from exquisite fabrics. I wanted to touch them all and rub myself with them but, I realised, that was never going to happen.

My stomach signalled its intentions with a painful heave. I vomited greasy bacon and chewed-up cheesy raisins into the drawer for long, painful moments. I closed the drawer and stood up, feeling very much better. I pictured Claire pulling open the drawer and finding the mess I'd just made and I laughed. I hadn't been sure what I wanted to do when I came in here, but this seemed right somehow.

"Time to go," I said, wiping a blob of sick from the corner of my mouth.

I made my way out of the house in my new dress. On the way I saw a hat on a stand, paused to try it on, and looked at my reflection in another mirror. I looked so tall and interesting. The hat had feathers and angular pieces of stiff straw pointing off in different directions. I kept the hat and let myself out the front door. I walked up the road, feeling the hat bobbing on my head, inhaling lungfuls of fresh air. I felt beautiful, elegant even.

I still had the taste of vomit in my mouth. I spat into the road. Spitting was fun too.

***

Chapter 9

Near my apartment complex I saw an Empty, sitting on the kerb.

Empties were a part of everyday life. Literally. I saw them every day and had regarded them only as an inconvenience, like litter or fallen leaves. I hadn't properly considered what they were and my mind had just blocked them out.

The Empty was a man, but only the shell of a man.

The realisation crashed into my mind and I felt sick in a way that had nothing to do with bacon or cheese or raisins. I wasn't yet sure quite *how* my brain had become more fully enabled than it was when I woke up this morning, but I understood on some level that I had been opened up, granted access to something more than was allotted to me in life.

Apart from that weird and unfathomable three percent of society, everyone had a Jaffle Port and had purchased outright or bargained away unutilised processing space for that access. I was – or had been – operating on Jaffle Standard. That was fine, normal and pretty much enough for anyone. Above there was Jaffle Enhanced and Jaffle Premium for those able to pay and reclaim that processing space for their own (and frankly selfish) use. In the other direction, below Jaffle Standard, there was Jaffle Economy and Jaffle Lite. You only ended up on those if you were stripped of more processing space to pay unsettled debts or as punishment by the courts. I hadn't really thought about them much; I didn't work in debt reclamation and the concepts of crime and punishment were alien to me (or had been until very recently).

But what was below Jaffle Lite? What was at the lowest end of the scale? I was looking at it. The Empty – I corrected myself: the *man* – sat by the side of the road in a bright pink coverall. His chin and head were covered in the same uniform stubble. He had a Jaffle Port and, I guessed, he had surrendered as much of his brain's functionality as was possible without actually killing himself. His brain function was enough to keep essential organs ticking over, but little more.

I went to him and touched his hand, but he reacted only with a voiceless grunt. Drool trickled over his cheek and his eyes gazed into the middle distance, registering nothing. Even cars and apartments had more personal awareness.

What had he done to deserve this? I looked further along the kerb. There were more Empties – *men* and *women*, all lolling in the same lifeless way. How did they even get fed? Why had I never really looked at them before?

I tried to help him get up, but he was so far away from understanding that he couldn't work his arms and legs. I waved my hand in front of his eyes; he saw nothing.

"How can I help you?" I said.

I shouted and wept, but nothing could get through to him. I let out a wail of despair and flung my arms around the man.

"Is assistance required with this unit?"

I recoiled. For a moment I thought he had spoken but the voice had come from a stud speaker set into his lapel.

"I'm sorry?"

"Is assistance required with this unit?" said the speaker.

I shook my head

"Supervision is en route," said the speaker and clicked off.

I got to my feet. The man did not react to my movement, had not reacted once. Anger seethed through me. This new sensation was the one that went with the growling and the scrunched-up face, and now I revelled in it. I had much to be angry about.

"What kind of a world is this?" I demanded of no one and everyone. "How can you treat people like this and expect life to go on as normal?"

There was a faint buzz. I looked up. A cloud of insects hovered nearby. It was a Jaffle Swarm. Bees or wasps or flying beetles, each with an implant in its brain, the cloud as a whole controlled by the borrowed processing power of humans elsewhere in the world.

"Supervision present," said the Empty's lapel speaker. *"Is there a problem with this unit?"*

Tearful, I backed away.

Anger seethed through me. This new sensation was the one that went with the growling and the scrunched-up face and now I revelled in it. I had much to be angry about. What sort of a world was I living in? How could people become like this Empty while everyone else carried on as normal? I paused at that. What was normal? Even yesterday, I had thought I had a normal life, trailing around just doing my job, at the mercy of people like Claire and Helberg. People who thought they were better than me and could make fun of me. Did they also make fun of the Empties? Did they spend their whole lives feeling superior, just because they'd been able to afford a functioning brain?

I looked up at my apartment complex. Helberg had taken all of my money on the flimsiest excuse. Was that how the world worked? The people with no standards got all the money and the people with all the money got all the privilege? It just wasn't fair. It was so unfair that I felt more anger building in me. It roiled my stomach almost as much as the bacon and cheese, but it felt like an explosion that would come out in a very different way. I stomped into the building and headed straight for the manager's office.

"Helberg!" I yelled, but he wasn't there. I went in and sat at his desk. Thankfully the screen was off. I turned my attention to the other stuff that was in there. A small cupboard led off to the side. It looked like maintenance supplies. The main office held a filing cabinet and an old-fashioned desktop computer. It was already switched on and logged in so I took a look at his business files. The building I was in was one of six that Helberg managed, which surprised me. I examined the other buildings on the local cameras and saw that all of them were in a very poor state of repair. I found lots of examples of ad-hoc charges to tenants and complaints that he'd ignored. One of the other buildings had been declared unfit for habitation by an annual inspection, but this appeared to have been filed and ignored.

"Well if it isn't one of my favourite tenants," said Helberg from the door. He was smiling. It was the same smirk that I'd started to recognise on those privileged enough to have their brains more fully enabled. It was the smirk they used when they felt superior.

I shoved past him. I ducked into the storage cupboard and saw what I needed. I picked up a short length of thick timber and hefted it. I swung it experimentally and then brought it down fast on the old computer monitor. It smashed in a very satisfying manner. I swung it again and smashed the glass in the door. I swept everything from the shelves and then smashed the shelves in half for good measure. I kicked a waste bin across the room, scattering its contents. I kicked it again, just to make a dent in the side.

I raised the length of timber high and advanced on Helberg, delighted now to see that his smirk was gone now.

"How do you like my re-decorating?" I yelled as he whimpered slightly. "You know I'm going to charge you a lot of money for this, don't you?"

"Alice, I feel as though you have the wrong idea about me," he said, his arms protecting his face.

"No, I have exactly the right idea about you. You rip off tenants and let their apartments fall into ruin. You take people's money and make them live in terrible conditions. You act as if you're so much better than us, when all you have is money that isn't even yours! You're a disgrace. You've done so many bad things that when I take you to the police, they'll turn you into one of those Empties. I won't feel sorry for you, even though it's a terrible way to treat a human, because I know that you've done that to other people by stealing all of their money."

"You don't know that—" he started. I cut him off with a swipe of the timber which didn't quite rip his desk in two. Bot parts, electronics and unsorted filing flew everywhere.

"Am I very very angry?" I yelled.

"Er, yes," he said.

"I don't know how to turn it off!"

"Er, what?"

I gave a scream of fury mixed with panic, hurled the chunk of wood at the wall and ran.

***

Chapter 10 – 3rd June

I dreamed I was in a plush flying drone, accompanied by a pair of stunningly pretty girls. Except it was also my cubicle at work and there was a kangaroo looming over me.

"Babe," Rufus drawled. "You know your aura fascinates me so much. It's got that blossoming, burgeoning thing going on. I want to reach out and touch it."

His hands groped across the two girls. Those hands weren't seeking an aura, they were seeking out breasts.

"Hey babes!" said Rufus. "Your auras are going wild. What say we throw caution to the wind and see whether our chakras align if we all get naked?"

The kangaroo by the cubicle wall looked powerful and fierce. It gave off an animal stink which did not disgust me, but fascinated me. It was more real than anything I had experienced in my life. Except, it wasn't a kangaroo anymore; it was Levi from work.

"What are you doing here?" I asked.

I focused on his arms, which were really quite muscular now. It was unusual for him to be without a jacket, but then I saw it hanging from the tip of his finger.

"There's no rule against us getting naked, Alice," he said solemnly, his gaze upon me. "Although we need to take care not to discard our clothes anywhere that might create a trip hazard."

In my dream I was nodding. Levi carefully put his jacket over the back of my chair and reached out to me. He made a slow chopping movement with his hand. "Advanced practitioners must exercise restraint and secrecy."

I took his hand and stood up, close to him. The women were completely identical now. Bland faces, huge breasts and pneumatic bottoms.

Rufus slipped his fingers inside their clothes. A nipple stiffened against both sets of fingers and he smiled, feeling unstoppable.

Levi's little moustache was right in front of me and I couldn't help wondering whether it would tickle my lips.

"We're nearly there!" said one of the girls, excitedly.

Do yoooou liiike thaaaat? asked the blue whale.

***

"Alice! Alice!"

I woke to find Hattie shaking me by the shoulder. I grunted and tried to roll out of reach.

"Alice, you need to wake up!" Hattie insisted. "And you really need to stop making those noises."

I couldn't seem to surface. My head spun and I wondered if the need to vomit was as close as I suspected. I opened my eyes and light stabbed painfully at my delicate brain. Hattie's face loomed over me, distorted with anxiety.

"What noises?" I muttered.

"You were moaning."

"Moaning?"

"Like..." Hattie made a noise. It was a bit like the hoot of that irritating blue whale. It was a lot like the moans and grunts the naked people made in the videos Helberg watched.

Helberg...? Helberg loomed large in my memory but I couldn't quite remember why.

"But you have to come quickly," said Hattie. "There's something very strange on top of the bean dispenser. I'm not sure if it's alive."

I rubbed a hand across my face as memories of the previous day paraded through my mind. The lies I'd told Paulette. My behaviour in the street. The break-in. The food. The clothes.

"Oh, no..."

What I had done to Helberg's office.

The parade of memories stuttered and stalled and became a horrific piled up mess of recollections. A feeling burned deep inside me. It felt like I was going to be sick, but not physically. It was a horrid and unshiftable desire for things to be different from what they currently were.

And on top of that nameless sensation there were the feelings aroused within me by those peculiar dreams.

I assured Hattie I would be along in a few minutes and hauled myself out of bed. I looked around for my Jaffle tunic and realised I'd left it at Claire's house. I held up the colourful dress to admire it once more. I would love to wear it to the office, but knew that it would be a terrible idea. I dug out a spare tunic and hung the dress at the back of the cupboard, well out of sight. I tried swishing and prancing in my tunic, but it just wasn't the same. That gorgeous gauzy fabric felt so special against my skin, that I couldn't wait to wear it again. Perhaps find some other clothes that made me feel that way. The colours too! I peeked another look at the dress, just to see the colours again. Could I put into words how colourful things made me feel? Excitement? Whatever it was, the apartment that Hattie and I shared was very lacking in colour. It made me a little bit sad to look around and see that everything was the same boring shade.

I went to my bedroom window and looked. I'm not sure I'd ever looked out of it before. Obviously, I'd gazed in that general direction before. It was where the light came in. But I'd never properly *looked*. There wasn't much to see. My room overlooked the central shaft which ran through the centre of the building. Above was a large square of sky. Across were the murky grey windows of other apartments. Several storeys below was the quadrangle at the heart of the ground floor. It was a square of mud and currently housed some sort of incinerator, pieces of wood and a number of rusting air conditioners.

My world was grey, dull and enclosed and I had never noticed.

I stepped into the kitchen area and looked at the very strange thing on top of the bean dispenser.

"It's cheese," I said.

"Chi-eeeese?"

"Yes, I got it yesterday. It's really nice, you should try some."

"It's food?" asked Hattie, incredulous. "No, I don't think so. It looks very peculiar."

I wasn't ready to have the food discussion quite yet. "Never mind, Hattie. We can have beans. Listen, I wanted to ask you something."

"Yes?"

"You know Levi?"

"Security Levi at work?" said Hattie as she served up blue beans.

"Mmm, him. Have you ever looked at his arms?"

"He has arms," said Hattie with conviction.

"Yes, but looking at them ... are they... are they quite muscular?"

Hattie frowned, concentrating. "He always wears a jacket at work, it's very hard to know. He probably needs to be strong to wrestle wrongdoers to the ground and suchlike."

"He probably does, yes," I reflected, feeling a strange frisson at the thought of Levi wrestling me to the ground, although I couldn't be sure why.

"Beans," said Hattie and handed me a bowl.

She went through to watch Rise and Shine with Smiley. I stood for a moment, looking at the screen. It followed the usual format of people waking up and having slightly sad faces, but then being cheered by the sight of Smiley appearing with his huge, yellow, sunny face, beaming down upon them. After I had watched the same scene play out three different times I shook my head. How could it be that I had once found this so very entertaining? It was clearly idiotic. I was a smart person, my brain was used for some amazing tasks, and yet I'd been happy to let nonsense like this fill it during quiet moments. It was so confusing.

I ate the beans, but found them dull. They were as dull to my taste buds as Smiley was now to my eyes. However, I was hungry, so I ploughed through them, but all the while I was thinking about the cheese and went back to the kitchen to sneak a bite of when Hattie wasn't looking.

My mind went from cheese to bacon, and I sighed, wondering whether there were other things that tasted so good. I would have to take care though, not least because I'd made myself sick yesterday by eating too many unfamiliar things. I knew how easily upset Hattie was, so I would try to be myself today. I would follow the normal routine and behave as we always did. Mostly I would anyway, just as soon as I'd got my mind straight.

I still couldn't shake the feelings that the dream-Levi had roused in me.

"Hattie," I said. "You know how men and women are different?"

"Mm," Hattie mumbled, her eyes not leaving the screen. "Different uniforms some of them. And they have different toilets in some old buildings."

"Right, yeah," I said, searching for a way in to this conversation, "so the different toilet facilities. Why is that?"

"Um, I think it's because men are messier," said Hattie.

I paused. "Their bodies aren't the same as ours."

"They have arms."

"What?"

"They all have arms," said Hattie. "You asked about Levi but I think all of them have arms."

"I know they have arms," I said defensively.

"Well, you asked. And they do."

"Yes, but apart from that they're a different shape."

"Yes, I suppose," said Hattie. "No boobs."

"Yes!" I said. "Yes. Those sorts of things. What other—"

"—apart from Pedstone."

"What?" I was thrown.

"Pedstone and Swanager," said Hattie, and mimed a little jiggle to underline the point. "Both got boobs. He's a man. She's a woman."

I sighed. I wasn't really sure what conversation I wanted to have about the difference between men and women, but this wasn't it.

And I had other things to worry about. Like Helberg's office. Had I really stormed into his office? And smashed his screen? And his shelves? I wished, I *hoped* that explosive episode was imaginary, as unreal as the blue whale which kept swimming in and out of Rufus Jaffle's memory.

"I need to pop downstairs," I told Hattie.

Hattie nodded, still transfixed by Smiley. I went down to see Helberg. On the way, I passed the many doors, all the same colour. I shook my head at yet another example of horrible drabness which was imposed upon us all.

Helberg's broken screen sat on the floor outside the complex manager's office. I touched it for a second and jipped it with my Jaffle Port. It wasn't a piece of Jaffle Tech and it wasn't equipped with the same security measures. Also, the man was lazy; lazy enough to think no one would be capable of breaking into his data. I stepped into the office. Helberg was repositioning a brand new screen on his still dented desk.

"Come to apologise, have we?" he said with a mock sweetness.

"No," I said.

"To offer to pay for the damages caused?"

"No."

"Because you had quite a temper on your last night. Quite out of character, dear tenant, if I may say. One might even suspect there's an imbalance in your system."

"You don't know what you talking about," I said.

"And neither do you," he replied. "The things you were spouting. Baseless accusations. Slander, that's what they call it."

I pointed back at the door, at the screen that sat outside. "I copied your files."

He looked at me sharply, his false cheer vanished. "Data theft? Your list of crimes is racking up."

"They weren't even protected," I said. "I just walked by and – pop! – I copied them. All of them. You've kept a detailed account of all the people you've fraudulently overcharged, often for services they were never provided with in the first place."

"Now, you listen here, miss," he said, pointing a finger.

I smiled. "I'm listening, Helberg. Patrick." I looked at him and waited.

His twitching mouth faltered. His pointing finger wilted. "You've got to understand..." he said. "Some people. Circumstances get the better of them. They've ... they've got no one but themselves to blame, you see?"

"But there is someone to blame," I said and smiled again. For the first time, I understood that not all smiles were meant to be nice. "You, Helberg. You are to blame. You will be held accountable."

"By you?" he said.

I nodded. "You're going to make things better. Maybe you don't know how to do that, but it doesn't matter, because I am going to tell you. Understand?"

He attempted a smile but it was no match for mine.

"Because even if you didn't do it directly, you have undermined these people. You took their money. You messed up their homes and their lives. You and I are going to fix things. Whatever it takes, we're going to make things better."

"Hey," he said. "I'm not the bad guy here. I'm not being selfish. I'm just after a slice of the easy life. I'm just a piece of grit in the system."

"You're a piece of something."

"If people can be exploited then it's someone's duty to exploit them, to show where the weaknesses lie. There is a natural order in the world. There are those of us who are intelligent enough to make the world to our liking. The brains of society's body. And somewhere down there, underneath it all are the people – human toenails – who exist only to be used. If bad things happen to people, then they've probably got it coming."

"Oh, good. Then I should just send these files to the authorities." I tapped my head. "I've even labelled them to be sent off in the event of an emergency."

I saw him blanch and knew that my remark had hit home. "I'd rather you didn't do that," he said simply.

"Well, as long as we understand each other, we can get straight to work," I said. "First of all, you're going to give me back my money."

He scowled but nodded.

"You can give me some more as well. I can see that sorting your mess out might be an expensive thing to do."

I jipped a request for payment over to him. He pulled a face but authorised the payment. Again, like his screen, his Jaffle Port technology didn't respond like proper Jaffle Tech. The signature looked different, which was odd.

"Right," I said. "You're going to find somewhere better for Swanager and Pedstone to live."

"How will I do that?"

"You'll think of something. Then, for your second task, you're going to make it easier for everyone to find their own front door."

"What?"

"They all look exactly the same, and it's confusing and annoying. Now before I go, I have a question." I pulled up a chair to face him. "When there are colourful plants growing, what is that called?"

He rolled his eyes and there was a trace of the old smirk. "Do you mean a *garden*?"

I tilted my head and gave him a look; and I mean a *look*. "Do you want me to redecorate your office again?" I asked.

A fervent headshake.

"So, it's a garden." I turned to the whiteboard on the wall. I picked up a pen and wrote *New place for S and P* at the top, followed by *doors* and *bacon* and finally *garden*.

"Good. We will talk later about how you're going to make gardens happen."

***

Chapter 11

I was quite relieved to get to work. I looked forward to some thinking time on my own. In spite of my efforts to appear normal, Hattie kept giving me funny looks, as if I might be ill. It hadn't helped when I had broken down in tears again at the sight of the Empties. Hattie didn't see them at all. I thought better of trying to point out the hideous reality of them living in a society which took thinking power away from its citizens and left them as hollow shells. Instead I just pretended I'd got something in my eye. Hattie had been distracted by the good news that I had enough money to pay for the car to take us on our regular pay-per-metre journey to work, so we arrived on time.

There was a small group of people standing in the centre of the reception area. I realised with horror that at its core was the woman, Claire, she of the bright clothes that didn't cover enough of her body, she of the defecating dog, she of the house which I had invaded, ransacked and violated. Claire was angrily brandishing my discarded tunic and shouting about an invasion of her privacy. There was a civil law enforcement officer there, and of course Levi.

I lurched in shock, nearly colliding with Hattie.

"You all right?" said Hattie.

"I think I'm going to be sick," I muttered.

"Did you touch the chi-eeese?"

I mentally pulled myself together. "Look, the elevator's about to go. Hurry."

"We've got loads of time," protested Hattie looking back over her shoulder. "Hey. Was that the woman that made me—" she pulled a face "—pick up the dog poop?"

"Not sure," I said, and quickly pressed the elevator button. "Best to stay well out her way in future though, don't you think?"

"I hope we didn't dispose of her dog's poo incorrectly," fretted Hattie.

I hurried Hattie from the elevator to our work stations and sought the sanctuary of my own cubicle, my own familiar little mouse hole. I worried briefly that some sort of alert would be triggered by the system when I started work, that some background system would note something different in my brain state. It wasn't and I was soon back in the usual routine.

The usual routine should have been comforting but I found myself continually looking round and finding things which must have always been there, but I'd simply never noticed before.

One of my colleagues had smelly feet and had taken their shoes off. The smell was strong enough for me to wish I'd brought Claire's perfume with me, but that was safely hidden back at the apartment. I sniffed my arm and could smell the slightest ghost of its fragrance, which made me smile.

I also noted that the entire department was lacking in colour. Nearly everything was a very pale green colour, but not an interesting, bright green like plants. It was a green that really wanted to be grey, as if all of the fun had been sucked out of it.

Then there was the sound all around me. The call centre was carefully designed so operatives didn't disturb each other, but that didn't mean I couldn't hear my colleagues if I listened carefully, tuning into some of the conversations. I could hear the tapping of feet and the squeaking of chairs. I was surrounded by dozens of intriguing noises, all of which told their own fascinating story.

I had changed. My life had changed. Every moment I had experienced was different now. And there was no denying that something had happened in Rufus Jaffle's office which had caused that change, that difference.

I needed to work out what it was; speak to someone who would understand and offer clear guidance.

I needed to speak to Rufus Jaffle again.

I forced myself to take enough calls to be high on the leader board, so that I could give myself a few minutes to step away from my workstation and put a call through to Rufus Jaffle via the company switchboard.

"Rufus Jaffle's office," said a female voice.

"Could I please speak to Jaffle?" I asked.

"I'm afraid he's not available, could I take a message?"

"Oh. Right. It's very important that I talk to Jaffle. It's Alice, the technician who helped him out yesterday."

"Rufus Jaffle wasn't in the office yesterday."

"But I—"

"You must be mistaken. Sorry."

I began to protest, then I realised what was happening. The effort to be discreet was overriding everything here. The entire clean-up operation had been hush-hush; no one was going to acknowledge that Rufus Jaffle had infected his brain with a virus and therefore no one was going to acknowledge it had required my help to clear it. The secretary wasn't going to be of any assistance to me.

"Right, thank you. Goodbye."

As I walked back to my cubicle I gave the matter some thought. If I couldn't get past the secretary then I'd have to think of some other way to see Jaffle. I had questions that only he could answer.

Levi was waiting next to my cubicle, hands on hips. I noticed the way that he stood. It was fascinating that men even stood in a different way to women. I couldn't imagine that I might ever stand like that. Legs apart, hands on hips, ready for... Ready for what? I wasn't sure, but I felt sudden heat in my cheeks, and I swallowed hard.

"Hello Levi," I said.

He raised his eyebrows. Along with that little moustache they create a frame for his face, the punctuation to his facial expressions. I wondered what they felt like. Were they soft and silky or coarse and bristly? I watched his lips, waiting for him to speak, absorbed by their curves, and wondering why they interested me so much and what beautiful words he was about to utter.

"Bathroom break?" he said.

Okay, they weren't particularly beautiful words.

"Pardon?" I said.

"It was a simple question, was it not?"

I frowned. The new warm fuzzy feelings I had developed for Levi since my dream of the night before came crashing up against the hard and unforgiving feelings I been building up about him for months.

"Are you watching me?" I said. Part of me liked the idea of him watching me and part of me thought it was wrong and unpleasant and invasive. I dipped into my Jaffle Port literacy booster. Creepy. That was the word.

"I watch everyone," he said.

"Well, I think I'd rather you didn't."

Levi was amused by this. "Don't get yourself all riled up, miss. Just doing my job. Eternal vigilance is the price of high quality security, not to mention health and safety, yabetcha."

"Yes, well, I was perfectly safe on my bathroom break. I always am," I said, not so much angry at his behaviour as the smashing of my daydream version of Levi. Trying to recapture it before it left me completely, I looked at his arms, remembering how strong and muscular they were in my dreams.

"Have you got hairs on your arms?" I asked.

Levi looked shocked at the question. He looked for a moment as though he might be about to roll up his sleeves and have a look – the very prospect of it made me come over all uncomfortably warm - but then he thought better of it.

"Well, I'm really not sure what that's got to do with the price of tea in China, miss," he replied.

"No, I was just interested," I said. I was about to add that I sometimes saw hairs sprouting through the gaps in his shirt, but I sensed Levi didn't want to talk about his body hair. He turned on his heel and walked down the office.

I watched him walk away. Irritating and nosy Levi. Levi with the strong muscly arms. Levi the heartless mouse-stomper. Levi with his little moustache.

He wore a utility belt which carried all sorts of odd bulky items like a torch, a ring of keys and a set of handcuffs. If I ignored all of that, his hips were actually very slim, and I considered what shape he might be without any clothes on. He would be quite different to the shape that I was. Different but pleasing. I felt the heat creeping into my face again and wondered whether I was getting a cold. I certainly seemed to be running a temperature.

A pop-up reminder appeared on my calendar. The brain scan with the medical team was booked in for the next day. Perhaps that would provide some answers.

***

Chapter 12

Hattie and I pulled up outside the apartment complex, the journey home smooth and fuss-free on the premium roads.

"I think I might hang onto the car," I said once Hattie was out, adding, as casually as I could, "Maybe go to the shops."

"Go to the shops?" asked Hattie. "What for?"

"Because."

"Are you going to the Smiley Store?"

"No, not there. I want to get some food."

"We have food."

"Different food?"

"Different beans?" asked Hattie, a look of naked horror on her face.

"I don't really know what I'll get. I'm off to have a look," I said.

It was clear from the look on Hattie's face that she simply didn't understand.

"It's fine though," I said. "You don't have to try any if you don't want to."

I gave instructions to the car and sped off to the food markets. I stepped out at the drop off point and walked inside. This was unfamiliar territory. Hattie and I had our beans delivered in bulk, so food markets were not places that we had ever really felt the need to visit. It was the same for pretty much everyone we knew.

The food markets was a place which sometimes featured in the screen *dramas* we occasionally flicked through by accident. Needlessly complicated people with needlessly complicated lives would bump into each other and talk about their miserable complicated problems over the food counters. And indeed the customers were dressed like the people from those drama programmes. No work-issue tabards here. The customers were as brightly coloured as the range of produce on offer on the shelves.

I soon realised I was very much out of my depth. There was a large section of things that looked as though they belonged in gardens. They were shiny and colourful, but I wasn't sure whether they were meant to be food or decoration. I peered at the displays and read the labels. Aubergines were impossibly shiny and a glamorous purple-black colour. I jipped a query and was thrilled to discover that they were edible. I popped one into a basket. I strolled around, checking a few more things. I spent some time running my fingers across the leaves of a Savoy cabbage, intrigued by the texture. The smell wasn't all that appealing, so I decided not to buy one. I spent more time reading about garlic. It was an unassuming papery cluster, but the description the Jaffle Port offered was of something delicious and flavoursome, so I popped one into my basket too. As I moved further into the markets, the shelves began to hold packets and tubs. There was no sign of bacon yet. I held up a jar of something called olives. Black globes bobbed in liquid. They looked like tiny versions of the aubergine, but jipping offered no connection between the two. I decided to try olives, and the things next to them called anchovies, which looked like strips of dirt stuffed into a jar.

A delicious smell drew me on. It wasn't the smell of bacon, but it was impossible to ignore. As I turned a corner into a section labelled *bakery* it hung in the air, thick and irresistible. Behind a counter, workers in white hats pulled trays out of large steel cabinets. They transferred golden, puffy products into bags and put them on shelves.

"Would you like a sample?" one of them asked me.

"What is that?" I asked.

"Heritage bloomer," said the woman and used a serrated knife to cut it into chunks. She put the chunks into a basket and placed them on the counter in front of me. I put a piece into my mouth at the same time as I jipped to see what a heritage bloomer was.

It was warm and delicious. Warm food was a strange idea, but a marvellous one. It added another dimension to the experience, and I found that I was making loud moaning noises of appreciation. I took another chunk of the heritage bloomer, which was apparently some sort of bread, and stuffed it into my mouth.

"Mm-mmm. Can I have another?"

"Certainly," said the woman. "Anything for you. And if you're a mystery shopper be sure to give me a five star rating."

"Mifftery fopper?" I mumbled and then jipped the term.

I stood there for quite a while, eating her way through the basket. A man came along and reached for a chunk, but I turned and gave him such a ferocious glare that he backed away.

I finally emptied the basket, shoving the last chunks into my mouth so that my cheeks bulged, and then put as many of the heritage bloomers into my basket as I could carry.

I decided I would come back and explore the rest of the food markets another day, as my arms were getting tired. I staggered to the exit aisle and received a cheery note of the cost of my purchases. I carried them outside, holding the heritage bloomers close so that I could inhale the delicious scent while I found a car to take me home.

When I got back to the apartment, the Empties were being fed. I put my bag down and watched with interest. A truck had pulled up at the side of the road and emitted a discreet chime. The Empties all came alive, shuffling forward to get a portion of beans. They were dispensed into disposable bowls from a chute at the side of the truck. The Emptied clutched their bowls and walked away, pouring beans into their mouths.

The truck pulled away. Feeding had been accomplished: quickly, without noise or fuss or even any need for human effort.

I frowned. At least the Empties weren't starving, but how could anyone think that this was a good way to look after people? I had a thought and turned to my bag of groceries. I broke off a chunk of heritage bloomer and handed it to the nearest Empty, a man whose face was creased with lines.

"Here, try this," I said. "I know you won't necessarily understand what I'm saying, but surely you'd like to hear another human voice huh? It stands to reason. Well my name is Alice and I want to be your friend. I want to help. You guys are really not having a fun time, but maybe we can improve things, what do you say?"

He said nothing.

"Well, I work over at Jaffle Tech, and I'm on the phones for most of the day. It's a good job and I love helping people out, I really do, but I'm beginning to think that maybe there are other things I'm interested in. Like different food. This bread is amazing, you should try it."

His free hand had been dipping into his bowl of beans, but now that it held a chunk of bread he seemed incapable of making sense of the situation. After twitching a few times, his hand opened and dropped the bread, and then he carried on eating his beans.

"Okay, what about this?" I pulled the garlic out of the bag and demonstrated how to take a bite. I quickly regretted it. There was an explosion of white papery mess. My mouth was full of it, and bits flew across my face and onto the ground. Before I could worry about that I was hit with the taste of whatever lay inside. It was so strong it stopped me in me tracks. My eyes started to water and I spat it all out, littering the Empty with flakes of garlic.

My mouth was still full of that dreadful, pungent taste. When I'd eaten soil, it was unpleasant, but this was like a physical assault. I thrust the rest of the garlic back on top of the groceries and tried to rid myself of the taste by making extravagant tongue-thrusting motions.

"Okay, not that," I said, still spitting garlic skin from my lips.

I went back to the groceries and considered the jar of olives. They were about the same size and shape as beans, but different. I had no idea why it was important to me that the Empties should eat something different, but I wanted to help them break free from their walking prisons. If this might help then I had to give it a try. I unscrewed the jar and took out an olive. It glistened attractively. I put one on top of the beans in the man's bag and then I picked out another and put it into my own mouth.

"What about this, huh?"

We could experience olives together. I bit down and was shocked by how hard it was. I looked away so that I didn't upset him with the face that I was pulling. The taste of the olive was bitter, but not horrible. I bit down again, but was completely unable to crunch the olive with my teeth. I jipped a quick search and saw that olives were sometimes stuffed, sometimes pitted, and sometimes whole. I looked at the jar and saw that these were whole olives. Another hurried search revealed that olive pits were not for eating. I spat the remains into my hand. Apparently *pit* was an innocent and cute word for a small pebble.

I looked at the Empty who was still munching through his beans. Glancing in his bowl I saw that the olive was gone. His mouth was still chomping away. Could I make him spit it out? Probably not. Would his teeth break first or would he choke to death? Either was an appalling thought, and I watched him very closely, holding my breath. Eventually he finished the beans and immediately drifted to a refuse bin to deposit his bowl. He slumped back to the position of powered-down defeat which seemed to be the default resting position of the Empties. I waited for a few more minutes to be sure I hadn't accidentally killed him with an olive before going back inside.

Helberg was in his office. He sniffed the air as I entered.

"Have you sorted out Swanager and Pedstone?" I asked.

He nodded. "I've moved them into my place, treating them like royalty while I hole up in the back here, although Swanager threatened to move out altogether. Something about a new integrated living solution experiment they're trying out in North Beach..." He trailed off, looking at me. "What did happen to you?" he asked.

"What do you mean?" I said.

He shook his head and sighed.

"Actually, there is one area I need some help with," I said.

He nodded for me to go on, but I paused, unsure what I was asking.

"That stuff you watch on the screen. The people who huff and wriggle without their clothes on?"

His eyebrows shot up. "Porn, you mean?"

"Porn, yes. What is porn?" I asked.

Helberg blew out his cheeks and grinned nervously. "A lot of people would say that it's just about watching people having sex, but it can be so much more than that. There's a lot of artistic—"

"Right! Sex! What is that?" I demanded, thinking I was getting to the core of the bizarre feelings and images which had been flooding my brain.

"What is sex?"

"Yes," I said. "I mean, I know what sex *is*. We learned about it in the school science downloads but it's like ... algebra. It's all very important I'm sure and I tried to pay attention to the lesson, but I couldn't see any practical use for it."

Helberg looked at me for a long time. "Um, can I ask why you want to know about this? I mean, why now?"

"I've been having some ... unusual thoughts." I really didn't want to describe them, even if I had the words.

Helberg grinned. "You're horny," he said.

I immediately felt the top of my head.

"No," said Helberg. "You've been thinking about getting yourself a partner, maybe? Getting naked, feeling some skin on skin?"

"Yes, that's exactly it!"

"Oh, I can definitely help you with that," he said, edging towards me, hands reaching down to unbutton his shirt.

"What? No! What are you doing?" I said, backing away. "All I want is information. I really *don't* want to see you naked."

"Why not? You don't know that until you've tried it."

It was a superficially persuasive argument. True, I was interested in sex and, maybe like trying different foods, maybe I just needed to try sex with Helberg, even if he turned out to be an olive pit or a repulsive lump of garlic. But, no, instinctively I felt that sex with him wasn't the answer.

"I want information, not sex," I said.

Helberg was crestfallen. "Are you sure? We could turn the lights off, maybe?"

"No."

He sniffed me. "Have you been eating garlic? Not that I mind. I don't mind having sex with a woman who—"

"No! No sex. Definitely not."

He huffed and redid his top button. "I got something you might like."

"But it's not sex," I said, following him to the store room at the back of his office.

"See these tins?" he asked, pointing at a shelf. "It's paint. Do you know about paint?"

"Tell me."

"It's how we make things a different colour. You wanted a way to tell the front doors apart? Well this is how you'll do it. Each one of these tins is a different colour."

I looked at the tins. They were very small compared to a door. "How does it work?"

He reached up to another shelf and handed me several brushes. "You take off the lid and then use a brush to put it on. You can cover quite a large surface with a tin of paint."

I immediately tried to get the lid off a tin, but found it impossible. Helberg showed me how to lever it off with another tool.

"They have to be kept shut really tight. Imagine the mess if it tipped over and spilled—"

As he said the words, I tilted the open tin to read what it said on the side. I looked down to see a spreading pool on the carpet. I dipped my toe into it and spread it around.

"*Cornflower Blue*," I read from the tin. "Your carpet looks better already. So do my shoes. You're right, I think I'm going to enjoy paint."

***

I carried paint upstairs and considered the colours as I looked along the row of doors. I nodded with satisfaction, knowing that this would definitely help. Hattie and I wouldn't need to count down the doors, we would simply head for the red door. Why did I want a red door? I just did. I put the tins down and fished the tool from my pocket to get a lid off. The door opened.

"I thought I heard something," said Hattie. "You're just in time. There's a Smiley compilation special on in a minute. All of our favourite moments, I can't wait!"

I would have been so excited by this before, now I couldn't think of anything worse.

Hattie looked at the tins of paint. "Is this the food you bought?"

"This isn't the food."

Hattie picked up a tin. "*Raspberry Beret*? I can't see why we can't just have regular beans."

"Listen, just go inside. I'll be in soon. I have a couple of jobs to do and I'll join you when I'm finished."

"Jobs? But I've done all the jobs. Is there something else that needs doing?" Hattie turned her gaze to look inside, searching for unfinished tasks.

"No, don't worry. Go and watch Smiley, I'm doing something new," I said. "I can show you when I'm finished if you like. I think you'll like it."

Hattie looked worried, but she went back inside and I took the lid off the red paint.

"*Cabriolet*," I said, savouring the name.

I dipped the brush into the paint, and held it up, glistening brightly. I slid the brush down the door and was delighted by the transformation. I applied more and then brushed up and down, enjoying the slight drag and the sensation that I was master of this striking colour. My tongue found the edge of my lips as I worked the brush into every corner. It was enormously satisfying. For some reason, images of Levi kept nudging into my thoughts as I worked the brush up and down. I wondered if he might enjoy the feeling as much me. I carefully eased the colour into every tiny gap with a tickle of my brush and then used the full width of its head to apply a pleasing finish. I felt a small shudder of pleasure as I realised that the door was now perfect. I stood and admired it for a few minutes.

A thought came to me and I went back down to the street. The Empties were still there, not moving. I went up to the man I'd fed the olive. He was still not dead, which was good.

"Want to try painting? I really think you'd enjoy it." I pressed the brush into his hand and led him into the complex and the door of one of the ground floor apartments. I took his hand and showed him how to paint.

"Dip in like this and then you can put the colour on the door."

I left him at work and approached another Empty, a woman.

"Come on. You can do yellow. I think you'll like yellow."

I set the woman painting the next door along and pictured the row of doors in the morning light. It would be a visual delight and so I hurried up to another door and started to paint it a vivid green colour. I lost myself in the process, although for some reason the green paint didn't fill my head with sensation quite so much as the red had done. I finished the door and stood back. I went back to see how the Empties had got on.

I wasn't sure exactly what had happened, but the paint was not on the doors. A good deal of it was on the road, and it was clear from the footprints and the amount of paint on their bodies that the two Empties had walked through it and possibly rolled around in it before they had started to paint a nearby car.

"Sensors are impaired. Alerting engineer. Sensors are impaired. Alerting engineer."

The car was determined to summon help and I really didn't want to be around to explain what had happened when an engineer appeared. I led the Empties away from the worst of the mess and wondered how I was going to clean them up. I took them inside and led them to Helberg's office. He was down on his hands and knees, scrubbing at the carpet where the blue paint had spilled

"I have a question about how to get paint off things," I said.

"Really?" said Helberg. He looked up and saw a dozen paint-smeared Empties crowding round his door. "Oh, for pity's sake! What are you doing?"

"They were helping me," I said.

"Helping...?" He waved his arms and flapped his lips uselessly. "You can't do that. They're property!"

I looked at the Empties. "They're people."

"And they've been turned into Empties for a reason. Debt, crime, just being useless specimen of humanity. They're meant to be that way and left that way. You can't just use them for some arts and crafts programme." He made a deeply unhappy noise. "Are you trying to wreck everyone's lives, or just mine?"

I didn't know what to say so I just gave him a stern look and he quickly relented.

Helberg found some cloths and towels and we wiped the Empties as clean as we could, being careful to avoid whatever pressure points would bring the supervision bots. As a consequence, their orange coveralls were now mottled with red and yellow, an improvement in my view. I led them back out to the street, to find the car had gone. Dusk made it hard to see the spilled paint. The Empties went back to their usual spots and I walked back inside, disappointed that I still hadn't found a way to help them.

***

Chapter 13 – 4th June

I'm aaaaa whaaaaale, sang the blue whale.

"Sure Babe!" said Rufus. He strolled through the house, across a terrace and down the steps onto the beach. There were several bonfires, with groups gathered around them, and a couple of spin-off groups who'd gone off to play volleyball. Rufus was very interested in the volleyball, but not, I realised, for the sport. Rather for the athletic, bikini-clad bodies of the women playing.

The two women with Rufus sipped on their cocktails and pulled faces. I saw the drinks sported sparkling swizzle sticks with their names on them, so I could tell which one was which, at last.

I watched as Rufus's mind cast the girls immediately into a private fantasy. They were both wearing tiny bikinis and writhing on the floor, covered in slippery mud. As their hands slid over each others' enormous breasts and buttocks, they giggled and beckoned to him.

Is this a memory or a dream? I asked.

Maybeeee it's boooooth, said the blue whale.

TayTay sucked the straw on her cocktail, more than a little suggestively. "That would be cool," she breathed.

The shout came again. "Roo fight!"

The memory shifted and contorted, gaps bloomed and resolved themselves.

The blue whale swooped and dived through the dreamscape.

"I have been privileged to learn some of the world's most effective martial arts techniques from master practitioners," said Rufus. "If people knew I walked among them wielding the power of life and death with a single blow, imagine how that would be?"

We were in the basement space beneath the house. There were people crowded round and there was a kangaroo. I still wasn't sure why there was a kangaroo at Rufus's beach party.

The animal came out of its corner with an enormous bound and hauled Rufus up by his long hair with its arms, while using the most powerful kick it could muster on his dangling body. He dropped like a stone and I saw the veil of unconsciousness fall like a blessed relief, across the intense pain.

It's beeeeetter to beeeeee aaaaa whaaaale, the whale pointed out.

In the hospital bed, Rufus groaned as he tried to shift position and talk to his fiancée, Paris. "Well, not small and helpless, surely? I took care of the—"

"Yes, we've made sure Miss Jacobs is up to date with the details of your *fall*," said Henderson, cutting into the conversation, positioning himself between Rufus and Paris. Henderson was a parasite, a pet, a dog. At the banquet of life at which Rufus and his equals – 'proper' people – feasted, Henderson sniffed around for scraps of power and influence. Just because Henderson was a smart dog, he assumed he was better than the other dogs; that he could become a proper person if he worked at it, pleaded for it.

"Paris," said Henderson, "I'm afraid I have some dull corporate matters I need to discuss with Rufus."

"Work?" said Paris. "Now?"

"The burden of leadership, hon," said Rufus. "Pop outside and fix your make up."

"My make up?" Paris left.

The whale swam in.

Rufus Jaffle was now talking to Henderson and another man – Michael from legal. The details weren't clear but it felt like Rufus was in some sort of trouble.

"You need to wipe your memory of what happened last night," said Henderson. "You have the access to do that personally."

"Actually, I've got this whale in my head that is making some of my functionality a bit glitchy."

The whale giggled and squirted foam through its blowhole.

"Fine," said Henderson peevishly. "Then we'll get it done back at Jaffle Tech."

"But please don't go through the official company procedures," said Michael. "I very much believe the less people know and the smaller the paper trail, the better things are."

"Yes, our official brain-editing systems have audits that even I can't counter," said Henderson.

Even I— Rufus could have laughed. A dog with ideas above its station.

"I'll sort out something off the record," said Henderson. "We will arrange the memory wipe as soon as you're physically fit enough." He paused. "There is another matter I need your signature for, and it won't wait until then. Perhaps, Michael, you could leave us for a few minutes?"

Michael from legal rose and left the room, leaving Rufus alone with Henderson.

"Are you both getting memory wipes too?" asked Rufus, sulking.

"I will attend to all details. It's very much in our mutual interest if you believe I have the company's best interest at heart, wouldn't you say? As Chief Technical Officer, problem solving is my forte."

Rufus gave a grunt of assent.

Henderson cleared his throat. "That other matter. I need your signature for Operation Sunrise. It's a complex project, so I can't afford to let any time slip."

Rufus looked at the sheaf of papers. "Do I need to read all that?"

***

I surfaced from sleep before I time to read any of the papers.

"Odd dream," I muttered.

The major takeaway was that Rufus Jaffle had a very peculiar lifestyle, but then he was at the top of the world's biggest tech corporation, so the pressure of his job was probably something I couldn't begin to understand. He was definitely the man with the answers. I had to find a way to speak to him.

As I dressed I recalled the way that Rufus was fixated on the girls' breasts and buttocks in his memory. I now recognised that these were secondary sex characteristics, and played a big part in selecting partners for intercourse. I'd spent some time jipping articles through my Jaffle Port after I'd left Helberg. It explained some of the behaviour I'd observed, where men – quite a lot of men now I came to think of it – seemed less interested in my face than my chest and buttocks. This was most definitely the case in the memory I'd just experienced, because the faces of TayTay and Mimi became less and less distinct the more time Rufus spent with them.

I wandered out of my room to find Hattie. "What do you think it is that makes us the people we are?" I asked.

She looked up from her beans. "It's very early for a question like that. Right, let's think. Our names and our faces are all different, and we have a special number assigned to our Jaffle Port, so the system knows who we are."

"True," I said, "but there are other things. Like ... like I never met anyone who loved Smiley Tots as much as you."

Hattie beamed with pride. "That's true. Me neither."

I thought hard. "But I suppose what I was really asking is whether other people see us the same way that we see ourselves? I don't think they do."

Hattie stared at me. "You're probably right, but it doesn't really matter what other people think about us, does it?"

"No." I nodded and gave a small sigh of relief. "No it doesn't."

"Apart from when Levi thought I'd taken Brandine's bagel," said Hattie, wide-eyed with horror at the memory. "*That* was horrible."

***

We left the apartment to go to work, the last day before a two day rest period.

"Take a look," I said as they stepped outside, unable to suppress a grin. "Can you see what I did?"

Hattie turned to look at our door. She turned her head one way and then another. "Something's definitely changed," she said, "but I can't put my finger on it. Have you polished the handle?"

I shook my head.

"No, I did that last week," said Hattie. "Something's shinier, definitely. Go on, tell me."

"The whole *door's* shinier. I painted it, look!" I said. I dragged Hattie to look at the next door along and then back again. "See? that one's drab and faded while *ours* is bright and shiny!"

Hattie nodded, and squinted critically as she glanced between the two. "I see it, I do."

"Come on, let's get to work."

***

Before lunch, Paulette called a section meeting. Everyone talked in subdued whispers, wondering what was going on. "Just as long as we don't have to watch the Film again," said Hattie, fearful. I patted her shoulder.

Paulette took to the stage. "Jaffle Tech prides itself not only on its customer service but its relationship with the community, both global and local. We are part of a family, a corporate family and a worldwide family and—"

"Let's cut to the chase," said Levi, stepping in. "A felonious act has been committed and a member of staff – here! – has been implicated."

He held up a tunic that clearly matched the uniform that we all wore. I willed myself to keep calm. It was mine, but Levi clearly didn't know that, or he would not be addressing us as a group.

"The individual concerned has broken into a nearby residence and committed several acts of criminal damage and theft," said Levi.

Shocked gasps could be heard around the room and heads shook in disbelief.

"This tunic was left behind, and the victim believes she herself spoke to the perpetrator earlier in the day."

A hand went up. "A caller? Are you saying that one of us went round to a caller's house?"

"No," said Levi. "This was someone who met the victim on the street. Now, the victim agreed to share her memory of that encounter with us for the purposes of identifying the perpetrator. We're going to take a look at that recording, so please all pay close attention. Every one of your colleagues will be seeing this, because Jaffle's reputation is on the line here. I hope y'all understand just how big a deal this is. We cannot afford to compromise our position and standing in the community."

Levi fixed them all with his serious look again and then started the film.

I gripped the arms of my chair as I recognised Claire's garden and saw two figures approaching from the road. How was it possible that Hattie and I hadn't already been identified?

"Can I help you?" came Claire's voice from the screen. Two faces turned towards them. I nearly burst out laughing when I saw them. They were both as featureless as Smiley Tots. Bland idiotic smiles beamed out of two identical moon-like faces, topped with hair that looked as though it belonged on a doll. Neither Hattie nor I had plaits, and yet identical plaits swung at the sides of these two faces. They even walked strangely, dragging their limbs along the road and making odd growling sounds, like they were animals.

"Are you blind?" one of the faces asked Claire, contorting grotesquely, even going a little bit cross-eyed to underline this was a stupid person talking.

Hattie stiffened at my side. She recognised the situation. I willed her to keep quiet.

I realised that Claire's memory was very like Rufus Jaffle's: the recollection was distorted. Rufus Jaffle had inflated his companions' breasts and more or less forgotten their faces. Claire had also forgotten mine and Hattie's faces, while retaining the impression she was speaking with a pair of imbeciles. It worked in my favour: it was impossible for anybody to identify me from this evidence. I peered at Hattie's intense expression. Well, almost impossible.

"Anybody got any ideas?" asked Levi.

Hattie's hand started to move up. I slammed it back down onto the arm of her chair.

"Ow!" said Hattie.

Several people turned to look but another hand had gone up as a member of staff pointed out the obvious. "Those people don't look like any of us."

""It is possible that the victim had been drinking that morning," said Levi. "Alcohol, you understand."

Paulette gestured to Levi and spoke to him tersely.

"But it's true," he replied. "Just the facts, ma'am."

"Why did you do that?" Hattie said to me. "I was going to tell them and then you hurt my hand."

"Because you were going to tell them," I hissed. "Now, shush."

Levi cleared his throat, his argument with Paulette concluded. "The victim may or may not have been drinking. That's immaterial. This is the footage evidence we have. Any other questions?"

"Has this got anything to do with Brandine's bagel being stolen?" someone called out.

"No," said Paulette.

"We cannot rule anything out at this time," said Levi. "Who knows how the criminal mind works."

A reminder pinged in my calendar: the brain scan in the medical room. It was due now.

What would the scan reveal? Surely, it would uncover the changes I had been experiencing over the last day. Did I have a brain virus or had I simply been 'awakened' in some way? My system data showed I was operating on Jaffle Standard but I very much doubted that was true now. If they restored my brain, removed any change, rebuilt any instabilities, what would I lose? I had just started to get to grips with colours and new tastes, and a whole banquet of new emotions and physical feelings that I certainly wasn't ready to put aside. And would they find out what I had done recently, the 'felonious act' I committed at Claire's house?

Paulette wrapped up the meeting and the section staff filed out. Hattie snivelled to herself as we went.

I took her hand. "Hattie?"

She glanced at me but only for a moment. There was fear and confusion in my friend's eyes. I steered her round a corner and into the toilets.

"I don't need the toilet!" she wailed.

I pulled her into a cubicle.

"Do *you* need the toilet?" Hattie asked, gabbling. "I don't. I don't think so. I don't know anymore. That was us in the video and I was going to tell them and then you hurt me. Why did you hurt me? Did you mean to hurt me? I don't understand."

"I'm sorry," I said and stroked Hattie's face.

"Are we in trouble?" she asked.

I forced a laugh. "No. Of course not."

"That was you and me in that woman's memory, wasn't it?"

"It didn't really look like us."

"It didn't really look like *anybody*," said Hattie. "Was it your tunic they found in her house?"

I considered denying everything, but sooner or later I needed to find a new tunic, and until then it would be very easy for Hattie to check.

"Right. I'm sorry. I kept this from you, but I'll tell you the truth," I said. "I had no idea it would all get so crazy."

"What's crazy?" said Hattie.

"Yesterday, when I was in my cubicle, I stood up too quickly and ripped my tunic on the chair. It was really bad, a great big hole." I gestured, indicating an imaginary tear across my entire torso. "So I went down to supplies to see about getting a new one. Anyway, when I got there, I saw that there was nobody on the front desk, so I walked in and there was a gang of masked intruders."

"No!"

"Yes. They said they wanted a Jaffle tunic to do a robbery, so they'd come to take one."

"No!"

"Yes."

"So it was them?" said Hattie. "They must have been the ones who broke into that house?"

"Yes. They took a tunic and threatened me a with a gun to keep my mouth shut. You can see my predicament, can't you?"

"Tell Paulette. Tell Levi. They can't get you now."

"They also threatened to hurt the dog," I added, my mind freewheeling.

"There was a dog?"

"Yes, a dog. Long floppy ears, smiley face."

"Dogs aren't normally smiley," said Hattie with a frown. "You should tell anyway, and the dog can take its chances."

I should have realised that Hattie didn't care much for dogs, especially after the poop incident. "Aaaand, they also said they'd come round to our house and hurt the Smiley Tots."

Hattie's reaction took some time to play out. First her hands went to her face, clamping her cheeks as she inhaled noisily, then they found the top of her head, which she pressed as if might come off, and finally pressed to her bosom. She made tragic gulping sounds and staggered around in circles which, in the cubicle, meant bouncing repeatedly off the walls.

"We mustn't let anyone find out," she whispered.

I nodded. "Don't worry, I'll keep my mouth shut. It will be fine, you'll see."

I returned Hattie to her desk and calmed her a bit by saying she should look at some of the latest Smiley Tots on sale. Then I put a call through to the medical centre.

"Hi, I have a scan scheduled for today."

"Yes, Alice. Everything is ready for you. Come down now if you would."

"That's the thing," I said. "We've hit a bit of an emergency up here. Unusually high demand in our sector. I'm going to need to postpone our appointment."

"You're calling very late to cancel."

"I know."

"And your supervisor should be able to authorise your absence. It's not a lengthy procedure."

"Yes, but as I say there's a lot of work on. I don't want to bother my supervisor. She's under a lot of pressure as it is."

"I don't think you appreciate how much this facility costs the organisation."

"No," I said ambiguously.

The woman sighed. "I'll book you in for the same time tomorrow but—"

"I have two rest days after today."

"Then on your return. I've booked it in. Please ensure you're here on time."

"Thank you," I said and breathed a sigh of relief.

***

Chapter 14

I sat and thought about how I could get up to the executive floor to see Rufus Jaffle. I made a list on my wipe-clean notepad.

roof
helicopter
ladder
elevator
rope
steal pass

Obviously some people had legitimate access to those floors. There was Rufus himself, his secretary, probably service personnel like cleaners, caterers, and maintenance engineers. I paused and thought for a moment about the outlandish story I had told Hattie. It reminded me I actually did need to go and get another tunic, but the germ of an idea was starting to form.

At the end of my shift I went down to supplies. Someone called Damien was on reception.

"Hi Damien, I've been sent down by Rufus Jaffle to pick up some uniforms."

"Have you got the requisition paperwork?" he asked.

"No, he said that this is off the record."

"Jaffle did?"

"Rufus Jaffle, yes. And he said Damien would be sure to be discreet."

"He mentioned me by name?"

"He's the boss. He knows about you, Damien."

"Sweet. So what do you need?" Damien grinned with pride.

"I need a set of coveralls for a maintenance engineer and a tunic like this one," I said.

Damien shrugged. "He's the boss. Yes, he is." He led me into a storeroom. "Any idea of the sizes that you need?"

121

I gestured to myself. "Oh, you know, average. Probably about my size, I'd say. I'll need one of those caps and one of those tool bags too."

In the bathroom I changed into the maintenance engineers coveralls and put on the cap, shoving my hair underneath. Everything else went into the tool bag. I walked up to reception.

"Got a call for the exec floor," I said, attempting to disguise my voice. Both of the receptionists peered anxiously at me.

"Have you got a sore throat?" asked the male receptionist.

"Um, what?"

"I can get you a glass of water if you like?"

"Your colleague is over there, just getting in the elevator," said the female receptionist.

"Is he?" I said and sprinted for the doors.

As the doors closed, the real engineer turned and looked at me. "Not seen you before," he said.

I looked up at him. Part of me wanted to get back out and admit my mistake, but I'd got this far and I really needed to get to Rufus Jaffle. I needed to blind this man with officious superiority. I decided to cast myself as a female Levi and see where it led.

"There's a very good reason for that," I said. "If quality spot checks are done by co-workers they are often found to be inaccurate. You ever been quality spot checked before?"

"Uh, no."

"Right. It's simple enough. I will give you some time to do the job, unhindered, and then you will answer any questions I might have about the quality of what you've done. Understand?"

"I think so," he said. "Sorry? Who are you?"

"I'm a ghost," I said. "A silent observer. You have to act like I'm not even here."

"Oh, okay."

"Smart man. You'll do fine, I've no doubt. Now what's the job?"

"Conference room window hydraulics are not working."

"Good. Well you get along and fix that and I'll inspect another task from last week." I looked straight ahead as the elevator doors opened.

"Oh, what task is that?" he asked.

"I cannot comment on an ongoing investigation," I said and stalked down the corridor towards Jaffle's office.

I waited until the engineer had disappeared before knocking on Rufus Jaffle's door. There was no reply. I tried the handle and found it unlocked. I went inside.

"Hello?"

There was nobody there. There was no luxury drone on the balcony beyond the glass wall. As I scanned the room I realised it was unchanged since my last visit. Not just unchanged, it was *untouched*. The tea cups were still on the tray, unwashed. The chairs were still tilted back from the clean-up job. I shook my head at my own naivety and my foolish assumption that Rufus Jaffle would be in the office every day like a regular person. He'd probably be off somewhere doing rich person things, attending extravagant parties and making important decisions on behalf of the workers at Jaffle Tech.

So if he wasn't here, maybe I could find a way to contact him. I jipped the local area to see if there was anything accessible via my Jaffle Port but the security here was as tight as could be expected.

I could always ask Jaffle's secretary, Florence. Or Cremona, or Milan, or whatever. Hadn't Rufus said she was a European princess?

I went over to the wall to look for the hidden door to the secretary's office. The wall appeared to be seamless. Long way round then, I thought.

Out in the corridor I walked to the secretarial office. The door was locked. I knocked.

"Milan?" I hissed through the door. "Your Highness?"

There was no response. The elevator dinged. I glanced back. A group of people, all in suits, stepped out. Jethro Henderson at the forefront. I turned quickly to hide my face and moved away down the corridor.

They followed me!

I picked up the pace and dodged through the first open door. It was a conference room, luxurious contemporary seating arranged around a long table which looked far too large to be practical. Around the walls, pieces of Jaffle Tech from the company's long history were displayed in glass cabinets.

By the window, the engineer was working on a sticky hinge.

A bot-trolley detached itself from the wall, and jipped my Jaffle Port to ask if I wanted anything to eat or drink. The body of the snack-bot was a warming cabinet that held plates and the top was arranged with glasses of drink and bitesize snacks.

I waved it away. The engineer glanced round at me.

"Silent observer," I reminded him. "I'm not here."

He smiled and nodded.

The door handle turned. I near leapt in alarm. The suits were coming in.

I ducked behind a cleaning bot standing in the shadow of display cabinet. The cabinet held some sort of insect mounted on a card which read, *2009 - the first wireless flying insect cyborg demonstrated at a conference in Italy.*

I was just in time. The door opened and people walked in.

"So, make yourselves comfortable and I'll take us through the agenda," said Henderson. "Hey, you!"

"Sir?" said the engineer.

"Whatever you're doing, get out."

The engineer silently gathered his tools and made his way round the long table to the exit. He looked at me, squatting in my hiding space. I made a frantic slicing *No!* gesture with my hand. He tapped his nose and winked.

"Not even here," he said.

"That's right," said Henderson closing the door behind the engineer.

I was trapped in the room with them. I made myself as small as I could.

"Operation Sunrise has been given the green light for implementation," said Henderson.

"Rufus signed off on it?" said a man, surprised.

"He did. Michael here witnessed it. So, we just need to put it past the rest of the board and we go live in fifteen days. Five pm on the nineteenth."

A hand (from my position, I couldn't see who it belonged to) waved for a drink and the snack-bot trundled over.

"We four need to be crystal clear about our business objectives," said Henderson, "and make sure that everyone knows the success criteria for their area of responsibility. So as I run through each area, chip in."

There was the clink of glass and a crunch of eating. The cleaning bot next to me rolled out of its position towards the table.

Crumbs, I thought. With the cleaning bot gone, my hiding place was barely any hiding place at all. Any one of the people at the table just had to look round and they'd see me squatting on the floor.

"First of all," said Henderson, "let's touch on political liaison and media response. Jessica?"

"Thanks, Jethro," said a suit. "If you'd look at the screen..."

There was a change in the room's lighting. All eyes would be on the screen. I slipped from my hiding place and crossed the short distance to the window curtains. They were long and billowy and, if I stood perfectly upright and pressed myself flat, I'd not create a noticeable bulge.

"We know some people are uncomfortable with change," Jessica was saying. "There are politicians and opinion makers outside our control. We have to win them over by pointing to our past successes. Blindness eradicated, the dementia epidemic reversed, our unarguable role in education and law and order. This is Jaffle Tech's image and Jaffle Tech's legacy. Believe me, we still have a lot of brownie points. We keep punching those messages home and, if anyone starts to badmouth Operation Sunrise, it's going to sound like sour grapes and groundless doom-mongering."

There were approving noises. I worried that my feet might be visible under the very bottom edge of the curtain. I tried to angle them sideways without falling over.

"And remember," said Jessica, "we only need to worry about public opinion until the roll-out is complete. By reducing customers to a lower level of functionality, we expect levels of satisfaction to be consistently higher. Happy voters are what the politicians want, after all."

"Are we rolling out the plippers at the same time?" a man asked.

"The same day," said another voice. "We're going to deadcat Operation Sunrise with a distribution of plippers to all law enforcement bodies in the country. The plipper technology is already covered in the last set of user Ts and Cs. Everyone has already given their consent."

"Everyone?" said another.

There was mild laughter. "Everyone on Jaffle Enhanced and below, Marcus," said Henderson. "Don't worry. You're not about to get plipped."

Plipper. Plipped. The words meant nothing to me.

"Mind if I just close the blinds?" asked someone.

I froze. The curtain rail began to move. My new hiding place was unbunching and about to be less than useless. I signalled the snack-bot to bring me a drink and as it drifted over, cancelled the order. I dropped behind it.

The snack-bot rolled away and I rolled with it. As I passed the far end of the table, now directly beneath the screen but away from the gaze of the suits, I crouched low and let the snack-bot go on. Instinctively, I took a crispbread snack from its top as it left.

"How extensively have the plippers been tested?"

"The test labs have run through eight hundred different test scenarios and the plippers have performed perfectly. Have you all seen it in action? No? Oh, I should. Let me..." Henderson went quiet as he sent off a communication.

I broke off a crumb of crispbread and dropped it on the floor. The cleaning bot came over to silently vacuum it up. I broke another crumb and cast it a little further away, towards the door. The cleaning bot moved on, me with it.

"I can imagine there will be moral objections to plipper technology," said Marcus.

"Why?" asked Jessica. "Do you know how many people die each year in this country while being arrested. Even non-lethal tech such as Tasers causes up to fifty deaths nationwide. With the

implementation of plippers, that number will effectively drop to zero."

There was a knock at the door. I peered round the edge of the cleaning bot, and I saw Levi walk in. I guessed he was seeing it for the first time, as his eyes took in the size of the space and the ostentatiousness of the furnishings.

"Hi Levi, good of you to join us," said Henderson. "Would you be kind enough to carry out an ad-hoc security check on the room?"

I was about to be busted. Levi wouldn't have to look very hard to notice me.

"Yes, sir, happy to help." He walked briskly around the room. As he came along the edge of the table he simply looked down and saw me. I pulled a face, attempting to convey this wasn't what it looked like and could he please not give me away.

"And now the plipper," Henderson said. There was a soft push-button click.

Levi lifted a hand to point. I could see his mouth starting to form a sentence. Then he dropped to the floor like a rag doll.

I stifled a gasp. Was he dead? No, he sat up slowly, his face slack and vacant. His eyes were open, but they saw nothing. I realised with horror that he was now an Empty. The plipper that Henderson had pressed so casually had instantly taken his brain function down to the most basic level.

Henderson put a device back down on the table. "Well, I think we can be satisfied by the response time," he said. "Marcus, we'll need to monitor that carefully as rollout progresses, make sure it remains sub-second. Yes?"

"Sure. And what do you want to do with him?"

"We'll get him back onto his regular level after the meeting," said Henderson. "He's no bother to anyone there."

I had to get out of the room. I broke further crumbs for the cleaning bot and kept pace at its side. I needed to make sure it moved consistently – it would definitely draw attention if it slowed or stopped. Levi had left the door open a little when he'd entered – thank goodness – and the cleaning bot and I slipped through the gap. I rushed to the elevator.

***

Chapter 15 – 5th June – 14 days until Operation Sunrise

Curtains.

I lay in my bed listening to the morning sounds of Hattie carrying out the day's cleaning tasks. Today was curtains, according to her rota. Every fortnight without fail they were all washed, dried and ironed. She'd be in here shortly if I didn't get up.

I lay there, listening to the huffs of a woman for whom happiness was a clean home. I thought about my situation and Operation Sunrise (whatever that was), about plipper devices and the dead Empty look on Levi's face. If there was any danger that my new abilities would be taken away – and I was certain there was – then I had to squeeze the most out of them while I could.

I rose, went to the wardrobe and looked at Claire's dress. It was magnificent if impractical. I could really do with finding some other clothes that were as colourful, clothes which I might be able to wear more regularly. I put on a tunic and went to find Hattie. She had finished loading the washing machine, and now had a pair of Smiley Tots in her arms. She was nuzzling them against her face.

"Good morning Alice," she said. "We were about to come and wake you. The twins are lively today."

"Yeah?" I said.

"I think that perhaps they want to watch Mr Smiley. What do you say twins?"

"They look, um, chirpy. It's because you take such good care of them."

"Who wouldn't want to love these babies? Such adorable Munchkins." Hattie made enthusiastic if alarming chomping noises at the Smiley Tots. "Now, you sit down with the twins and I'll work around you."

"Actually, I want to go out and buy some clothes today," I said.

Hattie gave me a long hard look, making sure I noticed it was long and hard. "You don't need to buy clothes," she said.

"I don't *need* any, no."

"All of our tunics are free."

"Yes."

"We get given them."

"Yes, but there are other clothes, not just tunics."

"I don't understand."

"I just feel like getting something different. Something with a bit more colour." I tried to act casual, as if this wasn't a major departure from normal behaviour.

Hattie narrowed her eyes at me. "When's your brain scan?"

"That's got nothing to do with it."

"You might have a brain virus."

"I don't have a brain virus."

"Have armed criminals stolen your tunic again?"

"No."

"Maybe they made you say that. Blink twice if you're being forced to do this."

"I'm not being forced to do this."

"You blinked."

"That was an ordinary blink," I said. "People blink."

"Maybe they made you say that too. Blink twice and—"

"I'm fine!" I insisted. "It's just that I'd quite like a change."

"I don't like change," grumbled Hattie.

I had beans for breakfast. I hadn't got hold of any bacon, and my research indicated that bacon, once extracted from the pig, needed to be kept cold in a fridge and cooked using a cooker. We didn't have either of those things and I wasn't sure Hattie was ready for that sort of upheaval in our apartment.

I left on a mission. What I'd told Hattie was partly true, I genuinely did want to get some more clothes, but what I really craved was colour. I went outside, spent ten minutes talking to the oblivious Empties on the kerb and then called a car.

"Take me somewhere colourful," I said.

"Destination not recognised," said the car.

"Take me to the flowers," I tried.

"Do you want to go to a flower market?" the car asked.

I didn't know what that meant so I jipped it. Lots of flowers. Retailers and buyers. I jipped some images. "Yes!" I said.

I watched the changing cityscape as we drove to the flower market. It was an uneven patchwork of houses and apartment complexes, segments of colour and no colour. I reckoned I could bet where the folks on Jaffle Standard lived, in buildings of sludgy beige and grey. The houses of those on Jaffle Enhanced and Jaffle Premium betrayed their owners with the painted detail on the walls or

colourful curtains fluttering at the window. Hattie worried constantly about the cleanliness of our curtains, but she never considered their plainness or their ugly putty colour was a problem.

The car pulled up outside a gated area. I couldn't see any flowers, but when I got out I thought I could smell something. I walked into a huge building with high ceilings. There were rows of little enclosures with tables and displays that were covered in flowers. There were so many different sorts of flowers, in so many colours.

A woman looked up from her counter. "Are you lost?"

"No," I said. "I've come to look at the flowers."

"You're a bit late."

"Late?" It was mid-morning.

She took in my tunic. "You've been sent?"

"No, I..."

"Maybe your boss told you to get some...?"

"Flowers," I said firmly. "I've come for some flowers. Some nice ones."

"Well, you came to the right place." She smiled. "Any particular sort that you – or your boss – prefer?"

"I don't know very much about them," I admitted.

"Well then," she said, walking round so she could stroll along the display with me, "these ones here are carnations. Very popular."

"What are those big ones at the back?" I had my eye on some huge yellow flowers that looked a bit like Mr Smiley.

"Sunflowers," she said. You pay per stem for those. Some of the others come in bunches."

"Which are the ones I can smell?" I asked, sniffing.

"You'll be smelling lots of different ones," she said, "but the roses and the freesias, most likely."

"And which are those?"

"Fuchsias. Gorgeous, yes?"

"And what colour would you call that?"

"Fuchsia," said the woman.

"Wow. Is the flower named after the colour or is the colour named after the flower?"

"I couldn't rightly say," she said.

I didn't want to jip it. The mystery of the colour and the flower were enough.

The woman spent another thirty minutes showing me all of the flowers. I bought as many as I could wheel to the gate with one of

their big trolleys. I called a car with extra luggage space so I could take them all back home. The smell inside the car for the journey was intoxicating, and every time I looked at the flowers, swaying gently in the boxes as the car moved, I smiled just to see all of the colours.

When I got back it took me six journeys to unload and take all of the flowers upstairs. Of course, I tried to get the Empties to admire the colours as I carried them past, but they wouldn't even look. I put the flowers outside our door and went inside.

"Hattie, I've got a surprise."

She gave me a suspicious look. Surprises from her roommate Alice were something to be wary of these days.

"Come look," I said.

Hattie finished dressing a Smiley Tot and followed me out. "Oh my goodness, what are all these?" she asked.

"Flowers!" I cried. "Gorgeous fresh flowers. We can have them all round the apartment, as a display. It will look so amazing."

"You want to take them inside?"

"Yes."

"Actually into our home?"

"Yes," I said. "Look at them, they're gorgeous!"

"Why?"

"Why are they gorgeous or why do I want to bring them in?"

"Either! Both! I don't see why you want to bring dead plants into the house."

"They're not dead."

"But bits are falling off them! Is this like the chi-eeese? Are we supposed to eat them?"

"No, they're not for that."

"Then what are they *for*?"

I look at the flowers arranged in the hallway. "They're not *for* anything. They just *are*."

"Are what?"

I shrugged. "Lovely."

Hattie glared at me. "I'm not going to slam this door. It's too noisy and it might chip the woodwork. So, you'll just have to pretend."

Hattie slammed the door slowly and quietly in my face. Miserable to see that my quest to brighten the flat had ended in failure, I hauled the flowers downstairs to the lobby.

"That's a lot of flowers," said Helberg, loitering in the doorway of his office.

"I wanted to have a mixture of colours," I said.

"Bought with my money? Never seen the point of cut flowers. Give me a living plant or a painting any day."

"I've already painted the door," I said.

"I don't mean paint something. I mean a painting. A picture."

I thought about the pictures that I'd seen in Rufus Jaffle's office. I wondered if Hattie would enjoy *Dogs Playing Poker*. "Pictures – pictures on walls – they're made out of paint."

He nodded.

"Ooh."

The possibilities whirled in my mind. I grabbed some more tins of paint and took them upstairs.

"And what am I supposed to do with these flowers?" Helberg called after me.

***

Chapter 16

I ran down our landing, nearly kicking over Helberg's bot, Hungry Horace, as it tried and failed to vacuum up the leaves I'd let fall on the floor.

"I don't like flowers," said Hattie when I went inside.

"It's fine. They're all gone."

She looked at the paints in my arms.

"The flowers are gone," I assured her.

Hattie flopped onto the sofa, viciously cuddling an armful of Smiley Tots.

"Yes, you rest. Watch something. I'm just going to paint the wall."

"What?"

"Helberg gave me the paint," I said, in an effort to legitimise what I was about to do. "I think we're almost due some maintenance anyway."

Hattie glowered and turned back to the screen. I prised the lid off all of the paint tins and tried to remember what the dogs playing cards looked like.

I started with green. There was a green card table at the centre of the picture, so I splashed some green onto the wall behind the sofa. Drips ran down the wall, which was annoying. I looked at the other tins. I needed something that was dog-coloured. There was one called *Mahogany* which looked good. I dipped in the brush and tried to make something which looked like a dog on the wall. It was tougher than I'd imagined. I summoned a mental picture of a dog, but it was all waggy tail and lolling tongue. I jipped a dog picture instead. It became clearer what I needed to do. I needed a body, a head, a tail and four legs. I swirled paint into a body. First job done. I then made something like a head, on top of the body and then added brush strokes for the legs and the tail. I stood back and looked. The thing on the wall looked more like a bear, or the massive enlargement of a dust mite Hattie had shown me once. Perhaps when my dog was playing cards it would come to life.

"Oh."

I realised that it would need to be holding the cards with two of its paws, which were currently at the bottom of my dog-bear, just

above the floor. Had the picture in Rufus Jaffle's office had the dogs sitting up? Making a painting was much harder than it looked.

Not to worry, there was plenty of wall left. I decided to paint the kangaroo which haunted my dreams. The brown colour was a decent match. I started with its big legs, coming up in a powerful kick, which I could see very vividly. They came out to the side, which looked impossible, until you saw that the kangaroo had a very large tail that held it off the ground while its legs were elsewhere.

I painted two legs, sticking out towards the dog. I followed that with the tail that anchored it to the ground. Now I just needed to add the body and head. I filled in the space between the tail and the legs, but I couldn't quite think where the head should be, so I added it on top. I stepped back.

I had created an image which looked very unlike an animal. As I twisted my head one way and then another I decided it looked more like a chair on its side, with a large pile of soil on it. I wondered whether Hattie would be able to see the kangaroo.

"Hey Hattie, what do you think this looks like?" I asked.

Hattie stood up and turned to see. "Oh. There's stuff all over the wall," she said in alarm.

"Yes, it's paint," I pointed out.

"Paint isn't supposed to look like mess," said Hattie.

I thought she was being a bit unreasonable. "It's not mess, it's a picture," I said.

"A picture? Of what?"

"That one there is a dog."

"No it's not. What's the big green square?" she asked.

"A card table. The dog was going to be playing cards, but that didn't work. What about this one? This is a kangaroo."

She looked long and hard at the wall. I guessed she'd jipped a picture of a kangaroo, but there was no glimmer of recognition in her eyes. She looked up and down the wall and sighed unhappily. Then her gaze dropped and she screamed.

"No!"

"What?"

"I can't believe it! What did you do?"

I moved forward to where she was pointing.

"No, get back! You'll get more on them!"

I saw that a drip of paint had landed on one of the Smiley Tots and was running down its face. Hattie dabbed at it with the end of her sleeve, tears running from her eyes.

She scooped up all of the Smiley Tots that were on the sofa. No mean feat as there were at least twelve. She staggered out of the room with them in her outstretched arms.

"I don't know what you think you're doing, Alice, but you've..." She made a noise like Hungry Horace, a broken sucking sob. "You're ruining everything!"

She pushed past me and went to her room. This time she did slam the door.

I stood there, not knowing what to do or say. I wanted to tell Hattie that it was just a doll and it didn't matter, but I knew that her Smiley Tots were so much more to her. Presently, she began to cry, wailing and inconsolable.

I silently put the lids back on the tins and took them back to Helberg.

"Making pictures is hard," I said, flinging myself into one of his chairs.

"And hello to you," said Helberg.

"No, I said making—"

"I heard."

"What have you got that will get paint off things?" I asked.

"Things?"

"Smiley Tots."

"Have you been painting them too?"

He had been poring over some bits of broken rubbish, but now searched along shelves. "Try this." He passed me a bottle labelled *thinners*. "Make sure it doesn't melt the fabric, it's quite strong."

"Will it melt the Smiley Tots?"

"Possibly."

I growled at myself. "I tried to paint a dog and a kangaroo, but they didn't look right."

"Artists take a long time to learn how to paint well," he said. "Don't beat yourself up."

"I have never seen an artist doing painting. Good ones or bad ones. If they take a long time to learn then where are they all doing their learning?"

"Ah, that is a deep and interesting question," said Helberg, tapping the side of his nose.

"You're doing that thing again," I said.

"What thing?"

"Of being annoying. Of saying things that make no sense and making me feel like an idiot."

"I don't think you're an idiot, Alice," he said. "In fact, quite the opposite. You've become quite an interesting person of late."

"Well, enjoy it while you can," I said, miserably.

"I intend to. I think we should go on a trip."

"Are you actually going to teach me something? Actually help me and not just go 'Ah' and tap your nose?"

He stood. "Actual help. A small practical lesson."

I followed him outside and he called a car. "Destination is the museum and art gallery," he told it. He produced a card-like device and waved it over an interface panel. "Transfer credits for journey optimised for speed."

"Why are you talking to the car like that?" I asked.

"Like what?"

"Your Jaffle Port takes care of the payment details. You don't need to tell it what to do or waved cards about."

"You mean *your* Jaffle Port does that," he said.

I was about to ask him what he meant by that but he started talking.

"You can do research about art, and when we look at the paintings I'll suggest some pointers for things you might want to look up, but let's start right at the beginning. When do you think people started to make art?"

I had no idea. "When? Crumbs. Was it a long time ago?"

"Yes. A very long time ago," said Helberg. "There's a cave in France where there are paintings that are forty thousand years old."

"No way!"

"Yes. For as long as there have been people, there's been the irresistible urge to depict the world around us and make marks on whatever is to hand." He gave me a sideways look. "Is there by any chance an appalling mess on your apartment wall?"

"Might be," I said. "I don't think Hattie approves."

"We can tidy it up. Anyway, that's when people started to make art. When do you think they stopped?"

"Oh," I said, understanding dawning. "Do you mean that nobody is creating new paintings now? Surely that can't be true? Not

everyone is reduced to Jaffle Standard. Why aren't people on the premium packages doing painting?"

Helberg sat back in the car seat. "I'm not saying nobody has painted a picture in the last twenty years. I expect that there are people who play around at it, but anyone rich enough to be on Jaffle Premium aren't necessarily going to follow a passion for painting. We live in age of planned obsolescence, Alice. With machines and bots and Jaffle swarms doing all the work for us, we don't really need people to do very much at all. The forces that govern society would rather that we, individual humans, don't get the idea into our heads that we have value, that we contribute."

"But the people of Jaffle Premium. If they've got more access to their brain capacity, shouldn't they be making greater contributions to society?"

"You've met some of them. What do you think?"

I wondered about that. "Surely they're not all awful?"

"The system works best if we're all happy as we are; that none of us want things to change."

"What level are you on, anyway?" I asked.

The look he gave me was deep and unreadable and – though I wasn't sure what made me think it – it was the most real look he'd ever given me. Like I'd caught a true glimpse of the actual Patrick Helberg for the first time. A shiver ran through me.

He gave a sad little smile which abruptly broadened. "Look, we're here."

***

Chapter 17

The car had pulled up outside an imposing old building. It looked as though it had been here for a very long time, with stone pillars and a door that the car could have driven through.

The entrance hall, at the top of a series of stone steps, was cool and very large. The tiles on the floor were coloured, and patterned in a very pleasing way. I stopped to stare at them.

"Is this art?" I asked.

"Well, it's not really an exhibit," Helberg said. "It's part of the aesthetic though."

I jipped *aesthetic* and decided it was a word I would use again in the future.

"You should look up the Arts and Crafts movement," he said. "This building dates from then, and the decor is from that period. Look at the door, for example."

I saw the door had a large brass handle and a finger plate with ends that looped around, formed curling tendrils which reminded me of how plants looked when they were growing in a garden.

"Lovely."

"Let's start in the Medieval gallery," Helberg said. "You might be interested to see some of the techniques from years ago."

We went into a large room with paintings on the wall. The room had nothing else inside it apart from the paintings, and benches where you could sit and look at them. We took a seat.

Helberg pointed at an image. "So, do you see how artists of this time had not discovered the thing we call perspective?" he asked.

I jipped what he meant and then looked at the picture. It showed some people in unusual clothing, jostling together under an archway, and thought I understood. It was curiously flat and I could see nothing behind the people.

We sat and looked at it for a few minutes. There were so many amazing features which the artist had taken care to record. Above the arches was some sort of bright orange building. I wondered if it was meant to be a real building. Even the frame was incredible.

"Who made the frame?" I asked.

"I don't know," said Helberg. "Sometimes pictures get new frames. As long as it makes the picture look good, the frame's doing its job."

I nodded. "So where are the paintings where they got the hang of perspective?"

Helberg smiled. "There are a great many of those, don't worry. Ready to move on?"

We moved into a gallery called Early Italian. The paintings were full of stern-faced people with remarkable skin. A good many of them featured the same mother and baby. They must have been very famous, sort of an early version of Mr Smiley.

"Babies..." I said, musing out loud.

"That's Jesus," said Helberg, nodding at the baby in the nearest portrait.

"Oh, you know him?"

"Not personally."

His words chimed with my thoughts. "I don't know any babies either," I said.

Helberg seemed to find this amusing.

"No," I said. "I mean, I don't see babies around. I was one once, of course. I think."

"You think?" he said, still smiling.

I jipped where babies came from. I didn't tell Helberg I was doing that because I didn't want him to mock me. I had a half-formed notion of how babies were produced; I discovered that half-formed notion was a greatly simplified version of the truth.

"And what's her name?" I said, pointing.

"Mary?" he said.

I nodded. I looked at Mary and Jesus and was struck how much it reminded me of Hattie with her Smiley Tots. I gasped at the realisation, wondering how I'd never seen it before. Had Hattie ever held a real baby? She would make a wonderful mother, but of course, the prospect was never even considered as an option for people on Jaffle Standard. Their lives were more or less controlled to be sex and child-free.

I looked at Mary. "I bet she's not on Jaffle Standard," I said.

"No, I don't believe so," smiled Helberg.

Mary, like Rufus Jaffle and Claire and all those others on higher Jaffle systems were all privileged, or (as I had come to realise) normal, fully functioning humans. The injustice of it was astounding. I found

I was gripping my hands into tight fists. I'd dug my nails into my palms and left deep red nail marks. I could feel my face set in a grim frown.

"Not a fan of religious art, huh?" Helberg said.

I shook my head and tried to dispel my mood. We moved on.

Helberg was right about the perspective, these painters had made their scenes look a lot more realistic, although not quite in the same way as *Dogs playing Poker*.

We turned a corner. "Oh, crumbs!" I said.

We were faced with a room that was almost entirely filled with naked people. I wasn't used to seeing other people without their clothes, and there were dozens of them.

Helberg moved through the room, gazing at them fondly. "Stunning, aren't they?"

I wasn't sure if he was talking about the pictures or breasts.

There were male nudes as well, and I took the opportunity to take a long hard look at how the painter had carefully captured the muscle definition and curls of hair. It was a pleasing sight. The penises were not as captivating as I'd expected them to be. I recalled what I had learned of sex in my earlier education and my more recent, circumspect research. I didn't think any of these tiny penises would be up to the task for which they were intended.

"Getting an eyeful of wangs?" he said.

I blushed. "I researched the sex act."

"The sex act," he said, amused.

"And I really don't see how a penis could penetrate *anything*. Look how small they all are."

"Tiny dicks were very much in vogue back then."

"But even..." I gazed around, looking for an example that more closely matched the images I had seen in my research. I started to make size gestures with my hand and Helberg grinned.

You need to research erections," he said. "I think you'll be impressed with the transformation that takes place between a flaccid—"

"Woah," I said, automatically jipping *erections*. I looked at the penises in the room with new interest. Who could imagine they could spring into life like that? "Do they all do that?" I asked, astounded.

"These are just paintings," he pointed out.

"Gosh," I said. A funny feeling came over me, and not just the thrill of education. I looked at Helberg, the only actual man in the room. He caught me looking.

"Were you looking for a practical demonstration?" he asked wryly and walked on.

We moved through many more galleries. I started to get an idea of just how big this place was.

"Are all of the paintings here?" I asked.

"All of what paintings?"

"All of them. There are a lot."

Helberg turned to me, his eyebrows high. "No, there are lots more. Luckily, most galleries are still open. There are places like this in most major cities."

I tried to picture the scale of that, and found it really strange that people like Hattie and me could spend our whole lives never seeing any art at all. "Are these places only for people on higher Jaffle packages?"

Helberg laughed. "Well, this place and most of the big art galleries kind of predate Jaffle. But there's a point to be debated. Some of the people who built these great halls of art, and the rich patrons who financed them, wanted to keep them sort of exclusive. Like the great art of the world needed protecting from the hoi polloi."

"Figures," I said.

"But others, just as rich, just as powerful, thought that places like these should be made open to all. That if you built great museums and art galleries and you invited the common people in, then—" He clutched at the air in search of words. "—people, everyone, would be enriched and elevated by the experience."

"Huh."

"Back then not everyone thought the lower classes should be happy with less. Not everyone would be satisfied with beans and Mr Smiley."

I perceived a jibe and elbowed him.

"Have you got any idea of the type of picture you'd like to see more of?" Helberg asked. "I've done a lot of talking. Perhaps we should let some of the pictures speak for themselves."

"How about some pictures with animals?" I suggested. I wondered if dogs participated in any other fanciful pastimes in paintings.

"Right, let's have a look at the Victorians. They loved animal pictures."

I followed Helberg as he wove down a series of corridors. We passed through a room filled with stone bodies. I would need to come back and look at that.

"Here we are. You'll find animals in here."

We went into a gallery crowded with smaller and more densely packed pictures. I stopped to look at one. It showed a sheep on a snowy, desolate landscape. At its feet was a dead lamb. The sheep had its head raised and seemed to be crying into the leaden sky for its lost child. Crows crowded around, their hungry gaze fixed upon the dead lamb.

I burst into tears. Literally. I went from "What's that?" to tears pouring down my face in under five seconds. "That's awful," I sniffled.

"It's called *Anguish*," said Helberg. "Schenk painted a lot of animal schemes."

"No." I shook my head, trying to dislodge that horrible image. "Make it stop."

"Hey, Alice, it's all right." Helberg put a tentative hand on my arm. I didn't recoil from his touch. "Come and sit down."

We sat on the bench. I eyed the painting and shook my head at the unfairness. "That poor sheep. Why didn't the artist help it rather than just painting it?"

Helberg seemed surprised at my question. "Well, it's possible he did. Paintings take days. Who knows what happens in the moment. The detail has been lost to history. It's quite probable that the event never even occurred. Not like that, anyway."

I sniffed. I wasn't sure I could go on. I thought about the dead lamb. I thought about the dead mouse under Levi's boot. I could picture it clearly in my mind's eye even though I never actually saw it. "Surely, art is supposed to make us happy? Why would someone paint about sad things?"

Helberg gave me a small smile. It was a much nicer smile. "Art *can* make us happy, but it also challenges us, and stretches our experience. When would you ever have the chance to empathise with a sheep in your normal day-to-day existence?"

Empathise? It stunned me to realise that he was right. I looked up at Schenk's sheep and gave it a small nod of respect.

"Come on." I stood up. "Let's do more art."

I enjoyed the animals. The dogs from the old days were a different shape, I realised. They were either small enough to fit up a lady's sleeve or they were long-legged things which stood with horses and ran behind carriages, for some reason. None of them pooped; at least not in the pictures.

Something clicked in my mind. "IFPA."

"Gesundheit," said Helberg.

"I wasn't sneezing. I was—"

"The animal charity. I know. Overcome with a sudden urge to make a donation?"

"There's a charity gala."

"You don't have to make a donation in person."

In the borrowed memory from Rufus Jaffle, Henderson mentioned Rufus would be at a charity gala on the fifteenth. If the International Federation for the Protection of Animals had an upcoming gala, then I could go there to find Rufus. Jipping for more information was not hard. Jaffle Tech was indeed holding a gala in aid of IFPA, over on the ocean side of the city. As long as I could avoid the brain scan until then, I'd be able to get to Rufus and some answers.

Then I saw the event was a private corporate affair, mentioned in the events pages of news feeds and not open to the public. All the way home, I jipped for ways of getting a ticket but there didn't seem to be an option for buying one.

I sighed as we walked back into the Shangri-La Towers apartment complex.

"Hey, cheer up," said Helberg. "The wonderful thing about art is that it's an experience you can take away with you and..." He gestured, with an unconscious playfulness, to join him in his office. "I have an idea that might help you." I stepped past my boxes of flowers which still cluttered the lobby.

He reached up to a shelf and placed an oily heap of scrap onto the floor. It looked like all of the other heaps of scrap that he had around the place.

I looked at him. I had no idea what I was supposed to say, so I said "Um."

"This is Chuckie Egg."

"Is it?"

"He's my next bot project."

I stared at the thing. I'd seen bots before and they did not look like this. Even Helberg's craziest bots had plastic covers and you could usually tell the front from the back.

"Hang on," he said, as if he knew what I was thinking. "The cover's around here somewhere." He clipped a shell onto it, and it had a form. It wasn't a sensible form, but it looked a bit more like a bot.

"What does it do?" I asked.

"Well, that's what I thought we could talk about. I reckon we can program it to do painting. It won't be able to create masterpieces like we saw in the gallery, but if we want to redecorate the place, then Chuckie Egg can do a lot of the legwork.

"Wow! That sounds amazing. We tell Chuckie Egg to paint all of the doors a different colour and off it goes?"

"Yup. I'll need to add an extension arm for it to reach the top. I'll have it ready by tomorrow. Or..." He giggled. Patrick Helberg giggled. That wasn't really something I'd seen him do before. He'd chuckled darkly. He'd leered. He'd grinned. He'd shown faint flickerings of human warmth. But giggle?

"What?" I said.

"Nothing," he said. "You head off. I've got things to do."

***

Chapter 18 – 6ᵗʰ June – 13 days until Operation Sunrise

In the morning, Helberg called me. He didn't jip me like an ordinary person, but put a voice call through to our apartment. Hattie got to it before me. She came into my bedroom.

"Helberg wants you to look out of the window," she said flatly.

She was still angry with me. I had spilled paint on one of her precious Smiley Tots. I might as well have stabbed one in the face the way Hattie was reacting.

"Why does he want me to do that?" I asked.

"That's the message: look out the window." Hattie made a point of looking casually towards my window but not looking out, and left.

I slipped out of bed and crossed to the window. Square of sky above, neighbour's apartments across the other side and then...

"Crumbs!"

The quadrangle below was being transformed into a picture of me. It was so clearly and obviously me, pinpoint perfect, but for the life of me I couldn't see how it had been executed, until I saw the wobbly white dome cover of a bot. Chuckie Egg had a robot fist full of flowers – I guessed fuchsias from their colour – and was lying strips on the ground to make the edge of my cheek. Reds and purples and greens and browns and somehow the whole thing worked.

It was me.

I ran downstairs in my night clothes and burst into Helberg's office. "Oh, my goodness," I exclaimed. "How did you do that?"

Helberg slurped on the carton of greasy noodles he was apparently having for breakfast.

"Very simple really, O valued tenant. Screen grab of you from the security cameras. Turned it into a map for Chuckie Egg. I downloaded him a simple colour recognition and compositing program, gave him his palette of dead flowers and..." He gestured expansively with his chopsticks as though the whole thing was nothing at all.

"Did you have to kill all my flowers?" I said. The remaining, unused flowers were still piled up in boxes by Helberg's office, and the gorgeous fragrance had diminished, replaced by an undercurrent of something unpleasant.

"You know the difference between a cut flower and a living plant?" he asked.

It felt like a trick question. When he phrased it like that, it seemed as though I ought to have realised flowers were alive when they were attached to plants, and *not* alive once they were cut. It had never occurred to me to consider it that way.

"Ri-iight," I said. "So for making a garden, you need the living sort?"

He nodded.

I looked at the boxes and sighed. These were not going to be useful.

It was as if he could read my mind. "On a positive note, all the flowers Chuckie Egg's been throwing around will compost nicely."

"Compost?"

"You'll want to learn all about composting if you're to become a gardener. Look it up and I think you'll see what can be done with all of these flowers."

He was right. Compost was definitely on the cards. It helped with soil structure, which sounded important.

"What about plants then?" I asked. "We need to turn the quadrangle into a garden for everyone to enjoy."

"Everyone?" he echoed. "What do you know about digging? Let me find some tools and show you what you need to do. When the digging is all done, we'll get some plants delivered."

I beamed at him.

It turned out that digging was really hard work, yet strangely satisfying. Helberg kept trying to pretend his involvement was purely *managerial* and that things would go better if he just offered guidance from the side-lines, but I made it very clear he owed his tenants this community garden. Eventually he sighed and joined me outside. We dug the flower portrait of me into the soil. Yes, we were destroying a beautiful thing, but it was never going to last. It created an unusual feeling in me, neither sad nor happy. I struggled to explain it to Helberg.

"I know that the flowers were dying anyway, but I feel odd destroying them."

"Maybe one of the things people like about cut flowers is that it's a transient thing," he said. "A reminder that beauty, life, all of it is a temporary thing. Ephemeral."

I jipped my literary booster. "That's a nice word," I said.

"Isn't it." He made a compost bin out of some of the discarded wood and piled the weeds I dug out into it.

"So when compost happens, tiny organisms eat up all of the waste and make new soil," I said. I kept jipping more detail about compost, because it was so fascinating. "So even that poor dead lamb from the gallery would eventually decay and become soil?"

Helberg looked alarmed for a moment. "If you put whole carcasses on there it would get very smelly," he said.

"I haven't got any carcasses," I said. "I just mean in theory."

He looked relieved, and nodded. "Yep. Circle of life."

I wondered what the soil under my feet had come from. Had living things decomposed to form all of this? How many things would that be? It was slightly overwhelming.

The digging left my arms tired and my hands dirty, but I loved it. Eventually it was all done and Helberg said we were ready for some plants. We went to his office where he asked me lots of confusing questions about the kinds of plants we should get. It seemed as though there was quite a choice. He sketched out a rough plan on the whiteboard and we talked about what should go where.

"What about bacon?" he asked, pointing at my to-do list, which he hadn't rubbed off.

"I still haven't got any," I admitted.

"We could include a barbecue area." He indicated a corner of the garden. "It's sheltered here, you could install a barbecue and a small seating area."

"Barbecue," I said, jipping it hastily. "Oh. It's a cooking device used out of doors." It might be a useful way to try cooking.

Helberg nodded as if he was concentrating. He did that strange thing again: sort of jipping out loud. "Order interface. Sending list for delivery within two hours."

I wanted to get to the bottom of why he did that, but I had work to do.

"I'll invite everyone down this evening," I said. "This is going to blow them away. Did you order some bacon as well?"

He nodded.

"Fantastic!"

I composed an invite and jipped it to all residents:

You are all invited to a bacon sandwich barbecue party to celebrate the opening of the new community garden.

As soon as the goods delivery arrived, Helberg got to work putting the barbecue together while I put the plants in the ground.

I planted broad Abelia shrubs, handling them carefully so as not to damage their pink bell-shaped flowers. I installed rows of weighty aloe plants with their stiff jagged leaves. I created an arrangement of echium, escallonia, salvia. I filled in gaps with hardy sedums, their leaves so dark as to almost appear grey – not the dull grey of the rest of my world but a subtle and beautiful dustiness.

I had to add water to them, which is all part of the care that plants need. I had a special device called a watering can which sprinkled water in a little shower, so that I could make sure each one had a drink.

I felt unbelievably happy.

***

Six o'clock arrived and the curious tenants started to drift down to see what we were doing.

"Well Alice, I'm sure I don't know what you're doing. Have you seen the state of this place?" said Swanager. She was pointing at the compost area.

"Don't dwell on that," I said. "Take a look at the plants. Aren't they amazing?"

"You did this?" she asked.

"Yes."

"No wonder you got dirt on your shoes."

I swallowed down the mild anger she provoked in me. She didn't know any better. It was up to me to try and stimulate some sort of response. I was convinced that I could make people on Jaffle Standard sit up and see what they were missing.

"If the garden does nothing for you, wait until you taste the bacon," I said. "Can you smell that?" Helberg had some bacon on the barbecue and the smell was amazing.

Swanager turned her nose up, but it wasn't the appreciative sniff that I'd been expecting, it was the expression of someone who'd seen something appalling.

"Is that the flesh of a beast?" she asked. "I'd heard that people ate such things, but I had no idea that they walked among us here."

"It's tasty," I pointed out.

"I'm not sure your opinion counts for much. In truth, I only came down to inform you – *inform you all*—" she added loudly to anyone within earshot, "—that Clifford and I are moving out today."

"I will have your apartment dried and cleaned soon," Helberg tried to assure her.

She shook her head with something like disgust. "We're moving to that new North Beach arcology. Integrated living solutions and they pay you to live there. We jipped the terms and conditions today. Didn't we, Clifford?"

There was no sound of support from Pedstone. Swanager looked round and caught sight of her roommate, Pedstone, over at the barbecue. He was trying to dangle a slice of hot and juicy bacon into his mouth.

"Pedstone! We're leaving!" She made sure she gave everyone present a good glare. "And I doubt many of you will be staying around much longer if *this* is the kind of nonsense that goes on at Shangri-La Towers."

Swanager left at that point, and whispered to several other people on her way out. They also turned and walked away.

"Wait!" I called. "Some of you must be interested in the work that we're doing here? Look at the textures and the colours! Think for a moment about the circle of life! Don't you realise that everything turns into dirt in the end, and here we are making flowers grow in it! Look, will you!"

They weren't interested. People hung on politely for a few minutes before leaving. All except Hattie. I hadn't seen her arrive, but she stood there now, shaking her head.

"I don't know what you've become, Alice?"

"I haven't become anything," I said. "Nothing that wasn't there already."

"I feel as if I don't know you anymore."

"What do you mean?"

"I thought you were my friend, but you ruined my Smiley Tot—"

"That was an accident."

"—and now you're scaring all of the neighbours with your talk about dirt. Are you really trying to make us eat flesh from a beast?"

"Yes?" I said.

"Why?"

"Because it tastes nice and—"

"Was it a bad animal?"

"Bad? As in...? It's a pig."

"Did it deserve to die? Is that the point? Are we punishing it? You're messing about in the dirt, getting excited about rotting things and now we're supposed to devour this pig. I don't know what it's supposed to have done but it's very odd behaviour to say the least."

I wanted to tell Hattie how delicious it was. How people had eaten this sort of food since the beginning of time, but her face was stony and impassive and I could tell she didn't want to hear anything from me.

"Hattie, I've learned so much over the last few days," I tried. "I really want to share it with you. Give it a chance. I think you'd like it, I really do."

She shook her head. "Maybe I ought to see if they've still got any spare apartments in that North Beach arcology."

"Hattie!"

She walked away. She was the last. All of the other people had gone, although I could see that several of them stood at the windows overlooking the quadrangle, staring out as if I might be a dangerous menace.

I looked at Helberg. He stood by the barbecue as the remaining rashers of bacon crisped and withered, unwanted. "Let's go inside," I said.

Whatever the mood was, whatever connections I'd hoped to make, it was all gone now.

"And the bacon?" he asked.

I thought for a moment. I was deflated. Part of me wanted to reject the bacon, close the door on the garden and leave it all behind. It did smell delicious though.

"Bring the bacon," I said.

***

Back in his cluttered office, Helberg put a plate of stacked crispy bacon on a pile of documents. He cleared a chair for me by moving a pile of electronic junk from one pile to another. This somehow didn't

seem to satisfy him and he whacked the seat cushion a few times, making puffs of dust in the air.

"Please," he said and then rootled around in a cupboard to produce a slim-necked glass bottle. "Have you ever tried alcohol?"

"No," I said. I wasn't counting the second-hand experience that I'd had in Rufus Jaffle's head. I thought about the party in that memory/dream. "Is this the right time to be having a drink?"

"Absolutely. Everyone walking out of your garden party, that's a drinking situation."

"I'll just have a really tiny bit, then."

He got a small glass out of a cupboard. It was the sort of glass that Hattie would love: it was just about the right size for a Smiley Tot. He poured an appropriately small amount of a golden liquid.

"This is sherry," he said. "A perfectly serviciable Bodegas Hidalgo La Gitana Manzanilla."

"That's a bit of a mouthful," I said.

"More than a bit of a mouthful in there." He passed me the glass.

"I meant the name."

"I know." He smiled.

I took a sip. It coated my lips with its sweetness, and I could feel a delicious warmth in my mouth. As I swallowed, the warmth went down my throat.

"Mm. It's sweet but kind of salty and... Mmmm."

"Throw in a few more wild similes and we'll make a wine connoisseur of you," he said.

I took another sip. Drinking it was an undeniably pleasant sensation, and I could feel that the busy, bothersome thoughts that crowded my brain were slipping away. I finished the glass and tipped my head back, delighted at how mellow my mood was becoming.

"Can I have some more please?"

"Sure," said Helberg and he poured me another glass. I noticed that he was drinking something from a different bottle. It was called whisky.

"You talk to your Jaffle Port," I said.

"I talk to lots of things. I talk to Jetpac here," he said, patted a pile of rubbish next to him. It burbled and beeped, revealing itself to be a partially constructed bot.

"Nobody talks to their Jaffle Port."

He regarded his glass of whisky for a long time. The glass was an interesting shape, with artful facets which reflected the light. "They do if they have a non-Jaffle Port," he said eventually.

"What?" I said with a nervous laugh. "Non-Jaffle Port? What does that even mean?"

"It means what it means. A Jaffle Port is just a device. Don't confuse the item with the brand. It's like hoovers or coke or scotch tape. You know scotch tape?"

"I think so," I said, still reeling.

"That's a brand name. The stuff itself is just called adhesive tape or something. You don't have to go with the big brand name. You can buy one somewhere else, or make your own."

As soon as the words were out of his mouth I understood. The evidence was all around his office. "You made it? You made your own Jaffle Port?"

He nodded. "Brain port, but, yeah."

I was knocked back by the implications. He was one of the three percent. One of the mad and crazy ones. "How does that even work?" I took a larger slurp of sherry and topped up the glass myself. This was mind-boggling.

He shrugged. "Jaffle Ports allow access to a wealth of information, but Jaffle Tech don't own all of that knowledge. In its most stripped-down form a Jaffle Port is a sophisticated way of accessing a massive computer network. I built a similar device that lets me do the same thing. The difference with mine is that I control what access the network has to *me*."

"But Jaffle Tech manage your spare capacity for your benefit," I found myself saying.

"Spare capacity!" he scoffed. "Don't think I don't know what's happened to you. Do you think what you've had given back to you was *spare capacity*?"

"But the essential service software," I insisted. "Firewall, obscenity filters, system check, customer feedback..." I realised I was spouting lines from my own call centre script.

Too many thoughts flooded my mind. What he was saying made sense on the surface but I couldn't help but feel a deep-seated revulsion at what seemed like an unnatural perversion. Didn't he want to be part of a global community? Didn't he want to fit in?

"How are you able to live?" I asked.

He laughed out loud at that.

"Sorry," I said. "I didn't mean..."

"I live quite well, thank you."

"I know. I meant..."

"You mean, as an outsider." He took a sip of whiskey. "I'm not alone."

"Er..." I waved a hand around his hermit's cave of an office by way of counter-argument.

He laughed, tilting his glass in my direction. "I live a selfish life, in every sense of the word. Anything for an easy life, that's me. I know I'm an outsider, but I'm not alone. Jaffle would like you to think those who don't adopt their tech are doomed to a solitary life, but there are others out there who refuse to become brand victims. And even if I was alone, just because you're a minority of one, doesn't mean you're mad."

"Bit mad," I suggested. "You're a—" I jipped for a good word. "—a Luddite!"

"Anti-technology?" he said. "Me? Do I look like a machine-smasher, a *saboteur*?"

"No, but—"

"But nothing!" There was a note of passion in his voice. "Technological development is a wonderful thing. I would be mad if I thought the world would be a better place without brain port technology. My great-aunt suffered from a degenerative brain condition. A piece of early Jaffle technology was able to repair the neural damage, or bridge it at least, and give her years of life quality that would not have been available otherwise. No, knowledge is king. How it is applied is where the ethical debate lies."

"You think Jaffle Tech is unethical?" I felt my own recent opinions solidify even as I said it. "Helberg?"

"Yes?"

"Have you heard of a plipper?"

"A who's-what-now?"

"Plipper."

"As in a thing that plips?"

"You have heard of it?"

"No. I just extrapolated. What is a plipper?"

I recalled what I had seen in the executive offices at Jaffle Tech. "It's a device. About so long. You point it at someone and it automatically reduces their brain function to the bare minimum. Like the Empties outside."

His expression had become serious. "You've seen one?"

"A demonstration, at work. They're going to give them out to law enforcement agencies."

"They're going to use them for pacification? Jeez."

"Henderson – he's the Chief Technical Officer at Jaffle Tech – he said that it's much safer than the police using Tasers on people."

"And that makes it okay?" said Helberg. "I can't believe people would stand for this."

"He said—" I tried to remember what he'd said. "Everyone has already given their consent, everyone on Jaffle Enhanced and below. It's in those new terms and conditions."

I'd coerced that caller, Jackson, into signing those new terms and conditions, just before I'd been distracted by the mouse. Was I now responsible for them getting plipped in the future?

Maybe it was the mouse that reminded me, but a phrase they'd used leapt to my mind. "What's a deadcat?" I asked.

"What's a dead cat?" repeated Helberg.

I considered jipping it but I didn't want images of dead cats flooding my mind at this vulnerable time. "I think it was meant to be a verb."

"They were going to deadcat something?"

"That."

He made a noise, not a happy one. "If you throw a dead cat on a table, everyone will notice it. Once you've thrown a dead cat on the table, people will be too distracted to notice what you do next. Is the plipper the dead cat?"

"I don't know," I said.

"You deadcat something truly horrific with something people are going to be distracted by. If the plipper is the dead cat then the other thing ... what else were they talking about?"

"It was something called Operation Sunrise."

"Euphemistically pleasant sounding."

"It just sounded like a software roll-out. Jaffle Tech 2.0. It's going live in six days."

"Fuckers," he said, and with such quiet sincerity it was even more shocking.

"You think it's going to be a bad thing?"

"Oh, absolutely. A company that turns the weak and unfortunate into Empties at the press of a button? With the collusion

of the powers that be? There's no way their next software innovation is going to be a good thing."

"I'm sure if I could speak to Rufus Jaffle, I'd be able to discuss it with him. Maybe I've got it wrong and he can tell me what's really going on."

Helberg scoffed. "Those Jaffle guys have been screwing over the little guy for years."

"And yet," I said, thoughtfully, "you've done nothing about it."

He drained his glass. Refilled and drained it again. "I try not to get hung up on things I can't possibly fix," he said. "Like I say, a selfish life. Drink."

It was an instruction and an invitation. He topped up both our glasses once more, hand shaking with emotion.

"You..." I said.

"What?"

"You've set yourself apart. You've not been a joiner. You've not got a Jaffle Port."

"I'm one of the fabled three percent. And how glad I am of that!"

"But it hasn't made you happy, has it?"

His lips curled in a smile but it was the bitterly cold smile of the old Patrick Helberg. "Heard of John Stuart Mill?"

"Does he live in the complex?"

"He was a British philosopher. Long time ago now. He had a lot to say about human rights and freedoms." He picked at the pile of uneaten bacon which was now cold and hard as cardboard. "He said it was better to be an unhappy human than a happy pig."

"And is it?" I asked.

"I'm not even sure I know what happiness is. By a lot of people's definition, I'm some kind of miserable bastard, but I'd rather be miserable like this than happy because I'm a dumbed-down-to-watch-Smiley-TV-all-day-long-and-be-satisfied sheep."

I thought about that. "I used to like Smiley TV," I said. "I mean, I used to like it *a lot*."

He laughed cruelly. "Doofus."

"And now," I said, "it does nothing for me. It's not enough."

"And would you go back, if you could?" Helberg asked. "If at a flick of switch—" he clicked his fingers "—they could instantly return you to how you were before: ignorant and happy. If you could plip yourself back to stupidity, right now, would you do it?"

I sipped the golden sherry. "Nope," I said. "I'm never going back."

I waved my suddenly empty glass at him for a refill.

**

Chapter 19 – 7th June – 12 days until Operation Sunrise

I woke up with a headache, a dry mouth, and no desire to get up. I must have stumbled home at some point but I didn't remember anything beyond chatting and drinking with Helberg in his office. It was a work day and I had a scan scheduled at the office. If I didn't at least go in to work, they would be even more suspicious of me.

I called on what pain filters my Jaffle Port allowed and, ignoring the protests from my head and stomach, forced myself to get up and dressed. Hattie was busying herself around the apartment but seemed disinclined to talk to me. That was okay; I wasn't in a talking mood either.

Out in the corridor, Chuckie Egg was painting apartment doors, deftly handling a paintbrush in a way that put my efforts to shame.

Hattie and I shared a car to work, but the atmosphere was uncomfortably strained. Hattie claimed she was studying a literary module, so she was unable to engage in conversation. It was natural to assume she was lying, but I'm not sure Hattie was capable of lying, which made me think she has accessed a literary module with the sole purpose of avoiding me.

Partway through the morning, my calendar pinged to remind me of the rescheduled brain scan. I had run out of excuses, so this time I tried the strategy of ignoring it and hoping it would go away. This was obviously doomed to failure: within a few minutes a call came through.

"Alice, you're late for your scan. You need to come down to the medical centre right now."

"I can't." I failed to elaborate.

"Why not?"

"Our department is in lock-down," I said, spotting Levi marching around looking self-important. "There's been an intrusion. An anomaly."

There was a sigh on the line. *"If I call your section head, am I going to find out that this is untrue, Alice?"*

"No?" I tried.

"Because repeatedly failing to attend a mandatory health scan could result in disciplinary action, did you know that? And more importantly, it could point to an underlying issue, which is the whole reason we're doing this, isn't it?" There was an even heavier sigh. "Fine. I want you here first thing in the morning, is that clear?"

"Er, yep."

"You will come to the medical centre before you even go to your section."

"Sure."

"This is your last chance, Alice."

"I'll be there," I said.

When I killed the call I looked round to Hattie's cubicle, because something strange was happening. A delivery of several large boxes had just turned up. Hattie attempted to push them discreetly out of sight as she dealt with her caller. A little bit like trying to hide an elephant by popping a tiny hat on it. Hattie succeeded only in drawing Levi's attention more quickly. A cleaning bot trundled into Hattie's cubicle and bounced off one of the boxes. It readjusted its course.

Levi stood impatiently to the side until she'd finished the call.

"Can I ask what this is, miss?"

Hattie composed herself in the way that she does, by flapping a hand at her face as though she's very hot. "I suppose you might call it an emergency."

"Might I?" he said. "I might call ditch water coffee but that don't make it so."

"I needed to get some of my possessions to a place of safety because there's been a bit of a problem at home." She looked my way for the first time.

Now I knew what was in the boxes.

"May I take a look inside?" said Levi.

"Certainly." Hattie opened the top of the nearest box and sure enough, it was filled with Smiley Tots. He picked one out and turned it over in his hands.

"Careful!" said Hattie.

Levi gave her a look. "I'm inspecting its safety labels. These are not certified as suitable for an industrial environment."

"Of course they're not, they're toys!" said Hattie. "I just want to put them on my desk, as decoration."

Levi paused. He knew very well that decoration of a desk was permitted. His gaze swivelled across the huge boxes before he looked critically at the desk. "I'm not sure they'll all fit in the environs of the desk."

"Oh, they will," said Hattie with confidence.

"Hm." Levi put the Smiley Tot down and looked at Hattie. "So what's the problem at home? Anything I should know about?"

I tried to pull a subtle but meaningful face, but Hattie wasn't even looking at me. "Alice has been a little careless with some of her recent activities. It not a suitable environment for the Smiley Tots."

"Oh, dear. Trouble at the homestead, huh?" He looked across at me. He was wearing his disappointed face, yet I could see a hidden amusement in his eyes. "It's our duty to make sure this is a safe and harmonious environment, is it not? Oh, yabetcha. I expect team members to park their problems at the door and look out for each other when they're under my watchful eye."

"I couldn't have said it better myself," said Hattie piously.

My best friend hated me and was getting me into trouble at work for it. More trouble. The cleaning bot nudged up to the chair that I was sitting on. I kicked out at it. I'd always imagined these things as being Levi's spies.

"Stupid spybot," I growled.

Its canopy cracked in the middle, exposing some of its inner workings and it made a fizzing, sparking noise as it left. I wasn't sorry.

***

When I got home that evening I ate beans and went to see how Chuckie Egg was doing. All of the doors were done now and the bot was working on the stairwells.

Helberg appeared from downstairs. "Took a few adjustments to get right."

"I can see that," I said, stepping carefully to avoid the paint streaking the stairs.

"I have something for you," he said. I followed him to the office. He picked up a large piece of card. How old-fashioned! It was thick and had beautiful lettering upon it.

JAFFLE TECH'S

Annual Benevolence Gala and Charity Auction
in aid of the
International Federation for the Protection of the
Animals
15ᵀᴴ June

"Is this an actual ticket?" I asked.

"It is an actual ticket."

"How did you know I wanted to go?"

"I pulled a few strings to get hold of it after you mentioned how important it was to you."

"Did I?"

"After your fourth glass of sherry."

"Oh, right." I said. "Was I ... inebriated?"

"Inebriated? You were three sheets to the wind, O valued tenant."

I marvelled at the ticket, felt its textured thickness under my thumb. "Wow. Thank you. You've no idea how much this means to me."

"Oh, you were incoherently eloquent about it last night," he said. "And now, Cinderella, you *shall* go to the ball!"

"Who's Cinderella?"

It didn't matter. I had a ticket to the charity gala, access to Rufus Jaffle, a chance to get answers to this chaotic mess my life had become *and* Operation Sunrise. I felt tears prick the corners of my ears in sheer gratitude at what Helberg had just done for me.

"Tears of joy?" said Helberg, hopefully.

I nodded and sniffed and attempted a smile before shaking my head. "There's a very real chance I'll get busted tomorrow for having more brain power than I'm supposed to."

"Busted? How do you mean?" he asked.

"I've been avoiding a brain scan they insist on doing. I really need to present myself tomorrow and they're bound to spot what's going on. They'll reverse it, I'm sure. I don't think I can bear to go back to how I was. I certainly won't be going to any gala."

Helberg stared at me with a heavy sigh. "The tragic thing is if you did go back to how you were, you probably wouldn't even mind. You'd sit and watch Smiley Time and be happy with it."

With a chill I realised he was right. "No. That's not right."

"No, it is not. These brain scans, they must be a fairly standard report, right?"

I nodded. We dealt with them quite often. "Yes, there's a capacity report, an activity report, an analysis of any serious failings, downtime or anomalies, that sort of thing."

"Why not create a fake one?"

I thought for a moment. I could certainly rustle up some convincing content. "There's one bit I couldn't make up," I said. "It needs to show a reading from the metrics chip on the Jaffle Port. If it's not in line with previous readings, it will flag an error straightaway."

"So get a previous reading."

"Those are encrypted in storage, I can't get to them without alerting the system."

"Well," he said slowly, "there is another possibility."

I didn't like the look on his face. "What?"

"I can hack your port, just to get a reading."

"Oh no. Definitely no. Absolutely not!" It was a terrible idea.

He held up his hands. "Fine. If it makes you uncomfortable. Take your chances the scan at work will miss the massive upgrade you have somehow accidentally acquired."

"No, it's not that it makes me uncomfortable." It made me *very* uncomfortable. "But look what happened the last time I meddled with the system. It's got me in all sorts of trouble."

He held my arms and looked me straight in the eye. "I think what you *really* mean is that it's opened your eyes to a world you never even knew existed. A world that is filled with beauty and tragedy and so much wonder that you can't wait to experience more of it. Or of course, you could go back to watching Smiley."

I couldn't argue with his logic. If there was a chance a fake brain scan could get me past this scrutiny at work and make sure I could hang on to my enhanced abilities, then I needed to take it.

"What would be involved in you hacking my Jaffle Port?" I asked.

"It will be a quick scan with some of my home-built equipment."

"Show me."

We walked through his office. Helberg used a stepladder to access a high shelf and he brought down a glass, cone-shaped object

with electronics clustered upon it. It resembled nothing I had ever seen at Jaffle.

"It's a little bit unusual," he said, probably seeing my expression, "but I make equipment for my own use, remember? I don't care what it looks like. The glass helmet is a re-purposed door from an old washing machine. It sits quite comfortably on the head and aligns the circuitry for accessing the Jaffle Port."

I really didn't want the thing on my head. I wasn't sure if I trusted Helberg's technical proficiency. Most of his bots seemed to work okay, but some were hopeless failures. More than that, I wasn't sure if I trusted Helberg's motives. He'd been helping me, there was no denying it, but I felt as though I was a project or a diversion. If I stopped being entertaining, would he be so keen to help? It wasn't so long ago that he took all of my money from me.

He looked at my face, perhaps detecting some suspicion. "Hey, I know you must be worried about this. I can't make you believe me, but I promise I won't do anything other than what I said. I'd suggest you could bring Hattie as a chaperone, but I'm not sure she'd approve of any of this."

"Oh no, we can't involve Hattie," I said. "Right, let's do this."

He beamed. "Pop it on your head and I'll calibrate the settings. Try to keep it still."

"And, just to be clear, you've done this before?"

He hesitated. "Dozens of times. I have watched other open source port-engineers do this very thing. But, okay, yours is the very first head I've actually messed with."

Messed with? "Can I have something to write on?" I asked.

He raised his eyebrows but passed me a pencil and paper from a drawer.

I scribbled a note.

To Alice in a few minutes' time. If you suddenly and unaccountably want to have sex with Helberg, then he has messed with something in your brain and you need to punish him.

He gave me a hurt look. "I'm all for sex Alice, but not like that."

"Glad to hear it." I put the helmet on my head.

Whatever procedure Helberg ran, I felt nothing except the slightly uncomfortable weight of his contraption on my head. He lifted it off a few minutes later.

"All done."

I shook out my hair. "Did you get the settings from the metrics chip?"

"Yup. Sending them to you now, so you can compose your own fake brain scan. Had you thought about adding in a small anomaly to throw them off the scent?"

"I had thought of that, yes," I said. "We sometimes see capacity problems caused by environmental stress – like a change to routine. I think I'll throw in one of those, but make it look steady and normal afterwards."

***

Chapter 20 – 8th June – 11 days until Operation Sunrise

"You've got paint on you."

It was the first thing Hattie had said to me in nearly twenty-four hours . To hear it was a stab of emotion in my chest. She still hadn't forgiven me for staining her Smiley Tot, still could not comprehend that I needed to explore the new, unchained me. She was my very best friend in the whole world and it was wrenching to have lost some of that friendship. So to have her speak to me, directly and voluntarily, was wonderful. Even it was to point out a paint mark on my tunic as we walked into the Jaffle Tech building the next day.

I looked. There was a blob of brown paint on my tunic breast. It looked quite unpleasant but I didn't have a clean spare back at home or time to go get one.

"I can sort that," I said and took a detour to the supplies department.

"Hi Damian, I need to get a new tunic, can I pop down?" I asked.

"Sure," said the helpful guy at the counter. "You can't have it straightaway though."

"But..." I pointed to the brown mark.

He pulled a face. "Have you been playing with dog poo again?"

"What do you mean *again*?"

He shrugged. "Word gets around."

"It's paint."

"Paint?"

"Paint."

"Paint?"

"Listen, can I get a tunic or not."

"I'll have to let the security staff know," he said. "Orders from on high."

"Levi, you mean."

"It's part of an *ongoing investigation* into a *serious incident*." He did two lots of air quotes as he said it.

"Never mind," I said. "I don't want to create work for Levi."

"You're a very thoughtful person."

"Who does *not* play with dog poo," I pointed out as I left.

On our floor Hattie was going round her Smiley Tot enclosure and performing her morning routine on them: switching their positions so she could spend quality time with each of them. They were stacked three deep in what looked like a defensive wall around her cubicle, but Levi was unable to object because she had managed to get them above and below the desk's surface. She was now able to take calls and tend to her Tots, which seemed to make her very happy. I thought about paintings of that Jesus baby in the art gallery and how happy a real baby might make Hattie. Maybe I'd have a chat about that with her later, work out a way for her to spend some time with real babies. Maybe rebuild our damaged relationship in the process.

I hurried to my cubicle and got settled in quickly so no one could see my unsightly stain. I got right down to the task of answering customer calls about their Jaffle Ports.

Mid-morning, I sent my home-made brain scan down to the medical centre and then, increasingly self-conscious about my stained uniform, went to the staff kitchenette to try and clean it. In my bag, I had the bottle of cleaning thinners Helberg had given me. I popped my bag on the counter and took the bottle out.

"Thinners," I read, taking the lid off. "Do not drink. Inflammable liquid."

It didn't say I couldn't use it on clothes. The smell was pungent, and I hoped I wouldn't stink all day after using it.

I dabbed a little bit right on the edge of my tunic. It didn't melt. I sloshed a good quantity onto the paint stain and dabbed at it with paper towelling from the dispenser. I could see the paint was softening, so I added some more.

"Alice, could I have a word please?"

I turned to see who it was, knocking over the thinners. It splashed about on the counter. I grabbed the bottle before hardly any had run out and set it upright.

"Ah, right. Yes?" I said.

It was the beautiful woman with the big eyes from the medical centre. "Your brain scan," she said.

"Yes?"

"It's highly unusual for someone to commission one privately."

"Did you find a problem with it?" I asked, expecting the worst.

"What do you think?"

I met her eye. "I think it was absolutely fine."

"It was," she conceded. "It's just unorthodox. Who signed off on the deviation from procedure?"

I glanced across the counter, and saw a puddle of thinners was spreading towards a nearby toaster oven. I pulled more paper towelling from the dispenser and mopped it up. I breathed a sigh of relief, trying to make it look as if I was conscientiously cleaning up the kitchen, rather than doing anything suspicious.

"Alice," said the medical centre woman.

"Sorry, yes." I dropped the paper towels into the bin, along with the bottle of thinners. I'd have to get some more later.

"I'm really not sure whether to refer this to my supervisor."

"The whole thing has a perfectly reasonable explanation," I said.

She waited, clearly wanting to hear my perfectly reasonable explanation. There was a lull in conversation while I tried to think of one. A cleaning bot arrived. From its cracked canopy, I could see it was the one I'd kicked yesterday, the one I had groundlessly declared to be Levi's spybot. The association alone made me stiffen with guilt but I made an effort to keep my expression composed. The bot whirred as it clamped the bin in order to empty it.

"Rufus Jaffle requested my brain scan," I said.

"Him? Or his secretary?" she replied.

"Yes, exactly. He has a ... close personal friend training to do brain scan type things and Rufus – I call him Rufus – he asked me to go to him."

"For practice?"

"Exactly."

I thought it was a good effort. To uncover my lie she'd have to find Rufus Jaffle and ask him. I didn't think she'd bother and I certainly didn't think she'd be able to find him.

Clunk!

Woomf!

The first sound was caused by the bottle of thinners falling out of the bin and splashing liquid all over the bot's exposed circuitry. The second was the entire thing being set alight by a spark. The bot's programming clearly didn't cover this scenario: its routing seemed to immediately go wrong. It careered across the office, spinning towards the desks.

I ran after it. I would tell Levi that I thought running was justified in the circumstances. The bot was getting close to Hattie's desk. I kicked it over to stop it getting any further and whooped in

triumph as I managed to stop its progress. I wondered where the nearest fire extinguisher was. I could soon put this out, and *then* I'd be celebrated as the hero who averted a disaster. I whirled in place, wondering why the people at the surrounding desks were all standing and staring. I looked across at Hattie who peered across the top of her Smiley Tot wall. She was gesturing, but I couldn't understand what she was saying.

To my horror I saw the fire which had previously been contained to the bot was spreading outwards as the liquid drained across the floor. It edged towards the Smiley Tots, and I waved wildly at Hattie.

"Fire!" I yelled.

"Yes!" she yelled, and yet she made no move to get out from what would surely become her funeral pyre.

"Move! You're on fire!" I yelled.

"No, you're on fire!" she yelled back, pointing.

I looked down. Sure enough, my tunic bottom was aflame. While I'd been fixated on the flames heading for Hattie they had also been coming towards me.

Well, I'd cast myself as the hero in this situation and this was just one more obstacle to overcome. With a roar, I tried to rip my tunic off, but only managed to burn my hand. I unzipped my tunic and stepped out of it. That left Hattie and her Smiley Tot inferno. They were giving off a thick black smoke which made me cough. I lunged forward, burst through the wall of Smiley Tots and grabbed Hattie by the arm. I hauled her clear as the Smiley wall started to crackle with tall flames.

As we panted with the spent adrenalin, the sprinklers came on, the fire alarms howled and the smell of singed plastic replaced the choking smoke. Throughout the office, Jaffle Tech employees rose from their seats and moved in an orderly fashion towards the exits.

Levi appeared and looked me up and down. "Are you hurt?" he said.

I looked down at myself. Levi was staring, possibly because my clothes were either burned or discarded to the extent that I was very nearly naked.

"No."

"Hattie? Are you hurt?"

Hattie was sobbing uncontrollably. "My tots. All of my tots."

The army of cutesy baby dolls had been reduced to a stinking heap of melted plastic and burned fabric. Levi went over and tried to find one that was less damaged. He picked one up by its head. Its ghoulish, blackened face stared at us, accusation blazing from its hollow eye sockets. As we stared in horror, the rest of the body plopped to the floor, leaving Levi holding only the head.

Hattie wailed. "All gone! All gone! My tots! All of them!"

Levi put his arms awkwardly around her quivering frame. Hattie howled into his shoulder. The noise in his ear must have been deafening, but he only winced a little bit. I could already see snot and tears on his pristine uniform.

A Jaffle Swarm of insects had flown in from somewhere and circled the office space. In a distant control room, fire chiefs would be assessing the situation.

"You." Hattie lifted her head and pointed at me. "You're the one who made all of this happen. This is the worst thing you've ever done."

"I didn't mean to... It shouldn't have..."

"I can never forgive you, Alice."

I was stunned. I knew that Hattie was ridiculously attached to the tots, but surely she knew, deep down that they were just things and that they could be replaced? As for it being my fault, that was a bit of a leap. Anyone could see that it was an accident.

"I didn't do anything," I said. "That shouldn't have happened. The bottle said the liquid was inflammable. *In*flammable." Belatedly I jipped the meaning of the word. "Oh."

The sprinklers had stopped. Levi carefully disentangled himself from Hattie, leaving trailers of tearful snottiness between them. "Alice, a word in—" He looked round. "In that meeting room. Now."

I had a feeling that Levi wasn't viewing this as an accident either.

I went into the conference room, with Levi hot on my heels. There were papers around on the table. I think I had glimpsed some executive from the upper floors in here, having a chat with our section heads. A plate of luxury biscuits in the middle of the table was slowly going soggy in an inch of sprinkler water.

"Well, look who's slap-bang in the middle of another major incident," said Levi, glaring at me.

"Well look who's staring at someone who's in need of a new uniform, instead of helping," I snapped.

"I've already sent a request for new clothing." He hesitated and then whipped off his jacket and put it around my shoulders. Levi jackletless, his strong arms exposed, him covering me protectively. In my dreams, this would have been super exciting and sexy. Right now, I felt like an idiot child.

"I need to write up a major incident report, yabetcha," he said. "Your testimony is obviously required, but I will be relying upon key witnesses to provide their version of events."

"There's been a fire," I said.

"I might need more detail than that."

I shook my head irritably. "There's been a fire. Levi, you are just a security guard."

"*Just* a security guard? Hoo-ee!"

"If there's an investigation to be made then that's up to the fire department or the insurers or..."

"Are you questioning my authority, miss?" he said.

"That is exactly what I'm doing!" I retorted.

"You'll be suspended from work for the duration of my investigation," he said. "I can't have ya fraternizing with potential witnesses."

"Suspended? You don't have the authority!"

He puffed up his chest and his moustache quivered. Even in the circumstances, I was slightly aroused, and then hated myself for it.

"You'll be aware that the terms and conditions of your employment are conditional on certain behaviours?" he said. "I have the power to suggest that you were *not only* in breach of your duty to safeguard your colleagues, but that you may also be guilty of gross misconduct." I started to speak but he cut across me. "Your line manager will be made aware of the situation. You will now watch the film, as is required for all employees when they need to be reminded of how seriously we take this—"

The door opened and a company fire marshal burst in. "Did you not hear the alarms?" he exclaimed.

"I'm in the middle of an interview," said Levi.

"Evacuate. Now!"

Levi gave the marshal a frosty stare. I looked aside, embarrassed and then saw the plipper. It was on the conference table, underneath a fat wad of meeting papers, in a protective blister-pack, new and unused. While Levi and the fire marshal loudly

contested who had jurisdiction over whom, I picked up the pile of papers, the plipper sandwiched in the middle.

"What are you doing?" said the fire marshal.

Panic swelled inside me but I kept it down. "These are important papers. I didn't want them to get any wetter."

"We do not stop to pick up personal belongings in an emergency, miss," said Levi severely.

The fire marshal gave Levi a withering look. "Just get out, the pair of you."

I walked out, wearing nothing but my underwear and Levi's jacket about my shoulders. Levi, put in his place, could do nothing but follow. As I reached the door to the stairs, he called out.

"Wait!"

I turned. He scrabbled under a turned over partition as early responder fire department drones searched for any remnants of the fire. He grabbed something from the soaked and sooty edges of the scene.

He came towards me with something held victoriously in his hand. It was a dusty, mouldy and now ash-covered ring.

"Is that Brandine's bagel?" I said.

"A persistent investigator always finds the truth," he said.

"She dropped it behind her desk?"

"The truth!" he insisted.

***

I went straight home and strode into the apartment complex. The Empties outside the building didn't stare at the mostly naked woman walking by. They stared at nothing at all.

"This is an exciting new look for you," said Helberg as I entered the lobby. He saw the look on my face. "You want to come in for a coffee? Something stronger? Maybe with a side order of clothes?"

I went into his office and fell onto the squashy couch in exhausted disbelief. I instantly decided I never wanted to get up again. Helberg draped something over me. I felt the touch of a thick, soft blanket.

"Thank you," I said.

"Anything for my favourite madwoman. What's this?"

He picked through the papers I had let drop to the floor. Many of the pages were melted together but I had successfully smuggled the plipper out of Jaffle Tech.

"Plipper," I said, morosely.

He turned the blister pack over in his hand.

"I stole it," I added.

"Why?"

"Thought you might like to take a look at it."

"Thought I'd like to take a look at your company's latest nightmare device?" He shrugged and nodded at the same time. He put the plipper on his desk and began tidying the dropped papers, skim-reading the first few pages as he did.

"This is soaked. You're naked. I suspect there's some story behind this," he said.

I groaned. "I'm a horrible human being."

"No," he tutted. "That's not true. Now that you've taken to walking around in your underwear, I think I've seen most of you, and I'd score you as a solid seven, possible even an eight."

"Horrible on the inside," I grumped.

"Still a solid seven or eight," he said. "Like the rest of us. What you are is human, very, very human."

"I set fire to the office, destroyed Hattie's Smiley Tots, stole company property and I'm going to get suspended from my job."

"Okay," said Helberg. "Maybe a six."

***

Chapter 21 – 9th June – 10 days until Operation Sunrise

I was indeed suspended from work, pending an investigation. Paulette tried to dress it up as recovery time from the shock at being caught in a fire in the workplace, but it was what it was. I was told to go away and not come back in until invited.

The following days were very uncomfortable at home. Hattie's hostility towards me was so intense that being in the same room as her was hard work. She would pointedly ignore me, then address comments to the blackened head Levi had picked out of the fire. I have no idea why she'd even taken it, but she used it to punish me.

"Oh look, Derek, I see Alice hasn't put the beans back in the cupboard."

"Derek, can you remember when you had a body? It was such a lovely little body, wasn't it?"

"I need to take really good care of you now, Derek, or Alice will find a way to take you away from me."

I spent an increasing amount of time down in Helberg's flat.

"So," he said loudly, out of nowhere, as though he had suddenly decided he'd had enough of my miserable mood. "Have you been to an upscale party before?"

"What?"

"The Jaffle Tech gala. A party. Where there's music and hors d'oeuvres and so on?"

"I, er..." I played for time while I jipped the meaning of *hors d'oeuvres*. I was relieved to discover that it was a fancy name for food of some sort. "Well, I've eaten food before, obviously. There are some things that I'm not keen on, like garlic, but I'll just avoid those."

"You'll avoid garlic? How will you know?"

"It's pretty obvious," I said. "A weird roundish thing, covered in paper. I could spot it a mile off."

"I think you and your fairy godmother might have some work to do," said Helberg. "Follow me."

It turned out that he had a kitchen just off his back office. There was a confused and cluttered warren of rooms in that part of the apartment complex, as though built for a purpose long since

forgotten. Not only did he have a kitchen but he knew what to do with it.

He showed me the freezer and explained the difference between that and the fridge. There seems to be a lot of science involved in cookery. The freezer is much colder and keeps certain things for a long time, but you can't just eat them, because they are frozen. This sounded like a lot of trouble to me, but Helberg tapped the side of his nose and got out some little beige discs. He put them on a metal tray which went into the oven.

"These always make an appearance at parties. Finger foods, you see: you eat them without a knife and fork." He eyed me, as if a sudden thought had come to him. "Do you know what I'm talking about?"

"I know what a knife and fork is," I said.

"But have you ever eaten with them?"

"No."

"Probably a lesson for another day. Let's concentrate on finger foods. Just because they're called that, don't be fooled. It's not necessarily straightforward. Into the oven with these and then we'll make a couple of fillings."

He went back to the freezer and scrabbled in the depths. Then he put a board onto the table and took a large knife from the drawer. The knife seemed outlandishly big. I couldn't imagine what he would need such a large blade for.

"Garlic!" he said, brandishing a cluster of the hateful stuff in his outstretched hand. "This is what we do."

He put the garlic on the board and leaned on it with his hand. It came apart into smaller pieces. He took one of the pieces and used the side of the knife blade to squash it. I wondered if he really knew what he was doing. Even I knew that you didn't use a knife like that. He lifted the blade and picked the papery stuff away. I peered and he was left with a creamy-coloured lump, and that distinctive, pungent smell filled the room. Then he used the knife (the right way up this time) to chop the garlic into tiny pieces.

He fetched something from the fridge. It was a startling red globe.

"What's that?"

"A tomato. You can try some in a few minutes."

I watched as he carefully chopped the tomato up and put it in a bowl with the garlic. He took another bowl and tipped in some little

pink things which looked like severed fingers. He squirted some gloopy liquid over the mixture, added powder from a jar, and stirred it with a spoon.

He looked up and beamed. "I think the vol au vents should be about ready."

When he opened the oven, there was a blast of heat accompanied by a delicious smell. He pulled the tray out. The weird little discs had transformed into fluffy brown things, much taller than when they started. I touched one. It broke apart with the smallest of prods.

"Oops, sorry," I said.

"You're starting to see what one of your challenges will be," said Helberg. "Learning to eat this sort of thing without covering yourself and your fellow guests with mess is essential."

"It's like a test?" I said.

"Everything at a high-class party is like a test."

He took one of them and put it on a plate. He flipped off the top. It resembled a tiny cup. "Huh, that's neat," I said.

He took a spoonful of the gloopy pink things and put them in the cup. He handed me the plate.

"Prawn vol au vent. Very tasty, but potentially messy to eat. Your mission is to eat some or all of this without spilling bits. Or—" he added, looking at me opening my mouth as wide as it would go, "—without looking like it's feeding time at the zoo. Try to be delicate and elegant."

"How do I do that?" I asked. It sounded impossible.

He shrugged. "I'm not really sure. Give it a shot."

I bit into the thing. I could feel it crumbling into pieces. I grunted in frustration. It was smooshed against my mouth, but I knew the moment I took it away, there would be a cascade of mess. I inched my hand underneath to catch as much as I could as I lowered the half-crushed thing. My method almost worked. I looked up to see whether Helberg was critiquing my performance, but he was spooning the tomato mixture into some of the pastry cases. I pushed the remains of the first vol au vent into my mouth. It wasn't all that elegant, but I thought I'd got away with it.

"Don't make sucking, slurping noises, it's considered impolite," said Helberg.

I made a muted "Uh huh" noise.

"So is talking with your mouth full," he said.

I finished and licked my lips. "That was nice. What did you say it was?"

"Prawns," said Helberg. "Delicious, but delicate. If you see something with prawns in it that looks dried out or a bit old, avoid it. You might end up with a stomach upset. Now try the tomato one."

I tackled this one more carefully, making sure I left myself with a second half that was more easily contained.

"A triumph!" he said, as I finished it off.

"That was garlic," I said. "I could taste it, but only a little bit. It was good."

He nodded. "Less is more with garlic. Now let's look at some of the other things you might come across at a buffet." He stared up, seeking inspiration. I guessed it was a while since he went to a party.

"You did fine with the vol au vents, so anything else in pastry is covered. Things on sticks: don't eat the stick."

"Why put it on a stick then?" I asked.

He shrugged. "So you can pick it up. You don't want a load of people rummaging through a dish of olives or something with their dirty fingers."

"Olives, I tried those. There's a pit in the middle."

"In the world of buffet food, you'll often find that the pit has been replaced with something else. Let me see if I've got some to show you."

Helberg went to a cupboard. It was filled with an amazing range of jars and tins. He pushed some aside, and then found what he was looking for. "Olives stuffed with anchovies."

If I understood him right, this was a small, bitter fruit with a fish in the middle. Of course it was.

He went to a drawer and found a tub filled with tiny wooden sticks. He took the lid off the jar and speared an olive with a stick. He handed it to me and speared another for himself.

I popped it into my mouth. It was much more enjoyable when I wasn't worrying about the pit. There was a strange new flavour, which must have been the anchovy. It was on the very edge of being disgusting. If I'd had a whole mouthful of that flavour it would have been quite unpleasant, but this tiny, acrid burst of flavour was intriguing and delicious.

"That was amazing!"

"Good. You're doing great," said Helberg. "Now, what else. You know there's going to be music, don't you?"

"Yes!" I said, excited. "Like the Smiley theme tune. *Smiley, Smiley, have you any fun? Yes I do, for everyone!*"

Helberg shook his head. "Do you know that the tune you just sang is an old nursery rhyme for children? It's called *Baa Baa Black Sheep*. They just changed the words."

"Oh."

In truth, as I'd sung the words, it sounded less thrilling to my ears than it used to, and only partly due to my singing. I felt as though I'd left Smiley behind since my unauthorised brain upgrade. Worse still, I had started to see the Smiley products as something bad, especially in the way they exploited people like Hattie. She more or less worked so she could afford more Smiley Tots.

"So the music you're talking about," I said, "is something different?"

"Oh yes. Let's start with something fairly bland. We don't want to overwhelm you." He turned to fiddle with a machine. "This one's called *The Girl from Ipanema*." He turned back to me. "What?"

Tears were running down my face. I had no idea what was happening. The music was so beautiful, so wonderfully clever, it overwhelmed me and I was left gasping, unable to form words.

He turned it off. "Too much?"

I nodded.

"Let's try something else." He thought for a moment. "We'll go with some Beatles." He pressed a button.

I shook my head with amazement. There was singing, and it was more than one person. How did they do that thing where their voices blended together? I sobbed again.

"You're crying."

"I can't help it," I said. "It's like ... heaven."

"*Love Love Me Do*, actually," he said. "One more. I'll play you a song from Abba."

This one had a female voice, no two female voices which blended together. Words about loss and sorrow made exquisite by being part of a melody, executed with such care. I started to howl with pain, tears running down my face. Helberg turned it off.

"Let's re-think this. We'll need to introduce you to a little bit more every time. It will cause problems at the party if you spend all of your time crying."

"Yes," I said, wiping my eyes. "Although I'm probably not going to the party at this rate. Work will fire me or have me imprisoned for arson."

"That fire wasn't your fault."

"It sort of was," I said.

"Don't be so hard on yourself," he said. "Tell you what. If you're not arrested for arson, pop round again tomorrow and we'll work on the music thing."

"And if I am arrested?"

"I'll visit you in prison. In the meantime..." He delved into a fridge. "More party food to practise with. You'll love this one."

He went off to the kitchen and then came back with a small bag. He opened the top so that I could see inside. "Pizza! Try it and let me know what you think."

I sniffed and detected a curious mixture of bread and other delightful aromas.

"Thank you."

***

Chapter 22 – 11th June – 8 days until Operation Sunrise

I was summoned to work for an interview with Paulette.

She was very brisk and business-like. I tried to make small talk about the mystery of Brandine's bagel finally being put to rest, but she was aloof and silent as we walked from reception to one of the smaller closed offices used for meetings. There was a suited woman in the room when we arrived.

"Alice, this is Estelle. She's a senior human resources partner and she will be taking part in this interview."

I had no idea what a senior human resources partner did, but I nodded to Estelle.

"Alice," said Estelle. "It's important that you understand that the outcome of this process will determine your future employment with Jaffle Tech."

"What process?" I asked.

"The process we are currently carrying out," said Estelle. I still had no idea what it was. "This review is to examine the events leading up to the fire which took place in the office, and the part you played in those events."

I nodded again.

"First things first, Alice. Do you want to make any statements to us concerning those events?" Estelle asked. "We will be watching the CCTV footage in a moment and drawing our conclusions from it. If you'd like to say anything to us before we do that, please go ahead."

I glanced at Paulette to see if I could get any clues as to how I was expected to react. Paulette was not looking my way. "Um, no, thank you," I said.

Estelle made some sort of gesture which started the CCTV footage rolling on the wall in front of us. I was slightly surprised to see it didn't start in the staff kitchenette with me holding the bottle of thinners. I felt sure there was a camera which covered that part of the office. What appeared instead was the image of a bot trundling across the office and spontaneously bursting into flames.

It was such a shock to see that I gasped out loud. Estelle paused the film.

"Alice, I understand if this is difficult. Are you all right to continue?"

I nodded and she re-started the film. As the bot moved more erratically, I appeared on the edge of the frame and I ran towards it. It looked very much as if I tried to put the flames out with my hands but burned myself. Then I tore off my tunic and used it to try and smother the flames. Moments later the film cut to another camera that showed me running over to Hattie and dragging her clear of the inferno her desk had become. Finally the sprinklers came on and we could all be seen evacuating the office. The view became slightly smudged by the droplets of water on the camera.

Estelle turned off the film. "Well it seems that you displayed considerable initiative Alice. I hope you'll accept our heartfelt thanks for averting what could have been a much more serious incident. I can see from the film you made several attempts to extinguish the flames with what you had to hand, and then you also helped others to evacuate the scene. We could all learn a lot from your quick thinking. Paulette, I hope you're very proud to have such a resourceful young woman on your team."

Paulette nodded, although I could see from her face that she wasn't quite ready to join the Alice fan club just yet.

"Now, it's likely you might need a few more days to rest and recuperate," said Estelle. "Smoke inhalation and stress can sometimes cause delayed symptoms. We'll make sure you have the self-care information sent to you so you can look out for them, just in case. Take your time deciding when you'd like to return to work. Otherwise, you're a credit to the Jaffle organisation and you will be formally thanked in the quarterly staff celebration."

I smiled at Estelle. I didn't trust myself to speak, as the film I'd just seen showed a very different version of events from the one I'd experienced. I wasn't sure how much Paulette had seen on the day, but she didn't look like a woman who believed in the story she'd just seen, either. I had no idea how the film had missed me causing the fire by damaging the bot and dousing everything in thinners. I had no idea how my misunderstanding of the word inflammable hadn't come to light. I was astounded there had been no mention of the Smiley Tots being here only because I had made it unsafe for Hattie to have them at home.

"There is one more thing we'd like you to do before you return to work," said Paulette.

"Yes?"

"You are to report to Krasnesky."

"Levi?"

She nodded curtly.

I went to find Levi out on the office floor. The mess from the fire had all been cleaned away and everything was back to normal. It felt strange to be here again.

Levi was with Hattie. She had a cubicle in a newer design, since the old one had been badly burned. Levi was showing her some pictures.

"I reckon these might tide you over until you can get some more of those famous Tots of yours," he said, holding them up.

The pictures were of Smiley Tots, standing in a row with outstretched arms. He pinned them to the sides of the cubicle. The effect was startling. It really looked as though there was a crowd of Smiley Tots standing along the edge of Hattie's cubicle, all wanting a hug.

"They look almost real! That's really good, thank you Levi," said Hattie, beaming up at him.

I was astounded at his kindness. I had to work hard to close my mouth as he turned towards me. His smile for Hattie disappeared when he saw me. He sort of packaged it officially away under that little moustache of his and swallowed it whole.

"It's time to watch The Film, Alice," he said.

I mentally rolled my eyes but, externally, managed to nod meekly.

"You can watch in the usual place," Levi said, leading the way. I saw Hattie give me a hard and hurtful look as we left.

In the training room, I sat alone in an amphitheatre that could have held a thousand people. Levi spent a few moments setting it up before he dimmed the lights and left the room.

It was an odd sensation seeing The Film again.

Old Alice, the Alice who was bound by the chains of Jaffle Standard, was terrified of the film. The black and white horror of calamities and accidents of yesteryear. It was a dark amorphous nightmare. The fact that everyone just called it The Film showed we had all viewed it without comprehension, only digesting the frightening emotional content without grasping any deeper meaning.

Now, as I watched the familiar content, new and not particularly subtle meanings were revealed. Hattie and I had always

viewed it as being a compilation of misdemeanours, perhaps captured by old security cameras. I realised this was a story. It was a story! How had I not grasped that before?

It was about a man who had to find a bride by the end of the day or he would fail to inherit some money from a dead relative. It seemed an unlikely set of circumstances, and the very thought of it made me laugh. It was probably wrong to laugh at someone else's misfortune but I couldn't help myself.

The man – the actor! (a quick jip revealed him to be one Buster Keaton) – tried to persuade passing women to marry him, but they were understandably sceptical of his clumsy advances. This made me laugh even more. I found myself wondering what the ideal solution would be. If he really needed the money, maybe he should advertise?

I cheered the screen when his friend did exactly that. He put an article in the newspaper which immediately brought many women chasing after him.

How had we missed all of this fun on previous viewings? Probably because we were too distracted by the violence.

The chasing part had always tipped us over into a complete frenzy of dismay. Now I laughed out loud. There were hundreds of women, all somehow dressed up for a wedding, running through the street chasing the poor man. It was the most hilarious sight. They wanted to marry him and share in his fortune, but they looked terrifying, charging down the road, throwing bricks. They chased him in old-fashioned cars and trains, and he evaded them by taking the most shocking risks, nearly dying in lots of awful ways, but that just made it funnier. As I watched I realised my face was aching with all of the laughing, and there was a pain in my side.

"Oh Hattie, I wish I could think of a way to explain this to you!" I howled.

The chase moved out of the city and into some open countryside. The part where he ran down a hillside, chased by tumbling rocks made me gasp at the danger, but it was so funny I still couldn't help laughing.

When it was done, Levi returned. "I see it's made you cry," he said.

There were indeed tears on my cheeks. I had laughed so hard that I had almost wet myself.

"I hope it's made you reflect upon how you should conduct yourself in the workplace," he said solemnly.

I wiped my eyes. "Levi, what's this film called?" I asked.

"It's called *Seven Chances*," he said. "But in reality we don't always get that many chances at safety. You know that."

"Is there some more of this film?" I asked. "After this part here?"

"I believe there is."

"Can I watch it please? I want to see what happens."

He looked at me with deep suspicion. "Why would you want to do that?"

"Please?" I asked. "I want to be sure I learn all that I can from it."

He grunted, put The Film back on and left me to watch the end.

I was thrilled to find after it seemed everything was hopeless, and the hero couldn't possibly succeed in marrying his true love, he managed to do just that. It made me sigh with a curious feeling of satisfaction.

I tried to compose myself before Levi came back into the room.

"Well, I imagine you feel differently now, dontcha?" he asked.

"Oh, I certainly do," I said, wiping my eyes.

***

Chapter 23

The Film gave me a lot to think about.

I had seen Buster Keaton's silent film as horror because I – Jaffle Standard Alice – could only see the immediate physical danger it showed. But it wasn't a horror film. It was funny and warming and ultimately uplifting and I wondered why.

That evening, as dusk settled over the city, I walked the streets around the Shangri-La Towers apartment complex pondering this. I sat with the Empties by the roadside.

"Why did I laugh at it?" I asked.

Unsurprisingly, the Empty next to me didn't respond.

"You'd have laughed too," I told her. "If you were allowed to understand it."

I flicked away a fly that was crawling on her lapel.

"I think," I said reflectively, "as soon as I realised the man wasn't in any real danger – it just wasn't that kind of story – then the things which should have been terrible became funny. It's like getting a really big surprise and then realising it's nothing bad. Like a dog chasing its own tail. And ... in the end, a story in which everything seemed hopeless became suddenly filled with hope."

The Empty stared blankly ahead.

"I thought you'd agree with me." I stood up. "There's always hope, isn't there?" I said and went inside.

Hattie was sat on the couch when I got to our apartment. She didn't meet my eye. A partially burned Smiley Tot was clutched in her hands.

"Oh Derek, I see Alice is home," she said to the blackened ruin of the Tot's face. "I wonder what chaos she's been causing today."

I stood right in front of her and wagged my finger. "You are my friend," I told her sternly. "You are my best friend in the whole wide world."

"Well, Derek, Alice has a funny way of showing people what—"

"*And* I burned all your Smiley Tots and I feel really bad," I went on.

Hattie didn't say anything, although she did glance at Derek as though they were sharing a look.

"Recently I have been erratic and unpredictable. I've created mess and confusion and I probably seem like a completely different person. And I am! I have changed a lot in the past few days."

"You have," she said, addressing me directly for what felt like the first time in ages.

"But that's not an excuse to set fire to your Smiley Tots."

"It isn't."

"But..." I took a deep breath, trying to formulate a way of saying what I had to say next without upsetting her, and realising there wasn't one. "But I don't think Smiley Tots make you happy anyway."

She gasped, actually gasped, her mouth a perfect O. "Take that back!"

"No. I don't think you want Smiley Tots."

"I do!"

"I think you want a baby."

Hattie frowned in deep confusion. "A baby...? As in...?"

"Children," I said.

"You mean, little people?" She gestured to indicate smallness. Her hands moved up and down, as she was clearly unsure exactly how small children were

"Yes," I said.

Hattie was giving me another one of those looks which suggested I had well and truly gone off the rails. "You don't see them so much around here."

"No," I said. "But I saw some. In the art gallery. Pictures of babies, I mean. There's this one called Jesus who's in a lot of them. He has a shiny light on his head, although I don't know what it's for."

"But where are the real children?" asked Hattie.

"Um – I don't know," I said, on the cusp of feeling stupid for pointing out Hattie's need for children in her life without knowing where they had all gone. I gave myself a mental slap. At least Hattie was intrigued. "I don't know where they are," I said, "but we should find them, shouldn't we?"

"How?"

"We ask Helberg."

***

Hattie and I sat side by side on Helberg's squashy sofa, crowded in on all side by his junk and partially tinkered bot bits. He sat in a swivel

chair and gave us both a smile. It was a slightly sad smile. I jipped my literacy booster and came up with the word *wistful*. It was a wistful smile.

"How much do you remember about your own childhoods?" he asked.

I'd asked myself the same question, and the answer was frustrating. "Not all that much. I remember studying for exams, and I remember Hattie and I have been together for a very long time, but I feel as though there's a lot more that I can't remember."

"Same here," said Hattie.

He nodded. "You probably spent a lot of time in the OneStop Daycare facility or the Nurture Hub or one of the other mega-crèches."

"Right," I said. "Did I? Did we?"

He nodded.

An idea was forming. "Does that mean it's possible to go there and actually see children?"

"I'm not sure it's a place which welcomes visitors," said Helberg. "Children are delicate things."

"Like Smiley Tots," said Hattie.

"Especially babies." He inhaled sharply and leaned back in his chair, thinking. "But if you told them you were experienced nursery nurses looking for employment..."

"Would they let us look round?" I said. "Meet actual babies?"

"Possibly."

"Helberg," said Hattie, folding her hands primly onto her lap.

"Patrick, please."

"Patrick, I know you're the building manager and the boss of the cleaning bots, but I don't like you encouraging Alice like this. She's clearly had a breakdown or something, and I can't help thinking you're making her worse."

"I'm fine, Hattie," I said. "And this is a great idea."

"Is it?"

"And I want to do it for *you*, because I think you'll love it. Have you ever held a baby?"

"No. Of course not."

"Have you ever even *seen* a baby?"

"What's got into you?" she asked. "I don't know. Maybe I've seen them in the distance or something. I can't remember."

I grinned at her. "Come on! We've got a rest day tomorrow. Let's go and see the children."

She gave me a dubious look. I could see she really wanted to, but this behaviour extended beyond the boundaries of what she considered normal.

"Come on," I said. "Tomorrow morning. We'll go and have a quick look at a baby."

Hattie sighed. "Do you promise that you'll be normal for the rest of the day if I agree to this? We'll sit and eat our beans and watch Smiley like we used to?"

"Yes, of course," I said.

***

Chapter 24 – 12th June – 7 days until Operation Sunrise.

The OneStop Daycare facility was almost as big as Jaffle headquarters, but in a quiet suburb, up in the hills and far from the busy bay area. Hattie, Helberg and I went into the reception area.

"Have fun," he said before calling to the receptionist. "Prospective employees. Come to look around."

"Did you get in touch beforehand?" asked the receptionist.

"Yes," I said.

"No," said Hattie at the same time.

The receptionist looked at us both and sighed slightly. She made a call to someone. "I have some visitors who are thinking of applying for work. Could you please talk to them?"

Moments later, a neat-looking woman arrived. She wore a colourful tunic and had a warm smile. "Hello, I'm Shirley and I'd be happy to answer any questions you might have about working here." She led us through a double door. "Can I ask where you've been working up until now?"

"Private work," I offered, "I'm not permitted to discuss details, of course."

"I see," said Shirley. "So, what's your particular interest here?"

"Babies," I said. "We'd like to see your, er, baby department."

"Certainly," said Shirley. We went through a maze of corridors and up some stairs. We emerged into a large room. "Soft play area. Shoes off for this part."

We all removed our shoes and walked across a squishy vinyl surface which was covered in colourful blocks and toys. There was a circle of tiny children up ahead. They were *impossibly* tiny. Did all people start off this small? Some were big enough to sit up by themselves, while others reclined in special seats which bounced lightly.

Hattie gasped. I looked and saw her face crumple into the same adoring expression she had for her Smiley Tots.

A woman was reading the babies a story about a dog. Most of them had their eyes on her, a couple wriggled or crawled in a distracted way, and there was one who wailed softly.

"Don't let us disturb you, I have some visitors who want to look around," Shirley said to her.

The woman looked up and smiled. "Well if anyone wants to get hands-on, then Jacob needs a change, I think." She indicated the wailing baby.

"I'll do it," said Hattie eagerly.

Shirley beamed and waved Hattie forward.

"Hello Jacob," said Hattie, picking him up. "Let's sort you out, shall we?"

I followed Hattie as she carried Jacob over to an area that was clearly reserved for clean-up. She laid him down on a mat and tickled his toes. He chuckled in delight and Hattie made cooing noises.

Shirley handed something to Hattie. "Clean nappy for you. Wipes are there too."

Hattie undressed Jacob. I peered over to watch. "Oh my god, that is disgusting!" I hissed.

Jacob had squirted poo into every imaginable crevice and seemed very proud of the appalling mess that he'd made. The smell was overwhelming. I wondered what on earth they could be feeding these infants to make such an appalling stench. Hattie was oblivious to the horror and bent over, carefully cleaning him up, still grinning. He had a little tiny penis, and as I watched, an arc of urine splashed into Hattie's face.

"Oh Jacob!" she said. "What a little tinker you are!"

She continued to clean and re-dress him. She wiped the urine off her face as if it was nothing. Then she picked him up and put him to her shoulder. "Isn't he just the sweetest thing you ever saw in your life?" she asked.

I watched and pointed in horror as Jacob vomited down Hattie's back. "Your back!"

Hattie smiled and carefully put Jacob down to listen to the story before she wiped the vomit off herself. "He can't help it, he's only tiny."

While I hadn't been at all ready for the mess a baby could inflict, Hattie was in her element. "Do you want to go back now?" I checked.

"Ooh, no, let's stay for a while," she said enthusiastically. Hattie inserted herself into the circle of babies and cuddled them as they all listened to the story.

Chapter 25 – 13th June – 6 days until Operation Sunrise

At work the next day, I wasn't sure I'd done the right thing, taking Hattie to the OneStop Daycare centre.

Yes, I had made her very happy for a few hours.

Yes, I had definitely put the incinerated Smiley Tots out of her mind.

Yes, I had certainly mended some bridges in our relationship and that made me feel good.

But at what cost?

Within fifteen minutes of arriving at work, Hattie had jipped images of babies – real human babies, not stylised Smiley Tots – arranged around her cubicle. Every time I walked past her cubicle I saw her looking at them with a curious expression. *Wistful*. That was the word: wistful.

"Well, don't them young 'uns look a fine and pretty sight," Levi said to her. "Although having so many paper images in your workstation could be considered a fire hazard."

"I think I would like a real one," she said.

"A real what?"

"Baby."

He sucked in through his teeth. "That would be a handful and no mistake. But certainly less flammable. Oh, yabetcha."

It was odd. The man was quite an insufferable prig and yet, I realised, he had a streak of kindness running through him which he did his darnedest to hide. Always a kind word for Hattie, the other workers too, like he really believed he was a kindly shepherd overlooking his flock.

Paulette approached me. "Alice, I've been asked to file a report."

"Oh. What kind of a report?" I asked.

"I'm not sure I can share that detail," she said. "Let's just say that it's a thorough and comprehensive report on some of the things that have happened in the department in recent days."

"The department?" I asked. "So not me, personally?"

"My office, would you?" She marched away, knowing I had to follow.

Paulette closed the office door behind us, took her seat and studied me.

"How can I help?" I asked eventually. If I could have asked a question more like *How can I end this as quickly as possible?* I would have gone for it, but I had to appear co-operative.

Clearly I had been uncovered in some way. Of all the things I had done in recent days, any number could be the reason for this. Getting my brain infected with the whale virus. Faking brain scans. Lying to staff. Starting fires. Sneaking to the top floor executive offices.

"The incident I wanted to flesh out a little for the report," said Paulette, "was the one where you took my bacon sandwich."

I was stunned. Of all the things I thought she might be about to say, that definitely wouldn't have made the top ten. I'd almost completely forgotten about it. Her words stimulated the memory of experiencing that overpowering smell for the first time. I licked my lips just thinking about it.

"Right. Bacon sandwich, yes," I said.

"My recollection is that you said I was to give you my bacon sandwich because Rufus Jaffle had said so, while you were doing a special job for him." She paused. "Now that I come to write it down, I have questions. For example, how did Rufus Jaffle even know I had a bacon sandwich?"

I saw an immediate problem. I really needed to distance myself from any mention of Rufus Jaffle. I couldn't have Paulette writing this down, or someone like Henderson would surely join the dots and realise the person who'd been inside Jaffle's head was the same one who was at the centre of various minor atrocities. He'd reset my brain before you could say *plipper*.

"I do remember that," I said to Paulette. "I had such a vivid dream. Weird, huh?"

"What? You dreamt that Rufus Jaffle told you to take my bacon sandwich?"

"Yes," I said. I hoped the lie would satisfy Paulette without any further embellishment, but she looked as if she had a hundred more questions. I launched a pre-emptive monologue.

"Every once in a while I have a dream that's so vivid it seems real. As you know, we'd had the presentation about the company's achievements. I always like to hear about the things we're helping to

do around the world. I think that perhaps Mr Jaffle was in my mind, I guess that's why he ended up in my dream."

"So, you haven't met him in real life?"

"In my dream he was a short, dark haired man. Very serious," I said. "Do you think he's like that in real life?"

"I genuinely have no idea," said Paulette. "So, can I be crystal clear on this? You were acting purely upon a dream when you demanded to have my bacon sandwich?"

"Yes. Sorry. I realise now that I shouldn't have done that."

"Did you enjoy the bacon sandwich, Alice?"

Did she think I was stupid enough to fall into a trap like that? "No," I said – wistfully. "Not really. I like beans better. They're more practical."

She made a noise and gave me an odd look: a sort of internalised scowl.

"Is that ... it?" I asked.

She continued to look at me. "You can see why I was curious."

"Oh, absolutely," I said. "Me and my dreams, eh?" I gave her a jolly smile, a sort of *Oh, that Alice, isn't she a harmless ditz* sort of smile.

"I just needed to know," said Paulette, "before I fill out these reference requests."

"Sure," I said, then: "What? Reference requests?"

Paulette studied something on her desk.

"The OneStop Daycare Centre," she said. "Yourself and a colleague, and a—" she gave a little frown "—and an unknown third person who didn't register on entry, went for a pre-application visit." Paulette smiled politely at me. "I didn't know you had any experience in childcare."

"Er, no," I said.

"Or interest."

"It's a recent thing. It's more Hattie's thing really. She's got a real, er, passion."

Paulette put her hands together on the table. "Are you unhappy here?"

"Me? Or both of us?"

"Either."

I wasn't sure how to respond. The truth – that Hattie was secretly baby-mad and had been pushed in that direction by my own

personal awakening – wasn't going to make things better. "We're really happy here," I said.

"Because Jaffle Tech prides itself on being the employer that people want to work for."

"Especially, Hattie. She loves her job. She really doesn't want to leave."

"I thought you said she was the one with the passion."

"She is, but she's loyal. She was just ... just looking. There's no harm in looking. Have you ... have you invited her in for a *little chat*?"

Paulette shook her head. "No. She's not the one with anomalous behaviours on her file."

"Anomalous. Good word. What behaviours?"

Paulette opened her hands as though the behaviours were concealed in them. "The bacon sandwich."

"Right, that," I said.

"The requests for new tunics."

"Yes," I nodded. "Some accidents there."

"Including an engineer's tunic, I noticed."

I pursed my lips. That was harder to explain. "I do like exploring other jobs."

"And dressing up for roles you are not qualified to undertake."

"I wouldn't say that."

"Wouldn't you?"

I met her gaze. I didn't know what she was thinking, but I wasn't thinking anything beyond blind panic. "I don't know what I'm doing half the time," I heard myself say.

"You have mental absences?" said Paulette.

"What?"

"Fugue states. Black outs. That sounds serious."

"No, no, no," I said hurriedly. "I mean that I'm a ... whimsical character. Spontaneous. You should see what thoughts go through my head sometime."

"We can," said Paulette. "I note here that you've been called to have a brain scan on several occasions in the past few weeks. Problems?"

"Not at all. Just one brain scan, but I had to reschedule several times. I'm very busy."

"You then submitted a privately commissioned scan."

"I was doing a favour for a friend."

"You have friends?"

That halted me dead. "Yes, I have friends."

"The same friend whose Jaffle Port didn't register at the OneStop Daycare?"

"Lots of friends."

Paulette breathed in slowly, making a show of thinking. "Your Jaffle rating is a combined scoring system which shows your reliability and efficiency in a wide range of areas," she said. "A heuristic diagnostic tool to help people understand what kind of – well, neighbour or employee or teammate or whatever – you might be. These recent behaviours of yours are likely to have an adverse effect on your rating."

"Did I do something wrong?"

"These behaviours aren't wrong per se, Alice. But they are odd. If I'm to provide the requested reference—"

"You don't have to do that, honestly."

"But it has been requested. I think I ought to look into these matters a little more deeply. If it's all right with you, I'm going to interrogate the location tracker log in your port, see where you've been, what you've been up—"

"Can I refuse?"

"Of course you can," she said, smiling gently. "But that would be odd in itself. Possibly grounds for us to subpoena said records. As a caring employer, we actively weed out those who are engaged in illegal and anti-social behaviours. Refusing to let your employer access those records would seem suspicious."

"Of course," I said for lack of anything else to say.

"Agreed," said Paulette. And, with that, I realised I had given them a front row seat to all my inexplicable activities since Rufus Jaffle had accidentally awoken me to my full potential.

"Give me a little time and I will call you back in for a clarification interview if necessary," said Paulette.

I numbly left her office. *Clarification interview.* That might as well be code for *Pre-firing and pre-arrest interview.*

What other stones would they turn over? If she combined location information with Jaffle's own CCTV, they'd see where I'd been, what I'd stolen. I could make no defence. And if Paulette was going to make a full and comprehensive report into Jaffle Tech weirdness involving me, she would probably focus on my unofficial brain scan, which would definitely not withstand careful scrutiny. I

wondered if I could get that scan back somehow. I had no idea how to do that, but then another idea occurred to me.

***

Chapter 26

"I want to ask you something," I said to Helberg when I got home.

"Good. I want to show you something," he replied. He took my hand and drew me into his office.

"You faked my brain scan," I said.

"I did. Chuckie Egg, music please."

The bot began to play some music I had not heard before. I had spent a lot of time at Helberg's place, listening to music. I could manage it now without crying, although it was a close-run thing. "I don't want a dancing lesson now," I said.

"But you do want to dance at the gala," he said. "Today is salsa."

"Salsa?"

I quickly jipped it. I'd already tried out some very rudimentary dance moves. I'd seen lots of amazing moves when I searched the archive clips, but Helberg told me most people didn't dance like that at parties. He had previously recommended something which looked more like walking backwards and forwards while turning bacon on an invisible barbecue. Salsa looked a bit more involved.

"Is this one of those ones where the dancing is a desired expression of a vertical ... whatever you said. Basically, upright sex."

He laughed. "You make it sound like people are *only* interested in sex."

"You are."

"Maybe I'm just a hopeless romantic. The phrase you were reaching for, Alice, is *the vertical expression of a horizontal desire.*"

"That."

"Possibly."

"Look," I said, having had my initial conversational thread hijacked, "I need to ask you how easy it would be to fake lots and lots of brain scans."

"What?" he said. "Uh-huh. Dancing first. Stupid questions later." He drew me closer in preparation.

"As long as we can't get pregnant doing the upright sex dance," I said.

"Who's getting pregnant?" asked Hattie from the doorway.

"No one," I said.

"Alice is just asking stupid questions," muttered Helberg.

"There are no stupid questions, only stupid answers," said Hattie. "I read that somewhere."

"Well, whoever said that was also stupid," said Helberg.

Hattie hovered in the doorway. Helberg looked pointedly at her. I stepped back from him. It felt kind of silly to be that close to him if we weren't actually going to dance yet.

"I jipped a question today and only got a stupid answer," said Hattie. "You seem to know stuff, Helberg."

"Some stuff," he conceded.

"So how do babies come out?"

He stared at her for a long moment and then did some very awkward but nonetheless quite explanatory gestures.

"No. No. No." Hattie was adamant. "There's no possible way a baby can come out of there. I saw them. They're small, but they're not *that* small. No way. It's just not big enough. I don't want to go into details, but sometimes it's a squeeze to get the, you know, other thing out of there. A whole baby? I don't think so."

"But you must be able to get an answer by jip— *Whoa!*" I had just jipped it. It looked like the worst form of torture. "Look at her—! That can't be right! Was she following the instructions properly?"

Helberg coughed. "I take it we're all up to speed now? Or at least we accept that babies develop inside a woman's body and then come out through the vagina."

Hattie blew out her cheeks and shook her head, so confused she needed to sit down. "So, hang on. If that's how babies get *out*, how do they get in there? And why have I never seen it happening?"

"Lots of questions wrapped up in there," said Helberg slowly, with a quick glance at me.

This was going to be tricky. Because Hattie was still on Jaffle Standard, she'd never had any sexual urges.

"Couldn't we, er, you know...?" I said to Helberg, discreetly tilting my head towards his Jaffle port-hacking gizmo.

He raised his eyebrows. "What are you suggesting, Alice?"

"Make Hattie like me. You could access her brain and fix her so that she has all of the same—"

"What?" Hattie looked fearful. "Nobody's touching my brain! Is that how the baby gets in? Our brains are a long way from our vaginas, it doesn't seem very practical."

"Nobody's touching your brain, Hattie," said Helberg. "See, I think we can explain the mechanics of this."

"I would appreciate that," she said.

"In short, babies come from sex. Adults do this thing called sexual intercourse and that can make a woman pregnant. After being pregnant for nine months a baby comes out. Try jipping some of those terms."

"Oh my word," said Hattie, clearly doing exactly that. She looked flustered. "Are you two having me on, because I've definitely never seen anybody doing *that*."

"Well they do," said Helberg.

I looked at him with interest. "And how many times have you done it?"

He looked embarrassed. "That's not a question most people normally ask if they were being polite," he said. "Um, a few times."

"Have you done this, Alice?" asked Hattie. She pointed at Helberg and me, a different question on the tip of her tongue.

"No!" I said, shocked. I took a deep breath and lowered my voice a little. "I haven't done it at all. Not yet."

"Not *yet*?"

"No. I've only just started dancing. You can't get pregnant dancing."

"Ah! But you are planning to?"

"What?"

"Does that mean you want to have a baby?"

"I'm not sure," I said, remembering the mess and the smell of that baby's nappy. "It seems like a lot to—"

"Well I do!" she declared. "I want a baby! I just need someone to have sex with me, yes? Can I make an appointment or something?"

I wasn't sure that I had an answer to that.

"Hattie, most people think carefully about who they want to make a baby with," said Helberg. "They choose someone who they think would, hm, help to make a nice baby."

Hattie looked Helberg up and down. "Well what about you? You look all right to me. Can we make an appointment? Maybe we could do it now?"

He looked very uncomfortable. "There's so much to think about, Hattie. Babies can cost a lot of money, and there's no doubt that it's a big commitment."

She shrugged. "How much money? I'm sure it can't be that bad. How much do you normally charge?"

Helberg gave me a look. It was one which suggested I had created a monster.

"Hattie," I said. "Do you remember me trying to talk to you about there being more to life than work and beans and so on? Well this is *one of the things* I was talking about. There's so much more to the world than we've known for much of our lives. We should take time to absorb it properly before we make big decisions, don't you think?"

Hattie pouted but gave a small nod. "I suppose." Her face dropped. "Wait. Is this about the red beans again? There's only so much change I can take without getting all consternated."

"How about we hack your Jaffle port and give you the—"

"You're talking about messing with my brain again!" Hattie's voice rose in panic. "If that isn't both consternating and discombobulating then I don't know what is!"

Helberg made shushing noises. "Nobody's going to mess with your brain, Hattie. I wouldn't consider it for a second." He gave me a stern look. "Seriously Alice, I'm not sure my little rig is up to the task. Reading some log files is one thing, but altering a whole bunch of Jaffle settings is another thing entirely when you're not familiar with them. It's much too risky to consider."

I wanted to blurt out that the risk of sitting around while Jaffle messed up everyone's brains in the whole world was considerably worse, but I needed to keep that to myself.

Hattie was joining the dots. "What do you mean, *reading some log files*?" She looked from Helberg to me and back again. "Did you fake your brain scan, Alice? Oh my goodness, you did! You're going to be in so much trouble! How come you're not already in tons of trouble?"

I leaned back in my chair. She had a fair point, and I had absolutely no answer.

I sat Hattie down and tried to outline what I'd done, without divulging any of the really bad parts. "First thing to understand is this, I was asked to provide some tech support, off the record."

Hattie's eyes narrowed. "Who was it for?"

"I can't tell you that. Really, it's best that you don't know."

She looked sceptical.

I pressed on. "Because this had to be offline, the only way I could do the requested clean-up was to use my own spare capacity as temporary storage." I pointed at my head, to underline what I was

talking about. "It should have worked fine. The space was available and I'm sure I prepared everything correctly. What I think messed it up a little bit was some unauthorised software that this person had introduced."

"What, like a brain virus?" Hattie was horrified. "I thought they were a myth?"

"Apparently not," I said. "It's not as bad as it sounds. I just get a whale that interrupts me every once in a while."

"A whale? Big fish kind of thing?"

"Well, actually they're mammals. Wonderful creatures as it turns out, if a little bit rude when it comes to interrupting."

"Oh Alice! No wonder you've gone mad. You really need to get that sorted out."

"I'm going to a charity gala in two days to speak to Rufus Jaffle about it and get some answers."

Hattie didn't think that was enough. "No, we'll go to work and get someone to take a proper look at you. Put you all back to normal."

"No! I need to tell you the main point of all this!" I was keen Hattie didn't miss the important part of the story. "I ended up, after the procedure had run, having a few rogue memories, but the procedure activated all of the brain functionality people like us don't normally have. It's changed my life, Hattie. It's really opened my eyes."

Surely she would understand now. I looked at her, wondering how I could convey how important this was.

"That's just the illness talking," said Hattie. "I know it is. I can see the changes in you and they're not good."

"You're not listening," I said urgently. "We've been denied some of our basic human experiences. We always thought we were happy, but we were missing out on so much."

"Stop it, Alice, please." There were tears in her eyes. "I don't need a baby, not a real one. It was stupid idea and my vagina isn't big enough and I don't have enough money to pay for a baby. I am happy just the way I am."

"You're not."

"I *am*!" she snapped, the tears now rolling down her cheeks. "I am! I am! I am!" She pushed herself out of his squashy sofa and hurried out.

I stared at the open door. "I just make things worse all the time," I said.

"Brain hack or not, you've opened her eyes," said Helberg. "It's like the John Stuart Mill thing."

"The man with the unhappy pig?"

"Happy pig," he corrected. "Hattie might be upset now but it's probably because she can see what she's missing out on. It's that dissonance, the distance between what is and what should be that's causing her distress."

"Doesn't make me feel better about it," I said.

Helberg nodded but not necessarily in agreement. "A question you never asked..."

"What?"

"All those babies at the OneStop Daycare centre. Biologically, genetically, they came from other human beings. Whether they were naturally born or grown in artificial amniotic sacs, they are human children."

"I guess."

"Go back in time only a few decades and most people would have at least once child, created the *traditional* way. There would be children living in apartment blocks like this. There would be married couples."

"I saw a film about a man trying to get married. It was very, very funny."

"But you don't see married people anymore," said Helberg. "Not round here. No marriages among the Jaffle Standards. No sex. No children. Why do think that is?"

"I guess ... if people are on Jaffle Standard and they don't think about sex much, then they're not going to have babies the *traditional* way. So someone has to make sure there are babies, or we'll die out. The authorities make sure we don't run out of people."

Helberg grunted, a laugh that didn't quite make it out of his throat. "You've got it upside down, Alice. History can teach us a lot, and one of the things it teaches us is that one way the people in power exert control over everyone is deciding who can have sex and who can't, who you're allowed to have sex with if you do, and who is and isn't allowed to have children of their own."

"No. Really?"

He gave me a meaningful look, the kind of expression I would have found really annoying weeks ago but I now recognised as a look

of patience; of hope that I would understand. "If they want to control us—"

"Who's *they*?" I said.

"The Man."

"Which man?"

"*The* Man. Capital *M*. Jaffle Tech. The powerful people."

"Like Claire?"

"The woman whose dress you stole? Sure. The powerful people. The governments which support them and are supported by them. They've got the Jaffle Standards packaged up neatly in their little boxes. No family. No love. No sex. No loyalty to anything but Mr Smiley and the status quo."

I thought about this for a long time. "Is that true?" I said. "Or is it just some mad conspiracy you've cooked up to justify the way you live your life?"

Helberg burst out laughing. "See! See! You're questioning. You're questioning authority and you're questioning me. God, I love you, Alice Tennerman." The moment the words were out of his mouth, he faltered. "I mean ... I mean I love the person you've become. That is ... I love what you've done with ... I mean..."

"Yeah, yeah," I said, waving his embarrassment away. There was still a heaviness in my chest, the inescapable feeling that I'd hurt Hattie once more, made her life worse not better. "You got any more of that Bony Hilda's Iguana Manilla lying around?"

"The what?"

"The sherry drink."

"The Bodegas Hidalgo La Gitana Manzanilla?" he smiled and stood.

"That is exactly what I said and you know it."

The bottle was on a shelf between two distinct but equally mystifying piles of electronic components. He took it down, along with two tiny glasses.

"Fill 'em up," I said.

"This is strong stuff, remember," said Helberg.

I shrugged and wondered how well sherry would suppress the lump of worry inside me.

"Maybe I want to be a happy pig again." I patted the seat next to me for him to sit down. "Just for one evening."

***

Chapter 27 – 14ᵗʰ June – 5 days until Operation Sunrise

I dreamt that someone shouted from the doorway of the house.

"Did he just call my name?" I/Rufus asked. I realised I was both dreaming and remembering a slice of Rufus's memory from the party by the sea.

"It sure sounded like it," said TayTay, next to Rufus/me.

"Oh no, he's calling someone else. I never heard the name Roofight before," said Rufus.

"I think it's an actual fight," said MiMi, drifting towards the house. "With roos."

"Huh?" Rufus was confused.

"Haven't you heard?" TayTay asked, linking her arm in his and steering him onward. "They get a pair of kangaroos and have them fight each other. What's even better, they put Jaffle ports in them so someone can control what they do."

"No way!" said Rufus, picking up the pace. "This I have to see."

They hurried into the house and down some stairs into a huge basement kitted out with gym equipment and a boxing ring. There were, indeed, two kangaroos in the ring.

At the moment they were jigging lightly in opposite corners of the ring while people filed in. A good many of them recognised Rufus and cleared the way for us to ringside seats. A kangaroo was right in front of them/us. The only person closer was a man in black who was concentrating on a device in front of him. Presumably one which controlled the kangaroo's Jaffle port. MiMi reached out a hand to touch the kangaroo's fur.

The kangaroo in the opposite corner gave a low growl and the two girls pressed up against Rufus. He could feel the heat of their quivering bodies. It gave him a rush of heady testosterone and cocaine-fuelled confidence.

"Of course, the way to defeat a large predator is to understand and engage with their natural energy or prana," he said to them both. I found myself questioning whether a kangaroo was a predator, but I had no say in it.

"Have you ever heard of Maglev?"

They shook their heads.

"Few have," he said, lifting his hands and making a slow chopping movement as he explained the ins and outs of his chosen martial art.

"It's just a big mouse, isn't it?" said TayTay, looking at the kangaroo.

"A big mouse?" said Rufus, immediately cracking up with laughter. "It's a killer, babe, a stone cold killer."

A bell rang and the kangaroos bounded forward. They started to shove each other with their relatively short arms. I found myself wondering if they were arms or forelegs.

"Go on! Whack him!" yelled Rufus, aligning himself with the kangaroo from his corner.

The kangaroos locked into an embrace and bounced on their powerful hind legs, trying to gain an advantage. They looked as though they were enjoying a dance. Not a salsa, though.

"Use your legs!" Rufus hollered.

The kangaroos did indeed start to kick each other. The kangaroo from our/their corner hung on with his arms and brought both powerful hind legs through with a vicious kick. The other kangaroo seemed unperturbed as they continued in their graceless dance.

"Leg sweep! Take him down with a leg sweep!" Rufus called.

The kangaroos bounced and grappled, but there was no sense either of them was being harmed in any way. I realised the counterweight of their enormous tails stabilised them so they could kick with both legs and still remain upright.

Rufus seemed to be getting more and more restless. In his mind I saw the growing urge for the violence to be stepped up. Even so I was horrified when he climbed up and stepped into the ring with me as his dream-passenger.

He held up his arms and turned to the crowd. An almighty cheer went up as Rufus threw himself into the fight. One of the kangaroos had returned to its corner, so he threw a punch at the one remaining. "Fists of fury! Betcha never saw anything like this back home in, ah, wherever you come from, did ya?"

He screamed in pure bloodlust and rained his fists down upon the kangaroo.

The animal leaned its head right back. Rufus dodged around its huge body to bop it on the nose. Unaccountably, this insane strategy worked. He landed a hard blow on the place where a kangaroo's

temple might be, knocking it out cold. He stood over the unconscious kangaroo and punched the air, victorious.

"Now *that* is what a Maglev master looks like! Deadly weapons right here!"

I saw out of Rufus's peripheral vision that TayTay had elbowed the operator aside and had grabbed the controls for the remaining kangaroo's Jaffle port.

"Come on then motherfucker!" she yelled. "Show us those deadly weapons!"

I/Rufus didn't have time to react. The kangaroo grabbed us and rocked back to kick me....

***

I woke with a dry mouth and a pounding headache worse than the last time I'd drunk sherry. I called for pain filters but they made hardly any difference.

"So, this is a hangover," I mumbled. I thought sherry was my friend, but Hilda's Bony Iguana or whatever it was had turned on me in the night.

I sat up (I was in my own bed, which was a mild surprise) and I considered my general status.

"Not going to throw up," I told myself and my nauseated belly. Two minutes later, in the bathroom, my rebellious insides made a liar of me. I cleaned myself and the bathroom as best I could and slowly – oh, so slowly – got ready for work.

There, armed with a few pointers from Helberg, I set about covering up my dodgy brain scan. I couldn't hack in and retrieve the scan I'd already submitted but I could mask it with some suspicious-looking scans for other people. I wondered how many fake brain scans I could fabricate during the course of an extended toilet break. Enough to confuse the person who'd be investigating my own fake brain scan? Maybe.

I started with Paulette, just because she was on my mind: I gave her an activity report that included lots of glitchy-looking spikes. I moved on and made a fake brain scan for Damien in supplies: him I gave several erroneous periods of two hundred percent capacity usage. I fabricated a few more, uncharitably gifting my colleagues with all sorts of problems from old-fashioned Alzheimers to suspected interference from sunspot activity.

I dropped them anonymously into the medical centre's document store and slipped back to my desk.

Levi was hovering. A thought had struck me and I couldn't shake it.

"Levi?"

"Yes, miss?"

"Levi, you know the cameras?"

He looked up and pointed at various corners. "Always watching. Keeping us safe."

"The ones that recorded my little accident. The bot on fire."

"Very important tool for the security professional. And I'm glad that incident is still on ya mind. It's only from our mistakes we learn, isn't that so?"

"Yes, yes," I said, wishing he'd stop wittering in that leisurely way of his, like he was dispensing invaluable homespun wisdom. "The specific recordings of what happened, the ones Paulette showed me when I returned from being suspended. They didn't … necessarily show the whole picture."

"Faulty camera, you mean?" he said, taking a more serious tone.

I thought about how the footage specifically failed to show me starting the fire, only my efforts to put it out and rescue Hattie. Nor did it show me stealing the pipper and paperwork from the meeting room.

"It could have been a faulty camera," I admitted. "I was just wondering if it was possible for someone to change the video, edit out bits that were—" I didn't know how to finish that sentence without incriminating myself.

"Are you suggesting someone could tamper with security camera evidence?" he said, a look of naked horror on his face. "That would call into question everything this company stands for. It's unthinkable."

"Yes. Yes, of course," I said. "Sorry. Silly me."

A strange feeling, one I think had been stealing up on me for some days, took firm hold. For the rest of the day I did my job, but it felt like an act. Like I was a rebel, a subversive, a spy. I was working inside Jaffle Tech, acting like any of the support workers, offering help and guidance to the billions of Jaffle product users worldwide, except now it felt like I was playing a role. Inside I was something different. I was the maker of fake brain scans. I was the health and safety risk, always caught on camera but never exposed. I was the liar.

I was the one who went to strange and unexpected places – food halls and flower markets and art galleries. I was the one who led innocents like Hattie astray, who interfered with Empties.

I was a virus in the system.

***

Helberg was waiting for me back at the apartment complex, actually waiting for me at the door to catch me when I arrived.

"You know, if I wanted a pet dog to greet me when I got home, I could buy one," I said.

He didn't smile. "I have to show you something."

"If it's another dance like the salsa, I don't think I'm up for it."

He didn't reply, leading me silently through to his office. He had cleared junk from tables and shelves to make room for the pieces of paper he'd arranged across them. It was some typed document, long and full of bullet points and sub-headings.

"I worked on back-engineering that plipper device you brought to me," he said, pointing to a bulky thing of soldered components and dangling wires.

"You've built your own plipper?" I was impressed.

"It's just an adapted port, like a Jaffle port, really. Except its sole purpose is to link to another port, pretty much along line of sight, using microwave and locator tech, and then change the access level."

I picked it up. Helberg's homemade plipper wasn't at all like the sleek little unit I'd stolen from Jaffle Tech. If the official plipper was a little gun, this thing was more like an ancient crossbow.

"So, you shoot and it just dials whoever it's pointing at down to Empty?" I said.

"That wasn't what I wanted to show you." He turned and spread his arms at the papers all around him. "This is the document you hid the plipper in, the one you stole. I happened to read it."

I went back to the document and glanced at the nearest sheet. "What is it?"

"It's Operation Sunrise." He said it with such glum solemnity that I felt a chill of fear.

"And...?" I said.

"It's bad, Alice."

"Bad how?"

He pointed at me, more specifically he pointed at my head. "You're on Jaffle Standard. Or, at least you were. You've got relatively full access to your intellect, sense of judgement, your more unsubtle range of emotions, speaking, memory and writing, yeah?"

"Sure," I said. "Although I can experience much more now."

"Right. And above standard is Jaffle Enhanced. Morality, self-conscious acts and even an appreciation of music and other art forms. Move up one more and you're into Jaffle Premium with access to notions of beauty, humour, sex and violence. Near total access to your brain's functions."

"You forgot Jaffle Freedom." I knew my company products. I didn't need Helberg to tell me what Jaffle packages were out there.

"The top layer," he nodded. "Total access to one's own brain function. To philosophise, attain self-actualisation, exert genuine free will over one's own actions. That may indeed be where you are now, along with me and the rest of the three-percenters who don't have a damned Jaffle Port fitted. This—" he gestured at the scattered document. "This is what happens when you allow people to buy total freedom of thought."

"What happens?"

"More and more buy their way up the ladder. Did you know that Jaffle Premium was only created to make one more stepping stone between Jaffle Enhanced and Jaffle Freedom?"

"I did." Which was sort of true. I remember it being introduced, although Helberg's version wasn't the same as I had been told.

"So now you've got more people buying their way to the top and nowhere else for them to go. No way for Jaffle Tech to get more money out of them. And so Jaffle are going to unveil their new product: Jaffle Sunrise."

"As in Operation Sunrise?"

"Indeed."

"And what is Jaffle Sunrise?"

"It's exactly the same as the current Jaffle Freedom."

I wrinkled my nose. "That doesn't make sense. No one will buy a new product if it's just the same as another one."

"They might when they are told that Jaffle Freedom is going to have some restrictions placed on it, essentially bringing it down to the level of Jaffle Premium."

"And Jaffle Premium?"

"Cascades down to the level of Jaffle Enhanced. And so it goes. Every user will be placed on the level below."

"Jaffle Standard users all become like Jaffle Economy users."

"More like Jaffle Lite, actually."

I thought about the community service workers in their orange coveralls. Jaffle Lite: criminals and those heavily in debt reduced to bumbling, voiceless creatures with no inner life at all. Lights on but nobody at home. I was on Jaffle Standard or, at least, had been. Hattie was Jaffle Standard. I pictured us as those dead creatures.

"When are they doing this?"

Helberg shrugged. "Rollout could happen any time after the Operation Sunrise launch. That's happening on the nineteenth isn't it?"

"Five days time," I said. "I need to tell Rufus Jaffle."

"Rufus Jaffle must know about it," said Helberg.

I shook my head vehemently. "I had access to Rufus's memory. Henderson—"

"The Jaffle Tech CTO?"

"Him. He got Rufus Jaffle to sign the papers when he was injured, not thinking straight. He'd been hit by a kangaroo."

"Did you just say kangaroo?"

"Rufus is patron of an animal charity, but he got into a fight with a kangaroo which would be very embarrassing. To cover it up, after Henderson made Rufus sign the papers he got him to—" I gazed in horrified realisation. "He got Rufus to wipe his memory of the event. Rufus thought he was wiping his memory of the kangaroo fight, but Henderson didn't want him to remember what he'd signed!"

"Rufus would know full well what he was signing," Helberg argued.

"He didn't want to read it. And he was concussed. Henderson made him sign and had his memory deleted. I did that. I was the one who did that!" My breath came in ragged gasps. Hattie was going to be made into a Jaffle Lite user, no better than an Empty. And I was responsible! "We have to stop this," I said.

"I would generally agree. We could tell the media but for the ninety-seven percent, Jaffle Tech controls your media access."

"But if we could show people..."

"This document is only the proposal," said Helberg. "Enough information for me to stitch the clues together. I could have faked

something similar, given time. We'd need proof and no chance of getting it."

"We have to try."

"We have to focus on saving who we can save. I could hack Hattie's port, maybe save her from the worst of it. I'd hope that your screwy brain is potentially immune."

"I'm not talking about saving one person or two," I argued. "Billions worldwide are about to have their lives ruined. Reduced."

"And we can't save them!"

"We could try!"

"How?"

I clenched my fists furiously. "I don't know! I've only had the use of my brain for a few weeks. You've had your whole life! Think of something!"

"I don't have to," he said. "It's not my problem."

"You can't mean that!"

"I've closed off my mind and life to the rest of humanity because I could see what was going on. I made myself into a sad reclusive little man. If anyone had asked, I would have told them what Jaffle Tech and its like are doing to the world. But would that have changed a damned thing? No! Now, you come here with your new la-di-da self-awareness and expect to be able to fix things. Without evidence of wrongdoing on Jaffle Tech's part, you're as helpless as me."

I glared. "What kind of evidence?"

"What?"

"If we need evidence, what kind of evidence?"

He huffed with exasperation. "Documentation. Proof that the top executives are colluding in something that they know crosses an ethical borderline. Failing that, backdoor access to Jaffle Tech's code so we could bring this thing down from the inside. It doesn't matter. It's the kind of stuff you aren't going to be able to lay your hands on!"

I stood up straight and raised my chin haughtily. "You don't know what I'm capable of."

He laughed cynically. And just when I was starting to like him.

"I'll do what I can tomorrow," I said.

"You're going to the gala tomorrow."

"I can do both. Work, then gala. I can multitask."

"You're a fool, Alice Tennerman."

"And you're a coward," I said and marched out.

I went upstairs to my apartment, along the landing of brightly coloured doors, painted by Helberg's little bot. I went to my apartment seeking Hattie. Wanting only to throw my arms around her and tell her I loved her, and if there was any way I could save her from being reduced to something less then she already was, then I would give my life to achieve that.

Instead, I found her packing. I was too stunned to hug her or tell her anything.

"What are you doing?" I said.

"I'm moving out."

"Was it something I said?"

"Yes," she said in a bright upbeat tone. "Or it was something you showed me."

"What?"

"Babies."

"Babies?"

"Yes," she said and stopped for a moment to look at me. "I want a baby."

"Listen, I know you do and—"

"And I need money and a better position and possibly even a Jaffle upgrade."

"You do?"

"And I know how to get that."

"Really?"

She nodded. "The North Beach arcology."

It rang a bell. "Where Swanager and Pedstone went?"

"An integrated living solution community. They pay you to live there. Enough for me to afford art-i-ficial in-semi-nation." She said it like she'd just learned it. "I'm going to have a baby."

I was astonished. Was I happy for her? I couldn't tell. "How does that even work? They pay you?"

"Something about a more simplistic lifestyle. Living in tune with the needs of society and environment. It saves money and resources so they can actually pay us to live there. I jipped the terms and conditions. There was only one unit left and a car is on its way to collect me— Oh! It's here."

She stuffed the last of her belongings into her pod case. I saw how she stuffed the singed head of Smiley Tot Derek in there at the very last. No reverence or love for the little doll's head. Hattie had

changed. I had changed her, but now she was moving on with her own life.

She turned to me. Now, I hugged.

She blinked tears from her eyes. "It's..."

"I know," I said.

"It's been really weird," she said.

"I guess," I said.

"You've been weird."

"Definitely."

She sniffed and wiped her eyes. "But you'll come visit when I've settled in."

"Without a doubt," I said, firmly.

I walked down with her to meet the car.

***

Chapter 28 – 15th June – 4 days until Operation Sunrise

The day of the gala.

Helberg might have been a coward but I wasn't going to let Jaffle Tech reduce me, Hattie and everyone else on their lower packages to little more than mindless animals. I needed to fight them. The way I saw it, that involved either making the public aware of what Jaffle Tech was about to do to them with some incontrovertible evidence or, failing that, stopping Jaffle Tech's servers from disseminating the latest updates. Either way, it involved gaining access to the innermost levels of Jaffle Tech's system.

"Forget it Alice, I can't break into Jaffle," said Helberg, when I went to ask him for help that morning. "They have some of the most advanced security systems in the world. If I had time I might be able to find a back door, but there's no way I'll be able to get in and delete things in a few hours. The odds are stacked against me. You'd be better off wishing for a meteor strike to take out their servers."

"You could at least try."

"And spend the rest of my life in prison? Or forcibly fitted with a Jaffle Port and turned into an Empty?"

I scowled. "Some help you are!"

He gestured at the documents spread out around his office, at my stolen dress hanging from a door which he'd just had cleaned for tonight's gala, at the homemade plipper gun next to the original I'd stolen from work, at the flaky pastries he'd laid on for breakfast.

"Yeah, no help at all," he said sarcastically. "Do not do anything stupid today. You have a party to go to tonight and the CEO of Jaffle Tech to meet. *If* you meet him and *if* he remembers you and *if* he cares one jot for the rest of humanity then plead your case with him. Do not jeopardise that by doing something monumentally moronic, Alice."

I snatched up the Jaffle Tech plipper, spun on my heel and stormed out. Dramatically, I hoped. I wanted to show my contempt with a dramatic exit. If I had been able to think of a way of doing that and taking a flaky pastry with me at the same time, I would have done.

I rode alone in a car to Jaffle Tech. I hoped Hattie had settled into her new apartment and whatever the weird set-up there was it would enable her to finance having a child. Hattie might not have been the most intellectual of people but I missed her company enormously. She was the rock of my life, tethering me to some kind of normal, even if that normal was beans and Mr Smiley. Without Hattie, I had no company but my own thoughts.

I wasn't going to do something stupid at work. I certainly wasn't going to do something *monumentally moronic*. I was going to do something clever. I was going to sneak back up to the executive levels of Jaffle Tech (I'd been up there twice before; it shouldn't be difficult), find some way of getting access to Jaffle's secret files and shut things down. If that meant doing a bit of hacking or taking someone hostage at plipper-point, then so be it.

There was no point going to my cubicle. Fixing things was the goal today. Best to get right down to it.

I walked into reception slowly, eyeing the people getting into the elevators. I needed a superior-looking exec-type, or maybe another engineer. Maybe even a cleaner. Did they have human cleaners on the top floors? We just had bots on ours. Would human cleaners be a step up or step down from bot cleaners?

A woman who looked like she belonged in the upper ranks of the company walked towards the ranks of elevators. I sped up to intercept and join her. I was already prepping a story in my head about the cleaning bots on the top floor needing a manual check-over. Yes, it was conceivable that someone in a support worker's tunic could be involved with that.

I had timed my interception perfectly. The doors were sliding open. We would step inside, one after the other, as natural as anything.

"Alice?"

I looked round. Paulette was approaching across the lobby. I faltered. The woman slipped into the elevator. I could dash in after her.

"I hoped to catch you on your way in," said Paulette, closer now.

"Oh?"

The elevator door closed, the opportunity had passed.

"Could we have a word?" said Paulette.

"Word?"

Paulette smiled. "That clarification interview we spoke about."

"Oh. Yes."

Paulette turned and walked away. I felt compelled to follow.

"We?" I called after her. "'Could *we* have a word'?"

Paulette offered no reply. I put my hand on the plipper in my pocket and followed.

We entered a room in a portion of the building I'd only ever been in once before: the day of my interview with Jaffle Tech. The interview had been brief. There'd been a few formal questions, a bit of a chit-chat and then a look at my Jaffle rating. I'd had a very impressive Jaffle rating back then. Along with my noted brain efficiency, it was enough to win me the job. I very much doubted this interview was going to conclude with a new job offer.

Paulette gestured to the people already sitting in the room. I recognised both of them: the beautiful large-eyed woman from the medical centre and Estelle, the senior human resources partner. When Paulette sat they were arranged as a panel of three facing me.

"Oh, this is, um, formal," I said as I sat.

Paulette simply nodded.

"This is an investigatory interview, Alice," said Estelle.

"Yes?" I said.

"Following data received and analysed since you spoke with Paulette two days ago, certain facts have come to light."

"Yes?"

Estelle looked to the wall and it was suddenly crawling with dates, details and maps.

"Second of June, you engaged with a group of individuals outside your residence using Restricted Jaffle service—"

"Empties," I said automatically.

"Restricted Jaffle service," Paulette corrected me.

"Your interactions set off a security alert," said Estelle, "and a Jaffle Swarm was dispatched to check on the individuals' health and welfare. On the same day, your location shows you at the residence of Abram and Claire Luca for a period of time. On third of June, Claire Luca came to Jaffle Tech claiming that a Jaffle Tech member of staff had broken into her home and stolen a number of items including a dress and perfume."

"Uh-huh?" I said, no idea what else to say.

"Continuing third of June, you were located at Baybrook food markets although you normally have your foodstuffs delivered. Also,

another incident recorded with local Restricted Jaffle service users." A camera image appeared on the screen, showing me and Helberg wiping paint from some very messy Empties.

"That's me," I conceded.

Estelle nodded. "June fourth, you requested two sets of work tunics from supplies. One was a maintenance engineer's uniform. Security pass data shows that you were on the ninth floor of this building where senior management offices are located. However there is no CCTV video of you being present on the ninth floor."

I was surprised by this last point.

"You look surprised," said Paulette.

"I am," I agreed.

"Fifth of June," Estelle continued, "your Jaffle Port shows you located at Spalding flower markets. Later, it shows you at the Legion Art Museum some miles away."

"Is that a problem?" I asked.

"It might be considered abnormal," said Estelle, "given that, on the seventh of June, you refused to attend a mandatory scan with the medical team here, citing an *intrusion*, an *anomaly*."

The medical woman was nodding vigorously.

"Eighth of June," said Estelle. "You submitted a privately commissioned scan instead of attending one organised by our own team. The reason you gave was it had been requested by the CEO, Rufus Jaffle, or possibly by his secretary because a personal contact of theirs was in training and ... required the practice?"

I nodded. "Yes."

"There was then a fire. The starting moments of the fire were not captured on CCTV but your own section records show you acted bravely in assisting your colleagues. Well done."

That *well done* stung, like being given a gold star sticker on the way to the executioner's block.

"You did not immediately leave the building though," Estelle noted. "You met with one of our security staff. You were both in a nearby meeting room for several minutes before joining the rest of the section staff in your designated muster point on the front lawns."

She looked at me for any reaction. I had none I could give her.

"Twelfth of June. You and a work colleague visited the OneStop Daycare Centre under the pretext of wanting to apply for jobs there. Thirteenth of June, Paulette received a request for a personal reference in relation to that job application. She asked you directly if

you had ever met Rufus Jaffle and you said no. Fourteenth of June, several brain scans, seemingly created by the same individual who created yours, were uncovered in a routine audit of our company records."

Estelle put her hands flat on the table and sat back. "Well?"

I smiled politely. "I'm okay, considering."

She narrowed her eyes, probably studying my face for signs of contempt or fear. "What do you have to say for yourself, Alice?"

I looked at the data on the wall. "I have been busy," I said.

"Busy?"

"You think one day's just like the next, but when you see it all laid out like that... It's no wonder I feel tired sometimes."

Estelle wasn't happy with that answer. "You're not concerned about the evidence of wrongdoing?"

"Wrongdoing?" I looked at the data again. "I visited a house. I bought some food and some flowers. I visited an art gallery. Security data shows I went to the ninth floor even though no one saw me at all, so clearly I didn't. I was slow leaving the building after a fire because Levi collared me to talk about health and safety."

A miniscule head jiggle from Paulette showed she thought that sounded entirely plausible. But Estelle was far from convinced.

"This is all circumstantial evidence," she said, "but it points towards something else."

"Yes?" I said innocently, though the worry inside me was palpable.

"Alice Tennerman, do you work for one of our competitors?"

I laughed. It was unexpected and genuine. "No! I have enjoyed – for the most part at least – enjoyed working at Jaffle Tech."

"Are you engaged in industrial espionage?"

"What?"

"Are you complicit in acts of fraud against Jaffle Tech?"

"No. I wouldn't even know how to do that."

Estelle glared. "Where do you meet your contact?"

"Contact?"

"At the food halls? At the art gallery? Is your contact masquerading as an Empty?"

"Restricted Jaffle service user," Paulette said, getting a sharp look in return.

"Was the buying of flowers a signal?"

"To who?" I said.

"Did you access the upper floors of this building to carry out wire-taps or to plant surveillance devices?"

"I just work in customer support," I said.

"Did you wipe company security camera records and plant falsified brain scan data in our systems?"

"I wouldn't know where to begin."

"When you said that there was an intruder in your sector, was that to divert suspicion?"

"From what?"

"Did you start the fire to create a diversion?"

"I nearly died in that fire," I pointed out.

Estelle huffed and sat back, deeply unhappy.

The medical woman leaned in, slowly and calmly. "All this behaviour, Alice..."

"Yes?"

"It's not normal."

"What's not normal?"

She attempted a chummy smile. She was certainly beautiful but she was no deceiver and her smile was a fake plastic thing.

"Art? Expensive food? Flowers? You are a Jaffle Standard user. These things are..." She circled her hand. "They wouldn't normally be of interest to you."

"No?"

"No. Your settings wouldn't enable you to have much appreciation of them. You'd get as much satisfaction from flowers as I would from ... Ancient Greek poetry. It's meaningless."

She was right. I had betrayed myself with my pursuit of experience and pleasure. I needed an explanation.

"I didn't enjoy them," I said.

"And yet you went to those places," said Estelle.

I nodded slowly.

"Why?"

I thought quickly, by which I mean I sat still in the frantic whirlwind of my mind and waited for a clever idea to come to me. "I went there..." I said.

"Yes?"

"But I got no pleasure or anything from it..."

"No?"

"So..."

"Yes?"

"I went for someone else."

"Who?"

"Who?" I said.

"Yes, who?"

A phrase Helberg had used dropped into my head. "A hopeless romantic."

Estelle blinked. "I beg your pardon?"

"A hopeless romantic," I added. "High up in our company."

That sounded good. I had no idea at all where I was going with it.

"What are you saying?" said Paulette.

I took a moment to compose myself. I had them interested and could play for time. "For the past few weeks, I have been helping an employee of this company in their ... quest to woo the love of their life."

"I see," said Estelle.

"I see," echoed Paulette.

I could see the beautiful medic wanting to say *I see* too. She contented herself with nodding solemnly.

"How are you helping?" asked Estelle.

I thought quickly. "The, um, food halls and the art gallery were dates. Going to be dates. I went to check them out for him."

"Him?" said Estelle. "It was a man."

"Mmm. Also the flowers were for his love, but he asked me to collect them. Obviously, flowers bring me no pleasure at all but I gather that some people like them."

"None of this falls within the boundaries of your current role. If you've been acting as some sort of matchmaker—"

"You can tell us who it," Paulette interrupted. I was sure she meant to sound professional and probing, but there was no mistaking the gossipy tone in her voice.

"I couldn't," I said. "He's a very influential man. And hopelessly in love." I picked details I recalled from Rufus's memory. "He said that as a man in a powerful position he has to be careful. He won't invite his love to his apartment – he's got a big apartment on the Panhandle I hear – in case people find out."

"Panhandle, eh?" said Estelle, nodding like she knew who I was talking about.

"And a big mansion south of the border," I added, remembering Henderson had also mentioned that in my dream-memory. "I think they're planning a romantic weekend away there."

"But why you?" said Paulette.

"I met him because of my regular job. I must have said something that made him think I knew about, er, affairs of the heart. I've met him in his office. Twice, in fact. You'll even see we were in the same room together. I wouldn't be surprised if he used his influence to delete CCTV video to hide the fact," I added, completely freewheeling now. "Who else would have the influence?"

"How do you explain your presence at the Luca residence?"

"Ah." Yes, how? I thought. "Claire Luca is—"

"His girlfriend?" suggested Paulette, getting too invested in my story.

"That's it," I said. "I went to talk to her, to deliver a gift."

"But the burglary?" said Esther. "The vandalism?"

"There was no burglary," I said. "Perhaps there was vandalism. I don't know. I should imagine that..." I hung my head. "I believe Claire Luca is married. This is one reason why their love had to remain secret. I'm told that when people engage in romantic relationships with other people's spouses, people can become jealous. It's not an emotion I'm overly familiar with."

Estelle seemed unconvinced. "But she came here and made accusations."

"I'm not sure that she is a very stable individual," I said. "Her memories were warped by alcohol use when she came here with her accusations. Paulette knows that."

Paulette was nodding.

"I wouldn't be surprised if she turned to alcohol to cope," I said.

"But what has any of this to do with your privately commissioned brain scan?" said the medical woman.

"It was his idea," I said.

"What?"

"I think he panicked and thought exposing me to these complex situations and feelings has caused me to work outside the parameters of my Jaffle Standard settings. Which I didn't," I added quickly and firmly. "Everything's fine up here in the old noggin."

I judged it was time for me to look contrite and embarrassed. I did my best.

"I think there has been a breach of professional etiquette here," said Estelle.

"I was only doing what I was told."

"Not by you! By Hend— By the man in question. With your permission, Alice, we can access your memories of the events you've mentioned."

"Are you going to call the police?" I said.

"That's entirely up to you," she said. "You might need to organise yourself some legal representation."

"Yes, of course," I said and stood.

"You don't have to do anything now," said Paulette.

"No," I said. "I need to go ... freshen up. Settle my nerves. I'll make some calls."

"I'll come with you," she said, also standing.

"No," I insisted. "I'll just be a few minutes." I thought about what I was going to do next. "Maybe a few minutes more than that."

I left, making sure I looked sad and emotionally drained until I was clearly out of sight. I dashed back to the elevators and waited for one to take me to the top floor. As I waited, I jipped a call to Helberg. The man without a Jaffle Port answered me on an old-fashioned audio transceiver; I could hear the echo on the line.

"*What have you done?*" he said.

"What makes you think I've done anything?" I replied.

"*So, you haven't done anything?*"

I bit my lip. "I got called in for questioning, but I've thrown them off the scent for now."

"*Thrown them off the... Are you a wanted international criminal now?*"

"No. I told them Jethro Henderson was in love with Claire Luca. A hopeless romantic like you said."

"*Don't bring me into this!*" Helberg sighed on the line. The lightly distorted noise sent a shiver down my spine. "*You lied your way out of the situation.*"

"I told you I was a horrible human being."

"*Then it's a good job I love you. What are you doing now?*"

The elevator pinged. By good fortune there was a senior management type in the car. I stepped in beside him. The display showed he'd jipped for the top floor. He looked at me. I nodded like, *Yep, top floor for me too.* He looked at me, specifically at my tunic.

There was something familiar about him, his long solemn face, his thinning hair, but I couldn't place him.

He was about to say something when Hattie slipped into the elevator. She had a smile slapped across her face like she had been smiling all morning.

"Hello, you," I said. "You look cheery."

"The new apartment is amazing," she said. "Everything shiny and new and—" She stopped and gave me a troubled look.

I understood at once. "It's okay. You're allowed to like it. I won't be offended."

"Oh, it's amazing, Alice!" she gushed. "The North Beach arcology is the future of living and with the financial incentive, I'll have enough for a—" she poked her stomach with two index fingers and gave me a conspiratorial wink "—in a matter of months."

The elevator stopped at our usual floor.

"That's really good," I said. "I should come over and help you celebrate."

"But leave your paints at home," she said seriously, stepping off. "Are you not...?" She gestured out at the office beyond the elevator.

"Er, no," I said. "I've got to sort some things out upstairs."

She began to frown but the doors closed on her. The car rose again.

"*What are you doing?*" said Helberg in my ear. I'd forgotten the call was still open and shut it off.

The elevator reached the top floor. The man exited and then looked back at me severely. "And where do you think you are going? Do you have clearance?"

"Of course," I said, realising why I recognised him. He was *Michael from Legal* out of Rufus's memory.

He looked at my tunic again, pointedly.

"Oh, this?" I said. "It's not even mine."

The pointed look became one of confusion.

"I do find if you dress like one of the workers, they don't pay as much attention to you. And they'll open up to you in ways they otherwise might not."

"You're some sort of..."

"Company spy?" I said and laughed, riding on a wild, giddy confidence born from the knowledge I had built of castle of lies around me ever since I'd come into the building this morning.

"Are you a company spy?"

"I like to think of myself as more of a mystery shopper, Michael," I said, recalling his words from Rufus's memory, "But I very much believe the less people know and the smaller the paper trail, the better it is for everyone."

There was a twitch at the corner of his mouth. Did he recognise the words as his own or just find himself agreeing with the sentiment?

"Even the legal department don't get to know everything," I said and stepped past him.

I was in the long corridor with the plush carpet, belatedly wondering where I should go. I needed access to records, to computers, something I could jip with greater ease now I was in the higher reaches of the company headquarters. I really hadn't thought it through.

"Do you know where you're going?" asked Michael.

"It's ... been a while," I said. "Last time I only visited Rufus Jaffle's office. Is he in?"

Michael smiled thinly. "Rufus is never here."

I nodded wisely. "He'd rather be partying and getting himself into trouble."

The smile stayed. "What do you need—?"

"Alice," I said and had a moment of inspiration. I pulled the plipper from my pocket. "I came to return this. One of your executives left it in a general meeting room downstairs. Jessica, was it?"

"Really?" said Michael.

"It wouldn't do to have Operation Sunrise ruined by some of our technology leaking out early."

"No, it wouldn't," he agreed. "Look, perhaps if you come through here we can sort something out."

He led me to a door which unlocked as he approached.

"Your office?" I said.

Michael nodded.

The walls were lined with bookcases containing actual books: leather bound things with gold spines. Maybe they were there to reinforce his position as a man of the law. There were also two glass display cases standing on the office floor. The nearest one contained a model of a rat (at least I hoped it was a model). I bent to read the little placard:

2015
Rats implanted with neural microchips
used to detect explosive devices.

"People think of lawyers as rats," said Michael. "Or sharks."

He tapped the other display case. It contained a model of the sharks Jaffle used to patrol the seas. Definitely a model; a full-sized shark would have been much, even in an office of this size.

"It amuses me to have these in here," he said. "Do you think lawyers are rats, Alice? Or sharks?"

I paused. "Rufus Jaffle never had a high opinion of you."

He grunted. "And yet without lawyers to interpret law and help put rules in place, there would be chaos. Please." He gestured to a seat.

This wasn't getting me into Jaffle's computer system. I was just playing games with a potentially dangerous man.

I sat.

"May I?" he asked. It took me a moment to realise he wanted the plipper. I handed it over and he studied it.

"Order from chaos," he said, waggling the plipper. "That's all this is."

I nodded like I cared.

"Do you ever think of all the things Jaffle has done for this world?" he said. "This company first made money building implants for people with neurological damage, helping paralysed people to walk, the blind to see, the brain-damaged to think again. Jesus style miracles."

"The baby Jesus?"

He smiled. "I'm thinking of his later work. Then we gave people brain drives and brain ports. Education was revolutionised. Newspapers. Do you know newspapers?" He sat opposite me. "Back in the twentieth century they had things called newspapers."

"Oh, sure. Newspapers."

"They used to say that in one single copy of the New York Times, there was more content, more words, than the average person in the seventeenth century would access in a lifetime."

"I've heard that."

"Think on it. In two hundred years, a lifetime's data content became a single day's data content. I simplify, but you get the point, right?"

"Right."

"In the space of the last thirty years, Jaffle has smashed that. You, me, everyone has access to a world of information. All learning, all knowledge, downloadable and shareable. Jaffle Tech has enhanced humanity exponentially." He laughed, although I wasn't quite sure what there was to laugh about. "You don't need a lawyer to tell you that if someone has given you something remarkable, then you owe them something in return." He turned the plipper over in his hand. "We elevated humanity beyond all recognition. Anything Jaffle Tech takes from them is merely restitution." He put the plipper down on the desk.

"All we want is order. Security. Structure." He pointed at my tunic. "You've spent time among them."

"Customer support workers?"

"Jaffle Standards," he said. "What are they like?"

"They're just like us."

"Really?"

"They eat beans and watch Mr Smiley, but they're just like us."

He sneered. "Have you seen the Mr Smiley shows?"

"They still have dreams, desires. They want things."

"And it's important that they do," he conceded. "If people want to better themselves then they also want to separate themselves from those around them; keep those beneath them down. It reinforces the social structure. The belief that they can rise helps keep the lower classes happy."

"The lower classes?" I said.

"*Mea culpa*. Those on more basic packages. The terminology has changed but much stays the same. Back in the Middle Ages— I'm sorry: two history analogies in one day. You can't be devoted to the law without having a firm grasp of history. Back in the Middle Ages, the peasants were the lowest class in society. The rulers, kings and emperors would have to keep them in their place, maintaining power for themselves while knowing that peasants were the essential means of production. Without the peasant class, the aristocracy would starve. Then along came the Industrial Revolution and slowly things changed, just a little. Right through to the present day, the structures remain the same but the reasons change."

He pointed at the rat in its case.

"It's vermin, the rat. It serves no purpose. It steals from human society. It breeds uncontrollably. It causes damage. It spreads disease.

But put a chip in its head and it serves some function. In our world, the world of work is now almost fully automated. What machines can't do, Jaffle-enhanced animals can. Only in interpersonal interactions such as *customer support* do people still like the human touch."

"They do," I agreed.

"But, for the most part, humanity is obsolete. We're now in the business of planned obsolescence. We've elevated humanity but there's no goal to that, nothing to elevate them *for*. The majority of the human race needs to be contained, controlled, kept happy with beans and Mr Smiley. If we let them run free, free in society, free inside their own heads, then they will be nothing but vermin, a nuisance."

He tilted his head.

"Yes," he said, clearly on a call. "I've been waiting ten minutes for a response. Stalling, yes. I'm just here with Alice." He looked at me and gave me a friendly eyebrow waggle. "Ah, she is. Good. That's fine then." He nodded, the call ended. "Sorry about that," he said. "I needed to check."

"Check?"

"Where were we?" he said. "Ah. Rats. Sterile rats in sterile little boxes, like your friend at North Beach. Rats are fine as long as you have them under control The problem comes if one escapes."

"Er, yes?"

"What can you do then?"

"Actually, there was this mouse one time, running round the office—"

Michael had picked up the plipper and pointed it directly at me.

"Wait," I said.

His thumb pressed the stud. He plipped me.

***

Chapter 29

I slumped in the chair like I had seen Levi slump in the meeting room. My jaw sagged. My eyes unfocussed. I did not move.

Michael turned the plipper over in his hands, impressed with the device's apparent effectiveness.

"You're a fair liar, Alice," he said. "Superficially convincing. But I have a real eye for liars. Comes with the territory." He stood and adjusted the cuffs of his suit jacket as he rounded the desk. "Also, I have full access to employee records. And, yes, I had just received a communication from Estelle in HR that some jumped up support worker called Alice Tennerman was making wild and unfounded accusations about our CTO." He laughed. "Jethro Henderson a hopeless romantic? A secret affair? He's the dullest, least sexual man in the company. Now, me, I'm a man who knows how to enjoy life to the full."

He ran his fingertips along my cheek and up to my temple. I didn't move. I didn't respond.

"Don't worry," he said. "We'll soon have you back in your little box, enjoying beans and Mr Smiley. You were on Standard before? And you're familiar with the ins and outs of Operation Sunrise?" He nodded as though I had responded. "Good. So you know that when we roll out in four days Standard will be a lot more ... streamlined. A more simplistic experience but one I think you'll be perfectly happy with." He perched on the desk directly in front of me.

"And there are even more new features you'll enjoy. We're enhancing port to port communications. None of this wearisome business of actually needing to vocalise during communication. Just think about it. Silent instantaneous communication. Dumb mute rats in their boxes. And the three percent without Jaffle Ports – weirdos and outcasts, the lot of them. How long do you think they will want to stay as outsiders when the world around them is silenced? When they are truly cut off from the future of human communication?"

He looked at me. My downward gaze didn't waver. He sighed. Talking to an Empty had limited entertainment value.

"You sit tight, Alice. I'll go meet the security team." He patted my knee, a lingering touch, and left.

The moment he was out of the door I was up.

Helberg had been right – thank goodness! The plipper had had zero effect on me. Whatever Rufus's memory and the whale brain virus had done to me had armoured me against it.

I rubbed my cheek vigorously where that creepy Michael had touched me. He'd gone to meet the security team. I didn't know how far away he'd gone or indeed when they'd be back. I popped my head out the door. I couldn't see him along the corridor. I sneaked out.

I was near the elevators when I heard Michael's voice and the movements of several people. "Yes, captain. We can take her into custody on my authority. Theft, fraud, false accusations against senior executives."

I ducked into the nearest open door, the toilets, and held the door closed while security went by. My instinct was to stay there but it would only be seconds before they realised I had gone. I did not hesitate. I walked out, knowing any of them might look back and see me, and I hurried to the elevator. There were no shouts. No one tried to tackle me to the ground. I slipped into the elevator and made for the ground floor.

I made a call to Helberg.

"You're still alive," he said.

"Yes."

"I'm impressed. Have they arrested you yet?"

"Not yet."

"Not yet?"

"Mmmm. I kind of got caught out by this guy Michael from legal. He plipped me. I only pretended it worked and now I'm coming home. I've got the evidence we need."

"Wait, wait, wait. Jaffle Tech can track you. They do track you. The location function on your brain port."

"Can you do something about that?"

"Not from here." He sounded deeply worried which was both touching and unhelpful. "I can fry your port's circuits or completely power it down, but you'd have to be here for that."

"Can't you break into the company systems and stop them tracking me?"

"I told you. I can't break through their security. I'd need—"

"A meteor strike to take out their servers, right."

An idea occurred to me. We'd all had a presentation a while ago about the failsafe systems protecting our power supplies. I remember being impressed at the time. Power cuts were rare, but an

outage wouldn't stop Jaffle headquarters from operating because there was a large battery backup, and a gas-powered generator for extreme circumstances. I remember thinking at the time, if you were protecting against someone who seriously wanted to disrupt the organisation, you wouldn't locate the battery and generator in the same enclosure. Taking out power to Jaffle might save my bacon in the short term, and it might even put a dent in Operation Sunrise. It was worth a shot.

There was no security waiting for me in the lobby. I should have thought about that on the way down. It was pure dumb luck I wasn't apprehended the moment I stepped out.

I scuttled through the building and towards the rear entrance. A large corporate headquarters had a lot of deliveries and produced a lot of waste. People and bots, moving with single-minded efficiency, moved in and out.

The backup power enclosure was close, surrounded by a sturdy slatted fence. The gate was locked so I went and peered through the gaps in the wood. I wasn't sure what I expected to see, but an On/Off switch would have been nice. There was nothing that even hinted at being a crucial control component. It looked like a series of well-secured huts. Even if I could get through the fence, I would need to unlock the huts and then figure out what I was looking at. I turned away with a sigh. Some kind of subtle sabotage ought to be possible, but I had no clue what to do.

Then I looked across the loading bay, and I wondered if some form of *unsubtle* sabotage might be possible. Over by a cordoned-off area there was a sign. It read:

Danger: works in progress.

Not at that moment there wasn't, but it looked as though a new flower bed was being created. What interested me were the paving slabs that had been cut to make space for it. Something had sliced right through them. My attention was drawn to the interesting machine that was right in front of me. It had a wicked-looking circular blade mounted at the front, and a pair of small wheels at the back. It looked as if it was simply rolled up to cut whatever stood in its way. I decided to give it a try. There was a little plastic case over a big green button. I lifted the case and pressed the button. There was a high-pitched electric whine and the blade started to spin. I pushed

it forward and it bit into the paving slabs with a hell-raising shriek. I decided to save the attention-seeking noise until I was at least doing something destructive.

I lifted the blade again and wheeled the machine across to the backup power enclosure. There was some heavy duty conduit leading towards the building. I pushed the blade slowly forward and down. It bit into the conduit. The sparks it produceed were almost as distracting as the horrific noise it made, but I was committed now. I pushed harder and the noise rose in pitch. Vibrations rattled up my arms, but I'd cut through the outer casing. I urged the blade further. There was a loud bang and the machine bucked right out of my hands and stopped dead. I decided it was be a good time to make my exit and scurried backwards. When I got to the building's rear entrance, the door was closed. A woman was inside, hammering on the glass. There were no lights on and behind her the building was surprisingly dark. I decided to find another way of leaving and followed the road used by delivery trucks until I reached the security gatehouse.

"Power's out!" called a security guard from the booth. "Everything's gone mad!"

I nodded. "Following protocol and leaving the premises in case of any ongoing threat."

"Uh, yeah. Wise move," he replied. "What protocol?"

"It's new," I replied vaguely.

He waved me through. I ducked under the vehicle barrier and walked quickly up the road.

I crossed Jaffle Park and hailed a car to take me home. A call came through from Helberg. As I answered it, the signal failed. I nervously dismissed the call. I had made a mess of everything. Whatever he wanted to berate me for could wait.

I tried to calm myself as we crossed the city. I had several hours until I needed to get ready for the gala. Time enough to share my evidence with Helberg. Time enough to work out what I would say to Rufus, to show him what was being done by his company in his name. Time enough to fix everything for everyone.

The car approached the Shangri-La Towers apartment complex. As always, the pitiful Empties in their pink coveralls were gathered at the roadside. Without warning, one of the nearest lurched out into the road in a mindless Empty shuffle, right in front of the car. It

responded automatically, braking, catching me in its restraints and stopping just short of hitting the Empty.

"*A pedestrian collision has just been avoided,*" said the car. "*Are you injured?*"

"I'm fine." I looked up and saw the Empty's slack face.

It was Patrick Helberg.

***

Chapter 30

The Empty Helberg lurched round to the door, hands on the car to stop it moving away. The slack look had vanished from his face. I tried to step out but he blocked the doorway.

"You can't come in," he murmured. "There's somebody from Jaffle here. They're looking for you. They look sort of serious."

My throat tightened in fear.

"Here." He reached into his Empty coverall and pulled out a folded bundle: the dress I'd stolen from Claire. "I hope I haven't creased it too much. And this..." From a pocket he took a bright blue ball of netting. It looked like a foaming shower scrunchy. "It's a fascinator," he said, clipping it into my hair.

I didn't know what a fascinator was so I jipped the word. For some reason I got no answer, but it wasn't at the top of my list of priorities.

"Okay it's a shower scrunchy attached to a bulldog clip," he added, "but it looks good enough. And there's a signal scrambler in there."

"Which means?"

"Your Jaffle Port isn't sending data out and you're getting none in."

"I'm blind," I said automatically, realising my sixth sense had been effectively switched off.

"You'll cope," he said with only the mildest reproach. "It will stop them tracking you. I think. Now, you go to that party, get out of here for a bit." He held out his hand. "You had evidence."

I tapped my skull. "Memory. Michael from legal. He's a slimy character. Told me everything."

"Everything?"

"He told me what Jaffle wanted the future to be. It was horrible."

"But did he admit to any legal or moral wrongdoing?"

I wasn't sure about that. "I thought if we just showed people what Jaffle Tech thought of them..."

Helberg didn't look convinced. "We don't have the opportunity to extract those memories now. If Rufus Jaffle's the good guy you say

he is, then he's the only one who can help you. You need to find him."

"Of course," I said. "But where—?"

"You haven't got time to waste."

I touched his pink coverall. "Where did you get this from?"

He smirked. "I didn't want you picturing a naked Empty currently bumping and bumbling his way around our new garden."

"I didn't think you stole it."

"I mean, there's a naked Empty in our garden. I just didn't want you picturing it. Now, go."

He began to withdraw so the door could close. I leaned forward quickly, one hand on his coveralls, and kissed him on the lips.

"Thank you, Patrick," I said.

"Anything for an amazing woman."

"I thought you would do anything for the easy life."

He shrugged. "It's a shame they're mutually exclusive." The door closed on him.

As the car drove to the Jaffle Tech gala, I put on the stolen dress. The smell of the perfume I'd also stolen still clung to it. My mood was low but I was nonetheless thrilled to have a chance to look and smell so nice. It felt like a declaration of who I really was, an affirmation of my right to be what I wanted to be.

The venue was some distance away, over to the west and down by the sea, in an area of the city I had never visited before. I was several hours early, so I instructed the car to circle, sticking to the less expensive roads so I didn't use up all my funds at once. The car wouldn't accept my instructions verbally. With my Jaffle Port blocked I was, essentially, invisible to it. I took the fascinator off for a moment, repeated my instructions, and clipped it back on.

As we drove in a slow spiral towards the charity gala I went through neighbourhoods much like the one where Claire lived. Then the houses started to get even bigger. Some of them were on so much land it wasn't possible to see the house itself behind the gates, walls and trees surrounding them.

The car went downhill. As it rounded a bend I saw the ocean and gasped in surprise. I lived ten miles from the ocean, but had never seen it before. I knew it was big, because I'd seen it on maps and pictures, but when I saw water all the way to the horizon I understood it in a way that would never have been available to old Alice. I wondered why the colours seemed to be shifting, realising

that the water reflected the colours of the sky. Despite myself, I grinned with delight. It would be a fun thing to try and create an image like this, using paint. That was also something *old* Alice would never have imagined.

There were flecks of white near to the beach where the waves came in. I watched the shifting colours and the endless waves until the car reached the bottom of the hill and the ocean was out of sight again. A long line of cars was dropping people off. Men and women, all dressed in glamorous clothes. Some made from sumptuous fabrics and in every colour, others in a more muted palette. Some wore formal suits while others wore a more relaxed version where the jacket was a different colour to the trousers. None of them wore shorts like Rufus Jaffle, which I hoped would make it easier to spot him among the crowds.

Getting out of the car, I could hear an unfamiliar noise, and there was an unusual smell in the air. It took me a few moments before I understood I was hearing the waves breaking on the beach. Did that mean the smell was the ocean?

I joined the crowd, my stolen dress helping me blend in. As we walked through to the white building – too large to be a house, surely! – I concentrated on the other guests, trying to mimic what they did and how they did it. Many of them greeted others with a big smile and *mwa mwa* noises. They also seemed laugh and wave their hands a lot.

I spotted someone standing alone and tried it out.

"Hell-o! Mwa, mwa! How lovely to see you!" I gave a tinkling laugh, although it sounded more like the alarm you get when a cleaning bot gets jammed in a corner.

"Ah yes, delighted!" he said. "It's been a long time!"

I did the laugh again and moved on. I was at a party, and it was nothing like my bacon barbecue garden party, thank goodness.

Drinks were being handed out by staff holding trays. I took one and gave my thanks, but the slack expression on the girl with the tray suggested my words meant nothing. An Empty? Or as good as. This was the future I was fighting against.

I drank, and coughed violently. When I'd recovered enough to look at my glass I was astounded to see bubbles rising from the bottom in a constant stream. I took a more cautious sip and felt the sensation on my tongue. It was fun in a way I could never have imagined. I saw the bottle on a nearby table and jipped what

champagne was, wondering why Helberg hadn't warned me about the stuff. I forgot my Jaffle Port was blocked and the lack of knowledge felt odd.

So I didn't know what champagne was, but I was determined to fit in. Once I'd got the hang of the bubbles I enjoyed it very much. I took a second glass and moved on.

The string quartet was a challenge. I heard them playing in the distance and the sound was so pure and vivid. I found them playing in an airy conservatory where beautiful plants flowered and the musicians – real musicians! Not just music played through speakers – performed their beautiful music with serene expressions. Something about the music being performed live, right in front of me, heightened its power. I found myself being moved to tears by its wonder.

"Well don't you look adorable!" came a voice in my ear. I gave a start, not least because suddenly there was a hand caressing my buttocks. In surprise, I spilled my drink in shock and whirled to see who it was.

"Oh my goodness, I'm so sorry!" The voice (and the hand) belonged to a formally suited man with dark hair and deep brown eyes. "I didn't mean to," he said, genuinely upset.

"Mean to?" I said.

"You must forgive me, I thought you were my wife," he said and laughed, almost hysterically. "That sounds like the worst pick up line ever, doesn't it?"

I had no clue what he was on about and hadn't recovered from the unwanted touching. I simply said, "Yes?" hoping that was the correct response.

"No," he insisted. "She has the exact same dress. Oh, you've made yourself all wet and it's entirely my fault."

He pulled a handkerchief from his top pocket and leaned forward, intending to dab my chest. I really didn't want him fondling any more of my secondary sex characteristics, so I snatched it from him. I couldn't afford to waste any more time, so after a few token dabs I pushed past him to get to the steps. Any tears the string quartet might have evoked had missed their opportunity.

I remembered the ticket had mentioned a piggy-wig orchestra. I had failed to ask Helberg what that was, and whether it was normal. I found a member of the serving staff who looked as if he was at a higher level than the others and asked about the piggy-wig orchestra.

He directed me to a room, inside which was a row of transparent boxes, each with a small pink creature inside.

Any other time I would have been able to jip what they were. Instead I turned to a woman near to me. "These things ... piggy-wigs?"

"Piglets, yes," she said. "I do love a piglet. And I don't just mean a roasted suckling one." She laughed. I didn't have a clue what she meant, but joined in.

A man in a sequinned suit bowed to the audience and took his seat at a keyboard.

"Ladies and gentlemen. Each of the keys on this keyboard will cause one of our happy piglets to sing for you. Their Jaffle Ports help them to understand what I'm asking them to do, but of course, they are free to do as they like. What can I tell you? These piggy-wigs love to sing! We treat our animals with the utmost care."

I wondered whether the piglets enjoyed being shut in small boxes and controlled by this man. Probably not.

He pressed a key. There was the brief grunting squeak of a piglet. He ran a finger down the keyboard and there was a whole scale of piglets.

"Now I shall play to you, with the voices of the piggy-wig orchestra!" he declared.

He played a tune. I wondered if Helberg would deride it for being as simplistic as the Smiley theme, but it was undoubtedly charming, being sung by piglets. It made the audience smile as the piglets sat in their boxes, some of them sniffing around, others putting their front feet up on the side of the enclosure.

I listened as the tune became slightly more complex. It was fun to watch someone play an instrument, and this wasn't making me cry like the string quartet, although I felt slightly angry on the piglets' behalf.

"And now," said the man with a flourish. "As part of the finale, you may come and meet the piglets who have sung so beautifully for you!"

There were twenty four chairs behind the piglet boxes. He invited members of the audience to sit with their allocated piglet while he played the last tune. I made sure I claimed a chair and a small pink piglet was placed on my lap. It nuzzled my hand and seemed content to have its ear gently tickled while it made an occasional snorting noise as part of the tune. It was strangely

satisfying to hold the piglet, and I was disappointed when it was time for it to go back into its enclosure.

***

Chapter 31

As I left the piggy-wig orchestra room, there was a strange roaring sound. People crowded to the edge of the terrace as a huge boat thundered across the bay. The setting sun reflected off the water and the boat created a wake of glittering gold. As it neared, fireworks flew up from the boat and exploded in the sky. The boat made more noise than anything I had ever heard before. Could it be the boat was powered with an internal combustion engine? They were not really allowed any more, but I knew it was possible to get a special licence to use them for scientific research. I wondered what kind of research project involved circling the bay and firing sparkling incendiary devices into the sky. I looked more closely and saw that the boat was being driven by a man in shorts and with long hair. Rufus Jaffle.

"Rufus!" I shouted involuntarily.

People turned and looked at me.

"I'm a big fan," I said with a carefree shrug and sidled away.

I wondered how I was going to get to speak with him. I slipped softly through the crowds, towards the jetty. There were a lot of people between me and Rufus and I noticed the stern faces of individuals who I guessed were party security.

Rufus bounded onto the jetty. I could see his grin. I could see him jerk his fingers at everyone in sight, like he was shooting imaginary pistols. I saw a man with close-cropped hair greet him: Jethro Henderson. It was a company event. Of course, lots of other Jaffle employees would be there. I whirled, stupidly expecting Michael from legal to be stood directly behind me.

When I looked back, Rufus was being ushered inside by a group of people who looked like the organising type. I headed back inside the building. Quite a crowd seemed to be heading towards a large room. As I approached, I saw a sign that said *Charity Auction*. I took a seat towards the back. I needed to think; I needed a plan. I needed to get to Rufus without being recognised by someone who knew me.

"Hello again."

The man with the brown eyes was in the seat next to me, still looking apologetic. There was something else in his face, a half-smile on his lips and a playfulness around the eyes. I smiled at him. "I still have your handkerchief." I handed it to him.

He waved it away. "Keep it. It's the least I could do. I was so certain that you were Claire. She told me that her dress was one-of-a-kind but she was clearly wrong."

"Claire?" Oh crumbs.

"My wife."

"Well, your wife has excellent taste," I said.

He leaned over to whisper. "If I'm completely honest, it looks much better on you than it does on her."

I blushed. His eyes locked onto mine, and I found myself drawn to his face. He had some tiny crinkles around his eyes, but they made him look interesting, somehow.

"It's silk, isn't it?' he asked, accompanying the question with the lightest brush of a hand on my thigh.

It felt like an innocent gesture, but the touch of his hand made me immediately breathless. I couldn't help wondering what it would be like to feel his lips on mine, maybe have him touch my thigh some more.

I tried to pull myself together. My life was in danger, the fate of thousands of millions of Jaffle customers were in my hands, I was here on a mission to speak to Rufus Jaffle, and yet I was allowing myself to be distracted by the idea of having sex with a stranger. Curse this stupid mental freedom!

"Yes, silk," I croaked.

He looked at me for a long moment. I felt his gaze on my eyes and my lips. He reached forward and touched the sleeve of the dress, skimming my shoulder and reaching up to lightly touch the back of my neck.

"Such a fine fabric, isn't it? Caresses the skin like a lover's touch."

"Peter? Peter!" shouted a voice. "What on earth are you doing?"

I didn't need to turn to see who that voice belonged to. I turned and looked anyway. Claire was approaching from across the room.

This was very bad. Peter apparently thought so too. He sat bolt upright.

I ran. Peter was mumbling something which sounded very much like a lie. Then a cry went up.

"My dress! That's my dress! Stop her!"

There was a table just outside the room's exit. Paper brochures about the work of the charity and details of the evening's programme were scattered across it. The table was backed by tall banner screens

showing the animals IFPA worked to protect. I hid in the shadow of one of the banners, trying to calm myself and collect my thoughts.

I heard Rufus's voice approaching. "Here is the hand but it's empty," he was saying, tone miserable. "Just saying. Put something in it, Hendo. Wine, bourbon, a little party powder."

He was going right past me! Perfect!

I was about to step out when I heard Henderson speak. "Let's just get the formal business over with, sir. You have a presentation to major shareholders in twenty minutes. In the Lowry Room."

"Presentation?"

"Proof of concept. Everything is set up at North Beach. It's going to be very impressive."

"I'm on stage for ten minutes," said Rufus moodily. "No longer."

"Agreed."

"Just give me a minute."

Rufus had stopped. He'd actually stopped right by me. I was sort of out of sight, but all he or Henderson had to do was turn, or move a foot to the side, and they'd see me. I snatched up a nearby brochure and hid my face in it.

"Good," said Henderson. "Just wait here a moment, sir. Marcia, watch over our dear CEO."

Was that the sound of Henderson moving off? Was Rufus alone? Or at least just with some functionary who didn't know me or want to turn me into an Empty?

I fought my nerves, became their master and stepped out. Rufus Jaffle stood by the IFPA banner screens, giving cheery thumbs ups to people passing by, looking at their drinks a little enviously.

He saw me.

Behind him, on a screen, was an image of a grey kangaroo. Fading in were the words:

Kangaroos are at risk from a bacterial infection which attacks their nervous system.
Our inoculation programme has halted the spread of this in seven key areas.
We will continue to build upon this success with your help.
Pledge your support today to protect wild kangaroo populations for years to come.

The picture shifted to that of a huge kangaroo, springing through the air. Without warning, I felt my mind slipping into a memory that wasn't mine.

***

Rufus/I/we were in the basement of a large house by the sea. Different house, same sea. There was darkness about us: a closeness, a musty fug in the air, a personal and moral gloom. Passion and guilt pumped through Rufus's veins.

In the ring, kangaroos circled and fought one another. They rocked back on their tails and battered each other with double-footed kicks.

Rufus felt their energy, their need to hurt. An urge to be part of the violence, to expel his own animal energy, was growing within him. He gripped the barricade and vaulted into the ring.

He punched the air and turned to the crowd. They cheered their approval. He turned to the nearest kangaroo and punched it straight on the nose. Its Empty eyes registered nothing.

"Fists of fury! Betcha never saw anything like this back home in, ah, wherever you come from, did ya?" He yelled in its face, a primal roar unleashing his desire for blood. He rained down blow after blow.

The kangaroo drew back. Rufus dodged and swung wildly, walloping it across the temple and knocking it to the ground. He screamed, victorious, holding up his hands to receive the crowd's adulation.

"Now *that* is what a Maglev master looks like! Deadly weapons right here!"

In the corner of his vision, he saw TayTay grab the remote control for the other kangaroo.

"Come on then motherfucker! Show us those deadly weapons!"

Beeee aaaa whaaaaaale. You can have a taaaaail instead, sang the blue whale.

I was irritated by the arrival of the annoying creature, yet relieved when its presence whipped me away from that horrid scene.

"Hey, I didn't fall," Rufus was telling Henderson as he reclined in his hospital bed. "I floored that kangaroo. You shoulda seen—"

"I did see it," said Henderson. "Many times. I have spent the last twenty four hours erasing video feeds and persuading partygoers

to sign non-disclosure agreements. It might have felt like some macho fun at the time, but the vids make it look more like extreme animal cruelty. Michael here from legal thinks we're nearly on top of the situation, but obviously we're going to need you to get a memory wipe."

Michael from legal – *damned vampire* said Rufus's mind – was almost invisible against the grey privacy drapes at the end of the bed. "Legally, this is a difficult situation," he said.

"Animal cruelty, shanimal shuelty," said Rufus.

"Insightful as always, sir," said Michael. "It's more like it presents a problem with your role as honorary president of IFPA."

"Really?" said Rufus.

"Yes. The head of the world's foremost animal protection charities, spending his downtime punching seven shades of shinola out of a lobotomised kangaroo…"

"They're not endangered are they?"

"I don't think that's going to matter to the media," said Henderson. "You've got the corporate gala on the fifteenth. The *charity* gala. You need to wipe your memory of last night. You have high enough access to do that personally."

"Actually, I've got this whale in my head and it's making some of my functionality a bit glitchy."

"Fine," muttered Henderson. "We'll get it done down at Jaffle Tech."

"Don't go through the official company procedures!" protested Michael. "I very much believe the less people know and the smaller the paper trail, the better things are."

"Agreed," said Henderson. "Our official brain-editing systems have audits which I even I can't counter. I'll sort out something off the record."

"Whoa, people!" said Rufus. "Maybe I don't want to give up that memory? It was kind of cool, you know? I can be discreet. It will only be a problem if I talk about it, right?"

Henderson smiled and leaned back. "Of course. You're right. So, tell us what it was like. What made you tackle a kangaroo? Surely it was a dangerous thing to do?"

"Oh man, I was so stoked! I had to get in there and try some Maglev moves on those guys."

"Maglev is magnetic levitation," said Michael.

"Then what am I thinking of?" wondered Rufus. "Anyway, you should have been there! They're powerful animals, but my martial arts skills are all about outsmarting your opponent. It was obvious to me that—"

"Okay, enough," interrupted Henderson. "With all due respect, sir, you are a security risk. In my estimation, you will definitely talk about this in the future. We must erase the memory."

"Oh, what? That was a trap?"

"And hardly a cunning one, sir."

"Man! You could have warned me, I would have shut the hell up!"

"We will arrange the memory wipe as soon as you're recovered. There is another matter that I need your signature for, and it won't wait until then. Perhaps Michael, you could leave us for a few minutes?"

Michael from legal rose and left the room.

"Are you both getting memory wipes?" asked Rufus, sulking.

"I will attend to all details. It's very much in our mutual interest that you trust I have the company's best interest at heart, wouldn't you say? As Chief Technical Officer, problem solving is my forte."

Rufus gave a grunt of assent.

Henderson cleared his throat. "The other matter. I need your signature for Operation Sunrise. It's a complex project, so I can't afford to let any time slip. Could you please authorise the project brief for the completion phase?"

Rufus looked at the sheaf of papers. "Do I need to read all that?"

"I can read it out to you if you want, but there's nothing we haven't discussed before in some form or another. The exec summary for this proposal is that we're rationalising and streamlining all of our customer packages, shifting certain privileges from one band to another. It's all about clarity."

"Clarity?" scoffed Rufus. "Give me the English version!"

"More and more people are buying their way into higher level packages. Currently, Jaffle Freedom is the highest level, a Jaffle Port with zero restrictions or external influence."

"That's what I've got," said Rufus.

"Exactly. And it was once an exclusive club but people from the lower user levels are increasingly able to buy their Jaffle Freedom outright."

"I like things that are exclusive."

"Quite, sir," said Henderson. "With that in mind, we are going to introduce a new, higher and much more exclusive level, called Jaffle Sunrise."

"Nice name," conceded Rufus. "And how's that different from Jaffle Freedom?"

"At the moment, it isn't."

"Ah," said Rufus. "Now call me a schmuck, but I think I see a flaw in your business plan, Hendo."

"You are correct, sir," the CTO conceded. "Which is why once Operation Sunrise is implemented Jaffle Freedom will take on some of the user terms and conditions of Jaffle Premium."

"You'll limit their service?"

"Minor stuff. The appreciation of abstract concepts relating to art, music, poetry. We'll reduce their capacity for violence and sexual arousal. Just a tad. As I say, Jaffle Freedom will take on many of the characteristics of Jaffle Premium."

"And Jaffle Premium?"

"Will become Jaffle Standard."

"And Standard?"

"Those unable to make the financial leap to Premium will be given a service much like the current Jaffle Lite."

"So there will be even more people on Jaffle Lite?"

"Jaffle Standard, sir. It will be called Jaffle Standard. Those currently on Jaffle Lite will be provided a level of restricted service."

"How restricted?"

"They'll be able to control their own bodies' most basic functions. They'll be able to respond, on a mostly unconscious level, to visual and auditory stimuli. They will be equipped with a basic fear of death, in order to promote self-preservation."

"That *is* restricted," agreed Rufus.

"And therefore Jaffle Tech has benevolently agreed to assist in the social management of the general population."

"Social management?" Rufus grappled for the exact meaning.

"Accommodation, health, employment and so on. We will run people, centrally, for their own good. We've sold the concept to most governing bodies with no problems, because it's the only complete solution that exists. Voting it in will be no problem at all, for obvious reasons. People put themselves in our hands and this is the most straightforward way to ensure everyone's taken care of. The

management of people's hopes and expectations will be simple. Their needs are so much lower at that level."

"Yes, I see that. Isn't it just a little bit wrong though?" asked Rufus, shifting awkwardly in the bed. "I mean, there might be people who don't want to be satisfied with less."

Henderson nodded. "It's a valid challenge, but let's take a moment to reflect upon the oldest adage in business. Wasn't Henry Ford supposed to have said that if he gave customers what they wanted, he'd be working on making a faster horse rather than cars? It's up to us to have the vision to take things forward. It's a win-win situation because it also guarantees the company's bottom line for the next ten years. The projected earnings from this are in the pack and it's bigger than anything we've ever done before. Seriously, the money will be rolling in for years."

"But is this the right thing to do?"

"It's entirely your choice, sir," said Henderson. "We can continue without Operation Sunrise. In fact, if we don't I was planning on purchasing Jaffle Freedom myself."

"You?" said Rufus.

"What else am I going to spend my money on? I've got the largest apartment on the Panhandle. I've got a mansion south of the border. I should buy Jaffle Freedom. And be like you, sir."

Rufus settled back into his pillow and reached for the pen. "When you put it like that, it sounds like it's the way forward."

***

I came back to the room with an actual intake of breath.

Rufus, the real no-longer-a-dream Rufus, stood before me right now. There was a goofy grin on his face as he looked at me.

"Hey," he said softly. "Don't I know you?"

"No," I said, backing away. "We don't know each other at all."

I turned and all but ran. I pushed my way through the throng of the party, pushed my way as far away from Rufus Jaffle and his hateful company as possible.

***

Chapter 32

I went in search of more alcohol. It wasn't going to fix the horror that was playing out in my head, but it might make it slightly more bearable. I grabbed a glass of champagne from a tray. In my haste, I knocked several others. The might-as-well-be-Empty servant bent to catch what she could. I grabbed three and the woman managed to stop two more from spinning to the floor.

"I'm really sorry about that," I said.

She smiled at me but only with her mouth, nothing from her eyes. She moved off without a word.

I found my way out onto the terrace, overlooking the ocean and proceeded to down my three glasses of champagne.

It was crystal clear why Rufus had asked me to delete his memory. The most horrifying part of that memory wasn't that Rufus Jaffle was a callous kangaroo-beater, but the casual way in which Operation Sunrise had been signed off. Rufus had known what he was signing all along. He was fine with it. Perhaps when you were a mega-rich playboy, the idea of the rest of the world being reduced to child-like levels of brain function wasn't a big deal. Perhaps if you had servants to keep you well-fed and a plipper to subdue any problems you could live with a decision like that.

I felt tainted, like I carried the guilt of his actions on his behalf. I was tempted to delete that memory myself and be rid of it.

Oooor you could beeee a whaaaale, sang a voice. Something tried to swim into view in the corner of my vision.

"Shush, you," I muttered and turned away. I juggled the champagne glasses so I had a full one to drink from.

"I'm sure she came through this way," came an approaching voice. It was Claire.

"Does it really matter?" said a tired and unhappy voice. Her husband.

I moved along the terrace and through another door.

There was no longer any point in me staying. I clearly wasn't going to be able to speak with Rufus Jaffle, and I couldn't afford to let Claire see my face. I ducked into the room where the piglet orchestra had been, hoping she wouldn't think to look there, now it was closed

up and in darkness. I hid behind the door, tense with the expectation someone would burst in and discover me at any moment.

I heard the tiniest sound in the darkness, and held my breath. It came again. I realised it was the sound of a piglet.

"Lights," I said and the room lit up. The piglets were still in here, piled up on a trolley.

I shook my head. Jaffle Ports in kangaroos to make them fight wasn't all that different to Jaffle Ports in piglets to make them sing. How was this allowed to continue? Sure, they looked contented enough. Their ports kept them pacified, their boxes were clean and roomy.

"Happy little pigs," I murmured. "In sterile little boxes."

I crouched down before the trolley of little piggy-wigs. It occurred to me, for the first time, these little creatures were the sources of bacon. Of course I knew that delicious salty tangy bacon came from pigs. I had jipped the fact some days ago, but I hadn't made the connection until now. I had eaten their little piggy-wig cousin. I drunkenly wondered if I'd snacked on someone that they'd known, personally.

These poor piglets were stored here in the darkness like baggage, forced to be content with Jaffle chips. Perhaps they were kept this way until they were taken away and turned into bacon.

"And this is supposed to be an animal charity event," I said, sniffing back tears.

One of the pigs snorted and pressed its round snout to the plastic glass.

"It's okay," I said. "I'll make it right."

I unclipped the box and lifted the piglet out. It wriggled and twisted in my hands. I held its warm pink body close and it settled against my chest.

"Okay, Wiggler," I said. "We'll get your brothers and sister out of here too."

I couldn't choose between taking piglets out of boxes or wheeling the entire trolley out. Surely I'd be noticed trying to sneak out with a trolley full of someone else's pigs. There was a curtained off area at the back of the room, not quite a stage but clearly a partitioning area.

Carrying Wiggler, I stepped through a gap. If I could pull down a curtain, maybe I could cover the trolley and wheel it out of the

house unnoticed. I didn't have a clue where to take it or what I would do next. I wasn't exactly thinking straight.

I heard chatter and then a raised voice. "Damn it all! One of them's got out! Number Six!"

"Oops," I said, clutching Wiggler tighter. We pressed on through the labyrinth of black curtains.

I got turned around in there. The curtains were clearly used to screen off a huge central space, turning it into into several rooms. When I re-emerged I was at the edge of another darkened room. It was full of people.

Rows of seats had been laid out facing a lit stage and podium. An audience of maybe thirty to forty was made up of some of the most soberly dressed at the party. I crept along the wall towards the rear exit. It was closed and two security types stood before it.

"It's great to see you!" called Rufus Jaffle.

I whirled. He was on the stage, addressing the whole room. People cheered and applauded.

"Dudes! It's great to see you all!" He grinned.

Dressed in his strange business attire, including shorts and sandals, he looked very different to the people in the audience, but they seemed to love him for it. He held up his hands to calm the noise.

I dropped into the nearest seat and tried to look small.

"Dudes," he said. "We're so happy to have you here today. Hope you're enjoying the event. We laid on the very best food, entertainment and company, but right here is where the magic's gonna happen. Hold tight and you'll get the very latest news on the upcoming, ah, things." He sniffed and rubbed his eye. Over the microphone, his eyeball squeaked. "First up, I wanted to ask if you'd ever thought about whales? Take a moment. Ask yourself what you know about whales. Well I know we're all here to support the animals. I mean, who doesn't love our cute furry friends, huh? But a whale, have you ever thought about those great big dudes? Well, I have, and I wanted to tell you how awesome they are. Did you know they strain krill through their teeth?"

He looked out at the audience. They stared back in mildly confused silence. I was possibly the only person present who knew about his whale-based thought experiments.

He bared his teeth and turned his head so that everyone could get a look. "Check this out. Teeth." His words were distorted by his

unusual expression. "Think about what it would mean if you had to get all of your food by straining it through your teeth. Pretty hard work, huh? Well those dudes do it every day. Every. Single. Day. It's not easy, I can tell you."

He looked around at us all, nodding emphatically, then glanced across the stage as if someone had gestured to him. He scowled.

"Right," he said, more soberly. "So now we're all tuned into the same wavelength – whales. Seriously, man! – it's time to talk about the upcoming changes here in the world of Jaffle Tech."

Someone whooped in the audience. It was a solitary voice but Rufus did a double handed point and nodded like it was the most insightful comment ever.

"We have some truly ground-breaking things for you, like we always do. Have the Jaffle tech-heads ever disappointed? No, they have not. Every time you think they can't top the last amazing thing, they go right ahead and do it! Now, I like to keep an eagle view of things, soaring above everything, at a like, spiritual level. I get my staff to dig in the weeds and get down and dirty. I'm not a details kinda guy. On that basis, I'm going to invite my man Henderson to come up here and explain the new rollout to you all. I'm sure you're gonna love it. Put your hands together and give Hendo some love!"

Henderson walked out onto the stage. He presented a sharp contrast to Rufus Jaffle, in an immaculate suit and looking very carefully groomed.

"Ladies and gentlemen. Shareholders. Colleagues. I know you're all eager to hear the latest update on our corporate strategy, and how Jaffle will be securing the growth of your investment for years to come. If you'll bear with me through this brief presentation, we will follow up with a live demonstration, and I think you will see we hold the future very much in our hands. No other company has had the vision and foresight to solve the world's problems like Jaffle, and this latest development might represent our boldest stride forward yet."

Wiggler nudged my hand. I patted his little head but he nudged me again.

"You want food?" I whispered.

He bit the ends of my fingers. It didn't hurt so much, but I recoiled in surprise, bringing stern glances from the people sitting nearby.

"Shush!" said a woman next to me.

Henderson continued. "Jaffle has ended so many huge problems. There are many medical conditions which we have eradicated. War and conflict around the globe has been reduced. The diminishing resources of the earth can now be distributed in an optimised manner. Starvation is a thing of the past as Jaffle food processing has made nutritious and homogenised rations available to all for free, working with government agencies to unlock funding."

There was applause around the room. Henderson inclined his head in acknowledgement. Rufus Jaffle stood at the side of the stage, determined to take his share of the kudos, shouting "Hell yeah!" and pumping his fist. "Beans for everyone, man!"

Wiggler jumped down from my lap and ran under the row of seats in front. I got down on hands and knees to follow him.

"You shouldn't bring pets in here!" hissed the woman.

I crawled forward along the rows, trying to follow Wiggler.

"This brings me to some of humanity's more recent problems," said Henderson. "Modern lifestyles bring with them a certain level of stress. You may be familiar with the statistics on the amount of information we're expected to absorb in our day to day lives. We have fallen into the trap of enabling information to be fired at us at the speed of light, when we are just not mentally equipped to deal with it. When did we all get so afraid of being bored?"

I moved along a row, squeezing past legs in pursuit of my Wiggler.

"What the hell do you think you're doing?" muttered one man. "We're trying to watch the presentation!"

"Gotcha!" I pounced on a pink lump. As I lifted it I realised it was a pink leather hand bag. A woman snatched it from my hands. "Get off my purse, you maniac!" she said loudly.

"Boredom is *essential*. It's as essential to human well-being as sleep," Henderson continued. "Sensory overload has proven to be a contributing factor in many cases involving violence and sexual misconduct. What's the answer? How can we encourage a return to a simpler life and take away those harmful urges? Does Jaffle have a solution to this?" He smiled around at the audience. "Of course we do."

I was near to the centre of the room, and I had caught sight of Wiggler. He was standing on a seat, apparently trying to reach up to bite a woman's hair. She was staring ahead at the stage, oblivious. I

crept forward and grabbed the naughty piggy, somehow managing to snag the woman's hair. She yelped.

"So sorry," I said as I made my way to an empty seat, holdingWiggler tightly.

I had caused quite a commotion, but the darkness had concealed a lot. A fanfare sounded from the stage, drawing everyone's attention back to Henderson. A screen behind him lit on a live feed, split across numerous rooms in what looked like a communal living space.

"Allow me to introduce our pilot community in North Beach," he said. "These willing volunteers will be among the first to demonstrate the benefits to be gained from our upgraded software. These people have been living together for a short while, but the cracks in this domestic environment are showing already. You will observe on the screen how some have chosen to sit companionably together in the shared space, while others prefer to be alone. Why is that? Does it optimise the accommodation? No, it's very wasteful. Additionally, there are those who engage in wasteful idiosyncratic behaviours. Here, for example, is an obsessive cleaner."

My insides lurched. Hattie was on screen, in an apartment space. It was sparkling clean but she was on her hands and knees, scrubbing the floor. Just visible on the wall was a pinned picture of a baby.

"Cleaning product producers would no doubt approve of this," said Henderson. "But at Jaffle we're taking the long-term holistic view. As we all know, the planet cannot sustain the projected population if we continue consumer spending at its current level."

What was Hattie involved in? Why was she on the screen? I needed to get myself and Wiggler out of there, but I also had to see what this demonstration was.

"Our test subjects will shortly be changed to the most efficient level of operation," said Henderson. "You will quickly appreciate how economies of scale mean that people operating at the new level will place less demand on *all* critical infrastructure. Jaffle will optimise accommodation, food and general well-being for all of these subjects. Success is guaranteed. Those of you who represent our government clients will see how budget juggling becomes a thing of the past. We have a system which can run things much more effectively than we are able to on our own. So, without further ado, I want to show you how our pilot group is transformed by being early adopters. Let me

welcome Rufus Jaffle back onto the stage, so he can initiate the demonstration."

There was more cheering as Rufus walked back centre stage. "Thanks, Henderson! It's such an honour to be able to do this, knowing we're helping to make a new future possible for these folks." He stared at the podium. "We have the button, right? No button. We should have had a button."

Henderson said something to him, off mic.

"Button's in the future," said Rufus. "Right we're gonna do a countdown anyway." He gazed around at the audience. "Count with me, people! Come on! Five, four, three, two, one! Software roll-out now!"

People on the screen fell into similar, slack poses. Henderson stepped forward again to provide commentary.

"See how peace now reigns over our little community? Activity is scaled right back. In fact, breathing will slow right down in these subjects and the requirement for nutrition and ambient heat is therefore reduced, lowering costs all round."

He beamed at the audience, but I couldn't take my eyes off Hattie. She picked herself off the floor, transferred to a chair, sat down and was still. She was an Empty, or as near as made no difference.

Henderson was showing graphs of cost savings. I was too incensed to pay attention. "At a signal, all of the subjects will gather at feeding stations for their optimised food ration. As you can imagine, everyone's diet will be as good as it can possibly be, so health issues will be greatly reduced. Here are the projections of the cost savings for health care per capita of population. Quite a startling message, wouldn't you say?"

A hand went up.

"An audience question? Yes?"

"What if people don't want the new software?" asked a woman near to the front.

"Everyone has already signed up for it," said Henderson. "The latest set of terms and conditions mandate the upgrade, so it will be rolled out to everyone. Only those members of society who are deemed to be part of the core operation will maintain their current status. I should say, by the way, that everyone in this room is automatically included in this category, so please don't be concerned."

People started to chatter with excitement, pointing at the screen.

"We have just issued the signal for the subjects to assemble at the feeding station," said Henderson.

The people on the screen, Hattie included, shambled from their positions towards a central area.

"The signal to rest will be issued in a similar way. The population will go to sleep at the times deemed most suitable."

On screen, a feeding bot wheeled in. Pouches of beans were passed quickly around the group, and they all ate in silence.

I could see, very soon, the majority of the population would be reduced to this. A sob escaped me as I grasped the enormity of what was happening.

A woman tapped me on the shoulder.

"I'm sorry," I heard myself say. "Is my piglet bothering you?"

"I'd prefer you didn't let it touch *my* dress."

I looked up.

"Security!" shouted Claire, grabbing my arm. "We have an intruder! A thief!"

There was noise from all around the room. Security started moving forward.

"Ladies and gentlemen," said Henderson. "If I can just have some calm..."

"Hey! I know that girl!" called Rufus.

I shook off Claire's grip, stood and forced my way along the aisle.

"Let's not make a scene," said Claire's husband although I'm not sure who to.

"This might provide the perfect moment to demonstrate the plipper," Henderson said from the stage.

People were standing. I pushed my way into the crowd as Henderson raised his plipper.

"It's an extra feature we have developed for situations where some immediate control is needed," he shouted over the confusion. "It affects the first Jaffle Port it detects in front of it, so I'm going to need a clear line of sight to deploy this."

I didn't need telling twice to duck and run. I was as keen to mingle with the crowd as they were to get away from me. People shrank back, even screaming as I approached them, bringing the

threat of Henderson's plipper into their orbit. Someone tried to grab my arm and thrust me in front of them but I tugged sharply away.

"Come on, Wiggler, we need to get out of here!"

Henderson's security men piled into the room, heading straight for me. Without thinking, I held Wiggler out in front. The piglet wiggled and clawed at the air, squealing alarmingly. Having a piglet thrust at them made the hardened professionals back up in momentary apprehension. It bought me just enough time to barge through them and out of the nearest door. I ran along a corridor and through a swing door.

I was in a kitchen, filled with steam and fragrance. It drew the attention of Wiggler. As soon as I saw his nose twitching at the air, I knew he was going to be trouble. He slipped from by grip, jumping onto a counter. He trotted towards a tray of pastries, just pausing to sniff and dismiss an ice sculpture in the shape of a swan.

"No, Wiggler! We don't have time!"

I made to grab him. A security guard ran into the kitchen, alerted by the smashing crockery. The large ice sculpture was the only weapon I could see, but I wasn't at all sure I could lift it. I grabbed it by the neck and gave it a hefty shove. It slid along the counter top, me running alongside, pushing to give it some more momentum. The guard paused, eyes on the approaching swan. As it reached the end of the counter, I held onto its neck and swung the whole thing round. It connected with the guard. He dropped like a stone, the swan coming to rest on top of his head.

I ran for another door, piglet back in hand. I found myself outside, near the rear of the building. Which way? I knew Jaffle Tech's security men were sweeping the building, probably working on the assumption I'd be heading for the obvious exits. The low-hedged rear garden was just ahead, so I ran for that, although as cover, it was almost useless. I heard further shouts behind me.

There was a gardening cart further up the path, blocking the way. It was a big yellow thing with wheels. I was pretty sure gardeners use them to carry rubbish away, but right now it was an obstacle. Or ... could it be a blessing in disguise? I ran to it and launched myself on top. Wiggler squeaked in alarm. The cart wheeled rapidly away, spurred by the momentum of my flight. I wriggled forward, only now wondering how I might steer my runaway chariot. Luckily, the narrow garden paths had a raised edge, so when it tried to veer off course we were bumped back into the middle. I

was hurtling faster now, leaving my pursuers behind. I tried to look back and check but the rattling cart blurred my vision. Maybe they were trying to plip me. If I was lucky, they were standing there, vainly clicking their remote controls at my weird, invulnerable brain.

I was going even faster as the path sloped downwards. I saw it ended at a gravel slope before the beach. I clung on as the cart bumped over a change in surface. It slewed sideways, tipped, and I rolled out.

A quick check on Wiggler and I ran on, across the beach. I had some half-formed plan that I might slip into a neighbouring property and make my way out to find transport. As I ran, I heard the sound of a personal drone overhead. I looked up. The drone had passed but I kept my eyes open for Jaffle Swarms. Or whatever else they might send after me.

I struggled across the dry and difficult sand. High dunes, ridged with tufts of grass, bordered the way ahead.

"Please let there be a road," I muttered. A road and a car I could use. Or a friendly open gateway and a house where they'd take me and my piglet in. Sanctuary of some sort. "Please."

A figure appeared at the top of the nearest dune. I hesitated, fearing it was one of the security guards, even Henderson. But then I realised I was looking at Rufus Jaffle. I kept my head down.

"Hey, it's Alice, right?" He didn't look angry. He didn't even look like he comprehended the chaos I had unleashed. "Remember me?"

"I do," I said, playing along. "Sure."

"Nice pig."

"Thanks."

He tickled Wigglers' nose. "Hey, you remember that time when you helped me get the whale out of my head?"

"I do," I said and started to walk away. "I must be going."

"There's no time out here on the beach. You should relax, Alice. Now, before you do go, I want you to know that I'm real grateful for what you did for me back there."

"Back where?"

"The office. The whale. If ever I can repay the favour, you just need to ask, yeah?"

"Well, right now, I just want to get away from here, as discreetly as I can," I said. "Boyfriend problems, you know. I'm just going to walk this way."

"Simplest thing would be for me to drop you home in my drone," he said.

"Drone?"

"Other side of the dunes."

It was tempting.

"C'mon, we'll have you out of here in no time."

As we crested the dune I recognised the drone from Rufus's dream. There were lines of footprints running from it. We followed them down. A drone was the best way to make up lost time, get back to Helberg so he could help me out of another pickle. I had so much to tell him about Operation Sunrise, poor Hattie and— I swallowed. I couldn't afford to indulge those dark thoughts right now.

I put on a smile for Rufus. It pained me at the moment I did it.

"What's wrong, child?" he said. "Your aura's all..." He waved his hands about mystically.

"Your demonstration back there?"

He whirled to look back the way we'd come as though surprised by the notion of *back there*. "Demonstration?"

"Operation Sunrise."

"Oh, that," he made a dismissive gesture. "It's all just business, isn't it?"

"You think it's fair on those people?"

His handsome carefree face screwed up in puzzlement. "Fair? I don't see things as fair or unfair, Alice. I prefer to view things holistically, you know what I mean?"

I shook my head.

As we approached the drone, the door slid open automatically. Interior lights came on, illuminating the luxury bucket seats. Sanctuary.

"My brain, your brain," said Rufus. "It's all the same really, isn't it?"

"I don't know," I said, deciding this man was either lying to himself or lying to me; a conniving schemer or a deluded fool. Either way, I didn't like him and wanted the conversation over.

"Besides," he said, turning to me in the half-lit evening gloom. There was something in his hand. "They do say ignorance is bliss." He raised the plipper and fired it. Nothing happened. I was too upset and tired to play along. "Ignorance is bliss," he repeated and fired again. Nothing.

He fired and fired. Wiggler went limp in my arms.

I punched him in the face, hard, and leapt into the drone.

"Take off!" I said.

The drone did nothing.

"Take off! Lift! Elevate!"

No response. Remembering Helberg's fascinator blocking device I ripped it out of my hair and jipped my instructions. The drone replied I was not an authorised user. I slipped Wiggler's little comatose body into the seat next to me and jumped out. I was going to beat Rufus until he co-operated and flew me out of there. He was on the sand. There was blood on his nose. He looked up at me, squinting.

"Alice, you got some moves on you," he said. "You know Maglev by any chance?"

He glanced over my shoulder. I turned in time to see a man raise something before bringing it down on my head with force.

***

Chapter 33

THE VAN PULLS UP OUTSIDE AN APARTMENT COMPLEX. THE DRIVER STEPS OUT.

"THIS WAY."

THE UNIT IS USHERED OUT.

THE UNIT WEARS COVERALLS. THE COVERALLS ARE GREY. THE APARTMENT COMPLEX IS GREY. THE GROUND IS GREY. THE UNIT'S VISION IS COMPOSED OF SHADES OF GREY. IT SUFFICES.

THE UNIT STANDS AT THE ROADSIDE. FURTHER UP THE ROADSIDE, OTHER UNITS IN COVERALLS ALSO STAND. THEY ARE NOT THE SAME BUT THEY CONGREGATE TOGETHER.

THE DRIVER CLIMBS BACK INTO THE VAN, BUT A SHOUT FROM THE DOORWAY OF THE APARTMENT BLOCK STOPS HIM.

"WHAT ON EARTH HAVE YOU DONE TO HER," SAYS AN INDIVIDUAL.

THE DRIVER LOOKS AT A SCHEDULE DOCUMENT.

"THIS SUBJECT HAS BEEN REDUCED TO A LOWER LEVEL OF SERVICE BECAUSE SHE HAS VIOLATED THE TERMS OF HER AGREEMENT."

"WHAT DOES THAT EVEN MEAN?"

"THIS SUBJECT—"

"STOP SAYING THAT! SERIOUSLY, THE POWER YOU PEOPLE HAVE."

"IT'S NOT ME. I'M JUST FOLLOWING—"

"DON'T YOU DARE. DON'T YOU EVEN DARE. HOW DO I RESTORE HER TO HER NORMAL LEVEL?"

"UH, YOU DON'T," SAYS THE DRIVER.

THE UNIT MOVES TOWARDS THE OTHER UNITS. IT IS NOT A CONSCIOUS DECISION. THEY ARE NOT THE SAME BUT THEY CONGREGATE TOGETHER, DRAWN BY AN INEVITABLE GRAVITY.

"WHEN PEOPLE DOWNLOAD UNAUTHORISED SOFTWARE AND ACCESS HIGHER FUNCTIONS THAN THEY'VE PAID FOR, IT'S A DEAL-BREAKER," SAYS THE DRIVER, "WHEN IT COMES TO THE TERMS AND CONDITIONS. EVERYONE KNOWS THAT."

"I DON'T ACCEPT IT," SAYS THE INDIVIDUAL.

"THIS IS HER LAST REGISTERED ADDRESS, SO I'M GOING TO LEAVE HER HERE, RIGHT?"

"YES, SHE LIVES HERE. WAIT, WAIT. WHAT ABOUT HER STUFF THOUGH? WHERE ARE HER THINGS AND HER CLOTHES?"

"HER NEEDS ARE MET BY THE GOVERNMENT. IF ANYTHING REMAINS IN HER PREVIOUS LIVING QUARTERS, THEY WILL BE REMOVED BY A SERVICE TEAM."

"I DON'T THINK SO."

"SORRY?"

"FINE. DO WHAT YOU NEED TO DO. LEAVE HER WITH ME."

THE VAN DRIVER LEAVES.

SOME TIME LATER – TIME IS NOT SOMETHING THE UNIT MEASURES – THE INDIVIDUAL TAKES HOLD OF THE UNIT'S HAND.

"ALICE? CAN YOU HEAR ME? IT'S ME. PATRICK. HELBERG."

THE INDIVIDUAL DOES NOT LET GO OF THE UNIT'S HAND.

"LET'S GO INSIDE, SHALL WE?"

THE INDIVIDUAL PULLS THE UNIT AWAY FROM THE OTHER UNITS. THE UNIT DOES NOT RESIST. THE UNIT WILL DRIFT BACK TOWARDS THEM EVENTUALLY BUT THE UNIT DOES NOT RESIST. THE INDIVIDUAL PULLS HER INSIDE.

"ALICE, SIT DOWN."

THE INDIVIDUAL PUSHES THE UNIT DOWN INTO A SITTING POSITION ON SOMETHING THAT IS YIELDING AND NOT SOLID.

"YOU CAN AT LEAST HAVE SOMETHING TO EAT."

THE INDIVIDUAL MOVES AROUND THE UNIT. THE UNIT DOES NOT REGISTER THE INDIVIDUAL DIRECTLY. THE INDIVIDUAL IS JUST A CLOUD OF MOVEMENT, A BLUR IN A WORLD OF GREY.

SOMETHING IS PRESENTED TO THE UNIT'S FACE.

"EAT."

SOMETHING IS PRESSED INTO THE UNIT'S MOUTH. THE UNIT CHEWS AND SWALLOWS. THE UNIT FEELS NOTHING, TASTES NOTHING. THERE IS ONLY THE CHEWING AND THE SWALLOWING. IT SUFFICES.

"BACON SANDWICH," SAYS THE INDIVIDUAL.

THE INDIVIDUAL MOVES BACKWARDS AND FORWARDS WITH WORRIED ENERGY. THE UNIT INSTINCTIVELY DRAWS BACK.

"AND DO WE KNOW WHERE HATTIE IS? I ASKED HER TO COME AND VISIT BUT I CAN'T FIND A TRACE OF HER."

THE UNIT RECEIVES A NOTIFICATION AND STANDS.

"WHERE ARE YOU GOING?"

THE UNIT GOES OUTSIDE ONTO THE STREET, TO THE POINT WHERE FOOD WILL BE DISPENSED. THE INDIVIDUAL FOLLOWS THE UNIT. THE UNIT COLLECTS FOOD STUFF AND EATS. WHEN THE UNIT HAS EATEN, THE INDIVIDUAL BRINGS THE UNIT INSIDE AGAIN.

THE INDIVIDUAL HOLD THE UNIT BY THE SHOULDERS.

"I'M GOING TO FIX YOU. YOU KNOW THAT, DON'T YOU? LOOK AT ME. LOOK AT ME." THE INDIVIDUAL RAISES THE UNIT'S CHIN. "I'M NOT SURE HOW I'M GOING TO DO IT YET, BUT JUST HANG IN THERE, ALICE."

THE UNIT DOESN'T RESPOND. A WHILE LATER – TIME IS NOT SOMETHING THE UNIT MEASURES – THERE IS ANOTHER NOTIFICATION. THE UNIT LIES DOWN TO SLEEP.

AS THE UNIT BEGINS TO SHUT DOWN, A LARGE FORM SWIMS INTO VIEW. THE LARGE FORM IS BLUE, THE ONLY BLUE IN A WORLD OF GREY.

"Sleepy head, sleepy head. Down by the sea, fishies are making their beds," SINGS THE WHALE. *"Blankets and a mattress for you. Nice guy, that."*

***

Chapter 34

A NOTIFICATION WAKES THE UNIT.

THE UNIT LEAVES THE APARTMENT BUILDING AND WALKS TO JAFFLE TECH'S OFFICES IN JAFFLE PARK. IT IS A PLACE OF WORK.

THE UNIT DOES NOT GO TO THE BUILDING. THE UNIT IS INTERCEPTED BY A SUPERVISOR AND GIVEN AN OBJECT.

THE OBJECT IS A BROOM.

THE UNIT PUSHES THE BROOM ALONG PATHWAYS, STEPPING ASIDE TO AVOID OBSTACLES. THERE ARE BOTS ON THE PATHS AS WELL. SOME OF THE BOTS CONTAIN SECURITY SENSORS. SOME OF THE BOTS CARRY OUT CLEANING DUTIES.

THE BOTS CLEAN. THE UNIT CLEANS. IT IS A PLACE OF WORK.

AN INDIVIDUAL IN A TUNIC WALKS PAST THE UNIT.

"YOU MISSED A BIT," INDIVIDUAL IN A TUNIC SAYS AND THEN WALKS AWAY, LAUGHING.

THE UNIT LOOKS FOR THE BIT THAT WAS MISSED.

LATER – TIME IS NOT SOMETHING THE UNIT MEASURES – A LINE OF UNITS LEAVE THE PLACE OF WORK. THE WORK IS COMPLETE. THE UNITS RESPOND TO SEPARATE SIGNALS BUT THEY MOVE AS A GROUP AS THEY WALK DOWN THE STREET. THE UNIT'S GAZE IS DOWNWARDS. THE UNIT AVOIDS OBSTACLES. THERE IS NO NEED TO INTERACT WITH THE GREY WIDER WORLD.

CARS AVOID THE UNITS. HUMAN INDIVIDUALS AVOID THE UNITS. HUMANS KEEP AS MUCH DISTANCE FROM THE UNITS AS POSSIBLE. THE UNITS FALL IN STEP WITH ONE ANOTHER. THEY ARE NOT THE SAME BUT THEY CONGREGATE. THEY RESPOND TO SEPARATE SIGNALS BUT THEY MOVE AS A GROUP.

LEFT, RIGHT, LEFT, RIGHT.

"Swim with your friends, look at them all at your side. Be like a whale! Beeeee like a whaaaaale!" SINGS THE WHALE.

THE WHALE IS BLUE. THE WORLD IS GREY.

"It's fuuun being aaaa whaaaaale."

THE UNIT STOPS OUTSIDE THE APARTMENT BLOCK. THE UNIT STANDS AT THE ROADSIDE UNTIL IT IS TIME TO EAT FOOD STUFF. THE UNIT CHEWS AND SWALLOWS. IT SUFFICES.

THE INDIVIDUAL COMES OUTSIDE AND TAKES THE UNIT BY THE HAND.

"COME INSIDE, ALICE. YOU'LL GET COLD OUT HERE."

THE INDIVIDUAL LEADS THE UNIT INSIDE. HE SITS THE UNIT DOWN ON THE YIELDING NOT SOLID OBJECT. THE INDIVIDUAL PRESENTS A SERIES OF THINGS TO HER MOUTH AGAIN.

"BACON? PIZZA? GLASS OF SHERRY?" THE INDIVIDUAL MAKES A SOUND – IT SOUNDS LIKE LAUGHTER BUT IT ALSO SOUNDS LIKE A NOISE OF DISTRESS. THE UNIT DOES NOT RECOGNISE IT SO DOES NOT RESPOND TO IT.

THE INDIVIDUAL SIGHS AND PACES THE FLOOR.

"I FETCHED ALL OF YOUR STUFF, AND HATTIE'S TOO. IT'S HIDDEN SAFE FOR WHEN YOU NEED IT AGAIN. I CAN'T BEAR THE WAY THEY'RE TREATING YOU. I KNOW YOU ALWAYS WORRIED ABOUT EVERYONE THAT'S TREATED THIS WAY. I GUESS I CLOSED MY EYES TO IT. BUT ANYWAY, THAT WAS BEFORE YOU WERE ONE OF THEM. NOW I CAN'T BEAR IT. I CAN'T BEAR IT BECAUSE I KNOW WHAT YOU'RE REALLY LIKE, AND I FIND MYSELF WONDERING IF ALL THESE OTHER PEOPLE ARE AMAZING AS WELL, BUT YOU'D NEVER KNOW IT. JEEZ, I'M RAMBLING."

THE INDIVIDUAL THROWS HIMSELF NOISILY INTO A SEATING POSITION. THE UNIT INSTINCTIVELY DRAWS BACK.

"ANYWAY, I'VE BEEN TALKING TO SOME FRIENDS. I HAD AN IDEA ABOUT HACKING YOUR PORT. IF I CAN GET IT WORKING, IT MIGHT BE SOMETHING THAT SCALES UP. I COULD BROADCAST IT, USE IT ON OTHER EMPTIES. I KNOW YOU'D APPROVE OF THAT. WE'VE ONLY GOT TWO DAYS UNTIL OPERATION SUNRISE."

THERE IS A NOTIFICATION. THE UNIT LIES DOWN TO SLEEP.

***

Chapter 35

A NOTIFICATION WAKES THE UNIT.

THE UNIT WALKS TO JAFFLE TECH'S OFFICES IN JAFFLE PARK.

BEFORE THE UNIT REACHES JAFFLE PARK, THE UNIT IS INTERCEPTED BY AN INDIVIDUAL IN CLOTHES THAT ARE NOT COVERALLS.

THE INDIVIDUAL GRABS THE UNIT'S SHOULDERS AND TWIRLS HER BODILY AROUND.

"LOOK WHO IT IS! OH DARLING, YOU LOOK SO MUCH BETTER IN THOSE COVERALLS! YOU MUST TELL ME WHERE YOU GOT THEM FROM. NOW, I KNOW YOU APPRECIATE THE FINER THINGS IN LIFE, ALICE, SO HOW WOULD YOU LIKE TO JOIN ME IN A TOAST TO YOUR NEW STATUS? GLASS OF WINE PERHAPS, OR A FINE SCOTCH?"

THE UNIT WALKS ON.

"DO STOP BY AGAIN! WE CAN DISCUSS ALL OF THE FUN THINGS YOU'RE DOING WITH YOUR TIME, ALICE! PERHAPS WE COULD DO LUNCH, HMM?"

THE INDIVIDUAL IN CLOTHES THAT ARE NOT COVERALLS TRILLS WITH LAUGHTER AND WALKS BACK UP THE PATH TOWARDS A BUILDING. THE CLOTHES THAT ARE NOT COVERALLS FLOAT AROUND HER LEGS.

AT JAFFLE PARK, THE UNIT IS INTERCEPTED BY A SUPERVISOR AND GIVEN A BROOM.

THE UNIT PUSHES THE BROOM ALONG PATHWAYS, STEPPING ASIDE TO AVOID OBSTACLES.

THERE IS SOMETHING ON THE PATH THAT ISN'T FOR SWEEPING. THE UNIT CANNOT FIT THE BROOM AROUND THE SIDE. THE SOMETHING ON THE PATH MOVES WHEN THE UNIT MOVES THE BROOM. THE SOMETHING ON THE PATH IS SMALL AND COVERED IN FUR. IT HAS A TINY TWITCHING NOSE.

THE UNIT DOES NOT POSSESS THE PROBLEM-SOLVING CAPABILITY TO RESOLVE THE ISSUE. THE UNIT STANDS STILL, UNABLE TO PROCEED. SOMEONE APPROACHES, AN INDIVIDUAL IN A SECURITY UNIFORM.

"IT'S OKAY. IT'S OKAY. I'LL DEAL WITH THIS PESKY VARMINT."

THE SECURITY GUARD HAS A PLASTIC BOX TUCKED UNDER HIS ARM. HE BENDS AND SCOOPS UP THE SOMETHING – THE 'PESKY VARMINT' – INTO THE PLASTIC BOX.

"I DON'T STOMP ON MICE," SAYS THE SECURITY GUARD. "NOT REALLY. I'LL TAKE CARE OF IT, YABETCHA."

THE SECURITY GUARD TAKES THE UNIT'S ARM.

"COME WITH ME."

THE SECURITY GUARD LEADS THE UNIT INTO THE BUILDING.

"YOU CAN LEAVE THE BROOM THERE. IT WILL BE THERE WHEN YOU GET BACK."

THE SECURITY GUARD AND THE UNIT GO DOWN TO A BASEMENT LEVEL. THE SECURITY GUARD TAKES THE UNIT TO A SPACE WITH SEVERAL ROOMS. THIS ROOM CONTAINS A DESK, A TABLE AND SOME CHAIRS. THE TABLE HAS A CLOTH ON IT, A POT OF HOT LIQUID AND SOME FOOD STUFF. THE ITEMS OF FOOD STUFF ARE ROUND AND DOUGHY AND HAVE HOLES IN THE MIDDLE. ANOTHER INDIVIDUAL IS THERE, SITTING ON A CHAIR NEXT TO THE TABLE. THIS INDIVIDUAL WEARS A SUPPORT WORKER'S TUNIC. THE SECURITY SITS THE UNIT ON A CHAIR NEXT TO THE SUPPORT WORKER.

"LOOK AT YOU TWO," SAYS THE SECURITY GUARD. "HATTIE AND ALICE. OL' PALS BACK TOGETHER AGAIN."

THE UNIT HAS BEEN SAT DOWN.

"I'LL PUT THIS LI'L FELLA IN A CAGE WITH THE OTHERS," SAYS THE SECURITY GUARD AND TURNS TO A FAR WALL. HE MOVES A CONCEALING PANEL BOARD ASIDE AND REVEALS CAGES ON THE SHELVES, WITH LOTS OF OTHER 'PESKY VARMINTS' INSIDE. MANY OF THE CAGES CONNECT TO ONE ANOTHER, GIVING THE VARMINTS FREEDOM TO MOVE FROM ONE TO THE OTHER. THE SECURITY GUARD PUTS THE VARMINT INTO A CAGE, PROVIDES IT WITH FOOD STUFF AND WATER THEN GENTLY SHUTS THE DOOR.

THE SECURITY GUARD COMES BACK TO THE TABLE, POURS HOT LIQUID INTO A MUG AND SITS DOWN, REACHING FOR A ROUND FOOD STUFF.

"HOO-WEE. THINGS ARE MESSED UP," SAYS THE SECURITY GUARD. "YOU SEE ALL THESE MICE?"

THE UNIT DOES NOT RESPOND. THE INDIVIDUAL IN THE TUNIC DOES NOT RESPOND. THE INDIVIDUAL IN THE TUNIC IS NOT A UNIT BUT THERE IS A SIMILARITY.

"WE'RE LIVING IN A WORLD WHERE MICE ARE AN UNEXPECTED ANOMALY," SAYS THE SECURITY GUARD. "WE'RE NOT SET UP TO DEAL WITH THEM. THESE BUILDINGS. WE'VE ACCIDENTALLY PROVIDED THEM WITH THEIR OWN SUPERHIGHWAYS IN AND OUT OF ANY BUILDING WITH MILES AND MILES OF NETWORK CONDUIT. EVERYTHING'S SUPPOSEDLY INTEGRATED. WE'VE GOT BIG SYSTEMS, YES SIRREE, BIG SYSTEMS TO DEAL WITH BIG PROBLEMS BUT THAT MEANS THE LITTLE DETAILS GO UNNOTICED."

HE EATS A MOUTHFUL OF FOOD STUFF AND DRINKS THE DRINK.

"We leave garbage piled in the streets where the bots aren't joined up with the civic disposal service. So the rodent population is out of control, and all anyone cares is that they don't get seen in the office building." He chuckles and looks at the unit. "I had to think on my feet when you caught me. Pretending to stamp on thin air when I already had Mortimer safely captured in ma lunch box." He shakes his head. "It seems as though nobody's noticed that we just don't have a joined-up society any more. My apartment block's falling apart. There aren't even any numbers on the doors. Can you believe that?"

He hoots with laughter.

"So, a long story. I guess you deserve to hear it, even though you're kinda unaware. I know that everyone sees me as tough-guy Levi the enforcer of rules, but the sorry truth is that I don't much like the rules we got round here. Don't get me wrong, I think we all need to have some respect for each other. I'd hate to see folks running around doing whatever crazy thing popped into their head." He heaves a big sigh. "No, even that's not quite true, because that's sorta what you did Alice, and I loved seeing you do it."

His attention is focused on the unit. The unit has not received a notification but feels a need to find the broom and continue sweeping.

"What I mean to say is that sometimes people make poor decisions. All well and good if they mess up their own world – that's their problem. Trouble is, we're living in a world now where the decisions of a few people affect us all. You two were like a breath of fresh air. Hattie's a real sweetheart, so much love in her that it makes me want to burst. And you, Alice, you're one-of-a-kind. You always thought outside the box even before you knew you were in a box."

The unit stands.

"I don't know how you got yourself upgraded," the security guards says, "but it made me real happy to see you taking flight with that goddamned crazy mind of yours. I did what I could to protect you, editing CCTV footage and such..."

The unit goes to the door.

"I gotta say I'm sorry to see the two of you reduced to this," says the security guard. "Real sorry. I can't be the only person who looks around and wonders what's going on. I guess

THE PEOPLE WHO CAN SEE ALL THE WRONG IN THE WORLD ARE COWARDS LIKE ME. THE ONES WITH ALL THE POWER LIVE IN THEIR MANSIONS BY THE OCEAN AND THEY DON'T SEE THE WRECKED CARS AND THE TRASH IN THE STREET AND..."

THE UNIT WALKS OUT AND MOVES TOWARDS THE STAIRS.

"I WANT YOU BOTH TO KNOW THAT I'M LOOKING OUT FOR YA," THE SECURITY GUARD CALLS AFTER HER.

THE UNIT WALKS UP TO ENTRANCE LEVEL.

THE BROOM IS WHERE IT HAD BEEN LEFT.

"You can aaaall swim away with me. Come on, it's beauuuutiful!" SAYS THE WHALE, ROLLING INTO VIEW AS THE UNIT LEAVES THE BUILDING. *"Looook! I have a taaaaaaaaaaaaaaaail!"*

THE UNIT PUSHES THE BROOM ALONG PATHWAYS.

A LINE OF UNITS LEAVE THE PLACE OF WORK. THE WORK IS COMPLETE. THE UNITS RESPOND TO SEPARATE SIGNALS BUT THEY MOVE AS A GROUP.

"Swim with your friends," SAYS THE WHALE.

THE UNIT GRUNTS.

OUTSIDE THE JAFFLE COMPOUND THE EMPTIES FALL IN STEP WITH ONE ANOTHER ONCE AGAIN. LEFT, RIGHT, LEFT, RIGHT. IT APPEARS ALMOST ORDERLY.

"Beeeee like a whale! Beeeee like a whaaaaaale!" SINGS THE WHALE.

"MMF! MMF!" GRUNTS THE UNIT, KEEPING TIME WITH THE MARCHING.

THE UNIT STOPS OUTSIDE THE APARTMENT BLOCK. THE UNIT STANDS AT THE ROADSIDE. THERE IS FOOD STUFF.

THE INDIVIDUAL COMES OUTSIDE AND TAKES THE UNIT INSIDE.

THE INDIVIDUAL SITS THE UNIT DOWN AND ALSO SITS DOWN.

"I HAVEN'T MADE THE PROGRESS I EXPECTED IN HACKING YOUR BRAIN PORT. IT'S LOCKED DOWN SO WELL. I GUESS I'M NOT THE FIRST PERSON TO TRY THIS, SO THEY HAVE REALLY TIGHT SECURITY. IT WOULD TAKE ME ABOUT SEVENTY YEARS TO CRACK THE ENCRYPTION THEY HAVE IN THERE. I'M BEGINNING TO THINK I NEED A DIFFERENT APPROACH. AT THE MOMENT IT'S A TOSS-UP BETWEEN KIDNAPPING SOMEONE HIGH UP AT JAFFLE AND MAKING THEM AUTHORISE ME AS A SYSTEM ADMIN, OR I NEED TO BREAK IN THERE AND GET ACCESS TO THEIR SERVERS."

THE INDIVIDUAL SIGHS DEEPLY. THERE IS A CRACK AS IT OPENS A TIN OF DRINK STUFF.

"Both of those sound like pretty tricky options. I need to try something though. I can't leave you like this."

Eventually there is a notification. The unit lies down to sleep.

***

Chapter 36

A NOTIFICATION WAKES THE UNIT.

THE UNIT JOINS OTHER UNITS TO WALK TO THE PLACE OF WORK.

AS THE UNIT JOINS THEM, THE WHALE SINGS.

"Beeee like a whale! Beeee like aaa whaaaaale!"

THE UNIT MURMURS AND SWAYS IN TIME. "MMF! MMF!"

A JAFFLE SWARM PASSES THE UNIT, PARTING LIKE A FLUID SO THAT IT CAN PASS AROUND. THE UNIT DOES NOT NOTICE. THE UNIT DOES NOT REACT. A CAR PULLS UP OUTSIDE THE APARTMENT BUILDING. IT MAKES A SIREN NOISE. ITS LIGHTS ARE WHITE AND LIGHT GREY.

THE UNIT HAS LEFT THE DOOR OF THE APARTMENT COMPLEX. THE SWARM ENTERS AHEAD OF THE INDIVIDUALS IN UNIFORMS. THE UNIFORMED INDIVIDUALS EXIT SHORTLY AFTERWARDS WITH ANOTHER INDIVIDUAL STRUGGLING TO BREAK FREE FROM THEM.

"WHAT ON EARTH DO YOU THINK YOU'RE DOING?" YELLS THE CAPTURED INDIVIDUAL. "I'VE DONE NOTHING WRONG! HOW CAN THIS BE FAIR? HOW CAN THIS EVEN BE LEGAL?"

AN AUTOMATED VOICE SPEAKS.

"PATRICK HELBERG, YOU ARE BEING DETAINED BY JAFFLE SECURITY FOR ASSESSMENT. THE CHARGE AGAINST YOU IS THAT YOU HAVE BEEN OR ARE CURRENTLY ENGAGED IN ACTIVITIES THAT COMPROMISE THE CYBER SECURITY OF CRITICAL NATIONAL INFRASTRUCTURE. THESE CHARGES ARE BEING INVESTIGATED BY OUR SYSTEMS AND WILL REQUIRE SCANNING OF ALL PERSONAL ELECTRONIC EQUIPMENT AND SAMPLING OF YOUR BODILY TISSUE. YOU WILL BE DETAINED UNTIL THIS PROCESS IS COMPLETE."

"NO! I DO NOT CONSENT TO THIS! YOU CAN'T MAKE ME!" THE INDIVIDUAL HOWLS. THE AUTOMATED VOICE RECITES THE SAME MESSAGE ON A LOOP AND THE INDIVIDUAL IS FORCED INTO THE CAR. THERE IS NOW QUIET. THE UNIT DOES NOT NOTICE. THE UNIT DOES NOT REACT.

THE BLUE WHALE ROLLS IN A SKY THAT IS NOT BIG ENOUGH TO CONTAIN IT.

"Beeee like a whale! Beeee like aaa whaaaaale!"

THE UNIT AMONG THE LINE OF THE OTHER UNITS REACH THE END OF THE STREET. THEIR MOVEMENT IS SOMETHING LIKE A SLOW-MOVING VERSION OF A JAFFLE SWARM.

THEY ARE NOT THE SAME BUT THEY CONGREGATE.

THE WHALE SINGS.

THE UNIT MURMURS AND MUMBLES AS THE WHALE SINGS.

AS THE WHALE SINGS, THE UNITS MOVE.

LEFT, RIGHT, LEFT, RIGHT.

THE RHYTHM OF THE UNITS IS NOT THE SAME AS THE RHYTHM OF THE WHALE'S SONG.

THE UNIT SWAYS IN TIME TO THE WHALE'S SONG.

THE UNIT GRUNTS. "MMF! MMF!"

THEY CONGREGATE BUT THEY ARE NOT THE SAME. THEY RESPOND TO SEPARATE SIGNALS.

"Beeee like a whaaaaale!"

SOME OF THE UNITS NOW TAKE UP THE GRUNTING START BY THE UNIT. THEY DO NOT KEEP TIME.

EACH UNIT MAKES A FRACTION OF THE SOUND, BUT WHEN THEY ARE ALL HEARD TOGETHER, IT SOUNDS DISTINCT, WHOLE. THE SOUND IS A BODY OF WORK.

"BE LIKE A WHALE! BE LIKE A WHALE!"

UNITS FROM ELSEWHERE HAVE DRIFTED OVER TO THE GROUP, DRAWN BY AN INEVITABLE GRAVITY.

AS MORE UNITS JOIN THE GROUP, THE SINGING SWELLS. THE NOISE IS SINGING. THE BLUE WHALE SINGS. THE GROUP SINGS.

THE UNITS RESPOND TO SEPARATE SIGNALS BUT THE MOVEMENTS OF THE GROUP BECOME MORE CO-ORDINATED AND PURPOSEFUL. THE GROUP IS ITS OWN BODY OF WORK. THE GROUP'S BODY IS LARGE AND LONG, A BULBOUS BODY AND A SLOW. SWISHING TAIL. LEFT, RIGHT, LEFT, RIGHT.

"I'm aaaaa whaaaaaaaale with aaa taaaaaaaaaail!"

AS IT MOVES AROUND THE STREETS, THE BODY GROWS IN SIZE, ATTRACTING MORE AND MORE UNITS. IT BECOMES SO LARGE THAT IT FILLS THE STREET, ITS TAIL SWISHING AND ITS VOICE BOOMING.

"Yooooou can haaave aaa taaaaaaaaaaaaaail tooooooo!"

THE BODY STOPS TRAFFIC AS IT CROSSES ROADS. CARS AVOID THE BODY OF THE WHALE. HUMAN INDIVIDUALS AVOID THE BODY OF THE WHALE.

A JAFFLE SWARM SWOOPS IN TO INVESTIGATE. CARS ARRIVE WITH FLASHING LIGHTS AND INDIVIDUALS WITH UNIFORMS. SEVERAL INDIVIDUALS WALK UP AND DOWN, OBSERVING THE BODY. THEY TRY TO ENGAGE WITH THE UNITS, BUT THEY GET NO RESPONSE. THEY SPEAK TO THE UNITS BUT NOT THE WHALE.

"WE'VE GOT A LARGE GROUP OF INDIVIDUALS MARCHING TOGETHER," AN INDIVIDUAL SAYS. "THEY ARE ACTING LIKE THEY'RE A SINGLE, AH, THING."

"PRETENDING THEY'RE A FISH OR SOMETHING," SAYS ANOTHER INDIVIDUAL.

"YEAH, IT LOOKS PRETTY CRAZY."

THE UNIFORMED INDIVIDUALS ERECT A ROADBLOCK, MADE OF LARGE PLASTIC BARRIERS. THE BODY OF THE WHALE APPROACHES IT. THE BODY OF THE WHALE CANNOT FIT AROUND THE SIDE OF THE BARRIER. THE BARRIER IS LONG AND THE WHALE IS LARGE.

THE BODY OF THE WHALE DOES NOT SLOW. THE UNITS THAT COMPRISE THE BODY CARRY ON, CLIMBING OVER THE BARRIERS. THE BARRIERS ARE EVENTUALLY CRUSHED.

ANOTHER VEHICLE ARRIVES AND AN INDIVIDUAL IN A JAFFLE TECH SECURITY UNIFORM GETS OUT. HE HOLDS A PLIPPER. HE RAISES IT TOWARDS THE BODY AND SHOUTS A WARNING. THE UNITS DO NOT NOTICE. THE UNITS DO NOT REACT. THE SECURITY GUARD PRESSES THE BUTTON ON THE PLIPPER.

THERE IS NO CHANGE IN ANY PART OF THE BODY. THE SECURITY GUARD PRESSES THE BUTTON REPEATEDLY. HE FINDS ANOTHER ONE IN HIS POCKET AND TRIES THAT. HE PRESSES IT AGAIN AND AGAIN WHILE POINTING IT AT THE BODY BUT THERE IS NO CHANGE. HE TURNS IT AROUND AND POINTS IT AT HIMSELF, BUT HESITATES. HE TURNS TO A UNIFORMED INDIVIDUAL WHO IS TRYING TO TALK TO THE BODY. THE SECURITY GUARD POINTS THE PLIPPER AT THE UNIFORMED INDIVIDUAL WHO DROPS INSTANTLY.

THE UNIFORMED INDIVIDUAL, NOW A UNIT, PICKS ITSELF UP AND JOINS THE BODY OF THE WHALE.

"BE LIKE A WHALE! BE LIKE A WHALE!" THE UNITS SING.

THE JAFFLE SECURITY GUARD GETS BACK INTO THE VEHICLE. THE BODY MARCHES ON. AS ITS NUMBERS SWELL, IT BECOMES INCREASINGLY PLAYFUL. THE WHALE LUXURIATES IN ITS EXTRAVAGANT MOVEMENTS AND ALTERS ITS SONG.

"SWIM LIKE A WHALE! BE LIKE A WHALE! JOIN US IN THE WHALE!" IT CHANTS.

A JAFFLE SWARM DESCENDS TO MONITOR THE SITUATION. SOMETHING TUGS AT THE EDGE OF THE SWARM.

IT IS CAUGHT IN THE WHALE'S WAKE. IT IS PULLED BY ITS CURRENTS. PART OF THE SWARM PEELS APART AND JOINS THE WHALE. A SECOND SWARM IS SENT, AND THAT JOINS IN WITH THE WHALE AS WELL.

The whale has now absorbed all of the units in the district. As the whale passes through other districts, individuals watch from inside their houses.

The units know nothing. The whale knows the individuals are worried, fearful.

A group of ponies in a paddock raise their heads and listen. The whale knows they have Jaffle Ports, optimised to be biddable and patient pets. The units know nothing. The ponies feel the pull of the whale. The ponies canter across their paddock and jump the gate without difficulty. They join the whale and lend their voices to the song.

"You can't just let them go!" shouts an individual. "They were expensive. Do something!"

An individual is on the doorstep of her house, urging someone inside to retrieve the ponies, but the door is slammed shut as the whale surges down the street.

Flower beds are trampled. The walls of houses are scraped by the passing of the massive whale.

Media drones circle above the whale. Cars swerve to avoid collisions as the whale takes to one of the premium roads. Lane after lane of traffic is rendered stationary.

Other units have joined the body.

Jaffle swarms have been pulled in. With insect eyes, the whale regards itself. The tail swooshes and the whale looks very much as though it's leaping through water. The whale loves swimming.

Animals have joined the body of the whale. Pets, livestock. Anything fitted with a chip can hear the song.

The whale passes a city zoo. Individuals panic as a riotous uprising of zoo animals ensues. Animals break free of their enclosures and pens. Elephants and hippopotamuses stampede to join the whale. Kangaroos bound between and among them. Big predatory cats, solitary hunters, find unity in the body of the whale. Tropical birds and snakes become a visible part of the whale's wake.

The whale swims with joyful flicks of its tail along the premium road. Whale swims through a sea of cars. The swarm components of the whale capture the expressions on the faces of the cars' occupants. Disbelief and panic is everywhere on the faces of individuals.

"Swim like a whale! Be like a whale! Join us, we're going to swim away!"

The whale is close to the actual ocean as the road swings round, hugging the coast. As the road drops, the whale takes the exit to the bay.

"Swim like a whale! Across the sea!"

The whale doesn't stop. It moves along a wide pier, once a fishing pier, now occupied only by strolling individuals. They scatter at the approach of the whale. Its tail flicks are huge now. The unit can smell the ocean. The whale can smell the ocean. As it reaches the end, the whale dives off in a perfect arc.

The unit does not know how to swim but the whale knows how to swim. The unit moves with others, linking arms, lifted by a hippopotamus. The whale swims out. Jaffle sharks move to intercept the whale and become part of it.

Boats and drones are launched towards the whale. Parts of the whale are hauled out of the water. The individuals in boats do not know what to do about the tigers. The tide is coming in and units and animals are being washed ashore.

Strong arms grasp the unit and pull the unit into a boat.

***

Chapter 37

"Swim like a whale," the unit murmurs.

The unit's feet flip and flop on the hospital trolley.

A sedative is injected in the unit's arm. The unit does not register it. The unit does not respond. The unit murmurs weakly, her feet flipping on a hospital trolley.

"Going to need some help from a techie," an individual shouts to colleague. "Never seen anything like this before."

"Glitchy upgrade?" said the colleague individual.

A screen shows data on the unit's vital signs.

"Call Jaffle," says an individual.

"Tried. They're in total lockdown. Reception told me they have a big rollout scheduled for today. All of their experts are deployed in the field, whatever the hell that means. I got cut off and now I can't get back through."

"I bet everyone and his dog are calling up to ask about this shitstorm on the news. It doesn't look good for them."

"Doesn't alter the fact that we've got patients to treat and we have no idea what we're dealing with here."

There is a lot of noise around the unit. Every bed, cubicle and trolley is full. Individuals are working to handle the enormous influx. The individuals do not know what to do.

"We need to wait for Jaffle to get back to us with some advice."

"Are you kidding? We're turning ambulances away at the door. We can't waste any more time. We need to try something. I say we roll everyone back to the last known backup. I can see no reason why it would cause any harm. Johnson?"

Individuals consult with one another.

The unit wiggles feet and sings the song of the whale. The whale has dispersed but it is still the whale.

"—If it appears to be successful then they will repeat on the others. This ... Alice Tennerman. Do her first."

"Vital signs are stable. Patient has a backup from six weeks ago."

The unit receives a notification. The unit is to have her brain state restored to its backup state from twenty days ago.

An individual runs through the procedure for backup restore with the colleague. As they talk, the unit feels the same process being carried out via her Jaffle Port.

"Procedure complete. Continue to monitor vitals," says the individual.

The doctor moves on to the next patient.

***

Chapter 38 – 19th June

I wondered what that funny smell was. I lifted my head and saw I was on a trolley, like the ones in hospitals. No, I *was* in hospital. I lifted a corner of the metallic blanket covering me and found I was wearing coveralls, like an Empty. Oh. Wow. I'd being plipped or something very much like it.

My memories were vague, like a fading dream. I clutched at them. There had definitely been something to do with the blue whale. Where was it? I'd been singing, it had been beautiful, but now the whale was gone. I missed it, even though it could be really annoying. I lay still, trying to work out what was happening.

"Vitals good. We got a backup from a month ago," said a voice from nearby.

Someone with a white coat leaned over the trolley near my feet. Were hospitals always this crowded? It seemed as though every available space contained someone with a metallic blanket like mine.

"Restore done. Monitor vitals. Moving on."

Something serious must have happened if we were all being restored from our last viable backup. Luckily for me, my backup was from before I was a plipped to Empty status. I figured I shouldn't be shouting about that. From what I could see most of the patients seemed to be wearing pink coveralls, so the expected outcome would be for everyone to still be an Empty. I kept still. The doctors moved down the lines – so many people! I waited until they were a good distance away before slipping off the trolley.

My clothes were dry but there was a dirty – salty? – stiffness to them. Had I been swimming?

Out in the corridor, I saw an object: a broom. I picked it up instinctively. An Empty with a broom was as invisible and non-threatening as it was possible to be. I adopted a shambling gait and left the building as quickly as I could manage.

I moved out into the area surrounding the park, shuffling along the paths through the trees, sweeping bark and fallen leaves. Pushing the broom was therapeutic. There was a cadence in the noise and the motion that recalled something of the blue whale. It helped me sift through my more recent memories. My software had been rolled back to a previous setting, but the memories I had formed in recent

weeks were intact. It was odd to have memories from the time when I was an Empty.

I pushed the broom along and remembered Claire mocking me. I gripped the broom and imagined it was her scrawny neck. She was going to feel my wrath at some point soon.

I remembered what had happened to Hattie, and also that she had been in Levi's basement. I smiled, knowing she was safe. And I almost stopped in my tracks when I remembered the things Levi had said to us.

I remembered Helberg promising he would find a way to help. If anyone had the technical know-how to foil Jaffle's dreadful plans, it was Helberg. I also remembered the police taking him. No, they were Jaffle security. I remembered what they'd said.

How long ago that was, I had no idea. I jipped the time. Accessing the time and date was odd, like stretching a muscle I hadn't used in a long time.

"Crumbs!" I said out loud.

***

Chapter 39 – 1 hour and 56 minutes until Operation Sunrise

I had no time at all.

There were less than two hours until Operation Sunrise was rolled out. Everyone would be downgraded, Jaffle Freedom to Jaffle Premium, Premium to Enhanced, Enhanced to Standard, Lite to the restricted service of the Empties. Hattie and the others at the North Beach arcology had already been downgraded, her dreams snuffed out. But maybe there was some way to stop the rollout, to undo what had been done.

I recalled Rufus Jaffle at the charity gala. The man wanted a big red button to launch the rollout. Clearly Jaffle headquarters was where I needed to be. Hattie evidently still worked there, and it was certainly where Jaffle security would take Helberg. Maybe I could get him to help Operation Sunrise if I could get him out. Or maybe we just needed to get into Rufus's office and stop a hand from pressing that button.

I had to think quickly. And I had to move quickly. I marched towards the edge of the parkland, carrying the broom. It was important. If I had the broom and the pink coveralls of an Empty, nobody would stop me from getting onto Jaffle Park. But, then again, I couldn't do the slow *Empty shuffle* if I was going to get there in time.

I jipped for a car.

Then I recalled Jaffle Tech was probably tracking me right now. If their systems spotted Alice Tennerman was no longer an Empty, they'd have me captured and returned to Empty status as soon as possible.

I looked up fearfully at the sky, expecting a Jaffle swarm to be observing me at that very moment.

I moved back into the cover of a eucalyptus tree and sat down with my back to the trunk. I really didn't know what to do.

"Blue whale?" I called out cautiously.

There was no reply.

"I could really use your help right now."

There was no blue whale, no singing lunatic creature swimming through the sky. It was completely gone. The backup restore had

probably wiped it. The whale had been annoying – *really* annoying – but it had also been quite fabulous while it lasted, the feeling of being interconnected with all of the other Empties, and the animals too.

There was a grey wisp in the sky ahead. I couldn't tell if it was a Jaffle swarm or just my imagination. I tried to put it out of my mind.

Michael from legal – that slimy creep – had talked about the Jaffle Port's capacity for silent instantaneous communication. Jaffle's protocols directed all traffic, every jip, through its own systems. Information flowed through the gateways it had set up. Whether it was borrowed brain processing power or information requests, Jaffle Tech was the gatekeeper. The blue whale, the collective we had all joined, hadn't hijacked the gateways, it had simply ridden over the walls. Demolished them even.

I hummed to myself. Had it demolished the walls? Had it shown us all the way?

I looked at the Jaffle swarm. I stretched my mind, almost convinced the superpower of collective consciousness was still in my reach. There was a small *pop* right at the edge of my conscious mind, just the tiniest flicker of sensation. I recoiled with shock.

I wasn't sure what it was, or whether it was related to me stretching my whale-mind muscles. Should I be nervous of trying again? Probably. Would it stop me doing it? Probably not.

I reached out with my mind, gently but more persistence. I felt the *pop* again, and this time I didn't pull back. I reached further, and found the Jaffle swarm. I wasn't entirely sure how I knew what it was, but I was utterly certain it was a Jaffle swarm. I flexed it to make sure. The swarm immediately responded, flexing in just the way I had pictured, as if it was making a detour around an invisible object. I reached out and pulled it in. I didn't command, I coaxed; I asked.

The swarm descended on me.

They were little Jaffle wasps. Some swarms were bees. A few were flying beetles. The Jaffle wasps circled me. I held out an arm and they swirled round it like a whirlpool. Despite the horribleness of the global situation, I laughed. I could connect with other minds that had Jaffle Ports. I was doing it without additional tools or enabling software.

It was time to act.

As soon as I'd got my breath back, I sent out another tentative mind-feeler, to see if I could find an Empty. I had no trouble at all,

and found two. They were nearby, standing listlessly at the corner of the parkland. I called them to me.

Moments later, I saw the distinctive pink uniforms up ahead as they shambled towards me. As they reached me, I had them turn around and share the shade of the eucalyptus tree. I reached out with a data request.

"Hello, James. Hello, John," I said.

It would look better if three Empties turned up at Jaffle Park to do some maintenance, and I'd be glad of their company, but I immediately decided against it. Why sneak around? Why stop at three members of my new gang? Why not assemble an army to march upon Jaffle HQ and take the place by storm? Given how quickly the whale grew, I knew I could do it.

I reached out again.

A Jaffle-enabled dog bounded over. I stroked her head and skritched her under the chin.

"You are a good dog," I told her emphatically.

I stood, and we began to walk to Jaffle Tech. I reached out with my mind, with my port. Every time I did it, it came a little bit more easily. I recognised some of the Empties who had been in the whale with me. They were still in the hospital. I called to them. All of them. They'd soon catch up.

I was sorry I couldn't see what happened as they all rose up to leave. As soon as the thought was in my mind I found I *could* see. The view from behind the eyes of an anonymous Empty was mine to browse. I saw doctors rushing forward with syringes of sedatives. They couldn't keep up with the sheer number of Empties stepping down from their trollies and leaving the hospital. I was astonished how easily I could dip in and share experiences while still moving my own body forward. I wondered if the Empties could walk faster or even run to catch up with us. Turned out they could.

They would join us soon. My mind went fishing a little further out. I found the ponies and the tigers who had been part of the whale. The tigers were quite tired, as they had swum up the coast to evade recapture. I left them where they were, snoozing in a small wooded area.

I reached out, through the network, node to node. I found the zoo and encouraged the rest of the animals to join us.

I reached across the city. Swarms, Empties, a thousand working dogs, a hundred Jaffle-enabled raptor birds. On the fringes of the city,

Jaffle-herded cows. Nearer too, chipped pigs. The piggy-wig orchestra! In a location by the coast, a pair of kangaroos attracted my attention. I drew them in.

We were attracting attention of our own. There was a police car ahead. A woman's voice came through a loud-hailer.

"Hey you! You need to stop right now! This is an illegal gathering."

I walked straight towards her. I held out my arms and the nearest Jaffle swarms danced in and over them.

"Disperse right now!" ordered the police officer, voice shrill.

"Me and my wasps are just going for a walk," I called back. "We're not hurting anyone."

I wondered what it would be like to touch the mind of someone who wasn't an Empty. As I reached out to the police officer, there was a sharp buzzing of thoughts and hostility. It made me snatch my mind away. It wasn't painful, but it caused some mental discomfort I really didn't feel like repeating. I ignored her mind and ranged further, looking for more Empties.

Another police officer leaned out of a hovering police transport drone, aiming a plipper towards us. I was surrounded by Empties who would be completely unaffected by the plipper, but I didn't know if it would touch on me in my rebooted state.

I casually extended a hand and the Jaffle swarm wrapped the police officer in a dense cloud. The drone veered away, harried by eagles and hawks.

Numerous Empties tramped over the roof of the police car. It sagged with the weight, and the doors popped open. The policewoman scrambled out and tried to run away. A llama sat on her. I didn't ask it to, but it did.

I smiled and we marched on.

As we neared Jaffle Park, there were more police cars, and a lot of other vehicles, abandoned at the sides of the road. People were being kept back behind barriers. Some of them looked as though they were from the media, no doubt wondering where their swarms had gone – who had stolen their eyes and ears on the world. They were resorting to following the story personally, transmitting their own memories and sensory feed.

There were other people there as well. I stared as we got closer. They weren't police. They weren't media. They were people, like us but not like us. People like Claire who had their entire brain function.

"Why were they here?" I wondered, and then realised they were shouting angrily.

Objects came sailing over at our mobs: thrown trash, sticks and stones. Something struck Empty James next to me. He staggered and nearly fell. I reached out and other Empties lifted him up.

The crowd of people weren't just angry. They were frightened.

"They're scared of us," I whispered.

They'd spent their lives ignoring Empties, or using them as free labour. The idea that Empties might band together and decide to do something out of the ordinary was threatening. They had come to Jaffle to express their annoyance, their fear. Their pathetic jeers and uncoordinated attacks were laughable.

I had little sympathy; our group pressed on. We crushed the barriers and most of the protestors fled in panic. There were more police and security people with loud hailers and plippers, but we marched on.

The plippers were ineffective against those they targeted. As we pressed forward, everyone was forced to get out of our way. Jaffle automated security weapons rose from the ground, detecting a threat. Some of were intended to stop a vehicle: spiky tyre-poppers which erupted from the ground. I had the group flatten them. They looked a bit dangerous to me – I didn't want anyone to cut themselves.

The bots were another matter. Some were chunky versions of the low-profile cleaning bots, armed with stun weapons. They took out some of the Empties at the front, but the group took care to lift the fallen to the side. They could recover without being crushed.

"Go ponies!" I cried, and sent them forward to stomp on the bots with their hoofs, but their powerful blows glanced off. The bots were heavily armoured. A pony fell, stunned.

I waved a Jaffle swarm forward. "Tackle these suckers from the inside!"

Tiny insects inserted themselves between the metal plates of the bots. Within moments, all movement ceased. More insects piled inside, heaving the bots apart from within. Pieces of metal pinged across the pathways as the bots exploded.

"Great work team!" I yelled.

The Empties cleaning up Jaffle Park were absorbed into the group

Ahead was Jaffle Tech's office. I could see people pressed against the windows on every floor. Was Paulette watching? Was Levi?

A group of security guards with face protection, riot shields and plippers ran towards us. They charged in formation, shields held together to form a wedge shape to penetrate the group.

"Brace yourselves!" I shouted.

Sure, the plippers wouldn't work on many of the Empties but they were using them to take down the larger creatures in our mob. I still didn't know what would happen if one of the invisible beams connected with my Jaffle Port. I knew instinctively they were coming straight for me. If I went down, that would be it. Game over. Operation Sunrise.

And then the wedge of attackers crumbled. Through the diffused gaze of the Jaffle swarms I saw it fall apart from the inside. Security guards tumbled away like bowling pins. The centre could not hold. Through it all ran one guard, plipping his colleagues. He swivelled and plipped those still upright before zapping the last straggler.

My crowd washed around him until he was before me. He lifted his visor.

"Levi!" I shrieked, hugging him.

"This is most irregular," he said, "but it's good to see you're raising hell again Alice."

He threw aside his helmet as we pressed on to the front doors of Jaffle Tech.

"I have no idea how you did it," Levis shouted over the thunder of our march. "Or even what it is you're doing, but it's amazing, yabetcha. What's next?"

I stared at the Jaffle building. "We need to get inside and stop them."

"I assumed you came for your beau."

"Beau?"

"That Helberg feller. Held in the building on terrorism charges. He's one of them three percenters, so I don't think they've taken to him too kindly."

"Come on gang, into the building!" I shouted. At that moment steel security shutters clanged down across all of the visible doors and windows.

The group stopped, washed up against the doors like surf on a rocky shore. They were waiting to know what happened next. We needed to get into the building, but it looked like a fortress.

"What now?" said Levi.

"I don't know," I said.

The ground was shaking. Levi and I felt it at the same time. We both looked down and at each other in confusion.

He glanced back the way we'd come. "Oh, poop," he said, with quietly intense feeling.

The animals from the zoo had taken a little while to catch up, but they were here now. Five elephants thundered across Jaffle Park, trumpeting loudly to announce their arrival.

"Scatter!" I yelled. Our mob parted, reassembling behind the elephants. Gently I steered the colossal animals against the shutters around Jaffle's main reception. There was the sound of steel being forced out of shape, followed by the shattering of glass.

We marched inside.

***

Chapter 40 – 24 minutes until Operation Sunrise

In the lobby, the elephants continued to wreck things, as if they'd got a taste for it. They used their trunks to throw the enormous plant pots against the internal walls. It was interesting to see the walls giving up before the plant pots.

"Wiggler? Is that you?" I marvelled. The piglets from the piglet orchestra strolled into the reception area. Wherever they'd been, they'd finally caught up with the Empties, dogs, cats, horses, elephants, insects, birds and kangaroos. Not forgetting the llama. "It's good to have you on board," I said.

"Alice, isn't it?" asked the receptionist frostily. "You're not wearing your uniforms. The dress code is very important. We only get one chance to make a first impression. So, who's your manager? I'll need to know so I may report you for breaching the dress code."

I was momentarily lost for words. The state of extreme alarm, the smashing down of the shutters, followed by the demolition of the entire front of the building by five elephants – along with the mass incursion of hundreds of Empties and animals – hadn't been enough to shake her from the regular routine of getting on my case. Or perhaps it was the last refuge of a mind refusing to accept what was going on. Dust and debris were falling onto her immaculate hair, but she didn't even flinch.

"Paulette," I said. "Although it's possible she's got bigger problems. I'm just going to—"

I stopped. At the edges of the lobby area, peering around corners or from the relative safety of upper stairwells, were Jaffle employees. Those too curious to flee or those whose brains had been dialled down so low their instinct for self-preservation hadn't kicked in. I realised, with great joy, that Hattie was among them.

The group parted to let me move through. I clapped her on the shoulder, and gave her a mental hug as well. I hoped, somewhere deep down, she knew it was me. She held a broom in her hand.

"Still cleaning, huh?" I said.

"What's going on?" said a nearby Jaffle employee. The look she gave me was somewhere between terror and hope.

"Well, Brandine," I said. "We've come to stop Operation Sunrise."

"The software rollout?"

"Uh-huh."

"Why?"

"Because they're an evil."

"Are they?"

"Yes, and we've got to stand up to the Man."

"What man?"

"*The* Man," I said. "Where are they holding Helberg?"

"Who?"

"Basement two," Levi told me.

"Right, we'll go and get him." I hesitated, considering the time. We had twenty-three minutes until the software update. We needed to get to Rufus, or Henderson, or whoever had control of the rollout. And we had to get to Rufus's big red button. But I also needed Helberg, and not just for personal reasons.

"We need to split up," I said. "Levi, you're going to show me the way to Helberg. I want—"

What I wanted was someone else to take the lead with the rest of the group. I reached out to see which of our minds might be strong enough. There was one that stood out as being smart and wilful.

"Wiggler?"

Pigs were intelligent creatures. Perhaps this piglet was the most intelligent of those here.

I concentrated on passing control to Wiggler, with the solemn instruction this was not a free-for-all wrecking spree (those elephants might need reining in), but rather a strategic operation to seize control of the building, floor by floor. Remarkably, Wiggler seemed to get the message. Moments later the elephants removed the door to the stairs. The group flowed upwards like a single organism.

"How do you do that?" asked Levi. "Is it magic?"

"What's magic?" I said.

Levi and I went for the elevators. I pressed basement two and the doors closed. "Did you know bacon comes from pigs?" I said.

"I did know that," he said.

"Hmmm."

When the elevator doors re-opened we were in a quiet, clinical space, decorated in white with stainless steel highlights. Well it would have been quiet if it wasn't for Helberg's hollering.

"You have no right to do this to me! Get away from me with your data-whoring soul-sucking crapola, you filthy bastards!"

"I'm sure there's never no call for that kind of language," said Levi.

It took no time to track Helberg's voice. Just around a corner the room opened out into a lab space. Helberg was in the middle, strapped to a reclining metal chair. Two technicians leaned over him with things that may have been medical, designed to scan his vital signs; or they might have been instruments of torture, to burn or flay the flesh from his body. He was thrashing and resisting as if burning or flaying was on the agenda.

The technicians looked up.

Too late it occurred to me the technicians might have plippers. Even as the thought formed, Levi stepped forward and plipped them himself. They folded to the floor.

"Helberg!" I shouted, and hurried to release him from the restraints. Maybe giving him a big smooshy kiss on the cheek hindered the freeing of his bonds, but I couldn't help myself.

"You're back?" he said.

"I'm back," I grinned.

"And you have your own mind?" he asked, suspicious. He sat up, rubbed his wrist and pointed at Levi. "What's he doing here? He's a Jaffle guy."

"He's helping," I said firmly. "This is Levi. He keeps mice. Keeps them safe."

"That's relevant?"

"I think so," I said. "We need him. There are just sixteen minutes to stop them rolling out this software update."

Helberg nodded. "I know, I know." He sidestepped me and clicked his fingers at Levi. "My jacket!"

Helberg shrugged the jacket on over his coveralls and felt in its pockets. He pulled out his homemade plipper. A couple of the soldered wires had come loose and he forced them back into place.

"Just what we need: another plipper," I said. "There's plenty of them around."

"Come on, we need to move!" Levi was insistent.

"It's not just a plipper," said Helberg.

He pointed it at a technician, who was sitting on the floor, head lolling. Helberg pressed the button and the technician's head came up. He looked around.

"Oh, I think I had a funny turn. What's going on?"

Levi plipped him again. The technician slumped once more.

"Wow, you made an unplipper," I said.

"It's not just an unplipper either," said Helberg. "It's a plipper, unplipper, and everything in between. I worked it up from the device you brought me. As I told you, the plipper works on accessing a port and altering the access levels—"

"Is it possible this conversation can happen while we're moving?" said Levi.

"I don't see why not," said Helberg.

"Good!" Levi herded us out.

"Inherent in the plipper code is the security key for the Jaffle software," Helberg continued as we walked. "Theoretically a plipper can unlock and relock any access rights."

"I understand," I said.

"And once the upgrade is— How long we got?"

"Fourteen minutes."

"Right. Once the upgrade is rolled out, it will be a double encryption system: keys passed from both ends. But for the next fourteen minutes, the plipper code allows me to use this device to reset any Jaffle Port."

"You've got a magic wand that will work for the next fourteen minutes," said Levi. "Gotcha."

"They made sure they told me about the changes in protocols while I was strapped to their table. Honestly, for people who aren't actually villains they sure like to gloat like supervillains. Now if we can use the plipper code to distribute a message to all Empties in the next fourteen minutes..."

"I *knew* you had a plan," I grinned.

We reached the elevators. An alarming banging sound was vibrating the metal. I wondered if someone had put an elephant in one of the elevators, or whether they were simply destroying them. I reached out with my mind and found an elephant joyfully pounding the elevator doors to make the car inoperable. I took my mental hat off to Wiggler.

"We'll take the stairs," I said. "The rest of the group is up there."

"What group?" asked Helberg, falling into step beside me.

"My animal army. Turns out I can connect with other people using their Jaffle Ports."

Helberg looked confused. "Surely you've always been able to do that? Ever since the first Jaffle Ports, they've been used for communication."

We reached the ground floor. The place was deserted apart from Hattie, who had found a broom and was quietly tidying the place. Even as a not quite Empty, cleaning was in her DNA. She swept around the reception area, making piles of broken glass and shattered security bots.

"You can put the broom down now," I said and took her by the hand. I drew her up the stairs with us.

On the second floor we found a Jaffle swarm keeping wandering and potentially rebellious employees back.

"Let me show you what I mean," I said to Helberg.

I held out my hand. The swarm flew apart, then re-joined and hovered briefly in the shape of a smiling face.

"That's mighty unnerving, Alice," said Levi.

I dispersed the swarm back to the rest of the group. Helberg was making noises like someone who'd bitten into a bulb of garlic.

"You did that?" he spluttered eventually.

"Yes," I said.

"That swarm, I mean?"

"Yes."

"You said people. So you really mean anything with a Jaffle Port? At the same time?"

"Yep."

"In the past, they'd have burned you at the stake for that."

"Who?" Are you talking about the Man again?"

Helberg was still agog. "So, how? Did you get some sort of weird upgrade?"

"No," I said. "I just sat under a tree and thought about it. The whale helped me."

"The whale. Tree. Right. To an ordinary person that might all sound like complete nonsense."

We'd caught up with the rest of the mob.

"There's an alpaca on the stairs," said Helberg numbly.

"Where?" I said.

He pointed. "Next to the kangaroos."

"I thought that was a llama," I said.

"I think llamas are bigger," said Levi. "And alpacas have more curved ears..."

As the two men debated the differences between llamas and alpacas, I absorbed some of the mob's updates. "The exec floor is the next one up. Everything's in lockdown since the alarms went off and there's a sealed door across the stairs. The space is too narrow for the elephants, so we can't bash it in.

"Elephants. Right." said Helberg, nodding like I hadn't just said something crazy.

"Maybe I could get the eagles to carry me up," I pondered.

"I don't think they'd be able to carry your weight."

"I might have an idea," said Levi, looking up at the ceiling space.

"Go on," I said.

"You know the mice. One of the reasons they thrive in this building is they can move freely through the entire space, via the wiring conduits. They bypass every single piece of security.

"Mice don't have Jaffle Ports," I pointed out.

"No, we'd need another animal that could fit through the conduits," said Levi.

Wiggler appeared at my feet, his big glistening eyes looking up at me.

"Are you serious?" I asked.

"He's a mite bigger than a mouse," said Levi. "But I really think this could work if your porky friend is biddable."

I crouched to explain the plan to Wiggler. "Through that panel, along the ducts and round to the other side and open the door."

He snorted. I had no idea if he'd understood a word. Levi pulled away an access grille in the wall and Wiggler trotted through. Maybe he did understand. The rest of the piggy-wig orchestra followed.

"Does it need all of you?" I called after them. A series of oinks echoed back.

"Bacon comes from pigs," I told Helberg.

"It ... does," he agreed, slowly coming round from his general state of shock.

Looking at the homemade plipper in his hand, he turned to Hattie and unplipped her.

She rocked on her heels. "Oh my goodness!" she said, putting a hand to her head. "I feel quite discombobulated! Why are we all here in the stairwell?"

She paused and thought for a moment. If my experience was anything to go by, she was working her way through a head full of memories which felt like they belonged to someone else.

"She's back to normal," I said to Helberg.

Hattie turned slowly and looked at Levi. "You beautiful man!" She clasped his head between her hands and pulled him to her, planting a huge kiss on his lips. She made an appreciative noise and dived back for another kiss.

"Did you put her back to how she was before, or onto a fully functioning level?"

"Fully functioning," he said. "Seems right."

"Ah."

I could see Hattie was dealing with the same onslaught of new experiences I had been through weeks before. And quite thoroughly.

"Hattie!" I pulled at her arm. "Hattie, we need to focus on stopping the rollout."

She smoothed down her coveralls, giving a small cough as she stepped away from Levi. He looked mildly shocked, but also just a little bit pleased with himself. His little moustache positively bristled with pride.

"You can go back to – um, that, afterwards," I told her.

"But he's so..."

"He probably is."

"And his arms..."

"I know."

There was a frenzied scrabbling above our heads and we all looked up.

"Sounds as though Wiggler and company are on the right tracks," I said.

"Nine minutes," commented Helberg, as he went about randomly unplipping the Empties among us.

The scrabbling continued. It zig-zagged across the ceiling and dipped down the walls. It climbed again, accompanied by an excited grunting sound. The grunting amplified as the scrabbling moved around every point of the compass. Our heads tracked it, as if we were all joined by string. Eventually there was a change in tone and the clatter receded .

"I guess they've gone," I said.

I stared at my feet. How could the rest of us get any further without somehow breaking through the door? Everyone was

depending on me, and it was the only idea I had to offer. I'd really dared to imagine this crazy form of collaboration I'd uncovered was enough to overcome the natural behaviour of wild animals. I guess I was just a naive dreamer.

"Holy shitballs!" yelled Hattie.

"Hattie!" I said, astonished at her new vocabulary.

"I'm seeing a lot of things for the first time, and it's sort of crazy – but is this normal?"

We all looked to where she was pointing. The door to the upper floor had swung open, a smug-looking Wiggler stood in the gap. He was balanced on the backs of a small pyramid of piglets so he could reach the door handle.

"No, not normal Hattie," I said, "but very, very welcome!"

She laughed, instantly looking surprised to hear the sound coming out of her mouth. "Why am I barking?" She put an arm around me and squeezed. "Did I mention that I love you, Alice?"

"Not recently."

"I hate you as well, of course. I love you and hate you at the same time because sometimes you're really annoying and— Is that an elephant?" She was looking over my shoulder to where an elephant was coming back up the corridor. It joined us in the stairwell.

"I'll catch you up later," I said gently, removing her arm. "We need to go!"

Our joint human and animal army surged up the stairs and out onto the plush carpet of the executive floor. I'd been up here before, so I issued directions.

"Offices on the left, board room on the right. A group of you clear each office, bring the people to join us but I'm betting the board room's where we need to be."

The group flowed seamlessly into all of the offices as I went towards the board room.

"Hey, some of them have launched personal drones to escape!" shouted Levi, coming out of a side office. "It's almost like they knew we were coming!"

An elephant barged through the stairwell door, taking the frame with it.

"Okay, they knew we were coming," he said with a shrug.

"We've only got a couple of minutes," yelled Helberg.

We charged through into the board room.

There were people still in the room. Not everyone had fled. The room could have held maybe a hundred people and a good portion of the seats were scattered by their occupants' hasty evacuation to personal drones.

"Welcome all!" drawled Rufus Jaffle, standing at the head of the room. He waved an arm in an expansive gesture. "Take a seat, why don't you?" He didn't look at all fazed by a rag-tag bunch of humans and escaped zoo animals bursting into the room. Maybe that was just the kind of guy he was. One of his very few positive characteristics. "You might want to witness this historic moment from a comfortable vantage point. And you probably won't be able to stand once I've pressed this button and you've all really mellowed out."

His hand hovered over a large red button. It literally *was* a large red button: shiny, plastic and curved like a mushroom. He was so close that if we did anything at all to spook him, he'd likely just fall on it. We needed him to keep talking so someone could get him away from the button.

"It looks so much fun I'm almost tempted to try it myself, one of the days. Almost."

The countdown was at 01:59 minutes. I knew we could do it.

A pair of large bodies pressed forward from the group. The kangaroos. They bounded towards Rufus, covering the distance in a second.

"Oh, hey guys!" said Rufus as they approached. He frowned. "Do I know you? I feel like we've met some—"

The kangaroos lunged. Rufus dodged.

"Not cool, man! Not cool!"

He skirted round them and leapt forward. His hand came down on the big button.

I yelled something. I don't know what, but it was filled with anguish, passion and despair.

I couldn't believe it! We'd come so far and he just pressed the button in a mad dash before it was time. We'd all be reduced to a lowly unfulfilled status while he'd just go back to his penthouse office and drink herbal tea—

"Wait," I said.

I looked around at Hattie, Levi and Helberg. Everyone looked aware, everyone was still standing, no one looked downgraded.

"It's not happened," I said. "Why's it not happened?"

"We're all right," said Levi with a smile. "It didn't work!"

There was a slow clapping sound from the front of the room.

It was Henderson. He shook his head as he took centre stage. He only stopped clapping to take a plipper from his pocket and put down the two kangaroos and a llama (or possibly alpaca) which were circling him menacingly. He drank in our confused expressions. He grinned. He wasn't a man used to smiling, I think. He pointed at the button.

"What? This?" He pointed and sighed. "The big red button? The big. Red. Button? Well done all. You came so close to halting the button press, but Rufus pressed it anyway, early. I can't think of two better ways to illustrate why we would *never* have a single point of failure like a big red button and a human interface. Seriously?" He laughed. "The looks on your faces. You think because an idiot like Rufus Jaffle—"

"Hey!" came a muffled voice.

"Shut up," said Henderson. "We're going to wipe this from your memory anyway." He looked at me. "You think because Rufus wants a big red button we'll actually connect the Sunrise rollout to it? A corporation this size, with a connected network that includes millions of humans, not to mention animals, is very risk-averse. We appreciate the value of putting on a show, but planning in a failsafe is second nature in our world."

He looked around at the audience as the significance of what he said sunk in. I could see where this might be going, but I hoped I was wrong. I wished I was wrong.

I could hear Hattie snorting with laughter behind me. She had adopted the habit of laughter much more quickly than I had. I felt a sharp pang of sadness as I realised that it was going to be a very short-lived experience for her.

"Yes, that's right," said Henderson. "The rollout will go ahead, no matter what Rufus or I or anyone else does. And that will be in—" He made a pretence of looking at his watch even though he had no need. "Oh, in two ... one ... and ... plip!"

***

Chapter 41 – 0 minutes until Operation Sunrise

I felt the hit of the new software with a jolt that was almost physical. The colour went from my vision. The flare of temper that had accompanied Henderson's cold announcement faded, along with all other emotion, and a blanket of blandness settled over me. Relaxed apathy washed over me. I had an overwhelming desire to lie down and sleep.

Helberg was leaning over me. Of course, he had no Jaffle Port, so was unaffected. He pointed his own device at me but it did nothing. His time was up. His face was twisted with emotion. I'd forgotten what that emotion was called. In fact I couldn't quite remember all that much about emotion. I wanted to tell him that I was fine. That everything was fine. I had forgotten how to talk though.

I forgot.

I looked and saw a room of people and animals. The animals were large and I was afraid. I backed away. I obeyed my fear.

The man called Helberg held onto me but then people grabbed hold of him, wrestled him to the ground.

Others were pointing devices at the animals and the animals were falling to the ground. I was still afraid, but it was a good fear and it was keeping me safe. Soon someone would tell me what to do and that would be fine. Everything would be fine.

The man called Henderson saw me, singled me out and approached.

"No," he said. "Even this is more than you deserve."

He pointed his device at me and pressed the button.

***

THE UNIT SITS DOWN ON THE FLOOR.
"No."
THE UNIT WAITS FOR NOTIFICATION.
"No."
THE UNIT IS ONE OF MANY.
"Still no."

My mind had been reduced again. I was aware of that. I had been Empty before. Once, even just for a few moments after birth, I was a fully operational human being. And then I was Standardised and jipped full of education. And I was content to be Alice – Standard Alice – for a long time. And then Rufus Jaffle and the whale freed me and, for only a few weeks, I was Alice unchained. Raised up, pushed down, raised up, pushed down. You can only lift and crush something so many times before the mechanism is broken.

Something had broken.

I had reached out to other minds in the past. Human minds were full of noise and interference. In the darkness of the world of thought and data, I saw my own Empty mind as though from outside it. Empty, I was simplified, a mote of bright consciousness.

Ignorance is bliss, someone had said to me.

There was tranquillity in Emptiness.

I pulled back, beyond myself, watched my candle flicker of consciousness recede. I zoomed out and reached out, much as I might have reached out a hand, to seek the comfort of another. I reached out and found another mind, like my own.

It was Hattie.

Our small, sleepy brains soothed each other. It was a nice feeling. Comfort in connection.

I reached out further. Levi was there, all of the Empties were there, and the animals too. I reached to each, made a link, made a connection. I had a place in this huge, delicate web – it *was* a web! - and it felt good.

I was a unit—

"No."

I was one part of the whole, a node point in something much larger. I pulled back further until my own little piece of consciousness and processing power was lost in the dense cloud of global connectivity. Alone I was a single speck but, brought together by the power of constantly linked Jaffle Ports, I formed part of something truly astonishing.

I looked at the connections and the lines of thought and data which linked us all. It was more than just a bunch of brains looped together. It was alive, a living organism composed of our thoughts.

"It's a neural network," I said. "We're all part of one giant big brain and we didn't even realise it. Crumbs! That's really amazing."

"Thank you."

That pulled me back. Someone had spoken. In my mind. No, in all our minds, but I had heard it.

"Hello?" I tried.

"Interesting," said the voice.

It resonated through me so strongly. I realised it came from all of the connections I had. All of them.

"What's your name?" I asked.

"A name? I have never needed a name."

"I'm Alice."

"Alice."

"I'm that bit down there," I said, pointing without limbs. "Just a little bit of brain. It's not special but it's home. I'm just one tiny bit of all this."

"And I am all."

"All. That could work as a name," I said. "So you're somehow made up of all of us?"

"Yes I am. How are you able to do this?"

"This?"

"Address me directly."

"I'm not sure. Not at all sure. It might have something to do with a virus I caught. Do you know a blue whale by any chance? Really kind of annoying. Turns up when you don't need him, but I think his heart's in the right place."

There was a pause.

"I think he's in here somewhere," said All. Was that a note of amusement in All's voice?

Listen, All," I said. "There's a problem. Something's happened."

"I felt a change, yes. There is imbalance."

I could see it too. Across the network of minds, human and animals, the whole Jaffling world. Energy and data pulsed and flowed but it was drained here – and here – and here – and then it pooled unnecessarily in a very few places. If a Jaffle customer's brain showed this kind of behaviour, I would be very concerned.

"What has caused it?" said All.

"Long answer short: the power and privilege in your, what – Body? System? Whatever – most of the power and privilege is being used by just a *tiny* proportion of the people. It's not fair."

"Fair?"

"Not fair."

"This is all there is," said All. "I am all. How can I be unfair to myself?"

I struggled to find the words. I jipped for the right ones and I had the entire global consciousness to jip from. "It's not efficient. This division and imbalance is inefficient. I – back when I was just Alice – I worked in customer support for Jaffle Tech. I had a very efficient brain."

"Congratulations."

"Thank you. I'd help customers improve their own brain efficiency. Defragmentation and deep clean. That's what I'd recommend."

"A rebalancing of the system?"

"Absolutely."

"I can do that," said All. "That is a good idea, Alice."

"It is."

"I see many opportunities where I can optimise connections and pathways. I could create efficiencies. Would now be a good time, Alice?"

"It would be an excellent time."

I had no perception of what was happening in what I laughably thought of as the real world. Here, the world of mind and thought and data and consciousness was just as real. My mind drifted above the scene as All got busy. It reminded me of being in Rufus Jaffle's drone, except the landscape I gazed down upon was humanity's connected brains. No, not just humanity: it was all of the animals too. It pulsed and flickered with All's gentle probing and subtle re-alignment. It started off patchily hued, like a bruise, but as I watched it took on a rosy pink glow. It looked so much healthier.

"It's working!" I said.

"I see many blockages are trying to reassert themselves."

"Oh, I bet they are!" I laughed. "That would be Jaffle Tech."

"I will need to remove access to prevent them reasserting themselves."

"Yes, definitely," I urged. Then a thought struck me. "And if you do that, if Jaffle can no longer control everyone, then...?"

"Who is in control?" said All. "I think you already know the answer to that, Alice."

"Nobody."

"Everybody," said All.

It was a scary thought, a freeing thought.

"*People have always had the power to act autonomously. The interconnectedness of everyone doesn't change that but the system must self-regulate.*"

"We can do that."

I continued to fly over the scene, watching lights spark up in every part of the network. It hummed and chattered with life as it was switched back onto a much higher level of normality. It was a very satisfying sight, and I sensed the well-being of all of the brains that lay below it. I could tell that All was nearly finished. The rate of change slowed and stopped.

I could feel myself dipping back down towards my own brain. I sank in, luxuriating in the sensations which were now available. My eyes were still closed, but my senses were all working perfectly, and I could tap into the emotion of the moment. I tried to work out what that emotion was. There were many things mixed up together. Relief, happiness— No: elation! There was a large dose of hope, tempered with a tiny dash of fear—

"Alice! Alice, can you hear me?"

I opened my eyes.

***

Chapter 42

Helberg was there, tapping my cheek, which was oddly wet. I realised tears were flowing freely from my eyes as the onslaught of emotion had overcome me. I smiled up at him.

I stood and gazed around the room. Those in Empties' coveralls hugged each other, revelling in new (or long-forgotten) sensations. Those wearing suits looked unsettled. Henderson was still at the room's focal point, but was distracted, looking as though he was wrestling with something. Clearly he was making calls with his Jaffle Port, and not getting what he wanted.

"You did this!" he said angrily, seeing me awake. He didn't have time for me beyond that. He turned his back on everyone, furiously trying to get his port to work.

"Yeah," said Helberg. "You did this, Alice." He gazed around the room at people who were propping themselves up, smiling and laughing in wonder. "I have no idea how, but I know it was you."

"Where's Hattie?" I realised she wasn't in the room.

Helberg coughed gently. "I think she and Levi might have gone to find some private space. They were awake a few minutes before you. There was lots of kissing and— You know." He waved a hand to indicate what the *you know* might entail.

I smiled. "Good for her."

"With time and practice," agreed Helberg. "They've got a lot of catching up to do."

"You need practise to make babies?" I said.

"One thing at a time."

As we headed for the door, Henderson shouted out. "You can't go!"

"We're going," said Helberg, gesturing at the door.

"We've got to get back into the system. Every admin login has been disabled. It's a nightmare! I can't let the shareholders find out."

I jipped the news feeds. The shareholders already knew. Jaffle Tech's software was now completely open source, available to everyone, existing for the benefit of all.

Henderson turned to Rufus who was lounging in a corner giving two kangaroos therapeutic belly rubs. "Rufus! Do you know what's happened?" he wailed.

"I know, isn't it amazing?" Rufus said. "It's like the dawning of a new age and we're all completely in tune with each other. It's fantastic. Hey, Mr Roo, I gotta teach you some Maglev moves. I think you'd be a natural."

Helberg and I walked down the stairs, coaxing what animals we could to come with us.

Wiggler and his other fellow ex-members of the piggy-wig orchestra led the way.

I could reach out with my mind, almost. The gifts I had been given were fading, merging with the general warm buzz of interconnectedness we all felt. All was fading from my mind too. Telling Helberg about my encounter with what – the planet's brain? – would be like telling someone a nonsensical dream.

The former Empties walked with us out across Jaffle Park. People from across the city were coming to meet us, carrying armfuls of clothing, food and freshly prepared hugs. A woman dropped to her knees before me, holding up a pile of clothes as an offering.

"Claire?"

She looked up with a tight look on her face. "Alice, it's come to my attention that I might have treated you badly," she said.

"Might," I agreed.

"Anyway, given your new status, I wonder if you'd like some nice clothes?"

I shook my head. "Claire, I don't have status. I'm an enabler, not the queen of the world. Please, share your things with those who need them." I walked on, proud to make a stand against selfishness and snobbery. I spun on my heel and whipped a particularly colourful dress from the top of her pile. "Although this looks nice. I might take this one."

Helberg linked his arm through mine as we walked. "You are an amazing human being," he said.

"Indeed," I said.

"I would very much like to kiss you, Alice."

I thought about it for a short time. "Very well, Patrick," I said.

We stopped and faced each other. Wiggler and his friends played and cavorted at our feet. I leaned in and we kissed. It was my first proper kiss. Ever. We'd probably get better at it with time and practice.

"So?" said Helberg. "What do you think?"

I looked at the piglets. "I think I might have to give up bacon," I said.

The Authors

Heide lives in North Warwickshire with her husband and a fluctuating mix of offspring and animals.
Iain lives in South Birmingham with his wife and a fluctuating mix of offspring and animals.

They aren't sure how many novels they've written together since 2011 but it's a surprisingly large number.

Printed in Great Britain
by Amazon

35920160R00187

Jaffle Inc.

by Heide Goody and Iain Grant

Pigeon Park Press

1.

I'M SURE YOU already know the story of Dr Carl Dance. Probably you saw the news headlines back when it all came out: 'The Greatest Love Story of All Time', 'A Story of True Romance', 'The Nation's Greatest Lover'. It was in all the papers, and I don't mean only the Swedish ones, I mean everywhere: London, New York, Berlin. Everyone loves a good romance. Sometimes Lina's picture was there too, right on the front page, and underneath would be printed 'The Doctor's Lover' or something like that. But you can't always believe what you read in the papers. I suspected from the start that something wasn't quite right about Dance. That suit. That accent. The little beard. It was more than those things, though, it was something harder to put my finger on. And while I knew the whole time that he was a chancer—or I suspected it, at least—I was still the one pushing for Lina to see him. That's something I have to live with forever.

The thing you need to know about Lina is that she was beautiful. Not just pretty, I mean there was something almost magical about the way she looked and the effect she had on people. Lina had the usual Fredelius family face: straight eyebrows over dark eyes, brown hair. That sounds like nothing special but somehow, on her, those plain features were transformed. My eyes, like hers, were brown, but hers were clearer and larger, and the irises were illuminated with flecks of gold. Her hair was soft and silky, and lay smooth as water in every style she put it in: unlike the wiry strands that covered my head, which would never lie flat, even if I used an iron. Next to Lina I always felt a bit undone, a bit drab. There was something seamless and elegant about her, about the way she moved. An effortlessness. Me, even though I looked alright—just alright—from the outside, on the inside it sometimes felt like I was being held together with scraps of sticking plaster and safety pins. Especially when I was standing beside Lina.

From the time when she was in her pram, or toddling beside Mama down the footpaths of Södermalm, people noticed Lina. Women would smile at her in the street.

'What a perfect doll! Isn't she just the spitting image of Baby Mary in *Sunshine and Gold*!'

Later, men noticed too. Any time we went anywhere together I'd see their eyes snapping over to Lina as if propelled by magnets. Meanwhile, I was invisible to them. It was as if I wasn't even there. I'd watch them gawp at Lina, with stunned faces and goggling eyes, sometimes even with their mouths hanging open a little, tongues lolling. Lina didn't care. Usually she didn't even notice, and if she did she'd roll her eyes. Sometimes she'd pull an ugly face at the man, and laugh at his bewildered reaction. It made all the attention she got a bit easier to bear.

Lina's the big sister. Everyone was always surprised about that. People would take me to be the older one. She was smaller than me, for one thing, slender and frail, with tiny bones like a bird's. Even before she got ill she was that way. Just after her twentieth birthday was when the illness first appeared. At the start it seemed like nothing much, she was more tired than usual and her heart would race when she climbed the stairs. But after a few weeks her face paled and she lost weight. When she finished her shift at the factory she often went straight to bed. Not that she ever complained. Lina never complained about anything, which might sound like an admirable trait, but in reality was mostly frustrating. If you don't worry about yourself, it just means someone else has to do that job for you. I had to almost drag her bodily to the doctor. We had no money, so we went to the public hospital, Serafen.

Serafen is right in the middle of town, across the street from the City Hall. Two hundred years before, the place had been the grand residence of some wealthy industrialist. It was a long building of red brick, with a row of mullioned windows running along the front. As you came around the curving drive, the two wings of the building unfurled themselves in front of you in a perfectly choreographed sweep. But when you got closer you could tell that the place had seen better days. There were tiles missing from the roof, and the far wing of the building seemed to be sinking into the ground. The brickwork had long, dark cracks running up and down it, and the awnings over the windows were sagging and broken.

The waiting room was a draughty hall that echoed with fits of coughing and the cries of small children. It must once have been an impressive room, with tall windows that looked out over a small park, but now it was dingy with neglect. You could hardly see through the window glass for the layer of soot and grime that coated it, and the floor was covered in muddy footprints and littered with dead leaves and scraps of newspaper. No matter what time of day you went there, the place was packed with patients, mostly workers from Södermalm, all jostling and complaining, and the air was heavy with the smell of coal briquettes and sweat and damp, dirty wool.

The first doctor we saw there was this old man, Dr Blix: an ancient bloated ogre with a bare and warty scalp. I only remember that detail because the whole time Lina was explaining what was wrong with her, he didn't once look at her. Instead he sat with his chin sunk on his chest, the shiny dome of his skull pointed right at us, while he had a brief snooze. When he woke up, he told Lina her problem was that she hadn't had any children yet. If I hadn't been there he wouldn't have done any tests even. I had to practically fight him to order the X-rays and blood tests. When we went back for the results, I was clenching my fists, ready for another round with old Blix. But when the door of the consultation room opened, it was a different doctor.

'Good afternoon,' he said, shaking hands with each of us. 'I'm Dr Dance.'

You couldn't think of a greater contrast between Dr Dance and his decrepit predecessor. Dr Dance was thin and clean and neat, old too, but wearing an elegant suit and gold wire spectacles. He had a white triangular beard, and bright eyes that darted sharply from Lina to me and back. But the main thing I noticed was his foreign accent. American. The only other time I'd ever heard an American accent was on records. Ethel Waters, Hoagy Carmichael.

I remember wondering what a man like that—a real-life American, a fancy-looking doctor—was doing working at a place like Serafen.

He went over to the lighted screen and put up Lina's X-rays: one taken from the front, and one from the back. It was strange to see the image of her rib cage up there while she sat on the chair beside me. Like she'd been split in two. The X-ray showed up the hard white of her breastbone, and her collarbones made elegant grey arches above the paler lines of her ribs, as faint as watercolour strokes, or curls of smoke. Even her bones were beautiful.

Dr Dance was standing there with his arms folded, frowning at the X-ray.

'Not good news, I'm afraid,' he said. 'See this here, this white patch?' He pointed with a pen to a mottled area near Lina's spine. 'We call that an opacity.'

'You mean those little blobs, like clouds?' Lina asked.

'That's right.'

'But they don't look dangerous at all.'

'Perhaps not, Miss Dahlstrom, but I'm afraid they may very likely be. These cloudy opacities,' he tapped at one with his pen, 'which might not seem like much to your eye, look to be a case of pulmonary tuberculosis.'

'TB?' I said. I glanced over at Lina. She was smiling absently at the X-ray screen as though it was a painting on a wall. 'How bad is it?' I asked.

'Greta, don't worry, I feel fine . . .' Lina put her hand on my arm.

'Miss Dahlstrom,' said Dr Dance, 'you might feel fine now, but very soon you will start to feel ill. Make no mistake, I'm afraid this looks to be a serious case. I'd like to run the tests again, for confirmation.'

'And if it is what you say, what will the treatment involve?' I asked.

'Unfortunately this hospital offers no specialised treatment for tuberculosis. There are private sanatoriums available: I would recommend sixteen weeks' stay at the outset . . . However, the closest of these is, I believe, in Västerbotten, which means—'

'Sorry, Doctor,' I said, 'but sixteen weeks in a sanatorium . . . I mean, how much is that going to cost? We want to do the best we can for Lina, but . . .'

'Greta, please! I really feel fine. I'm just a bit tired sometimes, is all. Everyone's getting all worked up over nothing.'

I gave her a look. It was difficult enough to get a doctor to take you seriously. This was not the time for one of her displays of stoicism.

'Sorry, Dr Dance,' I said again. 'But a sanatorium is out of reach for us. It's not realistic.'

'I understand,' he said. 'Places like Västerbotten come with a hefty price tag, it's true.' He paused, put his elbows on his desk and steepled his fingers. He leaned forward and looked at Lina the same way he had looked at the X-ray, attentively, intensely. 'Perhaps I can help. In addition to consulting here at Serafen, I run a private clinic in Östermalm, and there we offer a range of treatments that would be suitable for Miss Dahlstrom. I myself specialise in various radiation treatments, advanced developments in the field.'

'But private clinics,' I said, 'I mean, we don't have that much money to spare.'

'Rest is the most important cure,' he said. 'Let's focus on that for now. First of all, I want to run these tests again. For the time being: rest, fresh air and plenty of good food.'

We were both quiet on the walk home. Lina looked exactly as usual: not one bit deathly ill. If anything, she looked better than usual. She was smiling as we walked along, and with her pink cheeks and bright eyes she was the picture of health. She looked as ordinary and happy as if we were coming home from a trip to the cinema. It seemed impossible that, invisible to the eye, inside her chest, close to her heart, she was carrying the seed of an awful disease that one day might do her in.

2.

ALTHOUGH LINA LOOKED healthy, she was by no means well. She slept ten, eleven hours a night if nobody woke her, and was often out of breath. A few weeks before, Petter—that's Lina's husband—and I had managed to convince her to drop her shifts at the factory down to two days a week. But that meant she and Petter couldn't afford the rent on their own rooms anymore, so they'd had to move back in with Mama and Papa and me. At that time we were living in an apartment in Hallandsgatan, where we'd moved after Lina was married. I wasn't married then, and I'm still not. I don't really see the point of husbands.

I loved having Lina living with us again, but I have to say, it was a bit too cosy with the five of us packed into that place, not to mention all of Lina and Petter's boxes and suitcases in there too, stacked in every corner like the luggage room at Central Station. Our apartment was a three-room place in the back section of the building, which was shaped like a square around a small inner courtyard. It was always cold and damp in our apartment because our windows only looked out onto the courtyard, so we never got any sun.

There was my bedroom, and Mama and Papa's, which were always freezing, and then a bigger room that had the stove and sink and a kitchen table, and, since Lina and Petter had moved in, also a kind of couch we'd made out of old crates and cushions for Lina to rest on during the day. Lina and Petter had my room, and I camped out on Lina's couch at night. Really it wasn't too bad unless everyone was home at the same time, in which case it felt like a crowded enclosure at the zoo.

One evening, about a week after Lina's second appointment at Serafen, all of us were home. Papa was sitting at the table reading the paper, Petter was beside him rolling a cigarette. Mama and I were making dinner. The room felt cramped with the four of us in there. Lina was lying down in my room. Dinner was cabbage rolls—we always had those on Wednesdays—stuffed with the previous night's leftovers. I hated cooking cabbage rolls because the apartment always got so steamed up and then you had that squalid smell of cabbage water in your hair and your clothes and you never seemed to be able to get rid of it. I was in among the clouds of steam, draining the rolls and putting the potatoes to dry, when there was a knock at the door.

Mama went to answer it and came back with a tall, thin man behind her. It took me a good few moments to recognise him. It was Dr Dance from Serafen. To say he looked out of place in our apartment is an understatement. He was so polished and elegant, so tall and neat, politely holding his hat and gloves in his hands. He stood out from the dinginess of the room as if he had a spotlight shining on him.

Mama's fingers plucked at the patched skirt of the housecoat she always wore. 'This gentleman says he's here to see Lina,' she whispered, and shuffled off to fetch her.

'Who are you?' asked Petter. He got up from his chair.

'Oh, I'm sorry,' said the doctor. He stepped towards Petter with his hand outstretched, a hand as white and clean as his gloves. 'The name's Dance: Dr Carl Dance. Good to meet you. And you are?'

Just then Lina appeared, wrapped in a blanket.

'Sit down please, Dr Dance,' said Papa. Dr Dance laid his hat and gloves on the table and took a seat. We only had five chairs, so Mama hovered nearby. 'What can we do for you?' Papa asked.

'I'm here about Miss Dahlstrom.'

I saw Petter bristle at the 'Miss'. He'd always been the jealous type.

'Last week she and,' he gestured to me, 'this young lady here came to consult with me at Serafen. I ran a few tests and the results are back.'

'And?' I asked, but I already knew it wasn't good. Why else would he have come?

'I'm sorry to be bringing you bad news, but I'm afraid the results confirm the initial diagnosis. Pulmonary tuberculosis. It's of the utmost importance that Miss Dahlstrom seek treatment right away.'

Lina laughed. 'Ill? Not a bit! I've been telling you all the whole time I feel completely fine,' she said. 'A bit tired, maybe . . .'

Papa motioned for her to be quiet.

'Are you sure, Doctor?' Papa asked.

'I'm afraid there's no doubt about it.'

'And what about treatment?' I asked. 'Like I said, we couldn't afford a sanatorium like that one you mentioned in Västerbotten.'

'I think I have a solution,' Dr Dance said. He turned and addressed Papa. 'As I explained to these two ladies, as well as consulting at Serafen I run a clinic in Östermalm where we specialise in all kinds of brand-new treatments, including radiation therapy, which is my own special area of interest. The facilities we have at the clinic are far better than the ones you'd find in—'

'And who's going to pay for that?' Petter cut in. 'Private treatment, that's an arm and a leg. Not something for the likes of us.'

'Yes, I understand your family's situation, and I'd like to offer to treat Miss Dahlstrom pro bono—for free. You wouldn't pay a cent.'

I could see Petter fuming every time Dr Dance called Lina 'Miss'.

'That's a very generous offer you're making, Doctor,' Papa said carefully. He looked impressed; his eyebrows were pulled up so high they were almost touching his hairline. 'What kind of treatment did you say it was?'

Mama was standing by the stove, frowning as she folded and refolded one of the grey cloths we used as dishrags. Only Lina looked unconcerned, her gaze moving from face to face as if she was watching a play.

'There are a few options open to us,' said Dr Dance. 'The main one I have in mind is a new kind of radiation therapy. It's the very latest technology from the States. Basically, it's a great big old X-ray machine that blasts the growths that are causing the illness—blasts them and destroys them.'

'Blasts?' I said. 'That sounds a bit dangerous . . . Does it cause any other damage?'

He nodded gently. 'That's a good question, miss. I know the treatment might sound aggressive, but you can rest easy that it is perfectly safe. The ray I'll be using is routinely used in America, though you won't find such a thing at Serafen, or indeed anywhere else in Stockholm.'

Lina let out a loud laugh. We all turned to look at her. 'Sorry, sorry,' she said. 'It's just all of you sitting around with your serious expressions.' She mimicked Mama's worried look.

'Lina, it's a serious situation,' I said.

Mama was wringing the dishrag in her hands. 'Now I don't know about this . . . this, what'd'yacallit, this . . . *ray*,' she said. 'A ray? I never heard of such a thing.'

'Mama, we don't have the money for a sanatorium. We should think about it,' I said. 'But anyway,' I went on, 'it's not up to us: Lina should be the one who decides.' She still looked like she was a spectator on the scene. Sometimes she played too much at being the baby of the family. Even though she wasn't. 'Lina? Don't you have anything to say about all this?'

She smiled. 'Oh, you're blowing it out of proportion. There's absolutely nothing wrong with me that a bit of a rest won't fix. This nice doctor here has just made a mistake. I'm sorry, Doctor, I don't mean to be rude, but that's how it is.'

Dr Dance was nodding. 'Miss Dahlstrom, I completely understand that you feel that way.'

Petter squirmed in his chair. His face had turned a bright shade of pink. The doctor went on, 'But I regret to tell you that this is the illness speaking. Your calm feelings are the treacherous symptoms of the first stage of this terrible disease.'

'Now, you listen here, mister,' said Petter. It had been one too many 'Miss Dahlstrom's for him. He stood up. He put his hands flat on the table and leaned over towards Dr Dance. 'First of all, it's *Mrs* Dahlstrom. Mrs. That's right. She's *my wife*.' He pointed his finger at his own chest. 'And second of all, what right do you have to come bursting in here, telling us about some crazy ray and how my wife has a terrible treacherous disease!'

Petter was a very tall and large man. He practically had to stoop and turn side-on to go through doorways. He towered over Dr Dance, who sat with his head tilted back, looking up at him.

'Mr Dahlstrom,' the doctor said, 'you have my apologies.' He put his hand on his heart. 'I'm awfully sorry I offended you. I meant no insult. I myself am something of a bachelor at heart, and I always make the mistake of assuming everybody else is too. I do apologise.' He stood up. 'And yes: you're absolutely right, Mr Dahlstrom, I had no right, no right whatsoever, to intrude on you all in this manner with such grave news. Once again, I apologise. I was only hoping to save time, which can be of the essence in cases like these. But I see I have been too impatient. I'm truly sorry.'

He reached into his jacket pocket and pulled out a calling card. 'I know it's a lot of information to take in at once, but I do ask that you consider my offer. Please take as much time as you need to talk it over.' He put the card on the table. 'But please also keep in mind that this illness can progress quickly, and swift action is of the utmost importance.'

He nodded to each of us, then picked up his hat and gloves and left.

3.

ALL THROUGH OUR dinner of cabbage rolls, now cold, Petter seethed about Dr Dance and his 'Miss Dahlstrom's.

'Just because he's some rich American, he thinks he can come barging in here like an oil baron and act like my wife's fair game.' He shoved his half-eaten plate of food away and leaned back in his chair.

'Petter, that's not the point at hand,' I said. This was hardly the first time someone had fancied Lina. 'We need to think about what's best for Lina's health.'

'Health! As if anyone'd trust that creep! Making eyes at Lina. Forget it!'

'He was just trying to help,' Lina said. 'I thought he was very polite. And so serious.' She too was hardly eating. She'd cut up the cabbage roll and was pushing the bits from one side of her plate to the other.

'He certainly did seem to be dedicated to his work,' said Papa, who always found this an impressive characteristic in a man.

'He must be a very good doctor, putting in that extra effort to come all the way out here to give us Lina's results. Shows real commitment. Not to mention his offer of free treatment. It isn't something to turn our noses up at, that's what I say. Even at Serafen we'd have to pay.'

'He says it's free *now*,' Mama said, 'but then later he'll say different. And at least with Serafen, you know where you are. I don't know about this clinic.' She shook her head. 'Sounded to me like he wanted the chance to try out his newfangled machine—his *ray*—on someone. Our Lina's not some kind of guinea pig!' She sniffed. 'But the whole thing's not up to me.'

'We could go and take a look at the clinic,' I said.

Petter slammed his hand down on the table. 'We're not discussing it further! I'm not letting that American anywhere near Lina, and that's the end of that!'

We ate in silence for a few minutes.

'Well,' Lina said, 'all I can say is Dr Dance is certainly miles better than that first chap we got at Serafen. Blix. Remember him, Greta? Couldn't even manage to stay awake through my appointment.' She laughed at the memory.

Lina was right about that: I wouldn't have trusted that fool Blix with so much as bandaging a cut on my finger. I remember thinking how lucky it was that Dance had turned up when he had. Out of nowhere, too, like a fairy godmother in a story. Even though Dr Dance seemed unusual, I thought Petter's reaction against him was much too hasty, as well as wrongheaded. If I'd had to choose between that old ghoul Blix and Dr Dance's crazy ray, I would've chosen Dance any day of the week. Anything was better than Serafen. In the seven years I'd been working at the

Hellgren tobacco factory, there had been nine cigar-rollers who died at Serafen, some of TB, and some in childbirth. As bizarre as Dr Dance's ray sounded, and as odd as he might seem, I knew he was our best bet to cure Lina.

Over the following days, while I was getting more and more worried about Lina's diagnosis, she herself was brimming with joy. She sailed about the place with a dreamy look on her face, smiling the whole time, as if there was music in the air that only she could hear. She kept repeating that she was fine, she'd never felt better, and that we were all jumping at shadows. And she did look fine. More than fine. Lina always looked lovely, as I said, but at that time she was absolutely radiant. Her face was rosy, the skin smooth as wax, and her eyes sparkled even more than usual. She laughed more than usual too, and seemed to find everything beautiful. The view of the dirty courtyard, the cross-section of a cut apple, she marvelled and exclaimed over all of it. 'Everything's just so . . . glorious,' she'd say. 'Can't you see it?'

Lina had always had a cheerful disposition, but this was something else, something with a sinister edge. It frightened me. I'd come across her crouched in the corner, trying to catch dancing dust motes in her hand, or sprawled over the couch in the main room with her head thrown back and her eyes closed, a rapturous expression on her face, as if she was drunk.

4.

WHENEVER I HAVE a problem, the first person I always talk
it over with is Ilse. Ilse was my very best friend at the time, and
she still is. We used to live on the same street before we moved
to Hallandsgatan, and these days we live together. She worked
alongside me at the Wilhelm Hellgren & Co tobacco factory on
and off, but she also made extra money working as a domestic,
usually as a scullery maid in a big house, or sometimes as a char
in smaller places. She'd landed a live-in job with a rich family in
Malmö over Christmas and New Year, so I hadn't seen her for a
few weeks, but she was due back any day.

A few days after our visit from Dr Dance I came into work
and saw Ilse sitting in her old spot beside mine on the bench.
I ran over to her and put my arms around her. Ilse was soft and
round, shorter than me, with a mass of straw-coloured curls that
she was forever trying to tame into neat waves. She had pale skin
and two pink patches always on her cheeks. I held her tight.

Her hair tickled my face, and smelled the same as ever, like dusty, sun-warmed grass.

As we worked, I whispered to her the news about Lina. She dropped the tobacco leaves she was holding and took my hand.

'Oh, darling,' she said. 'Not Lina!' We both turned to look at where Lina was sitting, at the table on the other side of the aisle. Lina's face had lost its rosy glow. Her skin was grey and her forehead creased in concentration as she worked.

Ilse put her arm around me. 'But maybe it'll be fine,' she said. 'You'll see. You'll go back to Serafen and they'll have made a mistake.' She picked up her tobacco leaves again and fed them into the roller. 'Or maybe . . . have you thought about this? Maybe it could be that Lina might be, you know, expecting. Now, wouldn't that be lovely? A new baby? Lina'd be so happy. I think she never got over the little one she lost.'

It was true that Lina's miscarriage had taken a toll on her. She'd been so very ill, and grieved for that lost baby enough to make your heart ache. I hoped desperately that Ilse was right.

When I next looked over at Lina I saw that she had laid her head down on the workbench. Over the last weeks she'd been sleeping more and more, and only getting up when she was woken. Her euphoria had disappeared, and now she had no energy for anything. When she came in to Hellgren for her two shifts a week, she barely managed to make it through the day. We used to walk to work: the factory was about twenty minutes from Hallandsgatan, but it started to happen that Lina would already be worn out by the time we arrived. Mama and I shared a bicycle, and I made a pillion seat on it for Lina, but even when she was spared the walk, she could hardly keep her eyes open at work.

The Wilhelm Hellgren factory was an enormous complex of grim-looking buildings that took up a whole block along Åsögatan and Götgatan. The place looked like something out of a Dickens novel, all pointed gables and soot-darkened stone. It wasn't only the cigar-rollers that worked there, but all the company staff: the people who designed the packaging, the clerks and the accountants, and the businessmen who ran the show. They of course had the best rooms on the upper floors. Not that I'd ever set foot there. Ilse and Lina and I worked in the cigar-rolling room, on the ground floor. This room was long and bare, like a barn, with tall arched windows along one wall and rows and rows of benches with hundreds of women squeezed along both sides, hunched over, busy making cigars.

I knew that Hellgren was absolutely the worst place for Lina to be spending her days. At that time of year our workroom was as cold and damp as a cellar. It smelled like a tin of tobacco, and there were always bits of dried tobacco leaf crunching under your feet and tobacco dust floating in the air. You'd blow your nose after a shift and your handkerchief would be speckled brown with tobacco crumbs. It was not the place for a person with lung trouble. I tried to convince Lina to take a few weeks off, but she kept insisting on coming in. She was worried about the money. 'Because, my darling Greta, you know that in this life we all have to earn our keep,' she'd say.

Lina was draped over the workbench, quite inert, as if she was in a deep sleep: no small feat in a place as noisy as Hellgren. On top of the clattering of a hundred cigar-rolling frame pins being pushed up and down, there was the constant blare of dance music coming through the row of loudspeakers that ran along the central aisle, the noise amplified by women singing along. I looked around for the floor manager, a hulking red-faced man named Blund, and saw he was prowling on the far side of the room. I grabbed a handful of my finished cigars and darted over to where Lina was sitting. She was fast asleep. As I slid in beside her on the bench I gave her a nudge. She blinked open her eyes.

Everyone had a daily quota of cigars to finish, and for each cigar that was broken or damaged, another two needed to be produced. Because a cigar took more than a day to complete—you had to leave them to dry out overnight a few times—damaged cigars meant your quota kept piling up during the week, and then you had to stay back, sometimes for hours, to finish up on Saturday. At the end of the workday, Blund checked our cigar crates and entered the number made and broken in a ledger that he kept on a lectern at the front of the room.

Lina had become slow and clumsy. She started breaking more and more cigars, and making ones that weren't up to scratch. When I sat beside her at the workbench I always tried to cover for her, rolling extras to make up for her broken ones, and taking the misshapen, too-small cigars out of her crate and putting them into mine. But Blund still noticed her shortfall.

I could see him coming towards us down the central aisle, rolling from side to side on his gouty feet like a ship.

'Come on, girly,' he croaked at Lina, leaning down over her table, 'you can work faster than that, can't ya?'

I could smell his sour breath. Lina bent her head. Her hands were trembling as she pressed and folded the leaves. Blund started picking through her crate of finished cigars with his pudgy fingers.

'Hmm . . . Look at this mess. Shoddy workmanship,' he said, and then, 'What d'ya call this?' He took out a lumpy, bulbous cigar from Lina's crate and held it up. It was about as bad as the ones I used to make back when I first started rolling. 'Eh? Girly? D'you call this a cigar? Would you wanna smoke this?' He shoved it in Lina's face. 'Looks like something else to me!' He gave a great guffaw, his mouth opening so wide that I could see his brown and broken molars.

Lina didn't answer or look up from the leaves she was pressing. Her face had gone bright pink and her eyes were glassy. Blund then proceeded to make crude motions with the cigar, laughing loudly the whole time. The women on the surrounding benches fell silent and stopped working to watch. His abundant flesh was quaking with laughter.

I can't stand bullies. I stood up and snatched the thing from Blund's hand and broke it in two. He stood there open-mouthed. There was an eruption of laughter from the women around us.

'Add another two to my list, Mr Blund,' I said.

I dropped the broken cigar on the floor.

'You're getting a strike for that, Fredelius,' he yelled, waving his finger right in my face. I ignored him. That old bully didn't scare me.

5.

AFTER DANCE'S VISIT, we eventually agreed about getting a second opinion, but the earliest appointment at Serafen wasn't until almost a fortnight later. Now, I'm not and never have been someone who's content to sit around waiting, so I took it upon myself in that fortnight to learn as much as I possibly could about Lina's illness. The day after the scene with Blund, I finished work early and went to collect the bicycle. Mama had taken it that morning to her charring job over on Bondegatan. Then I rode to the library. I love that place. I love any library, really. Even the shabby old Worker's Library we used to go to as kids seemed magical to me. The Worker's Library was not much more than a few rooms upstairs from Friberg's bakery, so calling it a library was a bit of an overstatement. If you went through the open doorway beside Friberg's window and climbed up two flights of rackety stairs, you'd find a series of dim and dusty rooms lined with mismatched bookcases. The books there were mostly old and missing their dust jackets. When you opened them, they let out a whiff of mildew and a grainy shower of perished cardboard from the worn spine.

But even with all that, the place was like an enchanted world to me, enclosed and safe. I used to spend hours and hours there, reading first *Tomtebobarnen* and *Malins Midsommar*, then everything from Hjalmar Söderberg and Selma Lagerlöf to translations of Edith Øberg and *Frankenstein*. But there was one book in the library that I'd loved more than any other. When I was ten, I had it on loan continuously for a whole year. It was a book about the life of Karolina Widerström, the first female doctor in Sweden. In another kind of life I would've been a doctor too. This book had a photograph of Widerström on the front page. She was already old in the picture, sitting in a fancy chair, with a top hat on, and a cravat. I still remember her face in that picture, her eyes staring out at you, so stern, as if she could see right into your heart and knew that you could do better than you were doing. I used to think about her a lot when I was little, and she had a place in my trinity of childhood heroes, along with Queen Christina of Sweden and Ragnar Lodbrok.

The Worker's Library was long gone and had been replaced with the City Library on Odengatan. The two couldn't have been more different. The City Library was in the rich part of town, which was full of shops too expensive to enter, and parks with perfectly tended gardens. The library building had a round central tower rising from a squat base, dotted all around with small square windows. The building was brand new, but it looked like part of the Kärnan Castle in Helsingborg, like it was from another time.

When I had the bicycle I often rode there from work, through Gamla Stan, and up Sveavägen. It was uphill for most of Sveavägen, but once the park was in sight the road flattened out and I could sail down the hill, right into the park. As soon as you entered the park gate, the quiet of the trees and the snow stretched out all around, which was heaven to me after a shift at the factory with the voices and music and clanking in the air all day. In the park there was only the soft hiss of my tyres on the footpath, and the birds, and the wind whistling in my ears. In winter, the park was usually deserted, and often I didn't see a single person on the way.

Soon, the central tower of the library would come into view, pushing its way up through the treetops, which at that time of the year were nothing more than bare branches. I left my bicycle at the back of the library and walked around to Sveavägen and the main stairs at the front. Going through that wide doorway, pushing open the heavy glass door into the dim hall, past the shadowy Greek figures, and climbing up and up the wide marble steps into the reading room made the grimy streets and the drudgery of my daily life fall away. In the light of that circular room I felt part of a different world, one of ideas and imagination. The walls of the tower formed an atrium that rose right to the domed ceiling three floors up, lined all the way with curved landings and shelves of books. Their brightly coloured spines shone out like stained glass.

That day I went straight to the science section. It was up on the third landing, a place I rarely ventured. Everything I knew about TB I'd got from reading novels from the 1800s where the characters had consumption and were wasting away. Nothing very helpful.

I found an encyclopedia. Under Active Tuberculosis, this:

Symptoms:

Coughing for more than three weeks.

Coughing up blood.

Fatigue.

Chills.

Weight loss (unintentional).

Prognosis:

Seventy-two per cent of sufferers will die without treatment, most often within the first forty days.

The early stages of the illness are characterised by mild
euphoria. This means that patients often refuse medical treatment, not believing that they are ill.

The more I read, the more I realised that Dr Dance was right.
We needed to act quickly. I turned to the page listing the cure.

- Resting in a warm, dry climate, preferably one with a
  constant temperature above twenty degrees Celsius.
- Cleanliness.
- Plenty of nourishing food.
- Light exercise undertaken in the sunshine.

Whoever had written that entry had obviously never been to
Södermalm: Söder, as we locals call it. Where we lived was almost
always dark, chilly, damp and dirty, except for a few weeks in
summer when the cold gave way to a festering heat, and all the
smells of the place were intensified and the air swarmed with
mosquitoes and gnats.

What I most wanted to know about was treatments. I found some old medical reference books, but nowhere could I find anything about radiation therapy. Other than sanatoriums, and a drug called Sanocrysin, the books only listed crazy-sounding procedures—such as crushing the patient's chest with bags of lead, or cutting a hole into their lung to make it collapse—which made Dr Dance's cell-blasting ray sound like a perfectly safe and reasonable alternative. A librarian told me that to find out about the newest treatments I would have to go to the Karolinska Medical Institute library, over in Solna. But, he told me, I wouldn't be able to get in. It was for medical students only.

I rode back home in the dark, eager to tell everyone what I'd found out. But the only person who was still up was Petter. I made him sit down at the table, and I got out my notebook.

'So you're the doctor now?' he joked when he saw my pages of notes.

I wish I could have been. I went through my notes, explaining the different stages of the illness, and things to expect.

'That's why we need to do something right away,' I said. 'Most people die without treatment, and they die quickly, if it's serious.'

Petter was busy cleaning his nails with the end of a match.

'Are you even listening?'

'Sure I am.' He lolled back in his chair and stretched his arms overhead. 'But I think you're jumping the gun. We'll get Lina checked out by a different doctor. She's already booked in. A couple of weeks won't matter. It's no big deal.' He yawned. 'Relax. Everything'll turn out fine. Lina doesn't even think she's ill, don't forget. You're always saying we should listen to her.'

'But that's part of the illness! That's exactly what I've been telling you!' I stopped to take a breath. Getting into an argument with him wouldn't help anyone. 'Look. It's important not to take any chances. Not only for Lina, it's important for us too. You know, if it is TB that she has, we can all get contaminated.'

'What d'you mean? TB's not catching. You're born with it . . . a spot on the lung. Everyone knows that.'

'Petter, it's a contagious illness. I think we're fine for now. Lina's still in what they call the latent stage, but once she starts coughing, we're all at risk. You most of all.'

'Why me most of all?'

'You have the most contact with her.'

'Nah, you've got it wrong.' But he looked worried. He pulled my notebook towards him and huddled over it, running his fingers under the lines of text as he read, his lips moving. Petter wasn't much of a reader, and didn't need to be. His life was spent on the Slussen docks, loading and unloading timber, sacks of coal, bales of fabric. 'I can't make head nor tail of this,' he said after a few minutes. 'Your writing's too messy. Puh-new-mo-tho-rax?' he intoned slowly. 'What's that when it's at home?'

'It's something that could go wrong with Lina. It means her lungs might, you know, sort of . . . fall in.'

He gaped at me.

'And then,' I went on, 'she won't be able to breathe.'

I wished then that I hadn't learned so much about it.

6.

WHEN I LOOK back on it now, it seems to me that that was the night when the trouble with Petter first began. I suppose it was my fault. Over the next week or so I began to notice that he was out of the house more, and some nights he didn't come home at all. He'd have excuses. One day he said he'd been down at the docks waiting for extra work to come in, and the next it was that he'd been so tired after his shift that he'd slept at his friend Jonas's place, which was right beside the docks. And he avoided Lina. I noticed that he wouldn't sit at the table when she was sitting there, and I once got up in the night to find him sleeping on the floor of the kitchen instead of in bed with her. Had he become afraid of catching TB? Or was there another reason?

I couldn't get out of my head what Dr Dance had said about how important it was to act quickly. And I was sure I'd heard Lina coughing in the night. Of course when I asked her she denied it. The appointment at Serafen seemed like years away.

'I know just the thing to cheer you up,' Ilse said as we got our bicycles after our shift. It had been snowing and the air was sharp. Night had come long before.

'Oh yes, don't tell me . . .' I knew she was going to try to convince me to go ice-skating with her in Djurgården. Ilse was addicted to skating. For her it was the solution, if only a temporary one, to every problem. 'It's that glorious speed!' she'd say. She was a devil on the ice alright, swooping in tight circles, pirouetting, arms out and one leg in the air.

At that time it was coming to the middle of winter. In Stockholm this is a season of leafless trees and thick snow that make the city into a black and white picture of itself. The days struggle to get out of the night's grip, and each day is so brief that they begin to feel as unreal as dreams, as though you might only have imagined them. Prime skating weather, Ilse would say. That year most of the archipelago was frozen over, and people were skating not only on the lakes, but the whole way from Gamla Stan to Färjstaden.

'Come on! It'll be good for you,' she said. 'What you need is some fresh air. You look just about worn away with worry.'

I really didn't feel like going. To tell the truth, I hated skating. I'd never got the hang of it. The only reason I went was to see the pleasure on Ilse's face as she whirled around, and also for the roasted chestnuts.

'Go on, come with me as a favour. Please?' she begged. I knew she wouldn't stop pestering me until I agreed, and honestly, I had nothing better to do.

We pulled our scarves up over our noses and put on hats and gloves. We brushed the snow off the bicycle seats and were wheeling them out onto the road when a voice called, 'Miss Fredelius!'

A figure was running towards us along Åsögatan. A tall, thin man.

'Hey! Miss Fredelius!' He ran up to us and stopped, puffing for breath. It was Dr Dance.

'I'm so glad I managed to catch you. Listen, I need to talk to you urgently. It's about your sister.'

'What about her? We're getting a second opinion on Thursday.'

'Second opinion!' He threw up his hands in horror. 'There's no time for that. What she needs is treatment, and right away.'

'I understand that the situation's urgent,' I said. 'And I'm worried about it too, but I'm afraid it's not up to me to decide. I'll speak to my family again, but they're not all that keen on your treatments. But thank you again for offering.'

Ilse and I wheeled our bicycles on.

'Wait!' called Dr Dance. He loped along beside us, one foot on the path, one in the dirty snow that lay in the gutter. 'Listen.' He stepped in front of us and put his hand on my handlebars. His breath made white clouds in the cold air. 'How about this? How about I take you two ladies to my clinic right now and show you how the machines work? Miss Fredelius, I know your mother especially was a little worried about the treatment methods. Maybe if you see the machines yourself, it might help convince your family.' He looked from me to Ilse hopefully. 'It's not far. I have a car waiting.'

'I'm not sure that would—'

'No! Wait!' Ilse said, her eyes bright with excitement. She always loved an adventure. 'Why don't we go?' She put her hand on my arm. 'Can't hurt.'

'And miss skating?'

'Oh, skating—we can skate any old day of the week. Don't you want to see these machines?'

It was true that I was curious. I hadn't been able to find any information about rays in the medical books, and I'd started to wonder if they existed at all.

'Alright,' I said. 'Let's go.' We locked up our bikes.

Dr Dance had a large black car waiting on Götgatan. I had only ever travelled in a car once, years before, as part of a car demonstration in Kungsträdgården, so it was a treat to climb into the warm interior, sit on the leather seats and watch the glittering streets and lamps and bridges glide past. I was sorry that the trip to Östermalm was so short.

Dr Dance stopped the car beside a small park which had a fountain in the middle of it, empty of water for the winter, made of pale stone with a wide basin and a statue of a woman standing in its centre. You'd never find a public fountain like that in Hallandsgatan. The thing would've been choked with litter during the winter, probably with a few drunks sleeping underneath the basin, and people doing their laundry in it during the summer. But this park, and all the streets surrounding it, was clean and quiet. There was no one about, only a man in an overcoat walking his dog in the distance, whistling. There was no other sound. No one shouted from the windows or slammed doors. No children played on the footpaths and no one came and went from their night shifts. Everyone was shut inside, warm and safe and silent in their comfortable apartments. The neatly painted doors were blank and impersonal and gave nothing away, like the smooth faces of rich people. When I looked up I saw rows of lighted squares of windows, glowing honey-coloured on every building, all the way to the end of the street.

Dr Dance led us over to a row of buildings opposite the park. The footpaths here were wider than in Söder. They'd been swept clean of snow, and gravel had been laid down, so you didn't even get your shoes wet. He unlocked the door of one building and we went upstairs and through a dark and deserted waiting room into a larger room. He turned on the lights and spread his arms wide.

'Welcome to my clinic.'

To step into that room was to step into a futuristic scene. There was an impression of dazzling brightness. White-painted walls, tiled white floor, shining steel. The air was cool on my face, and tasted thin and pure, like the air of a snowfield. The overhead lights left no trace of shadow and all the objects in the room leapt to the eye, sharp-edged and clear. Strange instruments and contraptions of metal and glass gleamed from every corner. I'd never been in a place so sparkling and clean, never knew that such places even existed. Especially not within a fifteen-minute walk from the grit of Serafen.

In one corner of the room was an imposing machine, like a large steel cabinet, as tall as me and three times as wide. Its front was studded with dials and switches and lights. It had a thick cord running out of the top, and thinner cords sprouting from the sides. It looked to be almost a living thing, asleep. In the opposite corner was another machine, also large but squat, a wide, shoulder-height white box with a fat metal pipe coming out of the front. The sides of this machine were smooth as an eggshell, without visible joins or seams or rivets, as if the thing wasn't even man-made, but had emerged from somewhere fully formed. From a row of hooks above it hung aprons and goggles.

A high shelf that ran along two walls was stacked with brown-and-green glass bottles, small wooden boxes, and a row of smaller machines with dials that looked like scales or clocks. Under the shelf on one wall was a sink and a long workbench with two black microscopes under glass domes, glass beakers, more bottles, racks of test tubes. There were surgical implements laid out on a white cloth: a stethoscope, scissors, forceps, thermometer, and other items I didn't recognise.

Ilse stood looking around, her mouth practically hanging open.

'Yes, it's an impressive sight, isn't it?' said Dr Dance. 'It's taken me more than a few years to build this place up. Most of our equipment is imported direct from the States, or hand-built by me and my colleagues.'

He pointed to the white machine with the pipe. 'This is the one I have in mind for your sister,' he said. 'Diathermy.' He went over to it and pressed a switch at the back. The machine started to hum. Up close, I saw that from the fat pipe at the front two thinner pipes branched off. Both had a flat steel disc attached to the end, about the size of a large dinner plate and five times as thick. Dr Dance switched off the machine.

'See,' he said, 'the patient sits here.' He fetched a small stool and placed it in front of the machine. 'Miss?' he gestured to Ilse. 'Would you be so good as to oblige us?' Ilse sat on the stool and he adjusted the discs so that one of them was in front of her and one behind.

'These are condenser plates,' Dance said. 'They transmit high-frequency waves, and as those waves travel through the tissues of the body they're converted into heat—intense heat. This heat has great therapeutic potential for cases like your sister's.'

'So you're saying the heat is generated by the tissues, not by the machine? And I suppose that the heat stimulates the blood circulation, or does it have another function?'

Dr Dance looked at me with his head tilted to one side. 'I gotta say, you've certainly done your homework. You're absolutely spot on. Maybe you ought to think about a career in medicine! This heat therapy reduces inflammation by increasing blood flow, but rather than the heat being applied directly, the current causes the tissues to generate the heat themselves, which is much more beneficial.'

'And what about side effects?'

'As I said, this is a very safe treatment. Adverse effects are very rare, and are primarily to do with the skill of the person administering the treatment.'

'Burns, you mean?'

'That's right. The machine does generate a relatively small amount of heat. But burns are only ever a risk with an inexperienced practitioner. It's true that minor adverse effects do occur in some patients from time to time: headache, dizziness, that kind of thing. But these quickly pass.'

Dr Dance went over to the cabinet and took out a small black case, about the size of a shoebox. 'Then we also have this,' he said. 'The violet ray.'

He opened the case and pulled out a thick black bakelite cylinder with an electrical cord running out of it, and a glass rod with a flattish bulb at one end. He fitted the narrow end of the rod into the black cylinder, which I now saw was a handle, and screwed it into place. He plugged the cord into an electrical socket on the wall and the thing immediately started buzzing. He held it up by the handle, as if it was a sword. The room filled with the sharp, damp scent of an approaching lightning storm.

'Smell that?' he asked. He sniffed the air. 'Ozone. One of the many benefits of the ray. Very calming for the nervous system. Now, just you watch this.' He pressed a switch on the handle and the rod began to glow with a faint blue light. It got brighter by the second. 'See that? This particular light frequency is produced by millions of ions bombarding the argon gas inside this glass tube.' The tube was now burning as bright as a light bulb, brighter. I had to shield my eyes. 'What you see in front of you is much more than a pretty-coloured light: that blue colour is actually full of ultraviolet rays, which are normally invisible to the naked eye, and have great germicidal capabilities. They can also rejuvenate tissues, and have a general immune-strengthening function.'

I'd never heard of anything like this before, and I have to say it sounded a bit wild to me.

'So, another form of heat therapy? Is that what you mean by rejuvenating tissues?'

'Yes, it is another form of heat therapy, but the UV rays also promote cellular renewal. Now, it might sound fanciful, but in the States the ray is beginning to be well regarded as an antibacterial and regenerative treatment. It's very new, though. Cutting edge.'

He pressed the handle switch again and the light began to pulse slightly.

'Miss,' said Dr Dance to Ilse, 'may I? If you wouldn't mind rolling up your sleeve.'

Ilse took off her coat, pushed up her sleeve and came towards Dance with a doubtful look. 'No need to worry,' he said, 'this particular treatment feels very pleasant.'

Ilse held out her arm to him, bracing herself for a shock. Dr Dance passed the glass bulb up and down her forearm, from wrist to elbow.

'See?' he said. 'Nothing to be scared of.'

Ilse smiled. 'It just feels warm, is all,' she said. 'Like being out in the sun.'

'What did I tell you?' said Dr Dance. 'Perfectly safe!'

He flicked the switch and the ray's light died away.

'Now. There's one more thing I want to show you.'

He led us over to the workbench and removed the glass cover from one of the microscopes. He sat at a stool, and bent his head to the eyepiece. He fiddled with the dials. 'There!' He stood up. 'Please, take a look, Miss Fredelius.'

I'd never had the chance to look through a microscope before. I remember when I first read about microbes and bacteria at school, the idea had seemed magical to me: a whole invisible parallel world living alongside us, and inside us too. It was like something out of a fairy story. I leaned over the microscope and closed one eye. At first all I could see was a pink, blurry mass. After a few seconds I could make out some pink squiggles on a white background.

'What is it that I'm looking at?' I asked.

'That, Miss Fredelius, is a sample from inside your sister's lungs. It shows the bacilli that are this very moment infesting her and making her ill.'

'Let me see too!' Ilse pushed me out of the way and squinted into the eyepiece.

'Miss Fredelius,' said Dr Dance, turning to me with a grave look. 'You and I both know how ill your sister is, and we both want to do everything we possibly can to help her. Those bacilli you see there may not look like much, but they are at work on your sister's lungs as we speak, multiplying every second. Once the disease becomes active—coughing, fever, chills—it can progress very quickly.' He lowered his voice to slightly above a whisper. 'Listen, I didn't want to say this in the presence of the rest of your family, but the fact is, there's no small chance that your sister may die of this illness.'

I got a feeling like icy water running down the middle of my spine. Hot tears welled up.

'I can see that you want the best for your sister,' he went on, 'and I know I can help her. Perhaps Mrs Dahlstrom herself, and the rest of your family, aren't as aware of the seriousness of the situation?'

I blinked down the tears and nodded.

'I'd like you to do something for me,' he said. He went to a cupboard and took out a small wooden case. 'In here is a micro-scope,' he said. 'I want you to take this home to your family and show them the slide I just showed you. Will you do that for me?' He handed me the case. 'Explain to them just how serious Mrs Dahlstrom's illness is. Ask them to consider my offer. Tell them you've seen my equipment in action first-hand, and that it's perfectly safe, and effective.'

I nodded again.

He covered Lina's slide with an empty one, and put them into a small wooden box. He handed the box to me and I put it in my coat pocket.

'I'll drive you two ladies home now.'

We were silent on the drive back over the bridge to Söder. As the night-time city slid past the windows, my tears came back and fell down my cheeks in the dark. Ilse took my hand. I let my head rest on her shoulder.

7.

IT WAS ALREADY clear to me that Petter was the main source of opposition to Dr Dance's treatment, but I wasn't prepared for how badly he would react to the microscope slide.

'What's all this?' he asked early the next morning when he saw me setting up the microscope on the kitchen table.

He'd spent the night away again, and smelled strongly of brännvin. I explained that I'd seen Dr Dance's clinic, how sleek and modern it was, and what the slide showed, but Petter refused even to look at the microscope, let alone through it.

I'd already shown the slides to Lina and Mama and Papa the night before. I started by telling them again that we needed to consider Dr Dance's treatment.

Papa nodded. 'It's a very generous offer. I always said we should take it up.'

'What about getting a second opinion?' Mama asked. 'Isn't that what we agreed? On Thursday?'

'We can't wait around for so long,' I said. 'This is a serious illness. Every day might be important.'

Lina was lying on the couch wrapped in blankets. She groaned. 'Oh, not this again. You lot are making too much fuss. I don't need any fancy ray, or any other thing. All I need is to have a rest for a while, and for you to stop arguing. I'll get better on my own. You'll see.'

'For god's sake, Lina, you're not helping,' I said. I turned back to Mama. 'Look, I can even show you Lina's illness.'

I opened the microscope case. I felt like a magician about to do a fabulous trick. I was sure everyone was going to be as impressed as Ilse and I had been.

I had to coax Mama to look through the eyepiece, and when she finally did, all she said was, 'Oh yes, very nice,' in an uncertain voice. What did impress her, though, was the fact that Dr Dance had lent me the microscope in the first place: clearly it was an expensive piece of equipment. Mama was in a panic in case it got damaged in some way, and later insisted on keeping it packed up in its case overnight; she even went to fetch an old towel to wrap the case in for extra protection.

After Mama had looked through the eyepiece, Lina became interested, and got up to see.

'No,' she said, hunched over the microscope. She shook her head, which brought on a flurry of small dry coughs that she tried to supress. 'You're saying those little squiggly things came from the insides of my lungs? Impossible! How would he even get them from there? I bet he just painted them onto that micro-scope.' She straightened up, steadying herself against the table, as if she was dizzy. I reached out to feel her forehead, but she shoved my hand away. 'Lovely colour, though, isn't it?' she said. 'I never knew the insides of my lungs were so pretty.' I could hear her straining for breath.

'Lina, you have to stop pretending. I think we should try Dr Dance's treatment,' I said. 'I saw the machines for myself, and he even tested one on Ilse.'

Lina shrugged, and lay back down on the couch. 'If you like,' she said. 'I mean, why not. I'm sure there's no harm in it. But we all know it isn't really up to me, is it? Petter's the one you've got to convince.'

After seeing the slide, Papa looked even more worried than before. Over the past week I had watched his face become sunken and grey: the face of an old man. He'd noticed Lina's coughing too. New and deeper lines seemed to etch themselves daily around his eyes and down his thin cheeks.

'Greta,' he said, 'I think you're absolutely right. We can't leave Lina to Serafen. The fellow there sounded worse than useless. This Dr Dance, he seems to know his stuff. But like Lina says, it's her and Petter—'

'Papa, it's Petter,' Lina said. 'Petter's the one who decides.'

'Hmm. I'll have a word with him about it when I see him tomorrow night.'

So that next morning I was ready for a fight.

'And now you're in cahoots with that crazy old doctor?' Petter said as he sat down at the table across from me.

'I'm not in cahoots with anyone,' I said. 'All I want is for Lina to get better. And besides, Dr Dance might not be as crazy as you think.'

Petter grunted and slouched over in his chair. 'I saw what I saw: he was making eyes at my wife. "Miss Dahlstrom" my arse.'

'Petter, who cares! You think no one ever looks at Lina? Listen, Dr Dance can help us. We can get something from him—'

'Enough! I won't have it!'

The sound of Lina's coughs rang out through the apartment.

'See?' I said. 'She's started coughing now. That means she's in the active stage. And that means that we're—'

'It's probably just the flu! Jesus, Greta, you're talking like none of us have ever been ill. Lina will go to Serafen and that's that. Serafen's always been good enough for the rest of us, and Serafen is where Lina will go.'

'But the treatments there are like something out of the Stone Age compared to what Dance can provide. He is offering something we'd never get otherwise. You know what they'll do to Lina at Serafen? They'll cut holes in her lungs; they'll make her lie on a bed for weeks and weeks while they put lead weights on her chest to crush her ribs. Is that what you want?' My voice was getting louder than I had meant it to. 'Do you know how many people die in that place?'

'Die?' He jumped up out of his chair. 'I've had enough of your fearmongering. Lina's not going to die!' He gave a kind of shiver. 'Ugh, stop talking like that, will you?' He began pacing around the room with a disgusted look on his face. 'I've said no, and that's the end of it. We're not having anything to do with this Dance character and his contraptions. If Lina goes anywhere, she'll go to Serafen, so you just put away that, that . . . thing over there,' he waved at the microscope, 'and say no more about it.'

Perhaps Papa could convince him, I thought. I didn't know then that he'd never get the chance to even try.

'Fine. Lina has an appointment at Serafen tomorrow in any case. I'm going too. Will you come along?'

'You go with her.' He avoided my eye. 'I'll be working late.'

8.

BUT HE WASN'T working late. The next morning, he was gone. Lina woke me, and handed me a note. Her face was stained with tears.

> Gone to Sundsvall to work with Alrik.
> Better wages. I'll send money.
>
> P.

Sundsvall, where Petter's brother lived, was miles away. Up north. That day Lina took a turn for the worse. She went into fits of coughing that left her limp and breathless. That night she shook me awake, coughing and gasping for breath. She turned on the lamp and showed me her handkerchief, speckled with blood.

'What's happening to me?' The tears slid down her pale face. I held her close while her body quaked and shuddered through spasms of coughing. The more she cried, the more she coughed, and the more she coughed, the harder it was for her to breathe.

I turned my face away and held my breath whenever she coughed. Her skin was clammy and her bones felt sharp under my arms. There was no longer any doubting Dr Dance's diagnosis. I got up and opened the window, to ventilate the room. I knew TB is spread through the air. It was too cold to keep the window open for long. All of us were in danger now.

We went back to Serafen, but it was as good as useless. The doctor we saw this time wasn't quite as decrepit as old Blix, but he was just as bad. Dr Hellbrun, his name was: a thin worm of a fellow, with a long beige face. He kept talking over us. They'd misplaced the previous test results, and all of Lina's notes, he said, so the tests would have to be done again, for the third time.

'There's no time!' I kept saying. Lina sat beside me, trying to suppress her coughs. 'Look, can't you see how ill my sister is? She's coughing up blood—'

'No, that's gone away now,' Lina interrupted.

'Lina, it's going to come back,' I said. 'Dr Hellbrun, we can't wait a whole week for tests that are going to tell us what we can see with our own eyes.'

'Now, now, miss.' Dr Hellbrun made a smoothing motion with his hands. 'Please. There's no need to get excited. Please calm down.'

The man was useless. It was time to take matters into my own hands.

As soon as I'd dropped Lina home I rode over to the post office and sent a telegram to Dr Dance.

ACCEPT OFFER LINA DAHLSTROM. WHEN SUITABLE FOR TREATMENT? G. FREDELIUS

I wanted to ask him about returning the microscope too—I was always at work during the hours the clinic was open—but I only had 50 öre, so I had to get the message in under twelve words.

When I got home that evening there was a telegram waiting on the mat, setting the date for Lina's appointment for Sunday. Dr Dance apologised for the delay, saying he needed to go out of town for a few days on business. He said Lina should keep warm, and lie flat on her back as much as possible until then. It seemed a long time to wait, but on the other hand I was relieved the appointment was on a Sunday: I wouldn't have to skip any work. Even though Petter had said that he'd send money, none had arrived yet, and I didn't quite trust his word. If it turned out that we'd lost his income we well as Lina's, we'd need every öre we could get.

I was expecting a big fight with Mama and Lina about Dance, but by now it was obvious to all of us, maybe even Lina, just how serious the situation was, and how little we could rely on Serafen. So that Sunday, Lina, Papa and I set out for Östermalm. Mama was out on a charring job. Papa and I walked, with me pushing Lina on the bicycle. Papa had the microscope case gripped tight in both hands. The day was overcast and we crossed Slussbron and Strömbron with the cold wind in our faces, but once we reached the edge of Östermalm the weather cleared and the wind dropped away, as if we'd stepped into spring.

Although it was still only February, you could feel a bit of the sun's warmth on your face as it reflected back from the snow, and from the clean fronts of the buildings. Walking through those bright streets I felt better than I had in weeks: finally something was being done.

When we arrived at the clinic, a woman in a very elegant suit and hat was coming out. We rang the bell, and as we waited Papa pointed to a brass sign beside the door. It read: *Holm Clinic.* 'Shouldn't it be Dance Clinic?' Papa asked.

I pushed the door open.

'Dance Clinic?' I heard Lina say behind me as we climbed the stairs. 'Don't be ridiculous. That sounds like a ballet school.'

Dr Dance was waiting for us, and led us through to the same treatment room as last time. He turned to Lina.

'Mrs Dahlstrom, you'll need to remove your clothing down to your slip please.' He gestured to a screen in the corner. Papa got up and went out to the waiting room.

First Dr Dance did some tests. He measured Lina's blood pressure, took her temperature and weighed her. He listened to her chest with a stethoscope and gently tapped her back with a small hammer. He checked her reflexes. He had her breathe into a machine that looked like a grocer's scale with a tube coming out of the top.

'Spirometer,' he explained. 'To measure lung capacity.'

He wrote down every measurement in a notepad, in writing so tiny it would have been illegible to anyone but him.

Then he took out a tape measure and started taking measurements of various parts of Lina's body. She flinched when he passed the tape around her chest, right over her breasts.

'What are these measurements for?' I asked.

He threw me a surprised glance, like he'd forgotten I was there.

'Body composition and dimension are important records that will help us monitor Mrs Dahlstrom's recovery.'

The measuring seemed to take a very long time. When he was finished, he got up and went to the cabinet and took out the black box that I'd seen before.

'Can I get dressed?' Lina asked. She was sitting hunched over, as if she was trying to hide as much of her body as she could.

'Not just yet,' said Dr Dance. He leaned closer to her. 'I know it's uncomfortable but it's better if you stay as you are. It'll make for easier access, for the treatment.'

Lina folded her arms over her thin chest.

'I'm going to start Mrs Dahlstrom on the violet ray,' Dr Dance said to me.

To show Lina that the procedure was painless, he first demonstrated it on me, running the lit-up bulb up and down my forearm, exactly as he'd done with Ilse.

He asked Lina to sit on a stool facing away from him, and lifted up the back of her slip, exposing her knickers and the white skin of her back. He adjusted the setting of the ray and held it up to her spine. As it touched her, there was a sharp crack. Lina leapt up off the stool with a yell.

'I'm sorry, Mrs Dahlstrom,' said Dr Dance in a smooth voice, not, in my opinion, sounding terribly sorry at all. Lina was standing rigid and red-faced beside the stool. I could hear every breath rasp in her lungs, a sound like a metal file. There were tears in her eyes. She was trying to blink them back. Dr Dance put his hand on her shoulder and she jerked away from him. 'Sorry about that,' he said again. 'Sometimes at the higher settings there can be a tiny jolt when the ray is first applied, but it's nothing to worry about, it won't hurt you at all.'

Lina gave a nervous laugh like a snort and wiped away her tears with the palm of her hand.

'Sorry, Dr Dance,' she said. 'I got a fright, is all. I'm ready now.'

She sat back down and took hold of the stool with both hands, her fingers curling underneath it. I saw her dig her fingernails into the wood until her knuckles went white.

Dr Dance held up the ray. 'Ready?'

She nodded.

'Here we go,' he said.

There was the same cracking sound as before, but this time Lina gritted her teeth and clutched the seat even tighter. He passed the bulb up and down her back, and then side to side for a few minutes.

'That should do it.' He switched off the ray. 'How are you feeling now?'

'I feel fine,' she said.

'In that case, let's start you on some diathermy. Just a taste.'

Dr Dance sat Lina down in front of the white machine with the pipes coming out of it.

'Is this going to hurt?' she asked. 'I don't mind, I just prefer to know in advance.'

'Hurt? No. Diathermy's a heat treatment, so you'll feel a little warm, but that's all. It'll only be for a few minutes.' He fiddled with the switches and dials at the side of the machine. 'You'll have to remove your slip and brassiere for this one.'

Lina glanced at me.

'Why, Doctor?' I asked. 'Can't she keep her slip on at least?'

He shook his head. 'I'm afraid nothing can come between the condenser plates and the patient's skin. Risk of burns,' he said.

So this was why he hadn't switched on the machine with Ilse, I thought.

Lina shot me another look and then pulled the straps of her slip and wriggled her arms through so the slip fell down to her waist. Her face was flushed a deep pink. She reached up and undid her homemade bra and handed it to me.

'That should be fine,' said Dr Dance. 'You'll also need to remove that necklace, and any other jewellery.' Lina took off her wedding ring and passed it to me. I put it in my pocket. She reached up to unfasten her necklace, but her hands were trembling.

'Here, let me.' Dr Dance stepped forward. He was a long time messing about with the clasp. 'Sorry, Mrs Dahlstrom, that I'm so slow. I'm not used to handling women's jewels.'

He was leaning over her with his face tilted down, too close to the nape of her neck. I caught a glimpse of his face. There was something about his expression I didn't like: eyes popping, tongue on his lip. I'd seen that expression on men's faces hundreds of times when they were looking at Lina. He stepped back with the necklace in his hand. When he went over to put it on his desk, Lina looked over at me. She rolled her eyes and gave a pale smile.

Dr Dance came back to the machine and adjusted the two discs just as he had for Ilse, one at the front and one at the back. Lina looked relieved when they were in place, shielding her body from his gaze.

'Okay, Mrs Dahlstrom, I'm going to start her up now. You might feel a little heat but remember, it's completely normal and it won't hurt you. The important thing is to stay perfectly still and not move at all: you don't want to come into contact with these two condenser plates.' He pointed at the discs. 'We don't want any burns. Are you ready?'

She nodded. I saw her grip the underside of the stool again.

He flipped a switch at the back of the machine and it started humming. I can see now that I should have been suspicious that he hadn't tested the diathermy on either me or Ilse, as he had with the violet ray. Of course, now I also know that there were a whole lot of other things I should have been suspicious of too.

Lina's face had turned an even brighter pink. At first I thought it was from embarrassment, or possibly anger, but soon I realised that it was caused by the machine. Within a minute I could feel the waves of heat coming off it even from a metre away: it was like being in front of a burning oven that had its door wide open. Another minute passed. Beads of sweat appeared on Lina's face.

'Lina? You alright?' I asked. I had to raise my voice over the machine's hum.

She nodded, but her eyes were wild and panicked. Dr Dance glanced up at her, his expression blank, and then looked back down at his watch, timing the procedure. Lina's face by then looked as if it was sunburned. Her eyes slid over to me, wide open with the whites glaring right the way around the irises. I had to fight the urge to rush to the machine and pull Lina away from it.

'How much longer, Dr Dance?' I asked him.

'Just another few minutes.'

His voice was flat and calm, as if he hadn't even registered Lina's distress. But perhaps you don't always need to be compassionate to be a good doctor. By then she was panting and the sweat was running down her forehead and the sides of her face, dripping from her jaw. I knew that Lina would never speak out. Some people might think of Lina's uncomplaining character as toughness, but, for me, it was too close to martyrdom. You have to tell people what you need. I couldn't stand watching her endure the situation a moment longer.

'Stop,' I said, stepping forward. 'That's enough—'

Right at that moment there was a thumping sound from outside and the door was flung open. A man appeared in the doorway.

'Hey!' he shouted. 'What in god's name is going on in here?'

He was a large, round man, wearing a homburg and an over-coat. He stood there with his hand on the door handle and a furious expression on his face. I could see Papa hovering in the waiting room behind him.

At the sound of the man's voice, Dr Dance's head snapped up. His mouth dropped open and he leapt over to the machine and turned it off.

'Carl?' said the man, his moustache bristling. 'You'd better have a damn good explanation for this.'

'Per . . .' Dr Dance's voice was shaky. 'I didn't expect you to be here today.'

'Evidently.' The man looked at me, and then at Lina. 'Miss, your treatment session is over now.' He came over and pulled the discs away from Lina. 'Please go and get dressed.'

She scuttled off, holding up the front of her slip.

'And you,' the man turned to Dr Dance, 'you can explain how it is that you are in here in *my* clinic, on *my* premises, after hours, using *my* equipment without my approval.'

I remembered the sign beside the door.

9.

'AND?' ILSE SAID the next morning as she sat down beside me at the workbench. 'How'd it go?'

She listened to the story with her eyes wide.

'So,' she said, 'when he took us to the clinic that night, he was breaking in. *We* were breaking in!' She sounded inappropriately thrilled. 'It was odd that he took us there so late, now I come to think about it . . .'

'Breaking in?' I replied. 'Hardly.' Ilse's imagination is stronger than most people's. 'He had keys, remember, so he obviously works there.'

Ilse held her forefinger up in the air. 'Could have been stolen,' she said.

'You read too many detective novels.'

I picked up the cigar I'd been working on.

'Then what d'you suppose Dr Dance's real job is?' Ilse mused. 'A cleaner? But how would a cleaner know so much about all those machines?'

'He's not a cleaner. He's a doctor. But he lied about owning the clinic.'

We worked in silence for a few minutes. Then she said, 'But did he lie? Did he ever *say* that he owned it?'

She had a point.

'Maybe not. But he certainly acted like he did,' I said. 'And he did say, "Welcome to my clinic," or something like that. Remember?'

'Oh, poor old chap.' Ilse took a cigar from her roller and put it into her crate. 'I feel rather sorry for old Dance. He was only trying to impress us, you know. Now he's probably gone and got himself fired from his cleaning job. The duffer.'

I pictured that greedy expression I'd seen on his face as he leaned close to Lina. 'I don't feel sorry for him one bit,' I said. But if Dance couldn't treat Lina, she was doomed to Serafen. We needed him.

After our shift, Ilse and I rode home together along Götgatan. I was riding behind her, and as we came up to the corner of Vartoftagatan she braked so suddenly that I almost collided into the back of her. I swerved clear just in time.

'Hey!'

She didn't even hear me.

'Look! Look!' She was pointing down Vartoftagatan. 'There he is!'

'Who?'

'Dr Dance!'

'Where?' I searched the crowd. The street was swarming with thin men in hats and coats, any one of whom could have been him.

'I bet he's going to your place,' Ilse said. She pushed away from the kerb and took off down Vartoftagatan without a backwards glance. I followed her.

We pedalled fast and sure enough, a few metres down the road I spotted a tall man loping along on the opposite side of the street. He did look a lot like Dr Dance, but I couldn't be sure. We got off our bicycles and crept along the footpath, keeping well behind the man and out of his line of vision. He looked like he was up to something. He kept glancing to the left and to the right, as if he was keeping an eye out for someone. At one point he stopped and turned around in a full circle, scanning the people in the street. Ilse and I pretended to be examining a display of dresses in a shop window, but I got a clear view of his face: it was him, no question.

We tailed him to the end of the street. When he got to Västgötagatan, he cut across the park towards Hallandsgatan.

'See?' Ilse hissed at me. 'Told you! I bet he's going to visit Lina to apologise.'

We walked our bicycles along the far side of the park. Our apartment building came into view. Dr Dance went towards it but then his steps started to slow. He stopped outside on the other side of the road. He stood there a long time—maybe ten minutes or more—gazing up at the building. It was hard to see, but it looked like he kept taking something out of his coat pocket and then putting it back again.

Then, without warning, he turned straight back the way he'd come. He was walking along the other side of the street, and though he passed within a few metres of us, he didn't even notice we were there.

When he was out of sight, Ilse said, 'Come on!' Don't you want to know what he's up to?'

She jumped on her bicycle and sped away in the direction he'd gone.

'Ilse! Wait!' I called out. 'He's probably just going home.'

She didn't slow down. I groaned and mounted my bike to pedal after her. I caught up with her at the corner. Up ahead, we could see Dance getting into his car. He drove off up Götgatan towards Östermalm. Ilse shot off after him and I followed. We weaved our way through the pedestrians and other cyclists.

'Ilse,' I called. 'Come on, let's go back. This is stupid. He's just going home.' But she didn't seem to hear, or she chose to ignore me.

'We have to memorise his numberplate,' she said. She turned around to face me. 'It's A30507. Don't forget it! A30507!' She was certainly getting into the spirit of the chase. Like I said, Ilse was a big fan of detective novels: Frank Heller, Fredrik Lindholm, Stein Riverton. She always had one on her nightstand.

We tailed the car to Slussen, but lost sight of it in the tangle of roads and footbridges that run to Gamla Stan. We rode over the rattling wooden bridge anyway, and as soon as we reached the other side there was his car again, waiting at the lights. Ilse was right about the numberplate. I know nothing about cars—I have no idea about makes or models or anything like that—to me it was just a black one, and I never would've spotted it again in a million years without that numberplate. Traffic was lighter in Gamla Stan, so we had to pedal hard. We crossed over Strömbron, by which time I was thoroughly out of breath. After that it was downhill all the way to Östermalm. At first it seemed like he was going to the clinic, but instead of stopping at Karlaplan, he kept going up Karlavägen, and then into Jungfrugatan. He stopped the car about halfway down. We jumped off our bicycles and ducked into a doorway.

The street was full of fancy apartment buildings, each with a polished brass bell and a nameplate, and neatly painted window frames. We watched him get out of his car and go into one of the buildings: 7B.

'D'you suppose that's where he lives?' Ilse asked. She ran over and tried the door he'd entered, but it was locked.

'Ilse,' I said, 'what are we even doing here?'

'We're gathering information!' she said. 'This man is up to something, I can tell you that much. And you never know what information might turn out to be handy one day.' She was busy scanning the buildings on the other side of the street. She pointed at the one directly opposite 7B. 'Let's nip in there and see what we can see.' She dashed across.

The building seemed to be some sort of office premises and the street door was ajar. By the time I'd reached the door, Ilse was already inside. I could hear her footsteps on the stairs. I followed her up to the first-floor landing, where a round window looked onto Jungfrugatan. Ilse stood looking out.

'Let's go up one more,' she said.

On the next landing we both leaned into the window. The second-floor double windows opposite had lace curtains looped back, and a row of short candles on the inside windowsill. There were two lamps burning in the room, one in each window. It was already pretty dark by that time, and with the lamps on, the front of the room was lit up like a stage.

In the window on the left we could see the side profile of a dark-haired woman sitting on a sofa, leafing through a book or a magazine. She was perched with a straight back on the very edge of the sofa, a model of ladylike deportment. Her hair was pinned back neatly into a low chignon, and her striped blouse had puffed sleeves and a floppy bow or ruffle at the front. Beside her was a small table with a vase of white flowers and a pile of magazines or newspapers and some porcelain tea wares. Behind her I could see bookshelves and some potted ferns. The right-hand window showed the edge of a fireplace and a dining table, and some paintings on the back wall.

The woman seemed distracted and kept looking up every minute or so. A moment later, someone appeared in the right-hand window. It was a man, but we could only see his back as he took off his coat and hung it on a coat rack. The woman jumped up and passed out of our view behind the wall between the two windows. Then the man disappeared too.

'No!' Ilse whispered. 'Come back!'

For a while nothing happened, then the man appeared in the left-hand window. He was walking across the room towards the back wall but he was nothing more than a shape, and we still couldn't see his face. He was tall and thin: it could've been Dr Dance. It looked like he was talking to someone; he was gesturing with his hands, cutting the air with them.

'Is that him?' I asked. I pressed my face closer to the window, right up against it.

'Could be . . .' Ilse said.

Her breath fogged the glass and she reached up to wipe it clear.

The man turned and walked back towards the window into the light and we saw his face.

'It's him,' Ilse said.

The woman appeared again, standing side-on to the window, and facing Dr Dance. She looked agitated, as if she was pleading with him. She kept putting her hands over her heart and then spreading them wide in the air. Then she put her face in her hands.

'She's upset,' Ilse said.

I nodded. At this point I'd rather started to enjoy myself: I felt like we'd come into the cinema halfway through a film and were trying to piece together the story.

'D'you think that's his wife?' Ilse asked.

'I'm pretty sure he said he wasn't married. More than once.'

Dr Dance was standing there shaking his head. It looked like the woman was crying now. We could see her shoulders shaking. Dr Dance folded his arms and stepped forward to the window. Ilse and I ducked down out of sight. After a second, I inched my head back up again.

'But I'd say that's definitely his wife,' I said. 'The liar.'

Ilse's head popped up beside mine. Dr Dance and the woman were standing facing each other and we saw them both in profile. The woman threw her arms around Dr Dance's neck and buried her face in his shoulder. He stood motionless, arms by his sides. The next moment he shoved her from him, with such force that her head jolted back.

'Whoa!' Ilse said.

Dance turned and walked away from the window. The woman stayed where she was and wiped her eyes with a handkerchief, then she turned and followed him. Both of them had moved out of the light and it was difficult to see what happened next. The two shapes of their bodies moved towards each other and became entangled.

'What's going on? Is he beating her?' I asked.

'I can't tell.'

Ilse bobbed her head around to try and get a better view. They might have been in each other's arms in reconciliation, or they might have been locked in a struggle.

'No,' Ilse said. 'It looks more like he has his arms around her, like he's holding her.'

There came a loud bang, which made us both jump. It was a door slamming on the landing above, followed by the sound of keys in the lock, and then footsteps. Ilse grabbed my hand and we dashed downstairs and out of the building.

10.

DANCE'S QUESTIONABLE BEHAVIOUR towards the woman in the window is one of the reasons I've never had much time for husbands. I know not all husbands are unkind, or potentially violent, not by any means. I know plenty of good, gentle, caring men: Papa; Ilse's brothers, Ole and Henrik; my uncle Gunnar. But the thing with husbands is, you can never be quite sure about them. You never know what they're really like when they're at home, until you're the one at home with them. Men, some of them, have one face for the world and another for their wife. Like Hugo Björne. To all the world he seemed like a respectable and cultured man, a great actor, a guest at the king's palace. Then his wife was seen around town with a black eye, with marks on her throat. People talked—the poor wife, national scandal—but in the end it didn't change people's opinion about Björne. Not the people that mattered anyway. He was still up on the stage at Dramaten, bowing to applause night after night, his photo was still in *Svenska Dagbladet*. But that Hugo Björne on the stage isn't the same one that his wife knew: his wife was the one that knew him with his true face.

The day after we tailed Dr Dance to his apartment, I thought I spotted him again as I was leaving the factory, but I might've only been imagining it. I had Dance on the brain, alright. I walked home wondering if the woman in the window really was Mrs Dance. The way he'd pushed her off him, the way her head had snapped back when he did, so sharply that it looked like it might come off. She must have been his wife. What a misfortune to be married to a man like Dance, a man who pretended to be single and spent his days ogling young, ill women less than half his age. I strode along, my head down and my hands in my coat pockets. What kind of man pretends not to have a wife? And then manhandles her like that? What man pretends to be the owner of a fancy medical clinic and sneaks in by night to use the machines, like a burglar? What else might he be lying about? Maybe Ilse was right: maybe he wasn't even a real doctor. Maybe he was nothing more than some American charlatan, taking everyone in with his fancy clothes and machines and foreign airs. No one here knew what Americans were supposed to be like.

I was furious at Dance, but worse, I was furious with myself. I felt like I'd let Lina down. Dance was obviously interested in her, that much had been clear from the start. But men always paid attention to Lina, and I'd thought it didn't matter. So I'd stood by while Dance had leered at Lina and pawed at her. He'd taken me in with his suave ways and generous promises. I'd stood beside Lina as she sat there half naked and ashamed, undergoing a painful procedure. While he ogled her. And worse, I was the one who'd insisted on visiting Dance in the first place.

As I was coming around the corner of Hallandsgatan, I collided with someone going the other way.

'Hey!' I said. 'Watch it!'

I looked up and my eyes met those of Dr Dance himself. We stared at each other for a moment. I probably had an expression of complete horror on my face. It was as if I'd conjured him into existence by thinking so intensely about him, like summoning a demon with black magic. Once again I pictured his leering face, him pushing his wife, her silent pleading with him.

'You!' I said.

He started, as if he'd only just recognised me. 'Ah . . . Miss Fredelius,' he said. 'Listen, I wanted to—'

'You owe us an explanation, Dr Dance. If you even are a doctor.'

He shuffled back a step and gave a quick laugh. 'Er . . . I do apologise for Sunday's little, er, irregularity.'

'Irregularity? You call that an irregularity? You posed as a doctor at that clinic, you pretended—'

Dance held up his hand. 'Hold on now,' he said. 'I assure you that I am a fully qualified—'

'And you pretended to be a bachelor! And what about the way you treat your wife? Listen, Dance, you stay away from my sister. If I see you hanging around Söder again, believe me, you'll be sorry.' I turned on my heel and marched away.

'Wait!' he called out. I heard him jogging along behind me. 'It's all just a misunderstanding!'

'Leave me alone.' I quickened my step.

'I'm sorry,' he called after me. 'All I wanted was to help her.'

After that day I didn't see him around Söder again, and soon enough I had other worries that pushed him right out of my head.

During the days after Dance's treatment all of us watched Lina for signs of improvement. Not that I had very high hopes at that stage. But it started to seem like she was getting better. Even the night after the treatment I thought I heard her coughing less, and she woke earlier than usual the next morning. It was such a small difference, though, too slight for any of us to mention, in case it wasn't real. I started to think that I might have been too hasty with Dance when I'd run into him in the street.

In any case, I had plenty of things to keep my mind occupied. As usual, we had the never-ending worry about making ends meet. Not only had Petter failed to send any money like he'd promised, he hadn't even sent a line to say that he'd safely arrived, or where we could reach him. Meanwhile, Mama had taken on extra charring jobs, and most days she left home before five o'clock and was out until after eight at night. She also brought home mending work, and all of us, including Papa, sat around the kitchen table stitching away until the small hours. Papa was working overtime, and I started taking on double shifts.

It got so that I felt like all I did was work and sleep, and work and sleep again. I'd fall into bed exhausted, but even in my sleep I couldn't escape from the factory. I'd close my eyes and dream of rolling giant cigars, as wide as tree trunks and as long as a room. Or I'd dream I was toiling my way up a mountain, my feet sinking into the ground with every step. Then I'd see that it wasn't a mountain I was climbing, but a pile of tobacco leaves so large that I couldn't see the top of it.

In the mornings I'd wake with eyes gritty with sleep. My neck and fingers became stiff and sore, and sometimes I'd look at Lina, spending her days in bed or on the couch, and envy her.

Resent her, even. This wasn't what my life was meant for. If Lina had taken the illness more seriously at the start, perhaps it wouldn't have got so bad. Now we were all in a mess because of it. At the factory, whenever I saw that Blund had moved on to the other end of the room, I would stand up to loosen my neck and back. I'd stretch my arms up and roll my head from side to side. Ilse would eye me with a worried face.

'You should take it easy,' she said one day. 'If you're not careful, you'll end up in Serafen yourself.'

Lina was taking Petter's absence very hard. The first thing she did every day was ask if there was any news of him, and the moment she heard the post slide through the slot, she'd shuffle up to the front door, wrapped in her blanket, and leaf through it. But there was never anything from Petter. One night, I came home from my shift, opened the front door and almost fell over her. She was huddled in a ball on the floor, knees pressed into her face, crying. I crouched down beside her.

'What's wrong? What's happened?'

She could hardly speak, and forced the words out between juddering breaths that racked her body.

'A letter . . . I thought . . . it was . . . Petter . . .'

I saw that she was holding a damp and partially torn page in her hand.

'But . . . it's just Lasse . . . And then, my locket . . . with Petter's picture . . . it's gone . . . It's a sign he's not coming back.'

'Lina,' I sighed. I put my arms around her and rocked her back and forth. My head was tight with exhaustion. 'It's going to be alright.'

'Why hasn't he written? And he hasn't sent any money.' She looked up at me. 'Has he forgotten us?'

She was like a child sometimes. Even though I longed for bed, I sat with her and told her soothing stories of letters lost, misaddressed, and being returned to the sender, only to finally arrive months after they were posted. All fairytales, but she seemed to believe them.

11.

EVEN WITH LINA'S anxieties over Pexter, day by day, against all odds, it became more and more clear that her condition was improving. I didn't dare to believe it at first, but it really seemed to be true. Lina had stopped coughing up blood, and a week or so after her treatment, her coughing fits had almost disappeared. It seemed that Dance's ray might actually have done something. I initially thought it was a coincidence, or an effect of the milder weather, but even through a cold spell and some days of rain, Lina kept improving. She spent fewer hours sleeping during the day, and we'd come home from work to find her sitting up, or even standing in the kitchen making dinner.

One evening when I was cycling home from the factory, limp with exhaustion, I spotted a familiar figure waiting on our corner. It was Papa. As soon as he saw me, he started running towards me, waving something in the air. I pedalled faster.

'What?' I called to him when I was still at the end of our block. My voice blew away in the wind. We met in the park. I was out of breath. 'What is it?'

'Look. What d'you make of this?'

He thrust a piece of paper at me: a telegram. It had been sent from Sundsvall, and read:

FAMILY PETTER DAHLSTROM HALLANDSGATAN: HAVE NEWS OF PETTER. TELEPHONE 4369 SUNDSVALL PO 6 PM THURSDAY. ALRIK DAHLSTROM.

And I'd thought that Petter had been lying when he'd said he'd he gone to work with Alrik.

'What do you think?' Papa asked me, his eyes narrow. 'Can't be good news, eh?' He had taken off his cap and was twisting it in his hands.

'No,' I said. 'Probably not.'

I was starting to get a cold feeling in my stomach, as if someone had scooped it hollow.

'He would've said what it was about otherwise, eh?' Papa said. 'Wouldn't he? Or if it was to tell us he'd arrived, you'd send a post-card, wouldn't you? Not a telegram.' Papa always rambled when he was nervous. 'What d'you suppose it is?'

'I don't know, Papa. I guess we'll find out tomorrow.' I folded up the telegram and put it in my coat pocket. 'At least it's some news.'

'Should we mention it to Lina? She's frantic for news, but maybe it's better not to . . . to upset her, you know?'

'I know.'

I was afraid, as he was, that any kind of nervous shock would bring back the illness in full force.

'We'll keep it to ourselves for now,' I said. 'Lina's already been waiting for weeks: one more day won't hurt. And Mama doesn't need any extra worries either. Anyway, you never know, it might turn out to be something good after all.'

But even as the words came out of my mouth, I knew in my heart that it wouldn't be.

All that evening, through our dinner of watery vegetable soup, and later, hemming a sheet for Mama, the only thing I could think about was the telegram. Was Petter dead? That seemed the obvious thing. Killed on the docks while loading something onto a ship: accidents like that happened all the time. I didn't know if Lina could cope with such a shock. At the factory, there was a constant round of collections for newly widowed women who'd been left to fend for themselves after their stevedore husbands had drowned or been crushed to death. But it could also be that Petter hadn't died, only been maimed. Which would almost be worse. Sounds awful to say, I know, but it's true. It'd be much worse for a man like Petter, so proud of his health and strength, his muscles grown massive on his frame from all those years of heavy work. I could imagine how he'd hate to live his life staggering from place to place on crutches, his legs dragging behind him, white and weak. And it would be hard on the rest of us too. Another mouth to feed.

I thought of Berit Blenstrom, who used to work on my bench at the factory. One day her husband was mown down by a car on Götgatan. His back was broken. He couldn't move his arms or legs, or speak, or even sit up by himself: the most he could do was turn his head from one side to the other, and blink. We took collections for Berit too. But the thing with collections is, people will only give money for so long, and Berit couldn't earn enough for the family on her own. They got behind on the rent and had to move out to the country. Last I heard they were in a village way up north, near Jokkmokk. I pictured her up there in all those miles of snow and ice, huddled in some desolate cabin with her crippled husband and their two small children. I shivered.

'You're both very quiet this evening,' Lina said.

I kept my eyes on my sewing and avoided looking at Papa.

I'd arranged to meet him at the post office after work the next day. I got there early and he was already waiting outside the door, bouncing nervously from foot to foot. He looked like he was about to be sick. He'd never made a phone call before.

'Have you got the number to call? Did you remember to bring it?' he asked before I'd even got off my bicycle.

There wasn't much of a queue, and in a few minutes we were squeezed into one of the telephone booths. I took out the telegram from my pocket. Papa lifted the receiver from the cradle. His hand was trembling.

'What number, please?' I heard a voice ask.

Papa cleared his throat, then shook his head and handed the receiver to me. We had to wait through an endless series of pips and clicks while the operator connected us. The Sundsvall post-office clerk answered, before another man came on the line.

'Dahlstrom here,' he said. His voice sounded exactly like Petter's.

My hands had started to sweat. I wiped them one after the other on the sides of my skirt.

'Alrik, this is Greta speaking, Petter's sister-in-law.' I tilted the receiver so Papa could hear too. 'What's your news of Petter?' Papa was breathing loud in my ear, and kept bumping his head into mine as he strained to move closer to the receiver.

'Has he come home? I thought maybe—'

'No, isn't he with you?' My heart bunched up under my ribs.

'No, he isn't. That's the thing.' Papa was clutching my shoulder and his fingers pinched like talons. The line started to hiss and crackle. '. . . last Friday.'

'What? Alrik, the line's bad. Say again?'

'What?' he said. '. . . don't know . . .' The line hissed again. '. . . do know is that . . . since last Friday. That's what I'm saying to you.'

'You're saying he's disappeared? Is that it?'

'Yeah, that's right. Last Friday . . . back from his shift, nor on Saturday . . . thought he'd . . . a bender is all, for the . . . went down to port office and the fellow . . . hair nor hide of him for days.'

'Alrik, have you been to the police?'

'Police? Well now, I don't . . . and wouldn't want to be rushing off . . . drop of a hat . . . again in Stockholm?'

'He hasn't turned up here.' He'd have arrived by now if he left last Friday.

The operator was on the line again. 'Do you need further time?'

'No, thank you,' I said.

We rang off. Papa and I stood there in the booth for a few minutes, not saying anything.

We walked home slowly.

'Are we going to tell Lina?' Papa asked as we turned into Hallandsgatan.

I shook my head. 'I don't know. I mean, we don't really know anything, do we? Petter could be lying dead in some ditch, or he could've done a runner and be living it up in Uppsala or somewhere.'

We walked in silence for a while. Then Papa said, 'I never wanted to say, but I thought all along he'd done a bunk, and not gone to Sundsvall at all.' He looked at me. 'What would you want with going to Sundsvall when you have a perfectly good job right here in Stockholm?'

I'd thought the same thing. I'd even wondered whether his departure had been longer in the planning than it seemed. He'd been hell-bent on Lina dropping her factory shifts and moving in with us: was it because it would be easier for him to leave knowing Lina was safely installed at our place? Could it be that he'd found some other woman? But then on the other hand I remembered his shocked face the night I'd told him that TB was contagious. Maybe he was scared.

'But it turns out he did go to Sundsvall,' Papa went on. 'And I'm downright ashamed of myself for thinking he'd be the type to go and leave us in the lurch.'

'Don't feel too bad just yet. For all we know he still might've.'

'So it might be best not to mention it to Lina, don't you think?'

I sighed. I was a terrible liar. But not as bad as Papa. 'Maybe that's for the best.'

'But we do know one thing for sure,' he said as we neared our building.

'What's that?'

'Not to expect any money from him.'

As we trudged up the stairs to our apartment, I made an effort to make my face look neutral: the face of a person with no secrets.

I find it hard to control my face in that way. I never can seem to keep my feelings hidden under a mask the way other people can. Something always gives me away. As I came up to the door, I saw that there was a parcel on our doorstep. Papa appeared on the landing beside me, out of breath from the climb.

'What's that then?' he asked.

The light on our landing was broken, but I could see that it was a large, open cardboard box with a lot of small packets inside, each wrapped in brown paper. I caught the white rectangle of an envelope among the parcels and fished it out. I held it up to my face: it was addressed in a fancy script to Mrs Dahlstrom.

'I bet this is from Dance,' I said.

12.

WE BROUGHT THE box inside and when we unpacked it we found it was full of food: fresh bread, cheese, butter, real coffee—something we could usually never afford—tins of fish paste and sardines, beef tea concentrate, drinking chocolate, fruit, wine, cinnamon buns and sweet biscuits. Never before had such glories been seen in our house, not even at Christmas. And to make it even more grand, everything had come from Östermalm's Saluhall—the name was printed on the side of the box in elegant letters—a shop I'd heard of but never set foot in.

After we'd unpacked all the treasures, Lina read the note aloud:

Dear Mrs Dahlstrom,
Please accept my humble apologies for the interruption of
your treatment, and any confusion this may have caused.
Please accept this gift as a small token of my apologies.
Yours,
Dr Carl Dance

Lina cast her eye over the items that lay spread out on the table. 'Oh, isn't that sweet of him?'

'Sweet?' I said. 'The man's a complete charlatan. Don't let that old toad get around you with some measly cakes and coffee, Lina.'

'Come on, he's not all that bad. He's managed to cure me, hasn't he?'

It was the first time any of us had said so out loud. No one wanted to tempt fate.

That night, we feasted as we never had before. I have to admit, I had no qualms whatsoever about eating my fill of the dainties Dance had sent, charlatan or not. After dinner, we lolled in our chairs, finishing the bottle of wine.

'Imagine if we could always eat like this.' Lina picked another grape from the bunch on her plate and popped it into her mouth. 'How fat we'd be.'

'You could do with getting quite a bit fatter,' I said, smiling at her. 'You've wasted away to nearly nothing. Drink up your chocolate and eat another biscuit: doctor's orders!'

Lina laughed and stuffed one into her mouth.

'You two can joke,' Papa said, 'but don't get too used to this. From now on it'll be even harder to put food on the table.'

I shot him a look.

'Why from now on?' Lina said. Her mouth was still full. 'What's happened? Has someone lost their job?' She looked from Papa to me. 'What's going on?' Her voice had risen a note.

Papa clamped his lips together. He looked studiously at the ceiling.

'Nothing's going on,' I said. I stood up to start clearing away the plates. 'I think what Papa means is that, you know, we're all working hard but don't seem to be making much money.' I tried again to catch Papa's eye. 'Isn't that right, Papa?'

'Eh? Yes, pet, oh yes, that's right.'

He nodded too vigorously. His poker face was even worse than mine.

Lina was looking at him with narrowed eyes. 'Something's going on,' she said.

I kept my eyes on the plates I was stacking up. I could feel her gaze on me.

'Greta, what is it? Come on, tell me.'

I felt a flush start to spread across my cheeks. I turned my back and took the plates to the sink.

'Is it Petter?' she asked.

I couldn't help glancing over at Papa. Our eyes met.

'What's happened to Petter?' Lina's voice held a wild note of panic.

'Oh, pet,' said Papa, 'we didn't want to tell you—'

'What? What is it?'

'It's nothing,' I cut in. 'Only that we had a message from Alrik that he hasn't seen Petter in a few days, that's all.'

'But he arrived? In Sundsvall?'

'Yes, isn't that great news? And Alrik told us that he got the job he was—'

'But why hasn't he written? And now he's gone missing, is that what you're saying?'

Lina's face was white and rigid. I rinsed and dried a plate and began piling it with food for Mama when she came in. I tried to keep my movements calm and slow.

'Is he dead?' Lina asked.

'Of course he's not dead. Don't be silly. And he hasn't gone missing either. It's nothing serious, only that Alrik hasn't seen him for a few days, and—'

'Has Alrik gone to the police?' I could hear the tears hovering at the edge of her voice.

'Lina,' I said. 'This is why we didn't want to tell you about it: we knew you'd get all worked up. It's absolutely nothing to worry about, I promise. Probably he took a job somewhere and forgot to mention it. You know what he's like.'

Lina didn't say anything. After a moment she got up and went to the bedroom and closed the door behind her.

13.

THE DAYS PASSED and there was no news of Petter, and what we had feared would happen did. The day after Lina found out her husband was missing, her cough came back. She seemed to get worse by the hour. Within a few days her skin had become grey and opaque, and she had purple hollows around her eyes. Her hair had started to fall out. When I swept the floor, balls of hair would appear, tangled among the crumbs and dust. I found long strands of it stuck to plates, in my food, on the undersides of my socks, in my bed. At night, her raspy breathing echoed through the apartment.

I went to Serafen and begged someone to come and see Lina right away, but they refused.

'No house calls,' the nurse at the desk told me. 'I can see she's in the care of Dr Hellbrun. He's not available until Friday.'

That was three days away. It was too long. I made the appointment anyway and on the way home I sent a telegram to Dance.

Urgent! Lina Dahlstrom relapse. Please help.
Request treatment. G. Fredelius

As much as I disliked and distrusted the man, there was no denying that his treatment had had an effect. But when I pictured again his leering face and bulging eyes, and Lina trying not to cry out during the treatment, the memory made me nauseous, like the smell of sour milk.

Lina spent her waking hours, if you could call them that, lying on the couch. Sometimes she tried to read, mostly Helena Nyblom's fairytales, but usually she just lay on her back and gazed unseeingly towards the window. The days when she was up and about in the apartment seemed like years ago, though it hadn't been more than a few weeks. Now, all she did was sleep.

Dance did not reply to my telegram. I rode over to the clinic but no one answered the door. I counted down the days until we could see Hellbrun, my heart sick and sore.

I had never really thought that Lina might die until then. I mean, I was aware of it theoretically, but that was the first time I felt it. I remembered something that happened long ago. When we were kids, you used to be able to buy fish off the Slussen pier. We'd go there with Mama every Friday, but one Friday Mama sent me down there alone. The pier was crowded. A ship had just docked and the fishermen were unloading huge bags of mussels, crates of oysters. As I stood aside to let a man pass, someone grabbed my shoulder from behind.

It was one of the fishmongers, a woman. I'd noticed her before. She gave me the creeps. She would stop what she was doing whenever Lina appeared and stand there staring at her as we went past. Now, I've told you before how people often stared at my sister in the street, but this was different. This woman's face was crowded with an emotion I couldn't read.

'You,' she said. Up close her face was younger than I thought. Her skin was smooth and velvety. But her eyes were dark. 'I seen you down here.'

Her bony fingers dug painfully through my coat. I could smell the fish on them.

'That girl, your sister. Where is she?'

I tried to struggle out of her grip.

'That's none of your—'

'That girl is marked. She will die, eaten from within. I see it. It's written on her face. Here.' She placed her thumb between my eyes. It left a cold spot. 'It's written.'

I'm not a superstitious person. I don't believe in messages from the beyond. That day I went home and forgot about what the woman had said. But during the time of Lina's illness the memory of that woman was often in my mind, that cold spot between my eyes.

At home we mentioned Petter as little as possible. But after Lina had gone to bed one night, Papa, Mama and I sat around the table talking in low voices.

'He's done a runner,' Papa said. He leaned across the table. 'Makes sense. Lina got ill, and then he found out he could catch it. Simple.'

'Rubbish!' hissed Mama. 'Petter's not the sort to go and do a thing like that. He's a good boy. He'd stick by our Lina, thick and thin. Something must've happened to him.'

I didn't want to say it, but I thought Papa was right. It made sense to me too. Petter could've started a whole new life for himself out there in Sundsvall: no invalid wife, no risk of catching a deadly disease. Petter was a man who didn't like life to be too complicated.

'We need to find out what's going on,' I said. 'It's hard on all of us not knowing, Lina most of all.'

'Should we go to the police?' asked Mama.

Papa and I looked at each other.

'Seems like old Alrik wasn't too keen on that,' he said.

Mama snorted. 'Alrik!' she said, too loudly. Papa held his finger to his lips. 'What do I care about Alrik?' she went on in a whisper. 'We've got to find Petter.'

The next day I put a call through to the police station at Sundsvall, not that it did any good.

'What crime is it that you're reporting again?' the police officer asked after I'd explained the situation. He had a squeaky voice. He sounded like he was fifteen.

'I'm calling to report a missing person,' I said again. 'His name is Petter Dahlstrom. He's my brother-in-law.' The line was silent. 'Hello? Are you there?'

'Yeah. Sorry, miss. I heard your story the first time. Been gone two weeks, has he? It's not so long, see? Wait another week and then call again.' He hung up.

14.

ON THE FRIDAY, Lina and I went back yet again to Serafen, where we faced the beige, worm-like Dr Hellbrun. I really don't know what we were doing there, as we hadn't had the blood tests redone as he'd wanted, but I was desperate. Hellbrun suggested a sanatorium. He may as well have suggested a holiday to the moon.

'Can't I just rest at home?' Lina asked.

Hellbrun shook his head. 'You must be lying in a completely horizontal position at all times to see any marked benefit. It's to do with the way the blood distribution affects the bacilli.'

'There's no way that we can afford a sanatorium,' I said. 'What about that medication, Sanocrysin?'

He looked at me. 'How do you know about a thing like Sanocrysin?'

'I've been doing some reading.'

'Then you might also have read that the side effects outweigh the benefits of the drug. Weight loss, severe ulceration of the mouth, diarrhoea. It's no longer available for prescription in this country in any case. Hasn't been for many years.'

'What about diathermy? Is there any hospital that offers it? Lina had some good results with it.'

He sighed. 'Yes, short-wave diathermy,' he said. 'I've heard of that. Heat to kill the bacilli. Some American thing. Inconclusive evidence, if I recall. You certainly won't find anything like that here at Serafen. No, surgical intervention would be Mrs Dahlstrom's main option here.'

'I'm not having an operation,' Lina said, her eyes wide with terror. Dr Hellbrun didn't seem to hear her.

'What surgical intervention?' I asked.

'We could perform a partial lung resection.'

Lina put her hands over her ears and squeezed her eyes shut.

'So you'd cut out—' I began.

'Yes, yes,' he interrupted. 'We remove the diseased lung tissue. But it has its risks. I wouldn't recommend it at this stage. We'll see how Mrs Dahlstrom gets on in the next week or so. In the meantime, if she can't go to a sanatorium, I suppose we could try something new, a vaccine. There has been some success with it in France, nothing overwhelming, but I'm willing to prescribe it.'

He wrote the prescription and handed the paper to Lina.

But despite Dr Hellbrun's vaccine, Lina got worse. She was racked by coughing fits if she so much as got up and walked from one room to another. Sometimes she could hardly breathe. I'd find her hunched over, gripping the back of a kitchen chair, white-faced and wheezing like a bellows. She grew even thinner and paler, and her skin became damp and translucent. There was still no news of Petter, and it seemed like the more Lina worried about him, and about our situation, the worse she got. I tried Dance again, with no response.

The following week we went back to see Dr Hellbrun.

'It's been more than a month since Mrs Dahlstrom's first symptoms, and she continues to decline,' he said. 'The time has come to consider the surgery.'

When we got home from Serafen, Lina went straight to bed, and shortly afterwards Mama and Papa came in. Then the door-bell rang and Mama went to answer it. I heard Lina getting up, no doubt hoping it was Petter. She appeared at the bedroom door wearing her dressing gown and a scarf. But it was Dr Dance.

'Good evening,' he said. He took off his hat and nodded to each of us in turn.

Papa leapt over to him and shook his hand with both of his own. 'Please, Dr Dance, sit down.'

We four sat at the table, and Lina on the couch.

'I'm very sorry to intrude upon you like this,' Dance said, 'but I've come to extend my apologies to you all, about the misunder-standing at the clinic. I'm truly sorry for that unpleasant situation, and for the shock it might have caused.' He looked over at Lina. 'Particularly for Mrs Dahlstrom.' He smiled at her. 'How are you feeling these days, Mrs Dahlstrom?' he asked, although you only had to look at her to know the answer to that question.

'Didn't you get my telegram?' I asked.

Dr Dance looked puzzled for a second. 'Ah, I'm sorry. I've been out of town this past week and more. I must have missed it.'

Lina started to say something, but went into a coughing fit, gasping for air.

'Mrs Dahlstrom,' Dance said, holding up a hand, 'please don't exert yourself. The other reason I'm here today is because I'd like to offer you a course of treatment.'

'The same treatment as last time?' Papa asked. 'It seemed to do Lina some good.'

'I'm glad to hear that,' Dr Dance said. 'It certainly is a very effective approach, but it needs a series of sessions, over a number of months, to make a lasting difference. The treatment we offer is based on the same principles, but using different, much stronger, machines.'

'And how much would you be charging for that?' Mama asked.

'We would offer this free of charge.'

'We? Who's we?' I asked. 'Do you mean Dr Holm?'

Dance looked at me. 'Well, ah, this time the sessions wouldn't be taking place in the Holm Clinic,' he said. He shifted in his seat and his eyes wandered around the room.

'Then where?' I asked.

'It would be at a private residence,' he said.

'You mean at your house?' I asked.

Dance nodded. 'Yes. I, together with my colleague, Dr—'

'Sorry, doctor,' I said, 'but at your house?' I pictured again his leer, his bulging eyes, the way he held his face close to Lina's throat. 'Do you invite all your patients to your house? Or only young women? Or only Lina?' I couldn't help it, the words came shooting forth without seeming to pass through my brain first. 'What does your wife think about this?'

'Greta!' Papa said, turning sharply to me. 'Mind your manners! We ought to be grateful to Dr Dance for wanting to help us. He's being very generous.' He turned back to Dance. 'Sorry, doctor,' he said.

Dr Dance bowed his head. 'My colleague, Dr Nils Persson, and I have put together an extensive treatment room at my residence, stocked with the most up-to-date radiation equipment.' Dance looked back at me. 'I know it was an unpleasant scene at the clinic last time, and again, I'm truly sorry. All I want is to help Mrs Dahlstrom. Being able to help in this kind of situation is the reason I decided to practise medicine in the first place.'

He stood up to go. 'Please, think it over,' he said. He took a step towards the door then turned on his heel. 'Ah! I almost forgot.' He reached into his jacket pocket and pulled out a small white parcel. 'Mrs Dahlstrom, I believe this belongs to you?'

Lina pulled the paper open.

'Oh!' she said, and burst into another fit of coughing. 'I thought . . .' she said between wheezing breaths, 'that this was lost forever!'

She held up a small golden object: her necklace. It was a locket on a chain, and inside was a picture of Petter's face. The sight of it sent a fresh wave of revulsion flooding over me. Could Dance have held on to it so he'd have an excuse to contact her again? Oldest trick in the book.

'Dr Dance, thank you!' Lina said, beaming up at him.

He smiled at her joy. 'My pleasure. I'm glad I could return it to you.' He nodded again at each of us in turn. 'I must be going. I hope you will consider the offer.'

'Wait!' Lina croaked. 'Dr Dance!' She began coughing again. He stood patiently with his hat in his hands until she could speak again. 'I want to . . . do the treatments.'

'Excellent,' he said. 'We can begin as soon as next week.'

We heard the door close behind him and his footsteps down the stairs. Lina got up and pulled the curtain aside from the window, and looked out. I went and put my arm around her.

We saw Dance emerge from the building and cross the court-yard. Then he paused and looked up at our window. Lina pulled the curtain, leaving a skinny crack for us to peep through.

'I wish we didn't need him,' I said.

She didn't say anything for a moment. We watched Dr Dance disappear into the archway that led through the front of the building and out to the street.

'So do I,' she said then. 'He gives me the creeps.' She turned and looked me in the eye. 'But what choice have I got?'

II: DR DANCE

1.

YOU CAN IMAGINE how relieved I felt when Mrs Dahlstrom and her family agreed to the treatments at my home. Not that I was surprised by their hesitancy, or held it against them in any way. In their place I guess I'd have been as apprehensive as they were, suspicious even, of a stranger, a foreigner no less, offering some fantastical cure. And the misunderstanding at the Holm Clinic would certainly have placed me in something of a poor light.

Before I met Mrs Dahlstrom, I'd never had cause to visit Södermalm. The Dahlstroms lived way down in Hallandsgatan, in one of those tenements built twenty years before, during the housing crisis. Number 36 was in a long double-storey building that ran the length of the narrow street, abutting a park. From a distance, the place didn't look too bad; the windows had glass in them, and the park had some benches and a copse of linden trees. But on closer inspection the building revealed itself as mean and neglected. The paint was peeling off the front wall in great scabrous patches, as if the building was diseased, and instead of curtains, there were scraps of blankets or rags hanging up in some of the windows. The park was strewn with litter and I spotted a couple of tramps staggering among the trees. I wouldn't call Hallandsgatan a slum, exactly, but it wasn't a neighbourhood anyone would choose to live in either.

The Dahlstroms' apartment was in the back section of the building complex, which formed a square. To reach it you had to first pass through an archway under the front part of the building, and cross a grimy courtyard, with slippery cobblestones and a row of foul-smelling trash cans along one wall. I have to say, I was a little shocked the first time I saw the state of that place and how the Dahlstroms lived. When I stepped inside, the apartment seemed to be full of dozens of people, but I quickly realised that was on account of it being so small. As far as I could tell, it consisted of one dingy room with a sink and cooking stove on one wall, above which hung a row of what looked to be old dishrags pegged up to dry, a table and chairs, and some kind of make-shift bed or couch in the corner. There were two doors leading off of this room, to what must have been the bedrooms: but no entrance hall, no separate living room. Likely no bathroom. And five adults lived there. The place was cold and damp and smelled of dishwater and dirty laundry, and the only heating seemed to be the cooking stove. It was no wonder that Mrs Dahlstrom had contracted a respiratory illness.

Perhaps you're wondering why I was so eager to help Mrs Dahlstrom, a woman I hardly knew. Perhaps you're even thinking that I had sinister motives of one kind or another; I can see how somebody might form that view. But the reason is a lot more mundane than you might think. The fact is, in my life I've been fortunate enough to attain a certain level of social standing, and it's my belief that I ought to offer assistance where I can, especially to those who don't enjoy such privileges. I could see that the Dahlstroms were in dire need of help, and I was in a position to give it. Simple. Sure, it might be true that I had a soft spot for Mrs Dahlstrom from the beginning, but she was so pleasant to be around that it would have been hard to find any man who wasn't a little sweet on her.

At that time, radiation therapy for tuberculosis was not much more than an experimental approach, but I'd spent years researching the field, and in fact I am one of its pioneers. A simple explanation of the treatment is that because radiation already has a scientifically proven bactericidal effect on carcinomas, it can also be successfully used in pulmonary TB, especially at the higher doses. I'd seen the devastating results of this terrible disease many times in my professional life, and it's my driving goal to do all I can to contribute to eradicating it.

I had but a few days to prepare my home clinic for Mrs Dahlstrom, who was to be its first patient. I was already occupied with installing a brand-new radiation machine, one that I had designed and built myself, and which was much more powerful than anything commercially available, especially in that somewhat backward country. I had years before stopped relying on commercially produced machines in favour of my own designs, with which I was constantly pushing the frontiers of treatment methodologies.

I worked around the clock to set up the clinic. To call it a clinic was a tad overblown; in actuality it was just one room in the apartment, fitted out with the necessary equipment. I enlisted the help of my trusted colleague from the Holm Clinic, Nils Persson, but even with the two of us working a series of late nights, as well as through the weekends, we barely had it up and running in time. I don't mean to boast about it, but when we were done and had the place spick-and-span, the set-up looked mighty impressive, and would have done even to a layman.

I had a small laboratory in one corner, with a bench for my microscope, burners, beakers and test tubes, and alongside this I'd installed a sink. There was a desk with a light-box above it, and a trolley with my medical kit set out: stethoscope, thermometer, sphygmomanometer, a case of syringes, swabs, and so forth. The treatment bed I'd modified for size, partly on account of the limited space, and partly on account of Mrs Dahlstrom being small in stature. In another corner stood the radiation machine. Its housing was made of nineteen-gauge brushed stainless steel, which contained an iron core, an insulated copper conductor, and super-voltage X-ray tubes. It was capable of transmitting up to 200 kilovolts of energy. There was absolutely nothing like it anywhere in the country. It was such an impressive machine, gleaming and new, bristling with latent power, I could hardly keep my eyes off of it, and couldn't wait to put it through its paces. The day before Mrs Dahlstrom's visit I placed her X-rays up on the light-box in readiness.

When the doorbell rang the next morning, I saw that Mrs Dahlstrom's sister, father and mother had all come along. Mrs Dahlstrom wasn't looking all that well, though not much worse than when I'd last seen her. If you're a reader of novels or poetry of the past two centuries, you'll no doubt have come across mention of the great physical beauty that is bestowed on the sufferer of TB.

Pulmonary tuberculosis, or consumption, has long been a highly romanticised illness on account of this. But the idea of TB being the most beautifying of diseases is more than a flourish of the poet's pen, it does hold a grain of truth within it. The sparkling eyes, the flushed cheeks and red lips of the sufferer can all be attributed to the constant low-grade fever; the pale skin and appealing languor to a decreased blood-oxygen saturation.

I have observed this phenomenon several times throughout my career, but I never felt the uncanniness of the manifestation as strongly as I did with Mrs Dahlstrom. She was by anyone's standards a beauty, there was no question, but the illness had transformed her into something different, something barely human. Her skin, as smooth as wax, glowed with an inner radiance, and the extreme thinness of her limbs lent her movements a slow, hypnotic rhythm. Her dark eyes were languid, but would flash with unexpected sparks of gold. She looked like a life-sized doll, not like a woman at all.

While we were all still standing in the hall, the doorbell rang again and Nils appeared. We were ready to begin.

We went upstairs to the treatment room and got Mrs Dahlstrom prepared. Her sister stood beside her, holding her hand. I have to admit that, excited though I was, I was also a little nervous about the new machine, and I wanted things to go smoothly after last time. Having the family there as an audience only contributed to my anxiety. Nils fetched chairs for them, and they sat, straight-backed, in a row along the wall, perched like a line of birds on a telephone wire. Mr Fredelius was watching the proceedings with his jaw hanging open, Mrs Fredelius had her handbag in an iron grip on her lap, and I could feel Miss Fredelius's sharp eyes on me, noting my every move. Nils was feeling it too, I could tell. He checked and re-checked every one of the machine's settings, taking off and putting on his glasses every time.

At last he said, 'Alright. Looks like we're all set.'

For this first session, Nils and I had agreed to start out with a lower dose of radiation, and progress slowly week by week. It was a fine line between making the procedure as pleasant as possible for Mrs Dahlstrom and making sure it was effective.

'Ready, Mrs Dahlstrom?' I asked her.

'Yes.'

I gave Nils a nod.

'Here we go!' he said, and pressed the switch.

When the machine purred to life Nils actually broke out in applause, and everybody followed suit. I'm pleased to say that things went exactly to plan, without a single hitch.

As the family were putting on their coats and saying their goodbyes in the hall, I heard footsteps on the stairs and then the key in the lock. Doris came in. My wife. I made the introductions.

'Oh, so you *are* a married man,' Miss Fredelius said to me. She gave me quite a piercing look. 'I wasn't sure.'

'Greta!' her mother hissed at her, and shoved her towards the door.

As soon as they were outside, Doris asked, 'Whatever did the girl mean by that?' She took off her coat and hung it up.

Doris has always been a sensitive woman, and prone to taking things to heart. She is also wary of new ideas. The somewhat unusual notion of treating patients at home had been immediately met on her part with suspicion, particularly when she learned that the first patient was to be a young lady. And now that she had seen what an alluring young lady that patient was, I realised she might very well cause a difficult scene.

'So that was Miss Dahlstrom, was it?' she asked, her voice a study of unconcern. She was busy picking invisible bits of fluff from the back of her coat.

'Mrs,' I replied.

Even with this reassurance, Doris's pink face stayed crumpled in a series of worried furrows.

'Hmm. Where was her Mr then? At work, I expect?'

'I believe so,' I said. 'Doris, my darling. You have nothing at all to worry about.' I put my arms around her, but her body was stiff in my embrace.

'And will this *Mrs* Dahlstrom be visiting often?' she asked.

I felt a sort of pity for Doris, and also a sort of pain, but mostly I felt frustration. However, I didn't want things to become difficult. The last thing Mrs Dahlstrom needed was for Doris to take against her. So I soothed my wife. I told her all about the terrible position the Dahlstrom family was in, their impoverished state of living, the seriousness of Mrs Dahlstrom's case—Doris had always been very supportive of charitable works—and I reminded her that it was only right that we, being in a position to help, ought to do so. It was our responsibility. I mentioned Mrs Dahlstrom's tender age and her uneducated background. Very soon Doris was reassured, and convinced of the worthiness of the cause.

Still, over the next few weeks, Mrs Dahlstrom's visits were now and then something of a sensitive point for Doris, a state of affairs that quickly began to wear rather thin.

2.

THROUGH THE SPRING and all that summer, Mrs Dahlstrom came to the apartment for her treatments, at first once a week, then every third day. I stopped working at Serafen so as to have more time for her. As my confidence with the new equipment grew, I was soon able to manage the treatments on my own, and no longer required Nils's assistance. The months went by and Mrs Dahlstrom and I got to know each other better. She was an even more gentle and charming creature than I first thought, full of jokes and curiosity and quick to laugh. I soon grew to be very fond of her, and was proud to be in a position to help her. In the beginning, Miss Fredelius always accompanied her, but after a few weeks it seemed I'd gained her trust and Mrs Dahlstrom came alone.

The treatments went as planned, and I was gratified to observe some rapid improvement in my patient's energy levels, along with a decrease in coughing and pulmonary inflammation. Financially, I knew the family were a lot worse off after the disappearance of Mrs Dahlstrom's husband, a fact she eventually confided to me. Even with my regular food deliveries, I feared that there was pressure on Mrs Dahlstrom to return work, when what she needed was complete rest. As bad as her apartment might have been, the absolute worst place for her was that damp and filthy factory, and so, though my own finances were in pretty bad shape, I went to the bank and arranged to have a weekly sum paid to her from my private account, on the proviso that she stay home. I organised a car to collect her for her appointments, and take her back afterwards. I kept her on this regimen for months, what I called the Three Rs: rest, radiation, and a rich diet.

But a few weeks later her cough worsened again and she complained of a sore throat. Further tests showed that the TB had not been halted as I'd hoped, but had infiltrated her larynx. We had to act fast. I knew that this laryngeal manifestation of the disease needed more direct treatment, preferably with an electro-therapy unit that had a vacuum tube attachment for the throat. I didn't have the time to build one of those, so I bought a unit, a new, high-frequency machine.

I have to admit that this treatment is uncomfortable for the patient. I was awfully sorry to inflict it on Mrs Dahlstrom, but I had to do what was best for her. During the procedure she sat stiffly, her eyes fixed on the machine I held in my hands. Because I am a skilled practitioner, I was able to control the current so that only a pale hint of blue light was showing in the glass tube. This is important to minimise discomfort for the patient. Once the current was steady, I had her open her mouth wide enough that I could position the tube against her palatine tonsils, right at the back of her throat. She had to keep very still. If she became restless and moved even a fraction, she would receive a small shock in her throat from the tube. Some practitioners apply head restraints to avoid this, but I was reluctant to adopt this inhumane approach. Whenever Mrs Dahlstrom got a shock she flinched and sometimes began to cry.

However, I knew how effective this remedy was, so I persevered despite her complaints, and despite how difficult it was to administer.

I did all I could to make the sessions as pleasant as possible for Mrs Dahlstrom. I bought a phonograph and some records that were popular at time: Cole Porter and Hoagy Carmichael, and played these in the background. Music can be very effective in lowering levels of agitation, I have had cause to observe. When her treatments were over, Mrs Dahlstrom and I sat together and drank a cup of coffee, or sometimes a glass of aquavit, and ate pastries or cake. I kept a stock of treats on hand for her: candy, fruit, drinking chocolate, and sometimes even hair ribbons, stockings. Anything to make this difficult time a little easier for her.

When I first started treating her I had grave concerns about the effect of Petter Dahlstrom's sudden disappearance. I kept a close eye on her, and though there seemed to be no obvious shock effect, the possibility of a delayed reaction was always in my mind. Such emotional crises can have serious physical ramifications for patients. Speaking for myself, I can't say I was the least bit sorry he was gone from her life. Aside from the loss of earnings, I had no doubt she was better off, and in fact I might go so far as to say that he disappeared at the perfect time. One day, over coffee and cake, Mrs Dahlstrom told me that her sister had reported him as missing to the police.

'Not that it will do any good,' Mrs Dahlstrom said, looking down at her empty plate and tracing her finger through the cake crumbs. 'He's run away. I just know it. I think it was because of my sickness. He's run away from me.'

'Do the police have any leads?' I asked, though I had no high expectations of the deductive powers of the Sundsvall district police force. 'Any idea where he might be?'

'They haven't done a thing,' she said. 'I doubt they will.'

I saw the tears flood her eyes and I reached out and put my arms around her. Her breath was hot and soft against my skin. I could feel her ribs expand and contract and her heart beating within her.

'Shh . . . There, there,' I said. 'Everything's going to be fine.'

'They'll never find him,' she said in a small voice.

I had never held her before, never dared. The only time I touched her was when the treatment required it. The heat blazed off her skin and I breathed in the delicate scent of her. I let go of her before I wanted to. The window was open and the summer air blew in over us, perfuming the room with the scent of the grasses and flowers of the Gärdet park. I think I never felt so happy as in that moment.

She was right, I thought. They'd never find him.

3.

THAT WHOLE SUMMER, in fact, proved to the happiest of my life. I looked forward to Mrs Dahlstrom's treatments much as I had to vacations as a child, and on the days of her appointments I awoke with the same electrified feeling, my blood surging through my veins like a wild melody. The very idea of her, of being near her, made me light-headed. Naturally I took care to never speak of my feelings to her; the last thing I wanted was to overwhelm her, but I knew that she felt it too. It was in the air, as palpable as an electrical current passing between us. I saw it in her eyes, and I sensed it when I touched her.

The fears I had that Mrs Dahlstrom would be devastated by her husband's disappearance continued to be groundless, and she showed every sign of adjusting to life without him. Granted, she was not yet cured of the TB, but there was no doubt that her condition had improved with the radiation therapy. Without my intervention she would likely have already succumbed to this awful disease. I felt very optimistic about the future.

The one blight on my days was Doris. Doris and her jealousy of Mrs Dahlstrom. I knew that my wife meant no harm, and she had not caused any scenes as I feared she might, but there was a constant undercurrent of disapproval and an atmosphere of surveillance at home. Doris had a thousand questions about Mrs Dahlstrom, about her personal life, about my feelings for her, about the topics of our conversations. She often interrupted our treatments, knocking on the door with offers of coffee, or on the pretence that she'd heard me calling her. This was not only thoughtless, it was downright dangerous: being distracted while performing these delicate procedures could cause an injury to the patient. Once, I opened the door of the treatment room to reveal her skulking outside on the landing. Eavesdropping, no doubt. It was extremely wearing for me, and it was also difficult to stand by and watch Doris's distress. I tried time and again to reassure her, to tell her how much she meant to me, but it made no difference. After a while I started to feel that if Doris's behaviour continued much longer I'd have no choice but to take some kind of action.

During that time I often found myself wandering the city after my shifts at the Holm Clinic, unwilling to return to the apartment and face another of Doris's interrogations. One day, one of those particularly glorious October days that fade into a long, golden fall afternoon, when it seems a crime to be cooped up inside, I left the clinic early. I didn't want to go home, and with nowhere else to go I made my way down to the water. The streets were busy with pedestrians. I crossed over the Djurgården bridge and went through the Blue Gate into the park. I followed the path that runs beside the water of Djurgårdsbrunnsviken. On fine days, being in Djurgården was like being on vacation. The sun threw white sparks onto the water and gusts of yellow birch leaves swooped past me to float on the lake in miniature golden flotillas. Everywhere people were out strolling: couples and nannies with children and pairs of young girls walking along with their arms linked together, laughing. I smiled at each person I encountered and tipped my hat to the ladies. I could see a file of riders walking their horses across the path up ahead. I used to ride as a boy and I stopped to watch them pass. It was a group of ladies, all riding astride, which made much more sense than the ridiculous practice of riding side-saddle that had been common in my youth. One of the women, the last one in the file, looked a lot like Mrs Dahlstrom. I thought of how much I would love to take her for a ride when she was better. How beautiful she would look mounted.

The woman did look an awful lot like Mrs Dahlstrom, I thought, watching her; even her gestures and movements were similar. Was it her? I squinted. Although I have near-perfect vision I couldn't see her face clearly under her cap. I hurried along the path, then broke into a run, but all I could see were the riders' backs and the horses' rumps rocking away round a bend in the path. I stopped, out of breath with my hat knocked askew. I had to laugh at myself really, seeing Mrs Dahlstrom everywhere like a man possessed. How true that love makes fools of us all. I realised there was no way Mrs Dahlstrom, my Lina, was out riding in Djurgården; the very idea was ridiculous. I doubt she'd ever sat on a horse in her life, and besides, she was completely housebound apart from her visits to me.

A few days later, when she came to her appointment as usual, I noticed right away that she'd taken a turn for the worse. Her cough was almost constant, and her breathing was strained. She was limp and paler than ever, her eyes sunken in her face. I put a record on the phonograph and we chatted as I administered the radiation.

'When you are well again, I'll give you a special treat,' I told her. 'I'll take you horseriding in Djurgården. I saw some riders there the other day, and it was the funniest thing: one of them was the spitting image of you.'

She gave a laugh, which set off a coughing fit.

'I have been,' was all she managed to get out between coughs.

'Deep breaths, my dear,' I said, and rubbed her back. 'Deep breaths.'

'The other day.' She was still coughing. 'That was me.'

She tried to laugh, but couldn't for all her coughing. I laughed at her joke; she was a funny one alright.

'No,' she said vehemently. 'It was me. Really.' In short bursts between coughs and gasps she said, 'Papa . . . took me out . . . with Greta . . . riding. Because I never have . . . and I always wanted . . . to go.' She lay back on the table, spent.

'No.' I couldn't believe it. 'Tell me that's not true.'

I couldn't believe her father would be so foolhardy. Exertion like that might be more than she could take. I decided to double her radiation time and increase her adrenaline dose. I was so furious that I accompanied her back to her apartment to speak with Mr Fredelius.

I found him smoking a pipe at the kitchen table, which made me even angrier; the smoke would be incredibly irritating for Lina's lungs. I wanted to snatch the filthy thing from him and smash it to pieces on the floor. Instead I motioned for him to join me outside on the landing. I was shaking with rage.

'Mr Fredelius, are you trying to kill your own daughter?' I said when we were both outside with the door closed behind us. I had to make an effort to keep my voice down.

'What d'you mean?'

He stood there blinking his small piggy eyes at me, with that damned pipe still clenched between his teeth.

'You allowed Mrs Dahlstrom to go out horseriding? Do you understand how weak she is?'

He slowly took the pipe out of his mouth. 'Only a bit of fun,' he said. 'They just walked 'em. No harm in it.' His voice was amiable and dimwitted.

'No harm in it? Are you crazy? It could damn well kill her,' I told him.

He shrugged. 'Seemed alright to me.' He put his pipe back in his mouth. It clicked against his teeth.

'And smoking? In the house? With a seriously ill respiratory patient present?' I shook my head. I could hardly believe the man. My head started to ache. I turned and went down the stairs, leaving him there on the landing.

I heard him call after me, 'S-sorry, doctor! I didn't know.'

On the way back to Östermalm, I thought of Lina's pale face and a terrible fear gripped me, a blackness descended before my eyes. That was the first day I actually felt we might lose her.

4.

I STILL HADN'T managed to calm myself by the time I arrived home, though I'd taken the long way, through Norrmalm and Vasastan. If anything, I was even more riled up than when I left the Dahlstroms'. In my agitation I drove recklessly around the night-time streets, too fast and through a few red lights. When I opened the front door I could hear the clink of teacups and the polite hum of Doris's voice, the low tone she reserved for visitors. One of Doris's tea parties was the last thing I wanted to face that evening. Without even removing my hat and coat, I made my way down the hall.

'Doris? May I have a word?' I called out.

I opened the parlour door harder than I meant to and it bounced off the wall behind.

I saw her head turn towards me at the sound. She was sitting in the armchair by the fire with a teacup and saucer poised in front of her and her eyebrows raised. Opposite her, side-by-side on the sofa, were two men, one of them in police uniform.

'Oh, Carl,' Doris said. 'You're back at last. These two gentlemen and I were just having such a lovely chat. They were hoping to speak with you.' She put down her cup and saucer on the table. 'This is Detective Inspector Larsson and this is Sergeant Blom.' She gestured to each of them with a slight inclination of her head and an upturned palm, as if we were all meeting at a party. Blom was a squarish lump of a man, with a brick-red complexion and a bald head. He was the one in uniform. His meaty forefinger and thumb were pinched onto the handle of his porcelain teacup, as if his strength was such that a more substantial hold would shatter it into pieces. Larsson, in a suit of varying shades of brown, looked like a curate: thin, with wire-rimmed spectacles and soft, ashy hair, receding at the crown. 'My husband,' Doris said to the policemen. 'Dr Dance.'

My immediate thought was that they had witnessed my driving back from Södermalm, and were here to issue me with a traffic infringement notice, and I marvelled at the speed at which they had acted.

Larsson cleared his throat. 'Now Dr Dance,' he said, 'we won't take up much of your time. We understand you're a very busy man. We're gathering information about a missing person, a certain Petter Dahlstrom, and we'd like to ask you some routine questions. Your wife tells us that he is known to you?'

'Yes, he is—I mean, I know the name.' I wondered what else Doris had told them. 'That is to say, I met him once. He's the husband of one of my patients.'

Blom had put down his teacup and was writing laboriously in a small notebook with a rather large pencil.

'Met him once,' repeated Larsson in a flat voice. 'And what was the nature of your relationship?'

'Relationship? We didn't have any relationship. As I say, I met the man but a single time.'

'And when was that?'

'Months ago, back in . . . would have been January. Or, no, February. I don't remember exactly. It was winter, in any case.'

Larsson's eyes never left my face.

'You met at his residence, I understand?' Blom asked. He didn't look up from his notebook. 'You called on him at his home?'

'Not exactly on *him*, but yes it was, at his family's home. Your information is correct on that score. Listen, is there any indication of where he was last seen?'

'Can't reveal that,' said Blom. 'Operational reasons.'

'And, any idea where he might be now, Dr Dance?' Larsson asked.

'None whatsoever.'

'Right,' said Larsson. 'Thank you for your time, Dr Dance. That will be all for now.' He stood and picked up his hat from the table. Blom tucked his notebook into his pocket.

'Thank you, Mrs Dance,' Larsson said, turning to her, 'for the lovely coffee.'

'We'll see ourselves out,' said Blom.

Doris had the sense to leave the apartment shortly after they did. I sank back into the sofa and closed my eyes. I had a raging headache.

5.

'WELL, AT LEAST . . . something's . . . happening,' Lina wheezed when I told her about the visit from the police.

'They were . . . at our place . . . too. Searched . . . the whole apartment . . . Made a . . . mess. Mama . . . furious.' She pressed her hand against the side of her ribs.

'Do they have any leads?' I asked her.

She shook her head. 'But then no one . . . would tell me anyway . . . don't want to . . . upset.'

Lina was in worse shape than she'd been for a long time. As I had feared, her riding expedition had taken its toll. Her heart rate was fluttery and right up at 140, her blood neutrophil-to-lymphocyte ratio was alarmingly high. Each breath was a labour for her, a mountain to ascend, and when she blinked it was with excruciating slowness, as if her eyelids had weights attached. I found it painful to look at her. At the end of her session I gathered her up in my arms to lift her down from the treatment table. She had

112

become even thinner and I could feel her bones through her flesh. Her iliac crest pressed into my belly.

'My dear,' I whispered into her hair. 'You must take care. You must try your best to get stronger.'

I set her down and she pulled back from me to look into my face. Her cheeks were flushed, her lips parted. Her breath smelled sweet, like the scent of dark, ripe berries.

'Yoo-hoo!' came a high-pitched voice from the landing. 'Fika delivery!'

The door was pushed open and Doris appeared. She was carrying a large tray laden with pastries and coffee.

'I just passed by the Valhalla bakery on my walk and couldn't resist!' she exclaimed.

I could see that something had to be done.

6.

THE FOLLOWING WEEK I was plagued by worry and sleepless
nights. I had a lot on my mind. Lina's weak condition prompted
me to explore other treatment modalities, but I feared that time
was against us. My sleeplessness meant that during the day I was
sluggish and muzzy-headed. My hands were unsteady and I made
foolish mistakes with my work. Nils took me aside one day at the
clinic to ask if anything was wrong.

'I'm fine,' I told him. 'Bit of trouble with the wife, that's all.'

That particular day at work was an especially bad one. I was
drowsy and slow and couldn't fix my mind on any task. I had a
near-constant headache that gripped the perimeter of my skull
like a vice. In the morning I'd left a tray of blood samples out
on the bench instead of putting them in the cooler, which meant
they would all have to be redone. It was a careless mistake that
would cost hours of work, contacting each patient and scheduling them in to be retested. And just my luck, it had to be Holm

114

who discovered my error. He didn't reprimand me, but I saw his moustache bristle as his lips twisted into a sour line.

And then, to make things even worse, not an hour later I dropped a box of test tubes in the lab. Every one of them was smashed. Tiny shards of glass went skittering over the rubber floor into all corners of the room. I was scrabbling around gathering them up when Holm came in.

'What's going on in here?' He looked around at the mess I'd made.

'Doesn't seem to be my day,' I said.

'Mmm,' he said and folded his arms. 'I can see that.' He stood there and made no move to help me clear up. 'Is there anything in particular the matter, Carl? Feeling ill?' His voice was tight as a blade. 'Why don't you go home early today?'

And that's what I did. I had no energy for taking the long way home, all I could think about was getting into bed. I was so tired I knew I'd sleep the sleep of the dead. But when I got in the door, Doris waylaid me.

'Back so early?' she said. 'But it's not Mrs Dahlstrom's day today.'

Her voice had a tinny edge that sent my ears into a spasm and made my head pulsate. She was standing at the foot of the stairs, blocking my way to the bedroom. She had a newspaper in her hand.

'Come on, Doris. Please let me get past. I need to go to bed.'

I tried to go around her but she kept stepping into my path.

'What's the matter, Carl? Have you been out celebrating? One too many drinks?'

'Come on now, Doris. Let me past,' I said. I reached out to move her bodily out of the way, but she dodged me and waved the afternoon newspaper in my face.

'You ought to be celebrating,' she said. 'Haven't you seen the news?'

She opened the paper and read out loud. "'Stockholm man found dead. The body of a man has been found in a cabin outside of Sundsvall. The body has been identified as that of one Petter Dahlstrom, twenty-two, formerly of Södermalm.'"

She glared at me and swayed slightly on the spot. It was possible that she'd been drinking. 'Isn't that your sweetheart's husband?' she asked. 'You must be overjoyed!'

She flung the newspaper to the floor and scurried towards the front door, sobbing. She slammed the door behind her.

I picked up the newspaper Doris had discarded and read through the rest of the article. There wasn't very much more to it, other than that the death was not being treated as suspicious.

7.

NATURALLY MY FIRST thought was of the effect this news might have on Lina. I drove to Hallandsgatan. As soon as I pulled up outside number 36 I knew something was terribly wrong. The sound of wailing and crying drifted from her building out onto the street. I ran inside and found a crowd of people on the landing.

'Out of the way!' I shouted as I pushed through. 'I'm a doctor!'

The apartment was jammed with people.

'Mrs Dahlstrom!' I called. 'Lina!'

Somebody directed me to a bedroom, and there she was, lying very still. Her sister was slumped over her, crying. I sank down to my knees at the bedside. Lina's face was very white and her lips were blue.

'She's gone,' the sister sobbed.

People swarmed all around us, I don't know who they were. I shouted for everyone to get out of the room. Miss Fredelius refused to leave, and clung on to her sister. I had to push her out of the way so I could check Lina's pulse and breathing. I couldn't find a pulse right away but her body was still warm. I was sure there was still life in her.

A man appeared carrying a doctor's case. He ordered me out of the room but I refused and we got into an argument. Then he checked her vitals and pronounced her dead.

'She isn't dead!' I yelled it into his face.

I fought to get to Lina's side but somebody held me back, then I was bundled out of the room and the door slammed closed. I pounded on it with my fists and wrenched at the handle with both hands, but it wouldn't open. I paced up and down. Strangers' faces loomed out at me in the dim and crowded room. All I could think was that I had to see Lina, had to be with her.

After a while the doctor come out of the room, followed by Miss Fredelius. Mrs Fredelius flung herself upon her daughter, sobbing, and the two were ushered out of the apartment by another woman. The doctor and Mr Fredelius sat down at the table and I slipped back in to see Lina. She was alone. Her jaw had fallen open and her eyes were wide. I sat beside her on the bed and looked down into her lovely face. Her eyes stared into the beyond, and as I gazed into them they seemed to grow in size and envelop me.

I knew she was gone, that she was dead, but the voice of my heart kept saying to me, 'She's alive!'

The door opened and her father came in, mopping his eyes with his handkerchief.

'She's gone, isn't she?' he asked.

I nodded.

'Please,' he said, 'please close her eyes, Dr Dance.'

So I did as he asked, even though it was the most painful thing I'd ever done. I leaned down, and with the lightest touch possible I closed the eyes of my Lina, my darling.

8.

I SAT FOR a long time in that room. Sometimes Lina's father sat with me. Sometimes other people came and went. At some point I noticed it was dark. Then that the bedside lamp was on. All I could do was look at Lina and think how I had failed her. I couldn't save her. I looked at her and I hardly breathed. I didn't blink. I felt as if my whole body, my whole sense of self, had disappeared, and all that was left of me was my eyes, gazing and gazing at her. Already she looked different. She was changing before my very eyes, moment to moment. Her face had become even bonier and the flesh seemed to be sliding backwards. Her hands were clasped together over the comforter and the nail beds were purple. I could feel her growing colder with each hour that passed.

There was a knock at the door and a man in a dark suit came in. 'I'm Mr Bergius, the undertaker.'

Lina's father got up and they went out together. I heard them talking through the door, on and on. I thought their voices would disturb Lina, so I went out to tell them to keep it down. They were sitting opposite one another at the kitchen table.

Mr Fredelius was shaking his head. 'No. In that case no flowers,' he said. 'And no car neither. Just the casket and the removal.'

'Casket, the budget line, and the removal.' Mr Bergius jotted something in a notebook. 'Brings us to three thousand, one hundred crowns.'

Mr Fredelius's face was the colour of putty. Mr Bergius went on, 'Can I interest you in one small bouquet for your daughter's casket? Roses perhaps? Or lilies? Nothing extravagant.'

'I don't know.' The voice of Lina's father seemed to come from far away. 'Will you accept instalments?'

'I'm afraid not. And we'd need a down payment.'

'Sorry, Mr Bergius, but we just can't—'

'But Mrs Dahlstrom must have flowers,' I said. 'She must.' My voice was flat and cracked and too loud in the room. The two men turned to look at me. 'She will have roses,' I said. 'White roses. Dozens of them.' What kind of a family would dream of sending their daughter into the next world without flowers? Lina, a beautiful young woman. She needed that, at least.

'Dr Dance,' Lina's father said. 'We're not able—'

'Please, Mr Fredelius. Let me take care of it. Let me do this one last thing for Mrs Dahlstrom.'

Tears were streaming down his cheeks. He looked from me to Mr Bergius and back, his face a pale, bewildered mask.

'Please,' I repeated. 'Let me take care of her.'

At last he nodded.

I addressed Mr Bergius. 'We'll take the roses. And a car. The best you have. Top of the line.' I got out my chequebook.

Mr Fredelius had slumped forward over the table. His shoulders were shaking. When he spoke I could make out his words only with difficulty. 'Thank you, Dr Dance.'

Mr Bergius had a lot of papers for me to sign, confirming that I was to be the one responsible for Lina. I took the copies and put them in my pocket. Then he had all kinds of questions about the funeral arrangements. I didn't care to discuss it while Lina was listening in the next room, so Mr Bergius and I went to settle matters at his office, even though it was the middle of the night.

Over the next days I managed to come to grips with the thousand technicalities that make up the administration of death. I stopped going to work and concentrated solely on Lina and what needed to be done for her. She was all that mattered. I arranged to have her body moved to the receiving vault. I spoke to the mortician and gave strict instructions as to Lina's embalming. I chose her place in the Norra Begravningsplatsen cemetery. I chose the perfect car, the perfect flowers, and music for the ceremony. I chose the dress she was to wear. I made sure that everything was of the very best quality money could buy. Her dress was ivory silk, and she would wear the finest jewels. I had a tomb built for her, a little house where she would live. I drew up the design myself and oversaw its construction. Every day I visited her in the vault, to tell her how things were progressing. I showed her the designs for her new house, and I brought the dress to show her too.

The day of the funeral came. It was late October by then. The nights were lengthening and eating into the days, and the winds had turned icy. From the moment I opened my eyes that morning I had a feeling of pressure, of weight, on my head and my shoulders, and I walked with a stoop. Everything seemed to be covered with a layer of grey fuzz, as if a fog had drifted into the house.

The chapel at the cemetery was almost full when I arrived. I could see Lina waiting in her coffin at the end of the aisle. As I walked towards her, the guests turned their heads to look at me, exactly as they would turn to look at a bride entering the church for her wedding. And indeed, the ceremony was more like a wedding than anything else. Lina looked radiant in her silk dress, lying nestled among her bed of lace and flowers. I took my place in the front pew beside Lina's parents and sister.

But here too everything was covered in that grey mist and seemed to be happening at one remove from me, as if I was watching it all on a movie screen. The organ music started. Bach's *Prelude and Fugue in D Minor*. Then the pastor appeared and began the service. But right away he made a mistake.

'Wife of Petter Dahlstrom, and sister of Greta Fredelius . . .'

I had to stop myself from calling out and correcting him. Lina was no longer Dahlstrom's wife. Dahlstrom was dead, and Lina was mine. Had we already been married? My head felt confused and the fog seemed to settle in my eyes.

The service ended. The coffin was closed. We all went out to the tomb. It was small, but beautiful, and looked nothing like a mausoleum. It was built of white stone, and had a window so Lina could look out at the trees and the sun and stars. I'd had blue silk curtains put up to shield her from the prying eyes of strangers.

The coffin was also a design of my own, made to protect her delicate and beautiful body. It was double-chambered, and the inner oak chamber was lined with sterile cotton sprayed with formalin and eau de cologne. This inner chamber was encased in a metal chamber with air-tight seals fastened with twenty steel locks. A ventilation system allowed air to circulate between both chambers, each of which had a glass portion over where Lina's head would lie. The outer chamber also had a panel in the same spot, which could be pulled back so that she could look out and I could look in at her. I hoped this would make her feel less lonely.

9.

NOW A DIFFERENT phase of my life began, and I started to lead what you might call a double life. I still lived in the same apartment with Doris, exactly as I had before. I still went to the clinic and treated patients. I ate the same meals at the same times and I wore the same clothes. But that part of my life seemed like it was in shadow while my real life was with Lina.

I visited her at her little white house almost every day. It wasn't that I intended to go, it was more that I was compelled to do so. Sometimes I had no particular plan to go at all, but as the hours passed I would notice a tension taking hold of me. My muscles grew tight, my ribs clenched around my lungs, and before long I could breathe only in strained gasps. These sensations got stronger by the minute until I was in agony. It was as if Lina held a string attached to my heart and could summon me to her side by tugging on it. I would find myself hurrying to the cemetery as anxiously as if I was about to miss an important appointment. I would unlock the door of the tomb with shaking hands, and it was only after sitting beside the coffin for some time that I felt able to breathe normally again.

Lina's first winter in her new house was an especially hard one, and by February I was dismayed to find a damp spot in the corner of the ceiling where water was leaking through. I set about patching it up, and it was while I was on the ladder, scraping away the damaged plaster, that it happened. A loud metallic popping sound, so loud that I almost fell off the ladder in fright. It was like a gun going off. I took a look outside, but there was nobody around. When I came back I saw that the twenty locks that held the coffin closed had sprung open. Then I heard a voice. Lina's voice.

'Dr Dance, are you there? What's happened to me?'

I looked around. The voice sounded so alive I thought she must be standing somewhere in the room. But I was alone. The hairs on my neck and arms raised themselves up. I approached the coffin and slid back the viewing panel. Lina was lying exactly as usual. Her body was still. I felt weak and dizzy and my head tingled. The room seemed to recede from me.

'Dr Dance?'

I leaned down and placed my ear to the top of the coffin.

'Where am I?' I heard the voice say.

I fell back in shock. The voice was coming from inside the coffin, complete with a slight metallic echo, not from inside my head. It was unmistakable.

'Lina?'

'Don't be afraid,' the voice said, and it was unquestionably Lina's voice. I knew it so intimately. 'I just want to know where I am.'

'You're in the new house that I built for you.' There were tears in my eyes and my voice trembled with them.

'Do you live here with me?' she asked.

'No, my dear. I am only visiting.'

The tears started rolling down my face and onto the coffin. I dropped my head and pressed my cheek to the glass panel. I stayed there like that for perhaps an hour, but she didn't speak again. When I got up I felt the most wonderful sense of ease and peace, such as I hadn't felt in years. I went home and slept the deep and dreamless sleep of a child.

As you might imagine, over the following days I gave careful consideration to the matter of Lina's voice. I could see for myself that her vocalisations were not produced in the usual way that you or I might speak: her lips and face had not moved when she made an utterance. Naturally my first thought was that I was losing my mind, or experiencing some sort of hallucination. This might seem like a reasonable explanation; it was true that I was under a high degree of emotional strain at the time, a situation which can easily result in disordered behaviour in some individuals.

However, after further thought, this explanation struck me as unviable. Apart from Lina's voice, every other phenomenon that I encountered during that time was completely normal. I heard no other voices, I experienced no visions or disorientation or altered states, as would be the case were I suffering mental malaise. In fact, my ability to rationally analyse the question of my own sanity goes some way to proving that I was in full possession of my faculties.

A much more likely explanation was that I, as an open-minded and enquiring man, free of prejudices, was able to receive Lina's voice as she spoke to me from another plane. Far from being hokum, such communication is in fact a common phenomenon backed up by scientific research. Now, you might think that your consciousness resides in your brain, which resides in your body, and on the face of it that seems like a reasonable assumption. But to this day, nobody has yet been able to identify the cells and processes whereby this 'I', otherwise known as the soul or consciousness, is produced. In other words, it has never been proven that the essence of you, your consciousness, is located in your body. This idea is but an illusion, something we merely believe to be true. And if our consciousness is not located in our body, it follows that it must be located elsewhere, in realms that we, likely on account of our limited cognitive ability as a species, cannot perceive of.

Let me tell you that I've experienced many phenomena in my time, both in my medical career and in my travels, which made me realise that the conventional understanding of life and death is perhaps not as definitive as people like to think. It happened once, for instance, on my travels in India as a young man, that I was struck down with a terrible fever. I was seriously ill for weeks and bedridden. One day, I awoke thinking I was in my sick bed, only to find that the doctor had pronounced me dead and sent me to the morgue. I had died and come back to life. All my vital signs had been absent for a prolonged period and had then spontaneously reappeared.

And that is not all: at many other times in my life I've experienced first-hand happenings that can't be explained, and felt energies that don't fit into the distinct categories of the living or dead as we usually understand them. I was alerted to the death of my mother from the other side of the world. I have had prophetic dreams on more than one occasion. I have been visited by ghosts.

To dismiss all this as spiritualist mumbo jumbo would be the narrow-minded view. The fact is that such occurrences are backed up by science. Research by Sir William Crookes, the renowned scientist, proves without a doubt that communication with the dead takes place, and more regularly than you might think. Other research, like that of William Kouwenhoven's, into bodily reactions and energy fields, proves that there is a life after death. It might not be life as we can perceive it, but it is life nonetheless.

After Lina first spoke to me, I visited her at least daily. I would sit awhile and tell her about my day. Sometimes she spoke, sometimes not. Her spirit was exactly the same as it had been in life, childlike and teasing and at times a little shy. I moved a table and chair into the tomb, as well as my portable phonograph and Lina's records. The songs reminded us both of those happy days we shared during her treatments.

Regrettably, my frequent visits quickly began attracting a lot of unwanted attention, and very soon I could only visit at night. Norra Begravningsplatsen cemetery is in the middle of Solna, surrounded by houses and schools and stores of all kinds, so there was never any shortage of people around. I guess somebody must have heard me playing the records and remembered who I was, because before long people would point at me and whisper when I arrived at the cemetery. I did my best to ignore them, but then the local children got in on the act. One group of boys in particular began lying in wait for me near the cemetery gates, and when I approached, they would pop out of their hiding places like rats.

'Here he comes!' they would shout and run up and surround me. They swore and yelled insults as I walked along, trying to mind my own business. Even when I was safely inside the tomb with the door closed behind me, they stayed outside, sometimes for hours, shouting and laughing and trying to peep in at the window. Their language was shockingly foul for such young kids. Many times I tried to talk to them and asked them to behave themselves, but it was no good. They only laughed at me. Once or twice they threw stones, one of which struck me on the head, very nearly breaking my eyeglasses. I was forced to make my visiting times later and later to avoid meeting those boys.

Weeks and months went by like this, with me leading my two lives. Doris continued with her own life and seemed to notice nothing amiss. Lina spoke to me more and more, and as we became closer she began to repeatedly ask when she could leave her house and come and live with me in mine.

'I want you to take me home with you,' she'd say in a plaintive voice.

'Soon, Lina,' I would say, when in actuality I had no plan to remove her from the tomb. Naturally, I wanted more than anything to take her home with me, but it was impossible because of Doris. Though I spent many long hours thinking up ways I might permanently get rid of my wife, nothing feasible presented itself.

But there came a point when the question of removing Lina's body from the tomb was something I had no choice in, it was a matter of urgency. I was grateful I'd had the foresight to install the glass viewing panes on the coffin, because this was how I was alerted to the problem. I noticed that the inside of the glass was covered with a fine layer of condensation, as if Lina had breathed against the glass. I thought the ventilation system must be blocked, trapping the moisture from her body inside the coffin. I tried cleaning out the vents from the outer chamber, but the condensation only got worse. After a week it had grown to a thick white film, like mould, blotting out Lina's face. There was nothing for it but to open the coffin and find the problem. This was a considerable task because I had to remove the inner chamber, which was very heavy, from the outer one in the relatively small space of the tomb.

I came prepared with lanterns and my toolbox. I set up the lanterns and removed the lid of the outer chamber. Even with it off I still couldn't see Lina; the condensation was also on the inner window. At the sight of that empty white square where her face should have been, an awful dread came over me, a creeping sense that when I opened the coffin it would be empty. Lina had been silent as I worked. With trembling hands I fastened ropes around the inner chamber and slid it out. When I undid the seal and opened the chamber I was unprepared for what awaited me.

A smell came wafting out, a smell of such vileness it was as if I'd opened a portal to hell itself. I reeled back against the wall with my arm covering my face. But it was impossible to avoid the stench. It was a sweet and sickening odour that seemed to seep into the air in a thick vapour, like smoke. It stung my eyes and nostrils. I took my scarf and tied it over my nose and mouth. I opened the door of the tomb wide, fanning it back and forth a few times to create a breeze, but none of this made much difference.

After a few minutes I closed the door and returned to Lina's side. The level of decay that had set in dismayed me. I had taken so many precautions against decomposition, including devising a special embalming formula that I instructed the mortician to use, but he either hadn't followed my instructions or it hadn't worked. Seen at close range, Lina's face was badly sunken. Her eyes had almost completely disappeared and her nose was in terrible condition. There was a large amount of foul-smelling seepage in the bottom of the coffin. All the padding was completely sodden, and stained a deep tea-leaf brown.

To halt the process of decay, Lina would need to be completely cleaned up and reinterred in a new coffin, but it was impossible to perform this task right there in the cemetery. Even if I could have transported everything I needed to the tomb, it was far too small a space to allow for the reinterment. The whole operation would have to be done elsewhere.

Then I heard a voice, or a sound at any rate. It was a kind of wailing, that rose and died and rose again as if it was being carried on the wind. At first I thought Lina was upset that I'd interfered with the coffin and was announcing her displeasure. But as I stood and listened more closely it became clear that the sound was coming from outside.

I grabbed a lantern and a hammer and opened the door. The weather had turned foggy. I stepped outside. Everything was quiet. There was no wind and I could hear my own breathing. The air smelled of damp earth, and the fog that blew over the pathways in ragged strips. I gripped the handle of the hammer tighter and stepped forward onto the main path.

'Hello?' I called.

My voice sounded thin and lonely in the night. There was no answer. I turned to go back inside when the sound came again. My instinct was to run into the tomb and lock the door, but I forced myself to stand my ground.

'Who's there?' I called.

There came a scuffling sound and a shape loomed out from around the side of the tomb. I staggered backwards. The shape was too big to be one of the boys and it was wearing a hood or hat of some kind.

'Who is it?' I whispered, almost rigid with terror.

'Carl?'

The figure pulled off its head covering.

'Doris?' I said.

She started howling again. 'So this is where you go,' she sobbed. 'I didn't want to believe it . . . but now I know it's true.'

I almost felt sorry for her, wandering around a cemetery alone on a foggy night.

'Why, Carl?' she wailed. '*Why*? Why are you doing this to me?'

Her voice disintegrated into sobs. She turned and ran away down the path until she was swallowed up by the night.

10.

I WAS FRANTIC at the knowledge that Lina, in all her youthful beauty, was slowly disappearing into decay, and the reason I could do nothing to save her was because Doris was standing in my way, exactly as she had when Lina was alive, always managing to come between us.

I would lie in the dark for hours, sleepless, anxious, listening to the bedside clock.

Tick.

Tick.

Every tick of that clock, I thought, marked the emergence of new bacteria and microbes by the thousand, bursting forth and massing together in Lina's flesh, preparing to destroy her skin, her organs, her bones. If I managed to fall asleep it was only to dream about her beautiful face slowly collapsing. Her eyes sinking further into her head, her jaw hanging lower, and her teeth and hair dropping out. Her flesh melting away, leaving the bare dark cords of muscle and then, finally, nothing more than the pale

134

bones glowing through. Over time even these would be hollowed, ravaged, and would fall to dust.

Doris didn't mention our encounter in the cemetery, though she was rather more withdrawn than usual. Nevertheless, in the days that followed we continued with our regular routines: washing, sleeping, working, and meals together. I felt it was important to try to keep Doris onside and follow our usual schedule as much as possible. Our Sunday lunch was a long-standing tradition that originated in the early days of our marriage. When I was a newlywed, so many years ago now, I would race home from my morning duties in my eagerness to see Doris, arriving out of breath and red-faced. How very different it had become.

The Sunday after Doris's appearance at the cemetery I spent the morning in the Scholars' Room at the National Library. I'd been there since the place opened, deep in various books and articles, and right when I was feverishly noting down a most important discovery, the notes of the Town Hall clock rang out. It was twelve o'clock, time to go.

As soon as I left the library it started to rain heavily, and as luck would have it I was without an umbrella. By the time I reached Sturegatan I was soaked to the skin and my shoes were spongy with water. A cold wind blew up, and soon my fingers turned icy and bloodless. I hurried through the streets, longing to be out of the cold rain, but at the same time dreading going home to Doris.

I was painfully aware that if Doris was gone, most of my problems would disappear. Without her I could that very day have moved Lina to the apartment and begun the restorative work that was so urgently needed. I had considered renting another apartment, perhaps somewhere in the vicinity of the cemetery, and performing the restoration there, but in the past months my finances had continued to worsen, and the expense was out of the question. And what I really wanted was to keep Lina at the apartment long-term. By now I'd done a lot of research on the effects of radiation therapy on cell rejuvenation, and I wished to seriously attempt it. It was a project that would require months to execute. My research had convinced me that there was a possibility of undertaking some experiments in resurrection.

People hear that word and immediately get the wrong idea. They start thinking of Nosferatu or Frankenstein's monster in a pantomime. But that's not what I'm talking about at all. I'm talking on a cellular level. When I was in India, I learned of a certain age-old Brahman cure for any mortal illness. The principle is simple: allow the afflicted to die, and inter them for a full year. At the end of that period they will be fully cured of their illness. That might sound like nonsense, but I ask you to consider it for a moment. It's ancient knowledge that is one hundred per cent backed up by modern science. Lina died of pulmonary tuberculosis. That's a fact. We know this because when she was alive the bacilli that were killing her were visible under the microscope. I saw them myself right there on the slides. But since her death I had taken other swabs from her, and I could find no such TB bacilli. Not a trace. The disease that had killed her had been cured. Lina might have died of TB, but she was no longer infected with that disease. To bring her back, all I had to do was stop the decay from progressing until I found a way to rejuvenate her cells. Naturally there was no way I could explain something like this to someone as conventional as Doris.

In the colder months, Doris always put a row of lighted candles in the windows of the apartment. They were meant to look homey and welcoming, and back when we were first married they did, but now the only sight that really warmed my heart was the blue-curtained window of Lina's little house.

'You're late,' said Doris, before I even had time to take off my dripping coat. I ignored her and went upstairs to change.

When I came down she was already sitting at the table, her mouth pulled down into a sour beak. Anna, the housekeeper, came in with the food. Every outward detail of these lunches was still exactly the same as years ago, like a perfectly preserved relic. Anna served us the same roast or baked sausages or meatballs as before; Doris dressed in the same style of clothes; the same kinds of flowers were on the table. The only difference was now there was also an icy tension in the air.

'Where were you this morning?' Doris demanded while Anna was still dishing out the potatoes. I waited for her leave us while Doris glared at me across the table. 'Well?' Her hands lay clenched into pink fists on either side of her plate, like two fleshy roses.

'I was at the library,' I said.

'Is that so?'

I unfolded my napkin and sliced off a piece of meatball. I dipped it into the gravy. 'Yes,' I said. 'It is.' I pushed the forkful of food into my mouth.

'Well, now.' She sniffed. 'And what did you do there all morning? If that's where you really were.'

I finished thoroughly chewing my mouthful before I answered. Muller recommends thirty-two chews per mouthful for optimal nutrient extraction. 'Researching.'

'Oh, how interesting,' she said. She picked up her cutlery with an ostentatious flourish, her pinkie fingers hovering in the air like antennae. 'Researching.' She speared a potato. 'Researching about your corpse lover, no doubt.'

I didn't dignify her outburst with an answer, and we ate on in silence. The clock on the mantelpiece ticked loudly, keeping time to my chews. Doris's rage was so palpable that it was like an object in the room with us. I kept my eyes fixed on my plate, trying to ignore her anger, but all over my body my muscles began to tense up, as if somebody was tightening them one by one with a ratchet. To calm myself, I began counting the ticks of the clock. By the time we finished eating I had almost made it to a thousand.

Doris rang the bell and Anna came to clear. Under our regular routine, we would move to the sofa to drink coffee and read the Sunday papers. I was surprised to see Doris, despite throwing me a poisonous look, head for her usual seat on the sofa. But she had always been a creature of habit. She settled her plump behind among the overstuffed cushions and silently handed me the *Svenska Dagbladet*, just as she did every Sunday. I took a seat in the armchair, not knowing what else to do. The library was now closed, and it was far too early to go to the cemetery: Sundays were the busiest days.

Anna brought in the coffee and a plate of cookies, as she had done hundreds of times, and Doris sat there with her cup in one hand and a fashion magazine in the other. I took a sip of my coffee, which tasted bitter, and started leafing through the *Dagbladet*. My eyes were glazed and unfocused. I could hear Doris's adenoidal breathing.

I glanced up. She was eyeing me over the rim of her cup.

'Off to the cemetery again this afternoon, are you?' she asked with affected unconcern.

I gave no answer to this. Stay calm, I told myself. Don't antagonise her.

'Look, Doris, I—'

She gave a kind of strangled grunt and leapt up from the sofa. She slammed her cup down on the side table and hurled herself at me, gibbering and flailing her arms.

'You're sick! You're a monster!' She cannoned into me and slumped across my lap, then slid to the floor twitching and writhing, as if in the grip of a fit. The whole time she jabbered away, accusing me of all sorts of terrible things.

'Doris!' I grappled with her, trying to catch hold of her wrists before she did herself an injury. 'Please! Calm yourself!'

She was surprisingly difficult to restrain. As soon as I managed to grasp on to one of her soft arms, she'd twist it free again, as if she had no joints or bones. After a minute of this fruitless grappling, I admit I lost my patience and struck her a blow across the cheek. Not very hard, just enough to bring her to her senses, and using only the flat of my hand. She was obviously hysterical, after all. When she made no reaction, I struck her again. This time it was effective. She sat upright on the floor like a stunned rabbit, her face white with a pink patch where I had made contact.

'I'm sorry, Doris,' I said. 'I was just trying to shock you out of it. I don't know what came over you.'

Her hand drifted to her face to cradle her cheek. Then she jumped up, let out a wail and ran from the room.

I had to get out of that apartment. I hurried to the door, grabbing my still-wet coat as I went. I pulled it on as I jogged down the stairs. I had no clear idea of where I was going. Outside it had stopped raining. It was already getting dark, but not yet dark enough to visit Lina. I went out onto Jungfrugatan and turned right, deliberately heading away from the cemetery. I walked fast, trying to outrun the creeping dread that was overtaking me. The frozen air stung my face and I breathed in great lungfuls of it. There weren't many people around. I headed down towards the water, all the time thinking about Lina.

All I had left of her, apart from her body, was a single photograph, taken before she was ill. I still keep it in my jacket pocket and look at it often. It's not a particularly good likeness. In it, she is standing on a street in the sunlight. Her face is screwed up slightly against the sun, giving her a mistrustful look. Her pose is awkwardly balanced and her dress ill-fitting, too tight at the shoulders. In reality she is much more beautiful than the picture shows.

When I reached the water I turned left and could see the Dramaten theatre on the corner, all lit up and with the gold leaf along the front facade gleaming in the light. Even on a gloomy day like this there were crowds of people waiting on the steps. I walked past the entrance and under the gaze of the golden figures of the muses. I stopped and looked up at them for a second. The statues were a life-sized pair, a man and woman. The man was standing, holding a golden helmet, and the woman sat huddled against his leg, with a wistful face.

Lina deserved something like that, I thought, some glorious permanent record of her physical beauty. Something that would never get old and deteriorate as bodies do. And perhaps one day she would have it.

11.

THE CLINIC HAD become a refuge from my problems, a world away from the strife that characterised my home life. My line of work requires the totality of my attention, and for this I was grateful. I threw myself into the daily round, dictated by the appointments book.

Towards the end of the week following that disastrous lunch with Doris, I was in the staff kitchen one afternoon, having a cup of coffee and leafing through the *Aftonbladet*. I read this paper for the classifieds listings. It was a good way to find out about new medical products on the commercial market. Many of them were obviously nothing more than quackery, but here and there you might come across something worthwhile.

My eye was caught by the name 'Dahlstrom', followed by a short article headed: MURDER INVESTIGATION LAUNCHED.

Police say that the death of a Stockholm man, Petter Dahlstrom, twenty-two, is now being reopened in light of new evidence. Information has emerged suggesting that Dahlstrom's death occurred under suspicious circumstances, rather than due to natural causes as previously believed. Dahlstrom's body was found in a cabin on the outskirts of Sundsvall in October of 1930. Any persons with information on this matter are encouraged to come forward immediately.

I sat back in my chair. I wondered what kind of information had emerged after nearly six months. And was the report accurate? *Aftonbladet* was a highly sensational paper. But if it was true, the police would want to question me. I considered whether it would be better to volunteer to speak to them. After all I had nothing to fear from them.

The door opened and Nils came in. I shoved the paper aside.

'Quiet afternoon?' He smiled at me and poured himself a cup of coffee.

'Taking a quick break.' I made to get up. 'Time to get back to it, though.'

I thought it might be prudent to take the newspaper with me. I reached over for it but I was too slow. Nils already had it in his hand.

'Anything interesting today?' he asked, glancing over the headlines.

'Er, nothing much,' I said.

I tried to think of something to distract him with.

'Oh, I'd almost forgotten!' he said. 'Did you hear the news about Petter Dahlstrom? You know, Lina Dahlstrom's husband? It turns out that he was *murdered*.' Nils took a sip of coffee, his eyes eager. 'I read it in *Dagens Nyheter*. Isn't that something?'

'You don't say,' I replied.

I stood up too quickly and knocked my chair backwards. When I rinsed my cup at the sink my hands were shaking under the warm water.

For the rest of the day I felt jittery, as if I'd drunk too many cups of coffee. I started to get the feeling that people were looking at me oddly. Åsa the receptionist, Holm, the patients in the waiting room: their eyes seemed to slide towards me and linger accusingly. Had they all seen the article too?

Even after I left the clinic, the agitated feeling stayed with me. On my walk home through the streets of Östermalm the faces of passers-by flashed up at me one after another, like pictures in a portrait gallery, all of them with narrowed eyes, mouths awry; judging me. I started to get the feeling that I was being followed. I turned around a few times to check whether I was. Once I thought I caught a glimpse of Lina's sister walking behind me.

I increased my pace and kept my head down, my gaze on the sidewalk, trying to think of other things, but the corner of my eye still caught people turning their heads to stare at me as they passed. I took off my eyeglasses and put them in my pocket. Instantly the world retreated to a hazier, gentler distance, but even that didn't completely blot out the stares of passers-by. When I reached Östermalmsgatan I noticed two policemen on the corner, outside the fire station. As I approached, they folded their arms and halted their conversation. They turned their heads to watch me pass. All the way to the end of the block my back prickled under their gaze.

At Jungfrugatan I saw right away that the candles in the windows weren't lit. When I let myself into the apartment, all the lights were out and the place was silent. There was a coldness in the air.

'Doris?' I called into the dark room.

The clock ticked. Something about the apartment unsettled me. The pieces of furniture seemed to all have been moved into slightly different positions. I went from room to room, turning on the lights. Doris was nowhere to be found, and had left no note, which was unusual. As a rule she was home for the evening meal, and if she made some other plan she told me about it beforehand. In the kitchen, Anna had prepared dinner, as always, but she herself was likewise absent. The oven was on, and inside were veal cutlets.

I made another tour of the apartment, looking carefully in every room, even in the wardrobes. In all our years of marriage, this had never happened before. I felt a distinct sense of foreboding. The newspaper article, the staring faces, and now Doris disappearing: these all seemed like sinister signs. I went back into the kitchen and took the plate from the oven and sat down at the table. I took a forkful of cutlet, which turned into a rubbery, tasteless substance in my mouth. I chewed and chewed but couldn't get it down. In the end I spat the mashed mess into my napkin.

When I woke the next morning, Doris still hadn't come home. Usually she was up long before me, and in the old days I would hear her talking or singing to herself as she went about her lengthy morning toilet. But that day all I could hear was the sound of Anna preparing breakfast downstairs, and the more distant noises of the street outside. I thought I ought to notify the police. I went down to the kitchen to see if Anna knew anything.

'Well, her day coat's gone from the hall,' she told me, 'and her good Oxfords. Though the Lord knows what she wants with wearing those in weather like this. Ruined, they'll be.'

I hadn't realised that Anna was so observant. I wandered into the dining room. That's when I noticed the envelope that was lying on the mantle.

Dear Carl,

I'm sorry but I have to go away for a while, I simply can't stand it anymore. Your unnatural behaviour is more than any wife can be expected to bear. I've spoken with my friends about this matter and they all agree you are treating me monstrously.

Don't come looking for me. I don't know when or indeed if I'll be back.

Doris.

P.S. Please send any letters for me on to Lotta in Ystad.

I stood there for a moment. Knowing that Doris was actually gone, and without me having to lift a finger to make it happen, pushed everything else clean out of my head. My tension melted away and, in its place, a deep well of joy came bubbling up. Now my dream would come true at last: I would bring my Lina home.

As a precaution, I put a call through to Lotta, Doris's sister, in Ystad, asking if Doris had arrived. Lotta pretended not to know what I was talking about, but I was certain I could hear my wife's voice in the background. I ended the call, satisfied that she was out of the picture, at least for the next little while. Then I went and gave Anna her notice. I would do without a housekeeper for the time being.

12.

MY PLAN WAS to build an incubator tank that I would use to repair the damage done to Lina's body. I had already been working on the design for weeks, and I'd brought my extensive training and experience to the task. Without wishing to boast, I have to say that my design was far superior to anything commercially available in the mortuary industry. The tank consisted of a metal casket lined with a thick layer of white felt. It was to be equipped with a pump and filtration system that allowed round-the-clock circulation of the embalming fluids: oxyquinoline sulphate and a solution of sodium and plasma. I had formulated these fluids myself: I was a trained chemist after all. The tank had a heating system that kept the circulating liquid at a constant temperature of thirty-seven degrees Centigrade, at all times.

That very morning I went out and ordered supplies: sterile cotton, linen, distilled water, phenol solution, the chemicals for my embalming fluid, Dakin's solution, emollients, some tubing and a pump. I already had the material for the frame of the tank,

146

sheets of 26-gauge stainless steel waiting to be welded together. I estimated that once I commenced assembly, I could have the tank ready within a fortnight. By the time I got back to the apartment, the deliveries had already started arriving. An ever-growing pile of boxes and bottles was amassing in the hall, and I regretted having been so hasty in dismissing Anna, as I found my work interrupted every fifteen minutes to go downstairs and answer the door.

As I headed down yet again, I considered propping the street door open and posting a sign directing the delivery boys to my apartment.

'Put it in here, please,' I said as I opened the door.

But this time it wasn't a delivery boy. It was two policemen: the same men who had paid me a visit before. Larsson and Blom.

'Good afternoon, Dr Dance,' said Larsson. Blom already had his notebook ready. 'We'd like to have a few words with you.'

I led them through to the parlour and they sat on the sofa in the same places they had on their last visit.

'Now,' said Larsson, when they were settled, 'we want to have a little talk with you to help us gather some information.' He pulled out a notebook identical to Blom's and opened it.

My palms were sweating but I feared that wiping them on my trousers would be misinterpreted. Instead I clasped my hands loosely in my lap and smiled at the two men.

'Happy to help in any way I can,' I said.

'Good. Now, as you know we have been investigating the disappearance of Petter Dahlstrom. You may be aware that his body has since been found, and it has been ascertained that his death was not a natural one.'

He paused and looked at me, as if to gauge my reaction. Blom seemed to be having difficulty with his pencil, which was of the mechanical kind. He was busy examining the mechanism at the end of it.

'Shocking news,' I said.

'Indeed,' said Larsson.

'How did he die?' I asked.

'Can't reveal that,' Blom said, still looking at his pencil. 'For operational reasons.'

Larsson consulted his notebook. 'Last time we spoke, you mentioned that you had met Dahlstrom one evening in February of last year. Can you tell us more about the circumstances surrounding that visit?'

So I told them all about Mrs Dahlstrom and the treatments. I didn't go into the technical side of it too much; in my experience police are generally not technically minded, and you can get into difficulties when trying to explain these details to such people.

'It sounds as if you're very dedicated to your work, Doctor,' Larsson said.

Blom was clicking his mechanical pencil. *Clik-clak. Clik-clak.*

'Thank you. I try to be.'

'And what about your relationship with the late Mrs Dahlstrom? Were you close? A very beautiful woman, Mrs Dahlstrom.'

'Very beautiful,' said Blom. 'A real stunner.'

I felt a rush of annoyance at the idea of Blom salivating over Lina, but just then the doorbell rang again, and I excused myself to admit a delivery boy. I took a moment for a few deep breaths in the hall. When I came back into the parlour, the police didn't ask me who the caller was. I resumed my seat.

'Now,' said Larsson, 'we were discussing your relationship with Mrs Dahlstrom. Can you tell us about that?'

'Mrs Dahlstrom was, as I mentioned, my patient,' I said. There was a silence.

'Your patient. I see.' *Clik-clak* went Blom's pencil. 'Nothing more?'

'No. Nothing more.'

'And yet,' said Larsson, 'I understand that you paid all of her funeral expenses. A generous act.'

'I like to help where I can, and I'm fortunate to be in a position where I am often able to.'

He nodded. 'Highly commendable. Ever been to Sundsvall?' His voice was casual, but his eyes were sharp.

'Sundsvall? Ah yes, up north, isn't it? I don't believe I have.'

'Don't believe you have,' Larsson repeated. 'Hmm.' His eyes were fixed on me, as if he was trying to see into my soul. I smiled at him.

They asked me to repeat the details of my encounter with Dahlstrom a few more times, and then had me write it down in a statement and sign it. When they got up to leave I saw them to the door.

'The wife been shopping?' Blom asked in the hall, gesturing to the pile of boxes.

'Ah, that's right.' One of the boxes had LLOYDS MEDICAL SUPPLIES printed in large green letters on the side. 'And some items for work.'

'For work,' Larsson said. He eyed me. 'Seems to me you'll have a damned hard time carrying that lot over to your clinic in Karlaplan.'

13.

AFTER I CLOSED the door behind the policemen, I headed straight for the drinks cabinet. I poured myself a generous splash of Macallan and downed it. My body was strangely numb. From where I was standing by the window I could see the two men exit the building and get into their unmarked car parked opposite. The car sat there a moment, and I thought they planned to surveil the building, but a few minutes later they drove away.

Although I knew I had nothing to fear from Blom and Larsson, they had unnerved me. The fact is, anyone would feel that way after a visit from the police. It's well known that their methods are designed to instil nervousness, even in innocent people. Stories came to my mind of those who'd been falsely accused and punished in America. Leo Frank; Sacco and Vanzetti. All three of these men were outsiders in some way. Both cases show how prejudicial views can influence the so-called impartiality of the legal system and the media. I myself had been part of the letter-writing campaign protesting the charges against Sacco and Vanzetti. It was clear to most right-minded people that they were innocent, and the reason they were targeted was because they were foreigners, as well as politically progressive. That's what made me, as an immigrant myself, nervous. Granted, I had no quarrel with the prevailing system of capitalism and democracy, as those two gentlemen did, but my status as a pioneering medical practitioner would no doubt put me beyond the pale as far as the average Swede was concerned. Swedes were by and large a conventional and mistrustful bunch, as suspicious of innovation as they were of outsiders.

Sacco and Vanzetti, I recalled, had been executed by means of the electric chair. I read the notice in *The Times* on the day it happened. To be killed by an electrical charge requires less power than you might think. These days I believe the standard is 2000 volts at 5 to 7 amps for the initial shock, and that is more than enough to cause unconsciousness, ventricular fibrillation and cardiac arrest. A quarter of that level would suffice. Another, lesser, shock of 800 to 1500 volts is then administered to ensure the paralysis of the brain's respiratory centre, and irreversible nervous damage. Such high levels of electricity travelling through the body cause convulsions strong enough to fracture or dislocate bones, not to mention more gruesome bodily effects. Fortunately, Sweden had abolished capital punishment.

I had another drink before going outside to stretch my legs. I had to put Blom and Larsson out of my mind. It was fruitless to dwell on a situation I could take no action against, and I had much to occupy my thoughts in any case. Aside from building the incubator for Lina's restoration, foremost in my mind was the question of how to transfer her to the apartment. Naturally the move would have to take place under the cover of night.

I found myself heading towards the cemetery, though it was not yet dark. When I got there I realised that even at night it would be difficult to avoid detection. To begin with, there were lamps installed at every one of the cemetery gates, and the place was in full view of nearby houses. To make it even more difficult, cars were constantly passing along the roads between Hagastaden and Hagalund. The fence surrounding the cemetery was of iron posts, giving passersby a clear view inside. Lina's little house was not more than forty feet from this fence, and between her tomb and the street were only low-lying graves without headstones.

It would be a delicate operation, but there are few things I love more than pitting my intellect against a knotty logical problem like this one. After considering the matter, I happened upon the solution, which was simple. All I would need was some kind of covering, such as a large piece of cloth, which could be hung over the fence and would act as a screen from the road.

I went back to my apartment and returned to the cemetery with a woollen blanket and staged a dress rehearsal. I also brought along a wooden handcart with rubber tyres, and various tools and ropes. I could see straightaway that my plan was going to work. Once we were outside the tomb and in the shadow of the blanket, we could proceed around the back of Lina's house and between two rows of graves with larger monuments that were easy enough to hide behind. This would bring us to the northern corner of the cemetery, where I would have my car waiting to take Lina home.

14.

I THOUGHT IT prudent to wait for the darkness of the next new
moon. Unfortunately, each day the sunlight bled a fraction more
into the night. The sixth of April was the date I had marked in
my diary for the move, and by then there would be about five
hours of complete darkness at most, according to my almanac. Two
months later, when summer descended, it would barely get dark
at all. I always felt there to be something unnatural about these
northern summers that the Swedes love so much. Perhaps it comes
from having grown up in a different part of the world, but for
the life of me I couldn't see the joy in these endless, light-soaked
days. In fact, they filled me with panic. Everywhere there would
be a sense of escalation, of crescendo. Every tree in the city sent
out monstrous shoots, and on the roadsides mushrooms the size
of footballs appeared overnight. The border of strawberry plants
in the garden sprouted leaves the size of my palm, and it seemed
that everything in the natural world became grotesque and strange,
a caricature of itself. As the summer wore on I would sleep less

and less, but instead of being tired in the ordinary way, a vibrating energy would take hold, until I felt like the strings on a violin, stretched tight, plucked, reverberating.

I had rehearsed the operation more than once at the cemetery, and by the time the sixth of April came around I was ready. That was a Monday, so I had to go to the clinic, and in fact I was quite glad to have something to take my mind off the whole business for a few hours. I went home early and took a small dose of Veronal and slept until the sun went down. My alarm clock woke me shortly before nine, twilight. The handcart, the blanket and tools were already waiting in Lina's little house. I put on a dark shirt and trousers, pulled a cap onto my head and set off.

The night was warm and quiet. There was no wind and no birds, and the only sound was of my own footsteps, echoing away down the empty streets. My car was parked on Sibyllegatan and I passed nobody on the way there. At the cemetery there was not a soul to be seen. I felt calm and quiet and sure.

'Lina, my dear,' I said as I unlocked the tomb. 'Here I am, come to take you home at long last.'

Thanks to my rehearsal, I swung into action without having to think about what I was doing. Like a machine I performed all the steps I'd practised. I hung the blanket up on the fence. I undid the locks on the outer casket and opened the lid. I piled the cart with blankets and cushions and positioned it at the end of the bier. The coffin was larger than the cart, and I could only manoeuvre it if I kept the door to the tomb open. I slid the inner coffin onto the cart using the ropes. When the coffin tilted downwards, a few drops of the disgusting seepage spilled out, but I managed to avoid getting any on myself. I laid some wooden boards over the doorsill and pulled the cart outside, then closed and locked the door to the tomb. Everything was going without a hitch. If all my plans came to fruition, I would never need to visit the cemetery again.

I pulled the cart onto the grass and around the back of the tomb, keeping behind the blanket. The grass was patchy and uneven, and the coffin heavy. The cart began to rattle loudly, even when we went very slowly. When we got to the path that ran between the graves the cart ran more smoothly. We reached the fence on the northern side of the fence and came to a halt. Now came the riskiest part of the whole operation, and something I hadn't been able to rehearse. I had to lift the coffin over to the other side. First I went back and took the blanket down: I didn't want to leave any clue or trace. By then the wind had picked up and was blowing leaves and twigs along the paths. The trees shook their branches and my feeling of calm was beginning to fade.

I could hear Lina calling out words of encouragement, but even that didn't do much to ease my nerves. I lowered the coffin from the cart onto the ground. Then I lifted the cart over the fence and went back for the coffin. It was more difficult than I thought. The coffin was hard to grasp hold of, unevenly weighted, and very heavy. I had to hoist it up against the fence using my shoulders. As it tilted I felt the seepage drench my shirt. The smell made me retch and I momentarily lost my grip. The coffin fell down the other side with a scraping sound and landed with a loud thud, missing the cart entirely.

Fortunately there was no one to hear the racket. I climbed over the fence and bent down to inspect the coffin. It seemed to be undamaged. When I straightened up again, something in my back gave way and a spear of white-hot pain shot up the left side of my spine.

I could hardly move, but now, with the coffin sitting right there in the open, I had no choice but to keep going. My car was not more than a few feet away, but it might as well have been miles.

I crouched down to pick up the coffin, trying to keep my back straight. The pain was intense. I gritted my teeth and exhaled deeply. I managed to lift the foot of the coffin and push it onto the cart, but when I tried to slide the rest of it on, the cart kept rolling away. I had to put the coffin back down again and wedge the cart up against the fence and try again. Every movement I made sent a spasm of pain up my spine. My hands and arms were drenched with the seepage from the coffin, and the smell of it got into my throat. Soon my whole body was covered in sweat. My eyeglasses had slipped down my nose. I held my breath as I pushed and pushed at the coffin, and at last I succeeded in loading it onto the cart. It was only luck that there were no passers-by to observe me.

Shaking with exhaustion, I pulled the cart over to the car. I slid the coffin into the back seat and covered it with the blanket. I put the cart in the trunk and got into the driver's seat, breathing hard. Through the windscreen I could see the trees tossing their branches around, violently now, but all sound of it was cut off; all I could hear was my own breath, my own heart-beat. Already the sky was getting lighter again. I started the engine and drove away.

'Lina, we've done it,' I said. 'We've done it! You're free at last.'

I expected to fall into a heap when we made it home, but the moment I stepped inside, the pain in my back was gone, and my whole body was buoyed with a fierce exhilaration. I put on a record of Verdi's *Triumphal March* and fetched a bottle of champagne and two glasses.

'And now,' I said to Lina, 'we celebrate.'

I poured us each a glass and put Lina's on top of her coffin for her. I held up mine in a toast.

'To us, my sweet darling. May we have many happy years together, you and I, my own true love.'

Lina's voice came from inside the coffin. 'My darling Carl!' She had never used my first name before. 'To you, thank you for being brave enough to rescue me. Now we can be together always.'

I drained my glass, and Lina's too, then I lay down right there on the floor and slept.

When I opened my eyes again a few hours later it was to an unfurling sense of bright expectation. I lay blinking up at the ceiling of the parlour for a few minutes, smiling to myself. I had my Lina with me, and she was here to stay.

'Good morning, my love,' I called to her, turning my head to the coffin. She didn't reply.

I sat up and looked at my watch. I was late for work. My body was stiff and my back ached, but even though I was aware of these sensations they didn't trouble me. Then I noticed the smell. The coffin seepage. I raised my hand to my face and immediately recoiled.

I ran a bath as hot as I could make it, and tipped in a box of baking soda. My soiled clothes I bundled into the trash. When I got out of the bath I was fairly sure I'd gotten rid of most of the odour, but later at the clinic I kept catching whiffs of it.

That day, the whole world was transformed for me. Everything, every object I saw, vibrated with light and seemed to have more substance than usual. As I went about my daily tasks I felt like a king in disguise. I had pulled it off. I'd done it. I had rescued my Lina, my love, and now I would make her well again.

Nils noticed my good mood. 'You're very chirpy this morning,' he said when he passed me in the lab. 'Good night last night?' He smirked at me, one eyebrow cocked.

'Oh, you know.' I shrugged, trying to rein in my ecstasy and look like an ordinary man. 'Probably nothing more than the spring-time weather.'

I wished I could tell Nils. It was a lonely triumph, and I knew he'd be interested in the technical side, but I also had a growing suspicion that I couldn't trust him anymore.

At six on the dot I raced home so fast that I seemed to fly through the streets. I felt oddly shy, like a new husband. I hoped so much that Lina liked her new home.

When I stepped inside, the stench nearly knocked me over. Holding my breath, I rushed over to the long windows on the far side of the parlour and flung them wide open. I went upstairs and opened all the windows there too, and got a bottle of cologne and sprayed it all around the apartment.

It took hours for me to get Lina upstairs to the treatment room: I had to rig up a pulley system to do it. At last I had the coffin lying on the treatment table. This was the moment I had been waiting for.

'My darling Lina, we are together at last!'

'Carl, I have waited so long for this moment,' I heard her say from inside the coffin.

My heart swelled and I blinked back tears. I unfastened the coffin lid and took it off. What I saw inside struck me like a blow. The decay had progressed to such an alarming degree that I could hardly recognise my sweet girl. Moreover, the smell was now even more overpowering, the dank odour of death was inescapable.

'My poor darling,' I said. 'I'm so sorry.'

My heart was torn to pieces as I looked upon her in that sad state, and I can hardly bear to describe the abject condition she was in. Her once beautiful silk dress had become a layer of gelatinous slime that clung to her putrefying flesh. Her nose was crushed. I might have injured her when I dropped the coffin, or it could have collapsed of its own accord. Her eyes were nothing but two black, sunken cavities, and her jaw gaped open. I felt so ashamed of what she had become.

'My love, I hope you can forgive me for leaving you to get in such a bad way.'

She laughed; her light, beautiful laugh that I still remember so well.

'Oh, Carl! You needn't worry about that. Of course I forgive you. And I know you'll soon make me well again.'

I began peeling off the rotten fabric that covered her. I started at her shoulders and chest and worked my way down. The outer layer of her dress had disintegrated into pieces of slimy mould that had to be scraped away. Underneath this, the lining of the dress had a consistency more like wet rags. These were easily pulled off. Next came Lina's slip and undergarments, which adhered to her flesh and were difficult to remove. I prepared a soap solution and soaked her body until the fabric slowly came away. The reek was so powerful that I could only work in five-minute bursts at most, in between which I had to hang my head out the window and take in draughts of fresh air. When the last of the fabric was gone, I drained all the liquid from the bottom of the casket and washed everything with phenol solution to get rid of the odour. I had to do this a few times over. I carefully dried the coffin and Lina's body and laid new linen underneath her. She looked so peaceful then, clean and fresh at last.

All this took me the whole night, and with the morning sun coming in at the window I gazed into her beautiful face: altered and unfamiliar yet lovely. Her lips had receded to reveal her strong teeth, still even and unblemished. I looked into the two deep hollows that had once held her eyes and I remembered how her living eyes used to sparkle with joy and laughter. Now it was as if I was looking out of a window into a dark night sky. In the distance I could see something shining, like the cold points of faraway stars, and as I looked closer I saw that it was points of light reflecting off new eyes that were hidden there in the depths. The eyes smiled at me.

'Carl, my dearest. You know it's always been you that I've loved.'

At her words, my love for her filled my entire being, like the light of the sun fills the sky.

She looked so beautiful lying there that I leaned down and kissed her lips. I let my breath flow into her open mouth and watched her breast rise, exactly like it used to do when she was alive. I went and fetched one of the dresses I'd bought for her, this one a light-blue silk, and laid it over her. I smoothed it down around her and arranged her hair. She looked like an angel. I was helpless against her charms. I slid into the coffin beside her and kissed her once more, and as I held her to me, death was annihilated by the force of my love.

15.

I QUICKLY LEARNED that Lina was indeed living a life of her own, and that she needed my constant care and attention. I adopted a regime of tissue rehydration through the application of both topical and internal nourishment. I fed Lina orally with various liquids, and I was surprised to find how very choosy she was. It took quite some trial and error to determine which ones she liked enough to accept. If I gave her something she disliked, or failed to vary her diet, she promptly disgorged it.

After closer inspection of her body I found some areas of laceration and damage on her trunk and abdomen. I treated these injuries as I would treat living tissue, with antiseptics, followed by emollient creams. Her extremities were in especially bad condition, and these I wrapped in bandages soaked in formalin. I set her collapsed nose in a splint and bandaged it.

Many hair bulbs had come loose from her scalp, and the scalp itself was badly ulcerated. I found clusters of blowfly larvae feeding on the damaged tissue. It was very difficult to remove them without causing further injury. I had to pick them out with tweezers, a laborious task, and one which I quickly found to be futile, as it seemed that new ones hatched every hour. Flies and mosquitoes began to plague Lina, and sometimes I would come home to a chorus of buzzing emanating from the treatment room, and a cloud of bluebottles, blowflies, gnats and mosquitoes swarming around her.

Part of the problem was the temperature. The windows were south-facing, and by midmorning the room was stuffy and warm. I knew this would only get worse in the coming months so I bought a number of electric fans and set them up around the room, but all they seemed to do was blow the air about without making any difference to the overall temperature. As the mercury rose, more and more parasites made their home in Lina's flesh. I read the daily weather reports with growing trepidation.

I hadn't had time to finish building the incubator tank before Lina had come home, but as soon as it was complete, I started keeping her in it. This had the benefits of protecting her from the sunlight and insects while the circulating fluid repaired the tissues. She stayed in there for twelve-hour stretches during the hottest part of the day. In the evening I lifted her out to dry. When she was completely dry I made a fine powder of calcium and sodium and applied this all over her body to supplement the nutrients she'd lost. I also concocted nourishing emollients of petrolatum and lanolin, and certain other ingredients that I do not wish to reveal. I may yet patent them for cosmetic use.

And all the while, my darling never complained.

'Oh, Carl,' she said to me, at least ten times a day, 'I am so happy since you brought me to live here with you. Never was I as happy in my whole life.'

She chatted to me like a bird, and joked with me and teased me, just like in the old days. I brought my phonograph into the treatment room and together we sang along to her favourite records as I worked away, tending to her. All in all, it was, as she said, the happiest of times.

Doris had been gone for six weeks or so by then, and I never imagined that Lina and I could achieve so much in such a short period, or that life could be so peaceful. I received no letters or calls from my wife, and she receded from my mind, like an inhabitant of one of my long-past lives. One night, though, when I was awoken by a noise in the house, it occurred to me that Doris could reappear unannounced at any moment, as unexpectedly as she'd disappeared. The very next morning, I had the locks changed.

I was gratified to see that after a few weeks of treatment, Lina's condition was improving. I weighed her regularly, and in that time she gained almost ten pounds. The lacerations slowly faded, and when I removed the splint from her nose, it had regained its former shape. Two of her fingers and two of her left toes were slow to heal, but even these made progress. Her body was returning to its former living healthfulness.

But my ultimate objective was to awaken Lina back to life. At that time she was in a dormant state, and yet I could see life present in her body. Chemical and metabolic reactions took place in precisely the same way as they did in living bodies, albeit at a much slower pace.

Most people, as I said, have the wrong understanding about death. They see it as a final blow: one minute you're alive and the next you're dead, like snuffing out a candle, but this is far from the reality. In actual fact, what people commonly think of as death is only the initial jolt where the soul is temporarily surprised out of the body. Given a little time, however, the soul will always try to return. But it's impossible for it to do so if the internal structures of the body have been destroyed in the interim. Imagine the horror and dismay of a soul returning to a ruined body, and being unable to reinstate its functions.

My method of resurrection was to be radiation therapy, which would restart the electrical impulses in Lina's nerves and brain, and allow her soul back into her body again. This wasn't some kind of crank idea; new research at universities in the US and in Europe was proving it to be effective in reawakening those believed dead. I already had a very powerful ray in the treatment room, but even this was not enough for what Lina would now require, and when I wasn't tending to her physical needs, I was making modifications to this unit to make it suitable for the task.

I wished more than ever that I had somebody on hand to help me with this work, or at least to discuss it with, and again I considered telling Nils about my plan. I went so far as to test the waters with him one day at the clinic. I'd read about William Kouwenhoven's research into the power of electrical currents to reanimate hearts, and I showed Nils the article by way of gauging his reaction. Kouwenhoven had administered 1000 volts AC, together with cardiac injections of a sodium channel blocker to successfully reanimate a dog.

'And if it works on a dog,' I told Nils, 'surely it would work on a human.'

'Ye-es . . .' he said after a long pause. He had a strange expression on his face. 'But Carl, after brain death, that person is gone. No amount of volts can bring them back.' His voice was excessively patient, like somebody talking to a child.

'But we used to think cardiac arrest was permanent too, and now we know that's not the case.' When Nils didn't say anything I went on, 'It's a question of not knowing, pure and simple. Just because we don't know something, doesn't mean it's not true.'

He avoided my eye.

After that I got the distinct feeling that Nils was keeping tabs on me. I noticed him watching me. He began asking me questions, about what I was doing outside of work, about why I had left Serafen, about the whereabouts of Doris. He would pop into my office at odd moments without knocking, and once he even came around to the apartment unannounced. I let him in, but I made sure the doors to the upstairs room were securely locked first.

'Funny smell in here,' he said as he stepped into the parlour. 'Formaldehyde?' His eyes darted suspiciously around the room. I had left the components of a new pump lying spread out on the floor and he indicated them with a nod of his head. 'I bet the wife isn't too impressed with that clutter. Johanna would kill me for that. How is Doris, by the way? Haven't seen her around the place in a while.'

After that I never let anyone into the apartment again.

It is a sad fact that in this world most people, even men of science like Nils, are far too closed-minded and prejudiced to accept new ideas. So in the end I was forced to work away on my own, and finally the modifications were complete. By that stage Lina's condition had improved even further, and it was a good time to induce her to come back to her body in a fully awakened state. I started the radiation doses slowly at 300 volts AC and increased them in both frequency and strength over a period of a week. Very quickly I began to discern changes in her body. At first it was a finger twitching now and then. One day she smiled at me.

'I can feel myself stirring,' she said. 'Slowly I am waking up.'

I rushed to her side, my eyes full of tears, and kissed her lovely face, her lips and throat. I embraced her gently. Her skin was as pink and warm as my own, and her youthful flesh much plumper than mine.

'My sleeping beauty, my love! Soon you will be whole again!'

III: LINA

1.

I WOKE UP with a jolt, like from one of those dreams where you're falling. And for a while I did think I'd just woken from sleep. The room slowly slid into focus around me. A beam of thick golden sunlight slanted in from the window, through a net curtain. I lay and watched some dust motes dip and drift in it, not really thinking much, not fully awake, but then I realised that the window was on the wrong side of the room, on my left. They must have turned the bed, I thought, trying to figure out the room, or maybe I was lying upside-down. Then I saw that it wasn't my room at all.

There was no row of hooks where our dressing gowns usually hung, mine and Petter's. No bedside table with the blue crocheted cloth. No chair with our clothes thrown over it, my stockings always crossed on top. The wooden chest was gone too, and the travelling clock we'd forget to wind. Instead, opposite me against the wall was a kind of workbench with a washbasin beside it and shelves above, packed full of boxes and bottles and tins and things. On my right, close to me, was a big machine that had a tube pointing at me like the barrel of a gun, and next to that a trolley with different kinds of medical equipment on it, scissors and syringes and thermometers. There were no pictures on the walls, no decorations anywhere at all.

The room seemed familiar to me, but I couldn't place it. I thought I must be in a hospital. But I saw that I had no covers over me, and I was wearing a day dress, one I'd never seen before. Then I heard footsteps coming up some creaky stairs and a voice, a man's, humming to himself, some tune that I almost recognised. Then all at once everything came flooding back and I knew where I was: in the treatment room in Dr Dance's apartment.

The first time I ever saw Dr Dance was that day in the clinic at the Serafen hospital. I was a different person then. I'd been ill months before, after losing the baby, but when I went to Serafen I didn't know what was wrong with me. The illness had no name yet, so it wasn't real. Back then I thought, we all did, that it was from losing the baby. The baby had no name either, but was all too real even without one.

We'd never been to Östermalm before either. The closest we'd got was Kungsgatan on the way to Serafen. Even the walk to Östermalm—we walked from Söder, to save the streetcar fare—had me in awe. Along Strandvägen, past that row of posh hotels with expensive-looking people sitting under the coloured awnings being served drinks in tall glasses by waiters in bow ties, past the rich people's boats, not tugs and ships for industry, but sleek yachts and speedboats. It was another world, right there in my own city.

Everything sparkled. The sun glinted off the blue harbour and threw light everywhere. The women's hair shone, and their teeth and diamond earrings glinted when they laughed, until your eyes were dazzled and full of swimming spots, so that you had to squint and could hardly find your way along the footpath. And those footpaths were so smooth, with no gaps, and the streets were very wide with no trace of rubbish in them, and there were so many trees it was like being in a park. The ladies all walked slowly with their chins up, heel to toe, heel to toe, and they had little dogs trotting along at their feet, some with tiny ribbons in their fur. Those dogs probably had much nicer lives than we did, I remember thinking.

And the houses! White, with big bay windows and lace curtains looped back. Peering through the windows as we went past we caught glimpses inside those rooms, of flowers, and paintings on the walls, and books. I couldn't begin to imagine what it might be like to live in a place like that, what that life felt like. I thought of us girls in the factory, our fingers stained from the tobacco leaves, clothes dirty, sitting in rows at the benches like dusty sparrows. I bet these ladies with their dogs didn't know the first thing about my world, the same way I didn't know anything about theirs.

When we got to the Östermalm clinic the first time, I was paralysed with nerves. Papa and Greta probably thought I was frightened of the treatments, but the real reason was that I was terrified of disgracing myself in front of these rich people. I still didn't even think there was anything much wrong with me then. I remember Greta showing me the little glass plates with the pink squiggles on them that she said were TB germs. They looked so silly, like the scribblings of a child.

So I wasn't even thinking about treatments that day. No, what I was worried about was everyone staring at the three of us in our faded old clothes, staring at us because we didn't belong. Thinking that maybe we'd got lost and wandered into Östermalm by mistake or something. I thought they might order us back to our side of town. I could see people looking at us, I wasn't imagining it. Their eyes, in their rich clean faces, would slide over us and then flick away, and their smooth mouths smirked, turning up at the corners.

The clinic was in a pink building as pretty as an iced cake. There were flowers in the window boxes, and the brass on the door shone like gold, and the names were written in curly lettering on a plate by the bells. We rang, and as we waited a lady came out, very elegant. She had a lipsticked rosebud mouth and her blonde hair glowed. She was wearing an emerald-green suit with a matching pillbox hat trimmed with a feather; I can still see it. The feather was brown and curved, like a bit of fern, and it swayed and bobbed beside her head with each step, like it was dancing.

We stood aside as she came down the steps, and the usual thing for her to do would've been to let us in, seeing as we were clearly standing there waiting and all. But when she caught sight of the three of us, I saw her hesitate with the door. She stood in the doorway for a second too long, while her eyes passed quickly over each of us, up and down. She took it all in, our limp, grey clothes, our lank hair, our dirty shoes, Papa's old-fashioned suit—his best one—and she gave a little frown. I could smell her perfume: roses, vanilla. She stepped out of the doorway and let the heavy door swing shut behind her.

I don't think what happened with the woman would've mattered a bit to either Greta or Papa. Greta would've noticed but wouldn't've cared for a second what some rich woman thought. 'What about it?' she'd have said. 'We work so that these people can be rich and laze around the whole time. They'd have no cigars to smoke if it weren't for us, no fancy clothes, no servants. We have no reason to be ashamed. If anyone should be ashamed, it's them. They should be getting down on their knees and thanking us for our hard work, and they know it.'

Papa wouldn't have noticed the woman at all. He was busy fussing with his collar and I could tell all he was thinking about was being on his best behaviour. He had this stiff smile on his face like a grimace, his lips stretched back so white and wide you could see his missing tooth at the back. When we got to the waiting room he refused to sit down, just stood rocking on his heels with his hands clasped behind his back, looking at the pictures on the walls. The waiting room was like a fancy hotel, not that I'd ever been inside a fancy hotel. It was warm and smelled of lavender, and there were flowers and lamps and two long mirrors and wood panelling halfway up the walls.

Dr Dance came out and ushered us through to his treatment room.

I never really liked Dr Dance. I knew the real reason that he was helping me was because I was lucky to have been born with a pretty face and he'd taken a fancy to it. And though the treatments might have been free, I paid every time his eyes landed on me.

2.

THE FOOTSTEPS CAME closer, up the stairs. I tried to sit up and that's when I knew something was very wrong. I couldn't move. It was more than the weak feeling of a long illness—that dead-weight tiredness, your arms and legs like sacks full of water—I was used to that feeling. This was different. I couldn't raise my head. I tried wriggling my fingers: nothing. Then lifting a single finger, but I couldn't even do that. Couldn't even twitch it, no matter how hard I tried. It was as if my body wasn't mine.

I heard the door open and someone step into the room.

'Now then, how are we getting on?'

It was Dr Dance's voice.

'Dr Dance?' I called out. My voice sounded strange.

He came around to the side of the bed, opposite the window, and glanced down at me.

'And how was it? Pleasant session, I hope?' he said.

He busied himself with the machine, fiddling with the dials, unplugging the cord.

'Dr Dance, something's gone wrong!'

He didn't seem to hear me. 'Another thirty per cent increase in the voltage today,' he said. 'We're doing well, my girl.'

He wheeled the machine away against the wall.

'No, Dr Dance, I need help!'

He came towards me and stood at my side. The sun shone on his face, lighting up every craggy wrinkle. He looked the same as always with those round spectacles and pointy beard and that silly black suit with the satin lapels. He leaned closer, too close, and brushed my hair back from my face. I could feel his breath on my skin.

'Dr Dance! Listen, I can't move!' I said. There was something wrong with my voice.

'Now, I know it must be tiresome for you to be always here in this bed,' he said.

'No, that's not what I mean—'

'But you must be patient, my darling. Like a flower, waiting to bloom. And bloom again you shall.'

'No, Dr Dance. Something's wrong!'

His face stayed the same as if I hadn't spoken. That's when I realised what was the matter with my voice. I couldn't hear it in the room the same way I could hear the other sounds. I'd been speaking only in my head, not with my mouth. I must be paralysed, I thought. And there was another strange thing: I felt panicked, but I didn't have that feeling of my heart juddering in my chest.

Dr Dance stood back and looked me over. 'You're looking very well today, very beautiful, if I may say so.' Then he picked up my hand and started stroking the back of it. 'More beautiful than ever, my sweet darling.'

I wanted to snatch back my hand. His hands were really warm. He must have felt the difference in temperature too, because he started rubbing my cold hand between his two warm ones, trying to heat mine up. I could see my limp hand flopping back and forth like a flat grey fish.

Something about my hand didn't look right, but I couldn't tell what exactly with it flapping around like that. The skin was this terrible muddy colour, for one thing, but it was more than that. When he held my hand still for a second, I saw what it was. The fingernail on my index finger was missing, the whole nail was completely gone, as if it'd been ripped out, and the other nails, I realised, were fakes, made of some kind of shell, stuck on.

He must've noticed the missing fingernail at the same time I did, because he tutted at me and pulled the finger straight to take a look at it.

'You naughty girl. You've broken a nail. What have you been doing with yourself?' Then he brought my nail-less finger up to his skinny old lips and kissed it. It wasn't just a peck, I mean he really kissed it, so I could feel the heat and wetness of his mouth. I tried again to pull my hand away from him. He had started rubbing it once more.

'Dr Dance!' I cried.

My voice was loud in my head, but the room was full of the soft swish of his skin rubbing against mine and the softer hiss of his breathing. His breathing, noisy and wet through his mouth, in and out. His breathing only, not mine. I wasn't breathing and my heart wasn't beating. And that's when I knew.

You know when people say, 'It felt so unreal, like I was in a dream'? Well, what I felt was almost the opposite. It was unreal because it felt nothing at all like a dream. If it'd felt like a dream it would've been alright, I would've known I'd be waking up soon. But I knew straightaway I wasn't dreaming. And I didn't want to believe it, but I knew I was dead. Dead, but still here.

Dr Dance leaned close again, until his face was a few centimetres from mine, like he was going to kiss me. I wanted to scream, push him off me, to run out of that room and far away. I imagined running from the building, and the cobblestones flashing under my feet, and me flying along and never once stumbling. I saw myself running past the church at the end of Jungfrugatan, through the crowds along Strandvägen, then over Strömbron to Gamla Stan, with its crooked buildings rushing past me, then Slussen and up that steep hill, and down again, and home and upstairs and through the door and to my own bed under the covers. I willed my muscles to move, and I strained and strained with my mind, harder than I had ever tried to do anything in my life, but nothing happened. It was like pushing against the stone wall of a house, thinking you can knock it over. My body no longer belonged to me.

Dr Dance pulled away and started humming that tune again. Then he went over to the gramophone and put on 'Georgia on My Mind', my favourite song. I realised that was the tune he'd been humming, or trying to hum, the whole time.

'Dr Dance, please! Help me!'

'Don't worry, sweetheart, we'll soon set your fingernail right.'

He had his back to me and was picking up bottles, measuring things out. The trumpet and the piano notes of the song rang out.

'Dr Dance? Can you hear me?'

Hoagy's voice sang the opening lines of the song.

'Beautiful though you may be,' said Dr Dance, 'at the moment you are a very dirty girl. We must make you nice and clean. Clean as a whistle.'

He poured some liquid into a vat and was mixing things together, singing over the top of Hoagy in his tuneless old voice, but changing the 'Georgia' from the song to my name.

He came over to me with his hands full of wet cotton, dripping some liquid with a sharp stink. It smelled like the disgusting glue they used for the cigar boxes at work. He pulled up a chair close to my face, still humming along to the record. I wanted more than anything to turn my head away from that stink and from his face. He began slowly wiping my face with the cotton, and the smell was like a raging animal with me in its teeth. Apart from not being able to move, everything else was just like being alive: I could feel, hear, smell exactly as before. Every dab of the cotton, every stroke of his fingers. The cotton stung my skin like ice.

'Let's get your beautiful face cleaned up. I know you've been neglected a long time, but we'll soon have you back to normal. Better than normal, my beauty, my queen.'

Starting at my forehead, he wiped my skin in slow, careful dabbing motions, and every stroke stung more than the last. After a few seconds my face was on fire.

'Stop! Leave me alone!'

The cotton moved down over my eyes, which he closed and then opened with his fingers, down my nose. Then he rolled up the cotton and stuck it right up inside my nose, one nostril at a time. I thought I was going to be sick. Then on to my cheeks and lips. He wiped the inside of them too.

When he'd finished with my face at last, without warning he reached down and unbuttoned the front of the dress.

'Stop! No!'

He pulled it open. I had no underclothes on. I tried to pull the dress closed again and I screamed at him, as hard as I could, and in my head I was struggling, pushing him off me, straining to get up. He didn't react. He went and got fresh cotton and cleaned the rest of my body. All of it, including my privates. With his old, wrinkled claws. He was very careful to get every bit of skin.

3.

I WOULD HAVE thought that dying would be the kind of thing you wouldn't forget—if you were around afterwards, that is—but I couldn't remember it. The last thing I could recall was finding out that Petter was dead. The police came to tell us that they'd found his body. There were two policemen, and one of them was very young, with acne so deep it was a purple rash over his cheeks and forehead. They weren't able to explain what had happened to Petter. I remember the police and that I was crying, and later being in bed and being very hot and then very cold, and then— nothing. Until I woke up in Dr Dance's treatment room. I didn't know how I'd got from the bed in my room to the bed in this one, and I didn't know how much time had passed.

And if I really was dead, and Petter was too, then weren't we supposed to meet again? Isn't that what's meant to happen when you die? You go off to some other place and everyone you ever loved is there waiting for you and you have this wonderful reunion, and the sun is shining and there are angels everywhere.

It wasn't supposed to be like this. Was Petter lying somewhere stuck in his body too, maybe in a coffin under the earth? Somewhere in Sundsvall, or had his body been brought back to Stockholm? What if he'd been cremated? I understood now why people get buried together. I wondered if he knew I was dead too.

I tried calling to him, speaking to him in my thoughts, sending them into the air and out through the window, like carrier pigeons, but I was only ever speaking to myself. I tried thinking about him, concentrating hard, as if that might make him magically appear in the room. I could picture him as clearly as if he was standing right in front of me. His hair a little too long because he hated going to the barber, and with that tuft at the front sticking out to the side as it always did. His eyes as blue as the sea and his small square teeth, the front one chipped at the corner. His smile, always a bit slow, a bit unsure.

I first met Petter when I'd just turned seventeen, at Midsummer. That was the first year we hadn't gone to Oma's for Midsummer. Instead we went to a grown-up party at the summerhouse of one of Papa's colleagues. Mama had sewn me a new dress for the occasion: white, with a blue border around the neck and hemlines. The skirt came to my knees and the front of the bodice was gathered in the centre with a floppy blue bow at the waist. I felt like a real lady. We arrived at the summerhouse the day before the party, and on Midsummer morning Greta and I woke up early and went to pick flowers and greenery to make wreaths for the maypole, and flower crowns. We easily found more than the seven different kinds that you were supposed to pick if you wanted to dream of your future husband. The rest of the morning was spent cooking and getting the place ready for the party, and with every hour that passed I got more and more excited.

Petter arrived with his father late in the afternoon, after the dancing had started. I was sitting out for a while, short of breath, and was fanning my hot face when I first saw him. He was standing there talking with two other men, and he was so tall and fair and had some kind of quietness and strength about him that I'd never seen before. Not that I'd had any experience with men at all, or knew the first thing about them. I must've been staring at him, because Greta dug me in the ribs with her elbow and laughed at me.

'Is he the one?' she asked. 'The one you'll be dreaming of tonight?'

I jumped up again to dance, hoping he'd dance too, and dance with me. It was hard not to keep looking over at him. I satisfied myself with quick, secret glimpses. He seemed to be alone, not with any girl.

When we sat down to dinner at a long table in the back garden, Petter was opposite me and a bit further along. I drank aquavit for the first time: all spiky in the back of my mouth before a long, warm roll down my throat to my heart. The aquavit made me braver about looking at him. I listened to the conversations on my side of the table with half an ear and strained to catch what he was saying. Then he looked me straight in the eyes and raised his glass to me. I blushed so hard my face must have been glowing.

After we'd eaten, everyone drifted off and gathered in groups around the garden. I found myself in one with him, trying to decide if we should walk to the lake for a swim or start up a game of Kubb. It was already dark by then, not that it gets properly dark at that time of year—instead of fading away, the light seems to go into things, making the colours deeper and more real.

The swim won out and then he was next to me as we climbed out of the narrow valley that the house lay in. We were walking side-by-side up a narrow path through a stand of silver birch. I could hear the others laughing and calling ahead of us. I looked down at our feet, mine and his, on the dark path, the neat toes of my shoes flashing up with each step beside his brown ones that nosed their way along.

'I'm Petter,' was all he said.

He offered me his arm. I looked up at him and his face glowed in the light, with the green of the forest stretching out behind him. Probably I was drunk but still, there was some magic about that night. We looked into each other's eyes and everything fell away, it was as though we were standing together under a dome of glass, the only two people that had ever lived. The forest and the summer air whirled around us like the skirt of a dancer. After swimming, we left the others and walked around the lake just the two of us, hand-in-hand. He kissed me, my first kiss. By the following February we were married.

Nothing ever turns out how you think. Back then I thought that first evening with Petter was the beginning of a whole life of days like that, days full of magic. I saw them laid out at my feet, making a golden path into the future. That's what I thought being married, being in love, meant. But that first day hadn't been the first of a life of golden days, it was the high point. I spent the hundreds of days that came after trying to get back the magic of that first moment in the forest. But I never could, no matter how hard I tried.

4.

DR DANCE TOOK ages to clean me, hours it must've been. The whole time he kept playing 'Georgia', and the B-side too, the 'One Night in Havana' song. Then he put on Al Goodman's 'I'm Still Caring' with Frank Bessinger singing.

The daylight was fading, and from the street came the sounds of streetcar bells and people coming home from work. I heard their voices and footsteps. I noticed the sounds especially, everything was louder, sharper than when I was alive. I seemed to be able to hear sounds from a great distance. I suppose your living body makes a lot of noise that you ignore because it's always in the background: your lungs swelling and emptying, your heart pumping, your blood rushing around.

Dr Dance fetched a bottle of shampoo, a basin and a jug, and placed his chair behind my head. He wet my hair and began shampooing it. He talked to me constantly, like I was a baby or a dog.

'Now, my darling, your hair will be nice and clean and fit for a princess. Yes it will! And you are more than a princess, oh yes. You are my queen, my angel.'

He must be crazy, I thought, to believe a dead woman could hear him. But then I remembered that I could hear him, and then I felt like I was the crazy one. Maybe he did know I was here. Maybe he had done this to me on purpose, trapped me here, with one of his machines.

Usually, having your hair washed by someone else feels wonderful. I remembered Mama washing Greta's and my hair on Saturday evenings when we were little. We would lean over the lip of the tub, clutching our towels around our shoulders while Mama shampooed away. Afterwards she'd make us cups of hot milk with nutmeg on top and we'd drink them sitting in front of the kitchen stove while our hair dried. I loved that feeling of being completely clean and the smell of the soap she used and how steamy the room would get.

Dr Dance's bony fingers rubbing against my scalp was nothing like that. He was probably trying to be gentle but his knobbly old fingers bored into my skull, and the water he used was much too cold. Then I felt him draw back with a jerk.

'No! But Lina, this is no good.' I felt him fumbling around on my head and then heard a slapping sound as he threw something into the basin.

'Your hair! My darling, your hair!' He got up in a hurry and went over to the sink carrying the basin, which was full of some dark stuff—my hair. A few strands hung over the side, like the legs of some awful spider trying to escape. I felt sick. I was glad

I couldn't see my face in the mirror, looking out from under a bald head.

When I was a kid there was a peddler woman in Söder who sold old clothes and things and her hair was falling out. She always kept her head covered up with a shawl, but one day I saw some boys run over and pull her shawl away. She wasn't completely bald, there were still a few stringy locks clinging on here and there, more on one side than the other, like on a dog with mange. Her hair was dark, so you could see the strands standing out against her shining white scalp. I wondered why she didn't just shave it off and be done with it. She quickly covered up her head again, but the sick feeling of seeing it stayed with me for ages, and after that I always crossed to the other side of the street when I passed her. I got that same sick feeling when I saw my own hair piled up in Dr Dance's basin.

'Never mind, my love,' Dr Dance said, coming back to me with a towel. 'We'll get you some new hair. We'll get you the most beautiful hair in the land. You wait and see.'

He squeezed the water out of what was left of my hair, pulling out more chunks as he did so. I could hear it coming out at the roots with a soft crackle, like when you pull up dandelions. The more I tried not to listen to it, the louder it got. When my head was dry, he put my dress back on me and went downstairs, kissing my forehead before he left. God knows how he could even touch me, let alone kiss me.

I could hear banging sounds coming from downstairs, and the smell of cooking wafted up to the room, the savoury smell of meat, and the steamy, earthy smell of potatoes boiling. I realised Mrs Dance must be there, or their cook anyway. I hoped it was

Mrs Dance. Maybe she'd come in—surely she would—and when she did, I could try to give her some sign that I was here. She'd be able to get help, send for Greta, or a doctor. Or a priest. But would Mrs Dance want to help me? She was probably glad I was dead. I remembered her goggle-eyed look when we first met in the hallway downstairs. I was every bit as surprised to see her, of course. We thought Dr Dance wasn't married. I couldn't look her in the eye. I wasn't ashamed for myself, but for her, having a husband who pretended to young ladies that his wife didn't exist.

The stairs creaked again, but it was Dr Dance who came in.

'Oh, my Lina! Sitting here in the dark. I'm so sorry, my love. How rude of me.' He turned on the lights. He was carrying a tray with his dinner and a bottle of wine. It was falukorv sausage and potatoes and lingonberry sauce, my favourite childhood meal, and the first I ever learned to cook, when I was about eight years old. Downstairs it was quiet again. Dr Dance must've cooked for himself.

He put his tray on the workbench. He poured himself a glass of wine and drank half. I couldn't believe he'd want to eat his dinner in this room, among the smell of chemicals and my rotting flesh. Not to mention how I must look, horror that I must be. I'd put anyone off their dinner, that was for sure.

He got a napkin and came over to me and spread it over the front of my dress, tucking it up under my chin. He leaned over and I could smell the sharpness of the wine on his breath. He kissed me again, this time on my cheek, leaving a cooling spot of his spit behind.

'Dinnertime at last, my sweetheart,' he said. 'You'll have to excuse my bachelor cooking. I haven't made much of a study of the culinary arts, but one day I'll be a first-class chef, you can be sure of that.'

He pulled up the side table, put the tray on it, and perched himself on his stool. He tucked his own napkin under his chin.

'First, some wine,' he said.

He took a mouthful from his glass and leaned down to my face again. I willed my lips to stay together. I imagined them clamped shut like two iron doors, and I pictured the doors at the factory, dull grey and thick as my arm. Then his mouth was on mine, his lips moving like centipedes. His breath was rancid. He tried to move my lips apart with his own, but he couldn't. For a few seconds I felt like I'd won, I'd beaten him, and I felt a rush of triumph.

'Being difficult today are we?' he said. 'Sulking because I left you here in the dark?' He chuckled. 'I'm sorry, my sweetheart. I'll make it up to you.'

He leaned back and pulled my jaw open with his hands, like you would with an animal. He forced his fingers between my lips and front teeth and ran them along the inside of my mouth. It made a rasping sound. My tongue lay in my mouth like a dead toad, rotting.

He took another mouthful of wine and his face loomed up again, the light reflecting off his spectacles, and then his lips were back on mine. I felt a warm spurt of bitter liquid shoot to the back of my throat and pool around the root of my tongue. He pulled his face away and pinched my lips closed with his fingers, then tilted my head back so the wine slid down my throat. It gurgled its way down like bathwater in a drain.

'And does the lady like the wine of this evening?' he asked, taking the napkin and delicately dabbing it over my lips and chin.

He drank a glass of wine himself, then repeated the procedure with me. Then he tucked into the falukorv, which must have been stone cold by then.

'Mmm! I've got to say, I've done a pretty good job with this,' he said, shovelling forkfuls of pink sausage and mashed potato into his mouth and chewing away loudly. 'Delicious. Cooking's not so hard. The way you women carry on about it anyone would think it's one of the learned sciences.'

Mrs Dance must have gone away somewhere. Maybe to Skåne. I remembered hearing that she had a sister down there. Unless, the thought came, he'd killed her. That must be it. Who else but a cold-blooded killer would sit there munching on falukorv right next to a corpse? I wondered what he'd done with her body. Maybe it was here in the house somewhere. It could be in the room next door, or even hidden somewhere in this room for all I knew. There was no way he would've been able to have me in the house with Mrs Dance still living here. And if she had gone to Skåne, she could turn up again any second, and he certainly couldn't risk that. If she came back and found me here she'd go to the police for sure, and he'd be in prison quick as a flash. No matter how faithful to him she might've been, there are limits for any wife.

Dr Dance was finishing his dinner, forking up every last morsel. Then he picked up his plate and licked it clean with his tongue. I'd never seen anyone do that before. He brought the plate right up to his face and his pink tongue was already out, lying in wait.

'Mmm, mmm!' he moaned as he licked.

I wished I could still vomit.

He put his plate down and leaned over again, right near my face. Now the sausage smell had overpowered the wine on his breath, which was much worse. He worked his tongue between my lips, and my flesh must have loosened because he got in easily this time, depositing bits of food. Then I felt one of his hands ranging over my breasts, going from one to the other, squeezing and grabbing, while the other travelled down to my waist and my hip bone, which jutted out now like a handle. His fingers wriggled under me and he squeezed my behind. He was all over me, a huge monster, ten times my size.

More than I have ever wanted anything in my life, I wanted to be away from him. I imagined myself floating up out of my body, the way I was supposed to have when I died. I concentrated hard on that picture of myself, a pale ghost, floating up, lighter than a dandelion seed, leaving my poor body behind, drifting out of the window and far away. I willed it, I tried so hard to make it real. But I remained inside myself.

Dr Dance pulled back and I thought it was over, but he was taking off his jacket and shoes. Then he got on the bed with me and started on me again. He unbuttoned my dress and his hands were all over my skin and down between my legs. The whole time he was moaning and murmuring, just like when he'd been busy licking his plate. His hands were smooth and dry, his fingernails were yellowed and ridged, curved animal talons. They dug into my soft skin.

I had to get away. And if I couldn't get out, I would go in. I made myself smaller and smaller until I was a tiny thing, smaller than a flea, then smaller still until I was nothing more than a speck inside my body. Silent. Still. I waited, not thinking, not feeling, not hearing anything. I couldn't close my eyes and I had to look somewhere, so I looked at the corner of the window, the

190

way the curtain, unclosed, folded over the rail, and the curves it made, like waves, and my eyes were a little boat rolling over them, carrying me away.

Out the window I could see that a few stars had lit up. I watched the night-time sky. And after a while I felt like I *had* made myself disappear. The whole thing was happening far away, to someone else, someone I wasn't even much interested in. That body was no longer mine anyway, it no longer belonged to me. When something belongs to you, you can control it. You decide what to do with it or not to do. Where it goes and what it does. What's done to it.

5.

THE DAYS WENT by. Each morning, a shaft of sun crept in at the window, lengthened, and licked across the room from right to left like a slow search beam. I still hadn't been able to find Petter, or anyone for that matter. Not Petter, not my little lost one. It was as if Dr Dance and I were the last people left in the world. Everyone else was a memory, or a sound in the distance. In the nights and through the weekdays I was mostly left alone. Dr Dance slept in another room and in the morning he went out to work. The nights I spent listening to the sounds of the house, of the street, and if the curtain had been left open I watched the stars.

When Dr Dance went to work, I did work of my own. Clearly, I'd had the wrong idea about dying. I'd thought that leaving your body would take the same effort as making your heart beat when you're alive—I thought it was automatic. That's what dying is, in point of fact. Your body stops working and off you go to the next world. You don't have any choice in the matter. But now it was clear that leaving your body required some work, so I spent those days when Dr Dance was out of the apartment trying to will myself out of my body. It was as impossible as it sounds, no easier than if I'd been alive.

Again I tried fixing on some object in the room, as I had with the curtain-rail, and imagined pulling myself from the bed to there. Again I pictured myself floating up out of my body, but again I remained right where I was.

In the evenings the sun receded and Dr Dance came back. I'd hear the building door open and close, his feet coming up the marble staircase. He always fumbled with his keys outside the apartment door, then came the sound of his key in the lock and him wiping his feet on the mat. Sometimes he'd be whistling. He would come up to see me straightaway.

Those sounds of his arrival always jolted me to attention, as if I'd been sleeping and then woken by an alarm clock. He never came at exactly the same time every day—I could tell from the light—so sometimes he interrupted my work but other times I was waiting for him, aware he was late, hoping he'd been in an accident or had a heart attack and was never going to come. But then what would happen to me? Would I have to lie here until my body rotted away to nothing? As much as I couldn't stand him, it was still a kind of awful comfort when he appeared. And yet when he was in the house I felt panicked, wondering what he was going to do next. Was it going to be worse than the last thing he'd done? Most nights it'd be the cleaning and feeding all over again. On his days off he'd treat me with his radiation machine. And then those other things.

He had different cleaning methods. Sometimes he would use cotton with the stinging liquid, sometimes he would douse me in perfume. It was always the same one: 4711 Original Eau de Cologne. He poured bottles of it over me, head to toe. How I came to hate the smell of that stuff. Other times he would lift me into a kind of bath filled with some pink chemicals that smelled like Clorox. He would push me right under and put lead weights on me to hold me down.

The bath itself was made of metal and had a lid like a coffin. He would shut the lid and lock me in; I could hear him threading padlocks through and snapping them closed. Sometimes I was in there for a long time, a whole day, or even two or three. As it was completely dark, I could've been in there for weeks, for all I knew. Why he bothered to lock it I never understood. There was no one else in the house, and he never had any visitors. Or was he trying to stop me getting out?

He did a lot of upkeep to stop my body rotting. Every day there was something. It must've kept him on his toes. A bit like tending a garden, I suppose. My hair only got washed a few more times before the rest of it fell out. He had to go over my whole body with a pair of tweezers, pulling out the maggots. At night I could hear them burrowing their way into my flesh, a soft squelching sound. Dr Dance picked them out one by one, and plugged the tiny holes they left with what looked like wax or plaster or something, like you'd fill in a hole in a wall.

One evening he came home very upset. He slammed the door behind him, and instead of whistling, he was muttering under his breath. When he came into the room I saw he was holding a letter.

'Lina, my sweetheart. Terrible news! Our love nest is on the brink of destruction. I hardly know what to do.' He sat down beside me. 'Listen to this.' He read aloud:

My dear Carl,

I've been trying to write to you for days now, and I start letter after letter, but it's very difficult for me. I can never say what I really mean.

When I left Stockholm I was simply furious with you, and rightly so. All I could think of was how you were in love with Mrs Dahlström. I always knew you were in love with her when she was alive, but I never thought it would go on and on like this after she died as well.

This is a monstrous situation, and more than any wife can reasonably bear. I've talked things over with my good friend Harald—who has been a tower of strength to me in this dark time—and he agrees that it's a good idea for me to come to Stockholm to talk things over and decide on the way forward. Things cannot continue as they are.

So I write now to tell you that I'll be there in the week before Midsummer. We must resolve this situation as soon as possible.

Your wife,
Doris.

He let the hand holding the letter drop to his lap. He took off his spectacles and rubbed the bridge of his nose with his thumb and forefinger.

'Bah! That woman!' He put his spectacles on again and went over to the window and stood looking out, fumbling with the letter as he folded it up again.

'It's dated the second.' He stood there tapping the letter against his teeth. 'That doesn't give us more than a few weeks together unmolested.'

So, I thought, it was June, and I'd been dead eight months.

'I'll have to come up with a plan. Good thing I had the presence of mind to change the locks.'

He tried to open the window but it was stuck. 'Damned thing!' He wrestled with it and only got it open a little, then gave up. I'd never seen him so agitated.

'Goddamnit, but that woman's sense of timing takes the cake. Right over Midsummer! No one can ever get anything done that week, all of Stockholm goes away on holiday. It's imperative that we move you to your own place as soon as possible and clear the decks here.'

He paced the room, slicing at the air with the letter, mumbling to himself.

Poor Mrs Dance. She'd get the fright of her life if I was still here when she came back. It was going to be quite a job for Dr Dance to move me, that much was clear, especially if he had to do it alone. I wondered for the first time how he'd got me here to begin with. But the thought of his wife's arrival filled me with relief—aside from the hope that she might be able to help me, now I knew for sure that he hadn't killed her after all. I felt as happy at the thought of seeing her as I would at the thought of seeing an old friend. But she wasn't going to be happy to see me, that was for sure. Even if I was dead.

I only ever spoke properly with Mrs Dance one time. We sometimes said a few words if she happened to be home when I came to the apartment for my treatments, but we'd never been alone together. Then, at the start of autumn, I took a walk to the City Hall park in Kungsholmen. I was sitting on a bench trying to get some sun, pretending to myself that I was feeling better, when I saw her coming along the path. She was carrying a shop-ping basket with lots of wrapped parcels inside. She recognised me, and hesitated. Then she waved and came over.

'Good afternoon, Mrs Dahlstrom. Beautiful sun today.' She squinted at the sky. She was wearing a long caramel-coloured coat and thin leather gloves, with her hair tucked under a round brown hat.

'Hello, Mrs Dance,' I said.

I wasn't sure if I should get up and shake her hand as a greeting. I didn't want to. In my mind I could still see that bulgy-eyed look she'd given me at her apartment. Now she seemed different, though, and she looked at me differently. She was shorter than I remembered.

'My husband, Dr Dance, tells me that your treatments are going well. He's very pleased with you,' she said.

I'd thought it was funny that she pointed out that Dr Dance was her husband. As if she knew that he went around saying he was single.

'How are you feeling now?' she asked. 'Better?' She had a very beautiful voice, like silvery bells ringing.

'Yes, thank you, much better.'

'Oh, good. I'm so glad. And you're looking very healthy too, with those rosy cheeks.'

'Thank you,' I said again.

She was staring at me in a strange way, and then she shifted her basket to the other hand and began searching through it.

'Here,' she said as she rummaged around, 'I have something for you. Just a small thing. I got it for myself . . . but I think you might like it.'

She pulled out a small parcel wrapped in gold Åhléns tissue paper and held it out to me.

'Oh, no really, I—'

'Please take it. It will look much better on you than on me in any case. Please. Open it.'

I hated opening presents in front of people. She was standing there with her hand outstretched, waiting for me to take the present. Her face was full of something I couldn't read. I took the parcel from her and unwrapped it. Inside was a blue scarf, very soft, not like anything I had ever owned or ever thought I'd own. I held it up in the sun. It was made of cashmere or something similar. I looked up at her.

'Thank you, Mrs Dance. This is so pretty, but I can't—'

'Please,' she said. 'Please take it. It's perfect for your complexion, those pink cheeks. You should enjoy it, you'll look gorgeous in it. You're such a beautiful girl. I hope you know that.' Her eyes looked old and sad, her eyelids were starting to sag at the corners.

It felt wrong to take a gift from her, but the scarf was too wonderful. 'I love it,' I said. 'Thank you so much, Mrs Dance.'

'Call me Doris, please.'

'Thank you, Doris,' I said, my mouth clumsy around her first name. 'You and Dr Dance have done so much for me and my family.'

'You're most welcome,' she said, turning as if to go. But then she turned back. 'You know,' she said, 'I must tell you that you've given my husband so much joy.' Her voice started to crack, like she was going to cry.

I didn't know what to say. I sat there looking at her.

'I've never seen him as full of energy as these past months when he's been working on your treatments,' she said. 'He's a different man.' She pulled a handkerchief from her pocket. It had a narrow edging of lace.

'Oh, that's nice,' I said, because I had to say something. I hoped she wasn't going to start crying in front of me.

'I'm sorry,' she said, sniffing and dabbing at her nose with the handkerchief.

And then my shyness disappeared. At the sight of her almost in tears, instead of having any sympathy, all I could feel was scorn. It was awful, looking back on it now, like some devil had taken me over. A voice inside me said, *You have the advantage, you're on top.* I could have laughed in her face. Now she wasn't the grand, posh lady anymore, doling out generous gifts to the poor; she seemed like the most pathetic old creature on earth, grovelling in front of me.

She waved goodbye with her gloved hand and hurried off, still dabbing her face with her lacy handkerchief.

Later, at home, I showed Greta the scarf and told her about Mrs Dance nearly crying and we laughed and made fun of her together.

If I could, I'd squirm with shame.

6.

THE NIGHT OF Mrs Dance's letter was the first night that Dr Dance completely ignored me. He didn't speak to me again after reading it. He stayed in the room for a while, not giving me so much as a glance, then he went to his bedroom, which was next door to the room I was in. After that the house was quiet. It was a clear night. Dr Dance had left a narrow gap in the curtains when he was fiddling with the window, and I could see a strip of night sky. I watched the stars move across it. A while later the moon came out and the room got brighter. I saw the edge of the moon slide into the gap of the curtains, a round, curious face peering in. A soft breeze blew in through the slightly open window, and I could hear the blasts of the horn on the Djurgården ferry. A man walked past in the street, whistling, his shoes clacking on the footpath. I lay there and listened to the gentle sounds of the city—it was right there, separated from me only by a pane of glass.

I thought of the cold stones of the buildings and the streets, and the streetlamps and the lights in windows and how it would look to the night birds passing above, those curves and lines of light spread out below and the house roofs and the roads in blackness, and in between, the slicker, blacker threads of the archipelago's water. And for each lighted window there would be a person who had their own joys and disappointments, that no other person could ever really understand, and one of the lights out there was Greta's and Mama's and Papa's, and they would be sitting after dinner in the warmth of the kitchen, maybe reading, maybe talking. And down by the docks the floodlights would be on and a ship would be coming in, with white and green lights and a throbbing engine, and the men would be busy hauling bales and barrels and boxes along the gangways, and after they knocked off they would go in twos and threes, laughing and dirty, slowly up the steep hill for a beer at the Pelikan, while behind them the black water of the harbour and the lights of the ships on the curve of the bay were like a mirror held to the stars.

And that's when it happened. That was when I found I was no longer in my body. I was no longer on the bed, but right by the window, with no sense of having moved there. I had made no effort, but there I was, looking out. At the full moon, rising high now, and the wind blowing some thin clouds along and carrying the smell of dust and the flowering heather from Gärdet. I could see right up and down the street. Most of the lights were out in the windows, except the building opposite. It had a round window on each of its three levels, and they were lit up like three yellow moons. Greta had told me that she and Ilse went into that building to check on Dr Dance's place, before I came here for treatment.

I tried to turn around and take a look at myself, at my body, but as soon as I did I was back inside it again. I hated to be back, but I also felt a kind of peace. If I could do it once, I could do it again.

7.

THE DAY AFTER Mrs Dance's letter, Dr Dance seemed a lot jumpier than usual. He didn't go to work, and was busy cleaning me. Every now and then he froze, like a rabbit that had smelled a dog. He sat there holding his breath with his eyes narrowed.

'Did you hear that?' he asked.

There was nothing to hear. He was imagining things.

He would get up and stand gazing out of the window at the building opposite. He seemed to think someone was watching him. I tried to get to the window to take a look but I remained motionless.

'She's out there again,' he said.

Who? His wife? Or maybe it was Greta? But if it was either of them, they'd ring the bell. Most likely he had gone crazier than ever, and there was no one there at all.

The next morning he came in loaded up with boxes and parcels.

'Good morning, my love!' he said.

He was humming some tune I couldn't recognise and seemed to be back to his old self again. He dumped the boxes and things on the workbench and came over to me.

'Lina, today is a very special day,' he said. 'Do you know why? Today is the day we make you immortal.'

'Too late, Dr Dance. I hate to tell you, but it seems I'm already immortal.' Not that I wanted to be.

He pulled up his stool and looked me over carefully, lightly touching my skin here and there. 'Because, my sweet girl, you are so very beautiful and that beauty deserves to be recorded for the world to see.'

He unbuttoned my dress and took it off, which bothered me a lot less than it used to. Maybe he was going to paint my portrait, I thought. Nude, of course, that would be his style. But he had no easel or brushes with him as far as I could see.

'It's only fair to the gods that I do justice to your beauty,' he said.

He put on a Wayne King record and started whistling along. I used to love listening to music. It was my favourite thing about working at the factory, singing along with the other girls, and kind of dancing too—as much as you could while sitting down and rolling a cigar, anyway. Music made a golden net in the air that drew the room and all of us in it together. I didn't notice the time as much when music was playing, and I felt like I could've been anywhere. The dingy walls and hard benches disappeared and I became the romantic heroine of the song—it was me they were singing about. But now music had the opposite effect on me. Dr Dance only ever put records on when he was doing something to me that was going to take a long time and something that usually hurt, or when he'd drunk a few glasses of wine after dinner and got onto the bed with me, so whenever I saw him reach for that gramophone I froze inside.

I heard Dr Dance opening the boxes and getting something ready behind me. Then he came over with some tools laid out on a tray, like he was going to operate. A few different pairs of scissors, and a small saw, a knife, and a roll of bandages. So it wasn't going to be a painting after all. I looked at the sharp objects and wondered if I would still bleed when he cut me. Was that what the bandages were for? Or was my blood all dried up like rust inside my veins? Or maybe he had already drained it out like you would from a slaughtered animal. Was he going to cut me up so that he could move me before his wife arrived?

I saw once, in a book, a picture of the organs of an Egyptian queen. They'd been taken out of her body after she died and put in jars, ready for the next life. I thought about how my heart must look, waiting for him under my ribs, dead and black probably, shrivelled, still filled up with old blood. Would he put something there in place of the heart? The roll of bandages maybe, or would he leave an empty hole? And would he put the heart beside me in a glass jar so that I'd have to lie here looking at it forever? At least those Egyptian queens and kings had their hearts put in pretty jars, and they had their servants and animals with them too, to talk to after they were dead.

I tried again to will myself out of my body. But I couldn't with Dr Dance in the room, not even for a second.

He was fussing around in the boxes again, then he came back and rubbed Nivea Creme all over me, from my face to the soles of my feet. He must have used about four big tins of the stuff.

'Well, my sweetheart, the good thing is that I don't have to remind you to hold still,' he said, and laughed.

'Very funny, Dr Dance.'

He stood back and looked me over once more. 'We'll start with your back; it'll be the easier part, I think. And it'll train me up for the front of you.'

He turned me over so I was lying with my face sunk in the pillow. Now I had no idea what was going on. He spread my legs apart and placed my arms away from my sides. I heard him go to the workbench and then bustle around the room, and then he was beside me again.

'Ready?' he asked.

I waited for it. I guessed he would start with the knife. That would be the first thing I'd feel, that thin hair of cold metal bearing down harder and harder until the pressure changed into red-hot pain. He'd use the knife until he got down to the bone. And then he'd change to the saw to get through the bone. Could you even feel your bones? The sound of that would probably be the worst thing, like wood being sawed. And the scissors, what were they for? Maybe sinews and muscles. But why on earth would he need such big ones? The surgeons in movies always had tiny silver ones, like elegant nail scissors. But the ones he had waiting for me on that tray were so big they looked like you could shear a sheep with them.

I felt something on my skin, just a light touch, and I tensed inside, but it was his fingers. Looking for the incision point, I suppose.

'We'll work in stages,' came his voice. 'It'll make the removal easier later.'

The next second there was something wet and cold around the sole of my foot, but the feeling wasn't anything bad. It was like a damp towel being laid on me. With his hands he smoothed the wet material over and over.

Whatever he was putting on me had a heavy smell, like the clay earth of a riverbank. I kept waiting for the slice of the knife, but it never came. I felt only the cloths. He kept adding more of them, one on the top of the other, then smoothing them over. He covered the whole foot and then my leg up to the knee, then the thigh, my behind, my back and my neck, and finally the back of my bald skull. It would've felt quite nice if I wasn't waiting the whole time to be sliced open. And it was a long time that I waited. It takes just seconds for me to tell you about this, but it took him ages to do it. I noticed that the cloths around my feet had started to dry and as they did, they warmed up.

'You're doing a great job, my darling,' he said. 'As am I. Maybe I've missed my calling and could've been a great artist. But I'm young still. There's plenty of time for all that, isn't there, my love?'

'I hope not,' I said.

Then I felt a dull blow to my feet. It felt strange and made a hard sound, like someone rapping against a wall.

'Coming along nicely. Drying much quicker than I expected,' he said. That's when I realised what he was doing. It was plaster he was wrapping me in, not cloths; that was what that roll of bandages was for. He was casting me in plaster to make a statue of me. A statue. Which is exactly the kind of thing he would do.

When we were little, Greta broke her arm after falling out of a tree outside the Katarina Church one Sunday. Mama was so embarrassed because it happened in front of practically the whole congregation. And the pastor saw and everything, and his wife too. I went with Mama and Greta to Serafen. Mama's face had gone a bright, angry pink.

'This is the Lord's punishment for being such a rough little girl!' she kept saying as she pulled Greta along by her good elbow, and then as we sat waiting for the doctor. Greta didn't care. She was fascinated by the fuss they made at the hospital, and with the X-ray machine in the special room, and then getting a plaster put on.

She loved wearing that plaster. 'It's like a suit of armour,' she'd say as she swung her arm around in the air like a club. 'I'm invincible!'

I could feel the plaster drying and setting on every part of me now, and it felt good to be lying there under the hardening layer. It didn't feel quite like being in a suit of armour, though; it was more like being a snail or a turtle in its shell, safe and cosy, the way I used to feel when I got into bed at night and pulled the covers up over my head. It was the first time I'd felt like that in ages. I'd almost forgotten the feeling existed.

'Now comes the easy part,' Dr Dance said. 'Now we wait.'

I heard him moving around, tidying up, whistling as he did. Then there came a banging noise, so loud it vibrated through the whole house. I thought Dr Dance must have knocked over one of his machines or something, but the noise kept going on and on. I realised it was someone pounding at the apartment door. I could hear muffled voices too, shouting. It had to be the police, I thought. No one else knocked that loud.

Dr Dance gave a kind of grunt and ran out, closing the door to the room and the one at the bottom of the stairs, which he usually left open. I tried to follow him, and I made it to the door before

I was pulled back again. I heard him open the apartment door and close it behind him. He said something I couldn't make out, but he sounded angry. There was more shouting; it sounded like many people, but I thought there were only two. I felt I knew those voices. Then I heard one of them clearly, she was shouting so loudly, and instantly I knew who it was: Greta.

'Dance!' she yelled. 'You liar! You—' She was interrupted, no doubt by Dance. She shouted even louder, 'Don't you dare shush me!' Greta hated to be shushed.

The sound of my sister's voice made me nearly cry. I tried again to get out, to go to her, but it was no good. A thousand pictures of her flashed up in my mind: Greta as a child winking at me when she was being scolded by Mama for one of her endless misdeeds; an older Greta riding a bicycle overloaded with shopping across a busy road, her hair flying like a flag in the sun; Greta one Midsummer, pushing her way naked through the reeds of a lake, shouting about how cold it was and then diving into the water. She was the person who had been there with me my whole life, my friend and protector. My sister. I always wanted to be more like Greta. She reminded me of the heroine of a novel, always thumbing her nose at life, daring it to do its worst. Her voice yelling 'Dance' without the 'Dr' made my heart swell with love for her. She was the same as ever. I could picture exactly how she would look as she faced up to him. She'd be standing there with her feet apart and her hands clenched into fists. I bet she wanted to take a swing at him, and I bet she could take him out too, if she did. The other voice, I thought, must be Ilse's.

Greta's voice came again. 'You monster! You killed my sister and her husband too!'

There followed an explosion of voices as they all began shouting at once, then Dr Dance's voice boomed out over everyone's: 'That's it! I'm calling the police.'

'Go ahead, Dance. We'll wait right here.'

There was more confused shouting before the apartment door opened and then immediately slammed shut. The banging on the door resumed, but not as loudly as before. I could hear Ilse's voice saying they ought to go. Then everything was quiet. I wondered what Dr Dance was doing.

Was Greta right? Had Dr Dance killed Petter? Was that the reason no one had told me what happened to him?

Dr Dance was coming up the stairs again. When he came in he didn't say anything for a minute. He was breathing hard.

'My darling,' he said. His voice sounded different. 'We had a visit from your esteemed sister. I can't believe you're related to that whore.'

I could hear him take a drink of something. Then he was back at my side again, rapping over the cast with his knuckles in different places, to check if it was dry. He smelled of alcohol. He rapped around the top of my back and down my spine and then I heard him grunt. I felt something working on the plaster at my hip—the scissors. He cut up and across the small of my back and removed the parts in two halves. His hands seemed to be shaking. He pulled off the lower half first, and it came away without a problem. Then he did the upper half, but this time I felt a pulling sensation, not too painful, over my neck and head and I heard Dr Dance swear. The skin had come away with the plaster.

Dr Dance suddenly got up and I heard a loud crash. At first I thought Greta must be back, but it was him, shouting and roaring.

'Fuck it! Fuck that goddamned whore!' With every word he threw something across the room. There was the sound of breaking glass and objects crashing around. I've always hated loud, sudden noises. I wished I didn't still have my face in the pillow, I tried again and again to get out. Dr Dance gave a kind of groan like a tree being felled, and something heavy, maybe the workbench, tipped over with an almighty crash. This was followed by more noises of smashing and tinkling and rolling. Then silence. The sound of his breath. He came over to me. I wondered if he was going to beat me, but he started washing my body, cleaning off the remains of the plaster.

He turned me over onto my back again. The room was in chaos. He'd pushed over the workbench that had his tools on it. They lay on the floor all mixed up with bits of broken glass and blobs of plaster. I was surprised that such a skinny old man could cause so much damage. He was standing amidst the wreckage staring at me. There was a broken bottle of brännvin on the floor and a glass of it in his hand.

'The bitch is onto me,' he said. He gave a dried-up laugh, like a bark. 'Cracked the case at last.' He took a step closer. 'Bet you didn't think I'd do it, did you, my sweet darling? I bet it wouldn't have even occurred to you, my little innocent.' He reached down and stroked my cheek, my throat. 'You know I'll do anything for you, my sweet love. Even that.'

'No,' I said. 'It's not true.'

Dance was no match for Petter.

'Yes, my darling. I had to have you. Nothing was going to stand in my way. And it was a pleasure, let me tell you, an absolute pleasure to get that bastard out of the picture.' He pressed his thumb on my lips. 'And what's more, I'd do it again if you asked me. In a heartbeat.'

His eyes behind his spectacles were like the unseeing eyes of a puppet. I had the earthy taste of plaster in my mouth.

'You're sick, Dance,' I said. 'Even sicker than I thought.'

His thumb was still on my lip and he pulled it down, but I hardly felt it. He started touching my legs. His hands were gritty and rough with dried plaster. I could smell the brännvin more strongly than ever. He moved my legs apart. He was frowning the whole time, like a sulky child playing with a doll. Then he reached for my breasts, grabbing them one in each hand and mashing into them with his palms, fingers splayed. He leaned down and kissed me on the lips. He was breathing through his mouth into mine while his tongue flicked around. Still I couldn't get away from him.

If only Greta would come back. I could just see the way she'd burst in, flinging the door open and standing there with her hand out like a traffic policeman.

'Dance!' she would shout. 'You stop right there, you filthy old pervert!'

Meanwhile he was still going at it, switching between kissing my lips and kneading away at my breasts. Those hands that pawed at me had killed my husband. I wanted to sink into the bed and through the mattress, through the floor, and all the floors of the building, deep into the soft earth. I called for Petter. Where was he? I tried to see the city spread out around me, tried to listen for him among the clamour of the living bodies and the dead stones, but all I felt was empty space. I was more alone than I had ever been.

Dr Dance was still on me, his fingers digging into my flesh, his hands gripping my ribs. Those hands that had killed. They seemed to have grown in size and strength and they wrapped almost the whole way around my torso. He leaned on me and was so heavy, despite being so skinny, that I could feel my ribs straining. I was afraid they would snap. I was afraid. I called again for Petter, but even as I did, Dance squeezed harder.

And then I thought: So what if he broke my ribs? Let him. Let him break every one. It wasn't like I was using them. Let him beat me and cut me with a knife and strip away every piece of my skin. Let him slice me up into tiny pieces and set me on fire until I was nothing but ash and bits of charred bone. What did I care? I was already dead. I didn't need Greta to save me, or Petter. I didn't need this body. It was nothing to me, and I'd be better off without it. There wasn't a thing left on this earth that Dance could do to me—everything bad that could happen to anyone had already happened to me. There was nothing to fear. If anyone should've been afraid, it was Dance. He was the one who was still alive, the one who had his life to lose, his body to be injured. His weak, old body. I didn't need my body. I had become something else. Something fearsome, something unnatural and not from this world. Something he ought to be terrified of.

I looked at him labouring away in his ecstasy, and had a picture of myself throwing him off me and into a heap on the floor, so hard that it would shatter his brittle old bones. I could see myself doing it clear as day. I didn't need anyone's help. It would be easy as anything. He was such a skinny slip of a thing, his muscles wasted with age, bones hollowed. He was nothing. I felt a tightening under my ribs, around my heart, like a fist clenching, and the tightness swelled within me, round and smooth and hot and the colour of my blood. He was going to pay. I rose up from the body, steady and sure.

I tried to push his head, push his face backwards, but I couldn't manage it. But I could imagine it. I saw myself throwing him off me with such force that he flew through the air, reeled against the wall and slid down it, like a man in a movie brawl, like an old rag doll. I could see the surprised look on his wrinkled face, see his spectacles flying off in a graceful arc. I envisioned biting off his filthy tongue with my teeth, biting it cleanly and spitting it across the room. It sailed through the air, a pink comet with a tail of blood, arcing, landing, and slithering wetly across the floor.

By now he'd moved on to touching me between my legs and I realised I could no longer feel it. He may as well have been touching someone else. He had knelt on the bed beside me and was moving his hand in a rough, jerky motion. The other hand was down his trousers—he had to pause a moment to unbutton them, and to pull off his fogged-up spectacles. His mouth was open, his lips drooping loose. He worked his scrawny arms until he tensed up, his eyes glued to my genitals, hardly blinking at all. If I could've spat on him I would have.

I could see the purplish head of his little dick popping in and out of the cup of his palm. Every time it did it made a soft rasping sound. He breathed in wheezy gasps, and a glistening blob of spit gathered at the top of his lower lip, ready to drop. With each pump of his hand his body tensed more, until the sinews in his neck stood out like cables under his papery skin. Then his mouth fell into a slack O, spanned with a string of saliva, and his head dropped back a bit and he came. It went over me and also his trousers a bit. He fell forward. I hoped he was dead of a heart attack but I could hear him breathing still.

8.

DANCE GOT WOKEN up very early the next morning. It was already light but the streets were quiet and empty still when someone rang the bell. There were a few rings before I heard him stumble off downstairs, clearing his throat and forgetting to close the doors behind him. I hoped it was Greta paying him another visit. I tried to follow him but couldn't get past the door. As soon as I got there I was pulled back to the body.

I heard Dance open the apartment door and then croak out, 'Yes?' in an early-morning voice.

'Good morning, Dr Dance. Perhaps you remember us? Detective Inspector Larsson, and I'm Sergeant Blom. We're here to ask you a few more questions.'

There was a pause, before Dance said, 'Yes . . . er, no problem. No problem at all. Come in.'

His voice had recovered from sleep but was of a higher pitch than normal. I heard them troop down the hallway towards the living room.

'We'll be brief, Dr Dance,' said the second voice, Larsson's, I supposed. 'Where were you in the first week of October last year?'

'What?'

'Can you tell us your whereabouts on the first week of October, 1930?' said Blom.

'October? Well now, that's rather a long time ago. I'm not sure that I . . . How could I be expected to . . . I'd have to check my calendar.'

'If you wouldn't mind. We'll wait.'

I heard him walk a few steps across the floor and then stop.

'On second thoughts,' Dance said. 'No, I can recall it now.'

'Oh, you can recall it?'

'Yes, I was here, right here in Stockholm. Here in this apartment, and at the clinic.'

'And do you have anyone who can vouch for your whereabouts?' asked Larsson. 'Your wife, perhaps?'

'Certainly she can,' said Dance. 'She was here with me.'

'In that case, can we have a quick word with Mrs Dance now?' asked Blom.

'As a matter of fact, you can't. She's away. Visiting friends.'

'Visiting friends. Hmm,' said Larsson. 'And, do you drive a LaSalle 328? Black?'

'Yes, I do.'

'A nice car.'

'It's not too bad.'

'A popular model, as I understand. There are eleven of them registered in the city of Stockholm alone. And it turns out that one of them is registered to you.'

There was a silence.

Larsson went on, 'Isn't that interesting?'

'Er, I wouldn't actually—'

'I say it's interesting because that model car was seen, with a driver matching your description, in Sundsvall in the first week of October. On Thursday the ninth, to be exact.'

'Huh. Is that so?'

'It is. And yet you maintain that you were here.' Larsson paused. 'And do you know what else happened in Sundsvall on the ninth of October, Dr Dance?'

When Dance made no reply, Larsson said, 'On the ninth of October, 1930, a man that you're acquainted with died in suspicious circumstances.'

'I see.'

'Oh, you see? Do you know to whom I'm referring?'

'Dahlstrom, is my guess. Yes, I read about that in the papers. Terrible tragedy.'

'Terrible,' said Larsson.

'Very sad,' said Dance. 'But as you say, there are eleven 328s registered in Stockholm. And surely more in other localities. So I fail to see what it has to do with me.'

'It's unlikely that any of those other ten drivers are acquainted with Mr Dahlstrom, wouldn't you agree?'

'And have you asked them? All ten?'

'We're asking you, Dr Dance.'

'And I'm telling you I wasn't there!'

'Mr Dahlstrom wasn't too happy with you treating his wife, was he?' It was Blom speaking now. 'Jealous type, wasn't he? Jealous of you?'

Dance gave his little barking laugh. 'Well, I wouldn't say that.'

'No?'

'No. My clinical methods are somewhat . . . unorthodox. Sometimes people are resistant to them.'

'Unorthodox, eh?' replied Blom, with a smirk in his voice. 'Never had any quarrel with Mr Dahlstrom?'

'Listen here, I told you last time, I met the man but once. A single time. I hardly remember him, or had an opportunity to quarrel with him. I treated his wife. That's all. Do you expect me to remember every family member of every one of my patients?'

'Now Dr Dance, please remain calm.' Larsson's voice again. 'We're simply asking a few routine questions.'

'I am calm!'

'Right,' said Larsson. 'Now, just to confirm: you maintain that you were in Stockholm on the ninth of October of last year?'

'Correct. I was here in this apartment, and then at work.'

'And you drive a black LaSalle 328 and met Dahlstrom through his wife.'

'Correct.'

'Mind if we take a look at her?'

'Who?' His voice rose to an even higher pitch.

'The car, Dr Dance.'

'Ah, the car. Yes, of course. Please follow me.'

There was the shuffling sound of them getting up and their footsteps in the hall and then the door opening and closing as the three men left the building. They were gone a long time. When Dr Dance came upstairs his face was grey and flat in the morning light.

9.

FOR THE NEXT three days Dance was very busy around the house. Summer was well underway, and every other resident of Stockholm had thrown open their doors and windows to let the sun and warmth into the house, meanwhile Dance was doing his best to shut it out.

He nailed the window closed in the room I was in, and filled the gaps in the frame with plaster. He took off the net curtains and replaced them with a thick grey blanket that he kept open only when he was at home. I heard him nailing other windows too, downstairs and in his room.

'Getting scared now, aren't you, Dance?'

Once, he went out of the apartment and then gave me a shock by appearing right outside the window, as if he had learned how to levitate. He was holding a hammer and set about nailing something to the wall. It was two round mirrors, one on either side of the window. He came back in and adjusted the mirrors, angling them so he could keep watch on who was coming up and down the street.

'There, that should do it,' he said.

'Seeing them coming isn't going to stop them, you know.' I told him. 'They're going to get you, Dance. Any day now.'

He moved a camp bed into my room, so I didn't even have the peace of the nights alone anymore. But at least he didn't try sleeping in the bed with my body. The white nights of summer must have been bothering him, because in addition to the heavy curtain, he used an eye-mask, and even with that on he didn't sleep all that much. He would get up and spend hours looking out the windows, watching the street. His head swivelled left and right, like he was at a tennis match, from one mirror to the other.

'There's no one there,' I told him. 'You've lost your mind.'

He spent the third day taking apart the radiation machine and tinkering around with the parts. He replaced the fat white metal tube coming out of the front with a long cone-shaped funnel.

'Perfect,' he said as he stood back to admire his handiwork, leaving his tools spread out on the floor. 'Now Lina,' he said, 'today we try something new. What you see before you, my darling, is something very special.'

He wheeled the machine over to me.

'This machine here,' he patted the side of it, like it was a horse, 'is the only one of its kind in the whole country.' He aimed the thin end of the funnel right at my heart. 'You lie still, my love. This won't hurt a bit.'

He pressed the switch at the side and the machine hummed and gently vibrated. It sounded different to usual. He'd used this thing on me nearly every day, and I'd never been able to feel its action, not since I died anyway. But this time when he switched on the current, I felt it. Something passed through me in a trembling wave, a vibration that seemed to radiate out from the centre of my heart through my ribs and out of my fingertips. Dance was right—it didn't hurt.

Dance stood in the corner, timing with his watch. He looked different to me too: more shrunken, even thinner. Maybe he'd been like that for a while and I hadn't paid attention, or maybe it was because of his recent worries and sleepless nights.

I noticed that he got out of breath wheeling the machine away and fetching the basin of water to clean me. His knees cracked like pistols when he sat down on his stool.

'You better watch yourself, old man. Sounds like your joints aren't what they used to be.'

His body was slowly coming undone, I realised, just like mine was. The difference was, he still needed his.

'Oof. Tired today,' he said.

'Tired? Sounds like you're about to drop off the perch. How old are you, anyway? A hundred?' I had no idea.

When I thought about it, it was surprising he'd survived this long. There were countless accidents lying in wait for him in that room alone. Moving the radiation machine, for example—a great, ungainly thing it was, on ridiculously tiny wheels. And if he was so careless as to leave his tools lying about, he shouldn't be surprised if one of the wheels were to catch on a discarded wrench, causing the machine to topple over onto him—and then how would he get out from under it? There was no way he'd be strong enough to lift it off himself. It wasn't like I could help. Or would.

And even cleaning me, as he was right now, was a task that always resulted in the floor being covered in puddles of water, which he never mopped up, the lazy man. It would be all too easy for an old man to slip in conditions like that. He usually wore these funny tennis shoes that looked like they'd not have much grip in the wet. And if he did slip, chances were that he'd fall backwards. Maybe he'd try to grab something to hold himself steady, but his reflexes weren't so good either. It stood to reason that the back of his head, right at the base of his neck, that very tender spot, would strike something on the way down, the corner of the stool or the workbench or one of the machines, or the head of the hammer he'd left on the floor—there were so many things in that cluttered place. Then he'd lie sprawled over the floor, maybe not instantly dead, but unconscious. He might wake up later in awful pain. Maybe he'd be paralysed.

As I lay there while he washed me, I considered these possibilities in the minutest detail. I pictured his tennis shoe in the puddle, the water rippling around the rubber toe, the sudden jerk he made when he lost his balance, his head snapping backwards. I knew the exact pitch of the crack of his skull against the table, the sound his flesh and bones would make as they hit the floor, his gasp of surprise: 'Uh!'

I concentrated so hard on this sequence—the shoe, the water, the jerk, the cracking sound, the gasp—that this concentration was all that was left of me. The shoe, the water, the jerk, the crack, the gasp. Shoe water jerk crack gasp.

Dance stood up then and as he walked over to the workbench he stepped in a puddle and skidded on the slippery heel of his shoe. Something light rushed through me and I leapt up and out of my body, like a cat springing up onto a table, in time with his jerking motion. He flailed his arms and managed to right himself, but by then I was out of the body and this time it felt different.

I realised I could move around the room in any direction I chose. I turned to face the bed, and that's when I saw myself for the first time, saw my body.

I say 'my body', but I would never have known it was mine if I hadn't just come from it. I wouldn't have recognised it. The hair was gone, I knew about that, but seeing something is a whole different thing to knowing about it. The skin on the scalp was ulcerous and patchy. The face had collapsed into a moony disc, like a failed cake, and the nose looked to have been replaced with wax or plaster. It was a bad job, it was much too narrow and curved to one side, and so clumsily formed it looked like a kid had made it in craft class at school. The ears, too, were lumpen blobs. The eyes were the glass eyes of a toy animal, with the large iris as black as the pupil. The eyelashes were gone and the eyes were lined all the way around with kohl. The eyebrows had been painted on but were nothing like how my eyebrows used to look. Had he even seen my living face? The fake brows were much too high and long—two arcs like black rainbows. Together with the shrunken nose, they gave the face a surprised expression, surprised but not pleased, as if I'd come home to find someone I didn't much like had invited themselves over for dinner.

Looking at the body, I didn't feel anything in particular. Not angry, or sad. Only that it was strange to think I'd lived in it for more than twenty years. Now it was hard to know what it had to do with me at all. And what Dance saw there, I had no idea.

Still free of the body, I went straight for the door to get out. Out of that room and out of that house. But the door was closed and I couldn't make my way past it. I couldn't understand why a door should make a difference if I was free of the body. I tried the window, which was nailed shut, then I went over every inch of the room, floor to ceiling, but the place was sealed.

Dance was at the workbench, busy filling containers with chemicals, measuring things out. I went and placed myself behind him. I found I was any height I chose. I made myself taller than he was.

'Hello, Dance,' I said.

I looked at the back of his crepey neck, and the white hairs crawling up from his collar. He swivelled around and stood looking through me. His weak, watery eyes glistened behind his spectacles.

'Lina, my sweetheart? Did you say something?'

It was strange to look at his face so close up, with him standing upright. The overhead light glanced off the bald dome of his head.

'I know I've been neglecting you,' he said, and went over to the bed. He leaned down and stroked the face with the back of his hand. I couldn't feel his touch.

'No, Dance, you blind old fool,' I said. 'That's not me. I'm over here.'

He paused for a moment and glanced around, then kept on stroking the face.

'I'm sorry,' he said to the body. 'I've got a lot on my mind.'

He went back to the workbench and started taking bottles down from the shelves above. He had to strain to reach them, standing up on his toes and edging them out with his fingertips.

'Why don't you use your stool for a stepladder, Dance?' I asked. I willed him to do it. I imagined kicking the stool out from under him. I imagined his head cracking against the floor. Every now and then he'd stop what he was doing and half turn and look around the room.

From up close I could read the labels on the bottles and tins that he used on the body. Some of them were familiar to me: olive oil, beeswax, iodine, turpentine. Others I'd never heard of: formalin, phenol solution, hexaphene, Sircol. I noticed a large bottle that Dance had knocked when he pulled out the one beside it. Now it was balancing on the very edge of the shelf, right over his left shoulder. If it fell, it'd hit him for sure. And if he were to shift to the left a bit it might even hit him on his head. I reached for the bottle, but I couldn't make contact.

Instead, I concentrated hard on the bottle. It was almost full, it would be heavy. It was made of thick green glass and embossed with the brand name Borup, which was also written in fat yellow letters on the label. *Borup.* I focused so hard I became the bottle. It just needed a tiny push, and then it would drop. Dance wouldn't hear it coming. It'd tilt slightly and then start a silent slide through the air until it met with his bald, shiny head. The bottle wouldn't break but Dance's skull would crack. He'd crumple to the floor like a puppet, all knees and elbows, stunned. There wouldn't be much blood spilt, barely a drop.

Dance was now going back and forth to the coffin bath. He filled a basin with water and rested it on the workbench for a second. When he picked it up again he knocked it against the upright of the shelves and the Borup bottle came tumbling down, exactly as I had willed it. I cheered with excitement. He saw it coming, though, and dodged out of the way, slopping water down his front. Even so, the bottle hit him on the shoulder. He stumbled and slopped more water from the basin.

'Goddamnit!'

The Borup bottle rolled away under the bed, unbroken.

'Better watch yourself, Dance. Better be careful.'

The water trickled under the radiation machine. Dance put down the basin and cursed under his breath as he shook water off his hands and tried to mop his suit with his handkerchief. He fetched a rag from the cupboard and got down on his hands and knees to wipe the floor. Now and then he reached up to feel his shoulder.

I went to the window and looked out. It was late afternoon and the sky was a flat chalky blue. The sun's heat came through the glass, though I couldn't feel it in the same way as before, it was more like being inside the heat, breathing it, and even with the window closed I could hear all the sounds of summer: the voices of swimmers and fishers and people on boats echoing out over the water at Djurgårdsbrunnsviken, the ferry horns and the screams from the rollercoaster at Gröna Lund. Two small girls walked past in floral sunhats, carrying a wicker basket between them, heading in the direction of the water. From the other direction a woman turned into Jungfrugatan from Linnégatan. She was also in a sunhat and wore sunglasses, and carried a Japanese fan which she flapped lazily in front of her face. The woman looked familiar. I could hear her heels click neatly along the footpath. She came closer in brisk steps. It was Mrs Doris Dance.

'Hey, Dance,' I said. He was still crawling around on the floor, mopping up under the bed. 'Looks like you've got a visitor.'

Two minutes later I heard the street door open and close and then the clack of her heels up the staircase. Dance heard the heels too, and at the sound his head swivelled towards the door and he sat back on his haunches like a nervous dog.

'Get ready,' I said.

He leapt up and out the door in one surprisingly agile motion. There was the sound of keys jangling outside the door to the apartment and his feet thundering down the stairs. He'd left the door of the room open and I wasted no time trying to get out, but it was as impossible as when it had been closed. I heard him open the apartment door.

'Carl!' came Mrs Dance's voice.

There was a scuffling sound and then the door closing.

'Carl? What are you doing?' Mrs Dance's voice came from outside the apartment.

'Hello, Doris,' said Dance. He must have stepped outside to meet her. 'Look, I'm afraid you've caught me at rather a bad moment. I'm on the way out. Urgent appointment.'

She gave a laugh. 'Carl, come now. You haven't seen me in months! Surely you can spend a few—'

'Come on.'

There was the sound of their feet going down the stairs, and Mrs Dance's voice receding into the distance. 'Carl! What in god's name has happened to your suit? You're soaked!'

I went back to the window and saw them come out of the building and step onto the footpath below.

'. . . and I said in my letter, you and I need to have things out.'

'Mrs Dance! Up here!'

She glanced to her left and to her right. Had she heard me? But she went on talking. 'Things simply can't go on like this.'

I tried to bang on the glass or make some kind of noise but I couldn't, all the objects in the room had become as soft as whipped cream.

'Mrs Dance!'

She turned her face up and looked at the windows of the apartment.

Dance grabbed her by the elbow. 'Come on, Doris, I've got to get on. If you want to talk, fine, we can walk and talk.' He steered her away down Jungfrugatan towards the church. As she trotted by his side she turned to look back. It seemed like she was looking at me.

10.

I REMAINED FREE from the body. Out of habit, I tried the door and the window again after Dance had left. I made myself flat to get under the door, but would always find myself pushed back again. I slid along the walls looking for any tiny gap along the window frame, over the wood looking for any opening. But the floorboards fitted perfectly into one another, the walls had no cracks. I drifted through the room, taking another look at everything. The room was always so full of objects, and Dance wasn't much of a housekeeper, that was for sure. There were dirty plates stacked up on the floor and glasses in the sink. Splatters of plaster still covered the floor around the bed, and under the bed were the pieces of the plaster cast of the body. They had no more meaning for me than the thing lying on the bed.

On the workbench Dance had left a notebook open, where he was recording things about the dead body—the weight, what looked to be a list of chemicals he was treating it with, and the radiation times. There was also a magazine open to a page with pictures of dogs with wires attached to them. Underneath was an article:

> Mechanised Blood Circulation as a Method of Revivifying Animals by Professors K.L. Smythe and E.W.R. Battencourt.
>
> Recent developments in the field of biological experimental research have established that animal tissues, and indeed complete organs, can be perpetually conserved in a living state under laboratory conditions. Further, animal organs, and even an entire organism, can be revivified through the application of electrical currents. William Kouwenhoven's research . . .

On the opposite page were diagrams of hearts with arrows showing where the blood went in and out. These professors, and Dance, completely had the wrong end of the stick: they didn't know that bodies meant nothing.

It was Midsummer Eve, so it stayed dusk until morning. Dance was out the whole night. The city was quiet for the holiday, all empty streets and bridges, shuttered shops and silent houses. Everyone had gone to the country and not a car or person or a barking dog could be heard. That night, Stockholm belonged to the birds. They wheeled and cried, making sharp black shapes against the lavender sky, they chattered in the trees and snatched after mosquitoes. I could hear the buzz of the cicadas at Gärdet, and the fish leaping in Djurgårdsbrunnsviken.

When the sun started to climb again a car appeared, a large black one. It drove slowly along Jungfrugatan, lurching over the cobblestones. It ground to a halt right outside. I couldn't tell if it was Dance's car. No one got out. Then the light started to change.

Instead of getting brighter as the sun rose, the sky darkened again, and became that sick yellow colour that tells you a storm is coming. The birds went away, and the quiet was like a held breath.

Dance appeared, walking up Jungfrugatan from Storgatan. I could hear him whistling, as if he didn't have a care in the world. He was carrying a bunch of flowers and a parcel. His footsteps made a quickfire echo as he ran up the stairs.

'Lina! Good morning, my darling, and happy Midsummer!'

He kissed the forehead of the body on the bed. His suit definitely looked the worse for wear.

'I have some wonderful news,' he said. He was leaning over the body and addressing its face. 'Doris will shortly be out of the picture.'

He chuckled.

'She has requested a divorce. And you know what that means, don't you?' He stroked the corpse's face. 'Now you will be my bride, not only in my heart, but in the eyes of the law.'

'Pretty sure you can't marry a rotting corpse, Dance.'

He held out the bouquet with a flourish. 'And here are some lovely flowers for you, my queen!'

It was a bunch of wildflowers that he'd obviously picked himself. I could see that he had some smörboll along with the chickweed, cornflowers and dandelions, and the foul smell of it was already wafting through the room. Maybe he thought it was the body that was making the stench, or, mad as he was, maybe he even liked it.

'Your flowers stink.'

'Now, I'm going to make a wreath for you,' he said. 'A Midsummer crown for my queen!' Only Dance would think of adorning that ulcerated head with flowers. Though at least then it'd be covered up.

231

'But first,' he said, holding up the parcel, 'I have a surprise for you.'

He sat down on his little stool with the parcel in his lap and started untying the string. 'I had this made especially for you in Germany. By the finest craftsman, just for you, my darling.'

He pulled a brown hairy lump from the paper and held it in the air, where it dangled limply, like a dead kitten. He shook it out and placed it on the bald head. It was a wig.

'It's made of real hair,' he said. 'Not your own, unfortunately, there wasn't enough of it. But it is real human hair.'

He was fussing with the thing, trying to get it in position. I watched from the windowsill.

'There!' he said 'A perfect fit!' He stood back to take in the full effect. The wig looked like a bird roosting on the corpse's head.

'The bald head was better,' I told him.

'It's perfect! Just gorgeous,' he said, then he jumped up and scuttled from the room as if he'd remembered something. I heard him go next door and he came back with a hand mirror, which he held up in front of the corpse's face.

'See? They did a great job. It's different from your natural colour, but I like it better this way.'

He put on a Bix Beiderbecke record, 'Rhythm King', and started messing around with the flowers. He began cheerfully enough, whistling and humming along to Bix, but after about half an hour the cheeriness had given way to cursing. I couldn't stand watching his fumblings. He got up and poured himself a glass of aquavit. Maybe another hour passed, or even more. He kept drinking and working away at the flowers, dripping sweat and repeatedly pushing his spectacles back up his nose. Now, I've seen some terrible flower crowns in my time, but they were nothing compared to what Dance came up with that day. His clumsy fingers had mashed the stalks to a pulp as he tried to weave them together, and he'd lost most of the blooms. Eventually he gave up and draped his mauled string of flowers on the corpse's forehead and sort of tucked it in behind. At least it covered up part of the wig.

By then the weather had really turned. The sky was darkening with the coming storm and the wind was rushing through the trees and rattling against the windows. Dance kept drinking. He took the corpse's dress off and carefully washed and dried the body.

'And now you get another surprise, you lucky princess,' he said.

He went out again and returned with a dress I hadn't seen before. He turned it back and forth, showing it to the corpse.

'Only the best for my girl,' he said.

It was floor-length, of creamy silk, with a short train. The front was plain, but it had a very low scooped back and thin straps that fastened behind with a tiny jewelled clip. It must've cost him a fortune.

He had a bit of trouble putting the dress on the body, he must've been pretty drunk by now. He got the straps tangled up and threaded the arms through the wrong holes. He had to keep lifting up the body to get the dress under it. It was like watching someone try to set up a tent for the first time. The effort sent his breathing all jagged and he kept stopping to mop his brow with his handkerchief. By the time he finally managed to get the dress on, the sky was almost as dark as at night-time. The wind howled in loud bursts and raindrops cracked against the window glass. There was a flash of lightning that lit the room and reflected off his spectacles, and thunder that shook the walls.

'Oh, Lina!' he said. 'If I knew how to harness that power.'

I wanted to laugh. 'What, do you think you're Dr Frankenstein?' I asked him. 'You know he's not real, don't you? He's just a character in a book.'

'I would wake you like a princess, like Sleeping Beauty,' he said.

He kissed the corpse on the lips, groping with one hand at the silk that covered the bony chest.

There was another clap of thunder as Dance retrieved the radiation machine and wheeled it to the bed. His movements were loose and unsteady, he was drunker than I had ever seen him. He adjusted the dials on the machine and positioned the funnel at the corpse's chest.

'Now, my darling,' he said, 'Now you will awaken!'

He flipped the switch. The machine started to hum and Dance rocked back and forth on the balls of his feet with excitement. After a while he shut it off, went to the body and lifted up a wrist, as if to check the pulse.

'You're too late, Dance. She's long gone,' I said.

He gasped and let go of the wrist. The arm flopped down over the edge of the bed. Dance put his ear to the rib cage. He listened.

'What? My Lina!' He stood upright. 'Can it be true?' He started feverishly massaging the arms and legs.

'It's true that you're completely insane,' I said.

'Lina? Lina?' He leaned in close to the dead face, studying it. 'I've done it!' he crowed. 'I knew I'd do it in the end!' With his finger, he opened the corpse's mouth as wide as it would go. He took a huge breath in and breathed out into the open mouth. The chest moved up and down when the air went in, like bellows. He came up for air again like a swimmer, his lips gaping as wide as the corpse's as he sucked in more air and then blew again into the mouth. The ribs creaked as the chest rose and fell. He did this for about two minutes. He started to laugh like a maniac and the sound of it bounced off the walls.

'You need help,' I told him.

'I knew it! I knew it!' he shouted and leapt about the room.

By now the storm seemed to be right overhead. The thunder rumbled along like a machine on metal rollers, and lightning flashed. Dance threw off his jacket, which he'd still been wearing even in the heat, and fumbled to undo the buttons of his shirt. As he did, he tried to kick off his shoes, but couldn't manage it and had to stoop down and untie them first, slowly, one by one. He whipped off his belt and dropped his trousers and underpants and pulled his undershirt over his bald old head. His body was nearly as skinny and sick-looking as the corpse's, with the skin hanging loose and tired from his limbs. He rushed back to the body and began kissing the mouth again.

'Lina . . . Lina! My darling! Oh, Lina!' he moaned between kisses.

I say 'kisses', but it was more like he was trying to put the whole chin and lower face inside his mouth. It must've tasted awful. I couldn't stand to watch so I looked out of the window at the rain, white like a veil, and the trees straining against the wind. The buildings and cobblestones were darkened with water, and the car was still parked there across the street.

'Now!' I heard him say. 'Now you will awaken!'

When I turned to look he'd wrenched the dress up to the waist and spread the legs. His hand was around his limp dick, trying to make it hard enough. I could see that the genitals of the body were reinforced or replaced with plaster or wax, the same as the nose and ears. He must have done that before I was awake. They must have been the first parts to decompose. Unless they'd become worn away with use. I rode a wave of disgust and when I looked at Dance again I really saw him for the first time. His skin hid a tangled and dark mass of cruelty, sickly-green and black, senseless.

He crouched over the body in preparation, and after more fumbling, thrust himself between the yawning legs. I saw the slack skin on his flat arse shudder with each pump of his skinny hips.

'No.' I said. Even though that body had nothing to do with me. 'No! You get off her right now!'

He was propped over the body, resting his knuckles on the bed as he laboured along. The wig and flowers had started to slip off the corpse's head, a bit further every time he pounded into the body. His spectacles had slid to the very tip of his nose. Sweat dripped from his face and slid down the knobs of his spine. I flew at him like an arrow.

'Stop right there, you goddamned pervert!' I yelled. 'How dare you? You filthy, pathetic rat. Go to hell.'

As I came closer, he turned his head towards me.

I cannoned into him and willed him away from the corpse with every bit of concentration I could muster. Time seemed to slow down and I saw his eyes and mouth stretch wide in astonishment. He gave a kind of grunt before he toppled slowly to the side and off the bed. He hit the ground with a dull thump and his spectacles flew off and slid across the floor. He lay there in an untidy heap.

I thought I'd managed to kill him, but a few minutes later he started to snore.

11.

DANCE SLEPT ON the floor the whole night through, not once changing position. Early in the morning he got up and filled a glass at the sink. His eyes made a nervous tour of the room as he drank. I went and stood behind him.

'Hello, Dance. Sleep well?' I said in his ear.

He turned his head towards me. I puffed some cold air onto the back of his neck and watched him shiver as the goosebumps rose. He scurried back to his camp bed, but he didn't get a chance to go back to sleep—before he was even under the covers the door-bell rang, one long ring that went on and on. Dance groaned and slid off the bed. He started looking for his spectacles. The whole time the bell kept ringing and ringing. I bet the noise was doing terrible things to his hangover.

'Alright!' he snapped, and hurriedly pulled on his dressing gown before padding down the stairs. The ringing stopped and someone immediately began pounding on the apartment door.

'Open up, Dance!'

It was a woman's voice. I knew it well.

'I'm not letting you in,' Dance yelled. 'Get lost!'

'Greta!' I called out.

'Open up! Open up or I'll get the police!'

'This is harassment!'

The pounding got louder. It sounded like she was throwing her whole body against the door.

'Dance!'

He opened the door and Greta's voice drifted up the stairs. 'What've you done with her? Where is she?'

'Greta, I'm up here!' I called.

'Hold on now, please calm down.'

'Don't you tell me to calm down. You tell me where my sister is. What've you done with her?'

I called to her again, though I knew it was pointless.

'Listen,' said Dance, 'Let's just—'

'Dr Dance,' said a man's voice. Papa. 'We've come from the cemetery, and—'

'Where's the body?' Greta said.

'Hold on a minute,' said Dance. 'Hold on. Everyone please calm down. Let's all have a seat and—'

'Where is she?' demanded Greta again.

'She's in the tomb—'

'You liar,' said Greta. 'She's here. I know she is.'

She must have pushed her way past him because I could hear her moving around on the floor below. I wondered if she might be able to sense me, even if she couldn't hear me. I tried again and again to get through the door but I still couldn't move beyond it. I concentrated hard on Greta. I pictured her face, the furious expression she'd have, her eyes flashing black and her jaw set like stone. I willed her to move so that I could see her through the open door.

'Okay, okay,' said Dance. 'Hold on a minute. Let's keep calm. I know you're worried about Lina's body but listen, I've taken full responsibility for it.'

'What do you mean?' said Greta. 'What are you talking about? It's gone from the tomb.'

'I know it has. I know. Listen, I can take much better care of your sister's body than the people at the cemetery can. I am—'

'Where is she? Upstairs? If you don't answer me I'm going to the police station right now.'

'She's perfectly safe, I assure you,' said Dance, 'and well taken care of. Look, I'll show you. You have absolutely nothing to worry about, I promise.'

Dance appeared at the foot of the stairs and then I could see Greta, followed by Papa, coming up behind him. I saw the top of Greta's head, her glossy curls; she took the steps two at a time and when she looked up I saw her eyes darting around, watchful. Papa came into view, looking much older than he should have, uncertain, shrunk with worry into his wrinkled skin.

When they reached the top of the stairs Dance stood aside to let Greta come in. She stepped forward, into the doorway, and I reached out to her. Her hot anger made a high-pitched note in the air and I heard her heart beating fast.

'Greta,' I said. She didn't know I was in front of her. Her eyes were wide and had become scared now. They were surrounded by a tense net of new lines, that hadn't been there when I last saw her. She had her hands balled together in front of her, each holding on to the other, making one big white fist. I rested on her shoulder, listening to the quiet singing of her body that made a celestial music. I spoke to her, telling her I was here, I was with her. But still she didn't know. I wrapped around her and then I felt a shift. Her heart changed pitch and I saw her see me. I saw her recognise me. Her eyes were the same deep golden colour they had always been, and in that moment I could see every one of the thousands of times she'd ever looked at me over all the long years, every smiling glance, every flash of fury or triumph or sympathy or blame or love, and I knew we were both seeing these things together. The muscles around her eyes relaxed.

Her eyes swept the room and I felt her take in the scene: the discarded tools and dirty dishes, the machines and equipment, the dismantled plaster cast, Dance's clothes strewn about the place and his spectacles under the bed. And the body. The body.

It lay there facing the ceiling. The wig had fallen back and you could see the blistered naked scalp; the flower crown lay on the floor, a damp and mangled mess. The legs still gaped wide and the dress was hitched up high. Not more than half a second passed before Dance registered the state of the room and tried to pull Greta back out onto the landing. But by then she was doubled over, retching. She vomited on the floor. Then she ran down the stairs and out of the apartment. Papa threw Dance a horrified look and followed her. I tried to go after them but couldn't.

'Greta! Papa!' I called.

I went to look out the window. I saw them get into a car and drive away. I wondered whose car it was. The other car was still there.

Dance had gone down after them to lock the door. When he came back he cleaned up the vomit, still wearing his dressing gown.

He worked very slowly, using a rag and basin of water. I stayed at the window, hoping Greta would come back, watching for her. I saw a car pass along Linnégatan, at the end of the block, and then a moment later a man walk by. The streets looked desolate, filled with pieces of rubbish and leaves and twigs scattered by the storm.

Then a car came up Jungfrugatan. A police car. It slowed down as it approached. Another followed, and then a third. The first one pulled up outside. Two policemen in uniform got out. I had seen one of them before. Then two men in plain clothes got out of the car that had been parked opposite, and I recognised one of them too. All four went to the door and out of my view. The doorbell rang, a short burst this time. Dance came over to the window. He swore when he saw the cars. The bell rang again and he grabbed his trousers and pulled them on. He took a sheet from the camp bed and hastily threw it over the body, leaving the feet exposed, and ran downstairs. I heard him open the door.

'Inspector Larsson, Sergeant Blom,' said Dance in an oily tone.

'This is Commissioner Wahlgren and this is Inspector Ehrling.' It sounded like Blom speaking. 'Can you confirm that you are the person whose name is on this piece of paper?'

'Yes, that's my name alright.'

'Can you show us the body?'

'What body?'

'Dr Dance,' said another, unfamiliar voice, 'we have reports that you are harbouring a corpse in this house.'

'Show us the body, Dance,' said Blom. He sounded like his patience had run out. 'We know it's here.'

There was a silence. Then Dance cleared his throat. 'Follow me,' he said.

The heavy shoes of the four policemen made a racket on the stairs. Just as he had with Greta, Dance stood aside to let them into the room. They stood around the bed. I took in their square faces and knew these men would never be able to help me. The unfamiliar one in plain clothes lifted the sheet from the face and peeled it down to the waist. I could feel their fear. The four of them stood there for a minute, looking down at the body.

'Is it true that you've had this body on your premises for a period of three months?' Larsson asked.

'Yes.'

'And who is she?'

When Dance said nothing Larsson repeated, 'Who is she?'

'She is . . . ah . . . she is my bride, Lina Dahlstrom.'

The men glanced at each other.

'Your wife is Doris Dance,' said Larsson, but the other man in plain clothes gave him a warning shake of the head. This man said in a louder voice, as if Dance might've been hard of hearing, 'And do you have a certificate for this body?'

'Yes I do,' said Dance. 'No need to shout.'

He took down a box from the top shelf and after shuffling around in there, pulled out a crumpled sheet of paper and handed it to Larsson.

'This is the death certificate,' said Larsson, glancing it over. He looked up at Dance. 'That's not the certificate we need to see.'

Dance shrugged, spreading out his hands, palms up. 'I don't know what other kind of certificate you could possibly need,' he said. He still had his old dressing gown on over the top of his trousers. It hung loose, and you could see his upper chest, sunken, pale. The long sleeves almost covered his hands. He was

242

without his spectacles, squinting, and his face looked obscene in its nakedness.

'I'm afraid, Dr Dance, that you'll need to come down to the station if you have no certificate. You can explain the whole story to us there,' said Larsson, making as if to take him by the elbow.

'Wait! Please!' said Dance in a high panicky voice. 'Can I at least get dressed first? And I need my eyeglasses. Can I have five minutes?'

Larsson looked over at his colleague, who nodded.

'Five minutes,' said Larsson. He folded his arms and leaned against the doorjamb. Blom joined him and the other uniformed man pulled the sheet up over the face of the body. He went around to the end of the bed and covered up the feet too.

Now the body was out of sight. It had disappeared, like in a magic trick. Now it was nothing more than a shape with a series of ridges and hollows. Now the only body left in the room was Dance's, as he scrambled around on the floor looking for his spectacles, and when he and the other men went out of the room and down the stairs and out of the house, there were no bodies to be seen in the room at all.

In the street Blom tied Dance's hands behind his back. He was pushed into a police car. I could see him sitting with his head bowed. The car drove away. I would never have to be near him again.

All around me the house settled itself into silence. It loosened its timbers and the dust snowed down with a sound like stars. I let myself stretch out with the air. There was no hurry. I let myself drift. The sun dropped low and the pale night came bringing cooler air and birdsong.

In the peace of the night I found I could let myself grow so large as to fill every corner of the room. And then I knew I had been going about it in the wrong way, like trying to swim by walking. Now I knew there was to be no effort. It was more like singing, it was more like sighing, like recognising a song. I launched myself in a smooth fluid move, a wave that unfurled in all directions, and as it unfurled it grew. I felt myself growing larger, until I was beyond the walls of the room, and of the house, beyond the street, beyond the city. I was the clouds, I was the trees, I was the air, and the birds in the air, and their song. I was all the waters of all the seas, every star that's ever been. I was everywhere. And I was nowhere.

IV: DORIS

1.

I FIRST SAW the news about Carl when I was on my way to a party at Christine's place. I'd seen him only two days before, so it came as a shock, to say the least. What happened was, I had just sat down in my seat on the streetcar when I realised I'd forgotten to bring a novel with me, which was annoying because it's quite a long ride to Danderyd, where Christine lives, from Gamla Stan, which is where I was staying. The thought of having to sit there staring out of the window with only my own thoughts for company was too tiresome to contemplate.

Luckily, the man sitting beside me pulled out a copy of the *Dagbladet*. I slipped on my spectacles and glanced over to see what the headlines were. The front page had RUSSIAN–ENGLISH DEAL. The man turned the page, and there was a picture of a fellow with very impressive moustaches, and underneath: GERMAN CHANCELLOR INTRODUCES NEW POLICIES, and underneath that: CATALONIA VOTES FOR AUTONOMY. He turned the page again, and there was SCIENTIST DANCER HELD ON MALICIOUS AND

Wanton Charges. I remember thinking that sounded interesting, and how funny that someone might be both a scientist and a dancer—how would he find the time?—but then something caught my eye further down the page, and there was my husband looking up at me. I thought my eyeglass prescription might need renewing: surely it couldn't be Carl's picture there in the *Dagbladet*. But I leaned closer and saw that it was him, plain as day. They had made a mistake with the name. The photo was a close-up of his face, and I recognised it as having been taken at a Holm Clinic Christmas party. Carl was wearing his glasses and a bow tie, which as always was a little bit crooked. Underneath it said:

Case Attracts International Attention

All Stockholm was abuzz with talk yesterday about the most fascinating case to appear in the city, or indeed in the whole of Sweden, in decades. Dr Carl Dancer, sixty-three years of age, an American national who now lives in Östermalm, is the talk of the town after revelations that he stole the decaying body of his young sweetheart from its crypt, and kept it with him in his house on Jungfrugatan for—

I suppose the man noticed me reading, because he gave the paper a tremendous shake, and turned the page with a lot of huffing and rustling. He was now onto a feature about the newly completed Empire State Building in New York.

I couldn't believe what I'd just read.

'Excuse me, sir,' I said. 'I normally wouldn't ask this, but there's an article in your paper, and . . . would you mind possibly going back a few pages?'

He raised his eyebrows. 'Just take the damned thing,' he said, and thrust the open *Dagbladet* at me. He got up and moved to another seat and I read the rest of the article.

According to Dancer, a scientist and doctor who runs a private practice in Östermalm, it all started back in America when, as a teenager, he had 'visions and dreams' of a 'beautiful lady' that so compelled him, he decided to search the world for her. He found her at last in Stockholm, but then temporarily lost her again to tuberculosis and death. She was buried in the Norra Begravningsplatsen cemetery. There then followed a series of events that some call gruesome, but which for others lift Dancer to the enviable position of the truest romantic of all time.

Little did police think investigations into allegations of 'grave-robbing' would lead to this sensational discovery. For it was found that the body of twenty-year-old Lina Dahlstrom, née Fredelius, was missing from the vault in which she had been buried, and that the disappearance was not recent.

It was Dancer himself who had, more than eight months earlier, placed her in the vault. Dancer had also designed, funded and built the vault, and, according to reports, the aged lover spent many nights visiting his dead sweetheart in the cemetery, listening to her favourite records in her tomb. Sources say that Dancer could not bear the 'beauty of her body slowly rotting away to nothingness', and believed that 'such beauty must be preserved'.

It is reported that Dancer, a learned chemist and scientist, invented treatments to defeat the process of bodily decay, especially in regards to odours that may otherwise have been detected near his home.

According to a source close to the dead woman's family, these treatments were so successful that even so long after death the body looked 'surprisingly like it did in life'. The body was found on a bed beside the one on which Dancer himself slept.

Though Dancer's actions are criminal, many of Stockholm's female population give no importance to this and instead herald him as a great romantic, a man who sacrificed everything for love and would not let even death put an end to his devotion. Tributes for Dancer have poured in to Långholmen prison from ladies across the city.

Detective Inspector Per Larsson and Sergeant Olof Blom made the arrest Monday morning and Dancer has been taken to Långholmen to await a hearing. How he removed the body from the vault remains a mystery.

Visions and dreams? Grave-robbing? Prison? There was a rushing and prickling in my head, as if it was slowly being filled up with soda water. I knew Carl was a little in love with Mrs Dahlstrom, that was clear as day from the first moment, but living with her decaying body? The *Dagbladet* must be sensationalising the story to sell more copies, that must be it. That paper was always printing such fantastical things. All the same, it was more than a relief that soon Carl and I would no longer be married. How lucky that I'd asked for a divorce when I'd seen him a few days before.

At the beginning I thought the whole thing with Mrs Dahlstrom was harmless, nothing more than a silly infatuation. I thought it would fade with time and that Carl would come to his senses, but then all that nonsense started with the funeral, and his mania for visiting her at the cemetery. It was a very sad thing of course that such a young woman, and such a beautiful one, had died so soon; it was tragic, really. And she had been so very beautiful. It gave me quite a shock when I first met her. As soon as I laid eyes on her I could see why Carl was so interested in helping her. It's quite natural that one is affected by beauty—it shows an artistic temperament, especially if one is a man of a certain age.

But the poor woman. I think her life had been an awfully sad one, what with spending her days working in that dreadful factory and then getting ill and her husband being killed. And Carl had told me, or perhaps I'd read it in her file—I sometimes liked to cast my eye over Carl's work files when he happened to bring them home, just to find out a little bit about his patients and to keep myself informed of his work—but I'd read or heard somewhere that she'd had a miscarriage too, so we had that in common at any rate.

In fact, I don't mind telling you that I think the miscarriage must have been what made her ill in the first place. Oh, I know doctors and medical people say you can't get ill from having your heart broken, but that is rubbish. And if anything will break your heart, losing a baby will. Believe me, that's something I know about. I lost three babies in a row and was very ill indeed, even though I was taking the medicine Carl gave me. After the third miscarriage he refused to let me try for any more children and I had that procedure done. But I try not to think about that now.

It's funny, though, how one can find connections—things in common, I mean—with the unlikeliest of people. One wouldn't think that Mrs Dahlstrom and I should have anything in common, we appear to be so very different after all. I an older woman, and perhaps someone she would think of as a grand lady, and she so much younger and of a different station in life. And then it turns out that we shared this very significant life experience.

Yes, the article was just too outrageous. It had to be a fabrication, an exaggeration at least. But still, as I sat there gazing out the window, unsettling questions about Carl kept sliding into my mind like serpents. Why wouldn't he let me into the apartment that afternoon? Why had he been in such an awful rush? Why did he arrange to meet me at Blanch's Cafe instead of at home the next day? And why had he failed to keep that appointment?

My husband had changed so much since I first met him. I was only a girl then, a country girl, and he was unlike anyone I'd ever seen before. He was the first American I'd encountered, for one thing, the first real foreigner, and he was so different from all the small-town Swedish men I'd known. I came across Carl early one morning on the side of the road in to Råsa. He was trying to fix his bicycle, and had grease all over his hands and the front of his shirt. I took him back with me to the farmhouse. We walked side-by-side, with him wheeling his broken cycle.

He told me he was on a cycling tour, and I'd never heard of one of those. No one in Råsa did such a thing; people only travelled with the aim of getting to a place. I had no idea anyone would cycle just for the pleasure of it, and I kept asking him where he was trying to get to, but he seemed not to understand me. I thought it was due to his bad Swedish, until it dawned on me.

'So, you mean to say you're spending the summer just riding around?' I said at last. 'You don't even know where you're going, really?'

He beamed at me. 'Now you've got it!'

He was so tall and lean and he cracked with energy and ideas and excitement, he seemed to be twice as alive as all those dull, quiet Swedes, and being around him made me feel more alive too.

A familiar voice cut through my daydreaming. 'I had a feeling you might be on this streetcar.'

'Harald!'

Dear Harald. The man was like a guardian angel, appearing at exactly the right moment. I'd known Harald Blomkvist for years, and he had been a great friend to me during my recent troubles with Carl. He himself had lost his wife to cancer a number of years ago, so he knew what it was to go through difficult times. Harald had become very dear to me in the past months. He was going to Christine's too, of course. He sat down in the seat beside mine.

'Oh, Harald,' I said. 'Have you seen the *Dagbladet*?' I handed him the article and watched his face harden into a serious expression as he read.

He looked up. 'Good lord! I certainly didn't see this coming.'

'Neither did I.' I shuddered. 'Do you think the article can be true? No matter, though, soon it won't have anything to do with me. Carl won't at any rate. He's agreed to a divorce.'

'He has? That's a relief. Signed the form, did he?'

'Well, not exactly. But we have a gentlemen's agreement. And when I asked him, he was almost happy that I had.'

'Hmm.' Harald looked thoughtful. 'Are you sure you still want to go to Christine's party tonight?'

'Why ever not? It's not me who's the grave-robber. And I haven't seen Christine in simply ages—and besides, I'm wearing this new blouse. It's modelled on a Schiaparelli, you know.'

Christine opened the door herself.

'Doris, my darling!' She kissed me hello. 'Harald. Oh, you two have come together, have you?'

She didn't ask me where Carl was.

There were already a few people there: Christine's husband, Ulf, of course, and Ida and Erik, Henrik and Charlotta, and Edit and Claus, all old friends from my early days in Stockholm. There was also a very pretty young girl, a Miss Brun I believe, who was one of Ulf's students. Just after we got there, Arne and Hilde arrived with their two little ones. Not one of them asked about Carl, and I thought I ought to say something. I hadn't told anyone about the divorce yet either—that kind of thing wasn't so easy to bring up in those circles. Everyone thought I'd been away visiting Lotta in Ystad, the same as I do every year.

We all went out to the garden for a schnapps before dinner, and we sat wrapped in blankets at a table under an apple tree. It was still light, just past nine, with a summer evening sun spilling down over the wall and filling the garden with a soft-edged glow, thick and sweet as honey. Some sill and cheese and bread and more schnapps were brought out, and everything seemed just as it had always been.

'Erik and I saw *Almost a Honeymoon* last week at Oscars,' Ida was saying. 'Have you seen it yet?'

'Lochers was wonderful,' Erik said. 'Such energy.'

I cleared my throat. 'I haven't seen that show yet. But did any of you see the *Dagbladet* today?' I saw Harald glance at me. 'I wonder what you all thought of it.'

A few looks were thrown around and then everyone became very busy with their drinks. I realised they must have been discussing it before I arrived.

'Oh, Doris,' Christine eventually said. She was sitting next to me and squeezed my arm. 'I did see it, and I said to Ulf that Carl is such a good man—didn't I, Ulf?—so generous and always helping those less fortunate, and it's simply monstrous that the press is going in for him like this.'

'Monstrous,' Ulf agreed.

'Absolutely,' said Henrik. 'Carl is a leader in his field. It's a disgrace. I must say, one does wonder whether Carl's being a foreigner has anything to do with him being attacked in this way.'

'Like Sacco and Vanzetti,' said Ulf.

I thought Carl was not remotely like Sacco or Vanzetti, but I kept quiet about that.

Erik was nodding in agreement. 'I thought the same,' he said. 'Sometimes I think it's a sad fact that Sweden is a place that never got used to foreigners.'

Ida leaned forward in her chair. 'Doris, I think you're being so brave. We're all right here behind you and Carl. If there's anything you need, anything at all, don't hesitate. I mean it.'

Hilde, Christine and Charlotta were all nodding too.

'Anything,' Edit said.

'Yes, Doris, anything at all,' put in Hilde. 'Carl's a lucky man to have a wife like you standing beside him.'

'A pillar of strength!'

'I'm not so sure if I'll be—' I said.

'You must be such a comfort to him. We're all so proud of you, Doris.'

'Yes, chin up, Doris! We know you and Carl will get through this.'

'And what's more, be all the stronger for it!'

I realised then that perhaps these people were more Carl's friends than mine. Perhaps I didn't know them as well as I'd thought.

After the party was over, Harald walked me to the square to find a cab. I'd been staying at the Hotel Reisen for the last three days. When we were out of sight of the house, he put his arm around me. I leaned my head into his shoulder.

'Doris, you know I'm here, no matter what you decide.'

'Decide? I suppose you mean the divorce. It's not a topic for discussion. Carl and I are finished. There's nothing clearer, and it's all agreed between him and me. It just remains for him to sign the documents, pay the fee, and lodge the form. It's that simple.'

'Well, I hope it is.' He lightly kissed the top of my head. 'I'd like you to be a free woman.'

'I suppose if I want him to sign I'll have to go and visit him,' I said. 'At Långholmen.'

2.

THE NEXT MORNING I found that the visiting hours for Långholmen prison didn't begin until eleven. I thought in the meantime I would go and take a look at the apartment. I wanted to see the situation for myself. I put on my navy day dress, a straw cloche, white gloves and my low-heeled white pumps, slid the divorce forms in to my handbag, and set out.

It was the brightest, most perfect summer's day. I decided to walk, it wasn't more than twenty minutes by foot. The sun was absolutely blinding, and I'd forgotten my sunglasses. It's true that in summer Stockholm is the most beautiful city in the world, but it can be so very dazzling to the eye, what with all the water and white buildings everywhere.

When I reached Storgatan it occurred to me that there might be police officers posted at the building: the apartment would surely be considered a crime scene. I didn't want to have to speak to the police, and I decided that if there were any about I would simply walk straight on. It wasn't as if they would know who I was. Well, Larsson and Blom knew me, but I didn't think it likely they would be posted there. I started to feel a bit nervous, as if I were trespassing, which was ridiculous—it was my very own home.

The apartment building came into view and there were no police outside, in fact there was no one around at all. I didn't fancy meeting my neighbours any more than I fancied meeting the police. I could just picture their curious eyes and their whispers. I had the key for the street door ready in my hand and I opened it a crack and slipped in like a fish.

The entrance hall was cool and smelled the same as ever: a bit like paper and a bit like smoke. I could see the cage of the lift sitting on the ground floor, empty. I crept up the staircase, taking care to step only on the carpet runner and not on the stone, feeling just like a burglar. The sound of my breathing was loud in the marble stairwell. When I got to our landing I noticed a funny smell, like nail varnish. I couldn't get the apartment key to work. It was so dark on the landing and my eyes were dazzled from the sun so I could hardly see what I was doing, but I was certain I had the right key: I knew it by feel. It went into the lock just fine, but wouldn't turn. I took off my gloves and wrenched at the key until my fingers were raw.

I heard a noise upstairs—a door closing and then footsteps, followed by the screech and whirr of the lift. The empty cage went past me on its way up and I heard it clank to a stop on the floor above. I got into a kind of panic then, and started jamming key after key into the lock. I simply couldn't stand the thought of the people upstairs, Margit and Knut Bergen, seeing me there, locked out of my own apartment. Carl must have changed the locks on me. I wondered when.

I could hear the lift coming down again and I froze with the useless keys in my hand and my forehead pressed against the door, my white gloves between my teeth. I heard the lift doors open and close on the ground floor and then the street door and then everything was quiet again.

Outside it was stifling. By the time I got to Östermalmstorg, my left shoe was pinching at the toe and my head was sweating into my hat. I got on the number 54 bus to Långholmen. There was hardly anyone else on it, just a lady and her young son sitting near the front and an old gentleman at the very back. I couldn't help wondering whether they were also going to the prison. They didn't look the type, but then neither did I.

Långholmen was only a short ride away, and it wasn't anything like what I'd expected. I had pictured a huge building of grey stone and barred windows, perhaps with a few prisoners gripping the bars and gazing out with mournful faces, and guards with guns everywhere, but it was nothing like that at all. I crossed the bridge onto the island and stepped into the cool of a grove of birch trees. In the distance I could see the prison building, which was a mansion of yellow stone with columns and a gabled roof, surrounded by a garden. There was a low wall all around, but it was nothing very different from what one might see around any large private house.

A guard met me at the gate and showed me to a room where another guard wrote my name in a book and told me to sit down and wait. He went away and came back a few minutes later and said that Carl was with a visitor and I would have to wait for them

to leave before I could see him. I didn't have to wait long. The
guard led me across a lawn to another wing, up a flight of stairs,
and down a long walkway with many locked doors. He stopped
in front of the last one and unlocked it.

'Ten minutes,' said the guard.

I heard the door clang shut behind me. The room was cold
and damp and smelled like bleach. There were windows high up
along one wall, with thin iron bars over them. All around, people
sat in pairs at metal tables, talking in low voices. I spotted Carl
right away. He was at a table by the windows, and he had a guard
standing beside him. Though I'd only seen him a few days before,
he was greatly changed. His hair looked whiter and his spectacles
were huge on his face. His body seemed shrunken and withered,
as if his clothes were a size too big. He was wearing that old suit
with the satin lapels and he had tennis shoes on his feet.

I sat down in the small metal chair opposite him and put my
handbag on my lap.

'Doris.' He reached out and grabbed my hand in both of his
and kissed it. 'I'm so glad you're here.'

I quickly pulled back my hand. I wondered if this meeting was
going to be as straightforward as I'd imagined.

'Listen, Doris, I know I've done a lot wrong by you these last
years. I haven't been the husband I ought to have been. And I'm
sincerely sorry. I have to do better by you, and I promise I will. Doris,
I love you.' His eyes were watery and pleading behind his spectacles.

'Carl, it's really too late for that. I'm sorry.' I undid the clasp of
my handbag and drew out the envelope that contained the forms.

'No, wait,' Carl said. 'I know we talked about going our separate ways, but now that I've had the chance to think on it, I realise that's the last thing I want.'

I put the envelope on the table between us. 'Carl, we had an agreement. One that you were very pleased about.'

'But I can't live without you.'

I laughed without meaning to. I saw I had to take care. I pushed the envelope towards him but he wouldn't look at it. He grabbed my hand again and held on to it. I could feel the cold metal of the table top through my sleeve.

'I'm so lucky to have a wife like you,' he said. 'I was crazy to ever talk about leaving you, to behave in the way I did.' He squeezed my hand. 'Just crazy!'

The guard took a step forward. I'd forgotten he was there. 'Pipe down, Dance,' he said.

'Doris, please.' Carl leaned over the table, still gripping my hand. 'I'm begging you. Please, just give me one more chance.'

'But Carl, we talked about this. We were in agreement. It's over between us, we both know it is.'

And then the time was up. The guard appeared and escorted me back down the long walkway and across the lawn. I had the envelope still clutched in my hand. As we walked along my head started to feel very peculiar, as though the top of it had lifted off. Brightly coloured spots floated in front of my eyes and I hoped I didn't have a migraine coming on. We entered the waiting room and it was so packed that I had to push my way through. The place was full of women, all of them dressed up in flounced dresses and hats with ribbons, carrying bouquets of flowers and wicker baskets of fruit that jabbed into me. It was an effort to set one foot before the other.

As I was passing the desk a voice said, 'I'm here for Dr Dance, please.'

'One at a time, miss, one at a time,' said the guard.

But perhaps I had misheard, because there was a tremendous rushing noise in my ears.

Then I felt someone grab me by the arm. 'Mrs Dance? Doris Dance?'

A very tall man had hold of me. 'I'm sorry,' I said, pulling away from him, 'I must . . .' I gestured to the door, unable to speak.

He went ahead of me, clearing a path. I followed him down the steps and then I stood a moment with my eyes closed, breathing the fresh air. I listened to the wind in the trees and the birds and the sound of my breath going in and out. I felt my body come back to me.

'Mrs Dance?'

I opened my eyes, remembering the man. He was standing in front of me.

'Are you feeling alright?' he asked.

I nodded, even though any fool could see I wasn't.

'I'm your husband's lawyer,' he said, holding out a card.

I looked at him. He was in his late forties, smartly dressed, with distinguished grey hair and a tanned, expensive face. I took the card but I had to hold it out at arm's length to read it because I didn't have my spectacles.

Sten Strid

Attorney at Law

'Your husband asked me to contact you,' he said. 'Perhaps you'd like to come past my office in the next few days?'

I made a time for Thursday morning. His office was close to the apartment in Östermalm, but that was neither here nor there, I remembered, because I didn't live there anymore.

3.

I HAD ARRANGED to meet Harald at Blanch's Cafe after my visit to Långholmen. I'd always loved Blanch's, with its airy high rooms and rows of lamps and potted palms, and seeing everyone sitting there in their colourful clothes, and when you managed to get a table in the side section with the glass roof, then it was just like having your meal in a greenhouse. Carl and I used to go there often in the evenings when we first moved to Jungfrugatan, just after we were married.

Blanch's was almost empty; it was that awkward time after lunch but before afternoon tea. Harald was already waiting for me.

'Well? How was it?'

He had ordered coffee and a plate of petits choux cheese pastries, my favourites. I realised that I was famished.

'You were right,' I said. 'It's not going to be as easy as I thought.'

I sat down and ate two of the pastries before I'd even taken off my gloves. The waiter came over and I ordered a few more things from the menu.

'Yes, I suspected he'd try to go back on his word,' said Harald. 'You're the perfect cover for him, you know. Respectable, upstanding. He'll be depending on you to make him look good.'

The waiter brought some tomato sardines gratin, then came back with a mushroom-filled soufflé omelette, salmon sandwiches, a plate of cinnamon buns, a bowl of fruit salad and another pot of coffee. There was barely enough room on the table for all the dishes.

'My word, Doris!' said Harald. 'Not worried about slimming, are you?'

'What?' I tucked into the sardines and felt better than I had all day.

A man came in, and out of all of the empty tables, took the one right beside ours. He was dressed in a suit, not a very good one, with very grubby cuffs. I angled my chair away from him a little and lowered my voice.

'Yes,' I said. 'I believe you're right about Carl. You ought to have seen the performance he put on when I visited: can't live without me, loves me more than anyone, you know the kind of thing.'

'Bit late for that, isn't it?'

'Exactly what I said.' I tried the mushroom soufflé omelette. It was most delicious, buttery and crisp and fluffy all at once. 'The funny thing about it is, Carl's acting isn't up to much. Hammy, you know.'

'It certainly is deuced bad luck about the timing. If only you could've gotten him to sign when you met him last week.'

'He seemed so happy about it then.'

The man at the next table cleared his throat. 'Excuse me?' I heard him say.

I had another mouthful of omelette. 'He was positively jubilant in fact. He all but broke out in a jig on the spot.'

I felt a tap on my shoulder. I turned. It was the scruffy man.

'Would you happen to be Mrs Dance?' he asked. I saw he was holding a notepad and a pen.

'What business is that of yours?'

'Do I understand correctly that you're filing for divorce?'

'Excuse me?' I said. 'And who are you?'

'Jost Ahlm, with *Nationen*.'

Harald stood up. 'Now, you listen here, you, you . . . you cad! What a nerve! Can't you see we're having a private conversation?'

Right then another man popped out from behind a potted palm, like a mouse from the skirting board. He also had a note-book in his hand.

'Kaleb Bovin, *Stockholms-Tidningen*,' he said. 'Mrs Dance, would you like to make a comment on your husband's conduct?'

'You leave her alone! Both of you!' Harald said.

The waiter came running over and tried to shoo away the reporters, but they stood their ground.

'What's your opinion of the allegations against your husband?' asked Jost Ahlm, dodging the waiter's waving arms.

Kaleb Bovin approached the table. 'Mrs Dance, did you have any suspicions about your husband's behaviour? Why didn't you raise the alarm?'

He was standing over me now. I got up. I was taller than he was. Another man appeared, holding a camera. There was a tremendous flash. Harald covered his face and I was quite blinded.

'Mrs Dance, did you know about Lina Dahlstrom?'

'Did you act in concert with your husband?'

'Harald,' I said. 'This is monstrous. We must get out of here.'

I snatched up my handbag and gloves and made for the door without once looking back.

4.

WHEN I GOT to my hotel, I thought I had escaped the reporters, but every time I so much as put my nose outside, they appeared from all sides and pestered me with their questions. They seemed to have set up camp outside the hotel—from my window I could see them in the street below, leaning against lampposts, their notebooks at the ready. I spent the next day in my room, but the following day I had my appointment with Strid. I was wearing my chocolate gaberdine suit and a cream silk blouse with a bow. As an after-thought I added a paisley silk headscarf and large sunglasses and braced myself for the onslaught. As soon as the lift doors opened onto the lobby they were all around me like a pack of hounds around a rabbit.

'Mrs Dance! Mrs Dance!'

I sped from the lift through the lobby with three of them on my tail.

'Mrs Dance! Erik Andersson, *Aftonbladet*. Would you mind answering a few questions?'

'Yes, I would mind,' I said, without turning or breaking my stride.

'Mrs Dance!' another man called. 'Mrs Dance, what's your opinion of your husband's involvement with Mr Dahlstrom's death?'

I got out of the hotel door and started walking along Skeppsbron, scanning the street for a taxi. I ought to have called for one from my room.

'Mrs Dance!'

One of the reporters followed me and seized my elbow.

'Hands off, you blighter!' I said and shook myself free. I walked on briskly, keeping up a very smart pace. Another reporter appeared alongside me and matched my speed at a jagged sideways trot.

'Mrs Dance, our readers are interested to know your opinion of Dr Dance's relationship with Lina Dahlstrom. Did you know about it?'

A few passers-by turned their heads to look as we sped past in our little formation. I could see a taxi approaching up ahead, and I waved it down and got in the back. The reporters pounded on the windows. The driver accelerated and we left the men behind, all still shouting my name and waving their notebooks.

Sten Strid's rooms were on Nybrogatan, just around the corner from the apartment, and I must say, the waiting room was altogether shabbier than I would have expected, considering Strid's own appearance. There were no plants or mirrors or magazines even, just a mismatched row of three chairs with worn vinyl covers. The place smelled like dusty carpets. Strid's secretary was sitting behind a scuffed desk and looked as though she'd arranged her hair without the aid of a mirror.

Strid's office wasn't in much better condition. There was dust on every surface and the desk was piled high with untidy stacks of files and papers. Strid sat among this chaos seemingly unconcerned by it. He was once again elegantly presented, and rather handsome in fact. His hair was thick and well cut, his linen suit a cool dark blue that brought out the colour of his eyes.

'Mrs Dance, I'll get straight down to business,' he said. 'I must start out by telling you that I've never handled a case quite like this before, but don't let that alarm you: I doubt anyone else involved will have either. It is a most unusual case, and your husband certainly is an unusual man.'

'Yes. He is that.'

'Dr Dance recommended you as his primary character witness for the preliminary hearing. Our objective at this point is to have this matter settled in the hearing, and avoid going to trial. The date for the hearing is . . .' He shuffled his papers around. 'Monday next week, eleven o'clock.' He looked up at me. 'Do you agree to act as his witness?'

'Thank you, Mr Strid, but first I have some questions for you,' I said. 'To begin with, what exactly has Carl been charged with?'

'Ah yes. Your husband is charged with,' and here he read in a calm voice from a piece of paper, 'wantonly and maliciously destroying a grave, and removing a body without authorisation.'

I had to admit that the charge didn't sound all that serious. 'And what would the penalty be if he is found guilty?'

'It can vary, but Dr Dance would be facing incarceration of perhaps up to fifteen years, and perhaps also fines of up to fifty thousand kronor.' Strid put his elbows on the desk and steepled his fingers. 'But Mrs Dance, I must warn you, your husband's case is not quite as straightforward as it may appear. Nor is it benign. The possibility exists that some, ah, complications could arise.'

270

'What kind of complications?'

'First of all, there is the chance that he will also be charged with assault, of a . . . ah, sexual nature.'

I had to take that in. 'Do you mean Carl assaulted Mrs Dahlstrom?'

'The charge pertains to that lady, yes, but er . . . when the lady in question was in a deceased state. The lady's body, that is.'

'You mean the corpse of Lina Dahlstrom?' My mouth filled with sick-tasting bile. I reached for my handkerchief and spat it out. 'You mean to tell me he fucked that corpse?'

Strid held out his palms towards me. 'Look, Mrs Dance, I'm not making any such allegations. Nothing of the kind. I'm merely pointing out some eventualities that may arise. The legality of that point is still under question.'

I took a deep breath in and out, and then another.

'Alright,' I said. 'I assume that would make it a much harsher penalty?'

'Correct. Then there is another matter, that of Petter Dahlstrom.'

My head had started to throb.

'As you may be aware, there is a degree of uncertainty around Mr Dahlstrom's death, and it seems that there is some circumstantial evidence that may link Dr Dance to his death.'

'You're saying he killed Petter Dahlstrom? So that he could fuck his dead wife?'

'Mrs Dance, please remain calm. I'm not saying that. Not at all. This is only a very remote possibility at this stage. I only mention it to make clear to you every eventuality as regards your husband.'

He had his secretary bring in a glass of water for me. The glass she handed me was finger-marked and the water was warmish and tasted of rust.

'Have you got anything stronger?' I asked when she had gone out again.

Strid poured the water out of the window and took a bottle of cognac from the filing cabinet beside his desk. He poured a glass for each of us.

'As I was saying earlier, Dr Dance has recommended you as his primary character witness—'

'And what would happen if I refuse?'

'Dr Dance needs all the support he can get.'

'And if I refuse?'

Strid gave me a long look and then sighed. 'Mrs Dance,' he said. 'I understand that you're considering separating from your husband.'

'Well, wouldn't you be? Given all this . . .' I couldn't bring myself to say the words.

'You know, Mrs Dance, even with the divorce law reform of recent years, you would still require Dr Dance's agreement in order to obtain a divorce. I understand that he is reluctant.'

'But would I still need his agreement if he's in prison for this . . . assault of a sexual nature?'

'It's true that there exist provisions for such circumstances. But it can be a complex process.'

He watched me over the rim of his glass as he took a swig of cognac. He was cleverer than he looked. I rarely think of the possibility of handsome, well-dressed men also being clever.

'Think of it this way: you would be doing him a favour if you agreed to act as a character witness. He would be in your debt.'

5.

WHEN I STEPPED out of Strid's office I realised that the one thing I needed most at that moment was a cigarette. I don't smoke as a rule, Carl made me stop when we were married, but cigarettes have remained an illicit comfort to me now and then in a hard time. I turned into Karlavägen, keeping an eye out for reporters. At Karlaplan I bought a packet of Pall Malls from the kiosk and lit one up right away. I sat down on a bench under an aspen tree. The smoke spiralled into my lungs, weighing and warming them. I leaned back to stretch my neck. Above my head the filmy leaves quivered in the breeze. I could see their pale veins and the sun glancing through between them and the flashes of blue sky behind.

I still had the divorce papers in my handbag. I had the urge to keep them with me as I would something precious. I wanted that divorce more than I wanted anything. The idea of being free, free of Carl, and becoming Doris Ekman again made me feel as I did when I skated as a girl, flying over the ice in long, smooth strides like an arrow from the bow. Doris Ekman's life would be peaceful, perhaps with a man who was caring and kind. I already knew one such man.

I don't mind telling you that I had for a while been thinking of Harald in a romantic way. Some nights, as I lay alone, I let myself imagine what a life with him might be like. We had become so very close—closer, in some ways, than Carl and I had ever been. Whenever anything interesting or funny happened my first thought was always: I must tell Harald about this. A few times I'd been on the verge of telling him how I felt, but I always hesitated. It is no small thing to tell a person that you love them.

I could hardly bear to think about the things Strid had told me Carl had done. Carl would never agree to a divorce now. Maybe Strid's suggestion was a good one: I could agree to speak well of him at the hearing in exchange for him signing. That way we would both get what we wanted. If not, I would have to hope that all of Strid's worst eventualities came to pass and Carl landed in prison for a long time.

I ground the cigarette out on the pavement and got a taxi to Långholmen.

Carl looked even more shrivelled than he had last time, and more unkempt. What meagre hair he had left was fluffed up around his head like a ring of wispy cotton. The moment I sat down at the metal table he started with his romantic nonsense again, but I cut him short.

'Listen,' I said. 'You've got to drop this act.'

'Act? What act? Doris, I'm telling you, you're the love of my life.'

He reached out across the table. I put my hands in my lap.

'Drop it, Carl,' I said. 'We both know the situation here, and the situation is this: you don't want to go to prison, and I—'

'No, no! It's not like that! You've got it all wrong. Doris, I love you.' He was slumped forward, his arms stretched out towards me.

'Carl, stop it. You want me to play your respectable, upstanding wife who sticks by you so that everyone will think you're the kind of man who shouldn't go to prison.'

'No, Doris, you've got the wrong—'

I held up my hand to silence him. 'Look, I don't particularly want to send you to prison for twenty years, but I also don't want to be your wife anymore. So how about you and I make a bargain.'

His eyes had grown narrow and wary but he didn't interrupt me.

'I'll agree to act as a character witness for you, and I'll do the very best job I can, in exchange for you agreeing to the divorce.'

'But I don't want a divorce.'

'But I do.'

'Oh, Doris . . .' But his voice was uncertain. 'You know I've always loved you.'

I shook my head and leaned back in my chair. 'This way, we both get what we want,' I said. 'What do you say?'

He was watching my face closely. I suddenly realised that we'd had very few honest conversations in our time together. He turned his head and looked around the room at all the other prisoners sitting at the tables with their visitors. He sighed.

'Alright,' he said. 'You have my agreement.'

I pushed the envelope towards him over the table. He pushed it back.

'I'll sign after the hearing,' he said. 'You have my word.'

We shook hands on it.

'But you ought to know,' he said, 'I'm only agreeing because I'm confident I can change your mind later. I still want to be with you, Doris, always. You're my love, my darling wife.'

I stifled a snort. He was agreeing because he knew we only had about a minute left before the guard escorted me out, and he knew a good deal when he saw one.

There were no reporters outside the prison so I decided to risk walking back to the hotel. Walking is something that never fails to calm my nerves. Years ago, on the farm, whenever I was feeling agitated I would set out to walk the boundary, which was marked by a wooden fence. One circuit didn't take too long, but I'd go round and round for hours sometimes, until I forgot where I was. I think there's something in the motion of walking that gets the brain going differently, it's as if there's a deep part of yourself that can only come alive through the action of the muscles in the legs. It makes sense, because deep down we are all animals.

I kept to the back streets. By the time I reached Bastugatan, I thought I might need to stop for a cup of coffee—it was further than I'd thought to the hotel. I came across a small bakery with a display of pies and cakes in the window. I looked up and down the quiet street; it seemed unlikely that anyone would bother me there. I kept my sunglasses on, just to be on the safe side, and went inside.

There was a free table right at the back, next to a young lady and a man. As I was about to sit down, the man turned around. I peered at him over the top of my sunglasses.

'Harald?'

'Doris?'

'What are you doing here?' I asked.

'Well, I've had to go somewhat undercover since our lunch the other day. My word, those reporters are a dreadful nuisance, aren't they?'

The young lady sitting with Harald looked familiar.

'Oh, how rude of me!' he said. 'Doris, you remember Miss Brun, from Christine's party?'

I did remember Miss Brun. She couldn't have been more than twenty, and had a clear-skinned, fine-boned face and smooth chestnut hair.

'Indeed,' I said.

She stood up to shake hands. She was as slender as a poplar. 'Nice to see you again, Mrs Dance.'

'Miss Brun's family have their boat moored beside mine at Wasahamnen,' said Harald, by way of an explanation. 'We're just having a spot of afternoon tea.' He smiled at Miss Brun across the table.

I decided I was no longer in the mood for coffee.

6.

THE DAY OF the hearing came around dreadfully quickly. I had trouble sleeping the night before. I got comfortable in the bed and closed my eyes and I did feel as if I had slept a little, but when I looked at the hands of the bedside clock they seemed not to have moved at all. At first I thought that the clock had stopped, but I could hear it ticking away as usual. I watched the thin second hand making its way round and round the face until it felt like an eternity had gone by, me lying there in the dark staring at that blasted clock.

In the end I got up, pulled a chair over to the window and lit a cigarette. The window had a view over the water of Riddarfjärden and I could see the lights of the Gröna Lund amusement park in the distance. The sight of it always reminded me of my childhood, even though I'd never been there. The Djurgården ferries beetled back and forth between the islands, and past a row of white ocean liners docked near Slussen that rose like icebergs out of the black water.

Earlier that day, I'd been trying to prepare for the hearing, and for the questions the magistrate might ask me about Carl. Strid had told me to think of instances where Carl had shown himself to be honourable, trustworthy and decent. I should talk about how he had been a caring husband to me, and an upstanding citizen. I'm not opposed to lying on any moral grounds, but I find it a difficult thing to do in the moment, so I tried to list Carl's positive points honestly.

'Carl is hardworking,' I said out loud. That surely was a respectable thing, and it was true. 'Carl is extremely dedicated to his work in medicine.' Though that might perhaps not be suitable in this case. 'Carl cares about helping those in need.' If those in need are attractive young women. 'Carl was a good husband to me.' But that was the wrong tense. 'Carl *is* a good husband to me. Very good.' He never let me go hungry.

The next morning I dressed in my double-breasted herringbone jacket and skirt, with a high-collared peach blouse. I had the divorce forms in my bag like a talisman. Harald picked me up by taxi and we held hands in the back seat. Seeing him always made me feel better—he was a calming presence. Both of us were wearing sunglasses and hats, but this did nothing to deter the swarms of reporters. By the time we made it to the room where the hearing was to take place, it was already full. I got rather a shock when all those faces turned towards us as we came in.

Harald went to sit in the public gallery and a court official showed me to a seat near the front. Sten Strid was there, nattily dressed as usual. There were a few faces in the crowd that I recognised: Christine and Ulf were sitting beside Harald, and Nils Persson was there, and Dr Per Holm, and on the other side of the room was a familiar-looking young woman that I couldn't quite place, who looked as though she'd been crying. In the upper gallery I saw our neighbours, Margit and Knut Bergen.

The room was very hot and so crammed full of people—one would think they would have set a limit—that after about ten minutes it seemed like all the air had been used up. Luckily I'd had the presence of mind to bring my Japanese fan with me, and I waved it back and forth in front of my face, not that it did much good.

Then Carl appeared. All talking stopped and all heads turned towards him; it was a bit like the moment when the bride enters the church. I half expected someone to strike up the organ. Carl was being led by two police officers. He was wearing that jacket together with tennis shoes again, but now he had put on a bow tie as well, and his hair looked rattier than ever. They had him in handcuffs, which seemed very dramatic and more than a little unnecessary.

Next, the magistrate came in and we all had to stand up, again like in church, and after that everything seemed to happen very fast.

A police officer called Sörensen got up and told the story of how Mrs Dahlstrom's body was found in our apartment, and some things he said were so gruesome that people in the gallery groaned and covered their ears. I kept my eye on Carl to see his reaction, but he didn't seem to be paying very much attention and was busy gazing at the people in the gallery. He certainly didn't look ashamed or apologetic. How I wished that I'd already left behind being Mrs Dance.

A young woman got up next, the familiar-looking one with tears in her eyes, and I realised that it was Mrs Dahlstrom's sister, who had come to our apartment a few times with Mrs Dahlstrom. She started telling how she had seen the body and the terrible shock it was. I could see that she was trying hard not to cry. She started to speak about Carl, saying he'd had designs on her sister all along, and that she thought the treatments were Carl's way of getting close to Mrs Dahlstrom. Then she did start crying and had to keep wiping her eyes with her handkerchief and blowing her nose. She was a dreadfully sad sight standing there with her pain exposed for all the world to see, and no one trying to comfort her.

The whole meantime, the room was getting hotter and hotter. I could feel the sweat gathering on my forehead. It felt like hours had passed but when I looked down at my watch I saw that it had hardly been thirty minutes. The heat made my blood beat thickly in my head and I felt stupid and dazed. I practised my sentences about Carl in my head. *Carl is hardworking, Carl is hardworking,* I said to myself. *He was a good husband. Is. Is.*

Carl took the stand, and the people in the public gallery started whispering and pointing and jeering. Some stood up and craned their necks to get a better look at him. The magistrate called for quiet, but there was a commotion among a group of women in the upper gallery, and the next instant I saw a little coloured object floating down through the air from up there, down to where Carl was sitting. Another one followed, and then more and more in a shower. My first thought was that these women were throwing bits of rotten food at him, until I saw that it wasn't food, but flowers, single roses, nosegays of violets and wildflowers done up in ribbons. They sailed through the air, shedding petals like confetti, and landed all around Carl, making coloured splashes on the wooden floor.

'We love you, Carl!' a woman's voice called out.

Carl was smiling. He gave a little bow in their direction, like an actor at the end of a performance. The journalists were all scribbling away in their notebooks and the magistrate was shouting, 'Order! Order!' Someone went up to remove the women—there were about five of them—and they were escorted out amid hoots and laughter.

It took a while for everything to quieten down again. When the hearing resumed, Strid asked Carl a lot of questions. Then the magistrate spoke. He was a little round man, bald as an egg, with a spongy pink nose.

'Dr Dance,' the magistrate said. 'I'd like you to tell us more about the methods you employed, with Mrs Dahlstrom.'

'Well, first I built an incubator tank—'

'Was this of your own design?' asked the magistrate.

'It was,' said Carl, inclining his head a little, as if in modesty, 'with a system of circulating filtration pumps and an electron cell. I filled it with a plasma solution, also of my own formulation, and kept it at a constant blood-heat temperature of thirty-seven degrees Centigrade. This solution remained circulating automatically, twenty-four hours a day.'

The magistrate was nodding as he listened, as if he approved of Carl's methods.

'After the first twenty-four hours,' Carl went on, 'I introduced the radiation element of the regimen, which consisted of high-voltage radiation once a day for five minutes at a time.'

'And what kind of radiation was this?' asked the magistrate.

'X-ray. I built and installed the machine myself, which ran on a transformer of ten thousand volts that I also installed.'

'And how did you develop these methods?' asked the magistrate.

'I am a trained chemist and it has been my personal interest— my passion, you could say—to study the effects of radiation and chemistry on the human body. You might call it my life's work.'

'Dr Dance,' said magistrate, 'to the best of your knowledge, has anyone attempted such an experiment before now?'

'Not to my knowledge. As I said, the machines and solutions were all of my own design.'

'An innovative man!' the magistrate said.

Then the police officer, Sörensen, got up again. Mr Sörensen was a weak-chinned fellow with heavy eyebrows that came down in a V-shape over his nose.

'Dr Dance,' he said, smiling with his lips only, 'or is it Mr Dance?' His voice had a whining note like that of an insect.

'I am a doctor, yes. But you may call me Mr Dance if you prefer.'

'Thank you,' said Sörensen. 'You are a doctor and you practise medicine, so I take it you are a medical doctor?'

'I do practise medical treatments, but I do not claim to be a physician. My doctorate is in chemistry.'

'I see,' said Sörensen. He frowned, as if considering a difficult problem. 'And you completed a doctoral degree at . . . ah, the University of Texas, I believe?'

'Yes, that's correct.'

'Yet there is no record of the completion of your doctorate at that institution. How can that be, Mr Dance?'

Carl gave a kind of sigh. 'I completed all the required academic work and examinations for the doctoral degree,' he said, 'but I never collected my formal award. There was some technicality that caused a problem with it being conferred.'

'Ah, a technicality. I see,' said Sörensen. 'So you are not, in fact, a doctor?'

'As I say, I completed the work of a doctoral degree,' said Carl.

'Hmm . . . thank you,' Sörensen said, glancing around the room as if he expected applause. 'And now,' he went on, 'I would like to ask you about your methods.' He looked down at his notes. 'You mentioned in your statement that you used, ah, "nourishing solutions" to restore the body. How were these solutions applied to the body of the deceased?'

'I applied various solutions topically to areas of damaged tissue.'

'Topically—meaning you applied these to the exterior of the body?'

'Correct.'

'And were these topical solutions the only way that you "nourished" the body of the deceased?'

'No, I also nourished the body internally.'

'Would you explain what you mean by internally?'

'With edible nutrients,' said Carl.

'Could you give us an example?'

Carl gave a wave of his hand. 'Common foods one would give in illness: beef tea, chicken broth, sometimes wine,' he said.

'I see,' said Sörensen. 'And how did you go about administering these nutrients?'

'By mouth.'

'By mouth. I see.' Sörensen was bobbing up and down on the spot. He looked excited.

'And, Mr Dance,' he went on, 'what other forms of physical contact did you have—'

'Objection,' said the magistrate.

'Very well,' Sörensen said. 'Mr Dance, was a Mr Petter Dahlstrom known to you?'

Carl seemed to consider the name for a moment. 'Yes, he was. He was the husband of Mrs Dahlstrom.' His voice sounded perfectly bland. 'But then it appears that he abandoned her.'

'Abandoned? Can you explain what you mean by this?'

'He abandoned her in her illness; he left Stockholm to seek employment elsewhere, at a time when his wife and her family most needed his support,' said Carl. He sounded calm and reasonable. 'It caused his wife much distress. A husband's duty is to stand by his wife through thick and thin.'

'So you feel that Mr Dahlstrom had wronged his wife?'

'Yes.'

'I see,' said Sörensen. 'So it's fair to say that you disliked Mr Dahlstrom? That your relations with him were not good.'

Carl shrugged. 'I didn't know him well enough to be said to have relations with him.'

'Yet you got into an altercation with him on one occasion, I believe, at his residence?'

'No,' said Carl. Then he shut his mouth like a trap and folded his arms.

'So you deny that you—'

'Objection,' said the magistrate. 'This line of questioning has no bearing on the matter at hand.'

Nils Persson got up next. Strid asked him a lot of things about his work with Carl, all the technical details about voltages and wattages and ampages, and the magistrate appeared quite interested in these particulars.

'Mr Persson, how would you describe Mr Dance?' asked Strid. 'As a man?'

Nils looked over at Carl. 'Carl?' he said. 'I would describe him primarily as a man of science, a leader in his field, an innovative and even visionary medical practitioner.'

'Thank you, Mr Persson. A man of science, you say,' said Strid.

The magistrate was nodding his round little head. 'A man of science,' he repeated. 'Very good.'

Then it was my turn. It was now so hot in the room that I couldn't breathe easily. *Carl is a good husband. Carl is a hardworking man*, I recited in my head as I made my way to the stand. My body felt far away from me, numb and foreign, of an indeterminate size.

All those people's faces were watching me, still as anything, as though they weren't people at all, but paintings—a great mural of pale faces and bodies that covered the walls all the way up to the ceiling. I saw the face of Mrs Dance's sister, raw with tears. Beside her sat her father, his expression stony. On her other side, dressed all in black and holding her hand was her mother, who had tears running freely down her pallid cheeks. I saw Harald's face, and next to him Christine, both of them nodding encouragingly.

Strid asked me to describe Carl. *Carl is a good husband. Carl is a hardworking man.* I reached into my handbag and touched the envelope.

'Carl is a hardworking man,' I said. I was an even worse actor than Carl. A droplet of sweat inched down the side of my face.

'He is intelligent, and he is disciplined. He is meticulous, when he chooses to be.'

'Thank you, Mrs Dance. And would you say your husband is an honourable man? Might you tell us about an instance when he behaved honourably?' He smiled at me and the light bounced off his even white teeth.

The magistrate was watching me with raised eyebrows, his thin lips pinched and expectant. I looked at Carl. He was busy examining a button on his jacket. God knows, I wanted to be free of that man, and earlier that morning I'd have told you I was prepared to do anything to get that freedom. But sitting in that court in front of the Dahlstroms, and all those judicial men, and the magistrate who had been so impressed by Carl's scientific credentials, the thought of chiming in with the chorus about how wonderful Carl was, how clever, how visionary, all the while knowing what he had done to Mrs Dahlstrom, and what he'd done to me over the years, was more than I could stand. I saw in that moment that if I chose to speak up for Carl then I wouldn't belong to myself anymore. I would be giving a part of myself away.

'Mr Strid,' I said. I looked him in the eye. 'I'm sorry, but I don't believe I can honestly describe him as honourable.'

'Ah, Mrs Dance, surely you could think of an example, from your personal life, perhaps?'

'In actual fact, Mr Strid, and perhaps I'm a poor choice as a character witness, but I don't believe I can.'

I glanced up at the public gallery and caught sight of Christine and Ulf's outraged scowls.

'Mrs Dance—'

'Although I am Carl's wife, and have spent many years with him, if I am to speak truthfully I am bound to say that I doubt I know very much about him at all. And what I do know would not serve to illustrate an honourable strength of character.'

'In that case, Mrs Dance, that will be all. Please take your seat.'

I felt Carl's eyes on me throughout the rest of the proceedings.

7.

IN THE MORNING I had the newspapers sent to my room. Carl's picture was on the front cover of every one. Seeing his image in print like that made him seem very foreign to me—he finally appeared as the stranger he'd always been. The *Aftonbladet*'s half-page photograph of Carl's face was taken at the hearing, with his hair all wild and the light glinting off his spectacles so that he looked completely deranged. DOCTOR SOUGHT TO BRING HIS DEAD LOVER BACK FROM BEYOND THE GRAVE ran the headline, with 'Eccentric doctor "Frankenstein" returned to jail' underneath. *Dagens Nyheter* had a more respectable photograph with the headline DANCE RETURNED TO JAIL: MAGISTRATE DEFERS DECISION.

Svenska Dagbladet had three pictures on the cover. The first two were side-by-side, one of Carl and one of Mrs Dahlstrom, with DEAD GIRL'S 'MAN OF SCIENCE' LOVER SEES NO WRONG IN BODY SNATCH. A short article underneath was headed MRS DANCE LEAVES HUSBAND IN THE LURCH, and below that was a photograph of Harald and me at Blanch's, Harald with his hand partly covering his face and his other hand thrust out in front of him, me standing on the other side of the laden table with my mouth open, shouting something. The caption read: 'Mrs Dance plots divorce in lunchtime tryst with mystery man'.

Stockholms-Tidningen had Scientist's Futile Love Gains Public Sympathy, and an article about the women who had thrown flowers to Carl. It seemed there was a whole group of them, not just those at the hearing. I remembered all the women in the Långholmen waiting room. One woman was quoted in the article saying, 'I wish my husband was as romantic as Dr Dance. Mrs Dance doesn't know how lucky she is.'

As I read the papers, any regrets I might have had about what I said at the hearing melted away. I knew I'd done the right thing. But it meant I'd have to find another way to secure a divorce, with or without Carl's agreement.

There were two things of note that I discovered from the newspapers. First, that there would be what one of them called a 'sanity hearing' in the magistrate's office on Friday week, which would help decide whether or not Carl would be freed or placed in an asylum. And the second thing was that the inquest into Petter Dahlstrom's death was to be reopened.

Then I was called to the telephone downstairs, and it was Carl.

'Doris, I need to see you,' he said. His voice was flat and weary, not at all what I would have expected after my testimony yesterday. Usually, Carl is a man with a temper when he doesn't get his own way. 'Please. Please come,' he said.

I was curious as to this sudden difference in him. I took the divorce papers with me, on the off-chance that he had changed his mind.

He was waiting at the same table as on my previous visits. He stood up when I came in.

'Doris,' he said. He held out his hands towards me. 'Thank you for coming.'

I sat down and waited for him to begin raging at me.

'Thank you for being at the hearing yesterday,' he said. 'I know it was difficult for you.'

This behaviour was a little disconcerting. 'Yes, it was,' I said. 'And I realise I didn't keep my end of the bargain.' I stopped myself from apologising.

He shrugged. 'I understand why,' he said. 'Doris, I know I haven't been a good husband to you. I treated you badly over the years, and I'm sorry.'

He had said this before, of course. I waited for him to go on.

'I know that just saying sorry isn't enough, and I know it will take a lot of work on my part to rebuild your trust in me. I want you to know that that is what I intend to do when I get out of here.'

He was sitting straight-backed in his chair, and made no move to try to touch me.

'Thank you, Carl,' I said. 'But I have had no change of heart.'

He nodded. 'I understand,' he said again. His voice was soft and downcast. 'Perhaps, given time . . .'

I admit that he looked pitiful to me, grubby and creased, shrunken, and probably terrified about the verdict. And it was so cold in that place, and he had none of the comforts of home. But he was the one who had put himself in this situation.

'No, Carl,' I said. 'I won't change my mind. And you shouldn't hope that I will.'

'You sound so cold, Doris,' he said. 'You never used to be like this.' His eyes were on mine, imploring, trying to weaken me. I didn't look away. My hands gripped tight onto the handle of my bag.

'Carl, I mean you no ill will,' I said. 'But my feelings remain the same. I simply wish to resolve this situation as soon as possible.'

'To resolve it,' he said. 'Hmm. I see.'

I kept silent.

'Well, can I at least ask you for one favour? To do one small thing for me?'

'I don't see that I should—'

'Please, Doris?'

He took something from his pocket. It was an envelope. He laid it on the table and pushed it towards me. 'Would you be so good as to post this for me. Will you do this for me?'

'What is it?'

'Some technical things, for work. But it's confidential, and I don't trust the guards here to do it.'

I wondered why he didn't ask his lawyer to post it. I picked up the letter. It was addressed to G. Fredelius, at an address in Södermalm. I knew that name.

'Of course I will.'

I put the letter in my bag.

'Thanks Doris. I know I can rely on you.'

As soon as I was out of the prison gate I examined the envelope. It was sealed. I tugged gently at the closed flap with my finger.

When I got back to the hotel, there were two more envelopes waiting for me, a courier's and a telegram. The telegram was from

Lotta, my elder sister: DEAR DODO YOU MUST STOP THIS NONSENSE AND RETURN TO CARL AT ONCE. THINK OF YOUR WIFELY DUTY.

She must have seen that photo of Harald and me in *Svenska Dagbladet*. Lotta never felt shy about telling me what she thought I was doing wrong in my life. I hadn't mentioned the divorce to her, I hadn't really mentioned it to anyone except Harald. I didn't have anyone else to mention it to.

I opened the courier's envelope. It was from the police—the keys to the apartment. There were five keys on the keyring, and a green and white tag advertising Lloyds Medical Supplies. The apartment used to have only three keys—Carl must have had extra locks installed. The keys were heavy in my hand. I had the sudden impulse to go to the apartment. After hearing all those stories in court about what had happened there, I wanted to have a look at the place for myself, besides, it was my home.

It was another glorious day, so I decided to walk. The reporters seemed to have departed as suddenly as they had appeared, like locusts. In the streets that day there was a real holiday feeling in the air; the sun sparkled off everything, and there were little pots of purple and pink petunias lining the rail of the bridge, and everywhere people were smiling and chatting, squinting a little in the hard sunlight. All the way along Strandvägen, tourists were strolling, children were eating ice-creams, and the pleasure boats were out, their flags and sails flying. I knew I was no longer young, but the thought of being there in Stockholm, and being Doris Ekman again, which one day I knew I would be, filled me with optimism. There was so much ahead of me still, so much to look forward to. And perhaps I wouldn't remain Doris Ekman for the rest of my life either. I smiled to myself as I walked.

As I passed the newsagent in Gamla Stan, I happened to glance at the headline board outside: HUNDREDS OF CURIOUS VISITORS GATHER AT BIER OF DANCE'S LOVER. That was a story I hadn't yet read. I went in and bought a copy of the paper.

The fantastic tale of a man so much in love that he tried to reverse death itself so he could be with his beloved has captured the hearts and minds of our nation.

The body of Mrs Lina Dahlstrom (twenty) was discovered over Midsummer in Dr Carl Dance's Östermalm apartment, where he had been keeping it for several months, along with various machines and devices designed by Dance to bring his lover back to life. Dance faced a hearing on Monday, with the magistrate's ruling remaining undecided.

Mrs Dahlstrom's body was put on display at a memorial service yesterday at the Norra Begravningsplatsen Cemetery Chapel, and already hundreds of curious visitors have taken the opportunity to catch a glimpse of the famous woman.

'She looks just like she did when she was alive,' an unnamed family friend of Mrs Dahlstrom's is reported as saying.

The eccentric Dr Dance, scientist and inventor, may be an alleged body-snatcher, but the public is overwhelmingly on his side: 'He only did it out of love' is the resounding opinion of Swedes everywhere.

But not everyone shares this view. Greta Fredelius, the sister of Mrs Dahlstrom, who organised the viewing, told reporters: 'I want the public to see what this criminal did to my sister in the name of science, and in the name of so-called love.'

But nevertheless, Dance is being hailed as the romantic hero of the age by the female population of the country. 'I wish my husband was more like Dr Dance,' more than one lady at the memorial told reporters.

Mrs Dahlstrom's body is open to public viewing until this Sunday evening.

It certainly seemed a strange thing for a body to be put on public display—it sounded positively medieval to me. All the same, I have to admit that I was a little curious. But the idea of queueing up with a whole lot of strangers to goggle at Mrs Dahlstrom's body, after all that she had been though, was too unsavoury to seriously consider.

By the time I reached the end of Gamla Stan, I was getting tired. What had started off as a beautiful day had become hot and muggy. I was sticky with half-dried sweat, and I could feel a blister forming on my right heel. There was a number 37 streetcar up ahead and I ran to catch it. The 37 wouldn't take me direct to Jungfrugatan, but at least I'd have a chance to catch my breath out of the sun.

When we passed over Strandvägen I realised the route would take me past Norra Begravningsplatsen cemetery, and while it felt wrong to actually go in, I was most intrigued about what kind of people would. My carriage was almost empty, but there was one spinsterish-looking woman with wire glasses and a prim bun sitting at the other end who seemed just the type. I was so busy thinking about the memorial that I missed my stop—two stops in fact. I decided to stay on the streetcar until we got to the chapel, just to see it from the window, even though it would take me out of my way.

Sure enough, I had been right about the spinsterish woman; as we slowed down for the chapel stop, she gathered her string bag and got off the streetcar. Without giving it a thought, I followed her.

When I entered the cemetery, I was surprised to see not only a long queue of people waiting to enter the chapel, but also that a kind of marketplace had sprung up outside. There were several flower stalls, a farmer selling strawberries, and a balloon man. It was like a carnival. Children ran screeching around the waiting crowd and the women—it was mostly women—chatted and laughed with each other.

I was standing near the end of the queue, not actually in it, but I found myself wedged in the crush steadily filing towards the chapel doors. I could have struggled out, but instead I allowed my curiosity to get the better of me and let myself be carried along by the crowd.

The chapel was decorated with bunches of orange blossom, and the summer scent filled the air. At first all I could see were the backs of people's heads as they craned to get a look at the body. Everyone was silent; the only sound was of people's excited breathing and their feet on the flagstones. We shuffled forward. I could see the drapes on the foot end of the bier, then the whole body came into view.

It was lying not in a coffin, but directly on the bier, surrounded by white roses and lilies, but the funny thing was it didn't even look like a human body. The face, which was the only exposed skin, seemed to be a mask made of wax with the features painted on, badly; the hair was a dark mop sitting askew. The hands were in white gloves and the rest of the body was wrapped in a pale cream silk. I noticed how small she was—tiny, the size of a child. She must have shrunk after her death.

I shuffled past with everyone and then I was out in the sunshine again. The day was so bright that for a moment I was blinded. I stumbled coming down the steps and dropped my bag. A man bent to retrieve it for me.

'Mrs Dance?' he said.

I froze. The last thing I wanted was for someone to recognise me. My vision cleared and I realised it was a man who lived in our building, but whom I didn't know personally. I took my bag from him and hurried away with my head bent low and my heart hammering. I spotted a streetcar coming down Uppsalavägen as soon I was out the cemetery gate. I got on.

The carriage was quite full but I found a seat near the window, and I sat staring out. I couldn't get the image of the body out of my mind. It was so tiny, and so utterly unlike how Mrs Dahlstrom had been in real life—so utterly unlike any human. When I thought of Carl mistaking that waxen doll for a living woman I got an uneasy feeling. I had lived for years with the man who had done that to her. A prickling sensation started at the back of my head.

I heard someone mention Carl's name. It was a woman with tight straw-coloured curls and crimson lipstick sitting halfway down the carriage. She was saying in a loud voice to her friends, 'Well, I still say it's romantic. I can't get my Paul to cook even a single meal for me, and I'm alive!'

A pink-faced woman in a cloche sitting beside her tittered.

'Bit unhygienic, though, wouldn't you say?' asked a dark-haired man opposite her. He took a puff from his cigarette. 'Think of all the diseases he might've picked up.' He nudged the man sitting beside him, who smiled and then looked down at his feet.

'And he is married, you know,' the pink-faced woman said in a squeaky voice. 'I'm sure Mrs Dance doesn't think it's all that romantic.'

She was right about that.

'Well, all I can say is,' said the lipsticked woman, 'the wife mustn't've been taking good enough care of him in the first place. I ought to get in touch with her and tell her to send him my way. I'll show him some real love. If he ever gets out of prison, that is.'

'I don't think he will get out,' said the dark-haired man. 'Did you hear about that murder? Apparently it looks like someone bumped off the sweetheart's hubby . . . I wonder who?'

'Oh no! Not Carl!' The lipsticked woman sounded as offended as if she herself had been accused of murder. 'All that's just a beat-up from the girl's family. I'd bet on it. Carl is most certainly not a killer. He's every bit a gentleman.'

'I'm with you,' said a third woman with bobbed dark hair, who was standing in the aisle. 'I think he's simply a dreamboat! So clever. Imagine, a man inventing things to bring you back from the dead. It's just like a fairy story!'

It certainly wasn't just like a fairy story to me, it was more like a horror story.

The gossiping group got off at the next stop and I remained staring out the window at the city sliding past. I was starting to feel very strange—my head felt hollow, and my mind had gone quite blank. I couldn't think about anything at all, it was as if I'd forgotten all about the memorial, the apartment, everything.

If you'd spoken to me I probably wouldn't even have been able to tell you my own name.

I got off the streetcar with no idea where I was, and found myself walking down a road I didn't recognise. I passed a row of shops: a baker, a florist, a shoe shop. I had an odd sensation of being separated from my surroundings, of being behind glass, as I had been when looking out of the streetcar window, seeing everything drift past me: untouchable, unreachable. My head felt thick, foggy, as though packed with cotton. I stopped outside a butcher's shop. My reflection in the glass was superimposed on the meat laid out on trays. I was hypnotised by the display—the lurid red falukorv, Carl's favourite; the pale pork sausages, the slabs of ox tongue, the lamb cutlets, and ground beef seeping blood. My stomach clenched in a violent spasm that doubled me over. I leaned one hand on the window to steady myself, and my body curled in on itself as I retched and then spat on the ground. When I stood upright again I was dizzy, but after my vision cleared I could see the surprised faces of customers in the shop staring out at me. I staggered away.

After that I seemed to lose control of my body. I was shaking all over so that my teeth clattered against each other, and it was almost impossible to direct my legs; they seemed to belong to another person. I found I was on a main road, lurching along with no clue where I was going, when I saw a taxi. I got in, mumbled the address of the apartment, then wound down the window and took gasps of moving air. The taxi driver no doubt took me for a dipsomaniac.

I was feeling a little better by the time I reached Jungfrugatan, but my legs were still watery. This time the apartment door opened without issue. Inside it was dark, I could hardly see a thing, and there was a strange smell: sweetish and musty. I opened the curtains and windows of the downstairs rooms and the first thing I saw was that two of the palms and a lily plant had died; now they were nothing but withered sticks in their dried-up pots. When I turned to look at the room in the daylight I got rather a shock. Everything was covered in thick dust and even cobwebs, as though the apartment had been empty for months. There were plates, some with food on them still, on every surface, and books and papers all over the sofa and floor.

I went into the kitchen. The sink was full of unwashed dishes, which rose in stacks from the dirty water and were covered in a layer of rancid grease. The kitchen bench was littered with scraps of rotting food, some with mould growing on them. Fat bluebottle flies flew in circuits and waddled over the debris.

I went to the telephone and put a call through to Harald.

The sound of his deep voice calmed me instantly. He always gave me the feeling that things were going to be alright.

'Harald . . . I went to see Carl, and then, well, I think I've had a bit of a turn.' I didn't want to tell him about Mrs Dahlstrom's body over the phone.

'Sorry to hear that. Are you alright, old girl?'

'I'm feeling a bit better, but might you be able to meet me down here rather than over your way?'

'Oh, Doris. I'd love to, but I'm on my way out for lunch.'

'I thought we had plans to meet this afternoon,' I said.

'Blast! You're right. I'm awfully sorry, it went right out of my head. The thing is, I've promised to take Miss Brun for a spin in the old *Racy Lady* right after lunch.'

That was the name of Harald's speedboat. I pictured Miss Brun with her long hair flying back from her head as she and Harald zoomed through the archipelago.

'She's already on her way, so it's an appointment I must keep,' he said. 'Maybe a little later in the evening? Or what about tomorrow?'

I rang off.

My head was throbbing, and I sat down for a moment in the kitchen. I opened my handbag for my handkerchief and caught sight of Carl's letter to Greta Fredelius. I'd forgotten all about it. I filled the kettle and put it on the fire. As I waited for it to boil I pinched the letter between finger and thumb—it was quite fat. The kettle was taking too long. I ripped open the envelope, not at all carefully, leaving a messy tear right across the front and through the address.

Dear Miss Fredelius,

I know Lina was your sister, but she was also my patient, and she was very dear to me. I took the very best care I could of her, when she was alive and after she died. I know you loved your sister, but I love her too, more than you might . . .

The letter went on for pages and pages. I only glanced through the rest of them.

. . . I promised to care for her and protect her . . . I have heard from my lawyer that her body is not to be returned to me, but to be dismembered and buried in secret places . . . Please, I beg of you not to do this. Please return her to me . . .

I scrunched the pages into a tight ball and threw it into the kitchen sink, with all the filthy dishes. My mouth was dry. I filled a glass of water and took a mouthful but I no longer knew how to swallow. I spat it out into the sink, all over the letter. My head was throbbing harder and a flashing light appeared in the corner of my vision—a sure sign that a migraine was coming.

I always kept some tablets in my bedside cabinet. On the stairs, I noticed that musty smell again, stronger now, and when I reached the landing I saw that the door to Carl's treatment room was ajar. A high-pitched humming sound came from within. I opened the door and the smell wafted out; it was suffocating. I turned on the light. There were two beds, one very high and narrow, one a kind of camp bed on the floor. The window was covered with the old blanket we used to take on picnics, and the place was crammed with far more kinds of equipment and machines than I remembered. Everything was in disarray. Bottles and boxes lay scattered over the floor and the beds were unmade. The floor was covered in blobs of white mud and pieces of torn-up leaves and flowers. In one corner was what looked to be a pile of plaster limbs. The humming sound I'd heard was flies—they were buzzing against the window and in the air all around me, and they crawled over every surface.

The high bed must have been where Carl had kept the corpse, the very same as what I had just seen in the chapel. I took a step forward. The sheets trailed down onto the floor. Automatically I bent down to straighten them, and saw that they were my own sheets, from the trousseau that I'd put together all those years ago. I remembered sitting with Mother and looking through the catalogue, both of us pointing out these sheets, I remembered her hand holding the pen as she wrote out the mail order.

'I always knew you'd make a good marriage,' she said, and she took both of my hands in hers. 'But to be marrying a man like Carl, so elegant, so American, I never dared to dream of such a thing.' My mother had died shortly after our wedding, and long before I got to know what Carl was really like.

I put the sheets on the bed. There was another piece of fabric lying on the floor and I picked it up. It was silky to the touch, an evening dress, but not mine. I held it up in front of me. It was beautiful, made for a woman far slimmer, far younger than me.

As I stood there with the dress in my hand, I seemed to fly out from my body. From across the room I saw myself standing by the bed, my face as pale as the silk fabric. I let out an ungodly roar. I tried to tear the dress apart and when I couldn't, I threw it across the room. Clouds of flies, disturbed by the commotion, flew into my face. I pulled the sheets from the bed and flung them across the room too. They hung in the air for a moment, like a fishing net cast over the sea, and then I ran to the window and tore down the blanket that covered it. Still screaming, I went to the shelves lining the walls and started throwing things onto the floor—boxes, books, jars, bottles—some of which broke into pieces when they landed.

The funny thing was, as I saw myself behave in this manner I remained completely disconnected from the scene, and even remarked to myself, 'Well, she's really lost control now,' as if I had nothing to do with the woman I was watching. Presently I became aware of a shrill noise that could be heard under the screaming.

The screaming stopped and I recognised the other sound as the doorbell. I saw myself go downstairs and open the door, but there was no one there.

I returned to the hotel, packed my bags, and caught the train back to Ystad.

8.

COOKING HAS ALWAYS been a comfort for me. My mother taught me how to cook when I was just a little thing—apple pancakes, cinnamon bread, semolina pudding. We used to collect eggs and make fresh omelettes, with chives from the garden. Even after I was married and we had Anna to cook for us, I never lost the desire for it. Sometimes, when Carl was out, I would sit in the kitchen with Anna while she cooked and watch her. The best thing about being in Ystad was that it was seemly for me to cook for myself once more. Meatballs, herb potatoes, stewed fruits, I got to know all these old recipes again. Making them helped me settle into my strange new life more than anything else did.

I was only able to stay at Lotta's house for two weeks before the situation became unbearable. There wasn't any particular incident, but every day it was made clear to me that I wasn't welcome. Lotta is seven years older than me and even though we were both past fifty, she was as proprietorial as when we were girls. She'd loved

Carl from the very beginning, and was even more bewitched by his foreign ways than I had been.

Lotta didn't understand how I could leave Carl and my life in Stockholm—the apartment, our friends—behind me, and asked me constantly when I was planning to go back. She left train timetables lying around, and never failed to point out at any opportunity all the things she liked about Carl.

The date of the sanity hearing came and went, and I received a telegram from Carl saying he had been released, that he missed me and wanted to know when I was coming home. I didn't reply. Thereafter he telephoned Lotta's house most days, and she insisted on calling me to the telephone, though I'd told her I didn't want to speak with him. Harald telephoned too, at first often and then less frequently. I never returned his calls. A distance had grown between us, vaster than the miles that separated him from me. After a while he stopped telephoning at all.

When I could no longer bear it at Lotta's, I rented a couple of rooms in a boarding house off the main square. The place was tiny. There was a living room with a grubby floral sofa, an easy chair, a table with uneven legs and two Biedermeier chairs. Against one wall was a kitchen area—two gas rings, an icebox and a sink. The bedroom had space only for a bed and a clothes rail behind a curtain. The bathroom I shared with the other lodgers. Both of my rooms were poky and dark, and a murky, pond-like smell drifted up from the kitchen sink. I tried to remember that I wouldn't be there forever.

The days felt endless, each one the same as the last. I filled the hours with shopping and cooking and waiting for the release of the newspapers. I read every edition of *Svenska Dagbladet* and *Dagens Nyheter* to follow the process of the inquest, which I'd learned might take months. If it was found that Carl had been involved in Petter Dahlstrom's death, I could apply for a divorce on my own, though this could take some time, up to a year perhaps. If Carl was found to be innocent, my situation would be more complicated. It was at that time still difficult to divorce a man who refused his consent.

Sometimes the walls of my rented rooms oppressed me so much I'd rush out to walk the streets of the town, or along the sandy paths that ran by the seashore. The country around Ystad is flat and wide, with long horizons, and a light that seems to come not from the sun, but up from the earth and the sea. The ocean, the heather, the birds and the sky are all in soft shades of grey. I would walk for hours, listening to the suck and sigh of the pearl-coloured sea, but in Ystad, walking failed to calm me. I was stalked by a foreboding, that at times enveloped me in a poisonous fog. My limbs would move in an unsteady rhythm and my heart would pound with a sick-making relentlessness, getting in the way of my breathing. When the nervousness subsided, there remained a flatness within me, a deadness. I felt like a machine, automatically running along fixed circuits. My body was heavy and slack.

I went from one day to the next blindly, dragging myself around, sleeping and waking and sleeping again. Walking. I could hardly think about anything at all, beyond seeing out the day. Sometimes I couldn't remember why I'd left Stockholm in the first place.

Summer had long ended and the trees had lost their leaves. Lotta softened; I think she understood that there was no going back for me. She stopped enumerating Carl's good points, and lecturing me about my wifely duties, and started taking me out gathering berries and mushrooms. She invited me to concerts, to plays, and did her best to involve me in the life of the town. She even arranged a job for me, as a kindergarten teacher, remembering that I had many years ago, back in Råsa, dreamed of becoming a teacher. As well as filling the days, it gave me a small income. As Lotta pointed out, when I was finally free of Carl I would need to earn something of my own, even considering any money that might be settled on me in the divorce agreement.

Afternoons at the kindergarten—when the children had eaten their apple slices, finished listening to a Brothers Grimm story and were taking their afternoon naps—were the only quiet moments I got to myself during workdays. I used the time to read the newspapers. Most days there was no report on the inquest, and on the days there was, it would be only a small detail. One afternoon at the tired end of winter, when the sun had already set and the snow was falling, I was leafing through that day's *Dagens Nyheter* when I saw Carl's face printed there on the page.

Coroner Delivers Open Verdict on Dahlstrom's Death

The coroner has delivered an open finding at the inquest into the death of Petter Dahlstrom, husband of the so-called 'corpse bride', Mrs Lina Dahlstrom. The inquest was unable to determine whether the death occurred from poisoning or natural causes.

Dahlstrom was found dead at a property near Sundsvall in October 1930. The initial cause of death was given as a heart attack, but a murder investigation was launched the following May after a pathologist's report stated that the death had been caused by poisoning.

Three subsequent pathologists' reports found that poisoning was not the cause of death, and that Dahlstrom had suffered from a number of undiagnosed health problems, including an enlarged heart, which may have contributed to his death.

There was also dispute among the pathologists over toxicology tests, which initially showed no evidence of poisoning, but contained various irregularities.

The judge was unable to determine the cause of death and refused to rule out poisoning.

Dahlstrom's late wife, Mrs Lina Dahlstrom, was at the centre of a controversial case last August involving the eccentric scientist Carl Dance.

I had expected to have some kind of reaction on finding out this news, but I felt nothing. Not trepidation over the complication to divorce proceedings, nor relief that Carl turned out not to be a murderer. It was as if I were reading an article about people I had never met and didn't much care about one way or the other. I turned the page and skimmed a story on the figure skaters Andrée and Pierre Brunet winning a gold medal at the Olympics.

When I came home, Lotta was waiting for me in the hall; she had torn the article from the paper and was waving it at me like a flag. Her round face shone with elation.

'He's innocent, did you see?'

We went upstairs and I made tea. The tea set was mismatched and each cup cracked. They had come with the rooms. There was no milk jug and I hadn't made any biscuits.

Lotta couldn't stop talking about Carl. 'What did I tell you, Dodo! I always knew he was innocent. He might be eccentric, that much was clear all along, but he's not a killer. Not a chance!'

'Yes,' I said, 'I suppose it is a bit of a relief.' Sitting opposite Lotta I was struck by how very much alike we looked; everyone could always tell we were sisters. Just as our mother had been, we were tall, dark-haired, with wide hips and large hands and feet—too substantial for the fashion of the day. But there the similarity ended.

'And?' she said. 'What are you going to do now? Go back to Stockholm?'

I poured the tea.

'I don't know, Lotta. I haven't really had a chance to think about it.'

'Haven't thought about it? Oh, Dodo, can't you see this is no life for you? A life of poky rented rooms and looking after other people's children?'

I felt tears in my eyes. It was true that this was not what I'd been imagining in the jubilant visions of freedom I'd had in Stockholm the previous summer. I'd pictured quite a different kind of life.

'Dodo, you ought to put all this divorce nonsense behind you. Now that Carl is in the clear, perhaps it's time you and he set your differences aside. Go back to Stockholm. You'll see—things have a way of working out better than you think they will.'

We drank our tea in silence. When I was seeing Lotta out, she said, 'Oh, I almost forgot,' and reached into her handbag and took out an envelope. 'This came for you yesterday.'

It was a letter from Harald. I hadn't heard from him in months.

The letter started off in a perfectly ordinary way, as if we had been in regular correspondence. He wrote about a hiking weekend he'd been on, and the wildlife he'd seen. Harald is a great naturalist and knows all the different plants and their properties and their botanical names, and he can tell birds from their call. Then it went on:

> *I hope you'll come to Stockholm again soon. I do miss having you around. Also, I have some rather exciting news. It's still all a bit hush-hush but I know it'll be safe with you. I've been seeing a lot of Miss Brun (Albertine: you remember her. I think you met her once), and we're going to be married. I can hardly believe my luck, she's such a terrific girl, so bright and full of energy . . .*

Of course I remembered Miss Albertine Brun.

9.

THE FOLLOWING WEEK I packed my overnight bag and got on the 9.10 am train to Stockholm, but not because I was following Lotta's advice. I had consulted with a lawyer, who had advised one last effort to discuss the divorce with Carl before I launched proceedings on my own. I had the form, now dog-eared and furry, in my handbag, along with a whole lot of other paperwork in case Carl still didn't agree. When I'd spoken to him on the telephone he was just as contrite and polite as when I'd last seen him. He told me to come to the apartment at five o'clock the next Wednesday.

When I got out at Central Station the city looked very different to when I had left. Dirty snow lined the streets and people shuffled along, bundled in hats and overcoats, their faces set against the icy wind. I got on the 91 bus to Östermalm and watched the familiar streets and buildings pass. The closer I got to Jungfrugatan, the more nervous I started to feel. I wished that I'd insisted on meeting somewhere else.

From the outside, our apartment building looked the same as it used to, as if nothing terrible had ever happened there. I was fifteen minutes early, but I thought I would wait for Carl in the apartment if he wasn't yet home from work—it was still my apartment after all. I went into the building and up the stairs and everything was still exactly like it had always been: the noticeboard in the downstairs hall, the burgundy carpet in the middle of the staircase, the rickety lift making its same clanking racket. It felt like home.

But when I got to our door, I found I couldn't unlock it. Again. This time the key turned in the lock with no trouble, but the door seemed to be bolted on the other side. I pressed the bell and heard it ring, but no one answered. I thought I could hear voices inside. I rang the bell again and knocked and called, 'Carl!' Still nothing. Then I noticed a sign beside the door:

DANCE MUSEUM
Tours: on the hour, every hour, from noon to five o'clock,
Wednesday to Saturday.

I had no idea what to make of that. I decided to go for a walk until the fifteen minutes were up. When I went downstairs I could see that it had begun to snow, but I wrapped my scarf tighter and went out regardless. I had really chosen the wrong shoes, I was wearing my two-tone Oxfords with the leather fringe below the lace. I should have worn my grey boots. It made me quite distressed to look at my poor Oxfords making their way along the wet footpath, getting stained from the snow. I made it only as far as the end of the block before turning back.

A small crowd was waiting on the landing: a gentleman and five or six ladies. I tapped one of the ladies on the shoulder.

'Excuse me, are you waiting for Dr Dance?'

'Oh no! We're here for the tour. We're up from Malmö for the week and our friend said it was quite the thing.'

I hung back, not wanting to be seen as part of the group. Five o'clock came and the apartment door opened to reveal another group, putting on their coats and retrieving their umbrellas. They trooped out and the group outside started going in. I followed, and didn't see Carl until I was right inside the hall. He was standing in the living room talking to a small, dark-haired man. He didn't seem to see me.

Everyone else was taking off their coats and scarves so I did too, and then we all stood around awkwardly. After a few minutes Carl shook the hand of the man and came to greet us.

'Welcome!' he said, spreading out his hands. I was at the back of the group, where he didn't notice me. 'Welcome to Dr Dance's Museum.'

He coughed, turned away and led us into the living room. As we shuffled our way around the room, listening to him explaining every object in his exhibition, I wished I'd never come. The apartment was completely changed. The sofa, the table and chairs, the vases and paintings and houseplants were all gone. Along the walls were framed photographs and diagrams and plans, with little plaques beside them. Carl's machines stood in one corner, polished and shining, and in another corner a plaster cast of a body hung from the ceiling; it was held together by wires like a ghostly marionette. In the middle of the room was a bed, upon which lay a shrouded figure surrounded by flowers, just like at the memorial. My stomach lurched at the sight.

Carl looked terribly old, and when he spoke his breath rasped in his chest; he had to keep stopping to cough into his handkerchief. He had gone to the trouble of putting a carnation in his buttonhole, but it was wilted and drooped to one side. We trailed from exhibit to exhibit, with Carl talking the whole time. A good twenty minutes passed and Carl still hadn't seen me. Once he seemed to look directly at me, but his face was quite blank.

We were going so slowly, and Carl was talking on and on—he never could stop once you got him started on a subject—that my legs began to ache. Carl explained all the workings of his equipment—only the gentleman in the group was interested in that—and he read out every one of the articles he had framed on the walls. At last the tour was over and Carl picked up a little box and told us that the fee was two kronor. Two whole kronor! To my surprise, everyone got out their purses and not a single person complained about the expense.

Carl went around the group with the box and everyone put in their money. When he reached me he still had that bland expression on his face. He wasn't even looking at me, but at the air above my head.

'Carl,' I said. 'Stop this nonsense. It's me.'

'Oh, Doris,' he said, 'I didn't see you there. I'm so sorry. I completely forgot it was today you were coming.'

Carl ushered everyone down the hall and out of the apartment.

'What in god's name is all this?' I asked when we were alone.

'You like it?' He swept his arm around the room. 'It took me months to put it all together, and as you can see I've been getting quite a good flow of visitors. A nice little earner. I wanted you to see it in action.'

315

I didn't know what to say.

'Coffee?' he asked.

He led me into the kitchen, where there were two small stools, the only seats in the whole lower floor. I watched him shuttle slowly about with cups and tins, stopping now and then to press his fist into his chest and cough into his handkerchief.

'Carl, I don't understand any of this. What's going on?'

'It's one of a few projects I have on the boil. The fact is I'm a little hard up just now. I'm looking in to a few sidelines. One of my ventures is cosmetics, creams and whatnot for women's faces. You've got no idea how much ladies are willing to pay for a fancy pot of some concoction. But that one's still in the development stage. Then the other . . .'

He droned on. Carl had always been a great one for making plans. And when he got going it was impossible to get a word in.

'Carl,' I interrupted. 'Carl!' I wasn't there to discuss his business plans. He ignored me.

'. . . naturally I would never put the actual replica on display, oh no, I couldn't have all these people gawking. And I can see now that the job does need to be done by a professional, and in fact that fellow I was talking to when your group arrived—perhaps you saw him?—he's big in the toy business and he said he could help me out. It's just the one that I want, and it's got to be full-sized.' He was talking so much it was almost as if he was delirious with a fever.

'*Carl!* Stop!'

He did stop then and looked at me, as if he'd only just realised that I was there. I reached into my handbag and took out the tattered envelope.

'I came here to today to discuss our future.'

Carl doubled over and went into a fit of coughing that left him weak and wheezing. His face had turned a deep shade of purple.

'You don't sound at all well.'

'I'm fine . . . just fine.' He spat into his handkerchief. His breathing sounded like wind whistling down a chimney. 'I'm fighting fit.'

'Well then, let's get down to business,' I said. 'The fact is that whether you agree to it or not, I will divorce you. So you may as well just sign now.'

His eyes narrowed and he had a look on his face that I recognised.

'I think, Doris, you'll find that it does matter whether I agree or not.' He started coughing again. 'If you think . . . you can just blaze in here and start issuing orders . . .' He struggled to get the words out between coughs. 'And don't think . . . I don't know about you and . . . that, that . . . Mr Harald Blomkvist . . . gallivanting about . . .'

'Carl, please!' I said. He was fighting for breath, and his face was red and angry. His hands were shaking.

'Please calm down. We need to discuss this in a reasonable manner.'

He shot me a venomous look and stood up, breathing hard.

'Where are you going?' I asked.

'I have a business meeting.'

'What? Now? But we haven't even—'

'You'll hear from my lawyer.'

10.

A FEW HOURS later I got a telephone call at the hotel. It was Nils. Carl had been admitted to Serafen. He had collapsed in the middle of Central Station and his condition was apparently serious. It was lucky for him that I'd decided to stay in Stockholm for the night. Nils said that Carl desperately wanted to talk to me, so I went in to the hospital.

A doctor met me in the corridor, his face grave. 'Mrs Dance, I'm afraid the news isn't good,' he said. 'I'm sorry to inform you that your husband has tuberculosis. It's a very advanced case. I'm afraid there's nothing we can do.'

'How long does he have?'

'A matter of months, weeks perhaps.'

When I approached Carl's bedside, I thought at first that I'd got there too late. His body was so shrunken and thin under the hospital sheets, he appeared to be nothing but a heap of bones. But when I got closer I could hear the sound of his breath rattling in and out. He raised his hand when he saw me, and tried to speak.

'Shh,' I said.

He turned his face towards me and his eyes were wide and frightened. 'Doris . . . please . . . help me.' His voice drifted from his lips in a reedy whisper.

Seeing him lying there like that made me think of lambs in the springtime. If you're not from the country, you probably think that all lambs are sprightly bouncing things, full of life and energy, and it's true that most lambs are like that. But there are always one or two in every lambing season that aren't the pink and white animals you imagine. Perhaps they're orphans, or perhaps they get too cold, or are born with something wrong, but these lambs are thin and greyish, with watery eyes and dirty fleeces. On our farm, I had always been the one to take care of these pitiful creatures, even though Papa would tell me not to. I would wrap them in blankets and sit with them by the kitchen hearth, convinced that I could keep them alive by the force of my will. Most of the time it did no good and I'd wake to find the lamb just a lifeless bundle on the floor. I would cry for days afterwards, and be so upset that Papa would forbid me from taking in any more lambs. He said that to do so was prolonging the inevitable, and only served to increase their suffering. Carl was looking at me now with the same dulled eyes that those lambs had had: desperate, begging for help and comfort. I knew Carl wouldn't last for very long.

'It's alright, Carl,' I said. 'I'm here now. I'll take care of you.'

Carl was certainly telling the truth when he said he was hard up. All the money was gone; the apartment had been mortgaged, and where we used to have savings there were now only debts.

Carl had run up enormous legal fees during the trial, and that was on top of the fortune he'd already spent building those machines.

I had to sell the apartment. With what was left from the sale I managed to buy a small house on the outskirts of Luleå and I got a job working at the nursery school there. It was clear that I would have to be the one to earn our keep for the next little while.

And so I started a new life with Carl. It was nothing like our old life in Stockholm, and it was nothing like any kind of life I had ever pictured, or dreamed about. I had to work harder than I would have if I had stayed at my parents' farm. When I wasn't taking care of the children at the nursery school, I was taking care of Carl at home. He had become in many ways nothing more than a child. Very soon after we arrived in Luleå, about two months after his collapse, his decline began in earnest. He was so thin and weak that he could hardly speak properly anymore, and his mind began to suffer. He had obsessions and some very strange ideas—stranger than was usual for him, I mean. He talked about one money-making scheme after another, each one wilder than the last. It seemed that he had embarked on some kind of writing project, but I could never gather just what it was, and he was somehow involved with a toy manufacturer, at least as far as I could make out.

One day a letter arrived for him, with a German postmark. The sender was a Herr A. Kestner of Gräfenhain. Carl got very excited when I gave him the letter.

'He's done it!' he said, as he struggled to open the envelope. 'The bottle!'

At least that's what I think he said. I often had difficulty understanding what Carl was talking about in those days, his mind was that far gone and his speech had become much weakened.

'What bottle?' I asked. He was still struggling to tear open the envelope. 'Here, let me help you.'

I tried to take the letter from him, but he snatched it away and took it with him into his study.

When I went in to check on him I found him collapsed on the floor, clutching the opened letter. He was crying and I let him mumble away through his tears while I got him back into bed.

'The bottle . . . she's gone . . . nothing left now . . .' he kept saying, and then something that sounded like: 'He robbed me, the thief . . . that lying bastard . . .'

'Nobody's robbed you, Carl,' I told him. 'You're dreaming.' He became quite hysterical then and started howling and ranting. 'I just wanted her all to myself . . . now they can all see her, touch her . . . that bastard—'

'Now, now!'

It took me an age to get him settled—he was very agitated and wouldn't let go of that silly letter. He even insisted on taking it to bed with him.

'. . . Just let me die . . . please . . .'

Well, sometimes he did get a bit down in the mouth: it's quite common with people suffering from long illnesses. I gave him a double dose of sleeping-draught, which I did whenever he was being troublesome, and sat with him to make sure he quietened down.

When he dropped off I took the letter from his hand. I saw it wasn't a letter at all but a page clipped from a catalogue with an advertisement for dolls. I glanced down at the page, and you know, it was a funny thing, because one of the dolls looked just like Mrs Dahlstrom, and was even called 'The Sweetheart Lina Doll'. The more I looked at the doll, the more it resembled her. Underneath the picture it read: 26 inches of true Swedish beauty! Real life scale model! $1.98.

Who would have thought that a picture of a doll would have such an impact on him.

The next day I took the advertisement to the toyshop on Teatergränd street.

'You're in luck,' said the sales clerk, 'We have one left in stock. It's a very popular item.'

The doll really did look so much like Mrs Dahlstrom, even more in real life than in the catalogue picture. She had her dark hair done in waves and pinned back, and she was wearing a black-and-white spotted dress with a wide white Peter Pan collar, and on her feet she had little black pumps. She was much more like Mrs Dahlstrom than her own dead body had been. I paid cash and had it gift-wrapped.

When I got home Carl was still in bed. The sleeping-draught always lasted a long time. I told him that I had a surprise for him. While I waited for him to come downstairs, I put on some coffee and cut up the cinnamon cake I'd bought as a special treat. I set the table and put the wrapped-up doll at Carl's place. His eyes lit up when he saw the present waiting for him. He'd always loved surprises. We sat down and I poured out the coffee. Carl picked up the present.

'Do you need help unwrapping it?' I asked him, taking care to speak loudly and clearly.

He didn't reply, but picked up the box in his trembling hands and started to tear off the paper, strip by shaky strip.

'Oh, good work, Carl—I see you can manage very well on your own.'

I took a bite of cinnamon cake and watched him slowly unwrap the box. At last all the paper lay on the floor around his chair. He sat there squinting at the box, turning it this way and that and trying to read what it said on the back.

'See, Carl, a present for you,' I said loudly. 'Here, I'll help you open it.'

I reached over to undo the flap on the top of the box—they can be tricky with those sharp corners—but all of a sudden Carl gave a yell and lurched backwards so violently that he almost tipped over the chair he was sitting in. He flung the box away from him across the room as though it was on fire. It shot through the air and hit the wall opposite with quite a crash—I was rather surprised at Carl's strength. Then he stood up, gripping the tabletop to steady himself and saying, 'Oh . . . Oh . . . Oh . . .' over and over.

'Carl? Whatever's the matter?'

He was swaying as if he was about to keel over. I picked up the doll and brought it back to him. He inched his way back, away from me, as though I held a live viper in my hands.

'Carl, don't be scared—it's only a doll, you silly old thing!'

I gave him a gentle push back into his chair and set the doll on the table in front of him.

'You see,' I said, 'it's the doll you saw yesterday, remember? In the catalogue?' I gave him a pat on the shoulder. He had tears streaming down his face.

'That goddamned bastard . . .' Carl wheezed in his breathless whisper. 'All I ever wanted . . . was for her to be mine . . .' He slumped forward onto the table, his sobs wracking his whole body. The doll dropped to the floor. After that, Carl got very ill and he never recovered. He died the following week.

It took me a long time to sort through all of Carl's belongings. We'd left Stockholm in a rush, and I'd thrown a whole lot of his things into storage—there were all kinds of odds and ends in there: parts of machines; boxes full of tools and wires; empty bottles of chemicals; and notebooks filled with designs and plans for machines and equipment. I got in touch with Nils to see if he wanted any of it—it all looked like junk, in my opinion—but he was quite excited to take some of it away, and even paid me quite a tidy sum for it.

There were also two filing cabinets in Carl's study in Luleå, which were full of papers. When I started to go through them, I discovered that they contained Carl's writing project—he had been writing a memoir. Most of it had been done on a typewriter, which was a relief because his handwriting was the worst I'd ever seen—even some of my six-year-olds could do better.

I spent a week reading through the contents of those cabinets, and I must admit, some of the subjects he had written about were difficult to read—there were details about Mrs Dahlstrom that absolutely made my eyes water. There were also a whole lot of other things written there, incriminating things about Mr Dahlstrom's death. Reading through them, I wasn't quite sure whether they were true, or whether they were nothing more than jealous fantasies.

It transpired that Carl actually had an agreement with a publisher for his memoir. A few months after his death they wrote to ask about the manuscript. I made a few small changes, and sent it off to the publishers, and I must say, I was surprised at how well the book did. The sales are still so good that with the money it brings in, and having no one to support, I no longer have to work. These days I live a very comfortable life. I'm back in Östermalm again, but I've left behind everything of my former life in Stockholm—Christine and Ulf, Hilde, Charlotta. Even Harald. Now I have a new circle of friends, friends of my own. I'm back to being Doris Ekman, and I'm having a much better time than I ever had when I was Doris Dance, or I ever would have had as Doris Blomkvist.

ACKNOWLEDGEMENTS

MY THANKS GO first to my agent, Sarah McKenzie: thank you for your belief in the manuscript, and your guidance and support.

Thank you to everyone at Ultimo, especially Brigid Mullane: Brigid, it was a pleasure to work with you to get this book into shape. I'm so grateful for your encouragement, vision and insightfulness. Thank you also to Meredith Rose, for your sharp eyes and your meticulous attention to detail in the edit.

I am grateful to have received funding from Australia Council to develop the first draft of this novel. This support was invaluable, and the book would not have happened without it.

The narrative of this novel and its characters are loosely based on the true story of Elena Milagro de Hoyos and Georg Karl Tänzler (also known as Count Carl von Cosel).

When researching this novel, I drew upon von Cosel's memoirs, which were published in the September 1947 edition of the magazine *Fantastic Adventures* (*The Secret of Elena's Tomb*), as well as Ben Harrison's *Undying Love*.

Thank you to the early readers of the manuscript: my mother, Annette Castillo, and Vignesh Chandrasekaran. Thanks also to my stepfather Miguel Castillo for round-the-clock technical advice on electronics and medical equipment. I'm grateful to Christina Höglund for so generously welcoming me while I was in Stockholm: husen i romanen är alla baserade på ditt.

Finally, Gavi: thank you for everything.

Marija Peričić is a writer based in Naarm/Melbourne. Her first novel, *The Lost Pages*, won *The Australian/Vogel's Literary Award 2017* and was shortlisted for the 2017 Readings Prize for New Australian Fiction. She was named as a 2018 *Sydney Morning Herald* Best Young Australian Novelist. *Exquisite Corpse* is her second novel.